AF478606

MATT MULLICAN
RUBBINGS
CATALOGUE
1984–2016

jrp|ringier

MATT MULLICAN
RUBBINGS
CATALOGUE
1984–2016

EDITED BY
DIETER SCHWARZ

JRP|Ringier
Kunstmuseum Winterthur
Kunsthalle Vogelmann

Throughout his artistic career Matt Mullican has always actively engaged with the question as to how he should give visual form to his ideas. When the "what"—the theme of his work— was already crystallizing, the matter of the "how"—its execution— was still unresolved, because Mullican's ideas were not tied to any physical object: instead they concerned the ways in which human beings perceive phenomena and how these are arranged and combined to create a notion of reality. In conversation Mullican has described the first thing that really gripped his imagination as a young artist: "It was the idea that all I see are light patterns. I had deconstructed the world to simple patterns and I made artwork about light reflecting and light emanating. When you say that all you see are light patterns, you remove all subject matter. There is no difference between me looking at you and me looking at a ladder. They are the same because everything is simply abstract."[1]

On the one hand Mullican was acutely aware of the myriad light phenomena that arise from the visible world, on the other hand he knew of the invisible conventions as to their meaning— an irreconcilable dissociation. This is reflected in a work with comic fragments from 1973: *Details from an Imaginary Universe*. This seemingly random accumulation of details, which is presented as an illustration of part of another universe—as *pars pro toto*—immediately makes one wonder what else there is in this universe and what that fictive reality looks like. If this universe appears in comics, then other visual or material manifestations could also be read as representations of a fictive reality, which could be pieced together to give an overall picture of that reality. Whatever the case, there can be accounts of that reality— either as a narrative or in an image, for instance a drawing—like Mullican's seemingly factual pen-and-ink drawings in which he recorded his knowledge of "reality." This knowledge ranged from physical experiments that he had done at school to notions of life and death or heaven and hell that he had formed as a child. The crucial factor was that all these things could be drawn and thus verified on the basis of representation: "I also made line drawings of a place that did not exist and never would exist. But the comic book fragments and the drawings were detailed and that posed a problem: how does a detail exist of something that does not exist? My answer is that it exists because it is not about the physicality of the light pattern. It is about what the pattern represents. It is not about the physical world, but it is about the representation of the physical world, and I represented that world through line drawings. But if all I see are light patterns, then where is life in those patterns? Life exists in our subjective experience, in the senses. Therefore, pictured reality is equal to reality. The fictional is equal to the real. Or at least, such was my premise. Everything is abstract and it is only through our history and culture that we construct a reality."[2]

Basically these drawings of details of a fictional world are on a par with the construction of a coherent reality that every human being is aiming at by trying to reconcile the unconscious internal processes of human life with the experience of the outside world, that is, the gap between thinking and being. And it is the unbridgeable nature of this gap that fuels artistic representation. The notion that "Nothing should exist,"[3] which Mullican noted down as an argument for his work, is not intended as an imperative. In fact it follows on from the statement that, "It's really strange that anything exists"—a conclusion that has far-reaching consequences, since it includes the speaker, and invalidates any conventions about the existence of reality. However, this zero point also marks the beginning of the process of construction to which Mullican has since dedicated his entire oeuvre, with each individual work serving as a building block in his obsessive, undaunted determination to construct the model of a coherent world that takes in everything including the polar opposites—life and death, heaven and hell.[4] This construction, which spans the full range of the world's polarities, is achieved by means of representation, by the formulation of signs that connect one domain with the next.

With his experience of the real world thus having led him into the realms of representation, Mullican now turned his attention to different levels of representation and to the degree of reality that each is capable of conveying. At one end of the spectrum is photography, which captures a selected moment and is presumably closest to reality; the process of abstraction then logically leads the way to pictograms—the universally legible signs that guide us through the confusion of airports and cities—and ultimately to yet more symbolic signs that have become widely accepted without even looking like what they represent. Since entering this world of signs Mullican has devised all sorts of ways of using signs in different contexts, thereby giving those signs authority and connotations that go beyond what an artistic means such as painting, for instance, can achieve. In the late 1970s he chose the poster—a form with public appeal—as the medium to convey his notion of subjective reality. At the same time, however, he also had signs and charts etched into granite or transposed into decorative colored glass panes, thereby imbuing his images with the gravitas and timelessness of the materials. Mullican also discovered that he could make use of flags and oversized banners, of the kind that normally serve to publicize a symbolic message or to adorn public buildings. However, as opposed to the usual role of these mediums as vehicles for value systems and communication, Mullican's banners were no more than signs of signs, voids that alerted others to an idea rather than to a given. The comment, "Flags are faster than paintings," became Mullican's way of explaining why these wind-blown fabrics could better meet his needs than painting. At the same time as producing these various sign-bearing entities, Mullican was also always drawing—producing a body of works that is, however, very different to his carefully planned pen-and-ink compositions. Those other drawings were simply an extension of his normal volubility, that is to say, a rarely interrupted flow of drawing-writing, which served—like his early performances—to explain thoughts in pictures, to work out particular ideas, and to stand in their own right as diagrammatic outlines.

One constant in all of this is that the artist's extreme subjectivity finds a counterpart in pictorial works that avoid individual, personal handwriting or expression, and instead take on the appearance of a symbolic sign. Despite the widespread use of photomechanical image-production in the form of screen prints or offset prints, which took hold in the 1960s, Mullican has always preferred methods that are not used in commercial manufacturing. His flags were sewn by hand; the granite and the glass were worked by craftspeople in their studios. Mullican was not interested in the quantitative aspect of reproduction; he was fascinated, on a deeper level, by the sign itself, namely that one thing can be replaced by another and represented in this new form. This process is not a closed circle connecting the signifier and the signified, but the transposition of one thing onto another, which then sets a never-ending sequence in motion. Mullican's work—in terms of semiotics rather than psychoanalysis—is about the fiction of the Other, which is given a voice through the sign, which in turn gives us access to another reality that we can thus also experience in some way.

In Mullican's work representation is never unequivocal, because his symbols allow any element to be connected to any other. This opens up the possibility of modeling a concept in a material form without the direction that model takes being fixed: a model can just as easily prefigure as-yet unconstructed reality as it can sum up existing reality—but how does the viewer distinguish one from the other? In the cosmologies designed by Mullican there is also room for symbolism, that is to say, he does not only model a concept of the world, he also models the process of modeling. This in itself accounts for the fact that Mullican's

cosmological designs are neither prescriptive nor normative—
they do not describe the world as it is or should be, they address
modeling itself: "My cosmology is a model for a cosmology;
it is not a cosmology."[5]

Mullican devised his first cosmology in 1973. In it he developed
ideas he had already had as a boy as he tried to imagine his
future and make sense of his place in the world—"it deals with
what happens before birth and after death."[6] While that first
cosmology took the form of a narrative, the second, which dates
back to 1982—a model of five worlds—could be described
as a structure: "It tries to break down and decode the universe."[7]
In this cosmology there are five distinct yet interrelated worlds,
each with its own code—the green-tinged elementary world with
untouched materials; a blue-colored "world unframed," that is,
an instrumental world in which useful tools have been made
from the materials; the yellow "world framed," that is, the world
of the arts, in which things have become images and forms;
the black-and-white symbolic world, in which language represents things on the basis of abstract signs; and lastly the red,
subjective world, in which things and signs acquire an ineffable
significance. The quality that makes this second cosmology
particularly interesting is not the splitting of reality into separate
realms, which might have been an end in itself. The fact is that
these five realms are conceived in such a way that they inter-
relate and that every world represents a position, from which
the other realms can be read. From the perspective of the
symbolic world, all the other worlds appear symbolic; each world
defines the others in terms of its own qualities. Mullican has
called this effect "Five into One": "when you're in the green
world, all five worlds look green; when you're in the blue world,
all five worlds look blue; when you're in the yellow world, all five
worlds look yellow; and when you're in the black-and-white
world—the language world—it all looks that way."[8] A particular
image that symbolizes a world—in illustrations, for instance,
a boiler or generator as emblems of the "world unframed"—
therefore need not appear in the color blue, which is associated
with that world. On the contrary, it can appear in any of the
five worlds and is always read in the context of that world.
The occupation of a particular position within the syntax of the
cosmology causes the meaning of the other positions to change;
the cosmology thus itself functions as a generator, instigating
new combinations. As in the models, the worlds always imply a
two-way movement—on one hand the world is broken down into
ever smaller parts, on the other the five worlds synthesize to
form a new unit, which, as an individual component, becomes
part of a larger entity.

When Mullican uses his cosmology for diverse purposes—as
an underlying structure for poster designs or as the basis
of a script of his own—he is operating in the purpose-oriented

"world unframed." At the same time he is interested in confronting symbolic representation with indexical representation, that is to say, with the traces of real components. How could reality become manifest other than in the prints left behind by things, in physical traces? Displaying the same determination with which he pursued the symbolic, Mullican also sought to secure the indices in his works. These include casts after objects that Mullican created first in plaster and then executed in tin—working in the most primitive conditions in his own kitchen. The objects in question are present in these casts as three-dimensional impressions, with the originals being located in another place. The photograms made from described and denoted glass spheres are also part of this realm, because the exposed photo-paper directly displays the lines that were drawn elsewhere on a different surface.[9] There is even a place here for the artificial stones made in 1990 using laserography, and for the amphitheater from Mullican's computer-generated model of a city, because these are not likenesses, but rather the material realization of data sequences.[10]

The most extensive group in this series of manifestations of an assumed reality are the rubbings, which—due to the fact that they are executed on canvases or sheets of paper—are easily confused with paintings, drawings, or prints. They have their origins in the artist's need to find a way—other than drawing sketches—of creating a pictorial representation of his cosmologies. Initially he did this by drawing cosmological schemes in black oil crayon on small-format canvases. Although the recurrence of individual motifs and the strong contrast of the black planes and the red, green, yellow, blue, or white acrylic grounds made them appear less anonymous than the aforementioned, hand-painted posters, they were nevertheless closer to prints than to painting. In these works Mullican did achieve the visual effect he was striving for, but he had not yet found a suitable production process; as it was, the production process lacked the logic that he was seeking. The solution to this problem came to him purely by chance, on a visit to the Museum of Fine Arts in Boston, where he saw a Chinese stone with incised characters and, next to it, a rubbing taken from that same stone.[11] This technique had first been developed in China in the seventh century, when it was used to reproduce carved inscriptions. Paper was laid on the carved stone and impressions were made in the paper by rubbing. The paper was then inked, so that the indentations remained white and the characters stood out as a negative image. Now Mullican had his model: he had previously made glass etchings, but now—inspired by what he saw in the museum—he immediately went to his studio and laid a sheet of paper on a glass etching and made his first rubbing.[12] In this case the original etching still retained its aesthetic integrity as a work; subsequently, however, the master plates produced solely for the purpose of rubbings were relatively unsightly and not for display; it was only the rubbing that counted as a work. Mullican had thus established the intrinsic paradox of these works: it is not the original image, but the copy that is for show.

Mullican rapidly systematized this technique and from that point on it became a central part of his work. He found various ways of creating the source images in the masters: either by making a preparatory sketch with a drawing tool, or by projecting an image onto a picture carrier as the basis for a drawing. Whatever the case, this was always done manually and not with the aid of any photomechanical processes. The masters for the rubbings were then produced by using a knife to incise a drawing into the picture carrier; initially this was card, which was later replaced by MDF panels. The edge of the incision would be slightly raised, creating a sharp line that sufficed for the rubbing. Depending on how it was done, the outcome could be either just the drawing, as a positive, linear image, or the entire picture plane, as a textured surface. These rubbings were done on canvases (rather than paper) with a colored ground. The canvases were then attached to stretchers, in the manner of easel paintings, which occupy space in a different way to the works on paper. Mullican, having decided to standardize the formats so that these works could be used as modular elements, chose two basic types: a vertical, double square measuring 8 × 4 feet, and a shorter format measuring 6 × 4 feet. Although the canvases can stand on their own, they can also be placed, separately, side-by-side as diptyches or—more often—combined to create larger, wall-filling groups. Mullican himself coined the term "modular mix and match" to describe this additive and combinatory principle, which works equally well in exhibition designs and architectural projects.

In the encyclopedia arc described by Mullican's œuvre, the rubbings represent one of the oldest known methods of reproduction and could be seen as the polar opposite to the digital techniques that Mullican started to use around 1990 to illustrate the cosmologies and the related city models. But let us listen to Mullican's own description of the rubbings and their relationship to the original image: "There is a kind of fake history that occurs, because in my studio I have the master plate, the relief, and in the gallery you see the rubbing, but it is taken from another place. This relationship between the master and the print creates a kind of artificial history. The rubbing is not a painting, a drawing, or a print, it is none of them and all of them. It is a retinal image in the sense of Plato's shadow. When I look at something, what any eye sees is the retinal image, but the world is not that. What the rubbing represents is what the eye sees, the relief is it."[13] The rubbings are likenesses, as opposed to compositions; they are shadows of something that was literally hidden behind the canvas, with the result that the rubbing appears somewhat blurred and indirect. However, this shadowiness is also a structural property, which Mullican describes in terms of both Platonic idealism and physiological perception.

Not so very long ago in the history of art, Max Ernst introduced rubbings into the repertoire of techniques used by the Surrealists. As such it was probably the most logical response to André Breton's declaration in 1924 in his *Manifesto of Surrealism* that "it is not a matter of drawing, but simply of tracing."[14] Ernst created his frottages by laying lightweight drawing paper on textured surfaces. Using a pencil, he created rubbings of these textures, which were then interpreted as objectified, almost photographic images of details of the real world. "This technique was transposed into oil painting as grattage. Instead of applying graphite to the picture carrier, the artist created the image by removing oil paint from a canvas. He could use this technique in a wide variety of ways. Sometimes, having applied various paints to the canvas, he would scrape the surface, revealing hidden layers of color and textures in the underlying materials; sometimes he would apply thin paint with a spatula to create individual shapes; sometimes he would draw a comb or a serrated spatula across the surface, leaving a seismographic trace of the movements of his hand."[15]

As the son of practicing artists—Luchita Hurtado and Lee Mullican—Matt Mullican witnessed Surrealism and its aesthetics first-hand as he was growing up.[16] Even if Mullican, unlike the Surrealists, has never used rubbings to promote automatism, his approach to these shadow images is still related to the notion of tracing, and may remind the viewer of the fumage technique developed by Wolfgang Paalen, who created smoke patterns on canvas, calling to mind a flame or fire that had long since been extinguished. Echoes of works executed in a state of unconsciousness still resonate in Mullican's work, made under hypnosis as "That Person." However, as a student he became interested in the production of pictures as reproductions, as he saw Andy Warhol doing. Mullican particularly admired the fact that Warhol's use of screen prints to transfer an image to a canvas allowed him to put an emotionless distance between himself and the motif. Warhol himself always organized his image-making process as manual fabrication rather than industrial production, and Mullican has adhered to the same principle as he works with assistants on his own rubbings. Mention should also be made here of Jasper Johns, who—in the 1950s— was already using the letters of the alphabet and the numbers 0 to 9 as motifs in his "Figures," "Alphabets," and "Numbers" series. He used templates and prints to transfer his motifs to the picture surface. However, since these motifs do not represent physical realities but are pure signs in their own right, their "likenesses" cannot stand for themselves or for a thing; by definition they refer to an ideational realm.[17] This was just one aspect—highly significant for Mullican's work—of the much wider ranging ideas that Johns was pursuing with his traces of a reality that is not present in the finished painting. From bites taken out of the surfaces of oil paintings to casts and impressions of body parts, Johns devised ever-new strategies for conveying a tangible sense of the figure of the artist. However, unlike Mullican, for whom every individual fragment of reality found in a rubbing is given a place in a cosmology, Johns distanced himself from the idea of a presupposed order and always ensured that the meaning of the motifs in his works remained ambiguous.

If we consider Matt Mullican's rubbings in light of his cosmology of five worlds, they can be seen in the green world as objects made from wood, canvas, and oil crayons. In the blue "world unframed" they are panels that can be hung up to form walls; in the yellow "world framed" they are read as works of art, which resemble paintings, drawings, and prints, but are not in fact any of these. In the black-and-white world the rubbings are spoken and written—that is the world that we currently find ourselves in—and in the red, subjective world they become the fantasies that the viewer associates with their pictorial motifs. This means that although there are certain motifs in Mullican's rubbings that are significant in the context of his own work, the rubbings can also be regarded as self-referential, because—both materially and symbolically—they are always also components in his mental edifice. Bearing this in mind, it is possible to see how Mullican has used this medium over the years, and which motifs he has represented in his rubbings.

When Mullican first showed his rubbings in an exhibition—in 1984 at Mary Boone Gallery in New York—the presentation included both individual panels and large-format composite works.[18] Visitors could study the icons used for the individual worlds in the cosmology. These icons, which could not be adequately represented in posters or on flags, consisted of a series of elements and autogenic cells, boilers, steam machines, lungs as machines that change conditions, a cross-section through a steam ship as a metaphor for social order, and a cathedral as a metaphor for cultural and religious structure. In the larger, multi-part pieces, the cosmology of the five worlds was interpreted in visual terms. Mullican's use of recurrent motifs and differentiated black-and-white or colored versions, made it clear that the rubbings were reproductions and not originals, or paintings, in the usual sense.

The present catalogue of rubbings and the motifs depicted in them provide the reader with a concentrated overview of Mullican's work and an insight into how he works with his themes—how he develops new perspectives on them over the years. It is already clear from the first rubbings that

the structural affinity between frottage and collage referred
to by Max Ernst also extends, in different circumstances,
to Mullican's rubbings.[19] In 1986 Mullican pictured different
realms of the cosmology—namely the elements in a prehistoric
landscape, history and the arts, and the city—as individual works,
which he then presented as a continuous, vertical sequence
on a long length of canvas. Elements from the first rubbings
reappear in the realm of the city: the cathedral, the steam
machine, cutaways of a ship's hull, and of a house. By combining
whole master plates and connecting them to form larger works,
by taking details from the latter and then presenting these
adjacent to each other on a new panel, Mullican had found a way
to use rubbings to explore the combinatorics that are intrinsic
to his cosmology. Detached from their narrative context, the
symbolic positions of the first cosmology are clearly "portable,"
that is to say they can be introduced into the structure of the
second cosmology. In 1989 Mullican produced a series of works
(consisting of either one or two canvases) that are divided
vertically into two sections, in which already familiar figures—
anatomy, generators—are confronted with the elemental world
and are specified by the choice of colors; not long after this
more emblematic works followed, including *Paris Opera House*,
Generator Hall, and *Roundhouse*.

In 1987 this production method took on another dimension in
Dallas Project, which Mullican has described as one of the most
extensive print projects ever realized by an artist. The first
version of this project was pulled on yellow grounds and on red
grounds, signaling the world of the arts and the subjective world;
this was followed by another version in which different colors
allocated individual images to specific contexts. At the heart of
Dallas Project there is an image of a city. It is a real city with
buildings, and also a projection of the cosmology onto a surface,
as we can see from the schematic city charts that Mullican
drew at the time and that were then reiterated in rubbings.
In the city we see the worlds of pure material, the unconscious,
language, subjectivity, and the arts: "So the city becomes an
allegory, an allegorical chart that one could walk through.
The city is an interface between me and the concepts behind the
chart."[20] Mullican developed these ideas in the rubbings he did
in 1991–1992; he produced more city charts that either stand
alone, are placed side-by-side, are superimposed on each other
as interlocking schemes, or that take up the already familiar
pictorial world as elements in their layouts: symbols from the
cosmology, details from *Evolution Chart*, the machines, and the
explanatory representation of the five worlds. Ultimately the
development of cosmological panels and city charts led to the
abovementioned concept of "Five into One."

After a break, in 1996 Mullican started to use pages from
notebooks for his rubbings; in 2003 he returned to this.

The transposition of hand-written notations onto canvases changed the character of the rubbings. What had started as a private note now—through its transformation in much larger panels—became a definitive formulation; by the same token the large-format panels now became an arena for working out ideas and their ramifications. In 2007 Mullican's fictive alter ego, "That Person," also started to feature in the rubbings. Drawings done when Mullican was under hypnosis by that other, unknown person, are a separate strand of work in Mullican's output and, as such, distinct from the cosmologies. Whereas the latter are about modeling, that is to say, a conceptual approach, the drawings by "That Person" are about observation and deduction. We have no actual knowledge of "That Person," and we can only build up a picture of his world from the drawings and the written statements they contain.[21] For Mullican, learning from "That Person" means adding information to his own speculations concerning reality as it is experienced by others, that is to say, constructing the world through a different consciousness rather than by means of an abstract concept.

At the same time Mullican also continued to work on his cosmological charts and the city derived from the latter. In principle Mullican had already extended the city charts in the 1980s, creating a field within which cities were systematically combined and turned into abstract patterns. He also availed himself of techniques used in the applied arts and had the pattern woven as a carpet[22]; however, the rubbing technique made it much simpler to make charts exploring the many possibilities achievable by combining elements. The charts became grids, in which colored squares, rectangles, and semi-circles from the charts could be arranged in any order, so that the ensuing world revolved around the arts, language, the elements, or the subjective. In the linear version, in which adjoining schematic city charts form a square field, it is possible to produce yet more combinations: a wealth of imaginary orders that kindle new ideas. How could one conceive of a cosmology centered on the "world unframed"? What about a cosmology that was centered on the elements or on the subjective? And what does it mean when one of these worlds is constrained by another? In the rubbings Mullican did in 2012, the properties of a single world either partially or entirely occupy the cosmological chart. By contrast, the charts in the sequence of rubbings done in 2013 include details of images as symbolic representatives of reality in different positions and contexts. These material elements had already been introduced into the extensive series of small-format charts done a year earlier, where they appeared as individual images or as pairs of images, once again reminding the viewer of the status of these images as copies. And by using details from comics in these works, Mullican recalled the details from an imaginary universe that were alluded to at the outset of this essay. In his ever-inventive redeployment of his charts, Mullican reversed the circumstances yet again by now interpreting them as a perspectival representation of an interior, thereby creating a paradigmatic situation into which he introduced figures, things, and cosmological charts. At the same time Mullican realized another series of rubbings with self-sufficient, symbolic signs or words referring to figures in the cosmologies—God, Fate, Heaven, Hell, Elements, and so on. He did the same thing with the orders that govern ordinary life—the sequence of hours, days, and months, the daily round of mealtimes. This reduction to primary signs with their promise of clarification and regulation was the counterpart to the flood of details that the series of comic elements had brought into play. At the same time the cosmological charts were divided into a sequence of partial planes, small-format rubbings, which can also be read in their own right as potential orders.

It was not by chance that Mullican chose images of machines (that change the aggregate state of materials and that generate energy) as symbols of his own work, for his discovery of rubbings led him to a medium that is better suited than any other mode of representation to the transformation of pictorial materials of all kinds, and to the presentation of these materials for public view: a combinatory instrument that facilitates both reproduction and harmonization—in other words, "modular mix and match."

1 Matt Mullican, *Im Gespräch/Conversations*, with Koen Brams and Dirk Pültau, DuMont Dokumente, DuMont Buchverlag, Cologne 2011, p. 154.
2 Ibid., p. 154.
3 *Matt Mullican: Subject Element Sign Frame World*, Skira Rizzoli Publications, New York 2013, p. 121.
4 Allan McCollum gives a compelling account of this in his early essay on Mullican's work, "Matt Mullican's World," *Reallife Magazine*, no. 5, Winter 1980, p. 4–13.
5 Matt Mullican, "Interview Matt Mullican and Michael Tarantino," in *Matt Mullican: The MIT Project*, exh. cat., MIT List Visual Arts Center, Cambridge, May 12–July 1, 1990, Cambridge, Massachusetts 1990, p. 18.
6 Matt Mullican, *Im Gespräch/Conversations*, p. 152.
7 Ibid.
8 *Matt Mullican: A Drawing Translates the Way of Thinking*, "Drawing Papers," no. 82, exh. cat., Drawing Center, New York, November 21, 2008–February 5, 2009, New York 2008, p. 17.
9 See *Matt Mullican: Subject Element Sign Frame World*, p. 85.
10 Ibid., p. 177.
11 Holland Cotter, "Matt Mullican: Public Paradise," in *Matt Mullican: Banners, Monuments and the City, An Exhibition of Work for Public Spaces*, exh. cat., Goldie Paley Gallery, Moore College of Art, Philadelphia, September 11–October 18, 1987, Philadelphia 1987, p. 8.
12 Examples of these early rubbings are illustrated in Matt Mullican, *World Frame*, exh. cat., Contemporary Art Museum, University of South Florida, Tampa, October 30, 1992–January 9, 1993, Tampa 1993, p. 201–205.
13 *Matt Mullican: Works 1972–1992*, Ulrich Wilmes (ed.), Verlag der Buchhandlung Walther König, Cologne 1993, p. 116.
14 "Il ne s'agit pas de dessiner, il ne s'agit que de calquer": André Breton, *Œuvres complètes*, vol. I, "Bibliothèque de la Pléïade," Marguerite Bonnet (ed.) with the collaboration of Philippe Bernier, Etienne-Alain Hubert, and José Pierre for this volume, Gallimard, Paris 1988, p. 325. English in André Breton, *Manifestoes of Surrealism*, trans. Richard Seaver and Helen R. Lane, University of Michigan Press, Ann Arbor 1972, p. 21.
15 Jürgen Pech, in *Kunstmuseum Winterthur: Katalog der Gemälde und Skulpturen*, vol. 3. Dieter Schwarz (ed.), Kunstmuseum Winterthur/Richter Verlag, Winterthur/Düsseldorf 2011, p. 242–243.
16 For more on this see, *Mullican + Mullican*, exh. cat., Jonson Gallery of the University Art Museum, Albuquerque, April 4–May 26, 1989, Albuquerque 1989.
17 For more on this, see Roberta Bernstein, *Jasper Johns' Paintings and Sculptures 1954–1974: "The Changing Focus of the Eye,"* "Studies in the Fine Arts: The Avant-Garde," no. 46, UMI Research Press, Ann Arbor 1985, p. 21–27.
18 See *Matt Mullican*, exh. cat., Mary Boone and Michael Werner, New York, December 1–29, 1984, New York 1984.
19 " … in his own development the frottage occupies even more room than the collage, which, in his view, it is not fundamentally different from": trans. from Max Ernst, "Biographische Notizen (Wahrheitgewebe und Lügengewebe," in *Max Ernst*, exh. cat. Wallraf-Richartz-Museum, Cologne, December 28, 1962–March 3, 1963; Kunsthaus Zürich, 23 March–28 April 1963, Wallraf-Richartz-Museum, Cologne 1962, p. 28.
20 Matt Mullican, "Interview Matt Mullican and Michael Tarantino," p. 18.
21 For more on this, see Ulrich Wilmes, "That Person," in *Matt Mullican: Learning from That Person's Work*, exh. cat., Museum Ludwig, Cologne, March 19–June 12, 2005, Verlag der Buchhandlung Walther König, Cologne 2005, p. 15–21.
22 *Untitled (Field of Cities)*, 1986, wool, 114.5 × 58.5 cm, in *Matt Mullican: Banners, Monuments and the City*, no. 7.

This book lists all the rubbings on canvas done by Matt Mullican since 1984 that are known to the author. It does not include rubbings on paper, nor the rubbings on canvas—including preparatory works for the latter—that were conceived as multiples. However, even this list of rubbings on canvas may not be exhaustive, since the artist did not compile records or lists of these works at the time of their making. It has therefore only been possible to arrive at the present list by consulting visual materials, unsorted documents in Matt Mullican's own archive, and the galleries who represent him. A useful source of information was found in the images of early works in the photograph albums, previously stored in the artist's New York studio, which were relocated in the summer of 2015 to the Mai 36 Galerie in Zurich, where it was possible to consult these albums for the purpose of preparing this catalogue. Unfortunately there is virtually no information to be had regarding the rubbings that Matt Mullican produced as commissions for particular buildings or companies. There are no details of these in the artist's archive and all the author's efforts to discover more about these works proved fruitless, with new occupants in the buildings concerned or the companies that once commissioned the works no longer being in existence.

The current publication contains a list of the rubbings on canvas. However, it is not a catalogue raisonné in the usual sense with detailed provenances for the works, providing full background information on the works' owners, locations (frequently changing), exhibition history, and literature. Even if there had been time to attempt to research all the details, there are simply too many gaps in the documentation to make this worthwhile. Accordingly, this catalogue is intended as a practical tool that provides a detailed insight into Matt Mullican's work by focusing on the course that one particular strand of his art has taken over the last three decades.

The information on the rubbings is presented as follows:

Title: Since all these works are untitled, a brief indication of the nature of the image is given in brackets.

Date: Mullican rarely signs and dates these rubbings, which makes it all the harder to ascribe them to particular years. In addition to this certain motifs reappear, sometimes over the course of what must be several years. Some dates can be extrapolated from certain circumstances (such as the first public presentation of a particular group) or can be identified from the artist's own recollections. However, all dates are to be treated with caution. The rubbings are listed according to the year when they were made or as far these can be established; within any given year they are grouped according to motifs, since it is not possible to reconstruct the exact order of their making.

Technique: The medium for the images is always oil crayon. While the paints used for the grounds vary, they are never oils, only ever water-soluble acrylics or similar water-soluble substances. It was not deemed necessary to repeat this information for each entry.

Dimensions: Almost all these rubbings are done on standard formats, measured in inches and feet. Only some of the most recent of these rubbings, done by Matt Mullican in his Berlin studio, use formats measured in centimeters. The most common formats are 6 × 4 feet and 8 × 4 feet, i.e. 183 × 122 cm and 244 × 122 cm. For readers' convenience the table reproduced on page 39 lists equivalent imperial and metric measurements.

Location: The locations of works have not been included since it was frequently impossible to ascertain these with any certainty.

This catalogue has been published to accompany the exhibition of works by Matt Mullican on show in summer 2016, first at the Kunstmuseum Winterthur, Switzerland, and subsequently at the Kunsthalle Vogelmann in Heilbronn, Germany. Instead of publishing a standard, essayistic exhibition catalogue it seemed to me preferable to invest the funds at our disposal in a special publication that could serve as a resource for the future study of Matt Mullican's work. This in turn led to the idea of concentrating on a single medium in the present exhibition, as a way of exemplifying the processes that underpin Mullican's art. These processes and their significance are discussed in the catalogue text.

As the instigator and author of this publication, I would like to thank all those who have made it possible to compile and publish this catalogue in such a short space of time. First and foremost my thanks go to Matt Mullican himself, for his enthusiastic response to my idea and for the many pointers he provided in lengthy conversations, both as to how these rubbings should be understood and, on a practical level, as to where they might be found. I am most grateful for the trust he placed in me and hope this catalogue will express something of my appreciation of his generosity of spirit.

It would never have been possible to realize this catalogue without the unstinting support of the team at the Mai 36 Galerie in Zurich, who have represented Matt Mullican since 1988. My heartfelt thanks go to Victor Gisler for his willingness to collaborate on this project and for the information he provided so readily. I am also most grateful that his staff member, Justine Hauer, assisted me in my research. She took a keen interest in our project and resolved numerous issues, including the process of securing the reproductions needed for the catalogue. Thanks go also to Anna Caruso, Anna Bleuler, and Peter Baracchi. I am also very grateful to the other galleries that Matt Mullican has worked with in the past and who provided such useful information and so much visual material for this catalogue. My thanks therefore go to Brooke Alexander, New York; Silvia Dauder, ProjecteSD, Barcelona; Massimo De Carlo, Milan; Peter Freeman, Inc., New York; Cristina Guerra, Lisbon; Georg Kargl, Vienna; Michael Klein, New York; Martin Klosterfelde, Berlin; Capitain Petzel, Berlin; Micheline Szwajcer, Brussels; Johann Widauer, Innsbruck; Tracy Williams, New York. I would like to thank also the following people and institutions for their help: David Gray, New York; Peter Heimer, Berlin; Brigitte von Trotha-Ribbentrop, Berlin; Edward A. Vazquez and Margaret W. Wallace, Middlebury College, Middlebury, Vermont; Actelion Pharmaceuticals Ltd., Allschwil; AXA Konzern AG, Kunstsammlung, Cologne; Bonhams, Los Angeles; Christie's, Zurich; Cornette de Saint Cyr, Paris; Hirshhorn Museum and Sculpture Garden, Washington, DC; Kunsthaus Zürich; Lempertz Auktionen, Cologne; Los Angeles County Museum of Art, Los Angeles; Los Angeles Modern Auctions, Van Nuys, CA; Öffentliche Versicherung Braunschweig; The Progressive Art Collection, Mayfield Village, OH; Rago Arts & Auction Center, Lambertville, NJ; Sotheby's, Zurich; Three Star Books, Paris; UBS Art Collection, Zurich; Villa Grisebach, Berlin; Whitney Museum of American Art, New York. I should also like to express my sincere gratitude to Lionel Bovier and Clément Dirié at JRP|Ringier publishing house, whose wide experience has been of such benefit to this catalogue, and particulary Nicolas Eigenheer.

Lastly, I should like to express my deep gratitude to the Max Kohler-Stiftung for its very generous support for this exhibition of the work of Matt Mullican at the Kunstmuseum Winterthur and hence also for this catalogue. I am deeply grateful to the Foundation and its President, Dr Georg von Segesser. And I am also sincerely grateful to my colleague Dr Marc Gundel, Director of the Städtische Museen Heilbronn, not only for his interest in the exhibition but also for contributing to the funding for this catalogue.

Vom Beginn seiner Arbeit an stellte sich für Matt Mullican die praktische Frage, wie er die Gedanken, die ihn beschäftigten, materiell formulieren sollte. Als sich das „Was" – die Thematik der Arbeit – für ihn herauszubilden begann, war das „Wie" – die Ausführung – noch ungelöst, denn Mullicans Denken ging nicht von einem festen Gegenstand aus, es kreiste um die Wahrnehmung der Phänomene und darum, wie sich diese ordnen und zu einer Vorstellung der Realität fügen lassen. In einem Gespräch schilderte Mullican dieses erste ihn faszinierende Thema: „Es war die Idee, dass alles, was ich sehe, Lichtmuster sind. Ich hatte die Welt in einfache Muster zerlegt und machte Kunstwerke über die Reflexion und Strahlung von Licht. Sobald man sagt, man sieht nichts als Lichtmuster, schafft man alle Inhalte ab. Es gibt keinen Unterschied mehr, ob ich jetzt Sie anschaue oder eine Leiter. Es ist alles dasselbe, weil alles abstrakt ist."[1]

Einerseits sah Mullican sich konfrontiert mit der Flut von Lichtphänomenen, die von der sichtbaren Welt ausging, andererseits gab es das Wissen um die nicht sichtbaren Übereinkünfte über deren Bedeutung – eine unauflösbare Dissoziation. Einen Niederschlag fand sie in der 1973 datierten Arbeit mit Comic-Fragmenten, *Details from an Imaginary Universe*. Betrachtet man einen solchen zufällig gewählten Ausschnitt und versteht man die dargestellte Szene als Abbildung einer anderen Welt, als pars pro toto, dann stellt sich die Frage, was jenseits des Ausschnitts existiert und wie sich diese fiktive Realität konstituiert. Manifestiert sie sich in Comics, dann könnte man auch jede andere visuelle oder materielle Manifestation als Repräsentanten einer fiktiven Realität lesen und davon ausgehend versuchen, zu einem umfassenden Bild von dieser zu gelangen. Jedenfalls aber kann davon berichtet werden, entweder in einer Erzählung oder dann in einer Abbildung, beispielsweise in einer Zeichnung. So hielt Mullican in nüchtern ausgeführten Tuschezeichnungen fest, was er von der Realität zu wissen glaubte. Dieses Wissen reichte von physikalischen Experimenten aus dem Schulunterricht bis zu den Vorstellungen über Leben und Tod, Himmel und Hölle, die er sich als Kind gemacht hatte. Entscheidend war allein, dass sich all dies zeichnen und damit auf der Ebene der Darstellung verifizieren liess: „Ich machte auch Strichzeichnungen von einem Ort, den es nie gegeben hatte und den es nie geben würde. Aber die Comic-Fragmente und die Zeichnungen waren detailliert, und das stellte mich vor ein Problem: Warum gibt es ein Detail von etwas, das es nicht gibt? Meine Antwort ist: Weil es sich dabei nicht um die physische Existenz des Lichtmusters handelt. Es dreht sich vielmehr darum, was das Muster darstellt. Es geht nicht um die physische Welt, sondern um die Darstellung der physischen Welt, und ich stellte diese Welt durch Strichzeichnungen dar. Aber wenn ich nur Lichtmuster sehe – wo in diesen Mustern ist das Leben? Das Leben existiert in unserer subjektiven Erfahrung, in den Sinnen. Deshalb ist die abgebildete Realität dasselbe wie die Realität. Das Erdachte entspricht dem Realen. Das war zumindest meine Prämisse. Alles ist abstrakt, und wir schaffen eine Realität allein durch unsere Geschichte und unsere Kultur."[2]

Im Grunde lassen sich diese Zeichnungen von Details einer fiktiven Welt mit dem Konstruieren einer zusammenhängenden Realität vergleichen, das jeder Mensch unternimmt, wenn er die unbewusst sich vollziehenden inneren Vorgänge mit der Erfahrung der Aussenwelt, die Differenz von Denken und Sein, in Übereinstimmung zu bringen versucht. Aus der fehlenden Übereinstimmung resultiert das Bedürfnis nach Repräsentation. Der Satz „Nothing should exist"[3], den Mullican als Argument für seine Arbeit notierte, ist nicht gedacht als Imperativ. Vielmehr ist er zusammen mit der ihm vorausgehenden Aussage „It's really strange that anything exists" eine Feststellung von ungeheurer Tragweite, da sie den Sprechenden mit einschliesst und jede Übereinkunft über die Existenz der Realität zunichte macht. Von diesem Nullpunkt aus beginnt der Konstruktionsvorgang, dem sich Mullicans gesamtes Œuvre widmet, und jedes einzelne Werk lässt sich als Baustein in dem obsessiven und nicht abreissenden Bestreben verstehen, zwischen den Extrempunkten Leben und Tod, Himmel und Hölle das Modell einer kohärenten Welt zu errichten.[4] Diese Konstruktion, welche die Polarität überbrückt, geschieht mittels der Repräsentation, der Formulierung von Zeichen, die den einen Bereich mit dem anderen in Beziehung setzen.

War Mullican mit diesen Überlegungen von der Erfahrung des Realen in den Bereich der Repräsentation eingetreten, so fragte er sich nun nach den Ebenen der Darstellung und dem Grad von Realität, den sie jeweils zu vermitteln in der Lage sind. Von der Fotografie, die einen ausgewählten Moment wiedergibt und vermeintlich der Realität näher ist, führte der Abstraktionsweg der Darstellung folgerichtig zu Piktogrammen, die anhand universell lesbarer Bildzeichen den Weg durch das Dickicht von Flughäfen und Städten weisen, und weiter zu symbolischen, auf Konventionen beruhenden Zeichen, denen die Ähnlichkeit mit dem Dargestellten abgeht. Mit dem Eintritt in die Welt der Zeichen eröffnete sich für Mullican eine Fülle von Mitteln, Zeichen in verschiedenen Kontexten zu verwenden und ihnen auf diese Weise Autorität und zugleich Konnotationen zu verleihen, die über ein künstlerisches Ausdrucksmittel wie die Malerei hinausgehen. So nutzte er Ende der 1970er Jahre zunächst das Medium des Plakats, um in dieser an die Öffentlichkeit gerichteten Form die Idee einer subjektiven Wirklichkeit zum Ausdruck zu bringen. Zeichen und Pläne wurden aber auch auf Granitplatten geätzt oder in dekorative farbige Glasscheiben übersetzt, um ihnen die Offizialität und Zeitenthobenheit dieser Materialien mitzugeben. Einen weit verbreiteten Zeichenträger entdeckte Mullican in den Flaggen und überdimensionierten Bannern, die dazu dienen, eine symbolische Botschaft auf die Strasse zu tragen oder Gebäude damit zu schmücken, doch im Unterschied zu diesen Trägern von Wert- und Bedeutungssystemen waren Mullicans Banner nur das Zeichen eines Zeichens, eine Leerstelle, die nicht auf Feststehendes, sondern auf eine Idee verwies. „Flags are faster than paintings", war seine Devise, um klarzustellen, weshalb die wehenden Stoffe seinen Bedürfnissen besser als die Malerei entsprachen. Parallel zur Produktion dieser verschiedenartigen Zeichenträger zeichnete Mullican unablässig, doch unterschieden sich diese Blätter von der unpersönlichen Ausdrucksweise der sorgfältig geplanten Tuschezeichnungen. Sein Zeichnen war vielmehr eine Fortsetzung seines Redeflusses, ein kaum unterbrochenes Zeichnen-Schreiben, das wie die frühen Performances dazu diente, Gedanken bildhaft zu erläutern, bestimmte Vorstellungen auszuarbeiten und in der diagrammhaften Darlegung auch für sich selbst zu klären.

Konstant bleibt dabei stets, dass die äusserste Subjektivität des Künstlers ihr Gegenstück in Bildrealisationen findet, die den handschriftlichen, persönlichen Ausdruck abstreifen und denjenigen eines symbolischen Zeichens annehmen. Im Unterschied zu den zahlreichen Nutzungen fotomechanischer Übertragungen von Vorlagen auf Bildträger in Sieb- und Offsetdruck, wie sie in den 1960er Jahren entstanden, hielt Mullican an Verfahren fest, die auf nicht-industriellen Anfertigungen beruhen. Fahnen wurden einzeln von Hand genäht, Granitplatten oder Gläser in Ateliers handwerklich bearbeitet. Nicht die quantitative Dimension der Reproduktion war für Mullican ausschlaggebend, vielmehr die Faszination des Zeichens, also dass etwas durch etwas anderes ersetzt und damit dargestellt werden kann. Denkt man sich diese Bewegung nicht als eine in sich abgeschlossene, zwischen einem Zeichen und einem Bezeichneten kreisende, sondern grundsätzlich als Übertragung von einem Ding auf ein anderes, so setzt sich damit eine unaufhaltbare Bewegung in Gang. In Mullicans Arbeit geht es – nicht im psychoanalytischen, sondern im semiotischen Sinn – um die Fiktion des Anderen, das in den Zeichen das Wort ergreift, denn darin eröffnet sich eine andere Realität, und es lässt sich etwas darüber erfahren.

Repräsentation meint nicht Eindeutigkeit, denn die Symbolisierung erlaubt, jedes Element jedem anderen zuzuordnen. Damit ist die Möglichkeit gegeben, eine Vorstellung in irgendeiner materiellen Weise zu modellieren, ohne dass die Ausrichtung der Modellierung feststeht: Einerseits steht ein Modell für eine noch zu konstruierende Realität, und umgekehrt stellt das Modell die Realität in verkürzter Weise nach – doch wie lässt sich entscheiden, was jeweils der Fall ist? In den Kosmologien, die Mullican entwarf, erhielt auch die symbolische Ebene ihren Platz: Er modellierte nicht allein eine Weltvorstellung, er modellierte darin das Modellieren selbst. Deshalb geht Mullicans kosmologischen Plänen jeder präskriptive oder normative Anspruch ab – sie beschreiben die Welt nicht, wie sie ist oder sein sollte, sie handeln vom Modellierungsvorgang als solchem: „Meine Kosmologie ist ein Modell für eine Kosmologie; es ist keine Kosmologie."[5]

1973 entwarf Mullican seine erste Kosmologie; sie ging von Vorstellungen aus, die er sich als Kind gemacht hatte, um seine Herkunft und seinen Ort in der Welt für sich zu klären, sie „handelt davon, was vor der Geburt und nach dem Tod geschieht"[6]. War dies ein Narrativ, so entwickelte die zweite, um 1982 abgefasste Kosmologie mit dem Modell der fünf Welten eine Struktur: „Sie versucht das Universum zu zergliedern und zu dekodieren."[7] In diesem kosmologischen Plan lassen sich fünf aufeinander bezogene Welten mit ihren Codes unterscheiden – die grün gefärbte elementare Welt, in der die Materialien ungenutzt existieren; die blau gefärbte „world unframed", die instrumentelle Welt, in der aus den Materialien nutzbare Werkzeuge geworden sind; die gelbe „world framed", die Welt der Künste, in der aus den Dingen Bilder und Formen werden; die schwarze symbolische Welt, in der in abstrakten Zeichen von den Dingen gehandelt wird, und schliesslich die rot gefärbte Welt des Subjektiven, in der alles, Dinge und Zeichen, ihre unvermittelbare Deutung erfahren. Was diese zweite Kosmologie besonders interessant macht, ist nicht die Aufspaltung der Wirklichkeit in getrennte Bereiche, denn damit wäre der Plan abgeschlossen. Die fünf Bereiche sind vielmehr derart konzipiert, dass sie sich aufeinander beziehen und dass jede Welt eine Position darstellt, aus der die übrigen Bereiche gelesen werden können. So stellen sich aus der Perspektive des Symbolischen alle Welten als symbolisch dar; jedes Kapitel definiert das Ganze ihm selbst gemäss, ein Effekt, den Mullican „Five into One" nannte – „wenn du dich in der grünen Welt befindest, schauen alle Welten grün aus; wenn du in der blauen Welt bist, schauen alle fünf Welten blau aus; wenn du in der gelben Welt bist, schauen alle fünf Welten gelb aus; und wenn du in der schwarz-weissen Welt bist – der Sprachwelt – schaut alles so aus."[8] Ein bestimmtes Bild, das eine Welt bezeichnet, also beispielsweise Boiler oder Generator als Embleme der „world unframed", muss deshalb in Darstellungen nicht notwendigerweise in der entsprechenden Farbe Blau erscheinen. Im Gegenteil, es kann in allen fünf Welten auftreten und wird jeweils in deren Kontext gelesen. Mit der Besetzung einer Position innerhalb der Syntax der Kosmologie verändert sich die Bedeutung der übrigen Positionen, und so wirkt die Kosmologie selbst als Generator, als Erzeuger einer Kombinatorik. Stets ist man wie bei der Modellierung mit einer zwiefachen Bewegung konfrontiert – einerseits mit der Aufgliederung der Welt in immer kleinere Teile, anderseits mit der Synthese der fünf Welten zu einem neuen Gebilde, das als einzelner Teil in eine grössere Einheit eingeht.

Wenn Mullican die Kosmologie für verschiedenste Zwecke nutzte – als Grundstruktur für Entwürfe von Plakaten oder für die Konzeption einer eigenen Schrift –, so stellte er sich damit in die zweckgebundene „world unframed". Umgekehrt interessierte es ihn, die symbolische Repräsentation mit der indexikalischen, also mit realen materiellen Elementen zu konfrontieren. Wie konnte sich die Realität denn anders manifestieren als in Abdrücken, die ein Ding hinterliess, in materiellen Spuren? Ebenso konsequent, wie er das Symbolische verfolgte, suchte Mullican in Werken die Indizien zu sichern. Dazu zählen die Güsse nach Objekten, die Mullican erst in Gips, dann unter primitivsten Bedingungen in seiner Küche in Zinn ausführte. In diesen Güssen sind die dargestellten Objekte als plastische Abdrücke präsent, deren Original an einem andern Ort existiert. Ebenso gehören die Fotogramme nach beschriebenen und bezeichneten Glaskugeln in diesen Bereich, denn das belichtete Fotopapier zeigt unmittelbar die Linien, die an einem anderen Ort auf einer anders gearteten Fläche aufgezeichnet wurden.[9] Selbst die mittels Laserografie 1990 realisierten künstlichen Steine und das Amphitheater aus dem computergenerierten Stadtmodell Mullicans haben hier ihren Platz, denn sie sind die materielle Umsetzung abwesender Datenreihen und keine Abbildungen.[10]

Das umfangreichste Kapitel in dieser Reihe von Manifestationen einer angenommenen Realität sind die Rubbings, die aufgrund ihrer Ausführung auf Leinwänden oder Papierbogen leicht mit Bildern, Zeichnungen oder Drucken verwechselt werden könnten. Sie gehen zurück auf das Bedürfnis des Künstlers, für die Darstellung der Kosmologien neben Skizzen bildhafte Wiedergaben zu suchen. Zunächst realisierte er diese, indem er die kosmologischen Schemata mit schwarzer Ölkreide auf kleinformatige Leinwände zeichnete. Aufgrund der sich wiederholenden Motive und des harten Kontrasts der schwarzen Flächen auf der roten, grünen, gelben, blauen oder weissen Acrylgrundierung wirkten sie zwar nicht so anonym wie die bereits erwähnten handgemalten Poster, doch jedenfalls der Grafik näher als der Malerei. Zwar erreichte Mullican auf diese Weise die angestrebte visuelle Wirkung, doch hatte er dafür noch nicht den geeigneten Herstellungsvorgang gefunden, es fehlte die Logik der

Produktion. Ein Zufall führte ihn zur Lösung, nämlich ein Besuch im Museum of Fine Arts in Boston, wo er in der Sammlung einen chinesischen Stein mit eingemeisselten Schriftzeichen und daneben einen davon angefertigten Abrieb sah.[11] Diese Technik war in China im 7. Jahrhundert aufgekommen und diente zur Vervielfältigung von Texten. Man legte dafür ein Papier auf den Stein, rieb dieses in die Vertiefungen ein und überzog es dann mit Tusche. Dabei blieben die vertieften Stellen weiss und liessen die Schrift negativ hervortreten. Das Modell war damit gegeben: Mullican hatte zuvor Glasätzungen gemacht, und inspiriert vom Gesehenen legte er im Atelier sogleich ein Papier auf das Glas, machte einen Abrieb und erhielt so das erste Rubbing.[12] In diesem Fall besass die Unterlage noch ihre eigene ästhetische Bedeutung als Werk; die von da an eigens zum Zweck des Abriebs hergestellten Matrizen waren dagegen unansehnlich und sollten nicht gezeigt werden, denn nun zählte allein die davon abgezogene Kopie. Damit war das Paradox formuliert – in den Rubbings war nicht das Original zum Sehen bestimmt, die Kopie setzte sich an dessen Stelle.

Unverzüglich systematisierte Mullican die Technik des Abriebs und machte sie von da an zu einem zentralen Bestandteil seiner Arbeit. Bildvorlagen konnten auf verschiedene Weise auf die Matrizen gebracht werden: einmal durch eine direkte Vorzeichnung mit einem Stift, dann durch die Projektion einer Vorlage, die nachgezeichnet wurde, stets jedoch manuell und nicht fotomechanisch. Die Matrizen für den Abrieb wurden hergestellt, indem eine Zeichnung mit dem Messer in einen Karton, später dann in MDF-Platten geritzt wurde. Entlang der mit dem Messer geführten Schnitte war das Material leicht aufgeworfen, und es entstand eine scharfe Kante, die für den Abrieb genügte. Je nachdem konnte der Abrieb so ausfallen, dass allein die Zeichnung als positives lineares Bild erschien, oder es konnte durch Reiben der gesamten Bildfläche eine tonige Struktur geschaffen werden. Statt auf Papier wurden die Abriebe nun auf farbig grundierter Leinwand ausgeführt und diese auf einen Keilrahmen aufgespannt, um Tafelbilder herzustellen, die anders als die Papiere einen Raum besetzen. Eine Standardisierung der Formate war notwendig, um die Bilder als modulare Elemente zu verwenden; Mullican entschied sich für zwei Grundtypen, nämlich ein vertikales Doppelquadrat von 8 × 4 Fuss und ein etwas gedrungeneres Format von 6 × 4 Fuss. Die Leinwände konnten entweder für sich allein stehen, in Diptychen getrennt nebeneinander auftreten oder, noch öfter, zu grösseren, wandfüllenden Bildkomplexen zusammengestellt werden. Dieses additive und kombinatorische Prinzip, das sich nicht nur in der Gestaltung von Ausstellungen, sondern auch in Projekten für architektonische Situationen bewähren sollte, fasste Mullican in die Formel „Modular mix and match".

Im enzyklopädischen Bogen, den Mullicans Œuvre schlägt,
ist mit den Abrieben eine der ältesten bekannten Vervielfälti-
gungstechniken vertreten, als Gegenpol zu seinen um 1990
begonnenen Versuchen, digitale Darstellungsformen für
die Kosmologien und die daraus abgeleiteten Stadtmodelle zu
nutzen. Mullican beschreibt die Rubbings und deren Ableitung
von einem originalen Bild so: „Hier ist eine Art unechter
Genealogie im Gange; denn in meinem Atelier habe ich die
Originalplatte, das Relief, und in der Galerie sieht man den
Abdruck, aber dieser kommt von anderswoher. Diese Beziehung
zwischen der Matrize und dem Druck bildet eine Art künstlicher
Genealogie. Der Abdruck ist kein Gemälde, keine Zeichnung,
kein Druck, nichts davon und zugleich alles davon. Er ist ein
Netzhautbild, im Sinn von Platos Schatten. Wenn ich etwas
ansehe, sieht das Auge nur das Bild auf der Netzhaut, aber das
ist nicht die Welt. Ich sehe also den Schatten, und der ist nicht
das, was da ist. Der Abdruck ist das, was das Auge sieht,
das Relief ist das wirkliche Ding.“[13] In den Rubbings hat man es
nie mit einem Bild, sondern immer nur mit einem Abbild zu tun,
mit dem Schatten von etwas, was sich buchstäblich hinter
der Leinwand verbirgt, und daraus resultiert die Erscheinung
des Abriebs als eines etwas unscharfen, indirekten Bildes.
Ebenso ist das Schattenhafte eine strukturelle Eigenschaft,
die Mullican auf dem Hintergrund des platonischen Idealismus
wie der physiologischen Wahrnehmung beschreibt.

Blickt man in der Geschichte zurück, so ist der Abrieb eine
Technik, die von Max Ernst für die surrealistische Kunst nutz-
bar gemacht wurde. Er ist die wohl konsequenteste Antwort
auf André Bretons 1924 im *Manifeste du surréalisme* vorgetra-
gene Forderung, „es handelt sich nicht darum zu zeichnen,
es handelt sich nur darum durchzupausen“[14]. Für seine Frottagen
legte Ernst strukturierte Flächen unter dünnes Zeichenpapier.
Sie wurden danach mit dem Bleistift darauf abgerieben und
nun als objektivierte, fotografieähnliche Übertragungen von
Ausschnitten aus der Wirklichkeit gedeutet. „Als Grattage fand
das Verfahren auf die Ölmalerei Anwendung. Statt des Auftrags
von Graphit liess nun die Entfernung von Farbe die Bilder
erscheinen. Diesen Vorgang konnte der Künstler variations-
reich und unterschiedlich nutzen: Mal legte er die mit mehreren
Farben präparierte Leinwand durch Abkratzen partiell frei und
brachte verborgene Farbschichten und erhabene Strukturen
untergelegter Materialien zum Vorschein, mal erzeugte er mit
flüssiger, dünn gespachtelter Farbe einzelne Formen, mal zog
er Kämme oder gezackte Spachtel heran, um die Bewegungen
der Hand seismographisch zu übertragen.“[15]

Durch seine ebenfalls als Künstler tätigen Eltern Luchita Hurtado
und Lee Mullican war Mullican in einer vom Surrealismus
geprägten Umgebung aufgewachsen und mit dessen Ästhetik
vertraut.[16] Auch wenn sein Umgang mit der Abriebtechnik

im Unterschied zu den surrealistischen Verfahren nicht darauf ausgerichtet war, den Automatismus befördern, steht seine Formulierung des schattenhaften Bildes noch immer im Zeichen des Durchpausens und erinnert an Techniken wie etwa die von Wolfgang Paalen gepflegte Fumage, das Anbringen von Rauchspuren auf Leinwand, die auf ein nicht mehr präsentes Feuer verweisen. Reste der auf das Unbewusste gerichteten Arbeit lassen sich bis in Mullicans unter Hypnose vorgenommene Arbeit als „That Person" verfolgen. Während seiner Studienzeit wurde für ihn jedoch die Produktion von Bildern als Abbildungen wichtig, wie er sie bei Andy Warhol beobachtete. An dessen Werken bewunderte Mullican, dass durch die Übertragung von Bildvorlagen mittels Siebdruck auf die Leinwand emotionslose Distanz zum Motiv erzeugt wurde. Nach wie vor war bei Warhol die Bildherstellung in der Art einer Manufaktur und nicht als industrielles Verfahren organisiert, und Mullican sollte sich in der Arbeit an Rubbings mit Hilfe von Assistenten daran halten. Neben Warhol darf Jasper Johns nicht unerwähnt bleiben, denn bereits in den 1950er Jahren schuf er mit den *Figures*, *Alphabets* und *Numbers* Werkfolgen von Bildern, in denen die Motive, nämlich die Lettern des Alphabets und die Zahlen von 0 bis 9, mittels Schablonen oder als Abdrucke auf den Bildgrund übertragen wurden. Da diese Motive ohnehin keine materiellen Realitäten repräsentieren, sondern reine Zeichen sind, kann ihr „Abbild" nicht für sich oder für ein Ding stehen, es verweist notwendigerweise auf eine ideelle Ebene.[17] Dies war nur ein für Mullicans Werk folgenreicher Moment aus der viel weiter reichenden Auseinandersetzung, die Johns mit der Spur einer im Bild nicht präsenten Realität betrieb. Vom Biss in die Bildfläche bis zu Abgüssen und Abrieben von Körperteilen unternahm er immer neue Manöver, um die Figur des Künstlers vermeintlich fassbar zu machen. Doch im Unterschied zu Mullican, für den jedes im Abrieb vorgefundene spezifische Fragment der Realität seinen Ort in einer Kosmologie erhält, entfernte sich Johns von einer angenommenen Ordnung und hielt die Gewissheit darüber, worauf die Spuren verweisen, in der Schwebe.

Betrachtet man den Korpus der Rubbings aus der Sicht von Mullicans Kosmologie der fünf Welten, dann lassen sie sich in der grünen Welt als Material aus Ölkreide, Leinwand und Holz betrachten. In der blauen „world unframed" sind sie Tafeln, die aufgehängt werden können und Wände bilden, während sie in der gelben „world framed" als Kunstwerke verstanden werden, die Gemälden, Zeichnungen und Drucken gleichen und dennoch weder das eine noch das andere davon sind. In der schwarz-weissen Welt wird über die Rubbings gesprochen und geschrieben – aktuell befinden wir uns gerade darin –, und in der roten Welt des Subjektiven werden sie für den Betrachter zu den Phantasien, die er mit ihrer Bildwelt verbindet. Das bedeutet, dass Mullican in den Rubbings einerseits bestimmte

Motive präsentiert, die für seine Arbeit von Bedeutung sind, dass
sie aber zugleich selbstreferentiell begriffen werden können,
denn sie bleiben materiell und symbolisch stets Bestandteile
seines Ideengebäudes. Im Bewusstsein dieses Dispositivs lässt
sich verfolgen, wie Mullican das Medium nutzte und welche
Motive er darin zur Darstellung brachte.

Als Mullican erstmals Rubbings in einer Ausstellung zeigte, 1984
bei Mary Boone in New York, waren darunter sowohl
einzelne Bildtafeln wie auch grosse Schaubilder aus mehreren
Einzeltafeln.[18] Zu sehen waren die für einzelne Welten der
Kosmologie verwendeten Ikonen, die sich weder in Zeichnungen
noch auf Postern und Flaggen angemessen darstellen liessen,
nämlich die Aufreihung der Elemente und die autogenen Zellen,
Boiler, Dampfmaschine, Lunge als Maschinen, die Zustände
verändern, der Querschnitt durch das Dampfschiff als Sinnbild
sozialer, die Kathedrale als Sinnbild kultureller und religiöser
Ordnung. In den zusammengesetzten Schaubildern wurde
die Kosmologie der fünf Welten bildhaft interpretiert. Anhand
der Wiederholung von Motiven und der Differenzierung in
schwarz-weisse und farbige Versionen demonstrierte Mullican,
dass es sich bei den Rubbings nicht um Originale wie bei
Gemälden, sondern um Reproduktionen handelte.

Folgt man dem hier vorliegenden Katalog, so erhält man
anhand der verwendeten Motive eine konzentrierte Übersicht
über Mullicans Werk; man begreift, wie er mit den von ihm
entwickelten Themen arbeitet und wie sich im Lauf der Jahre
neue Perspektiven darauf ergeben. Bereits in den ersten
Rubbings wird klar, dass die von Max Ernst erwähnte strukturelle
Verwandtschaft der Frottage mit der Collage[19] unter verän-
derten Bedingungen auch für die Rubbings Gültigkeit besitzt.
So produzierte Mullican 1986 einzelne Bereiche der Kosmologie,
nämlich die Elemente in einer prähistorischen Landschaft,
die Geschichte und die Künste und drittens die Stadt als Einzelbilder und vereinte sie danach als vertikale zusammenhängende
Sequenz auf einer Leinwandbahn. Im Bereich der Stadt wiederum finden sich erneut die aus den ersten Rubbings bekannten
Elemente, nämlich die Kathedrale, die Dampfmaschine, die
Querschnitte durch den Schiffsbauch und durch das Innere
eines Hauses. Indem Mullican ganze Matrizen kombinierte und
zu Schautafeln zusammenfügte, indem er Ausschnitte daraus
wählte und diese auf einer Tafel unmittelbar nebeneinander-
setzte, hatte er einen Weg gefunden, um die der Kosmologie
inhärente Kombinatorik in der Herstellung der Rubbings aus-
zuspielen. Die symbolischen Positionen der ersten Kosmologie
erschienen, aus dem Narrativ gelöst, als disponible Figuren,
die innerhalb der Struktur der zweiten Kosmologie eingesetzt
werden konnten. 1989 entstand eine Reihe von vertikal zwei-
geteilten Arbeiten aus einer oder zwei Leinwänden, in denen
die bereits eingeführten Figuren – die Anatomie, die Maschinen

für die Gewinnung von Energie – mit der elementaren Welt konfrontiert und durch die Wahl der Farben spezifiziert wurden; wenig später sollten mit der Pariser Oper, dem Generatorraum und dem *Roundhouse* weitere emblematische Bilder folgen.

Eine erweiterte Dimension erhielt diese Produktionsweise mit dem 1987 realisierten *Dallas Project* – Mullican zufolge eine der grössten je von einem Künstler realisierten Druckarbeiten –, von dem eine erste Version auf gelben und roten, die Welten der Künste und des Subjektiven signalisierenden Bildgründen abgezogen wurde, danach eine mehrfarbige Version, in der die einzelnen Bildtafeln durch die Farben spezifischen Kontexten zugewiesen wurden. Im Zentrum des *Dallas Project* steht das Bild der Stadt. Sie ist eine reale Stadt mit Gebäuden und zugleich eine Projektion der Kosmologie auf eine Fläche, wie sich anhand der schematischen Stadtpläne erweist, die von Mullican um diese Zeit gezeichnet und in Rubbings verbreitet wurden. In der Stadt sind die Welten des reinen Materials, des Unbewussten, der Sprache, der Künste und des Subjektiven verbildlicht: „Die Stadt wird so zu einer Allegorie, einem allegorischen Plan, durch den man gehen kann. Die Stadt ist der Punkt, an dem ich die Konzepte hinter dem Plan berühre.“[20] In den Rubbings von 1991–1992 entfaltete Mullican diesen Gedanken, indem er weitere Stadtpläne entwarf, die entweder für sich standen, nebeneinander gestellt wurden, einander als verschachtelte Pläne überlagerten oder dann die bereits bekannte Bildwelt als Grundrissbestandteile in sich aufnahmen – Symbole aus der Kosmologie, Ausschnitte aus der Evolutionstafel, den Maschinen und aus der exemplarischen Darstellung der fünf Welten. Schliesslich führte diese Fortentwicklung von kosmologischer Tafel und Stadtplänen in die bereits erwähnte Vorstellung des „Five into One“.

Nach einer Unterbrechung begann Mullican 1996 damit, Seiten aus Notizbüchern für Rubbings zu verwenden; 2003 setzte er dies fort. Mit der Übertragung von handschriftlichen Aufzeichnungen auf Leinwände änderte sich der Charakter der Arbeiten: Was zuvor private Notiz gewesen war, wurde durch die Transformation auf Schautafeln zur definitiven Formulierung und umgekehrt wurden die grossformatigen Tafeln nun zum Schauplatz der Entwicklung von Gedanken und ihren Verzweigungen. 2007 trat Mullicans fiktives Alter ego, „That Person“, in die Rubbings ein. Die während Hypnosesitzungen geschaffenen, dieser anderen, unbekannten Person zugeschriebenen Zeichnungen sind ein von den Kosmologien getrennt verlaufender Werkstrang. Hat man es dort mit der Modellierung, also einer konzeptionellen Haltung zu tun, so hier mit der Beobachtung, also einer Deduktion. Über „That Person“, jene Person, liegt keinerlei Wissen vor, anhand der Zeichnungen und der darin geschriebenen Aussagen, die sie hinterlässt, entsteht eine Vorstellung von ihrer Welt.[21] Lernen von jener Person bedeutet für Mullican, den Spekulationen über die von anderen erlebte Realität Informationen zu unterlegen, das heisst, die Welt nicht mittels eines abstrakten Entwurfs, sondern durch ein anderes Bewusstsein zu konstruieren.

Unberührt davon ging die Arbeit an den kosmologischen Plänen und der daraus abgeleiteten Stadt weiter. Im Prinzip hatte Mullican schon in den 1980er Jahren die Stadtpläne zu einem Feld erweitert, innerhalb dessen die Städte systematisch kombiniert und zu abstrakten Mustern wurden. Damals entlehnte er die Darstellungsweise der angewandten Kunst, indem er das Muster als Teppich weben liess[22]; nun konnten mittels der Rubbing-Technik auf viel einfachere Weise die durch die Kombinatorik freiwerdenden Möglichkeiten auf Bildtafeln durchgespielt werden. Die Pläne wurden zum Gitterraster, in dem sich die farbigen Quadrate, Rechtecke und Halbkreisflächen frei anordnen liessen, und je nachdem war die daraus konstruierte Welt auf die Künste, auf Sprache, Elemente oder das Subjektive zentriert. In der linearen Version mit den zu einem quadratischen Feld gefügten schematischen Stadtplänen liessen sich weitere Kombinationen herstellen, eine Fülle von imaginären Ordnungen, die das Denken anspornten. Wie könnte man sich eine auf die „world unframed" zentrierte Kosmologie denken, wie eine Kosmologie, die auf die Elemente oder auf das Subjektive zentriert wäre, und was bedeutet es, wenn eine dieser Welten von einer anderen begrenzt wird? In den 2012 folgenden Rubbings besetzten die Eigenschaften einer einzigen Welt den kosmologischen Plan auf Teilflächen oder zur Gänze, und im Gegenzug fügte Mullican in der Sequenz der Rubbings von 2013 Bildausschnitte als symbolische Repräsentanten der Realität in verschiedenen Positionen und Kontexten in die Pläne ein. Diese materiellen Elemente hatte er im Jahr zuvor in der umfangreichen Reihe von kleinformatigen Tafeln eingeführt, als Einzelbilder und als Bildpaare, um erneut auf den Status der Abbildungen als Kopien hinzuweisen. Mit den dafür verwendeten Ausschnitten aus Comics knüpfte Mullican an die eingangs erwähnten Details aus einem imaginären Universum an. Im Spiel mit den Plänen kehrte er die Voraussetzungen ein weiteres Mal um, indem er sie nun als perspektivische Darstellung eines Interieurs interpretierte und auf diese Weise eine paradigmatische Situation schuf, in die er Figuren, Dinge und kosmologische Pläne einfügte. Zugleich realisierte Mullican eine weitere Reihe von Rubbings mit den für sich stehenden symbolischen Zeichen bzw. den Wörtern für die Figuren der Kosmologien – *God, Fate, Heaven, Hell, Elements* usf. – und ebenso mit den Ordnungen, nach denen sich das alltägliche Leben vollzieht – mit der Reihenfolge der Stunden, Tage und Monate, dem Tagesablauf mit den Mahlzeiten. Die Reduktion auf die primären Zeichen mit ihrem Versprechen von Klärung und Regelung war das Gegenstück zur Flut von Details, welche die Reihe der Comic-Elemente ins Spiel gebracht hatte. Zugleich teilten sich die kosmologischen

Pläne in eine Sequenz von Teilflächen auf, kleinformatigen Rubbings, die in sich wiederum als potentielle Ordnungen gelesen werden konnten.

Nicht von ungefähr hatte Mullican die Bilder von Maschinen, welche die Aggregatzustände von Materialien verändern und Energie generieren, als Sinnbilder für seine Arbeit gewählt, denn mit den Rubbings hatte er ein Medium gefunden, das adäquater als jede andere Darstellungsweise der Transformation von Bildmaterial jeglicher Art dienen und es für die Präsentation auf Schautafeln aufbereiten sollte, ein Instrument der Kombinatorik, das Vervielfältigung und Vereinheitlichung erlaubte – eben: „Modular mix and match".

1 „It was the idea that all I see are light patterns. I had deconstructed the world to simple patterns and I made artwork about light reflecting and light emanating. When you say that all you see are light patterns, you remove all subject matter. There is no difference between me looking at you and me looking at a ladder. They are the same because everything is simply abstract." Matt Mullican, *Im Gespräch/Conversations*, mit/with Koen Brams, Dirk Pültau, DuMont Buchverlag, Köln 2011 (DuMont Dokumente), S. 44, engl. S. 154.

2 „I also made line drawings of a place that did not exist and never would exist. But the comic book fragments and the drawings were detailed and that posed a problem: how does a detail exist of something that does not exist? My answer is that it exists because it is not about the physicality of the light pattern. It is about what the pattern represents. It is not about the physical world but it is about the representation of the physical world and I represented that world through line drawings. But if all I see are light patterns, then where is life in those patterns? Life exists in our subjective experience, in the senses. Therefore, pictured reality is equal to reality. The fictional is equal to the real. Or at least, such was my premise. Everything is abstract and it is only through our history and culture that we construct a reality." Matt Mullican, *Im Gespräch/Conversations*, wie Anm. 1, S. 44–45, engl. S. 154.

3 *Matt Mullican: Subject Element Sign Frame World*, Skira Rizzoli Publications, New York 2013, S. 121.

4 Eindrücklich schildert dies Allan McCollum in seinem frühen Aufsatz zu Mullicans Werk, "Matt Mullican's World", *Reallife Magazine*, Nr. 5, Winter 1980, S. 4–13.

5 „My cosmology is a model for a cosmology; it is not a cosmology.", in: „Interview Matt Mullican and Michael Tarantino", in: *Matt Mullican: The MIT Project* [Ausst.-Kat., 12.5.–1.7.1990], MIT List Visual Arts Center, Cambridge, Massachusetts 1990, S. 18.

6 Matt Mullican, *Im Gespräch/Conversations*, wie Anm. 1, S. 42, engl. S. 152.

7 Ebenda.

8 „[…] when you're in the green world, all five worlds look green; when you're in the blue world, all five worlds look blue; when you're in the yellow world, all five worlds look yellow; and when you're in the black-and-white world – the language world – it all looks that way." *Matt Mullican: A Drawing Translates the Way of Thinking* [Ausst.-Kat., 21.11.2008–5.2.2009], Drawing Center, New York 2008 (=Drawing Papers, 82), S. 17.

9 Vgl. *Matt Mullican: Subject Element Sign Frame World*, wie Anm. 3, S. 85.

10 Vgl. ebenda, S. 177.

11 Holland Cotter, „Matt Mullican: Public Paradise", in: *Matt Mullican: Banners, Monuments and the City, an Exhibition of Work for Public Spaces* [Ausst.-Kat., 11.9.–18.10.1987], Goldie Paley Gallery, Moore College of Art, Philadelphia 1987, S. 8.

12 Beispiele für diese ersten Rubbings sind abgebildet in: Matt Mullican, *World Frame* [Ausst.-Kat., 30.10.1992–9.1.1993] Contemporary Art Museum, University of South Florida, Tampa, Florida 1993, S. 201–205.

13 „There is a kind of fake history that occurs, because in my studio I have the master plate, the relief, and in the gallery you see the rubbing, but it is taken from another place. This relationship between the master and the print creates a kind of artificial history. The rubbing is not a painting, a drawing or a print, none of them and all of them. It is a retinal image in the sense of Plato's shadow. When I look at something, what any eye sees is the retinal image, but the world is not that. What the rubbing represents is what the eye sees, the relief is it." *Matt Mullican: Works 1972–1992*, Hg. von Ulrich Wilmes, Verlag der Buchhandlung Walther König, Köln 1993, S. 116.

14 „Il ne s'agit pas de dessiner, il ne s'agit que de calquer", André Breton, *Œuvres complètes*, I. Édition établie par Marguerite Bonnet avec, pour ce volume, la collaboration de Philippe Bernier, Etienne-Alain Hubert et José Pierre, Editions Gallimard, Paris 1988 (Bibliothèque de la Pléïade, 346), S. 325.

15 Jürgen Pech, in: *Kunstmuseum Winterthur: Katalog der Gemälde und Skulpturen*, Bd. 3, hg. von Dieter Schwarz, Kunstmuseum Winterthur/Richter Verlag, Winterthur und Düsseldorf 2011, S. 242–243.

16 Vgl. dazu *Mullican + Mullican* [Ausst.-Kat., 4.4.–26.5.1989], Jonson Gallery of the University Art Museum, Albuquerque, New Mexico 1989.

17 Vgl. dazu Roberta Bernstein, *Jasper Johns' Paintings and Sculptures 1954–1974: „The Changing Focus of the Eye"*, UMI Research Press, Ann Arbor, Michigan: 1985 (Studies in the Fine Arts: The Avant-Garde, 46), S. 21–27.

18 Vgl. *Matt Mullican* [Ausst.-Kat., 1.–29.12.1984], Mary Boone/Michael Werner, New York 1984.

19 „[…] sie [die Frottage] nimmt in seiner eigenen Entwicklung einen noch grösseren Platz ein als die Collage, von der sie sich überhaupt, wie er glaubt, nicht grundsätzlich unterscheidet." Max Ernst, „Biographische Notizen (Wahrheitgewebe und Lügengewebe)", in: *Max Ernst* [Ausst.-Kat. Wallraf-Richartz-Museum, Köln, 28.12.1962–3.3.1963; Kunsthaus Zürich, 23.3.–28.4.1963], Wallraf-Richartz-Museum, Köln 1962, S. 28.

20 „So the city becomes an allegory, an allegorical chart that one could walk through. The city is an interface between me and the concepts behind the chart." Matt Mullican, in: „Interview Matt Mullican and Michael Tarantino", wie Anm. 5, S. 18.

21 Vgl. dazu Ulrich Wilmes, „Jene Person", in: *Matt Mullican: Learning from that Person's Work* [Ausst.-Kat., 19.3.–12.6.2005]. Museum Ludwig/Verlag der Buchhandlung Walther König, Köln 2005, S. 8–14; engl. „That Person", S. 15–21.

22 *Untitled (Field of Cities)*, 1986, Wolle, 114,5 × 58,5 cm (*Matt Mullican: Banners, Monuments and the City*, wie Anm. 11, Nr. 7).

ANMERKUNGEN DES HERAUSGEBERS

Der vorliegende Katalog umfasst die von Matt Mullican seit 1984 geschaffenen Rubbings auf Leinwand, die dem Autor bekannt wurden. Rubbings auf Papier ebenso wie als Multiples konzipierte Rubbings auf Leinwand und die entsprechenden Vorarbeiten sind darin nicht enthalten. Der Katalog kann bezüglich der Rubbings auf Leinwand nicht den Anspruch auf Vollständigkeit erheben, da keine Aufzeichnungen oder Werklisten des Künstlers existieren. Bei der Erstellung des Katalogs war man deshalb auf Bildmaterial und andere, nicht systematisch geordnete Unterlagen im Archiv des Künstlers oder auf Angaben seiner Galerien angewiesen. Hilfreich war, dass die Photoalben mit frühen Werkaufnahmen im Sommer 2015 aus dem New Yorker Atelier in die Mai 36 Galerie in Zürich verbracht wurden, wo sie für die Bearbeitung dieses Katalogs zugänglich waren. Eine Lücke besteht besonders hinsichtlich der Rubbings, die im Zusammenhang mit Aufträgen für bestimmte Gebäude oder Firmen entstanden. Im Archiv des Künstlers fehlen dazu jegliche Angaben, und verschiedene Recherchen verliefen ergebnislos, da die Gebäude heute anders genutzt werden oder da die Firmen, die damals als Besteller auftraten, nicht mehr existieren.

Was hier vorliegt, ist eine Auflistung der Rubbings und kein Catalogue raisonné. Für eine solche Publikation, die zu jedem Werk einen Apparat mit Angaben zu den Eigentümern der Werke und den oft wechselnden Standorten, zur Ausstellungsgeschichte und zur Literatur enthält, fehlte sowohl die Zeit wie die Dokumentation. Der Katalog versteht sich deshalb als praktisches Instrument, um Mullicans Arbeit und ihren Verlauf über drei Jahrzehnte anhand eines bestimmten Werktypus näher kennenzulernen.

Die Angaben zu den Rubbings sind wie folgt gegliedert:

Titel: Die Werke sind alle ohne Titel, doch folgt in Klammern eine Ergänzung, welche die Darstellung kurz umschreibt.

Datierung: Die Rubbings wurden von Mullican kaum signiert und datiert, was die Zuordnung zu den Entstehungsjahren

zuweilen erschwert. Zudem erscheinen bestimmte Motive
mehrfach und über längere Zeitdauer. Manche Datierungen
konnten aus bestimmten Zusammenhängen – etwa anhand
der Erstausstellung von Rubbings-Gruppen – erschlossen
oder aufgrund der Erinnerung des Künstlers angegeben werden. Aufgeführt sind die Rubbings nach dem angenommenen
Entstehungsjahr; innerhalb eines Jahres sind sie nach
Motivgruppen geordnet, denn die tatsächliche Reihenfolge
der Entstehung lässt sich nicht rekonstruieren.

Technik: Alle Rubbings sind auf grundierten Leinwänden ausgeführt. Medium ist stets ein Ölkreidestift. Den verwendeten
Grundierungen ist gemeinsam, dass es sich nicht um Ölfarben,
sondern um wasserlösliche Farben auf Acrylbasis oder um
ähnliche Fabrikate handelt. Deshalb konnte auf eine Beschrei-
bung der Technik bei den einzelnen Werken verzichtet werden.

Masse: Mullican arbeitete stets auf Standardformaten in Inches
oder Fuss. Erst die letzten Rubbings, die im Berliner Atelier
realisiert wurden, basieren teilweise auf Formaten in Zentime-
tern. Die häufigsten Formate sind 6 × 4 bzw. 8 × 4 Fuss, d.h.
183 × 122 cm bzw. 244 × 122 cm. In der untenstehenden Tabelle
sind der Einfachheit halber die Umrechnungen der angelsäch-
sischen in europäische Massangaben abzulesen.

Standort: Es wurde darauf verzichtet, die Standorte der Werke
anzugeben, da diese sehr oft nicht eruierbar waren.

Anlass zur Publikation dieses Katalogs ist die Ausstellung von
Matt Mullican, die im Sommer 2016 im Kunstmuseum Winterthur
und anschliessend in der Kunsthalle Vogelmann in Heilbronn
stattfindet. Anstelle des üblichen Ausstellungskatalogs schien
es sinnvoller, die zur Verfügung stehenden Mittel in eine beson-
dere Publikation zu investieren, die über den Anlass hinaus
für das Studium von Mullicans Arbeit nützlich bleibt. So kam
der Gedanke auf, sich auf ein bestimmtes Medium zu konzen-
trieren, um daran exemplarisch das Vorgehen des Künstlers
darzustellen. In der Einführung zum Katalog ist dazu Näheres
nachzulesen.

Der Herausgeber möchte allen danken, die es ermöglicht haben,
innert kurzer Zeit diesen Katalog zusammenzustellen und zu
veröffentlichen. In erster Linie geht mein Dank an den Künstler,
der meinen Vorschlag begeistert aufnahm und mir in langen
Gesprächen zahllose Hinweise zum Verständnis der Rubbings
und zum Auffinden der Werke gab. Dankbar bin ich für sein
Vertrauen, und ich hoffe, ihm mit diesem Katalog etwas zurück-
geben zu können.

Es wäre nicht möglich gewesen, diesen Katalog ohne die
tatkräftige Unterstützung der Mai 36 Galerie in Zürich zu

realisieren, die seit 1988 Mullicans Werk vertritt. Victor Gisler
danke ich für seine Bereitschaft zur Zusammenarbeit und
für die Informationen, die er mir ohne Umschweife zur Verfügung
stellte. Dankbar bin ich auch dafür, dass seine Mitarbeiterin
Justine Hauer mir bei meinen Recherchen assistieren durfte.
Enthusiastisch arbeitete sie an diesem Projekt mit und
nahm sich zahlreicher Fragen und des Zusammentragens der
Abbildungen an. In den Dank möchte ich auch Anna Caruso,
Anna Bleuler und Peter Baracchi einschliessen. Dankbar bin
ich ferner allen Galerien, mit denen Mullican in den vergangenen
Jahren gearbeitet hat und die ebenfalls mit Informationen
und Bildmaterial zur Erstellung dieses Katalogs beitrugen,
nämlich Brooke Alexander, New York; Silvia Dauder, ProjecteSD,
Barcelona; Massimo De Carlo, Mailand; Peter Freeman, Inc.,
New York; Cristina Guerra, Lissabon; Georg Kargl, Wien; Michael
Klein, New York; Martin Klosterfelde, Berlin; Capitain Petzel,
Berlin; Micheline Szwajcer, Brüssel; Johann Widauer, Innsbruck;
Tracy Williams, New York. Ebenfalls danke ich folgenden
Personen und Institutionen für ihre bereitwillige Hilfe: David Gray,
New York; Peter Heimer, Berlin; Brigitte von Trotha-Ribbentrop,
Berlin; Edward A. Vazquez und Margaret W. Wallace, Middlebury
College, Middlebury, Vermont; Actelion Pharmaceuticals Ltd.,
Allschwil; AXA Konzern AG, Kunstsammlung, Köln; Bonhams,
Los Angeles; Christie's, Zürich; Cornette de Saint Cyr, Paris;
Hirshhorn Museum and Sculpture Garden, Washington, D.C.;
Kunsthaus Zürich; Lempertz Auktionen, Köln; Los Angeles
County Museum of Art, Los Angeles; Los Angeles Modern
Auctions, Van Nuys, CA; Öffentliche Versicherung Braunschweig;
The Progressive Art Collection, Mayfield Village, OH; Rago Arts
& Auction Center, Lambertville, NJ; Sotheby's, Zürich; Three Star
Books, Paris; UBS Art Collection, Zürich; Villa Grisebach, Berlin;
Whitney Museum of American Art, New York. In Lionel Bovier
von JRP|Ringier und seinem Nachfolger Clément Dirié fanden
wir für dieses Projekt die geeigneten Verleger, und in Nicolas
Eigenheer einen engagierten Gestalter.

Dankbar darf ich schliesslich erwähnen, dass die Max Kohler-
Stiftung mit einem grosszügigen Beitrag die Ausstellung
von Matt Mullican im Kunstmuseum Winterthur und damit auch
diese Publikation unterstützte, und ich danke der Stiftung
und ihrem Präsidenten, Dr. Georg von Segesser, herzlich dafür.
Meinem Kollegen Dr. Marc Gundel, Direktor der Städtischen
Museen Heilbronn, danke ich für seine Bereitschaft, sich nicht
nur auf die Ausstellung einzulassen, sondern auch diesen
Katalog mitzutragen.

CM	FEET/FUSS	INCHES
76	2.5	30
91.5	3	36
122	4	48
127		50
142	4.5	56
183	6	72
213	7	84
228.5	7.5	90
244	8	96
274	9	108
305	10	120
335	11	132
366	12	144
488	16	192
508		200
609.5	20	240
731.5	24	288
762	25	300
914.5	30	360
975	32	384
1036	34	408

CATALOGUE

1984–2016

1984

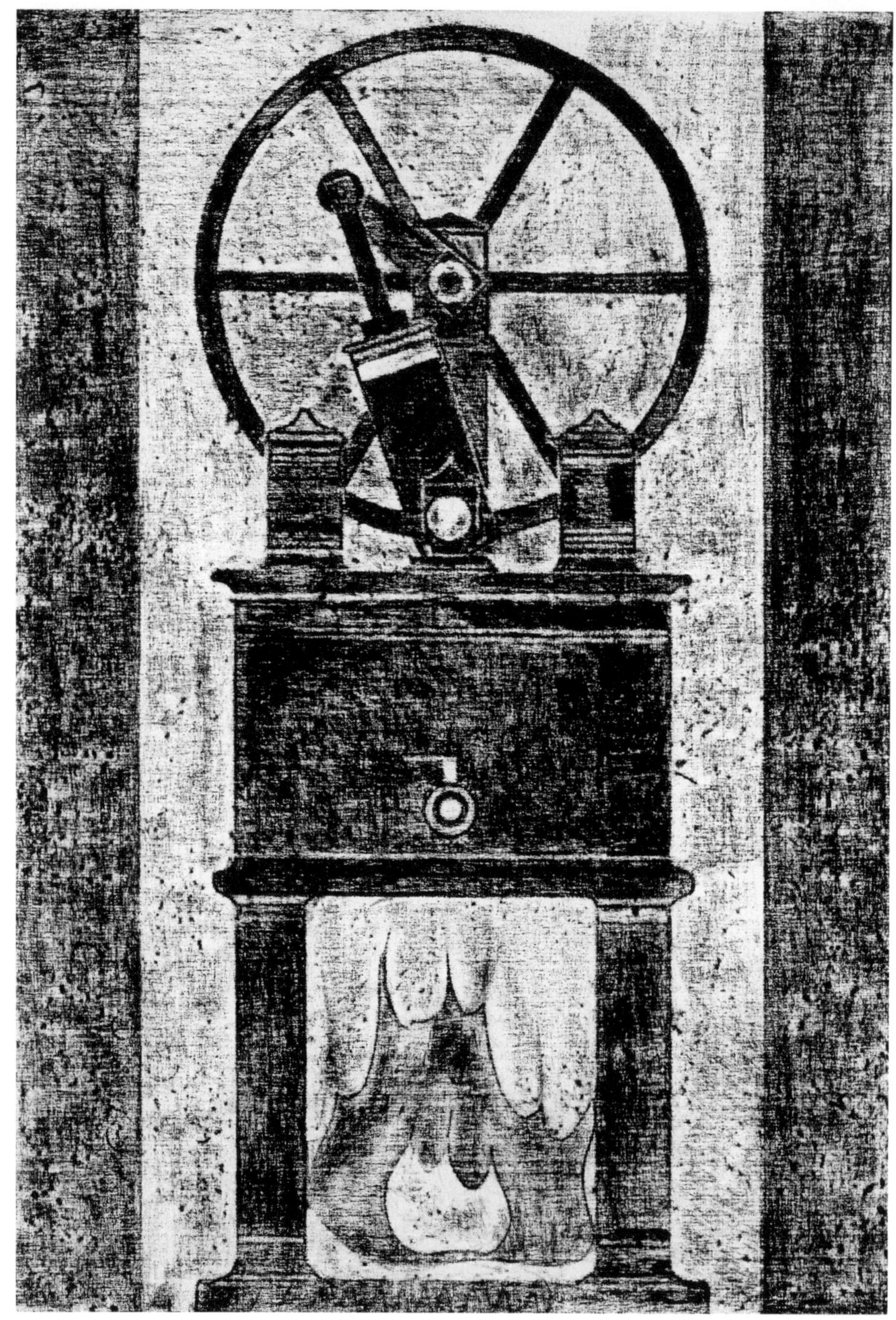

1984.1 Untitled (Steam Machine), 183 × 122 cm

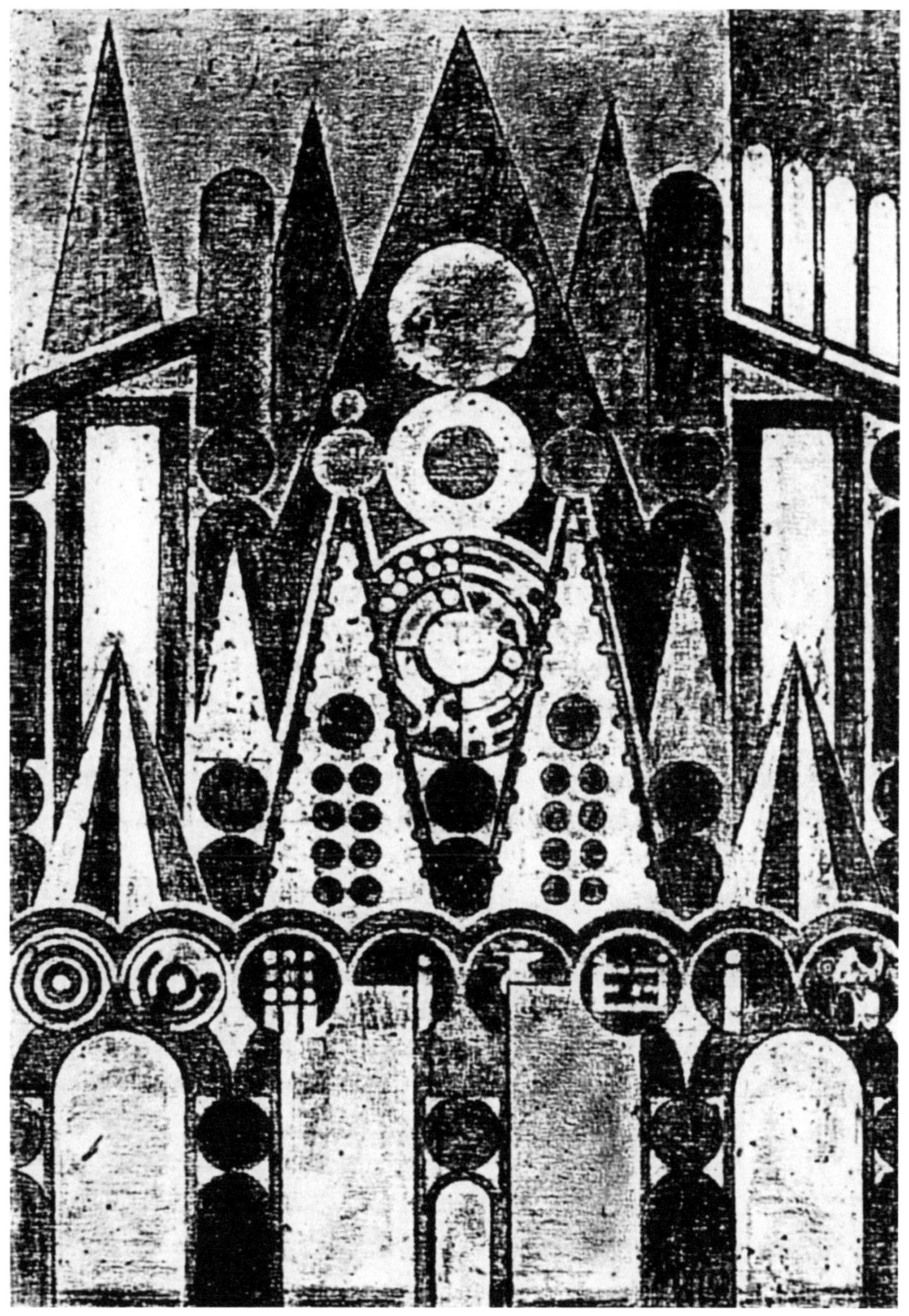

1984.2 Untitled (Cathedral), 183 × 122 cm

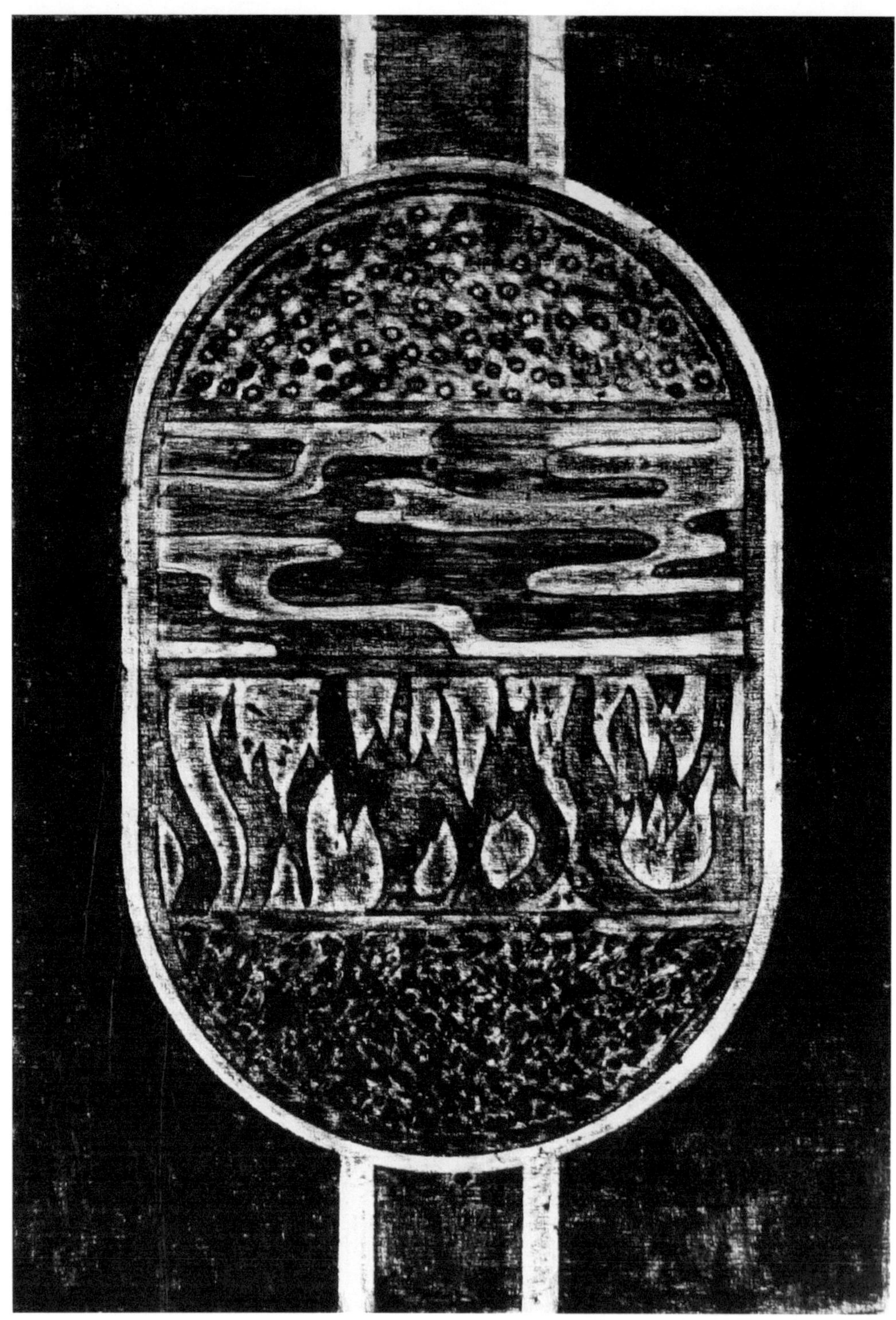

1984.3 Untitled (Boiler), 183 × 122 cm

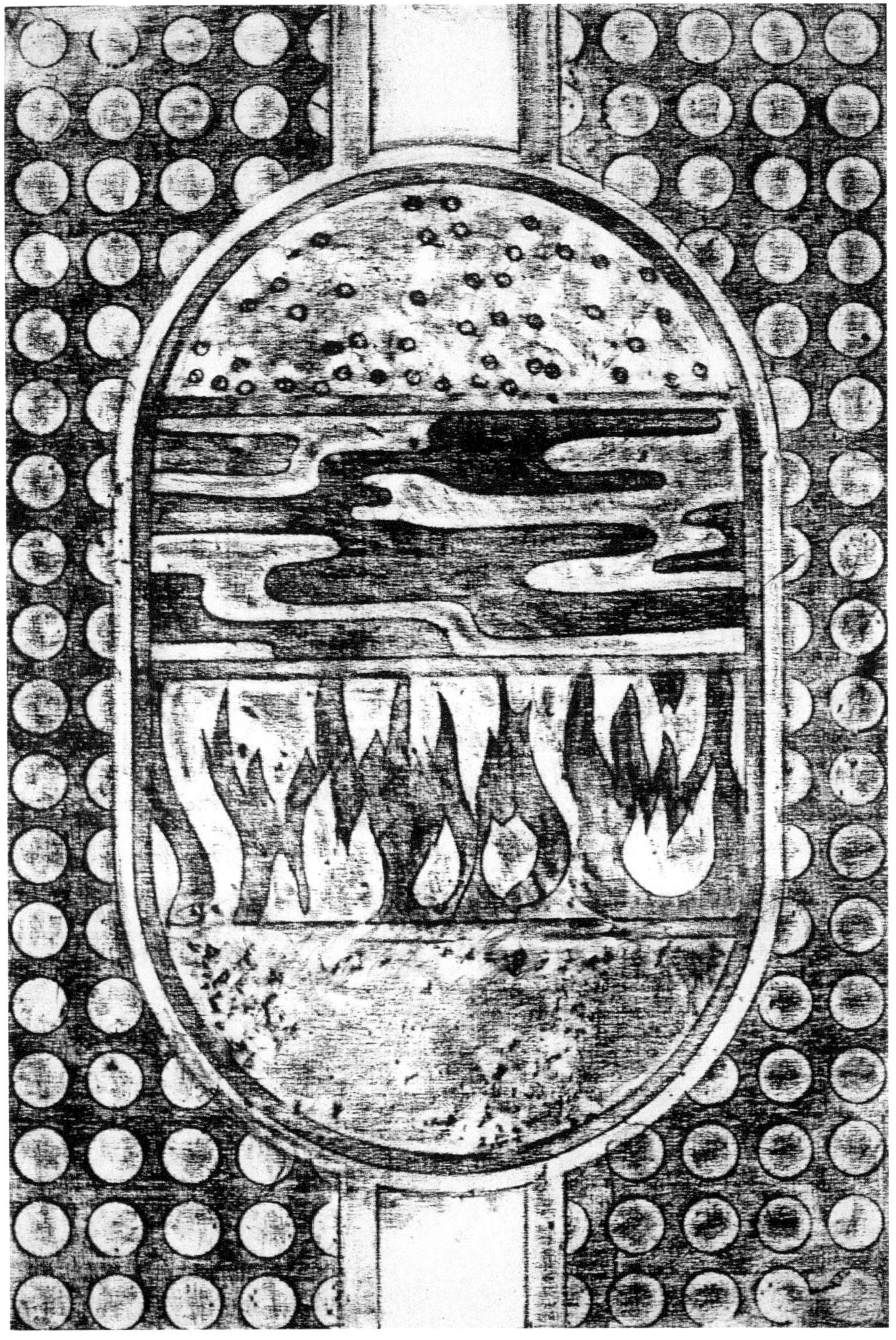

1984.4 Untitled (Boiler), 183 × 122 cm

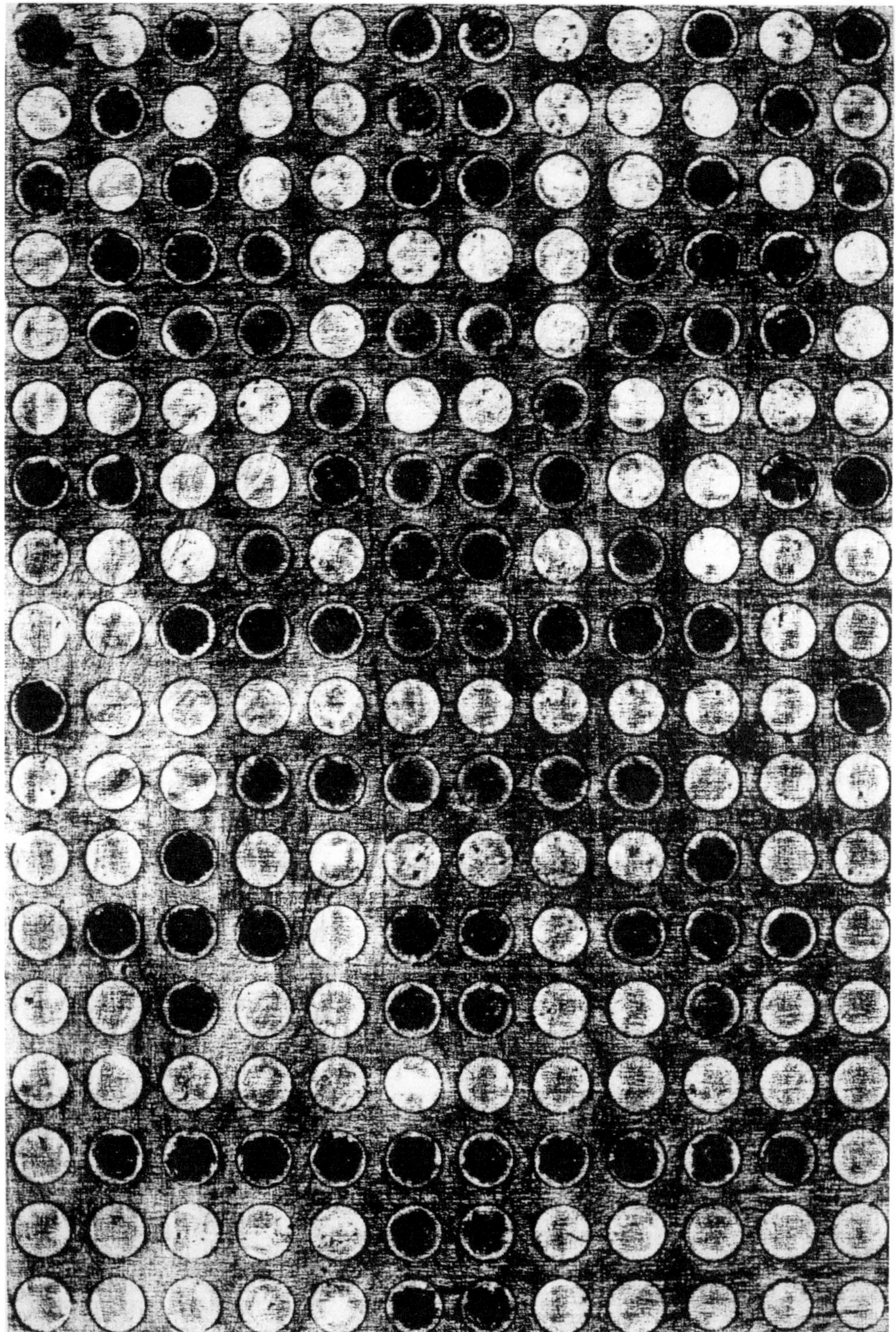

1984.5 Untitled (Elements in Patterns), 183 × 122 cm

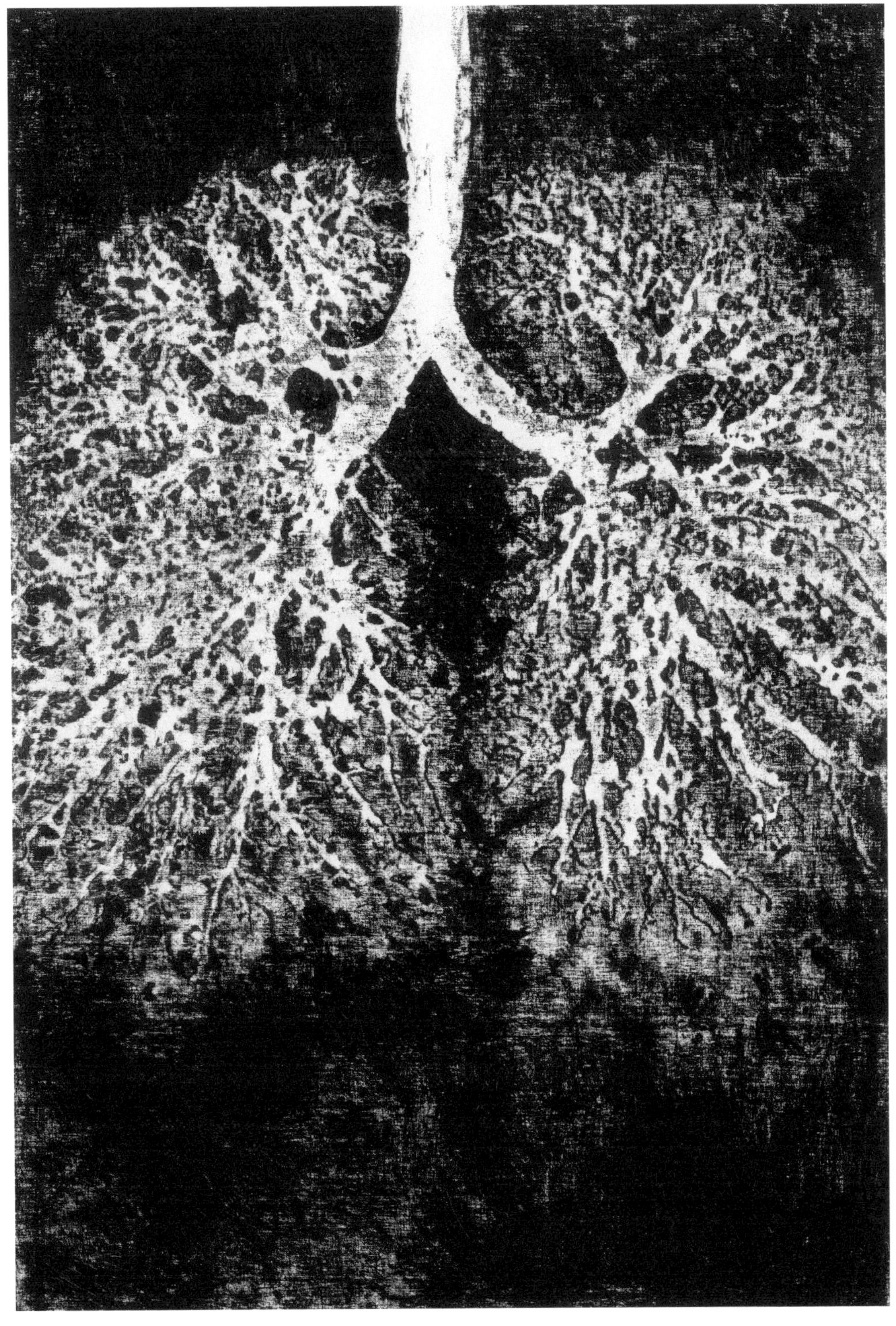

1984.6 Untitled (Lungs), 183 × 122 cm

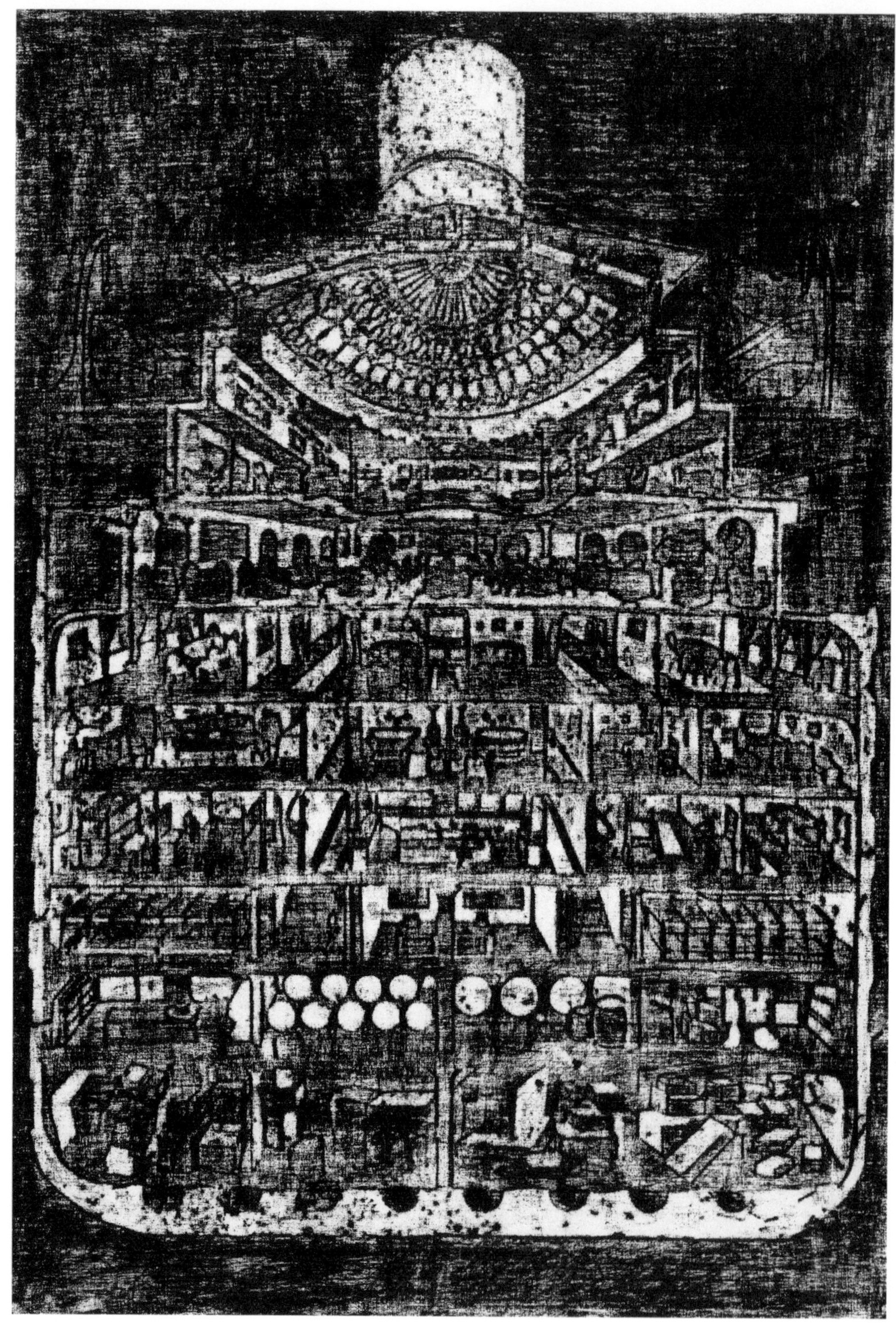

1984.7 Untitled (Steamship Cutaway), 183 × 122 cm

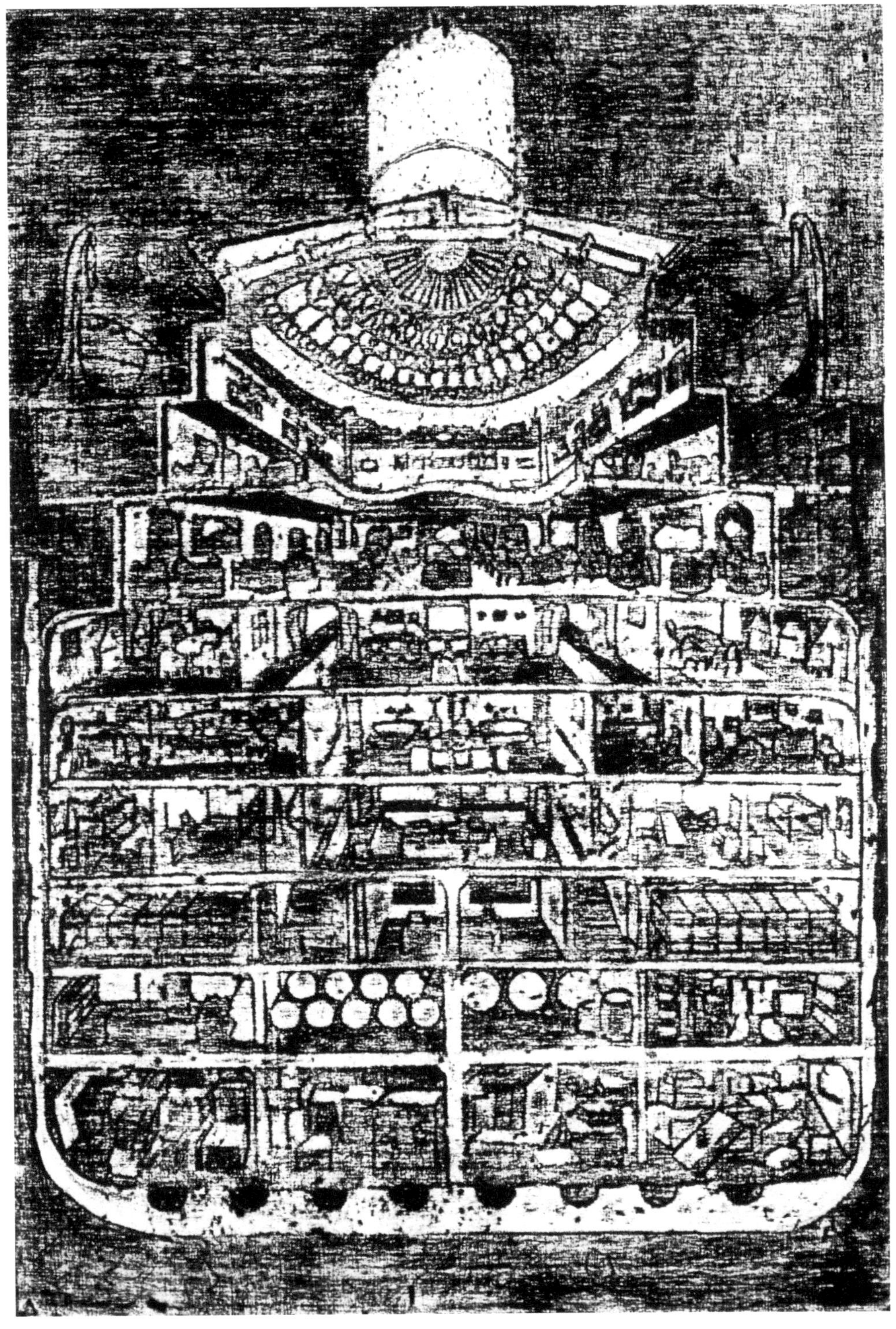

1984.8 Untitled (Steamship Cutaway), 183 × 122 cm

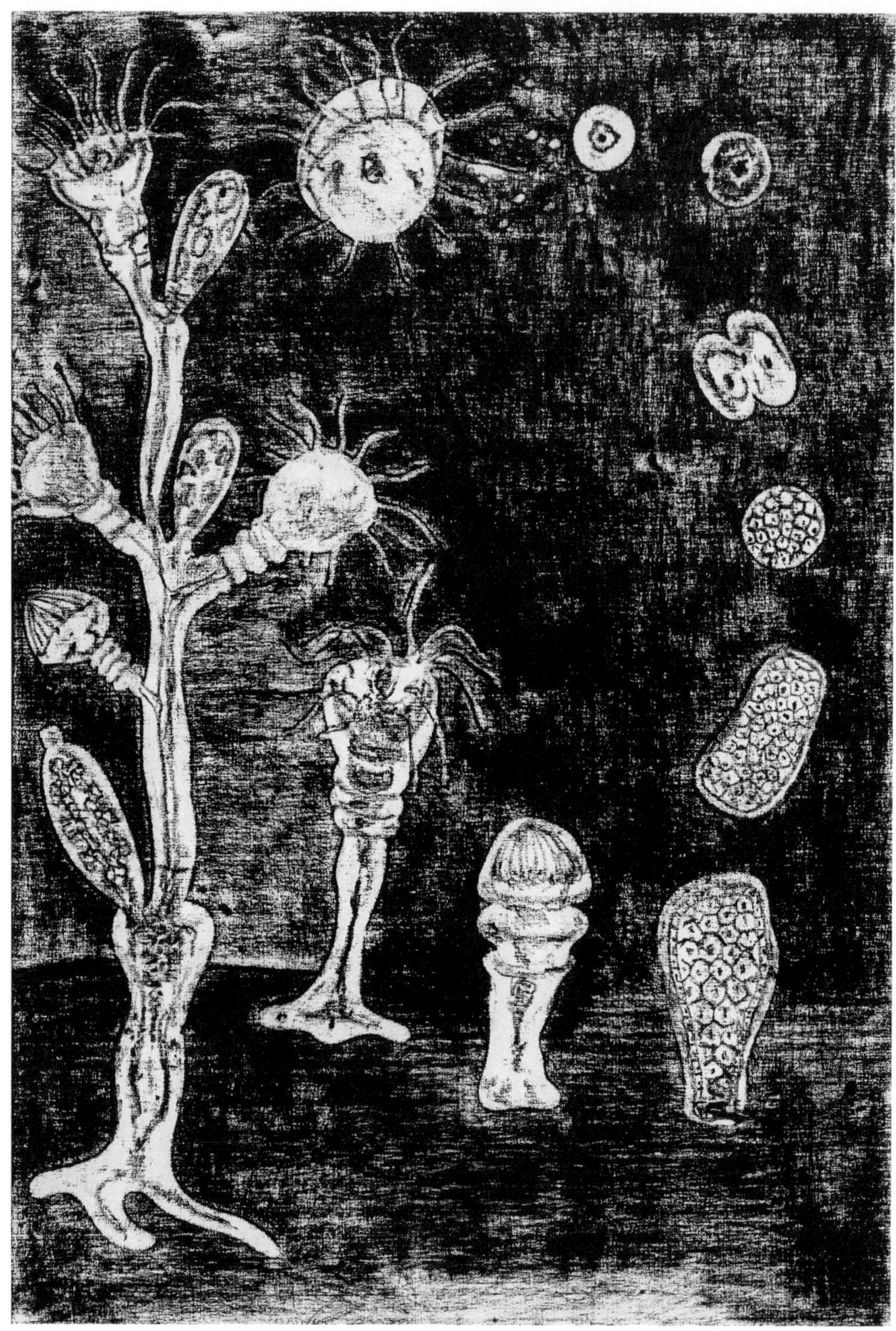

1984.9 Untitled (Autogenic Cells), 183 × 122 cm

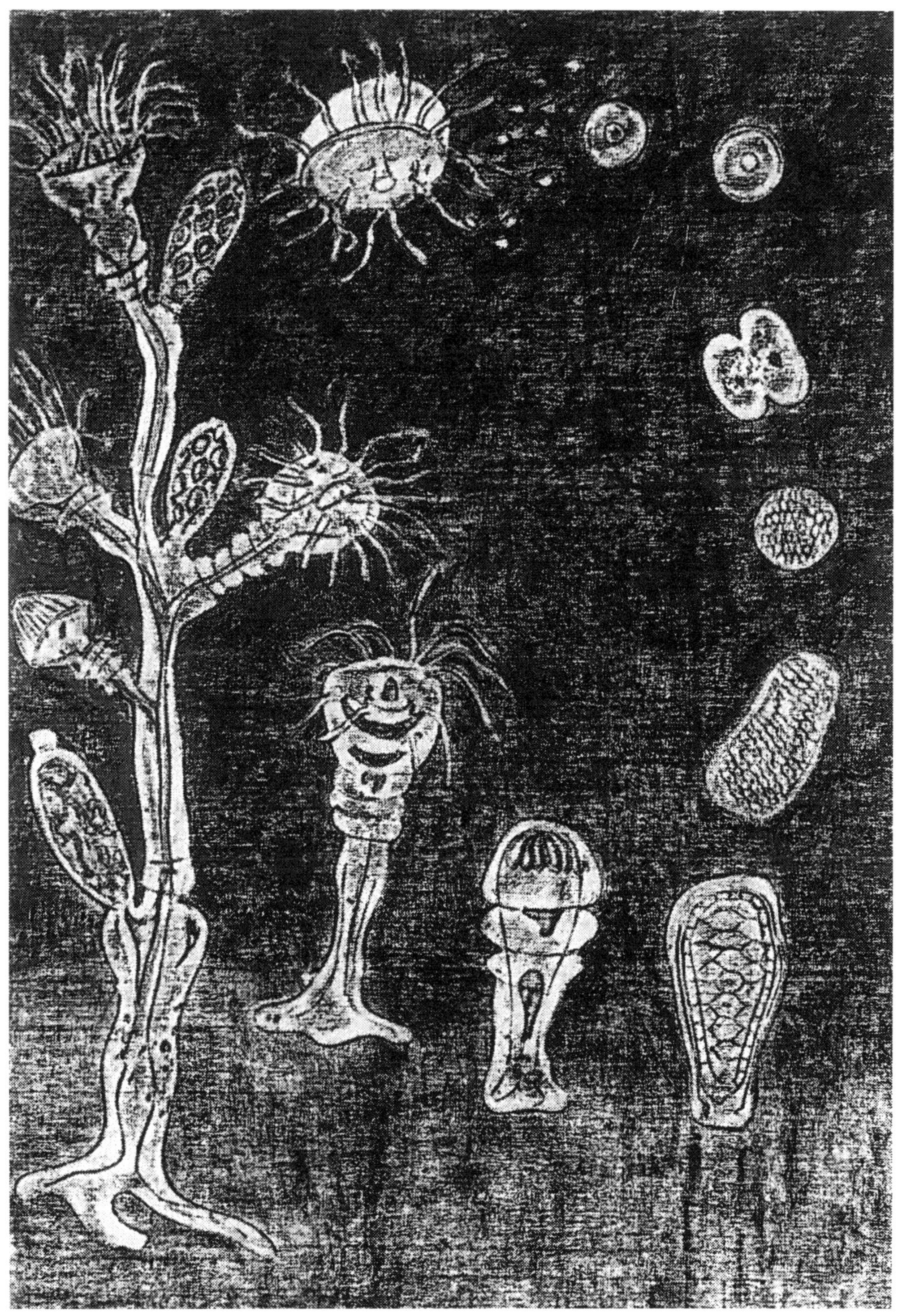

1984.10 Untitled (Autogenic Cells), 183 × 122 cm

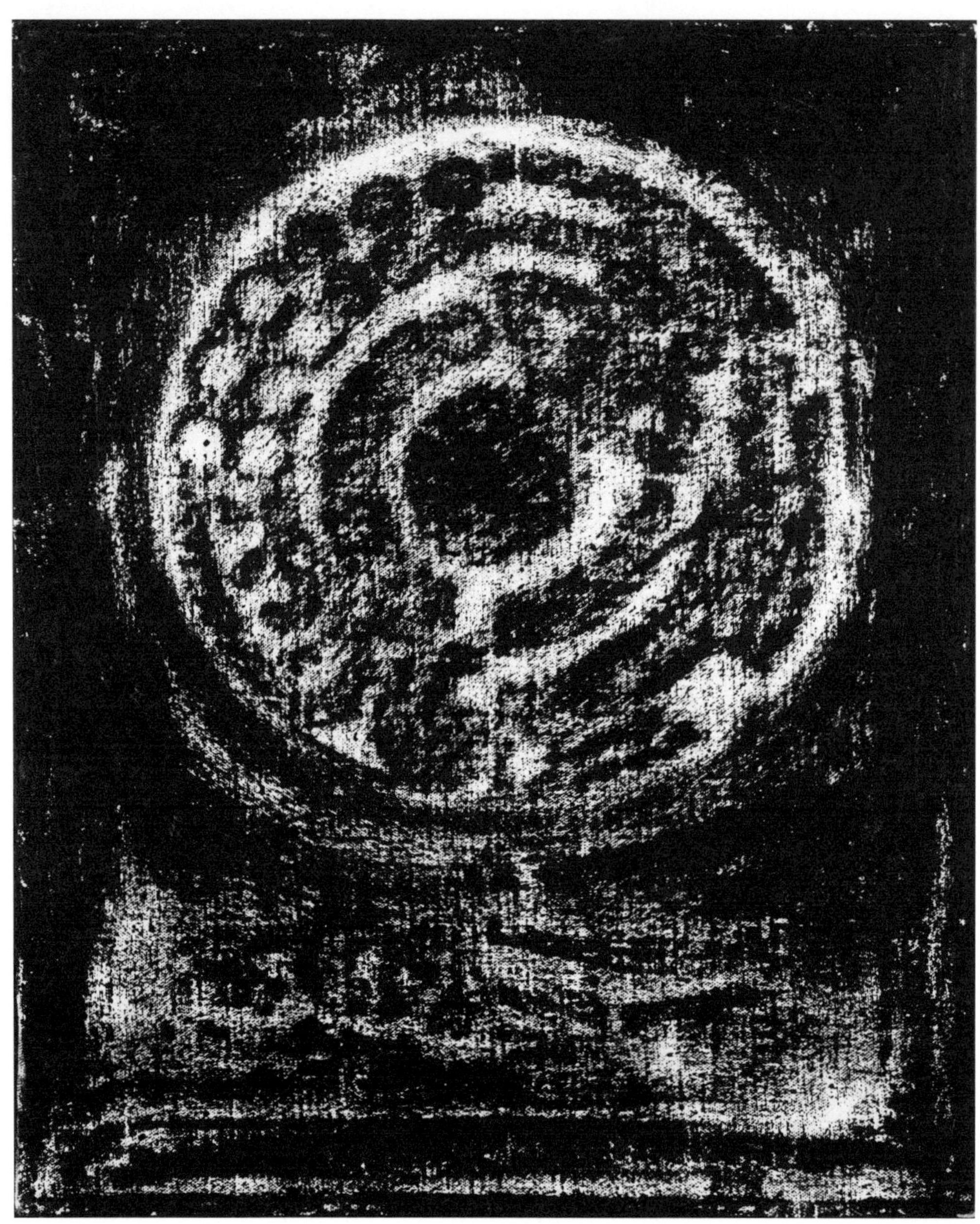

1984.11 Untitled (Cosmology over Death), 50 × 40 cm

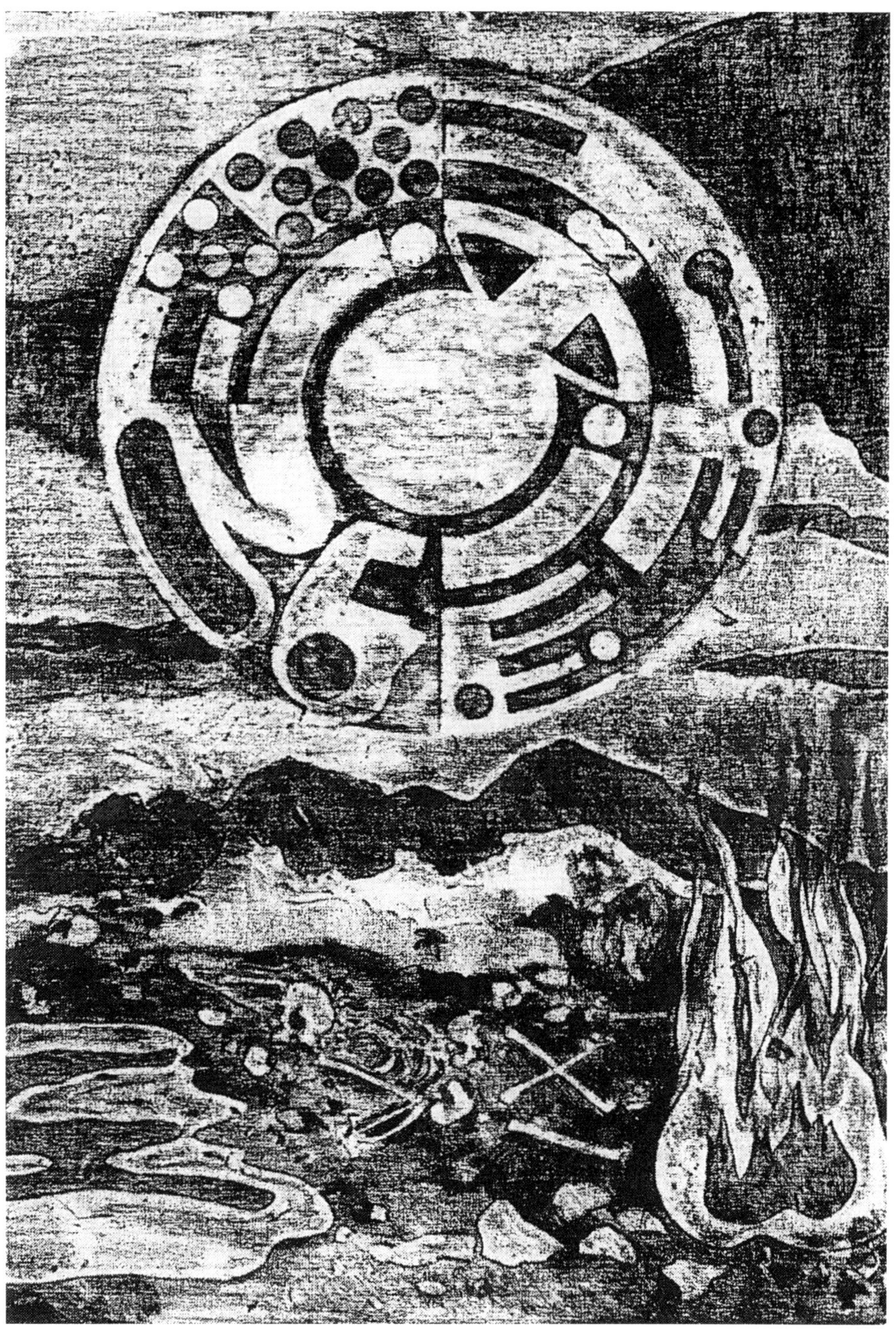

1984.12 Untitled (Cosmology over Death), 183 × 122 cm

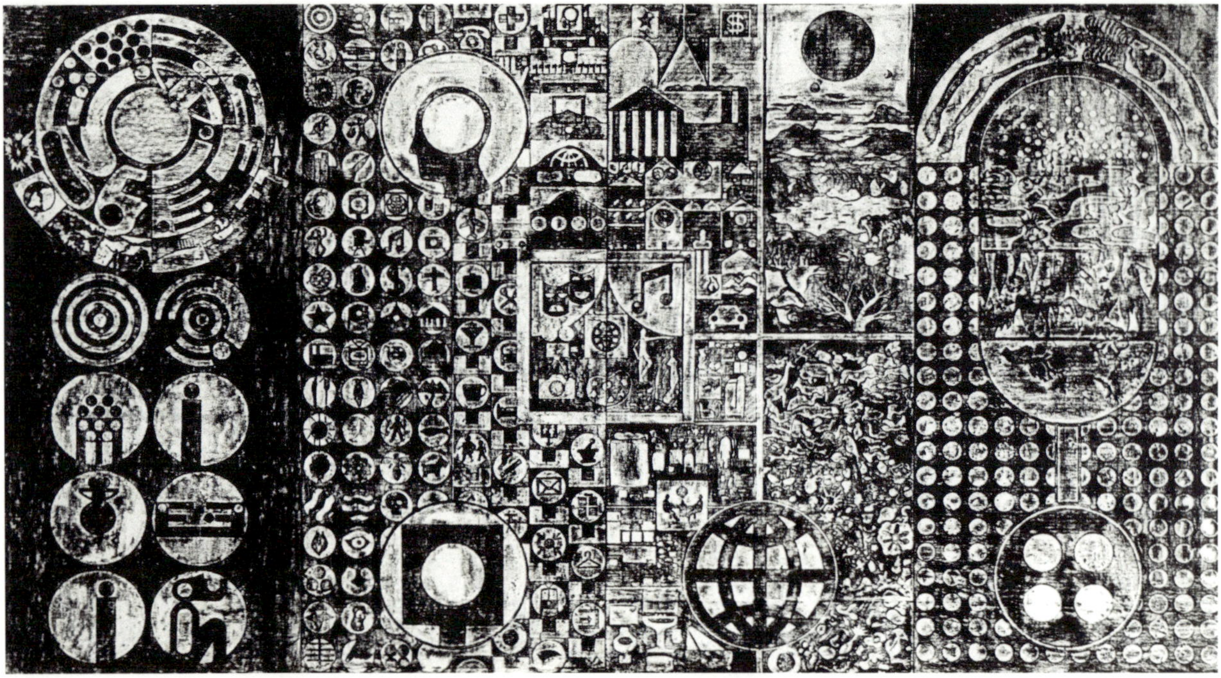

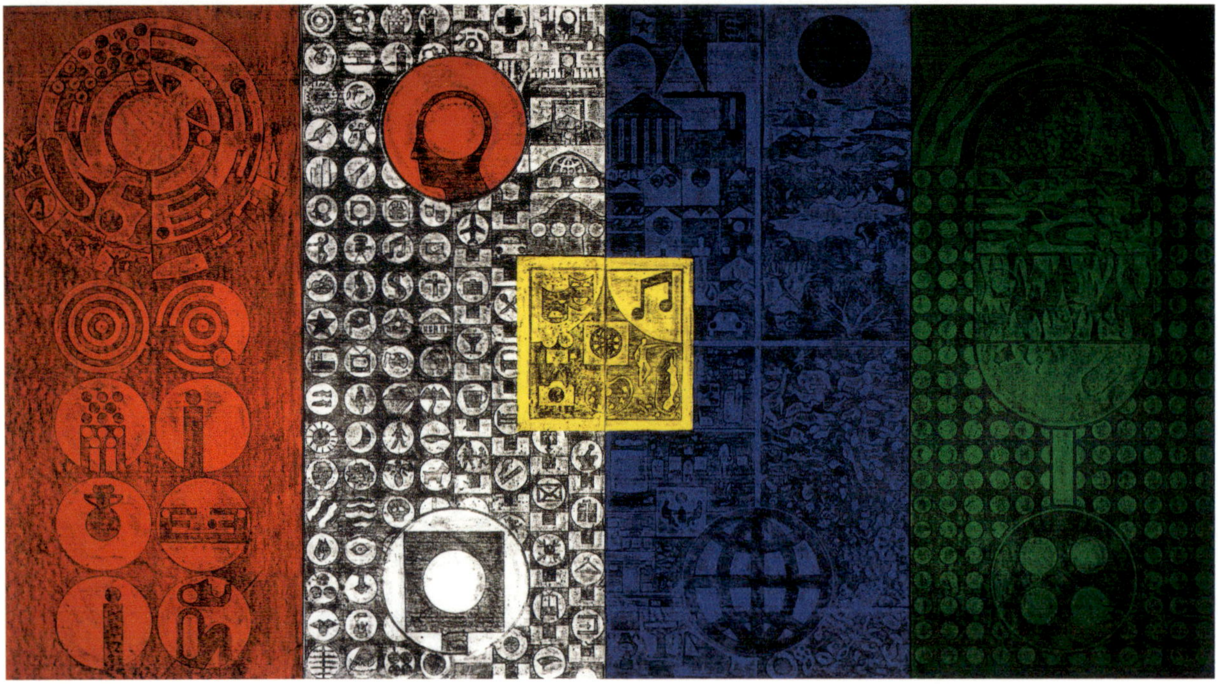

1984.13 Untitled (Big Chart), 274 × 488 cm (4 parts)
1984.14 Untitled (Big Chart), 274 × 488 cm (4 parts)

1985

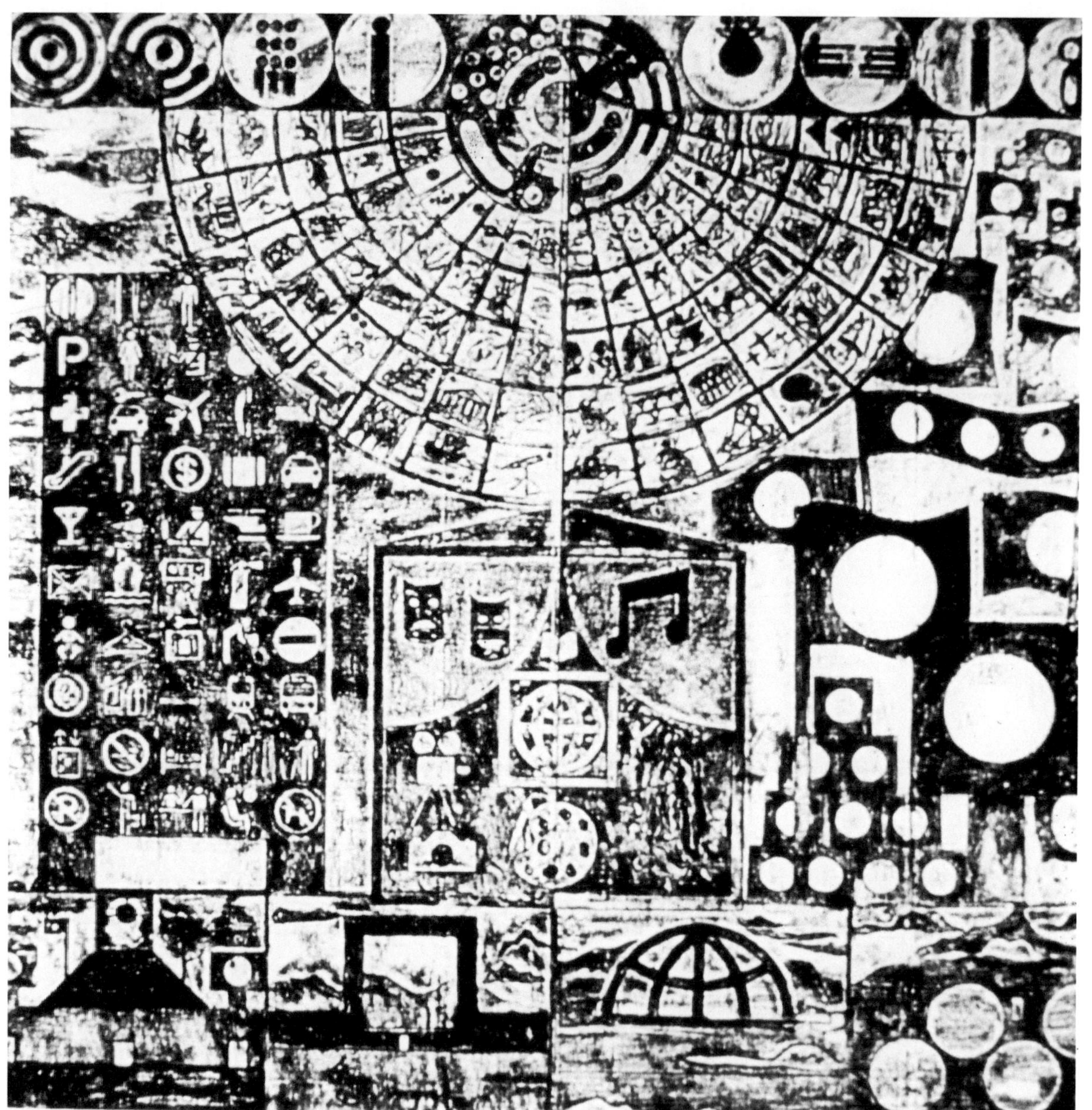

1985.1 Untitled (History over the Arts), 305 × 305 cm

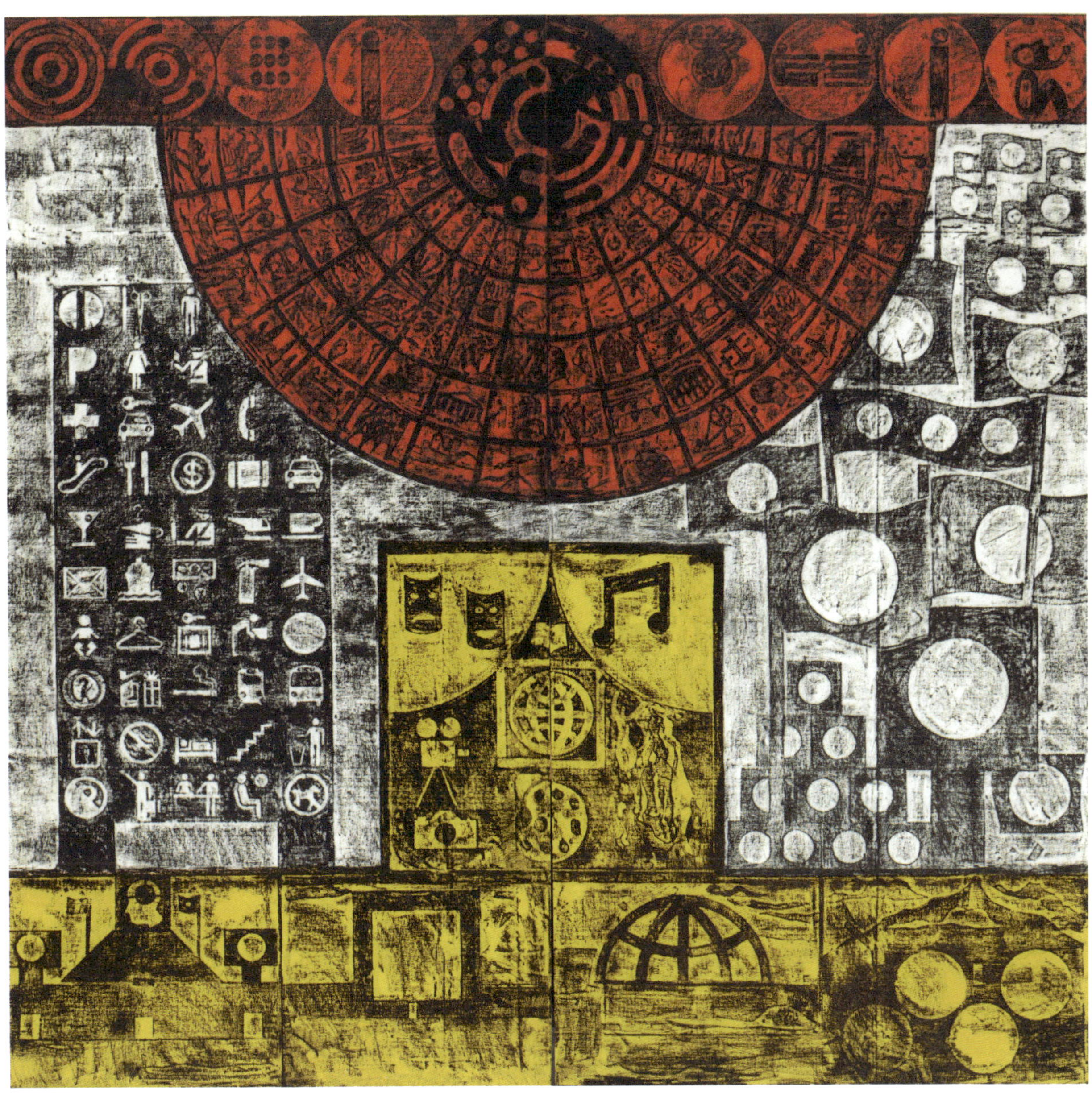

1985.2 Untitled (Subject, Sign, World Framed), 305 × 305 cm

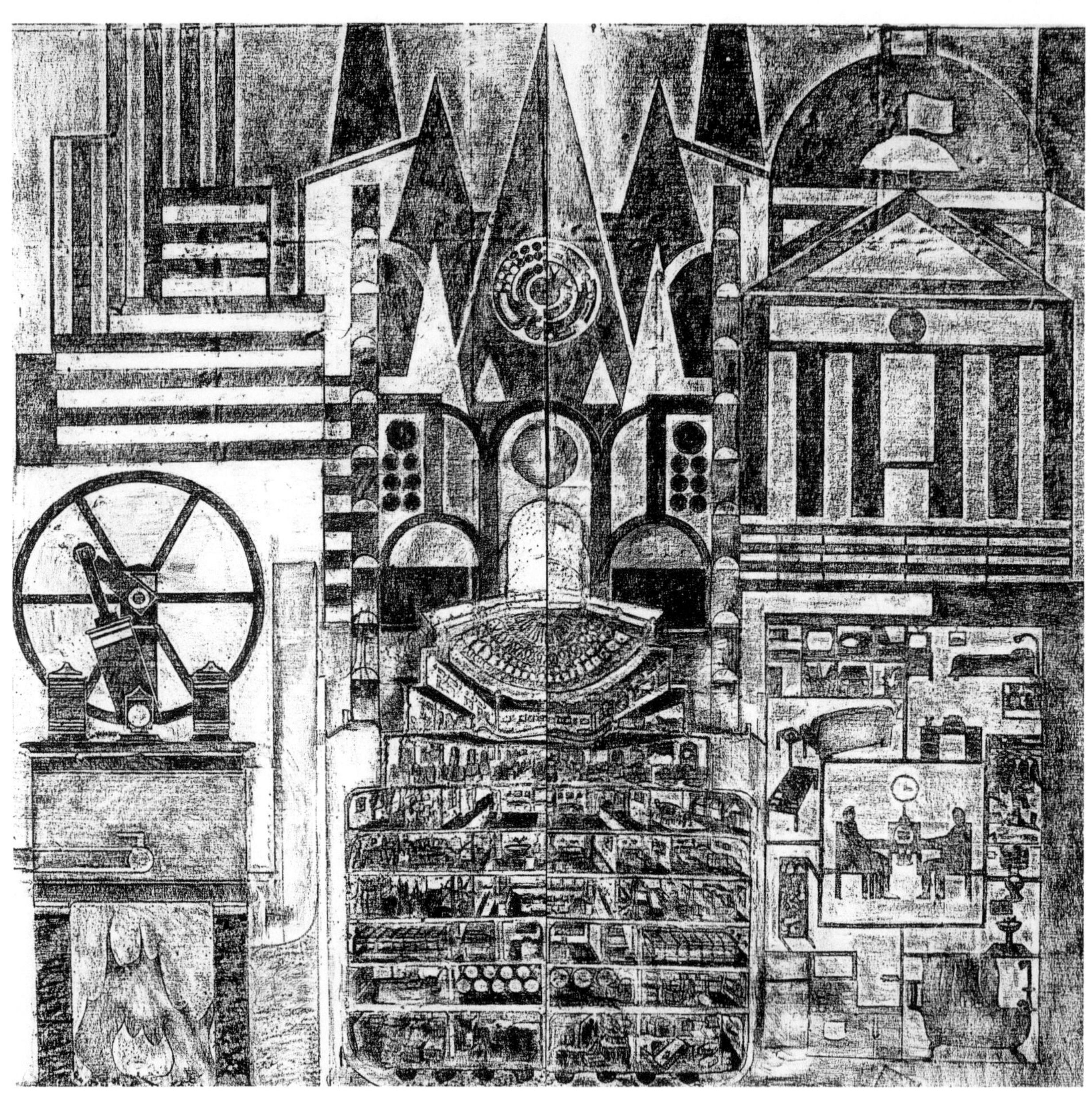

1985.3 Untitled (City), 305 × 305 cm

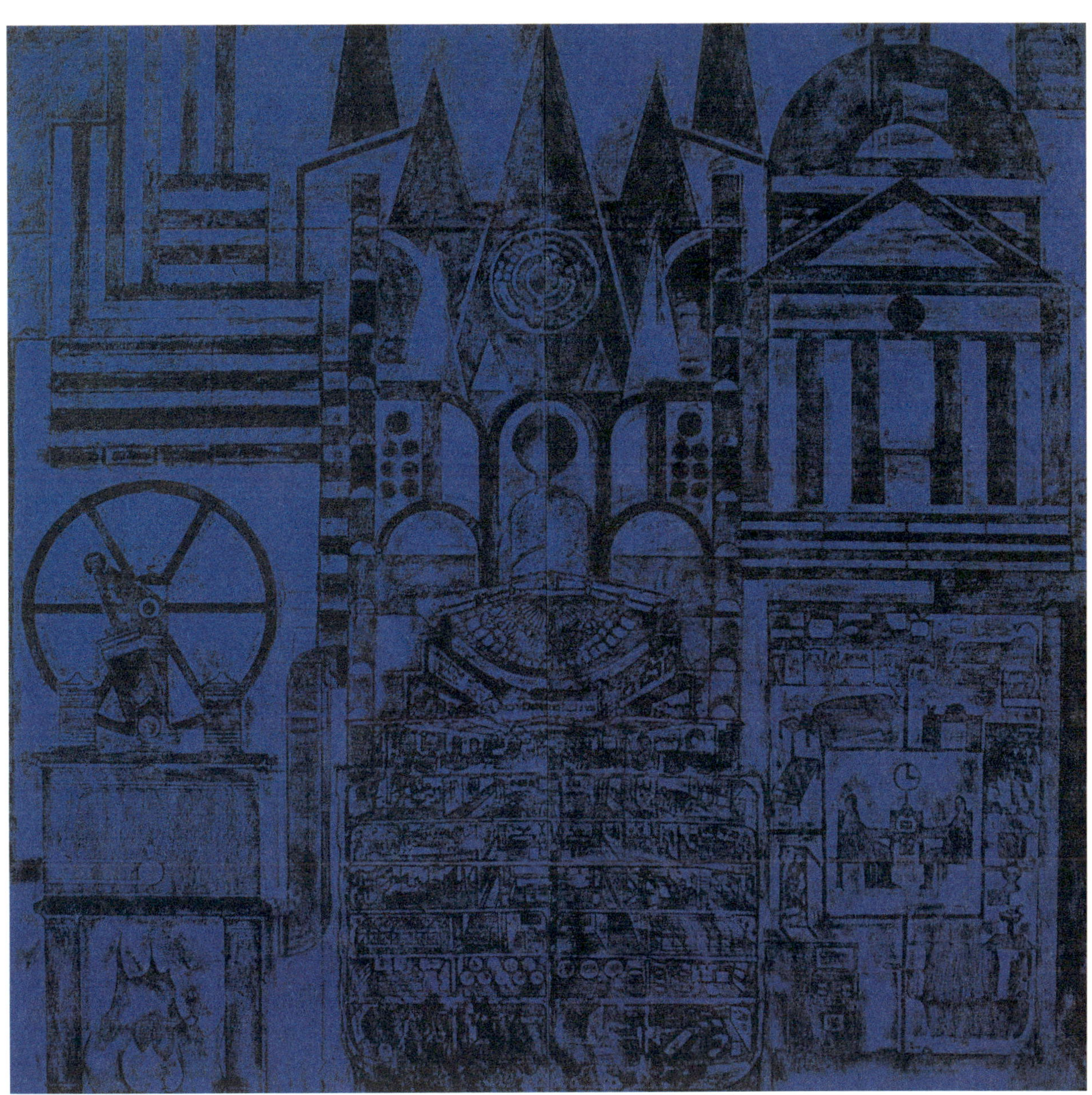

1985.4 Untitled (City Blue), 305 × 305 cm

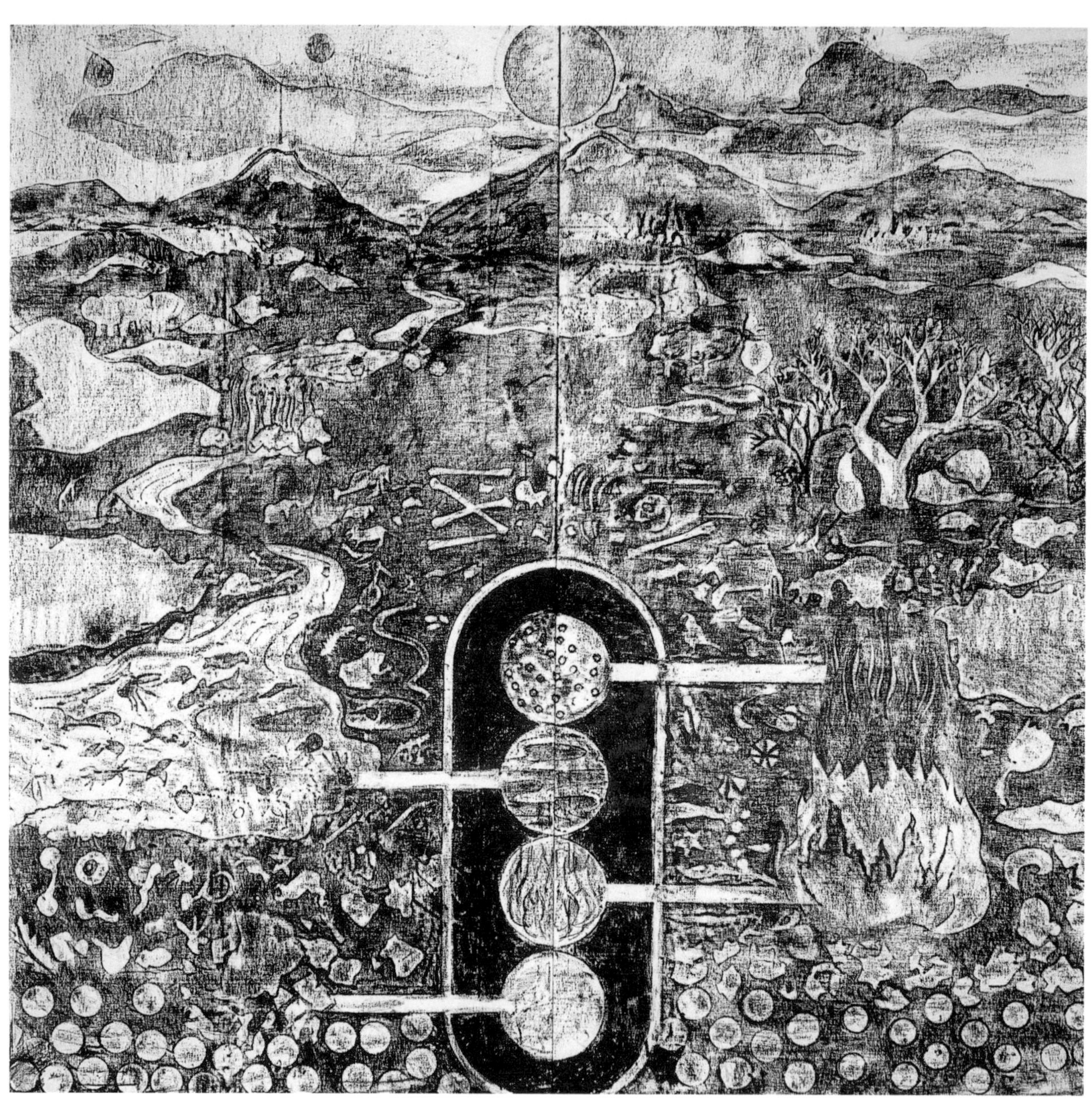

1985.5 Untitled (Elements), 305 × 305 cm

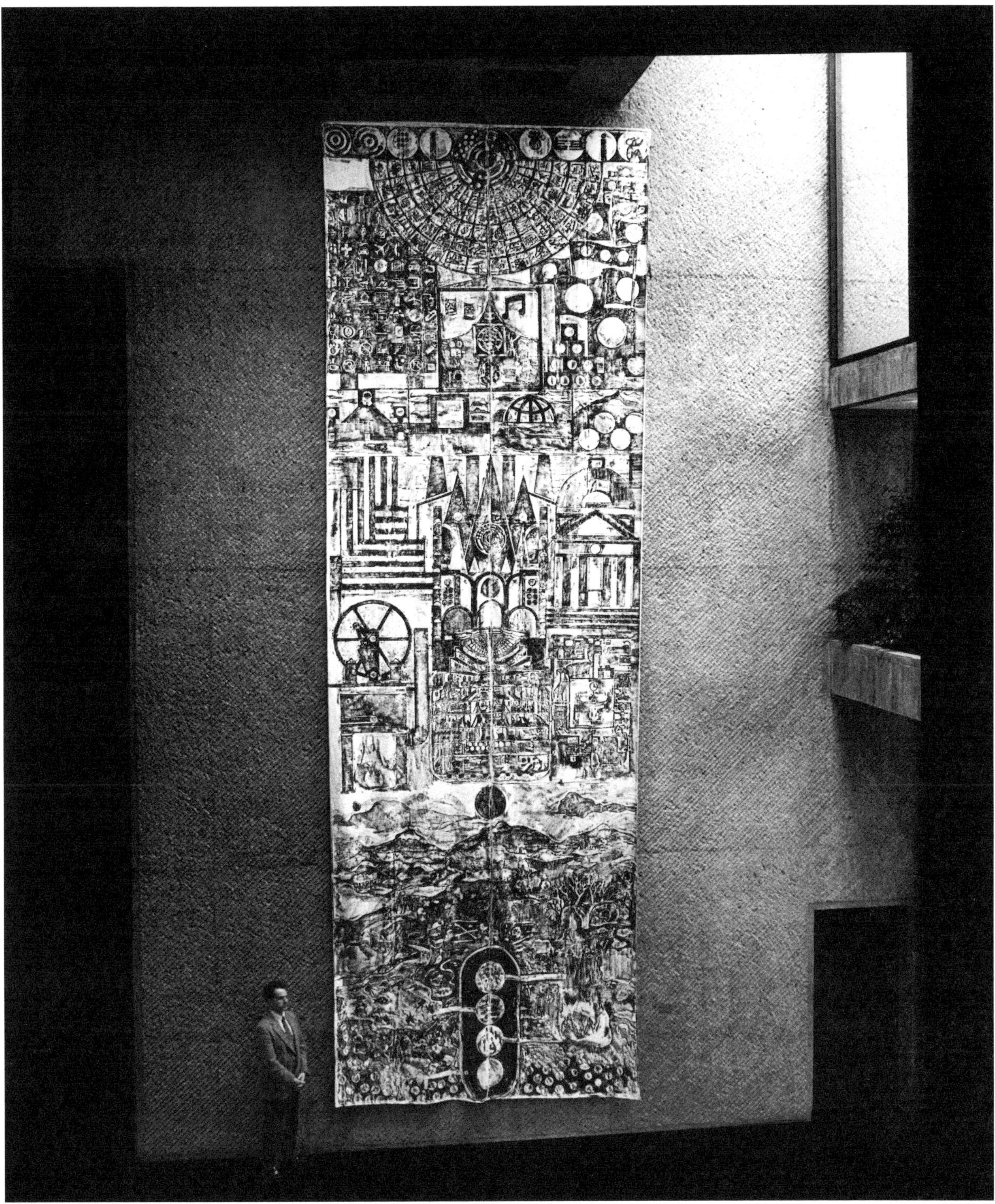

1985.6 Untitled (Vertical City), 914.5 × 305 cm

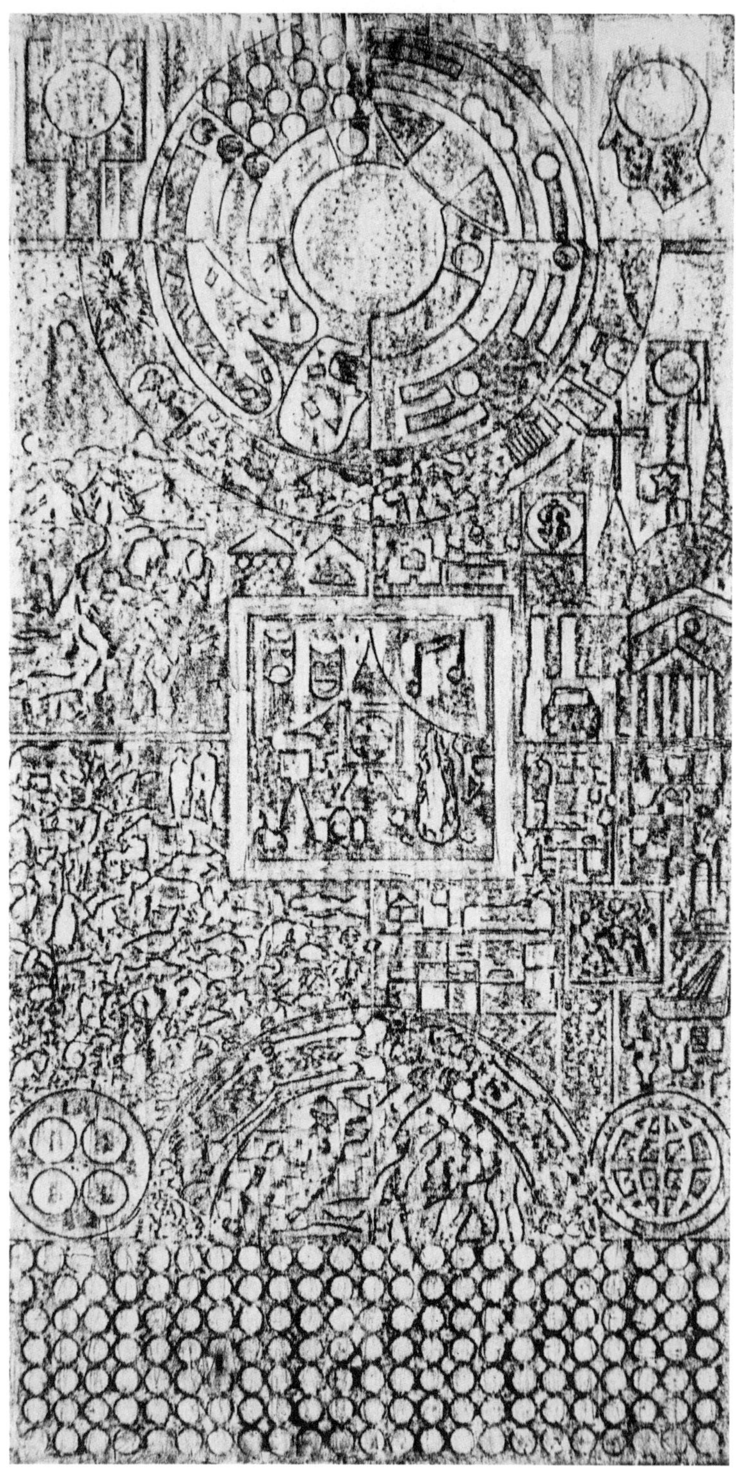

1985.7 Untitled (Big Chart—B&W Version), 244 × 122 cm

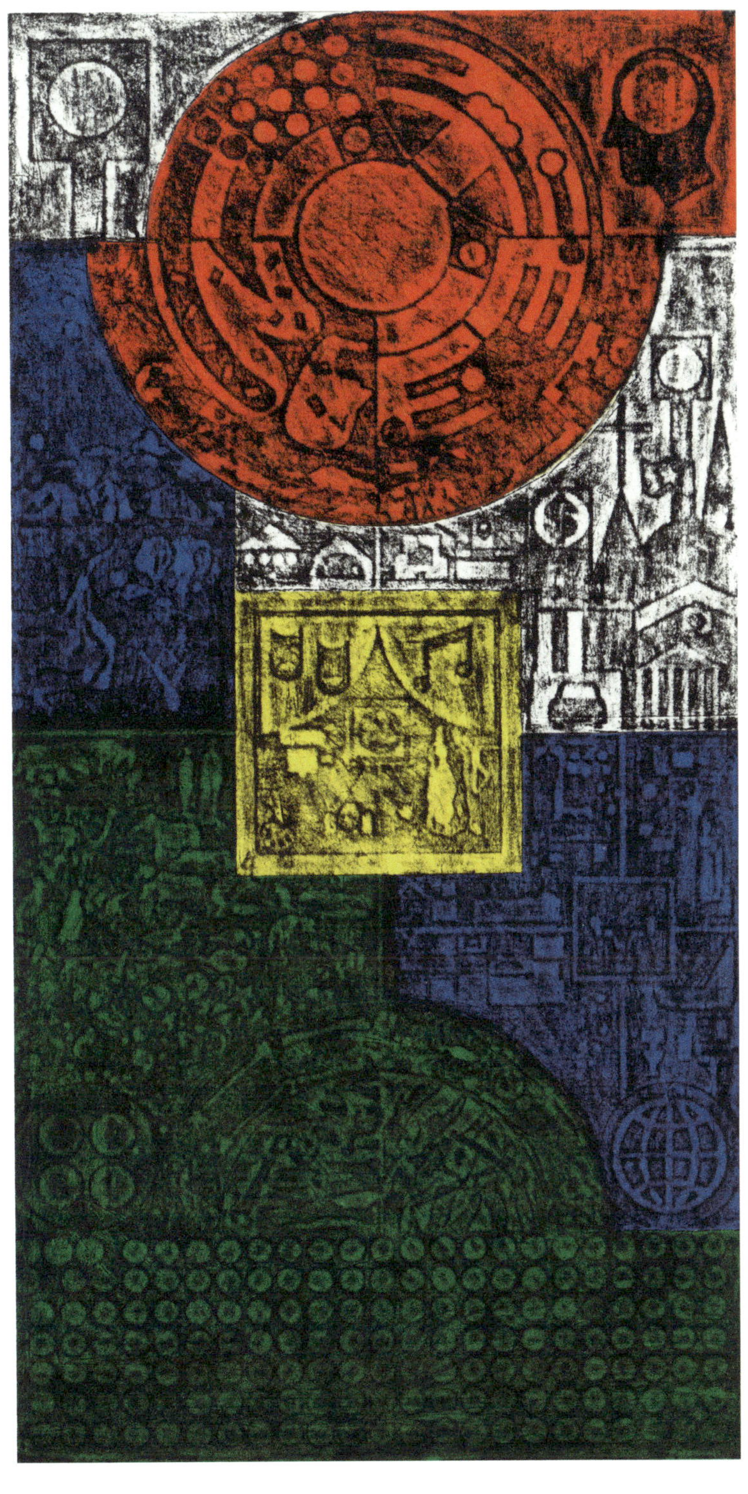

1985.8 Untitled (Big Chart), 244 × 122 cm

1986

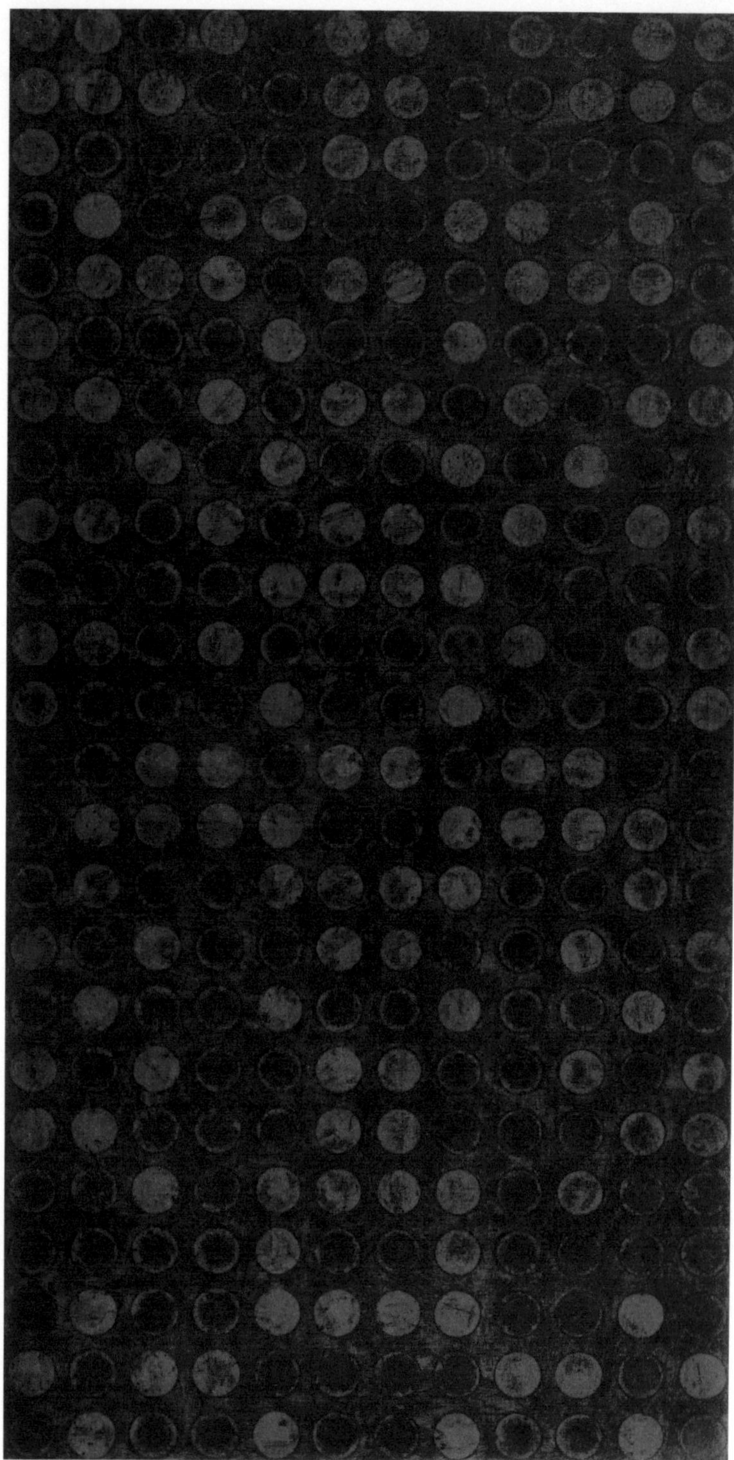

1986.1 Untitled (Elements Green), 244 × 122 cm

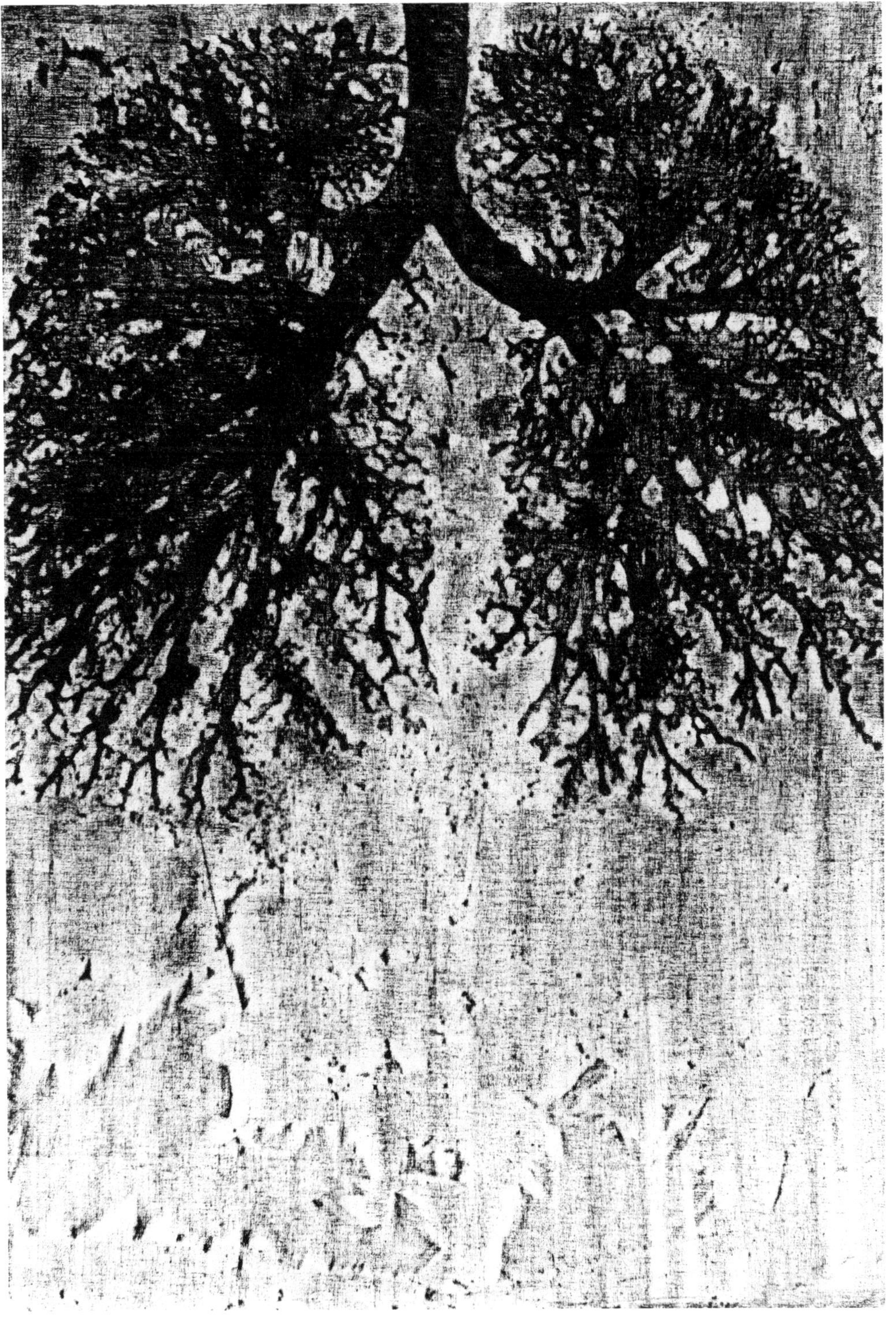

1986.2 Untitled (Lungs), 183 × 122 cm

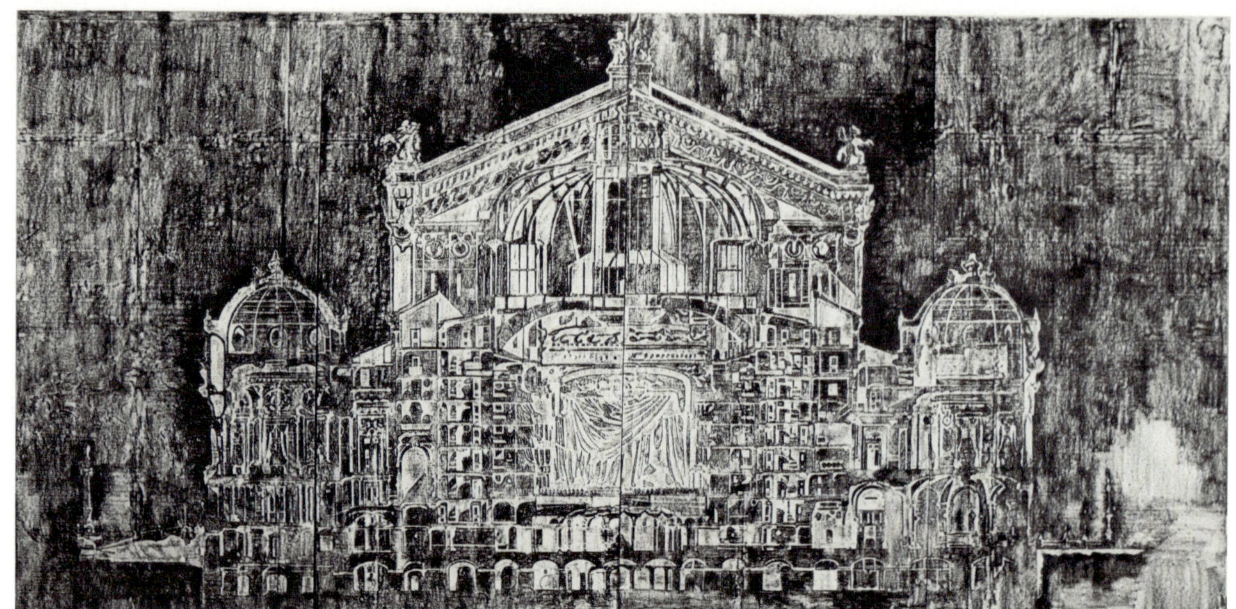
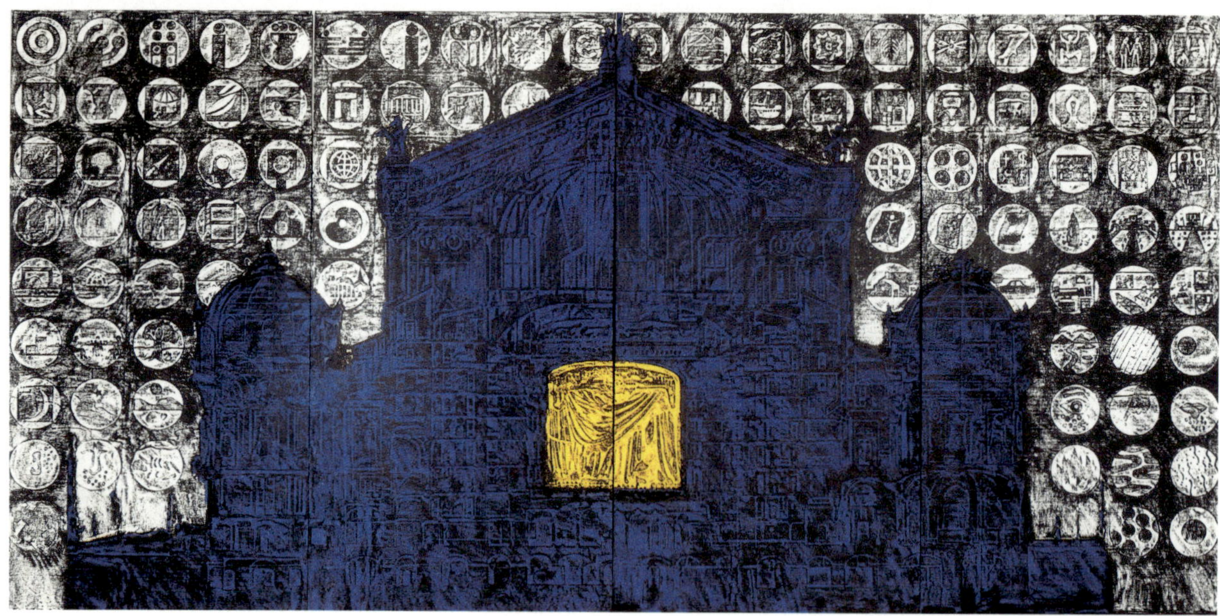

1986.3 Untitled (Paris Opera House), 305 × 609.5 (4 parts)
1986.4 Untitled (Paris Opera House), 305 × 609.5 (4 parts)

1987

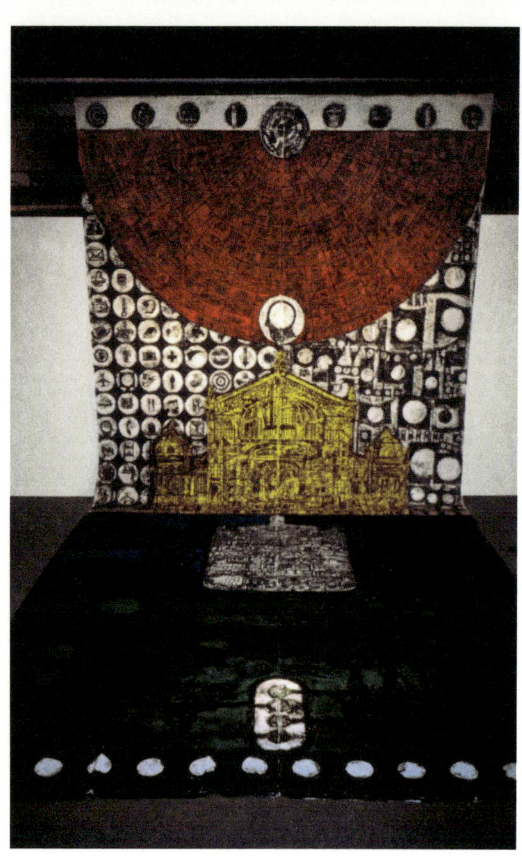

1987.1 Untitled (Cosmology), 1036 × 480 cm

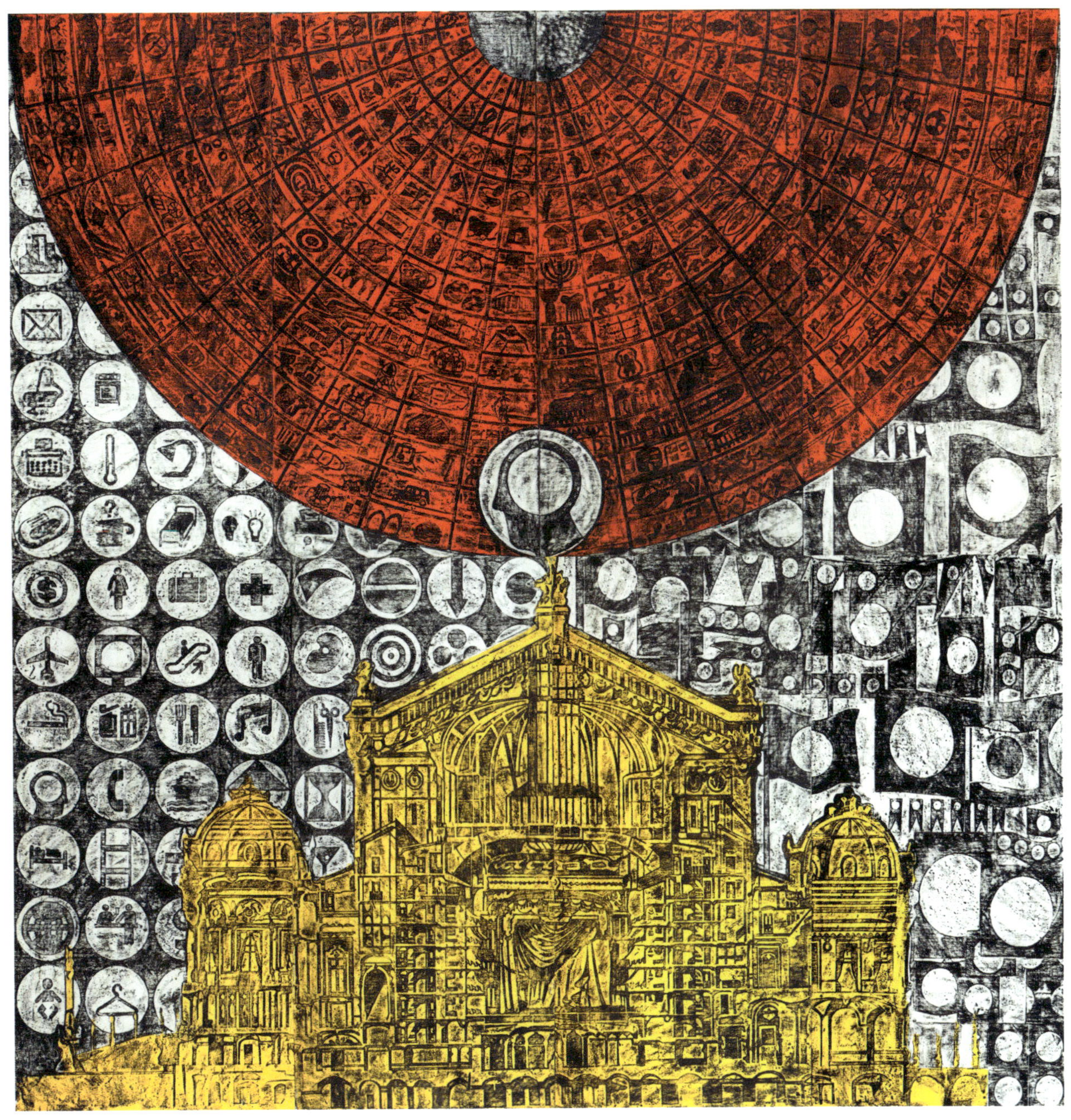

1987.2 Untitled (History over Opera House Surrounded by Signs and Flags), 488 × 488 cm (8 parts)

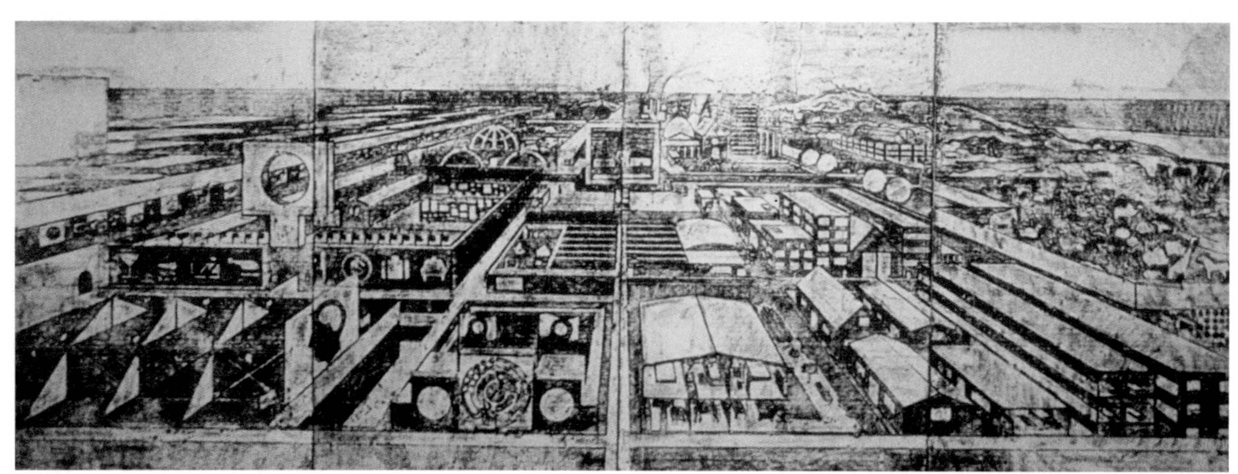

1987.3 Untitled (B&W City), 183 × 488 cm (4 parts)

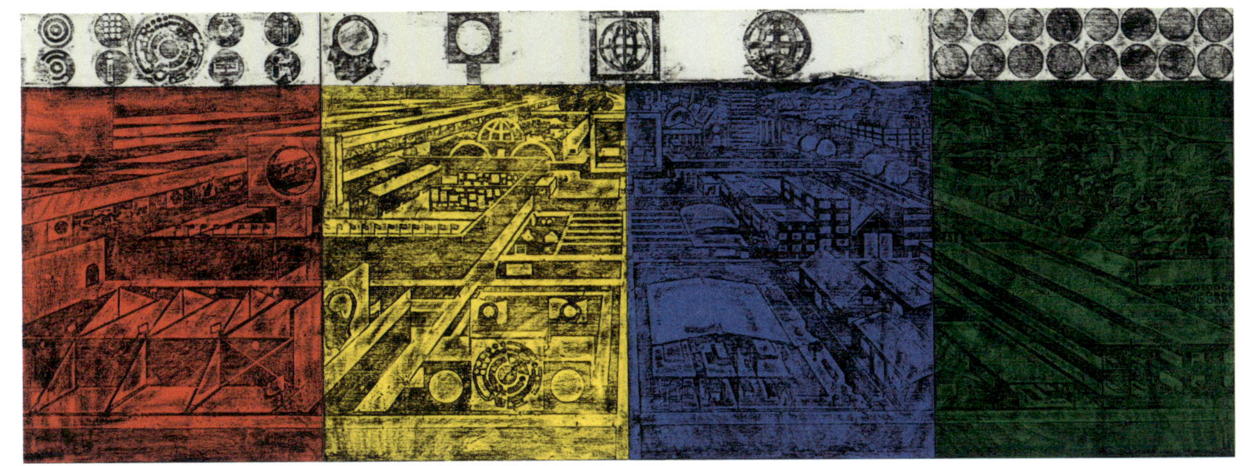

1987.4 Untitled (Colored City with Signs), 183 × 488 cm (4 parts)

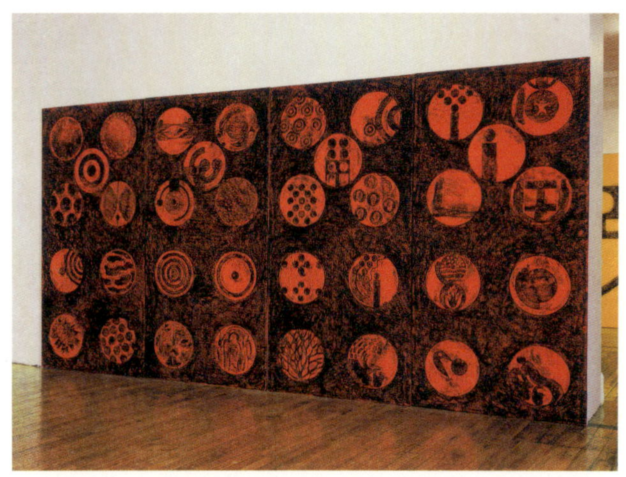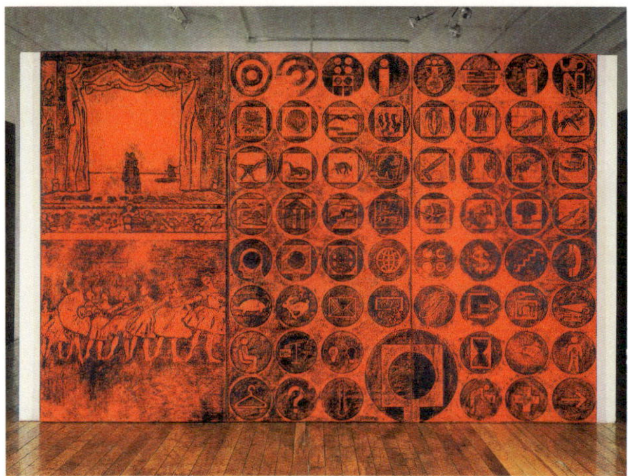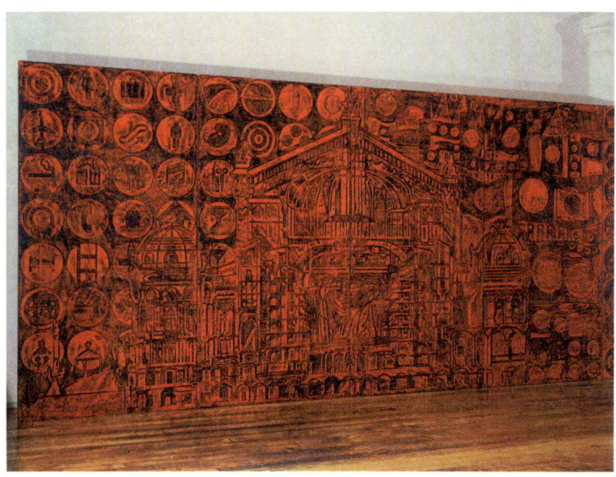

1987.5 Untitled (Dallas Project First Version), 244 × 3779.5 cm (31 parts)

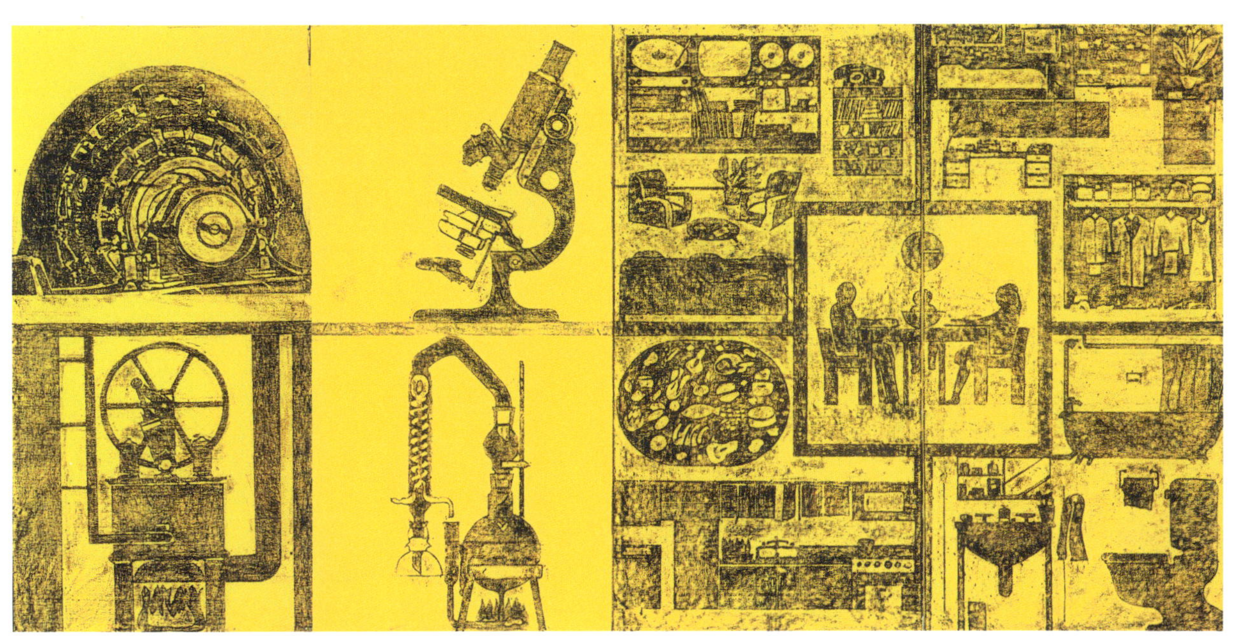

1987.5 Untitled (Dallas Project First Version), 244 × 3779.5 cm (31 parts)

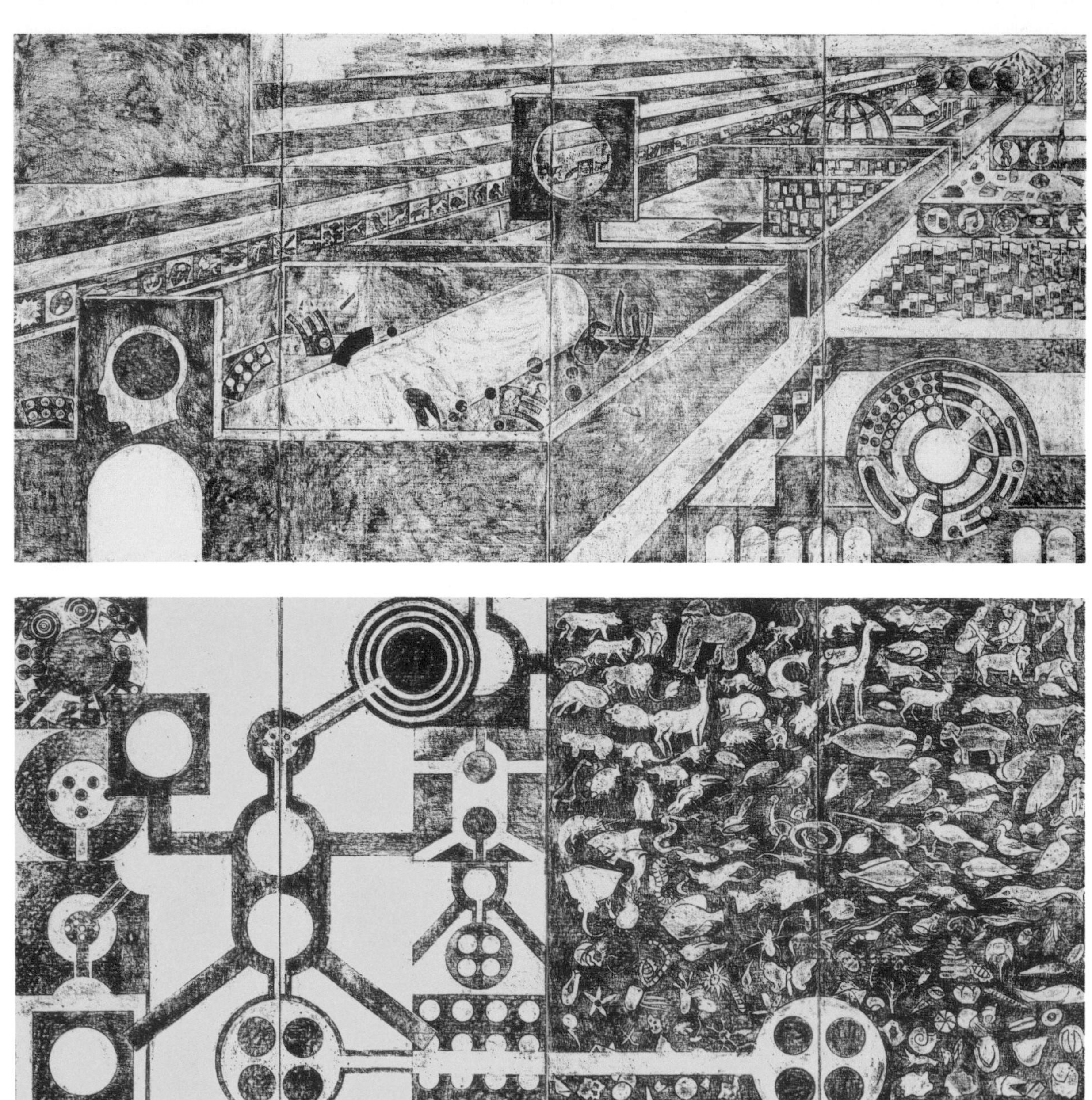

1987.5 Untitled (Dallas Project First Version), 244 × 3779.5 cm (31 parts)

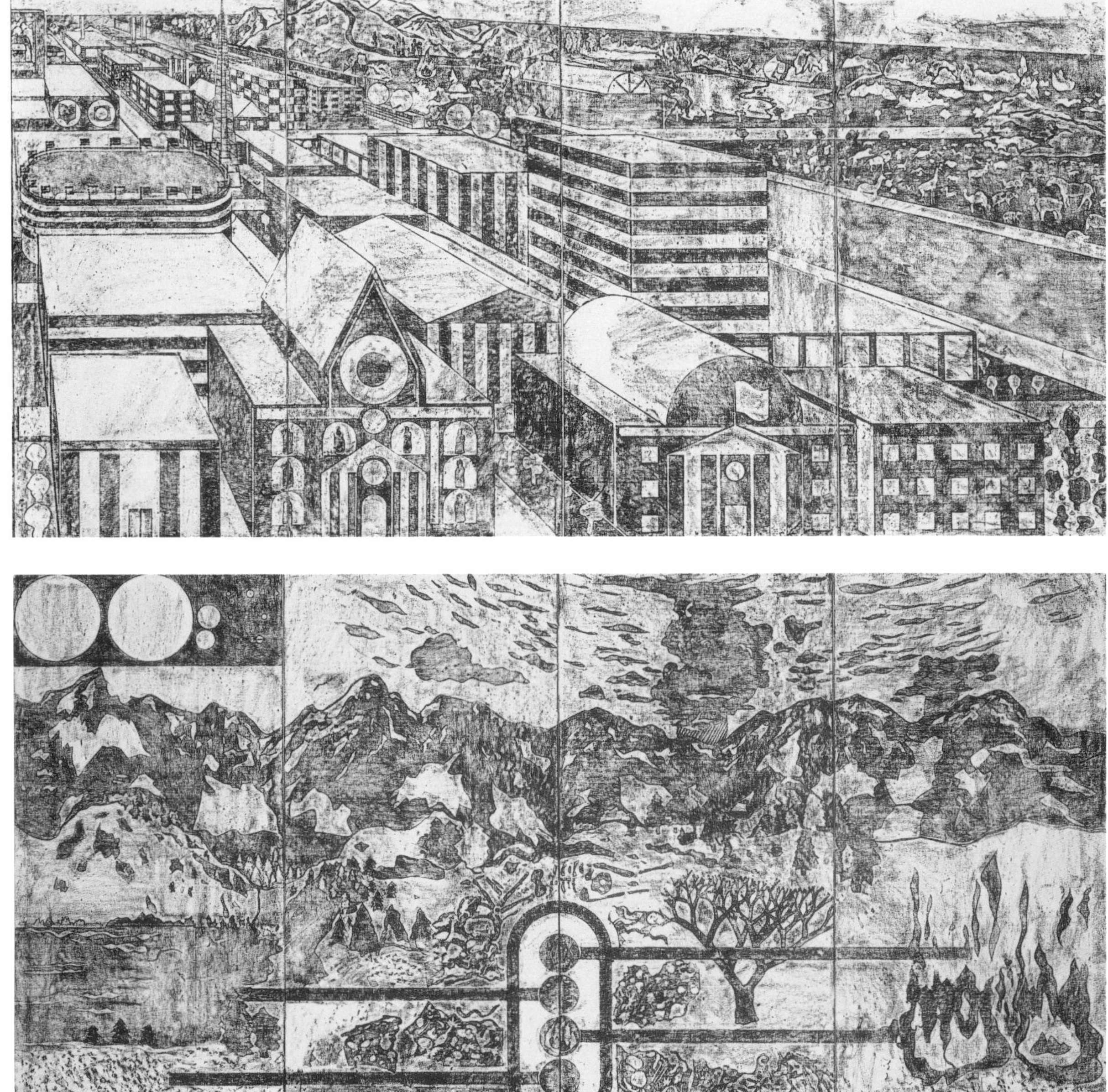

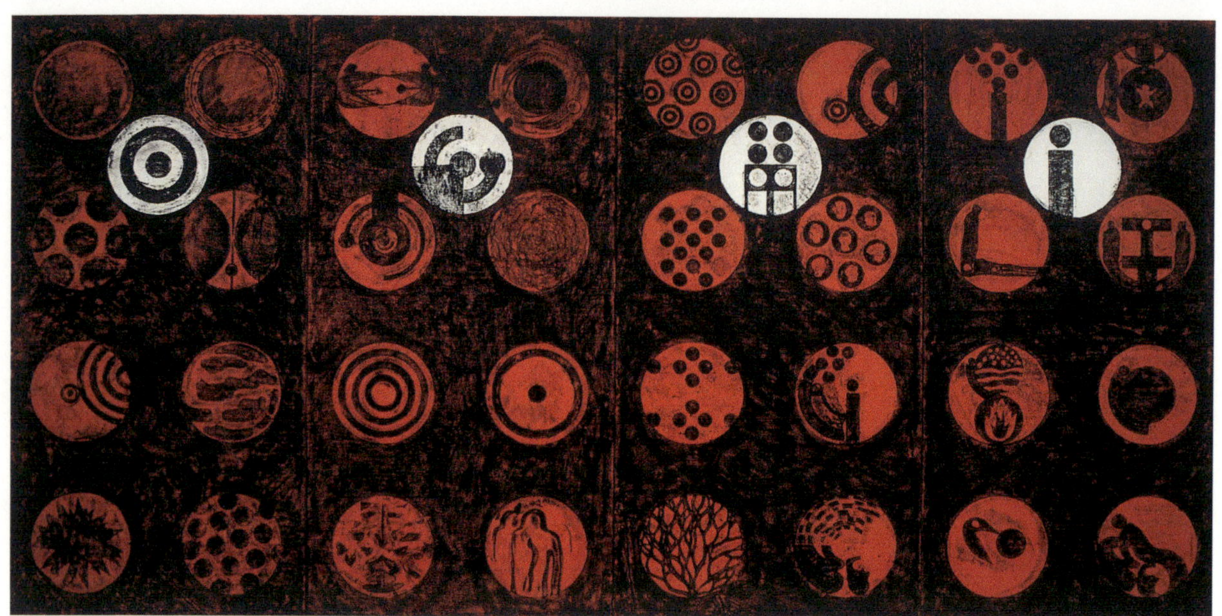

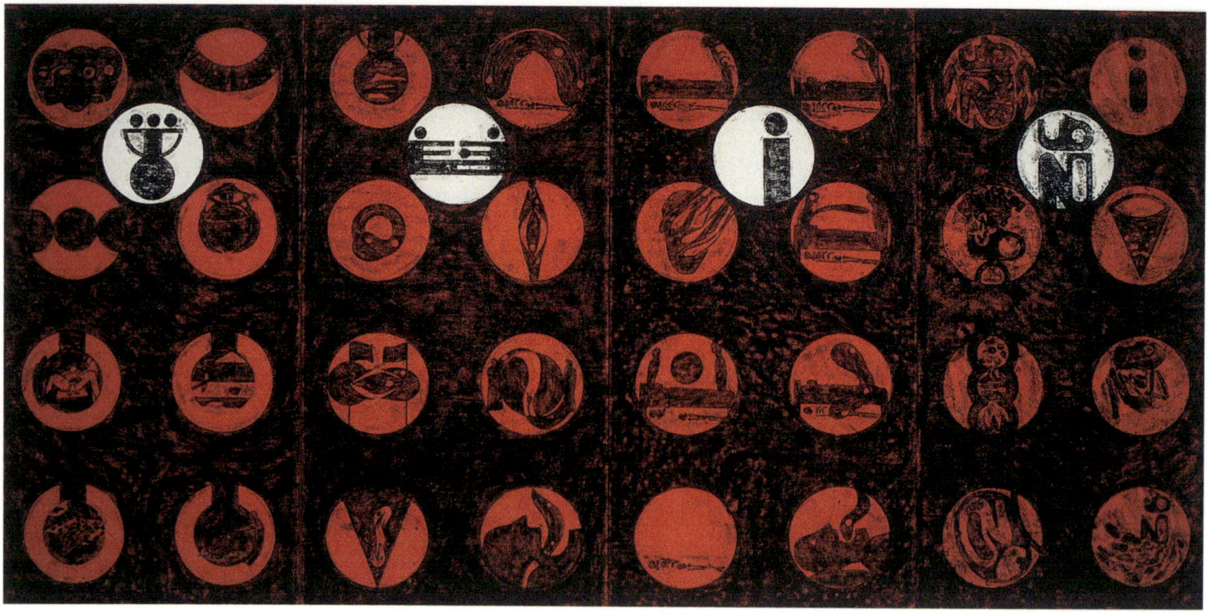

1987.6 Dallas Project (Panels 1–8: Cosmology Model), 244 × 976 cm (8 parts)

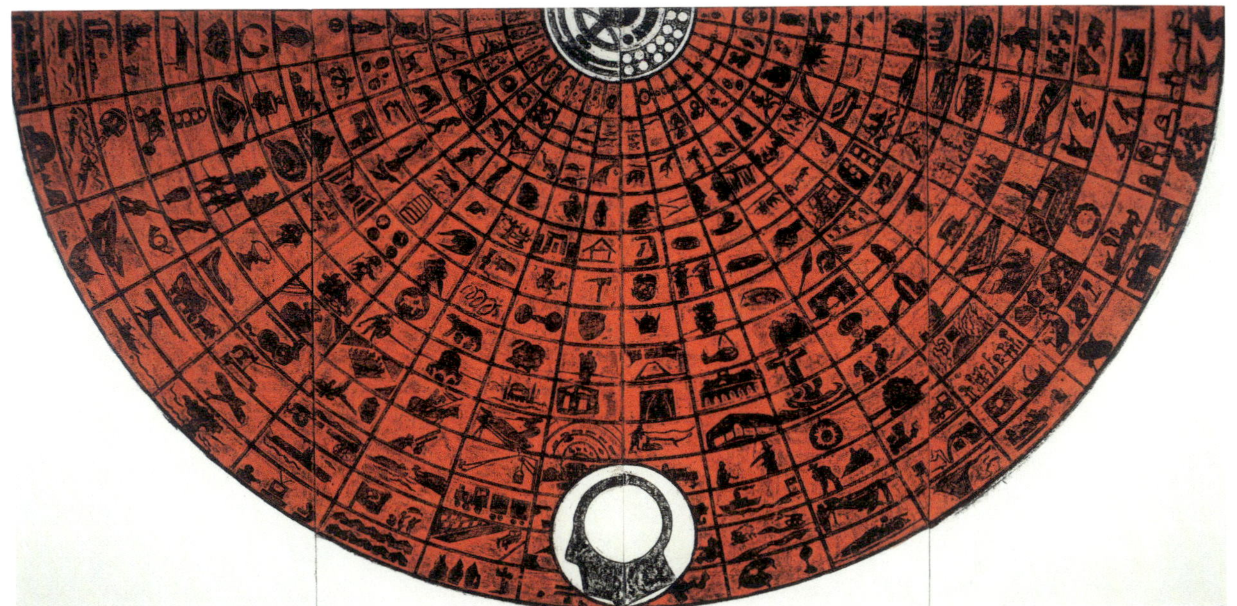

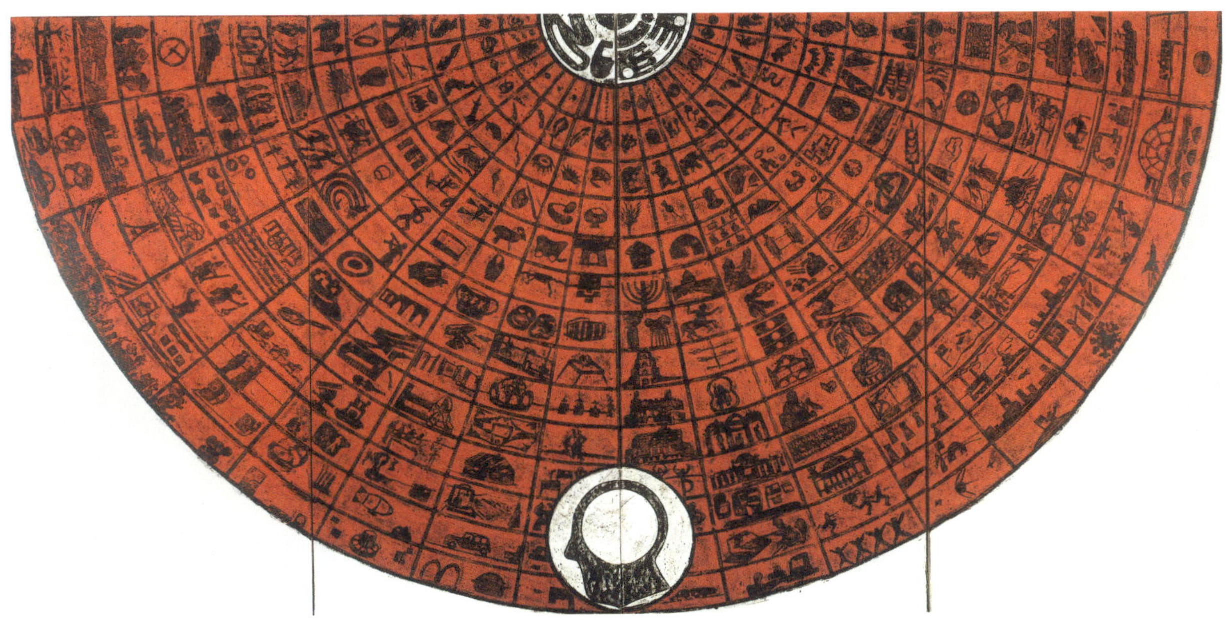

1987.7 Dallas Project (Panels 9–16: Subjective History), 244 × 976 cm (8 parts)

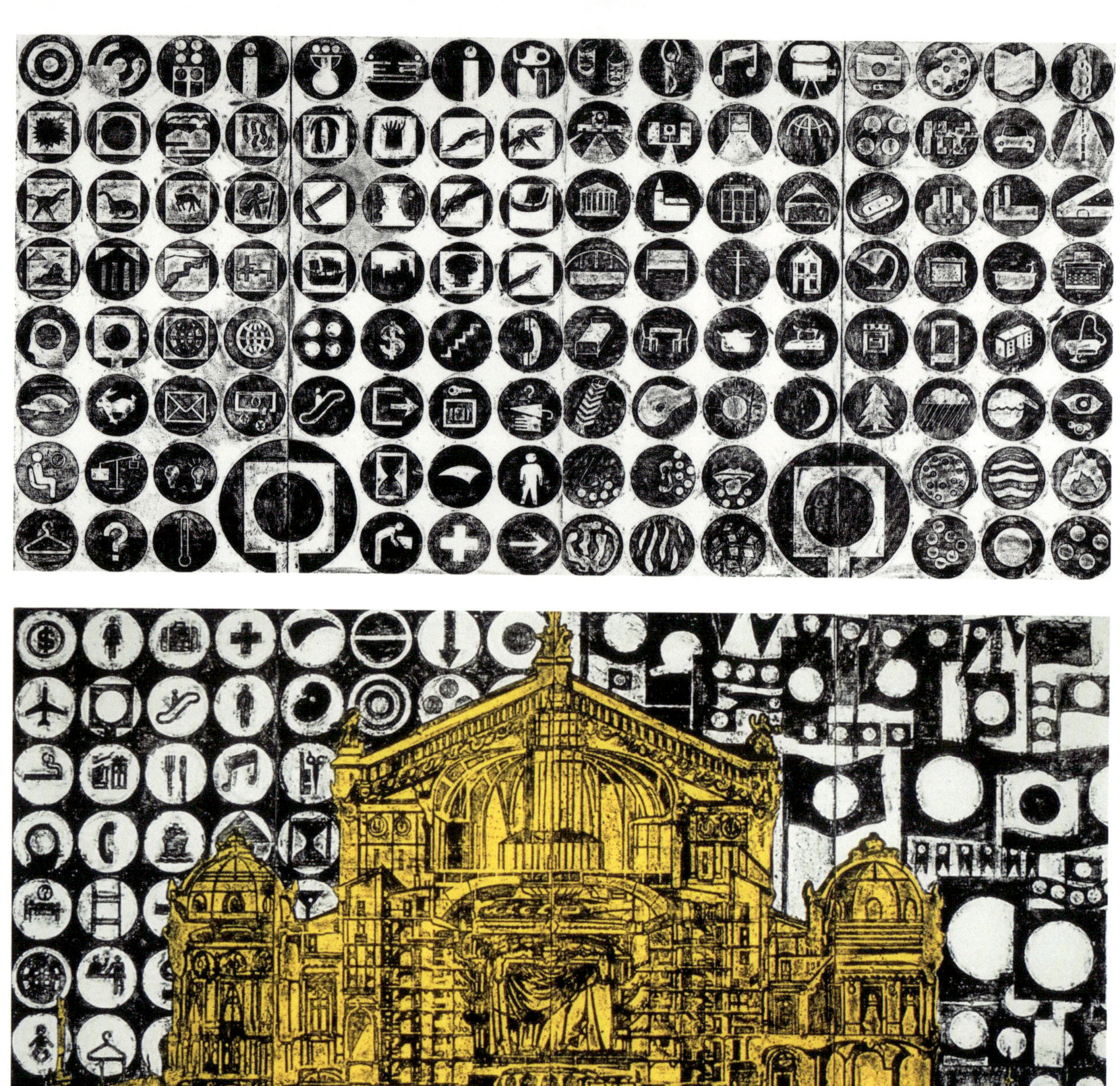

1987.8 Dallas Project (Panels 17–20: Signs), 244 × 488 cm (4 parts)
1987.9 Dallas Project (Panels 21–24: Paris Opera House on a Field of Signs and Flags), 244 × 488 cm (4 parts)

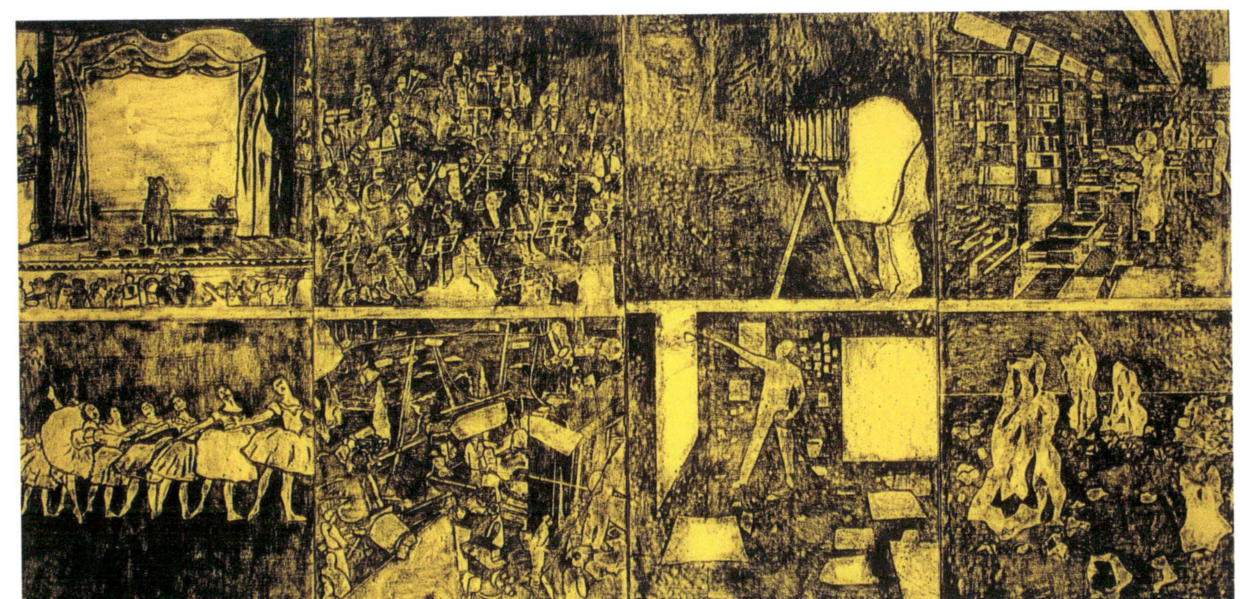
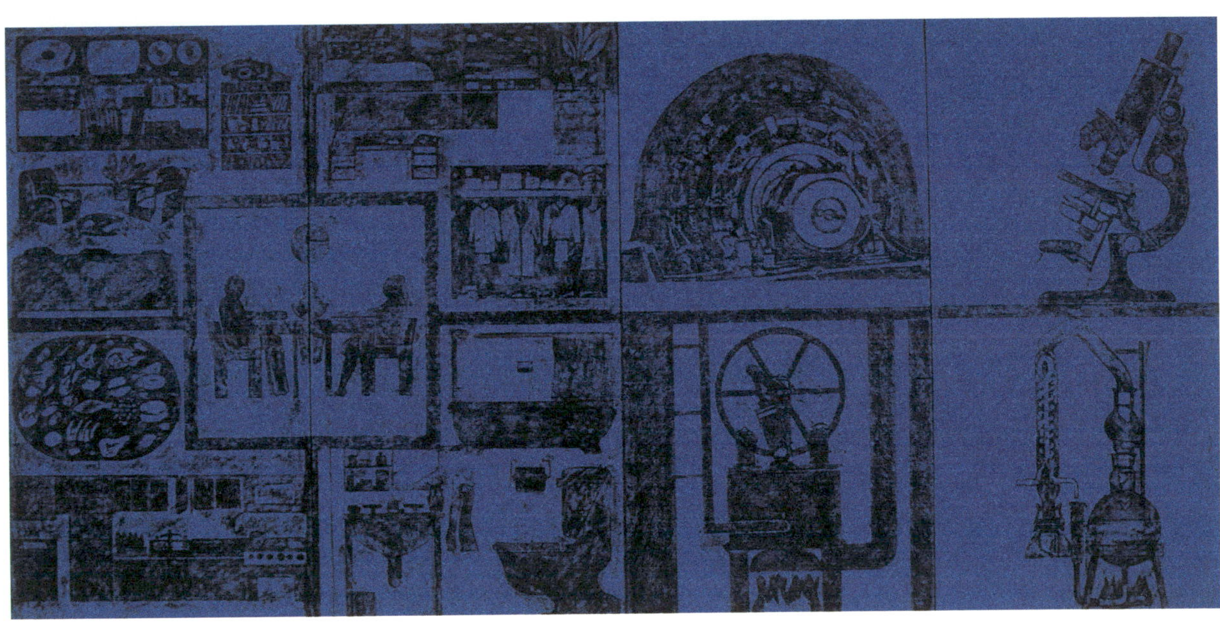

1987.10 Dallas Project (Panels 25–28: Pictorial and Performing Arts), 244 × 488 cm (4 parts)
1987.11 Dallas Project (Panels 37–40: House and Machines), 244 × 488 cm (4 parts)

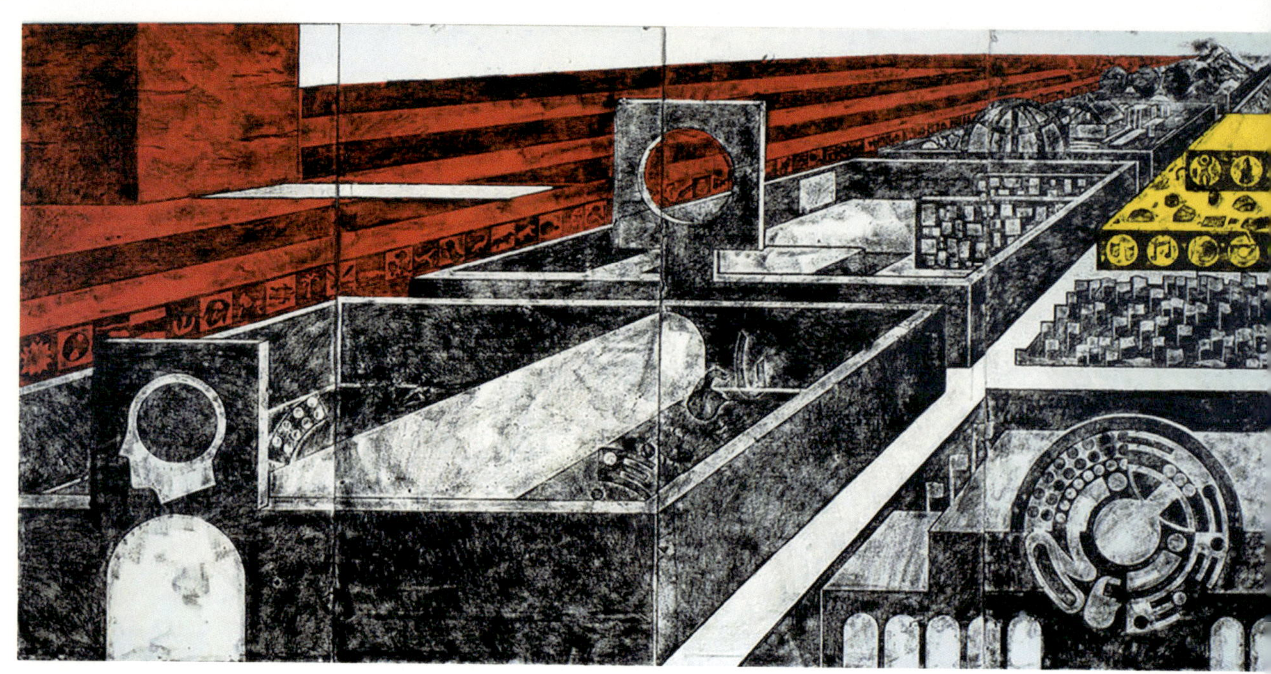

1987.12 Dallas Project (Panels 29–36: City), 244 × 976 cm (8 parts)

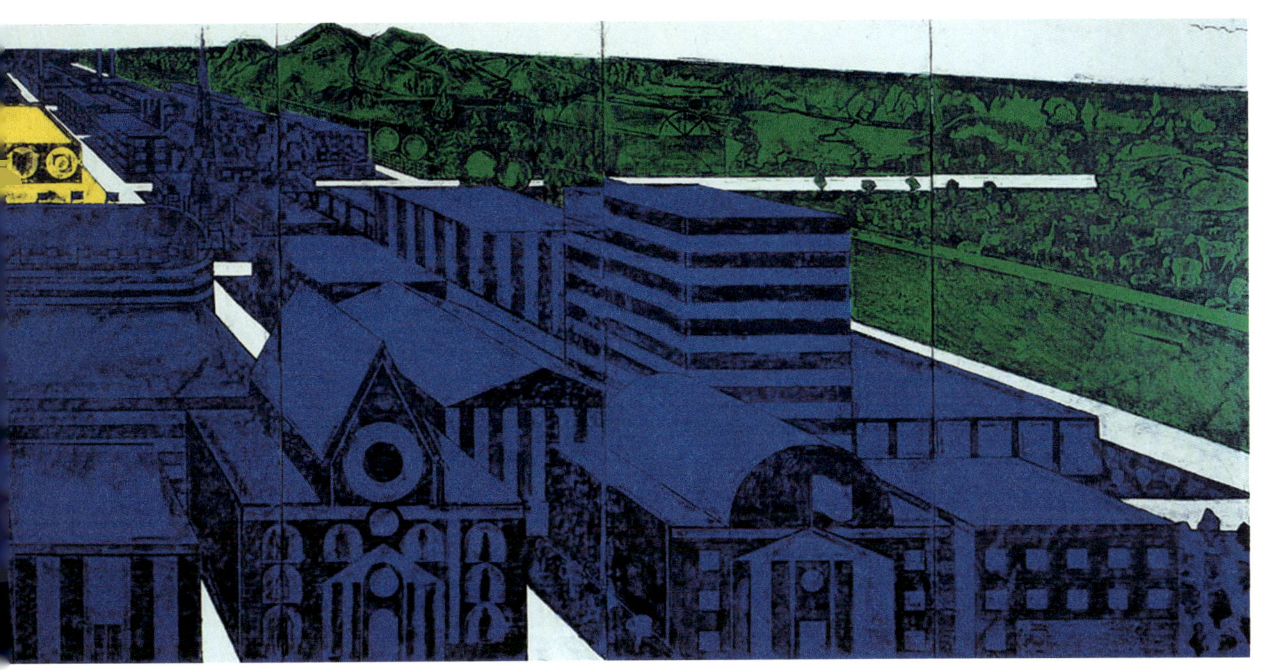

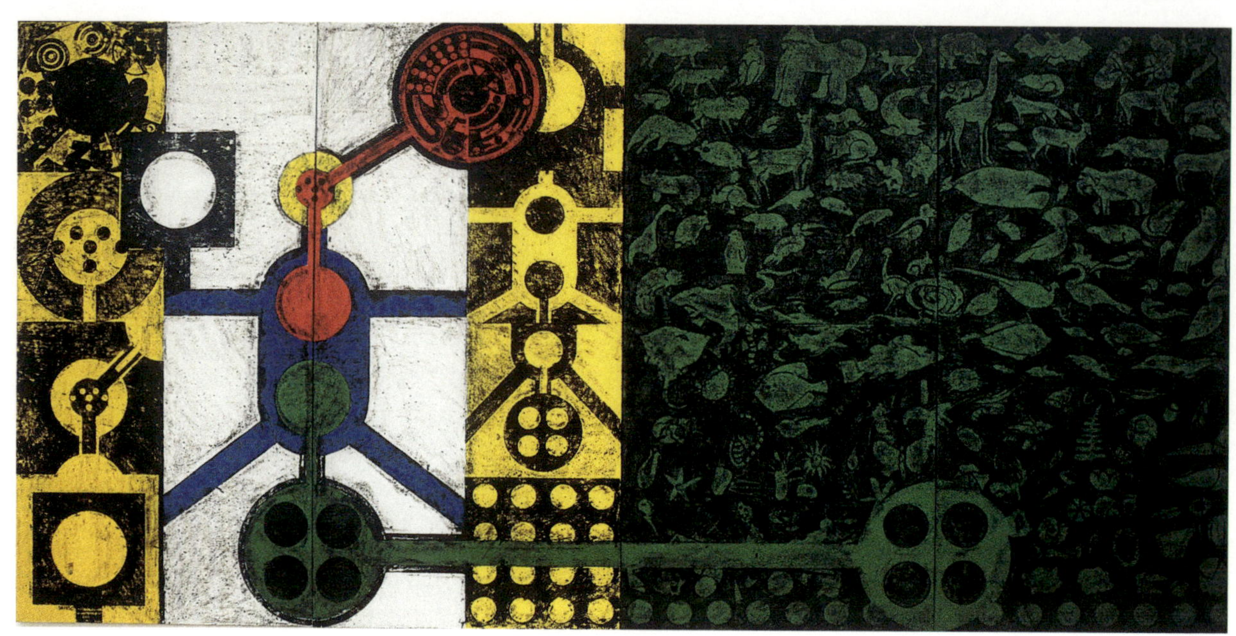

1987.13 Dallas Project (Panels 41–44: Anatomy and Evolutionary Chart), 244 × 488 cm (4 parts)

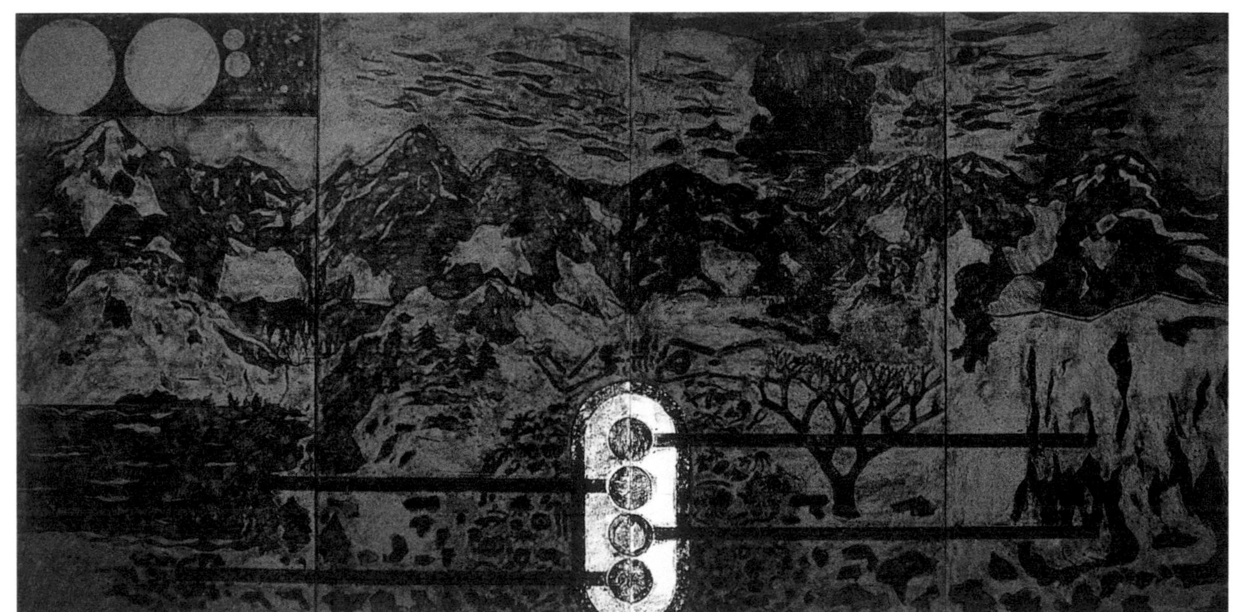

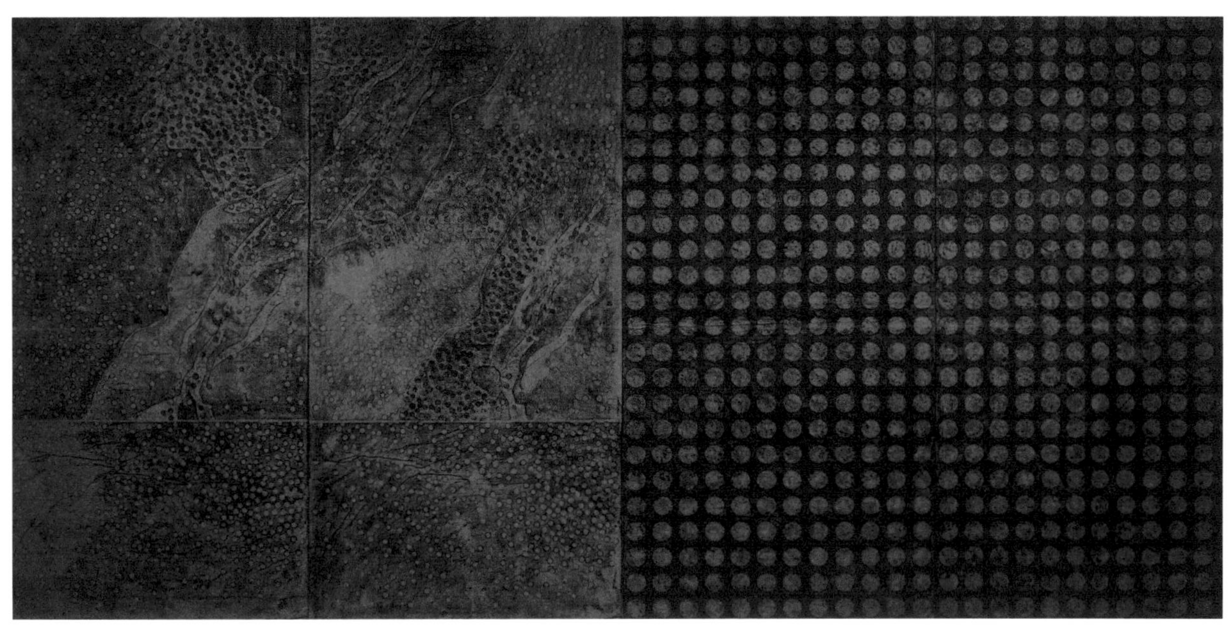

1987.14 Dallas Project (Panels 45–48: Boiler on Landscape), 244 × 488 cm (4 parts)
1987.15 Dallas Project (Panels 49–52: Weather Cycle and Elements), 244 × 488 cm (4 parts)

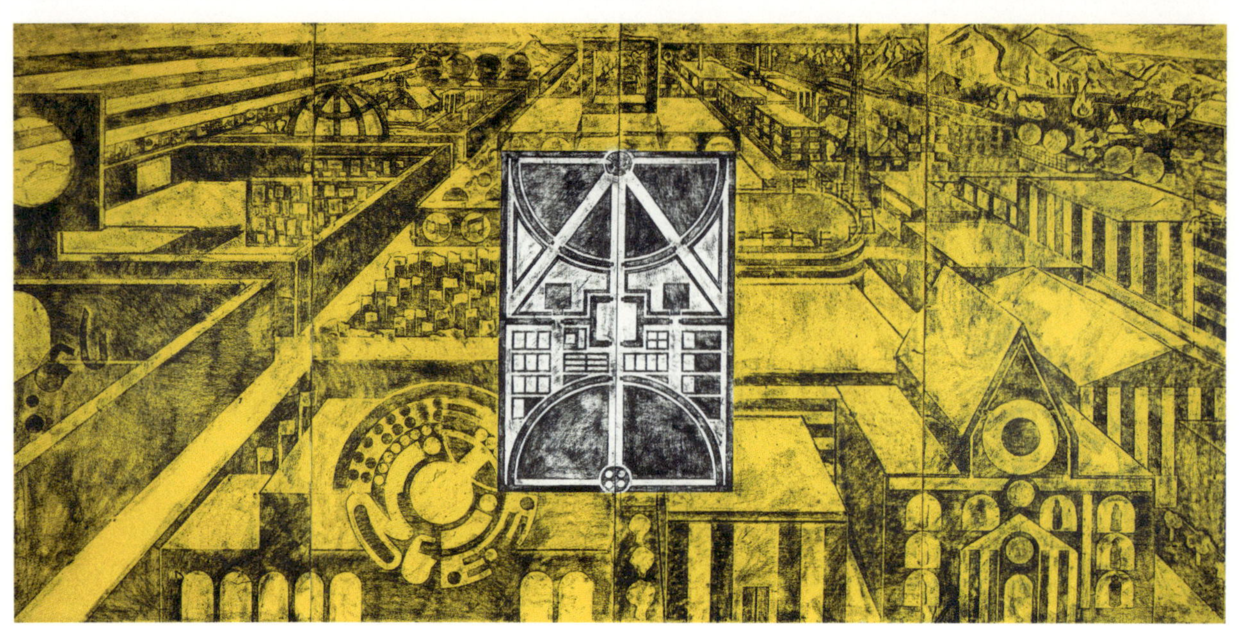

1987.16 Dallas Project (Language, World Framed and World Unframed), 244 × 488 cm (4 parts)

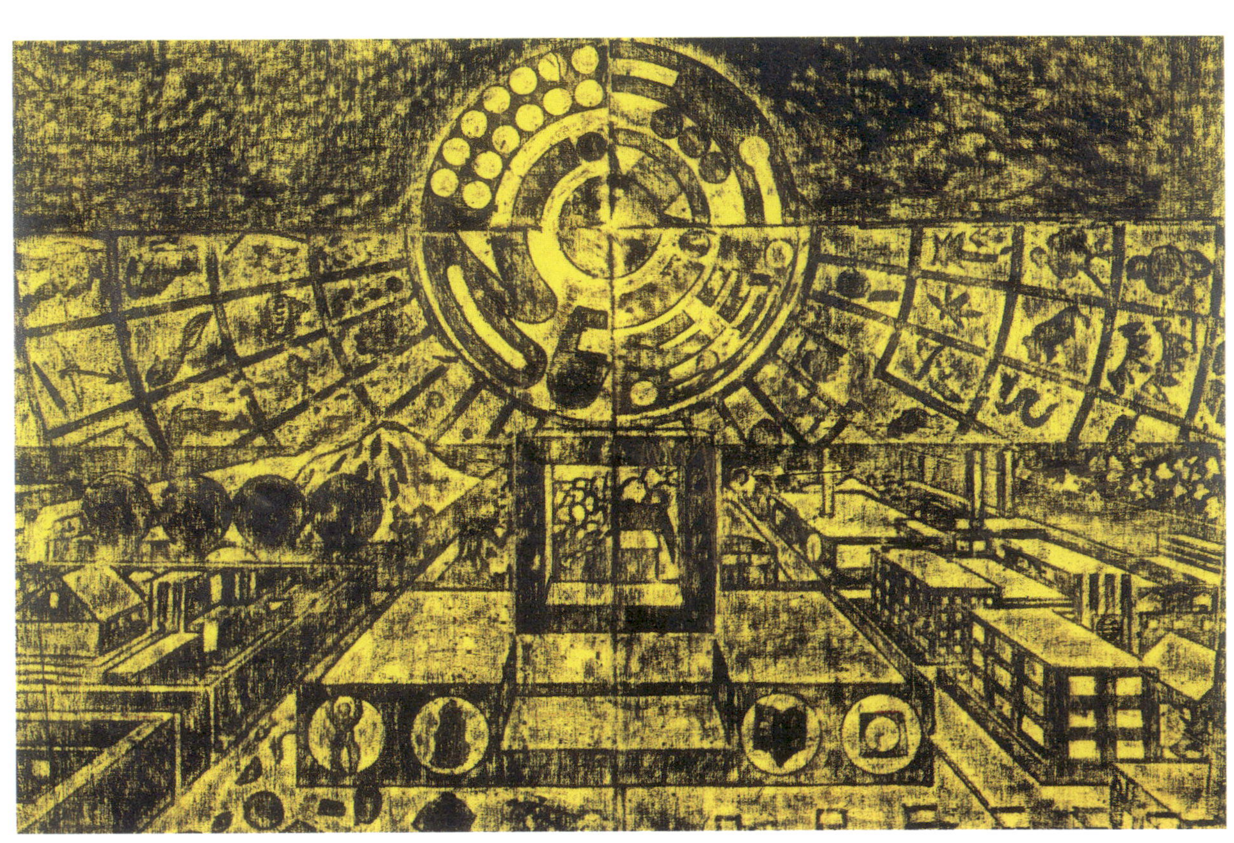

1987.17 Untitled (Cosmology over City Surrounded by History), 122 × 183 cm

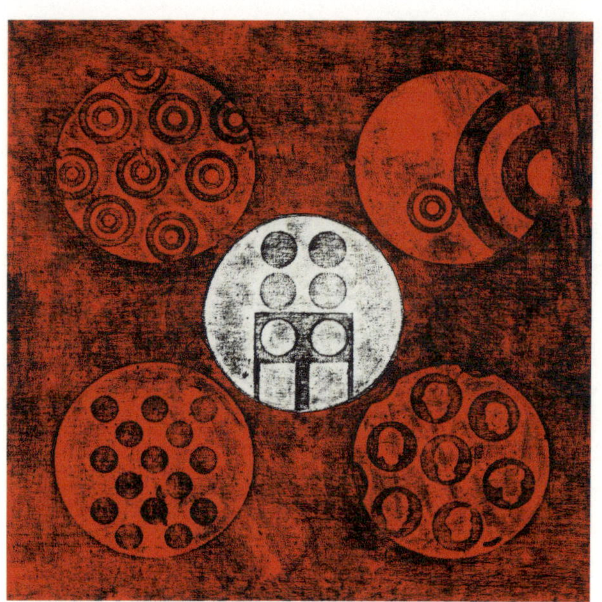

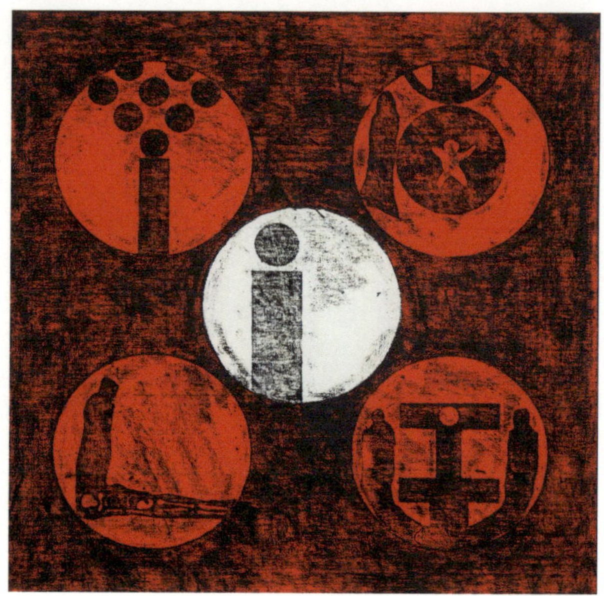

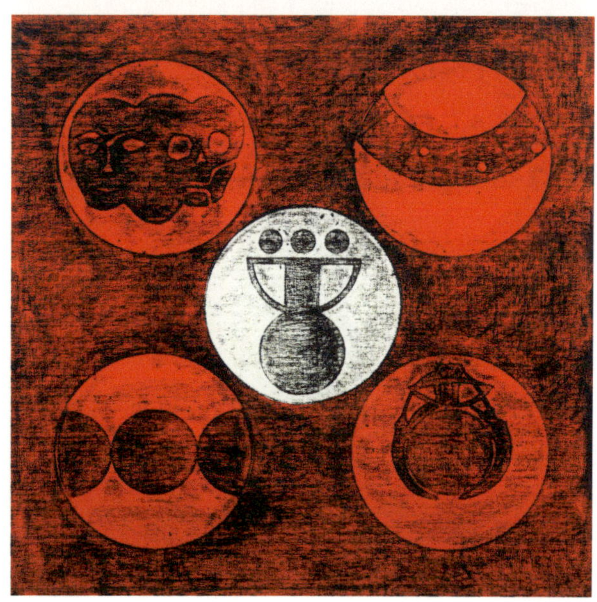

1987.18 Untitled (Before Birth), 122 × 122 cm
1987.19 Untitled (Life), 122 × 122 cm
1987.20 Untitled (Faith), 122 × 122 cm

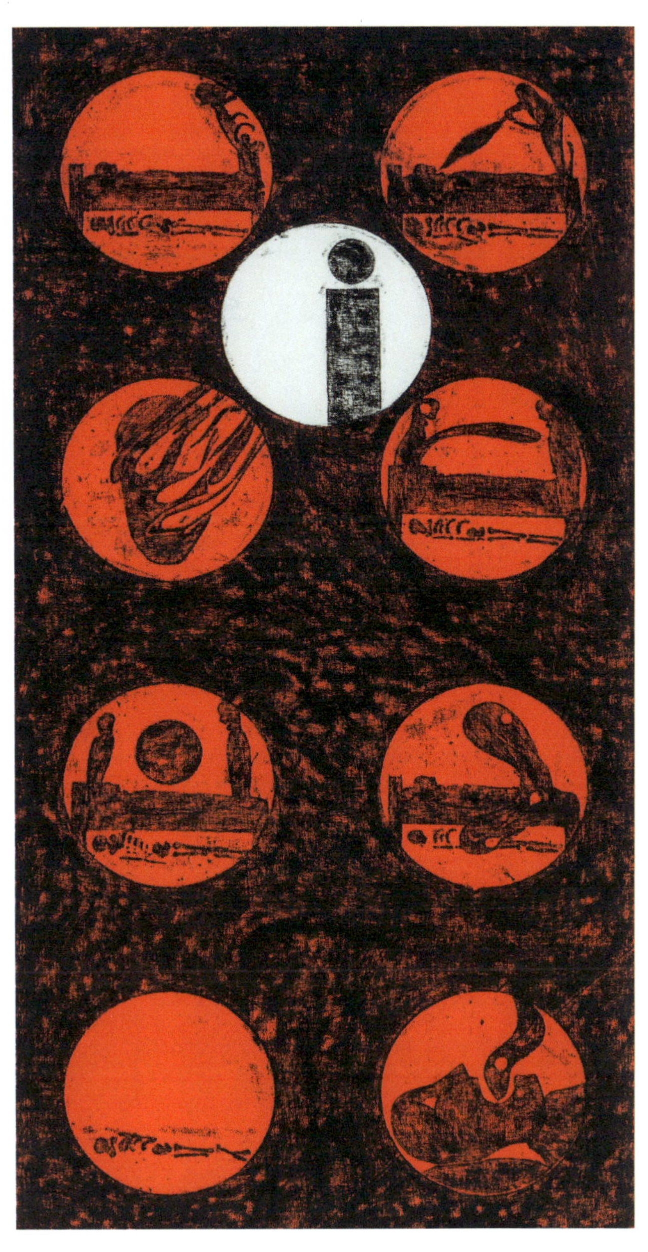

1987.21 Untitled (Death), 244 × 122 cm

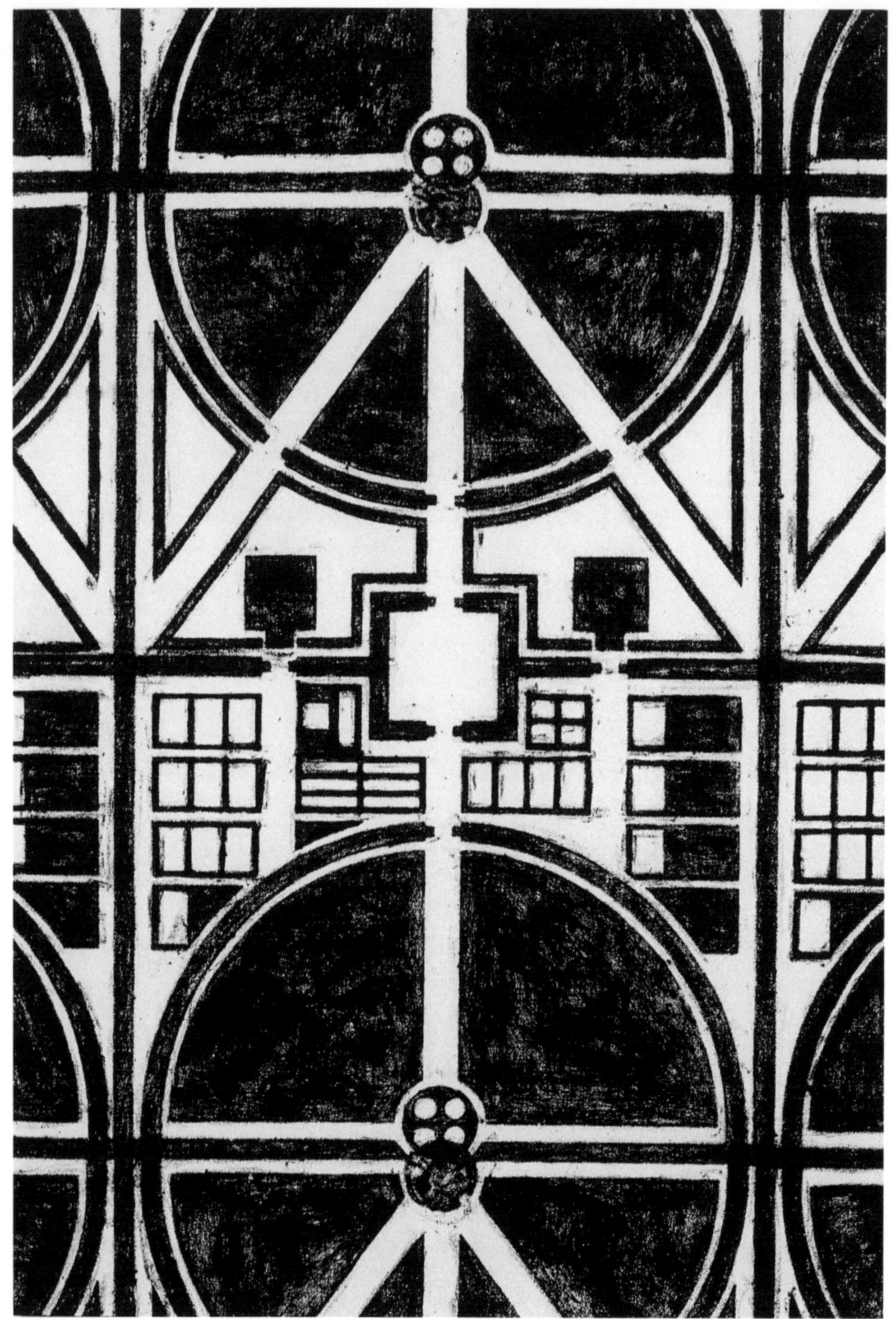

1987.22 Untitled (City), 183 × 122 cm

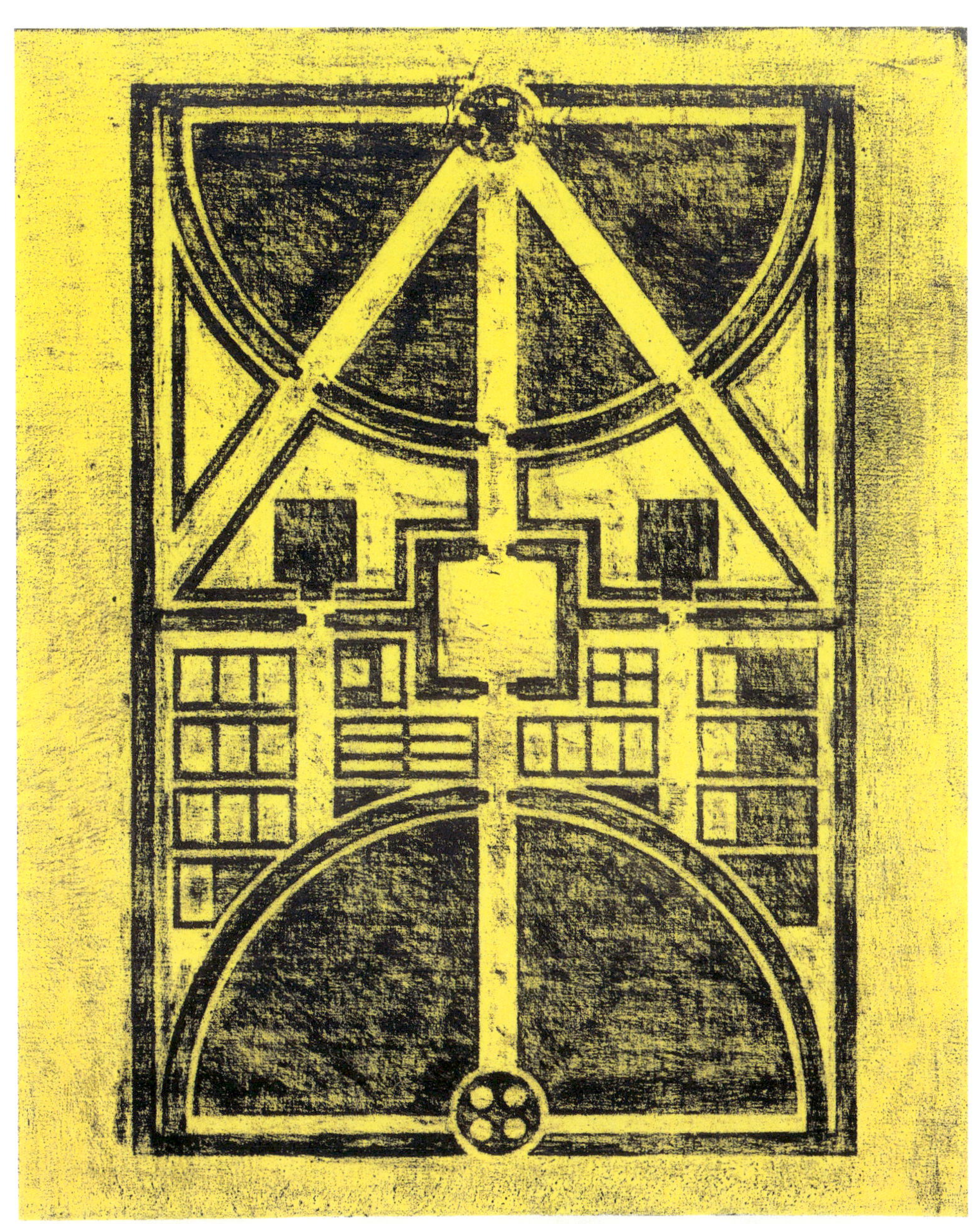

1987.23 Untitled (City), 183 × 122 cm

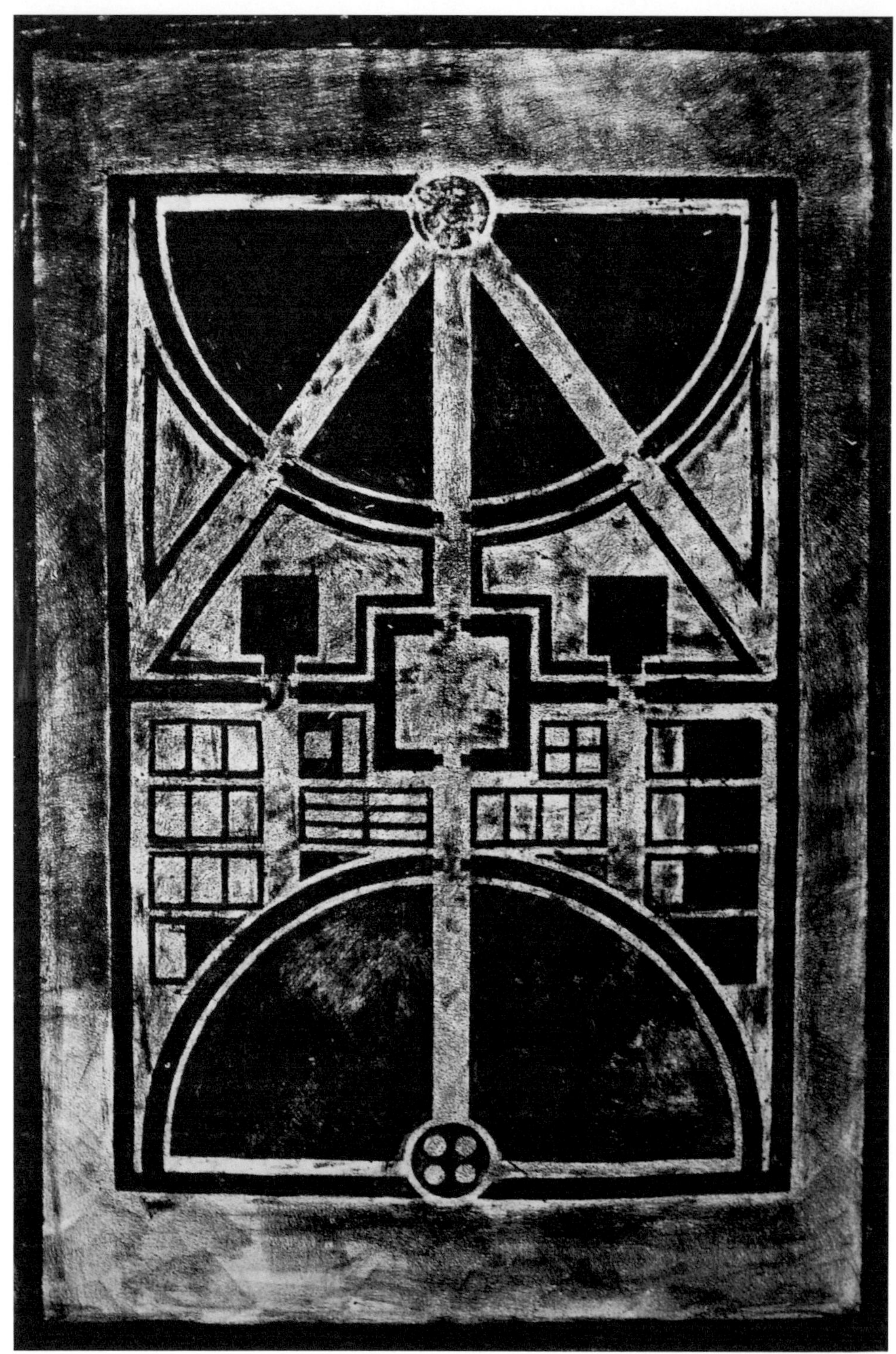

1987.24 Untitled (City), 183 × 122 cm

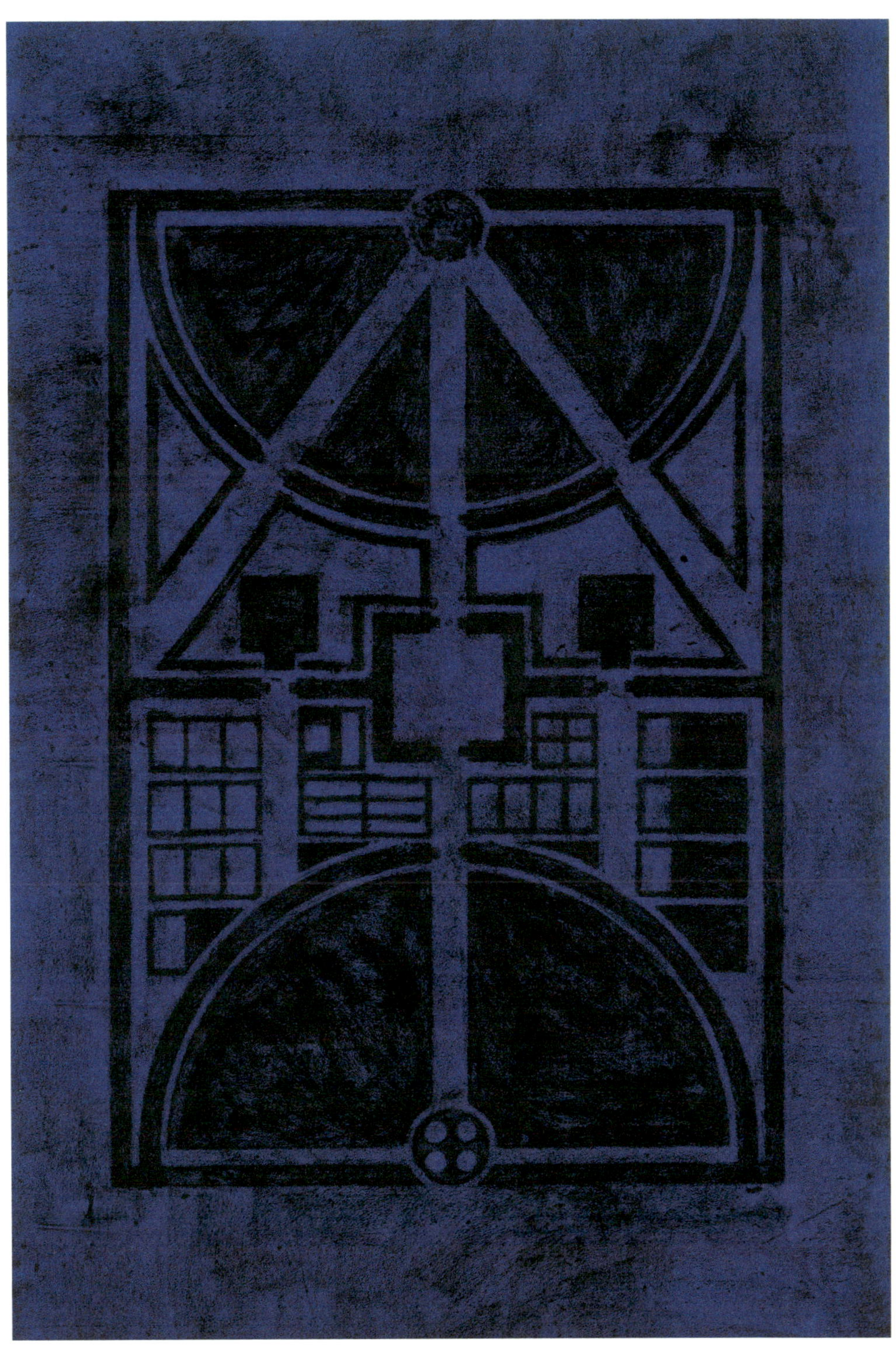

1987.25 Untitled (Blue City), 183 × 122 cm

1988

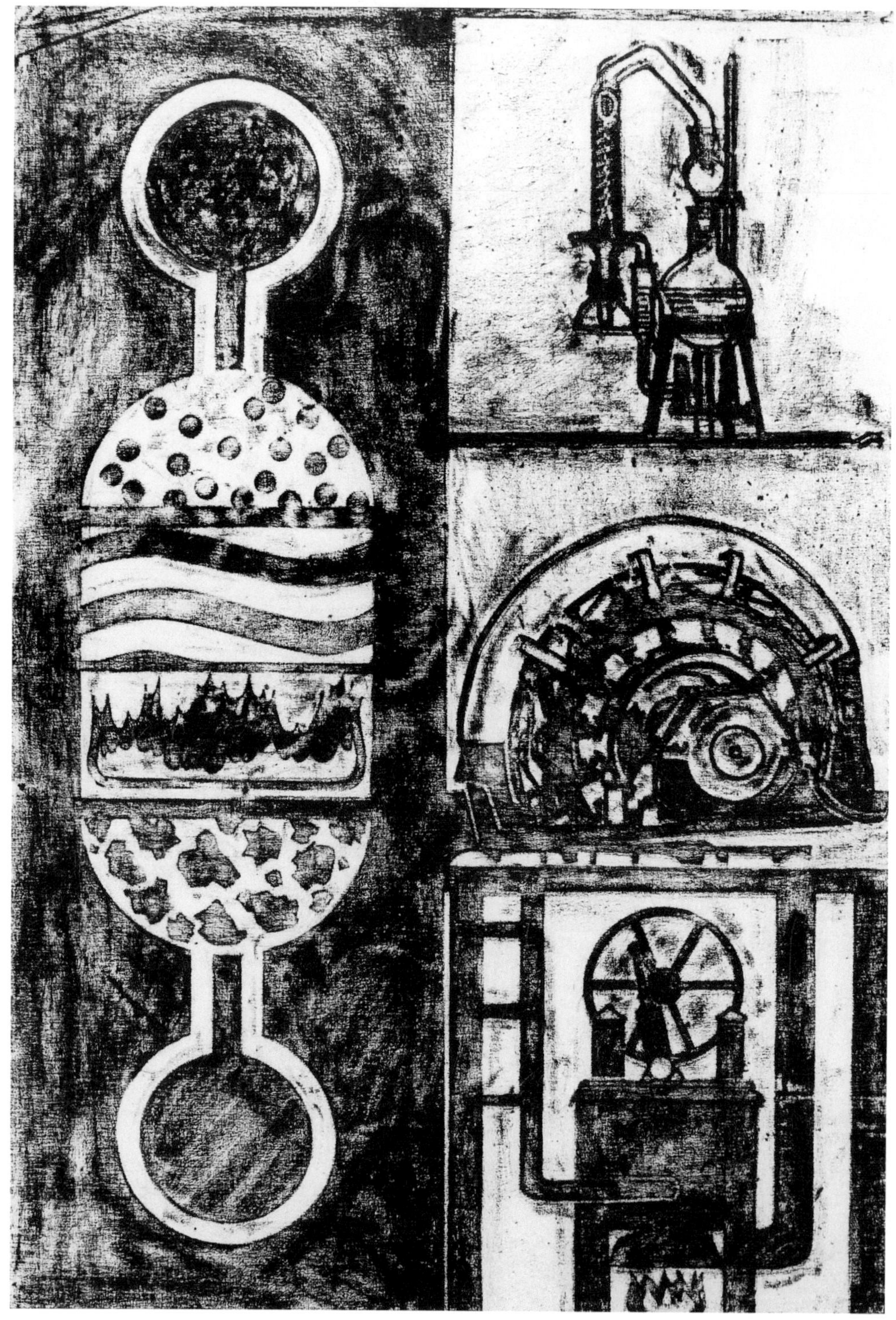

1988.1 Untitled (Boiler–Distiller, Generator, Steam Engine), 183 × 122 cm

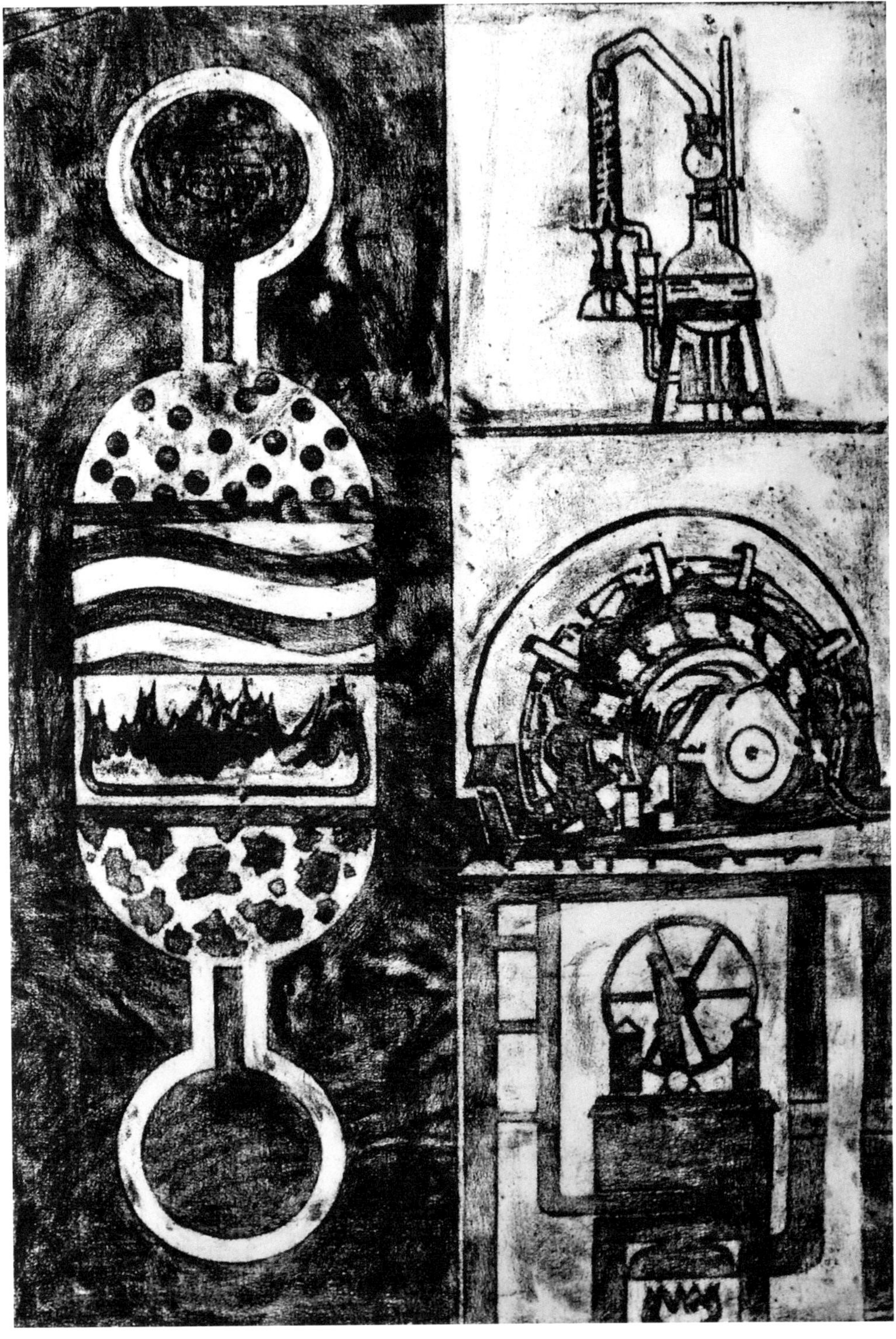

1988.2 Untitled (Boiler–Distiller, Generator, Steam Engine), 183 × 122 cm

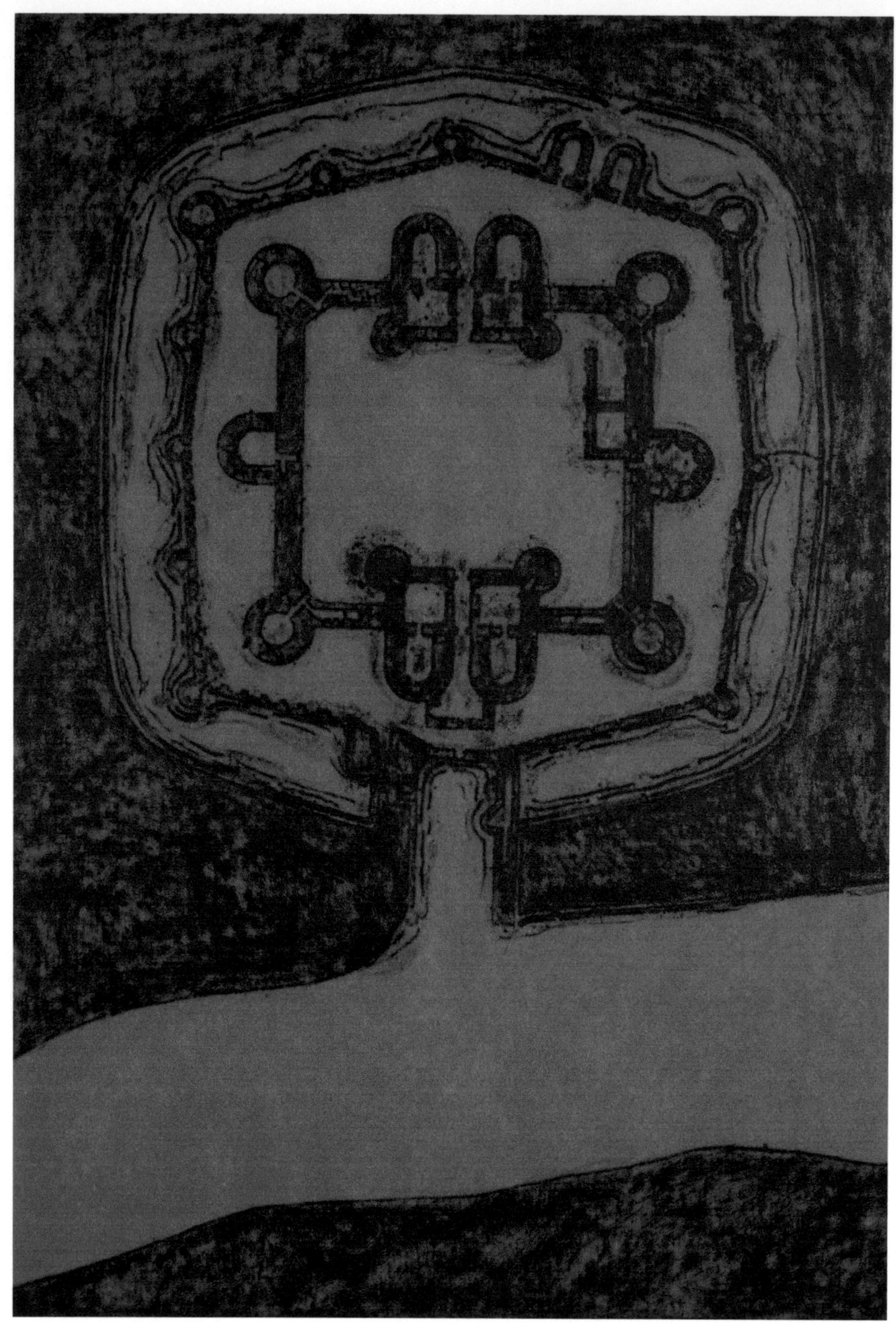

1988.3 Untitled (Castle), 183 × 122 cm

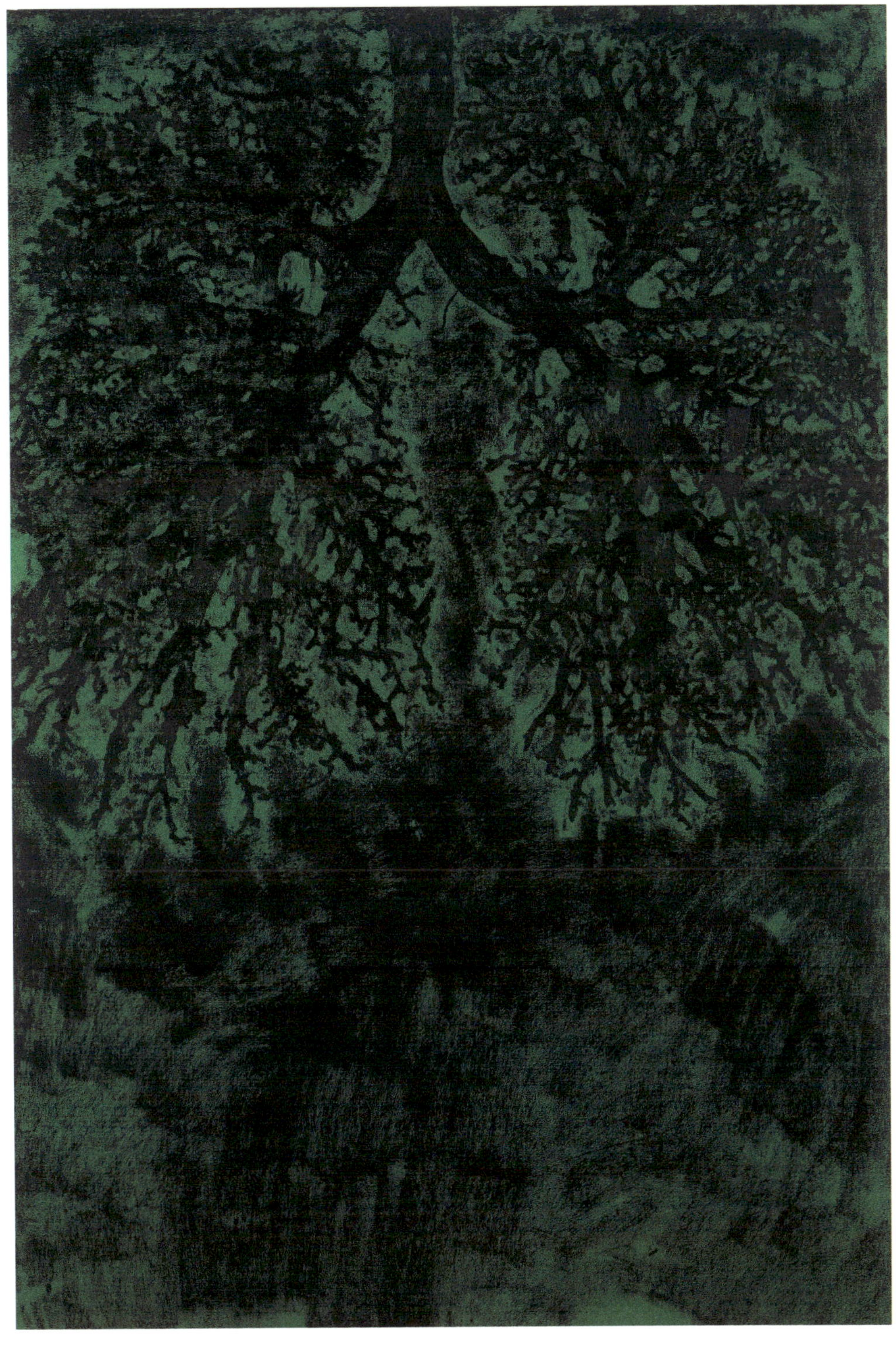

1988.4 Untitled (Green Lungs), 183 × 122 cm

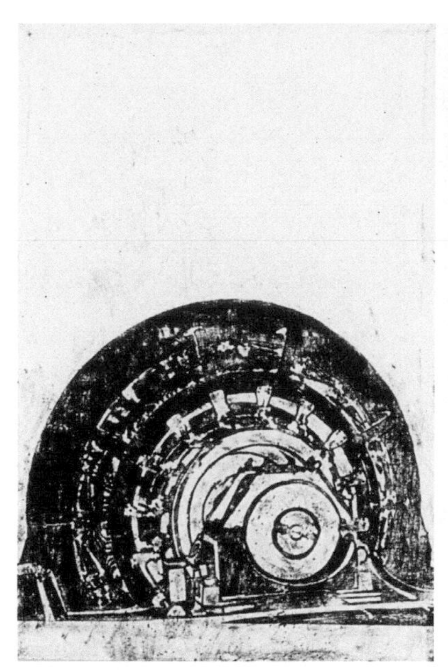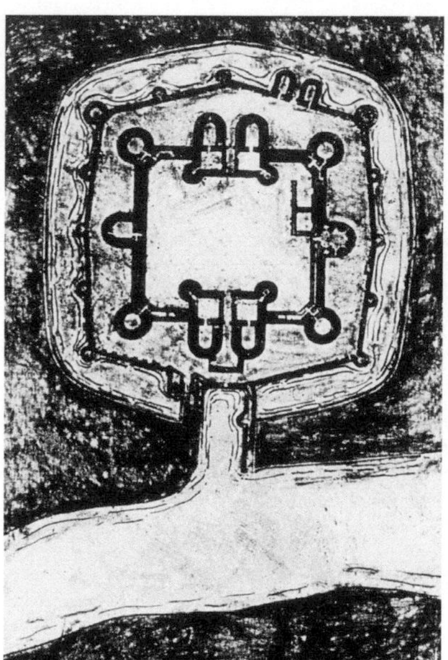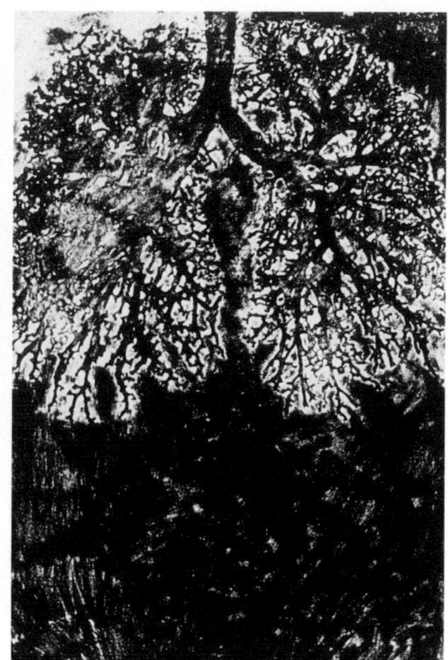

1988.5 Untitled (Generator, Castle, Lungs), 183 × 122 cm each (triptych)

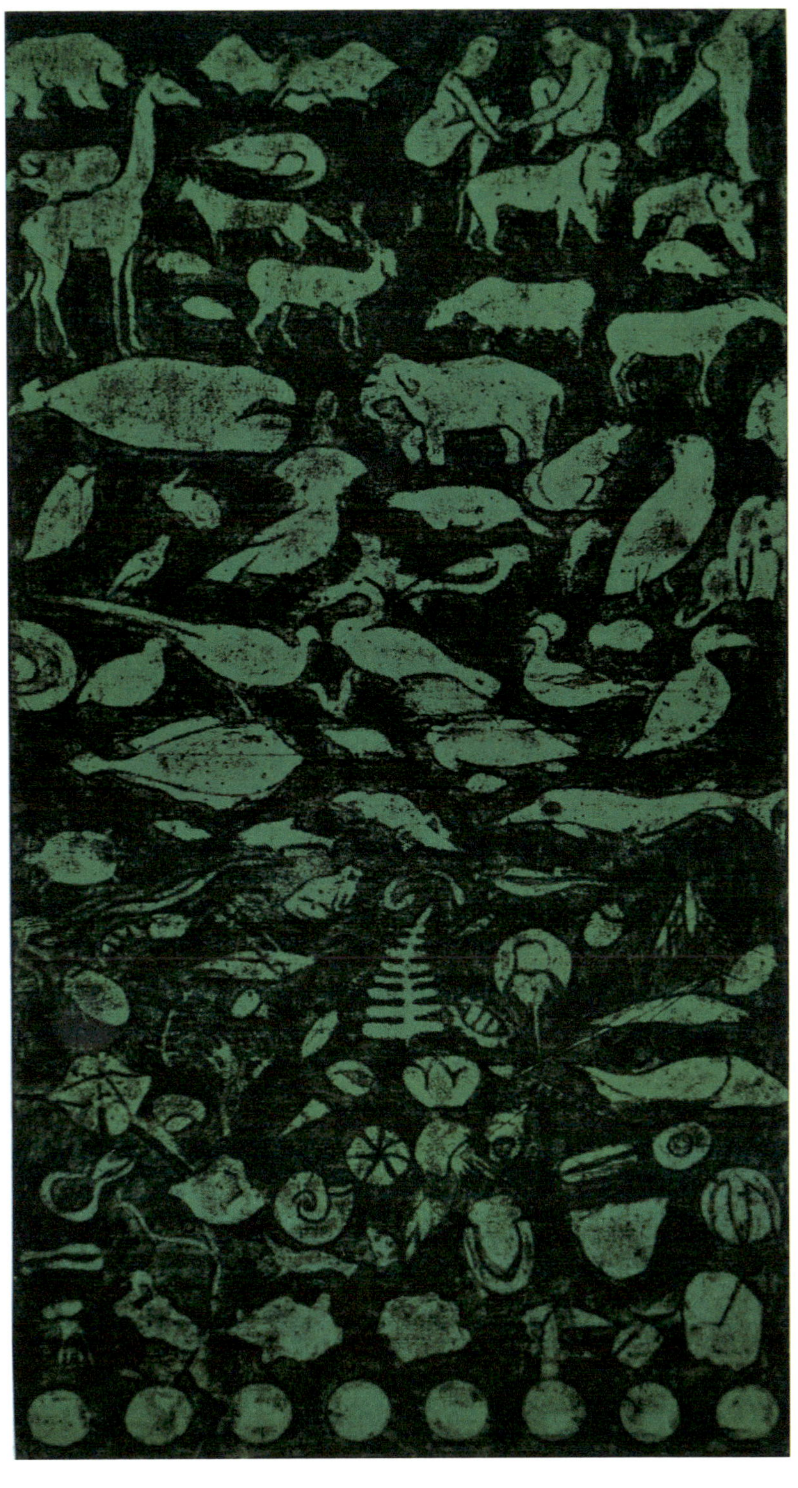

1988.6 Untitled (Elements Green), 244 × 122 cm

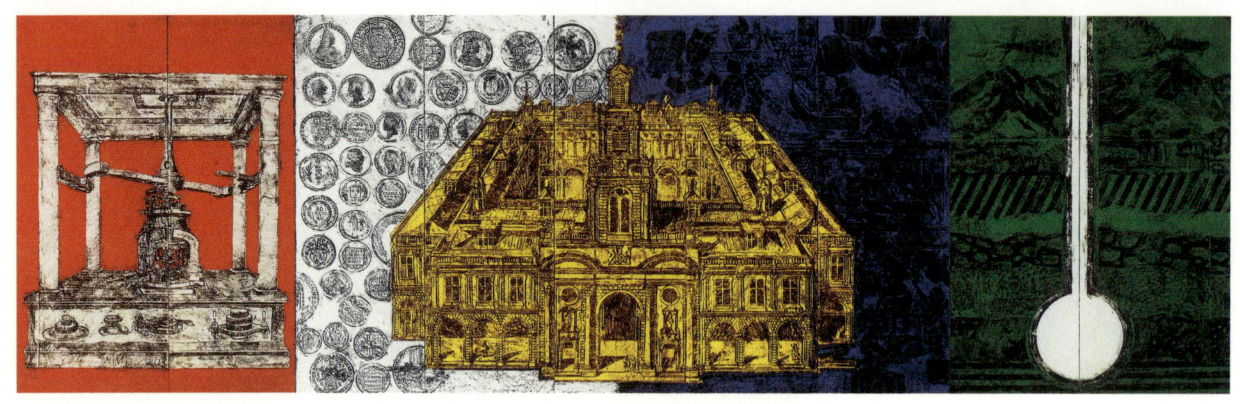

1988.7 Untitled (Bank), 366 × 1098 cm (9 parts)

1989

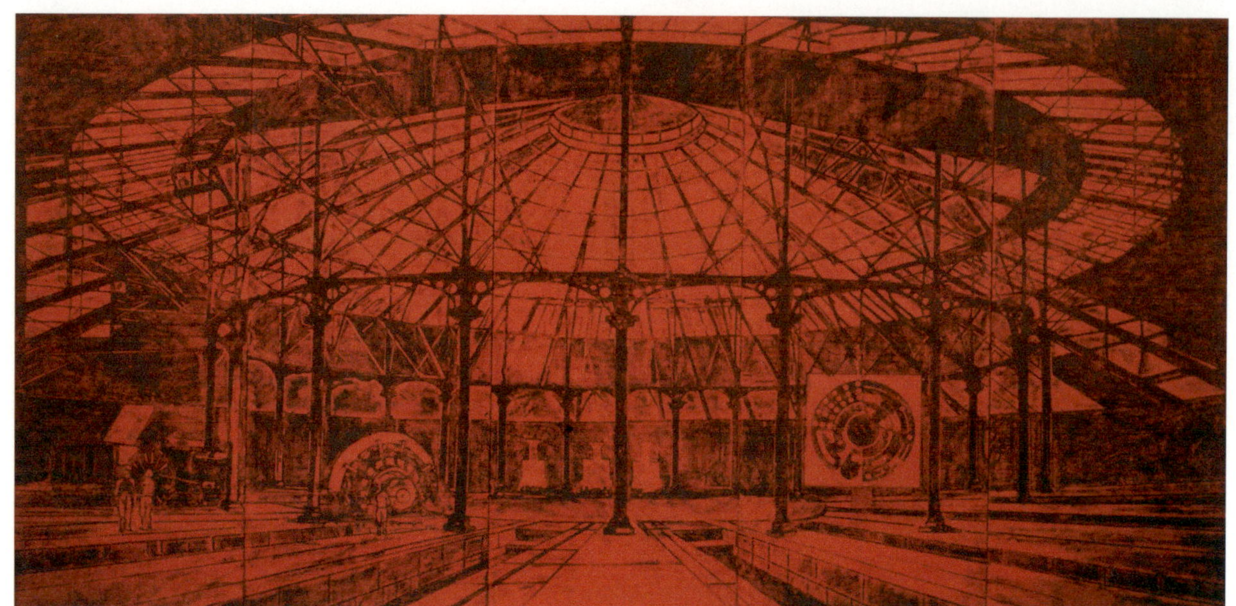

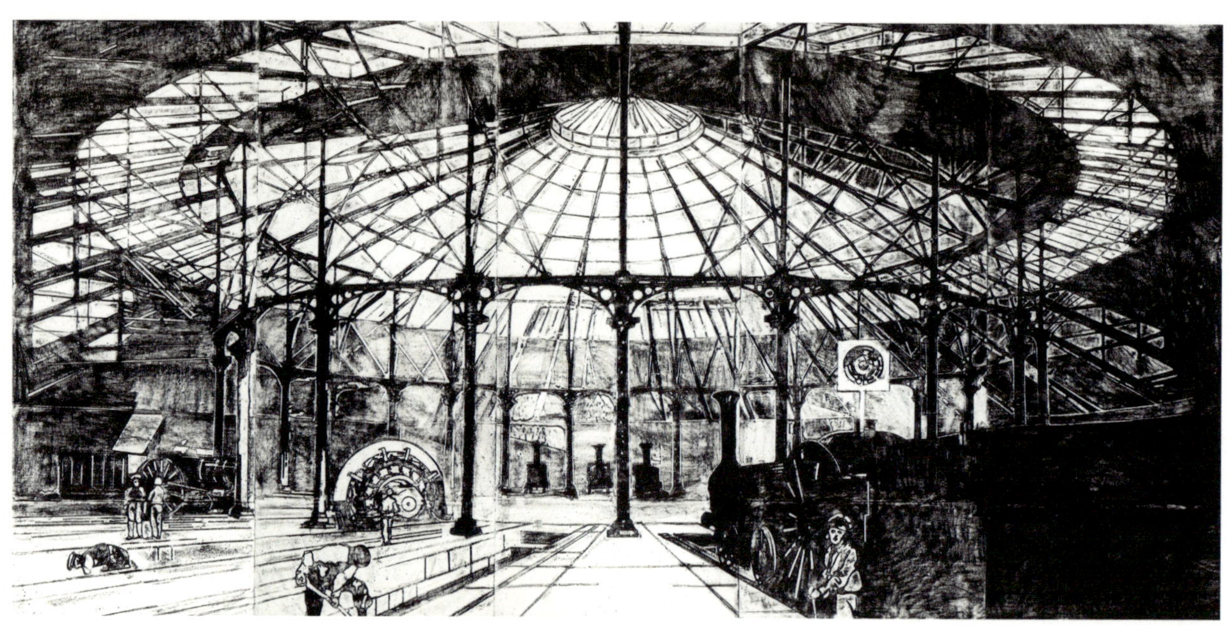

1989.1 Untitled (Roundhouse Red), 305 × 609.5 cm (5 parts)
1989.2 Untitled (Roundhouse B&W), 305 × 609.5 cm (5 parts)

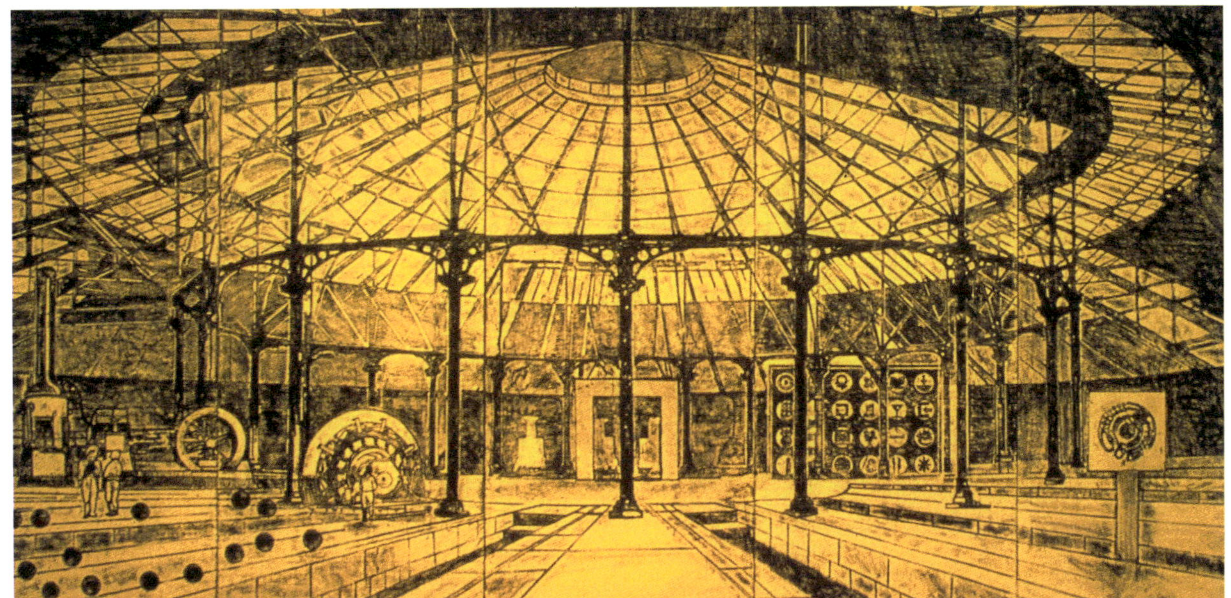

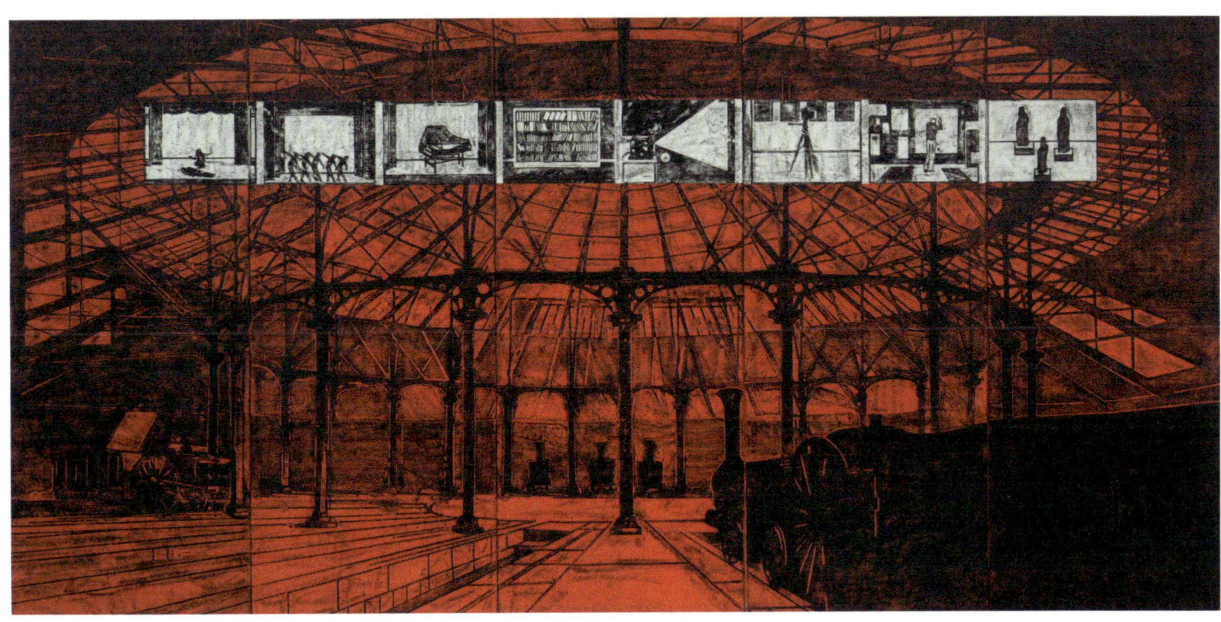

1989.3 Untitled (Roundhouse Yellow), 305 × 610 cm (5 parts)
1989.4 Untitled (Roundhouse of the Arts), 1989/2001, 305 × 609.5 cm (5 parts)

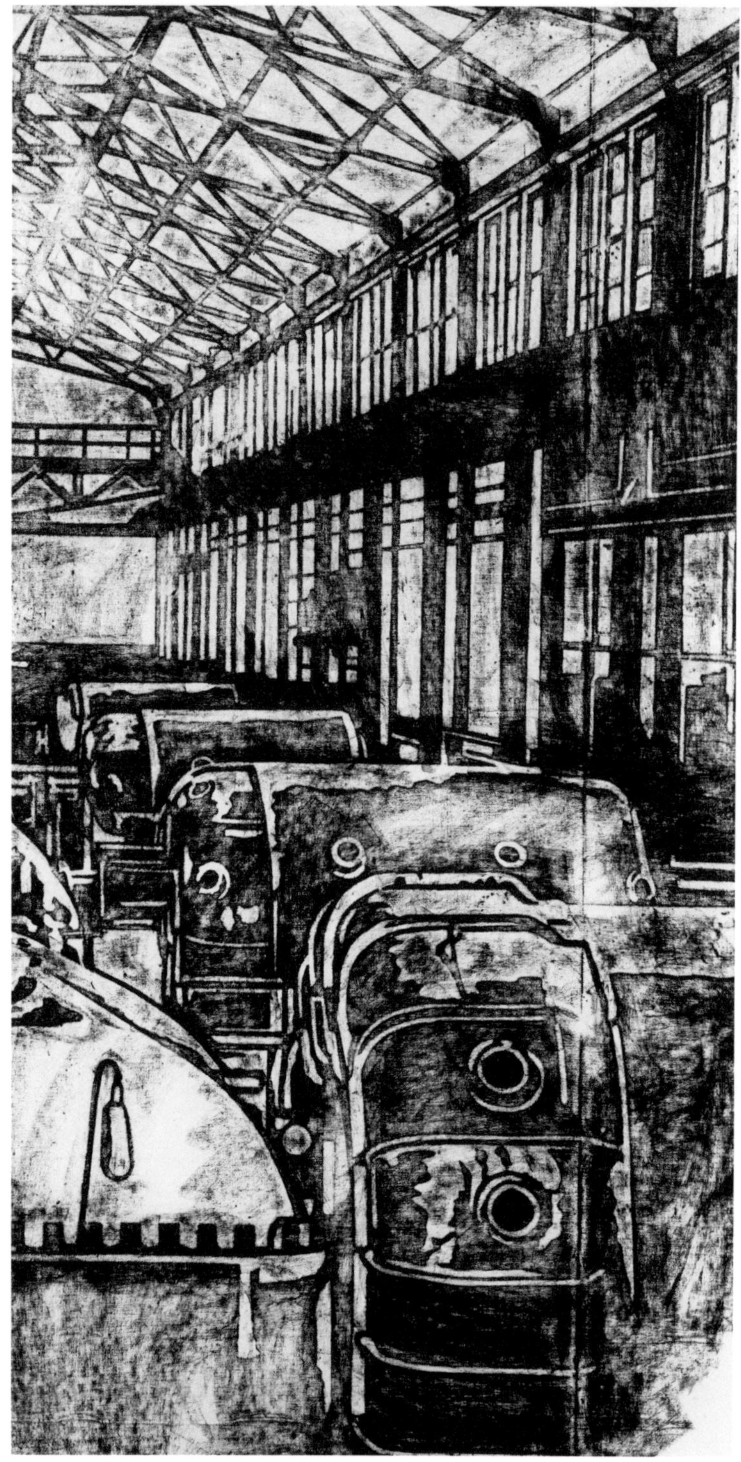

1989.5 Untitled (Generator Hall, Detail), 244 × 122 cm

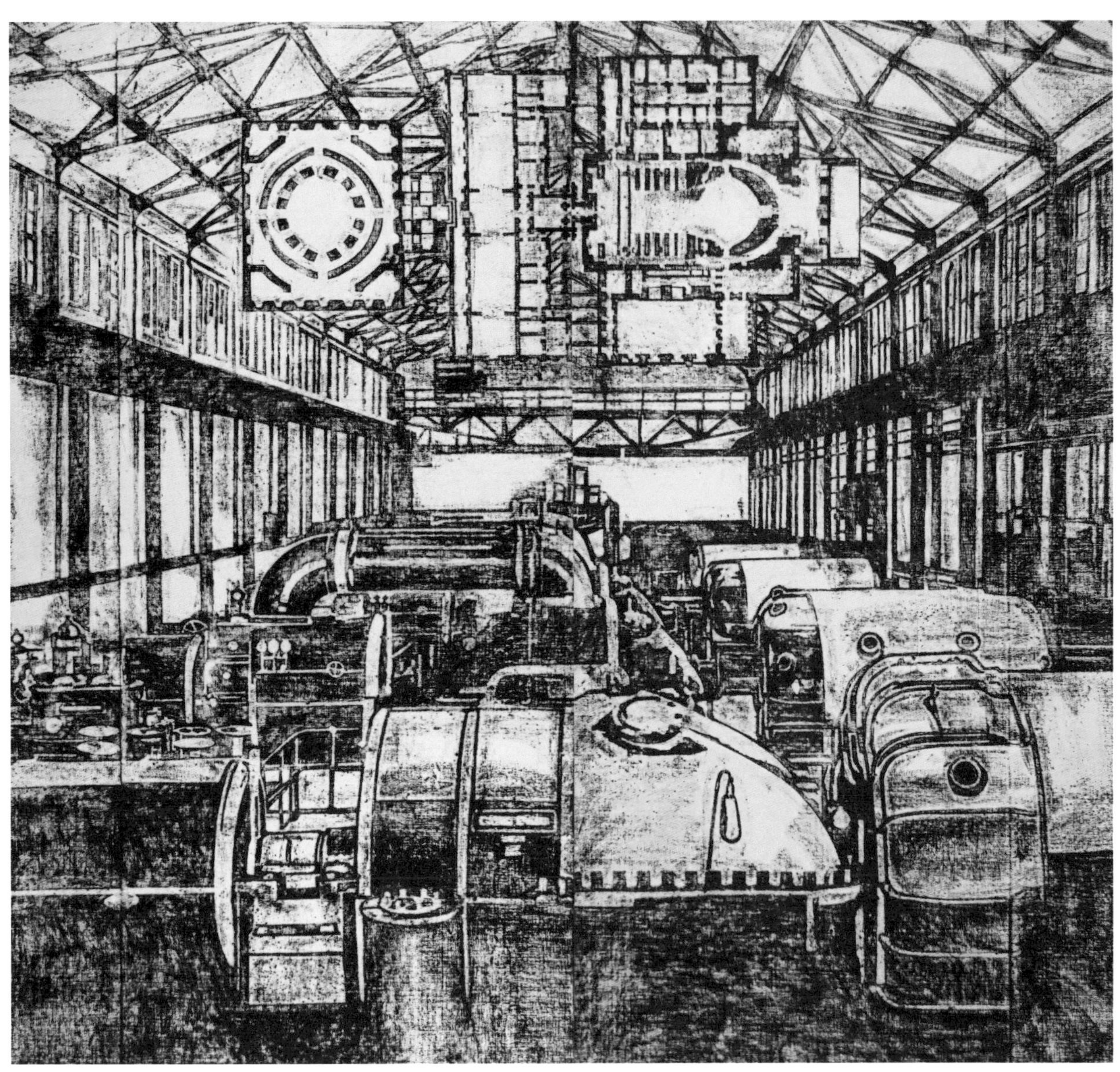

1989.6 Untitled (Yellow Generator Room), 305 × 305 cm (2 parts)

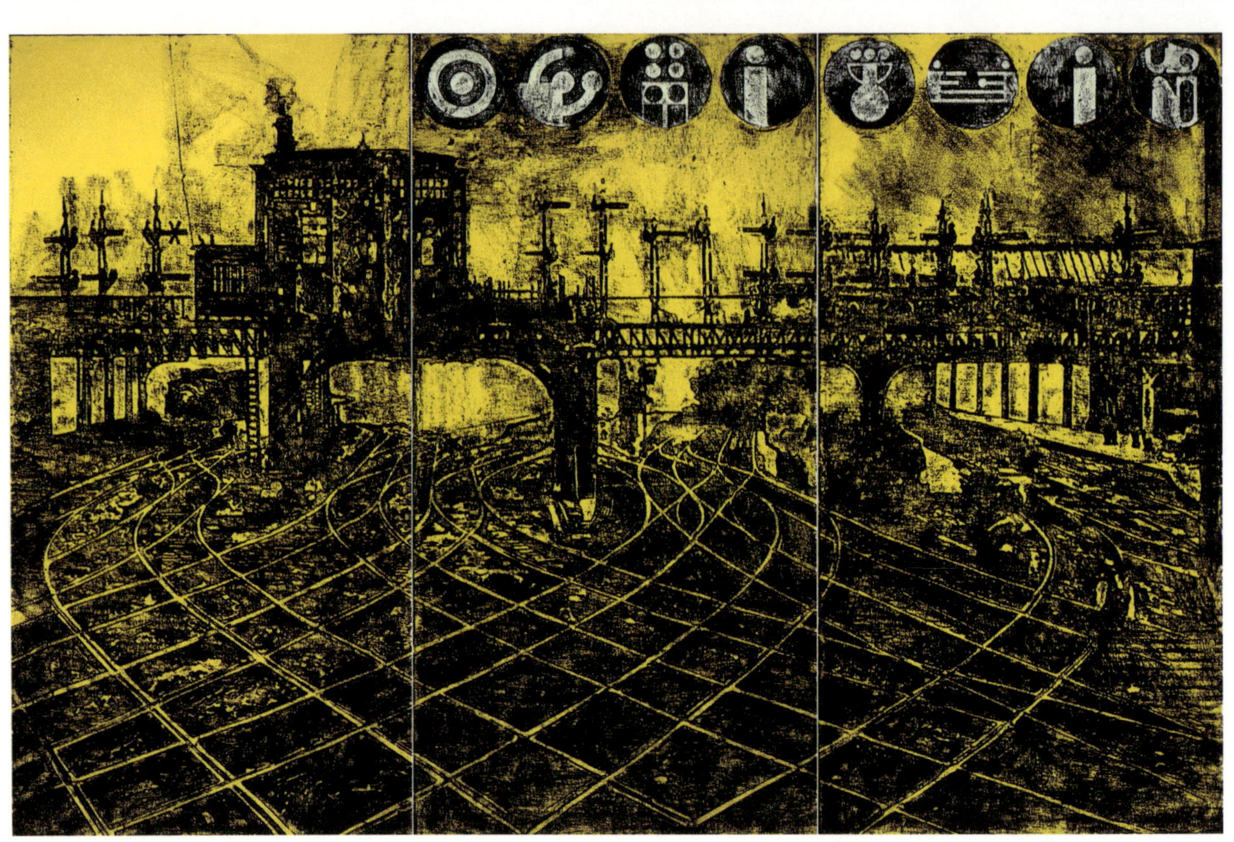

1989.7 Untitled (Train Station with Cosmology), 244 × 366 (3 parts)

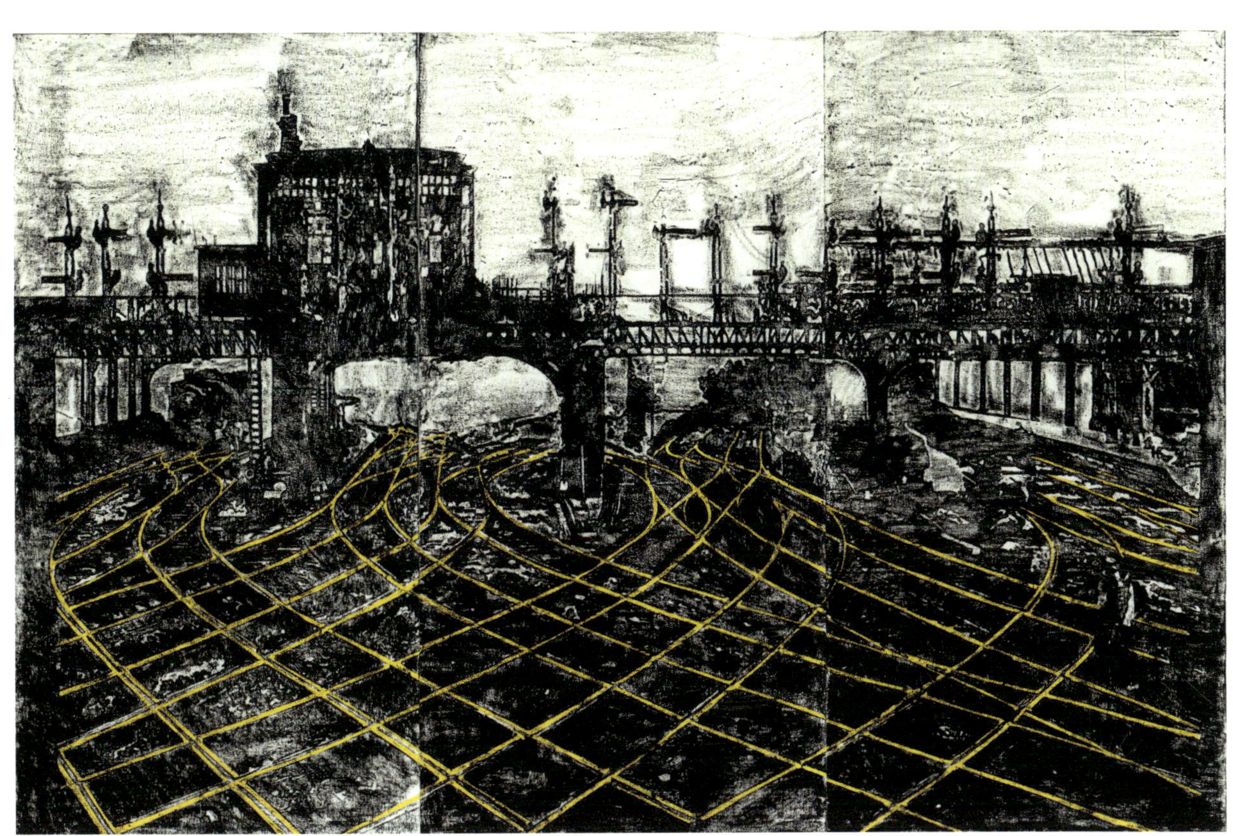

1989.8 Untitled (Train Station), 244 × 366 cm (3 parts)

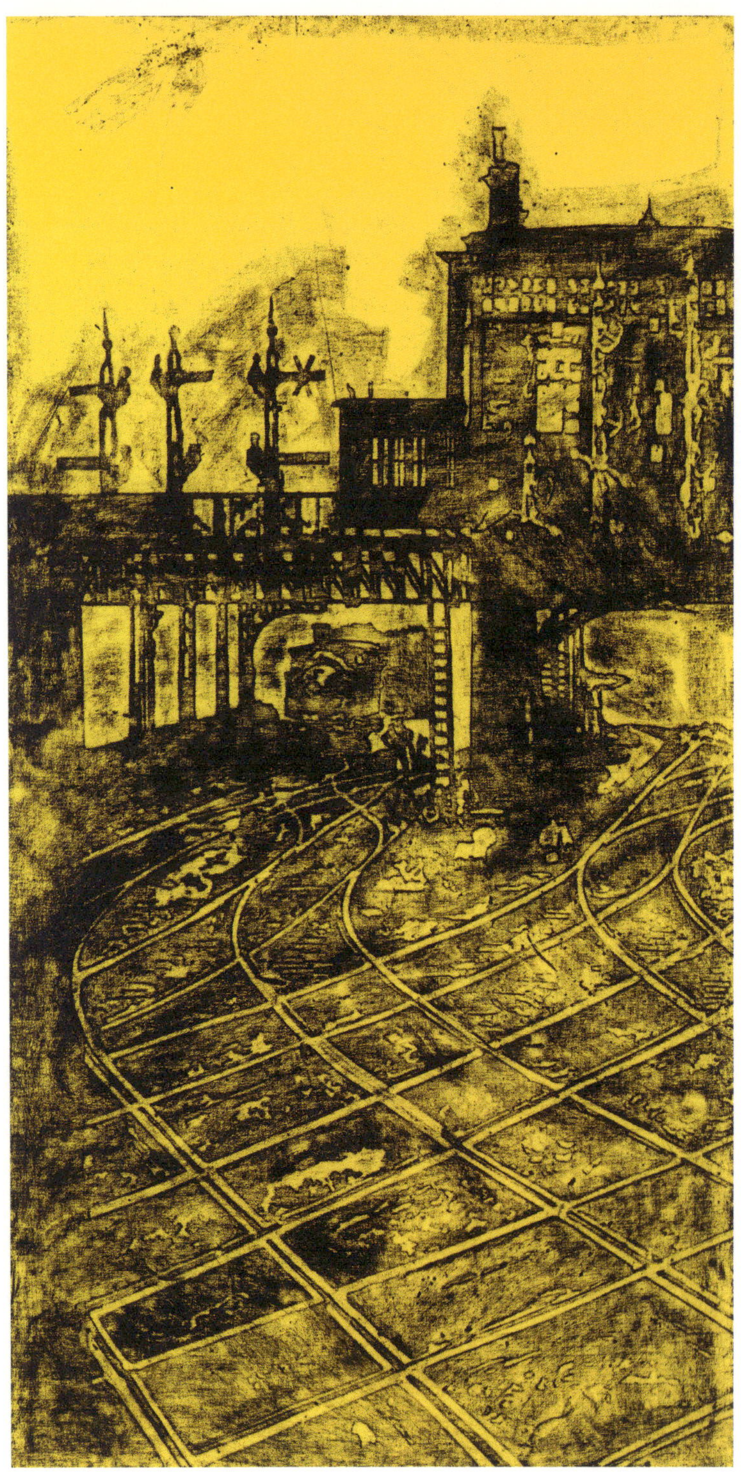

1989.9 Untitled (Train Station), 244 × 122 cm

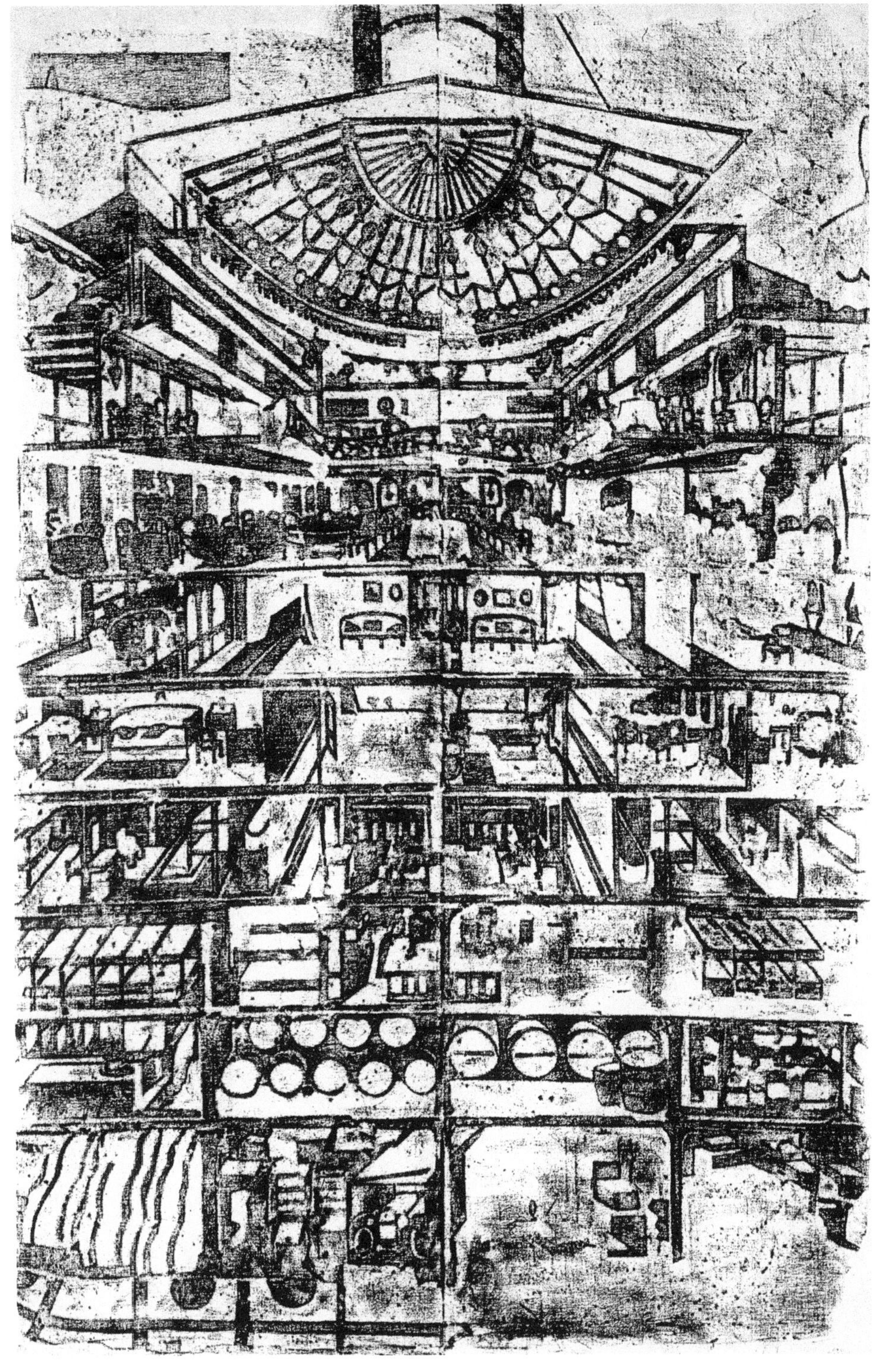

1989.10 Untitled (Ship's Interior), 183 × 122 cm

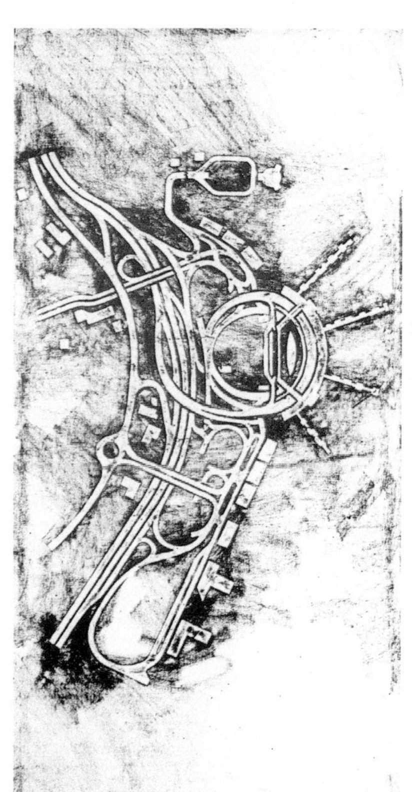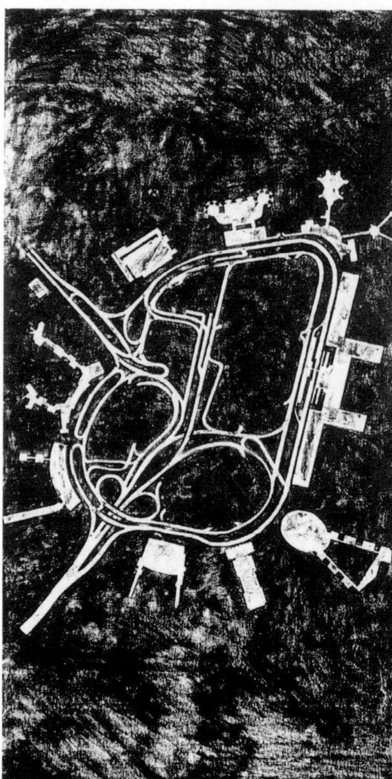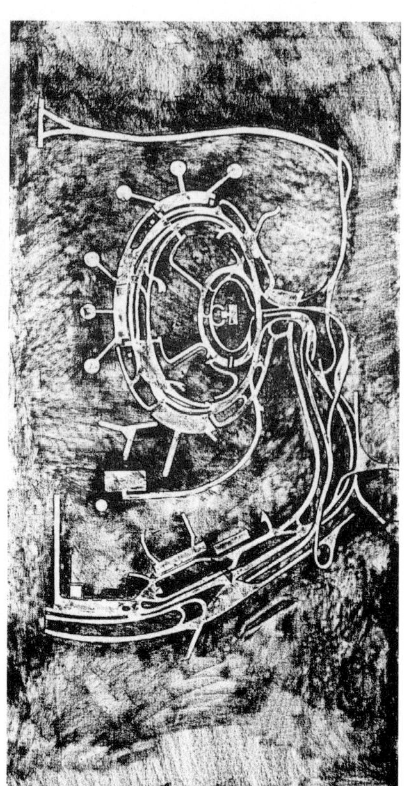

1989.11 Untitled (Airport), 244 × 122 cm each (triptych)

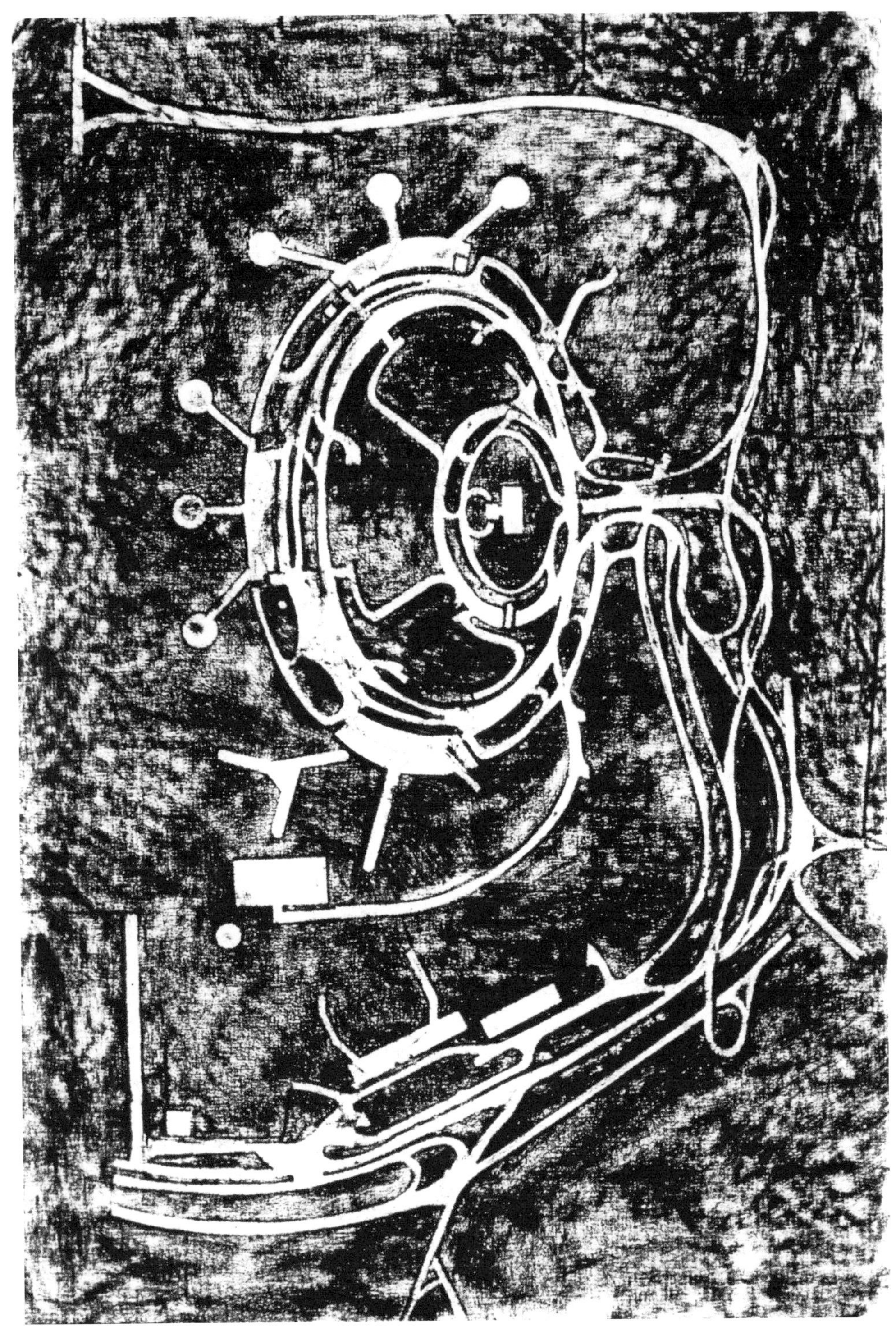

1989.12 Untitled (Airport), 183 × 122 cm

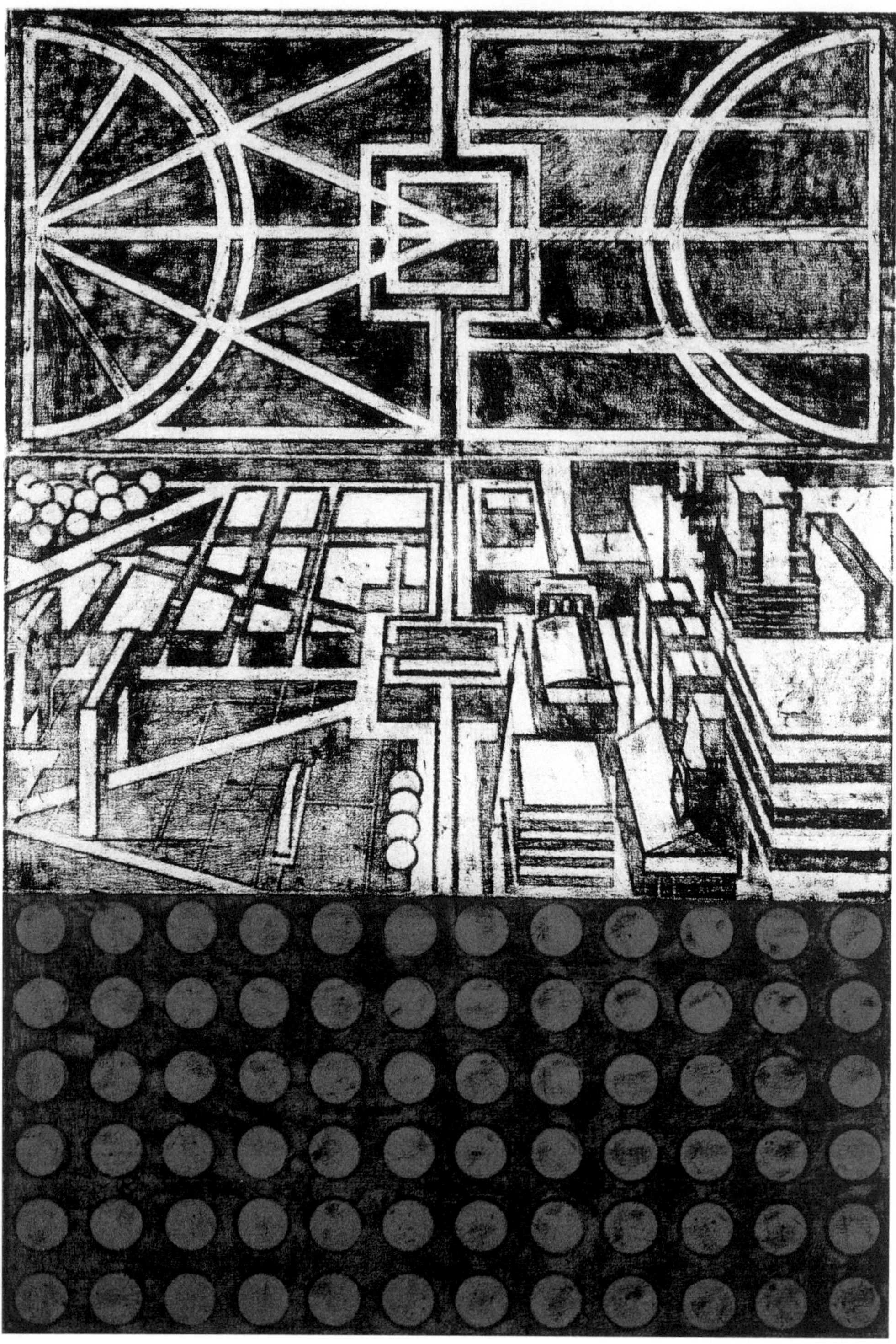

1989.13 Untitled (City into Elements), 183 × 122 cm

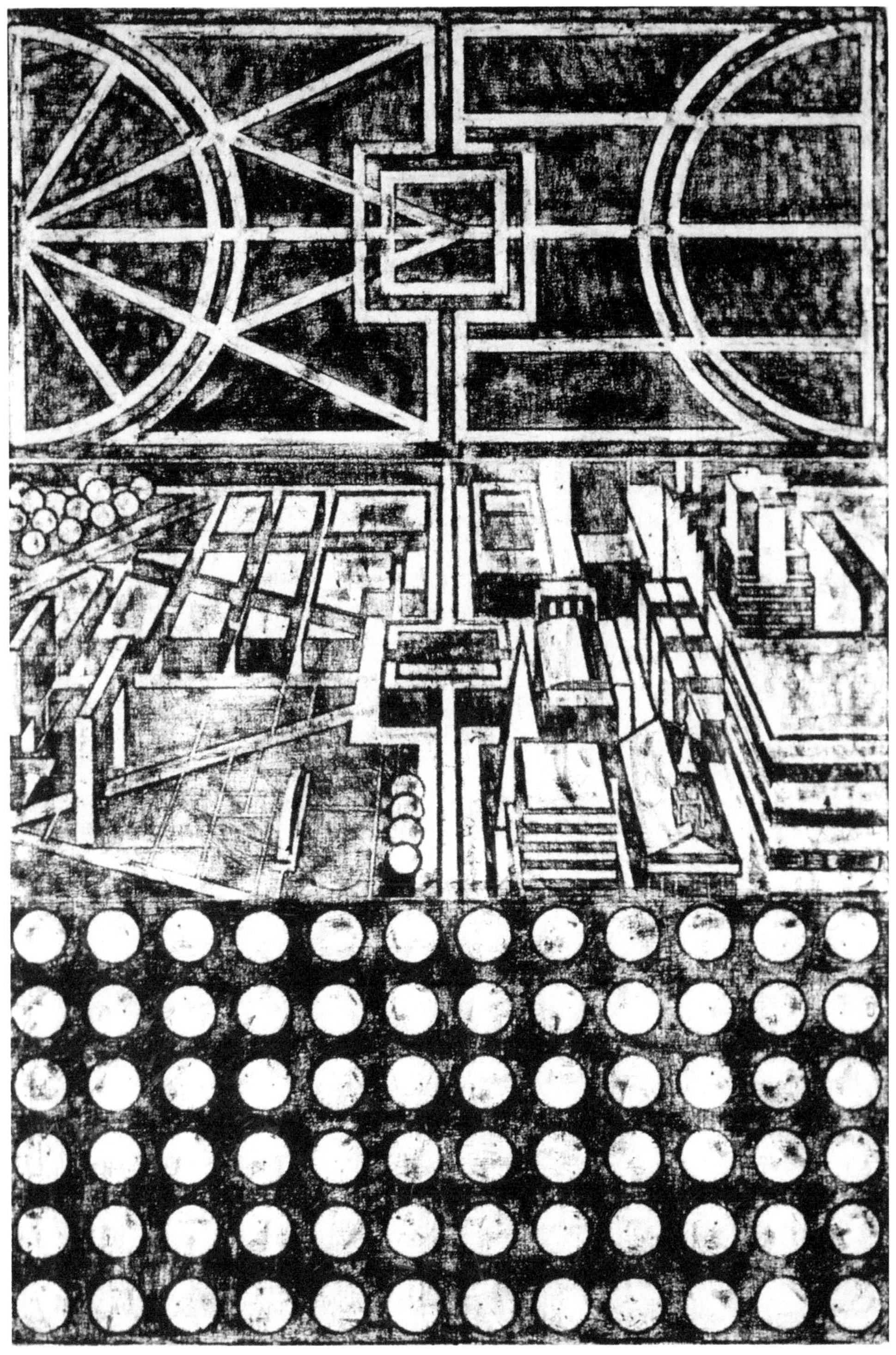

1989.14 Untitled (City into Elements), 183 × 122 cm

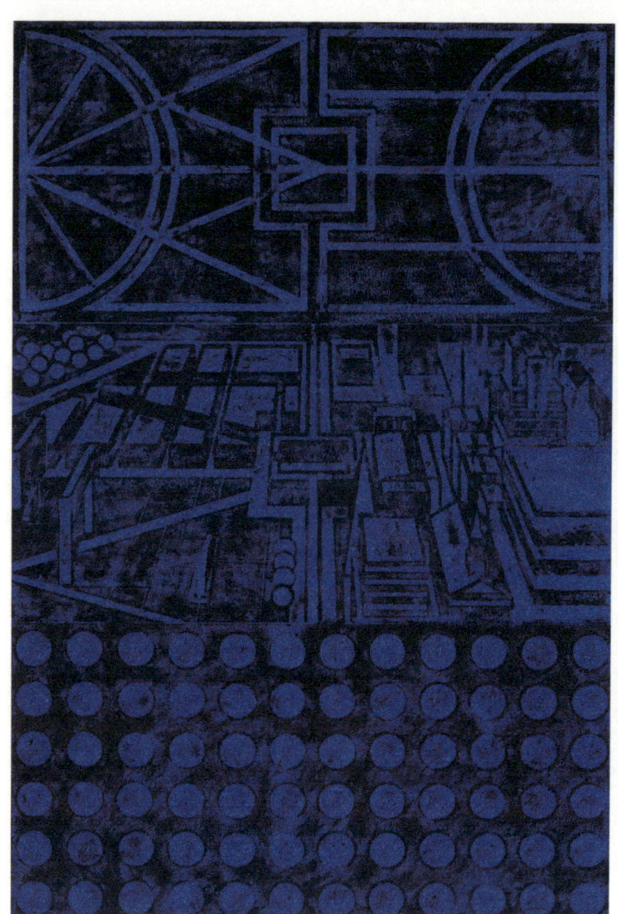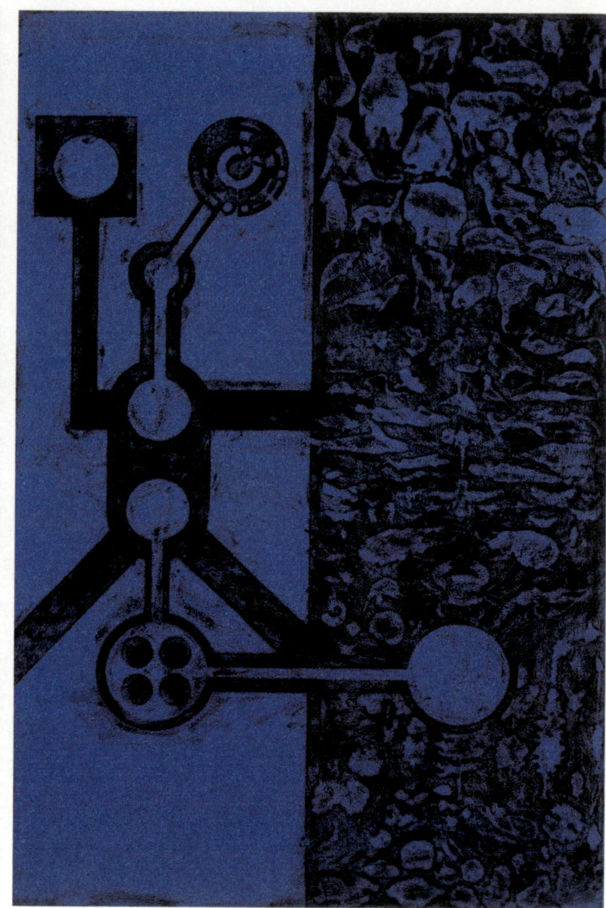

1989.15 Untitled (City into Elements—Anatomy and Evolution), 183 × 122 cm each (diptych)

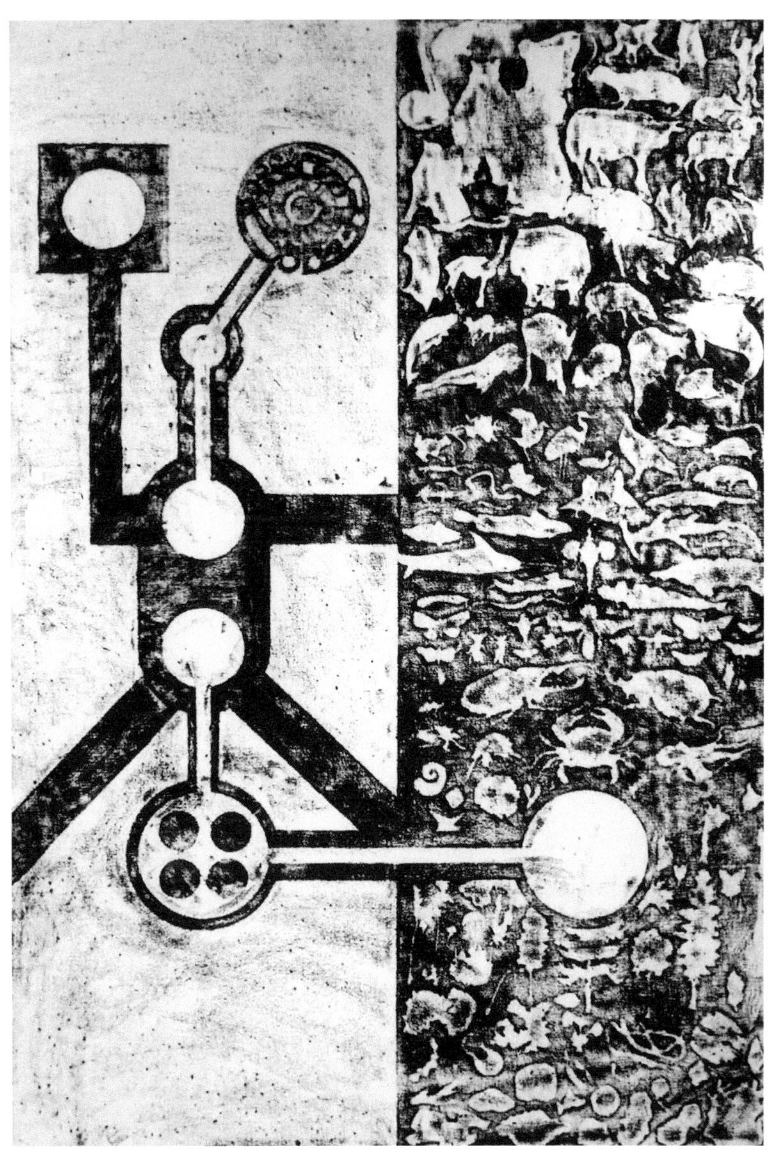

1989.16 Untitled (Anatomy and Evolution), 183 × 122 cm

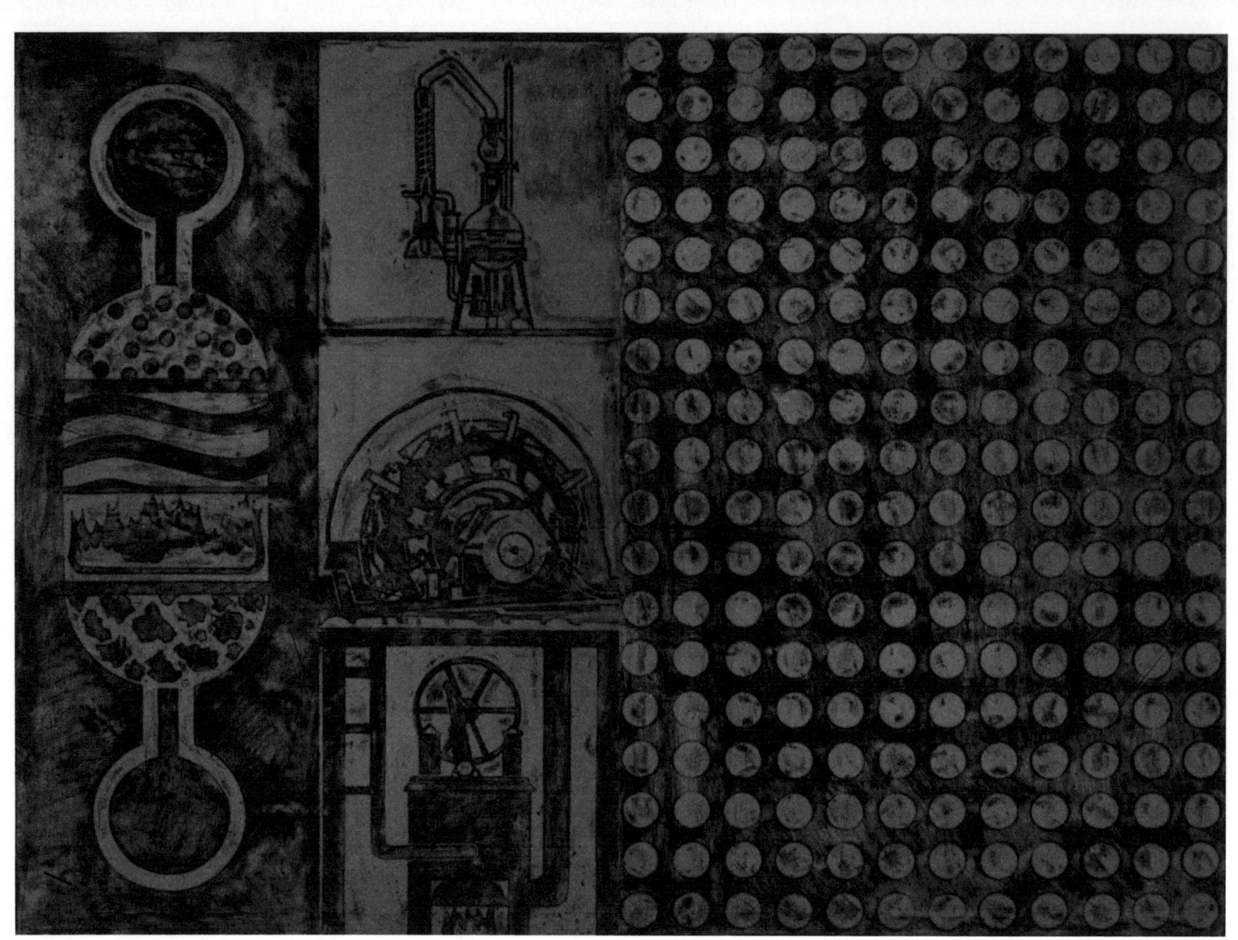

1989.17 Untitled (Boiler and Distiller, Generator, Steam Engine—Elements), 183 × 244 cm (2 parts)

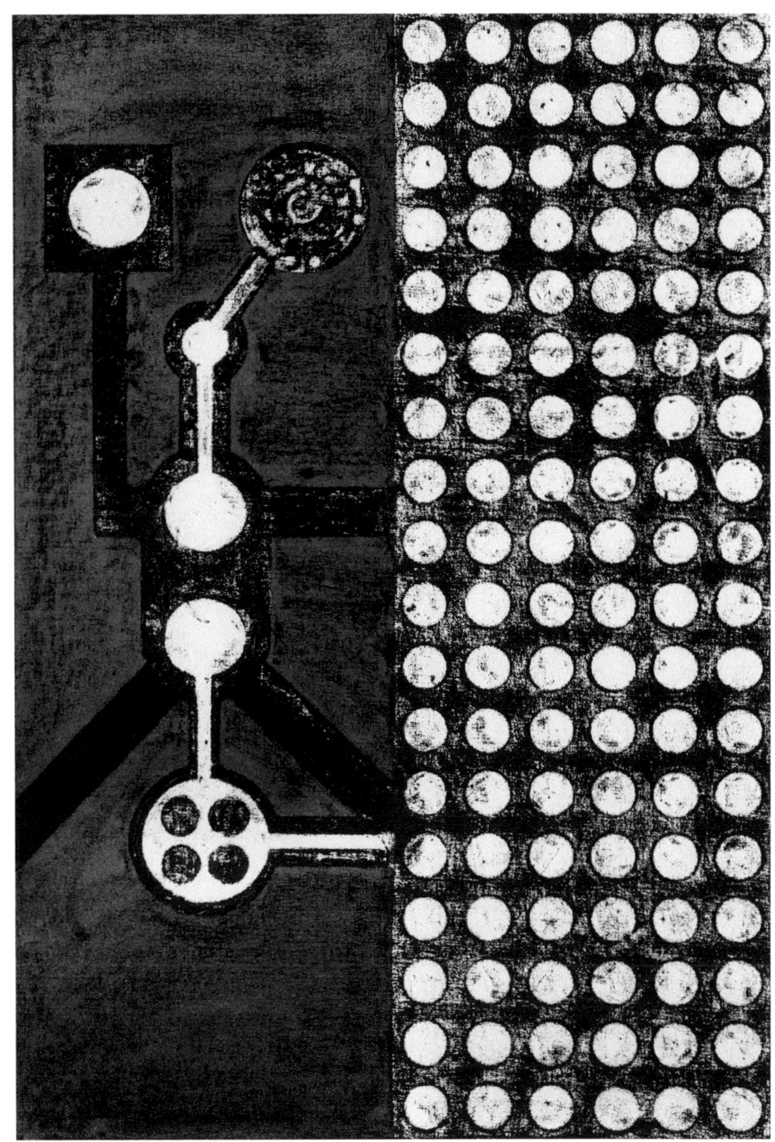

1989.18 Untitled (Anatomy and Elements), 183 × 122 cm

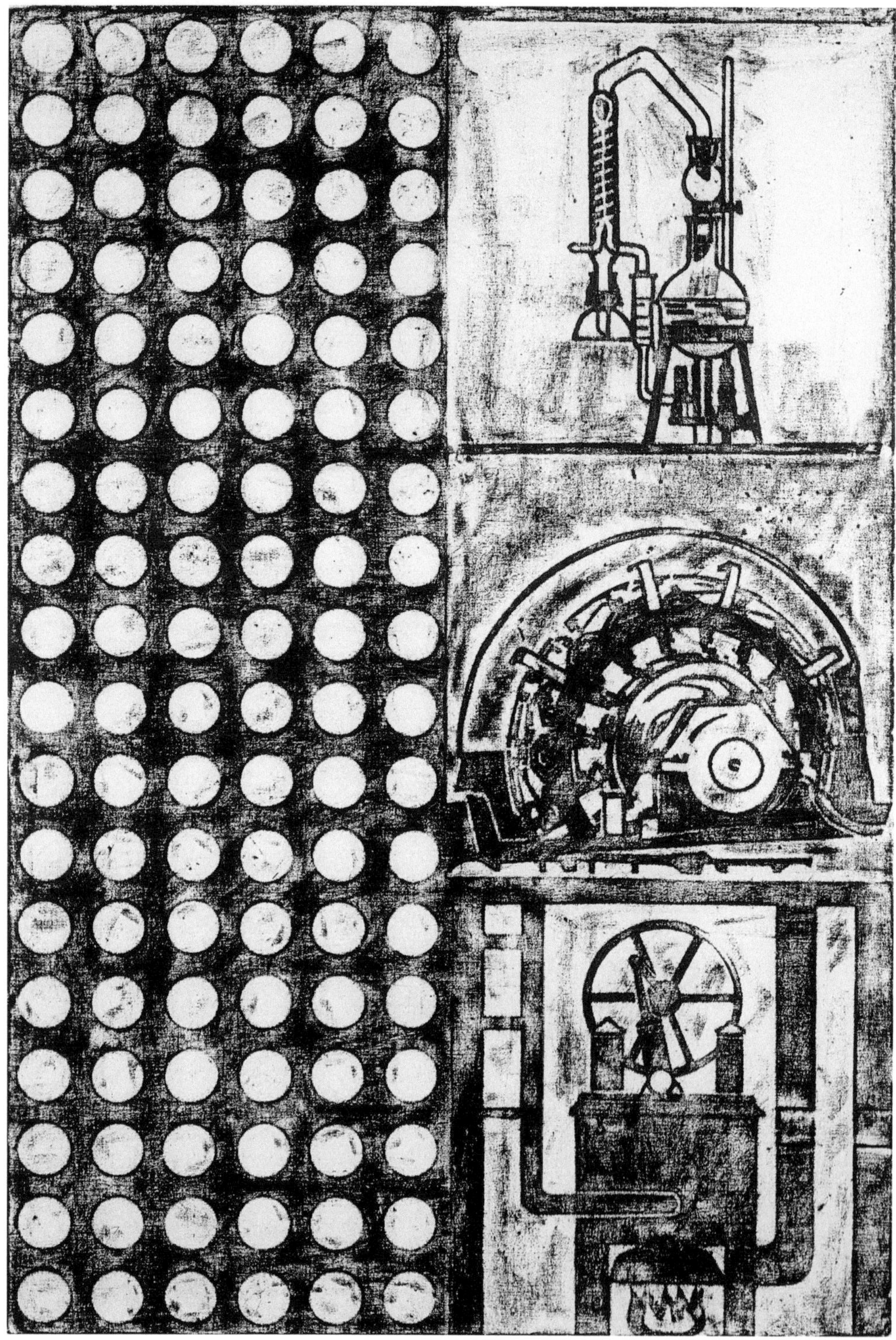

**1989.19 Untitled (Elements–Distiller, Generator, Steam Engine), 183 × 122 cm

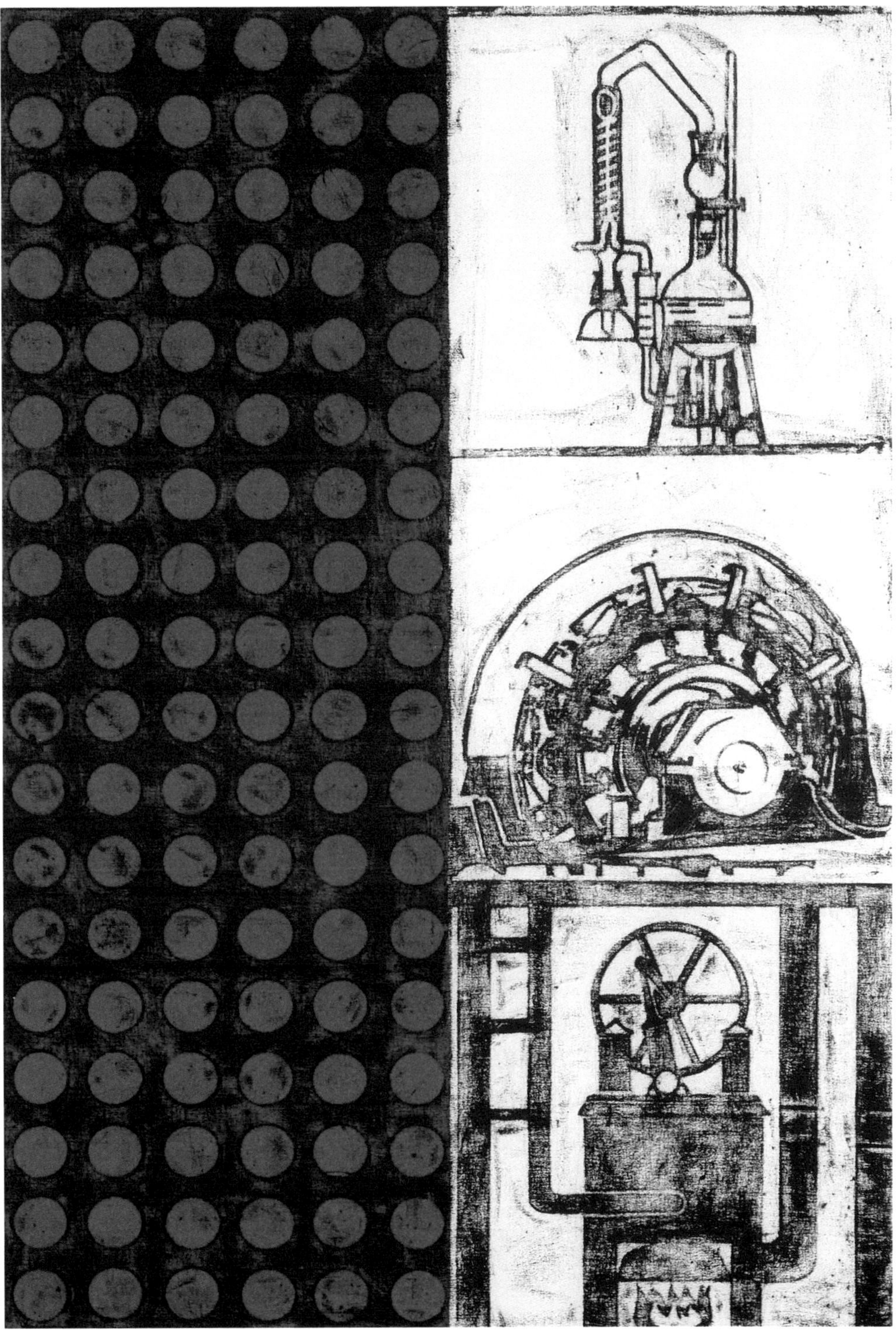

1989.20 Untitled (Elements—Distiller, Generator, Steam Engine), 183 × 122 cm

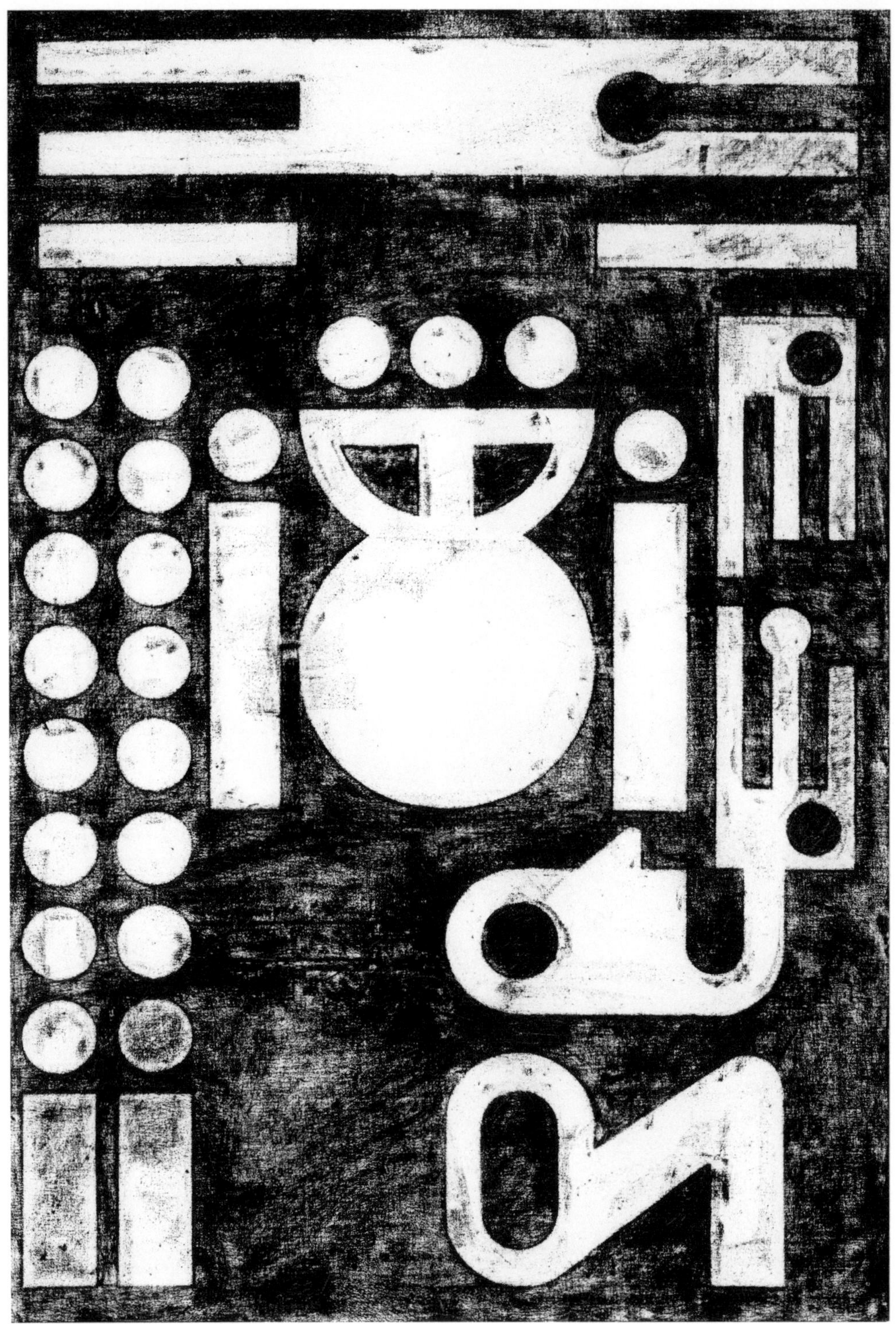

1989.21 Untitled (Cosmology), 183 × 122 cm

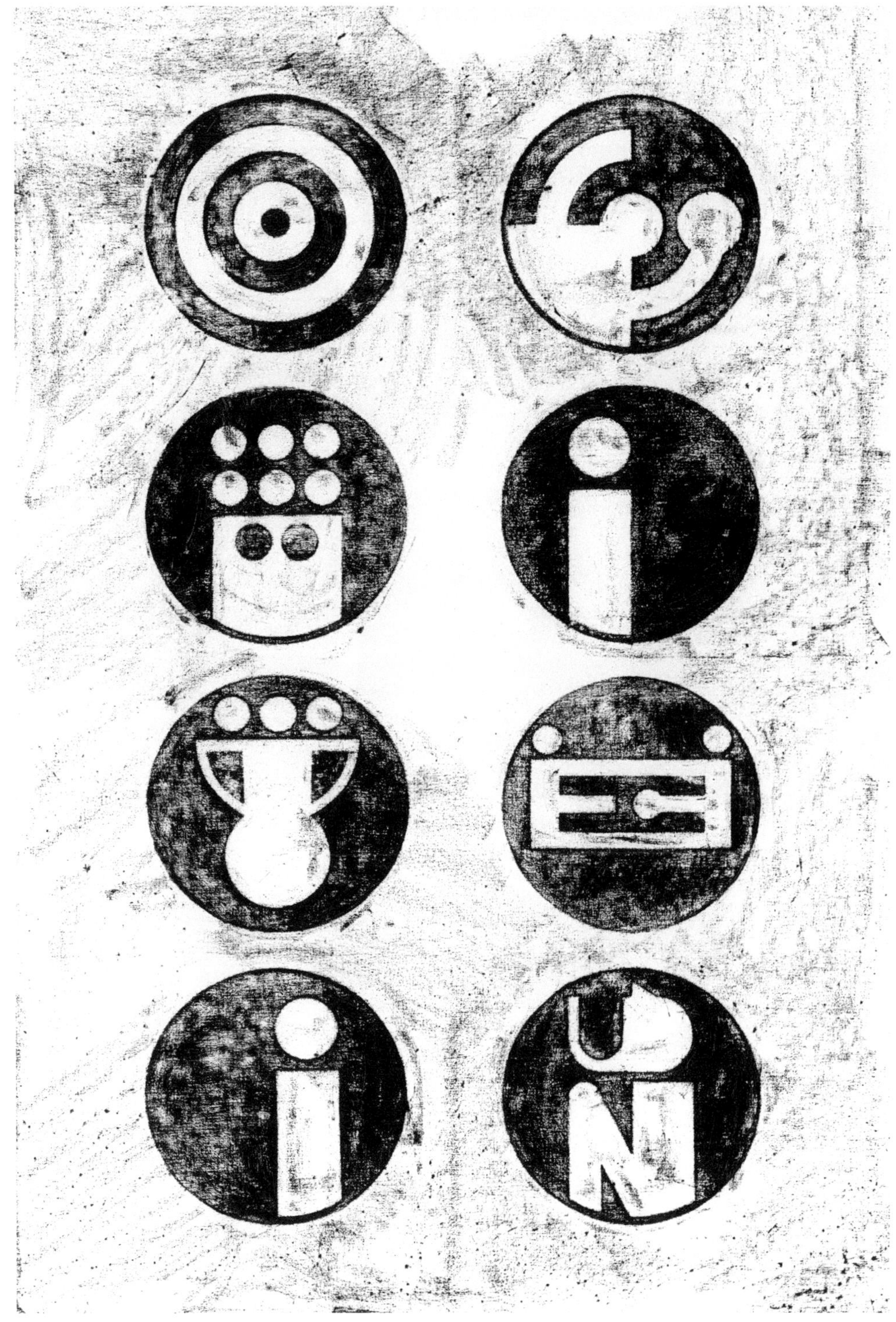

1989.22 Untitled (Cosmology), 183 × 122 cm

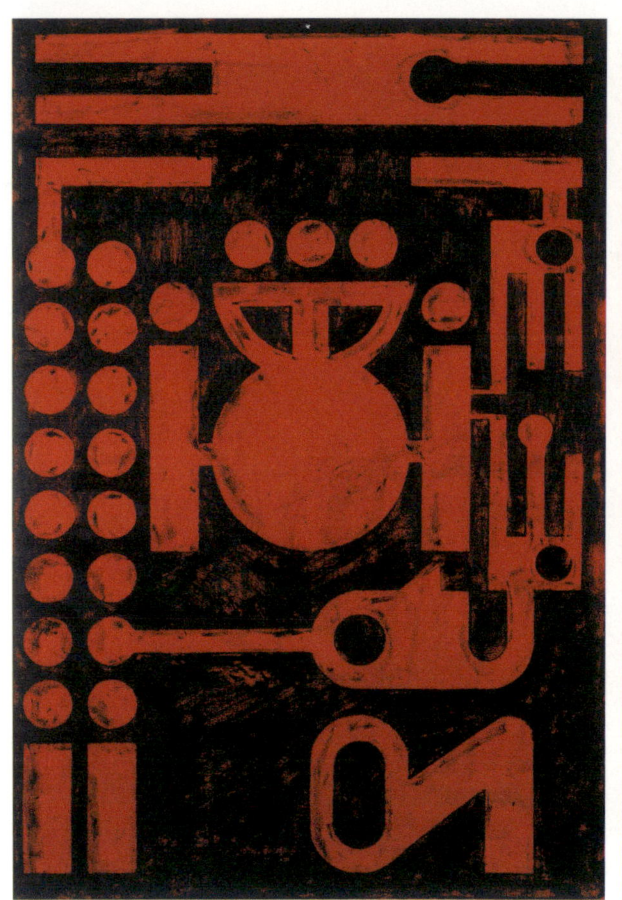 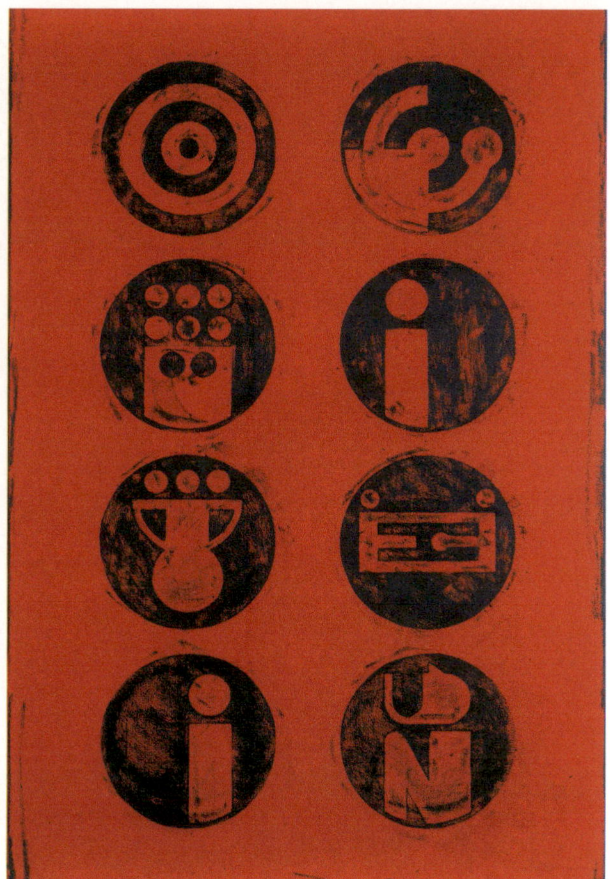

1989.23 Untitled (Cosmology), 183 × 122 cm each (diptych)

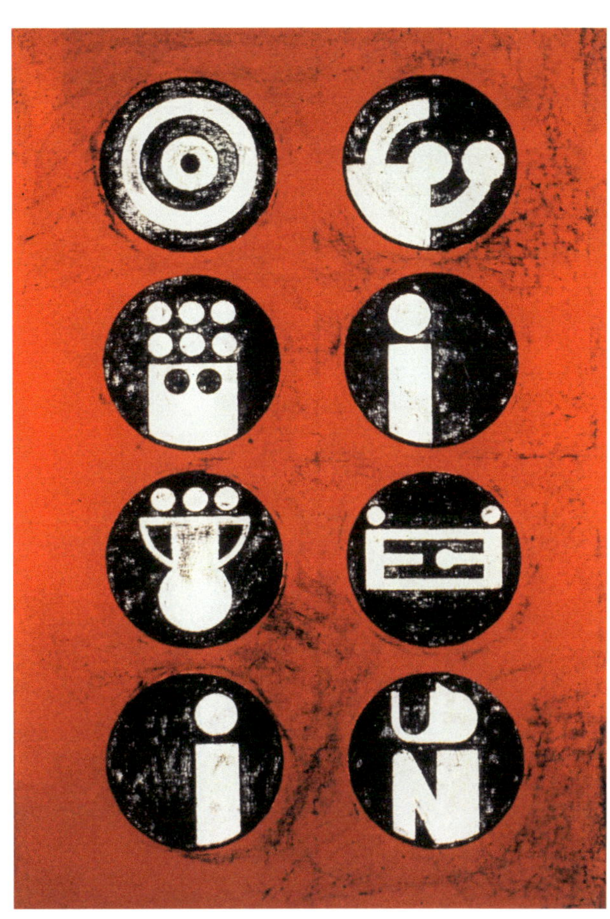

1989.24 Untitled (Cosmology), 183 × 122 cm

1989.25 Untitled (Signs), 183 × 122 cm

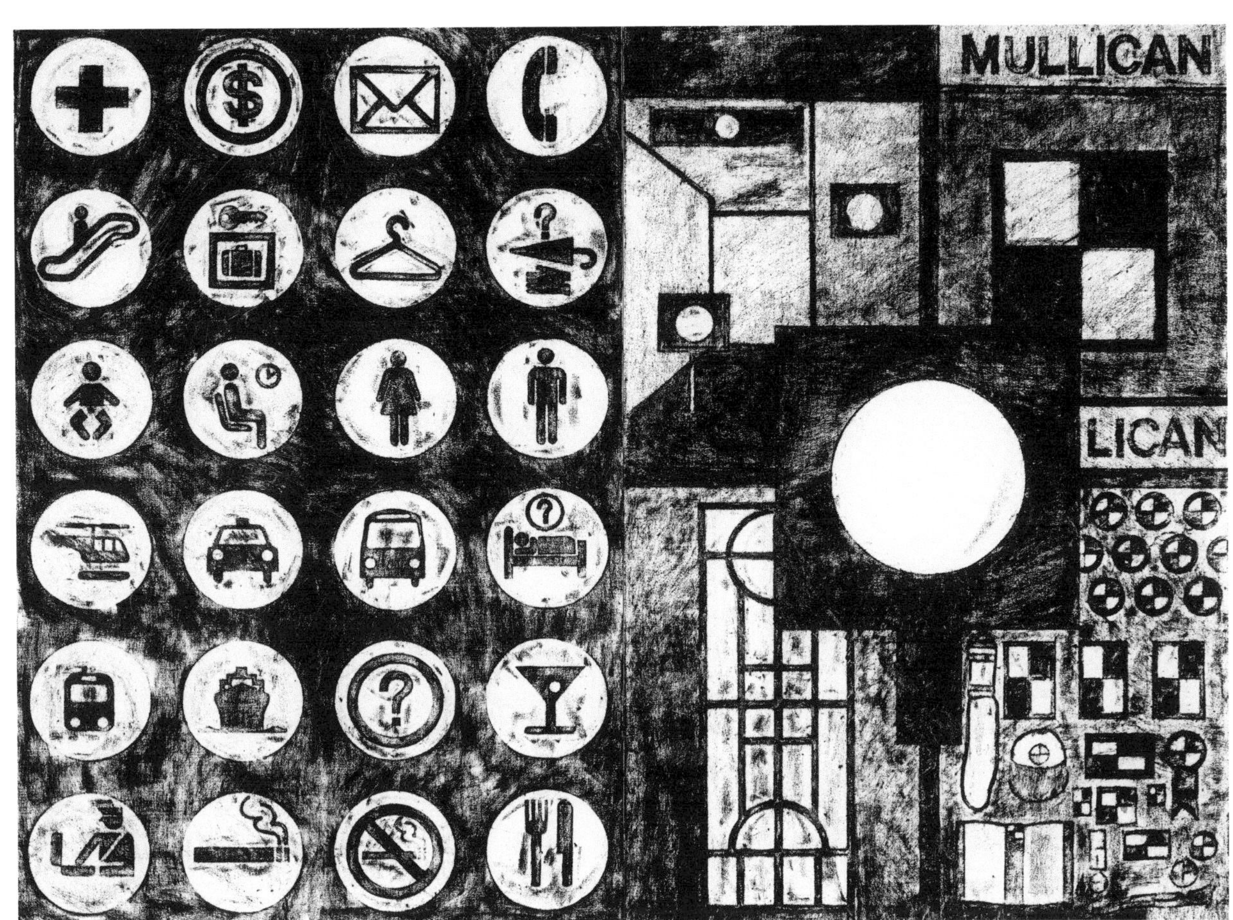

1989.26 Untitled (Signs), 183 × 244 cm (2 parts)

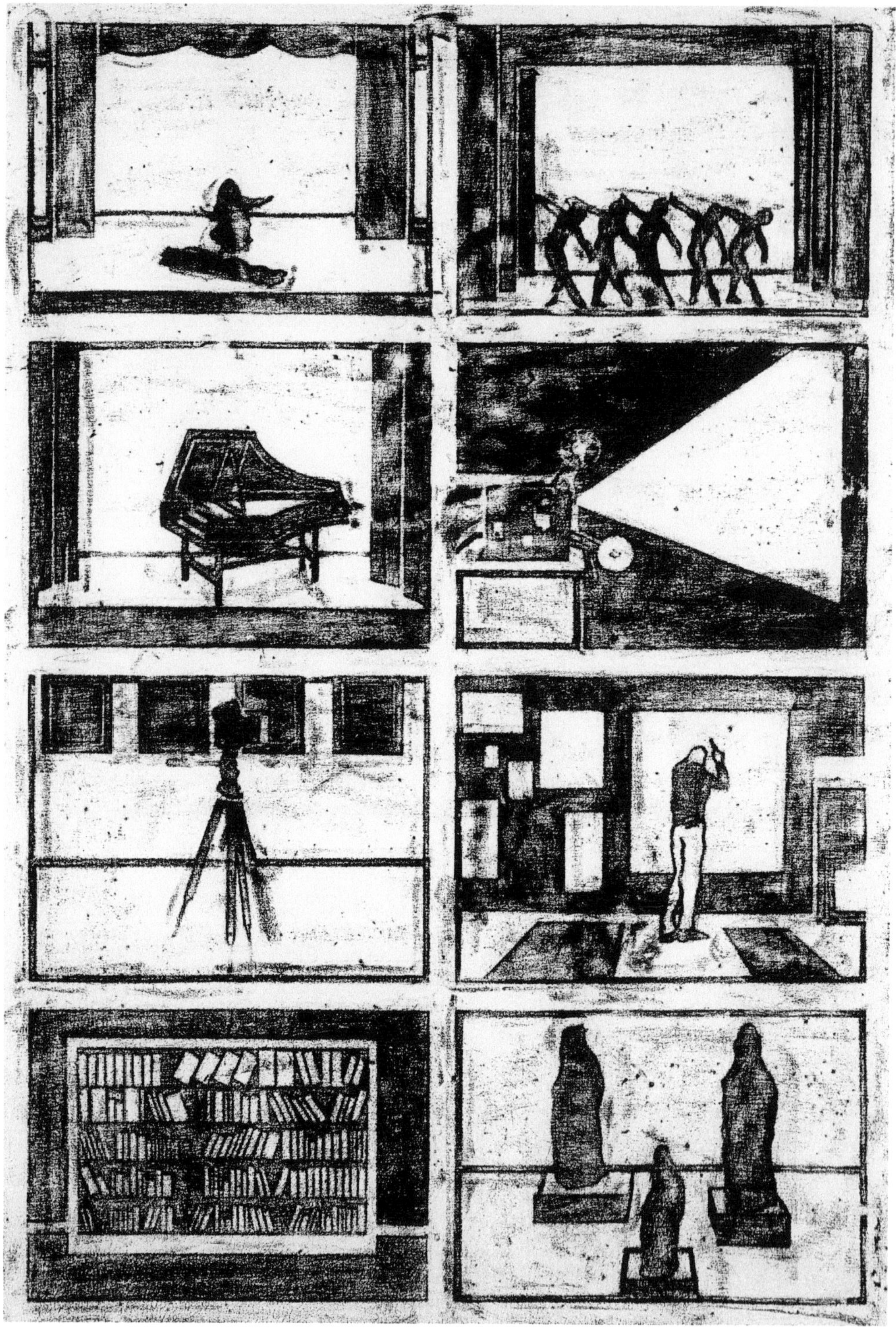

1989.27 Untitled (Arts), 183 × 122 cm

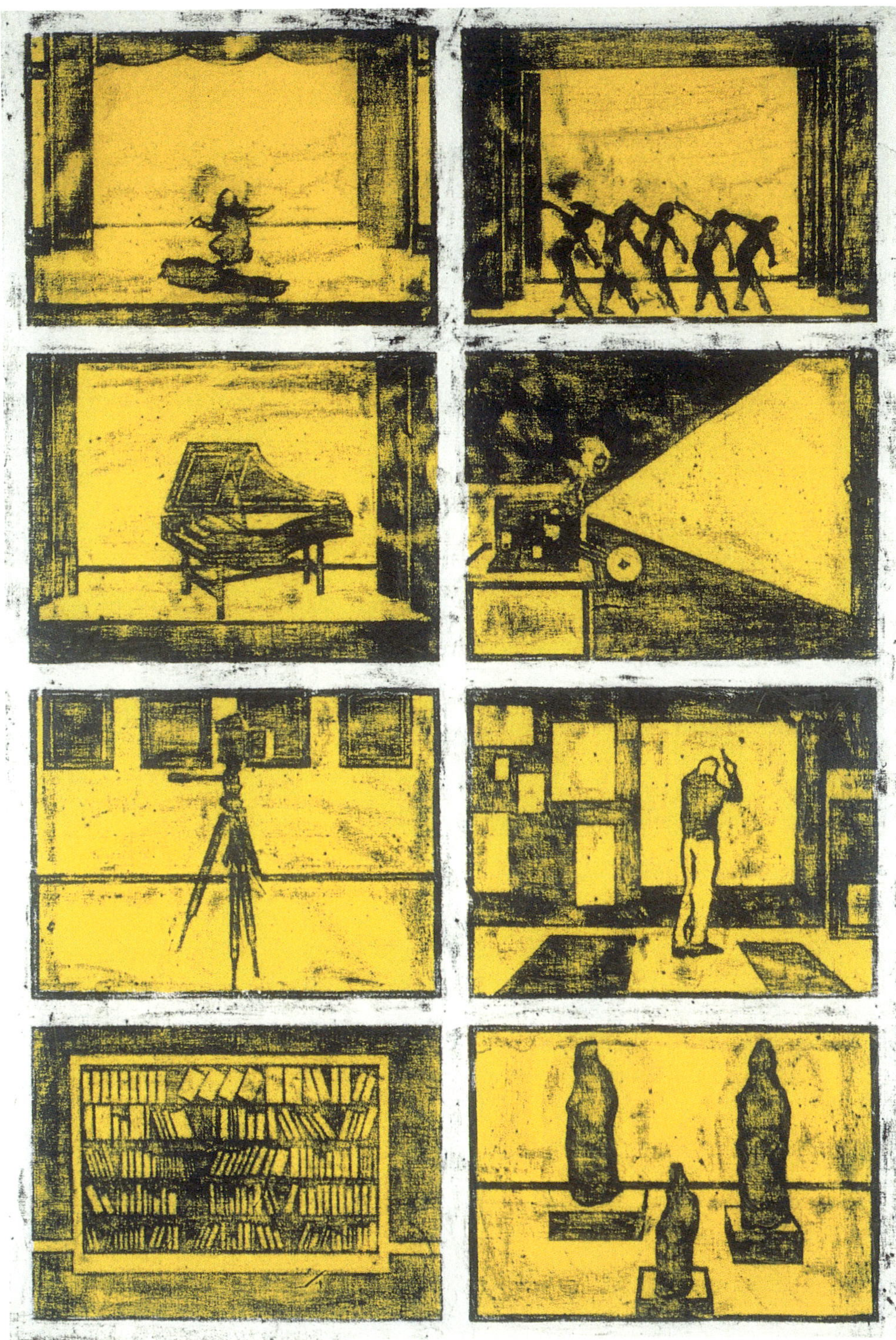

1989.28 Untitled (Arts), 183 × 122 cm

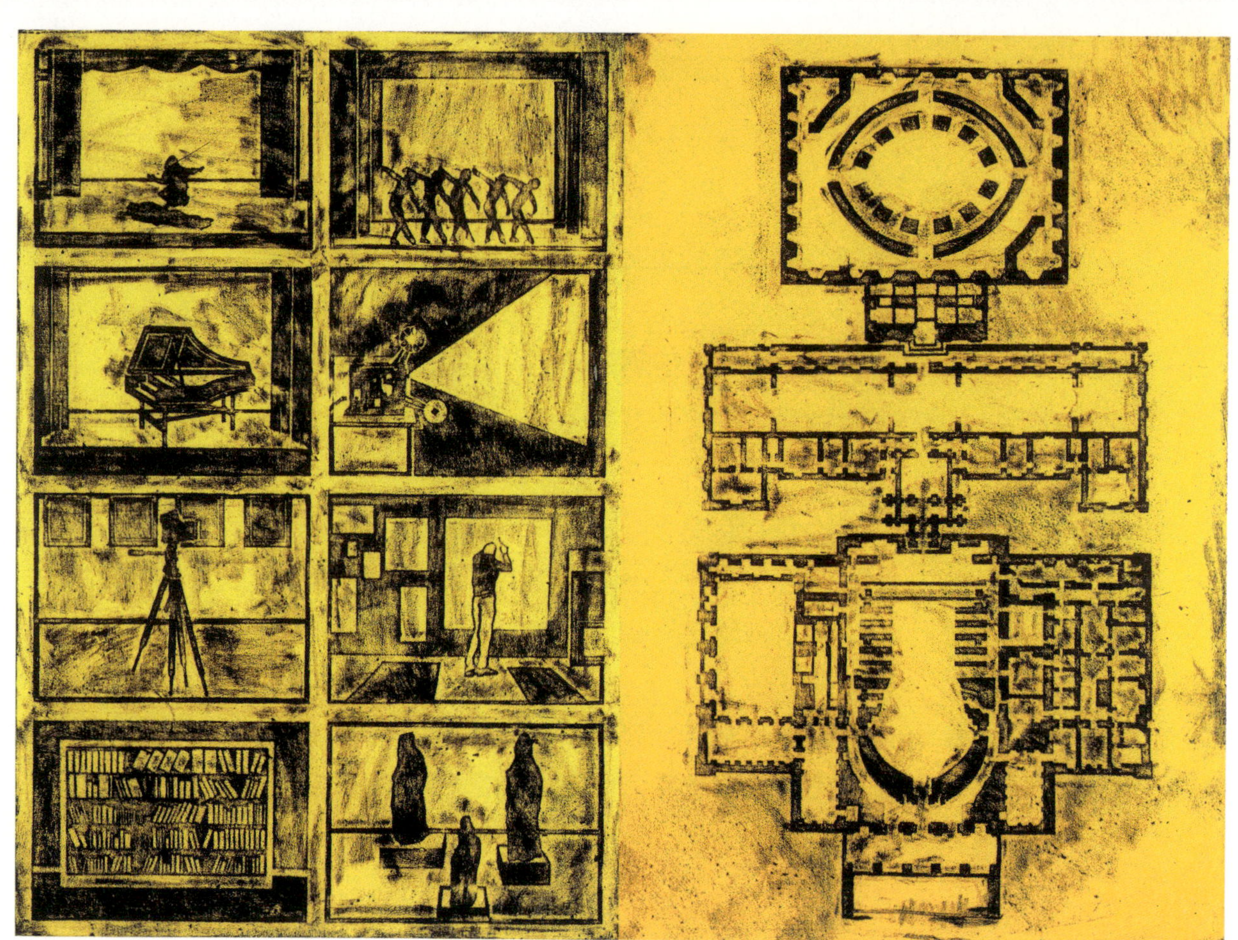

1989.29 Untitled (Arts), 183×244 cm (2 parts)

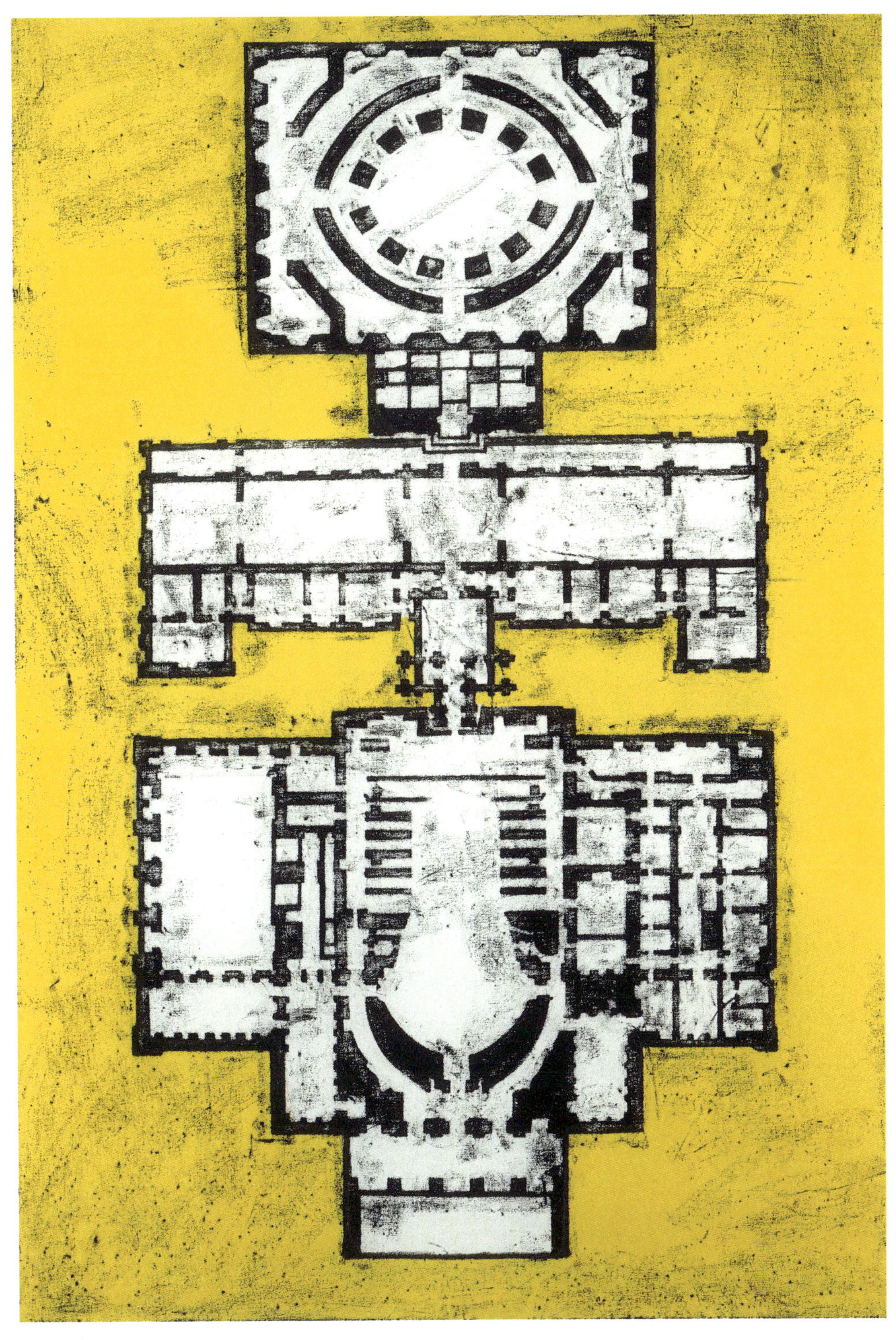

1989.30 Untitled (Theater into Museum into Library), 183 × 122 cm

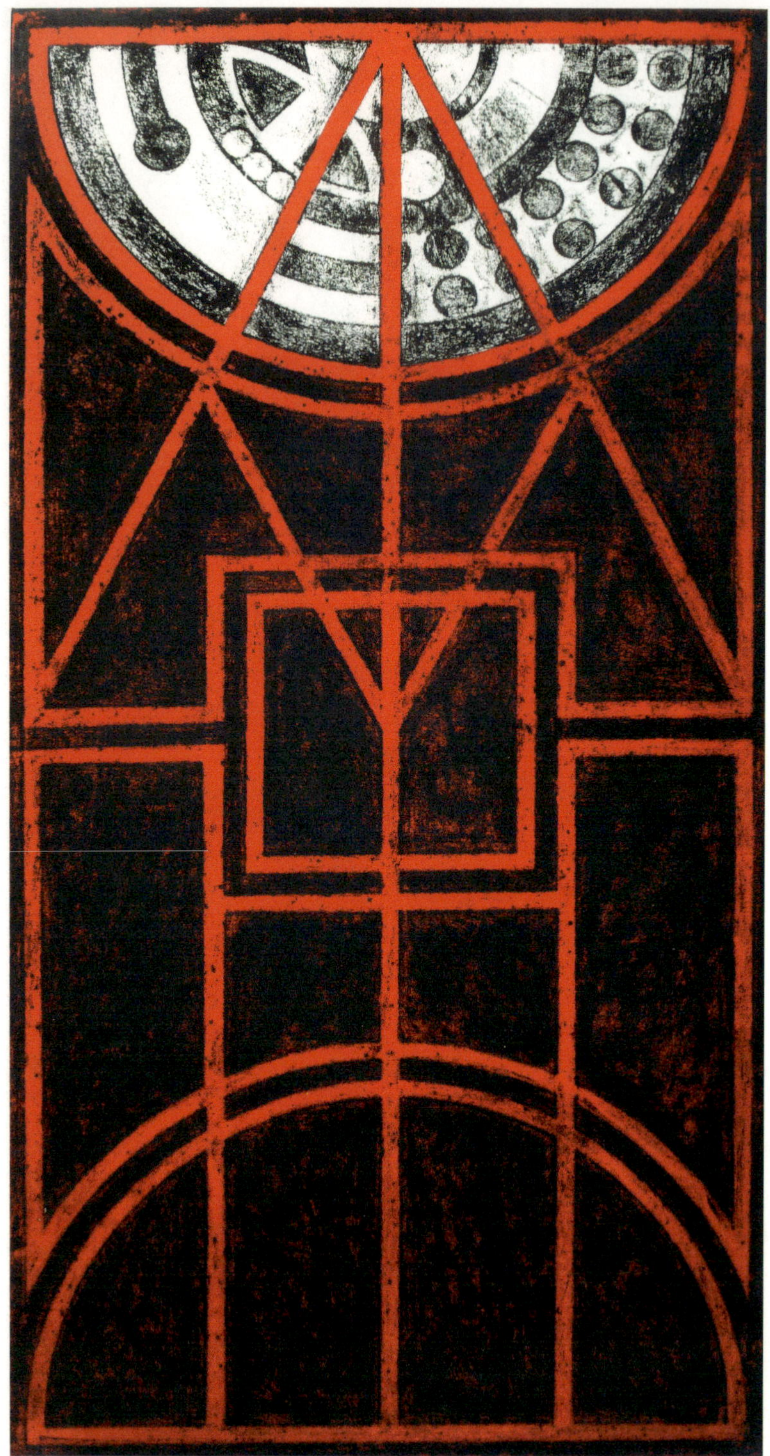

1989.31 Untitled (Subjective), 244 × 122 cm

1990

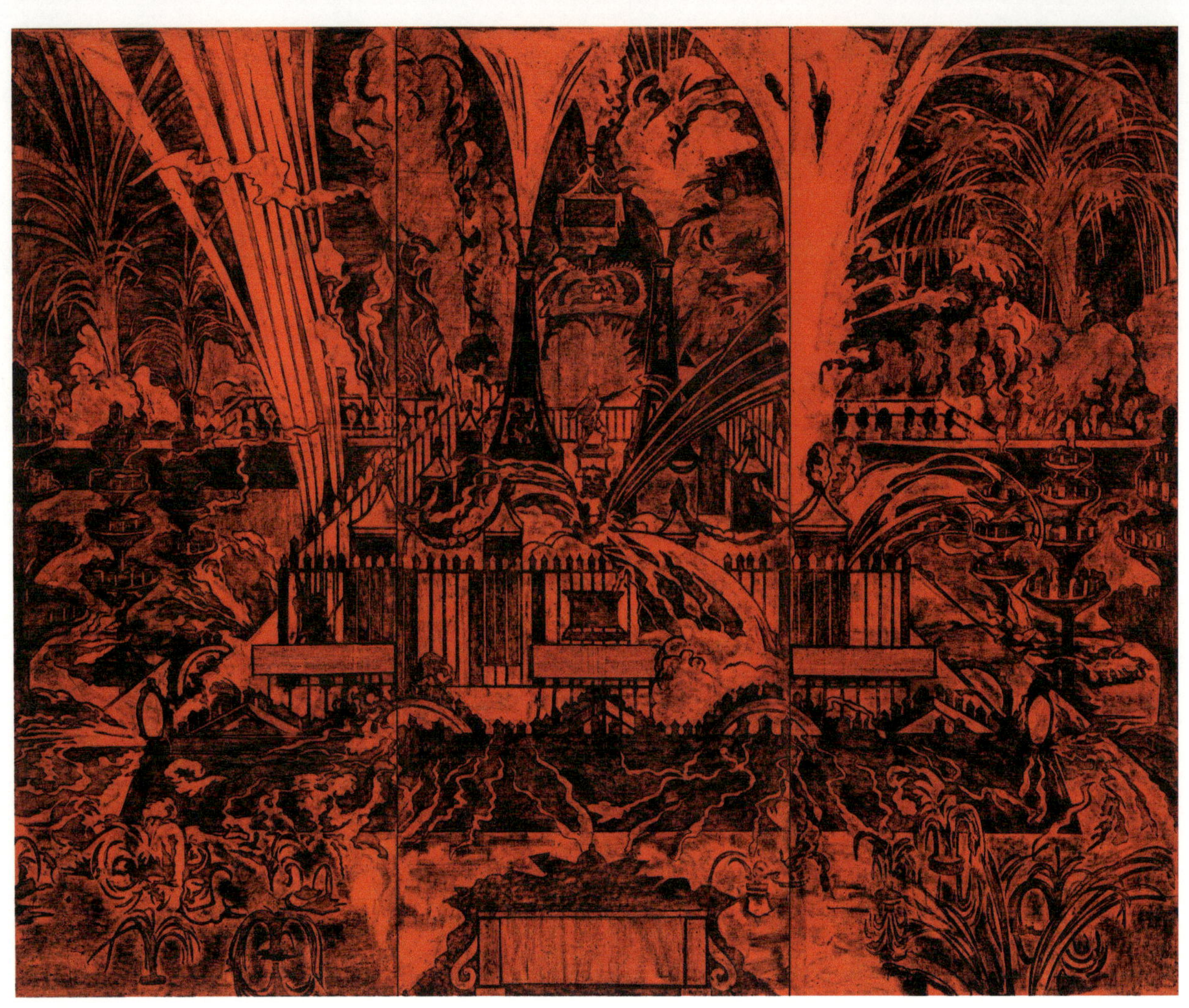

1990.1 Untitled (Fireworks), 305 × 366 cm (3 parts)

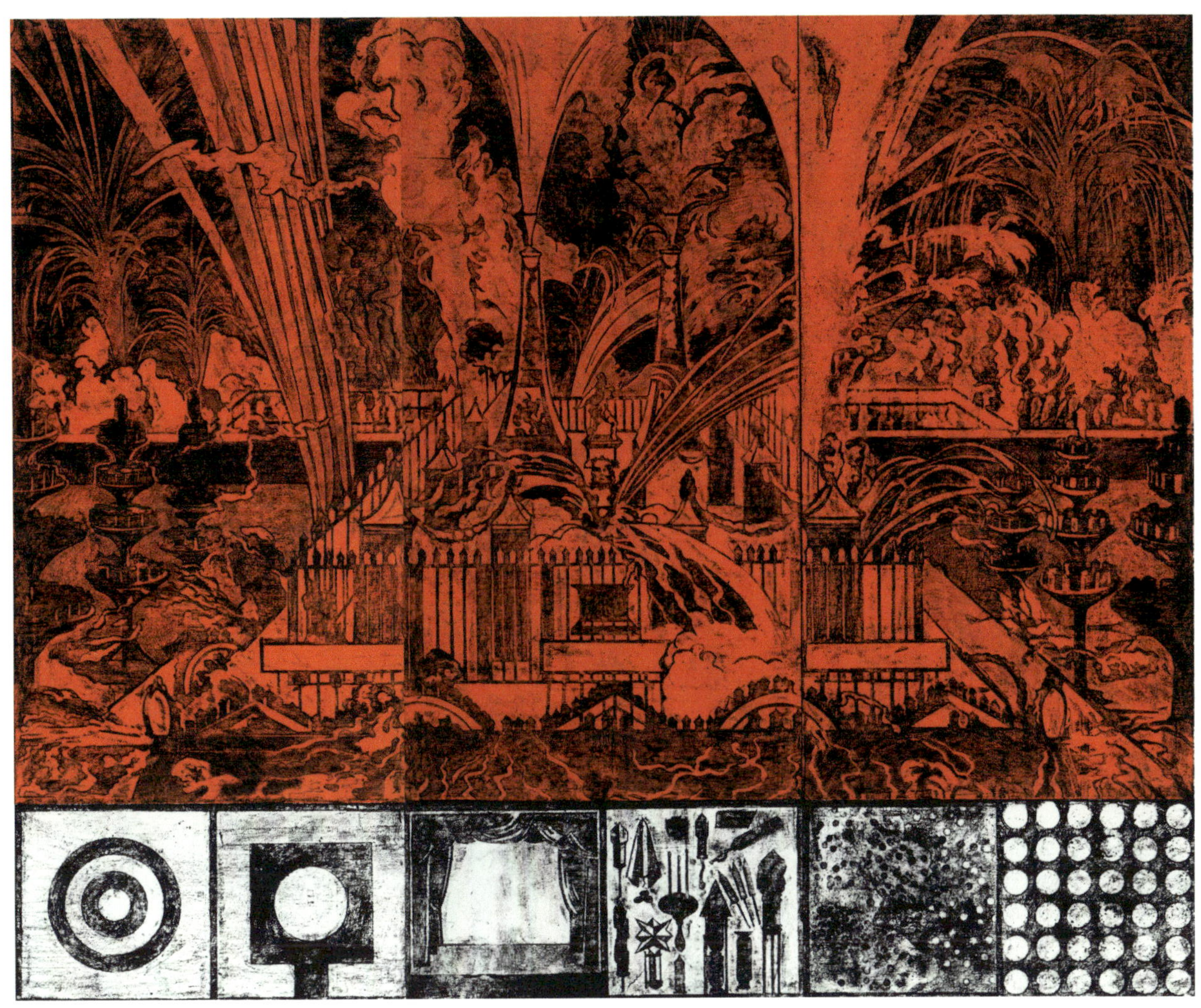

1990.2 Untitled (Paintings), 305 × 366 cm (3 parts)

1991

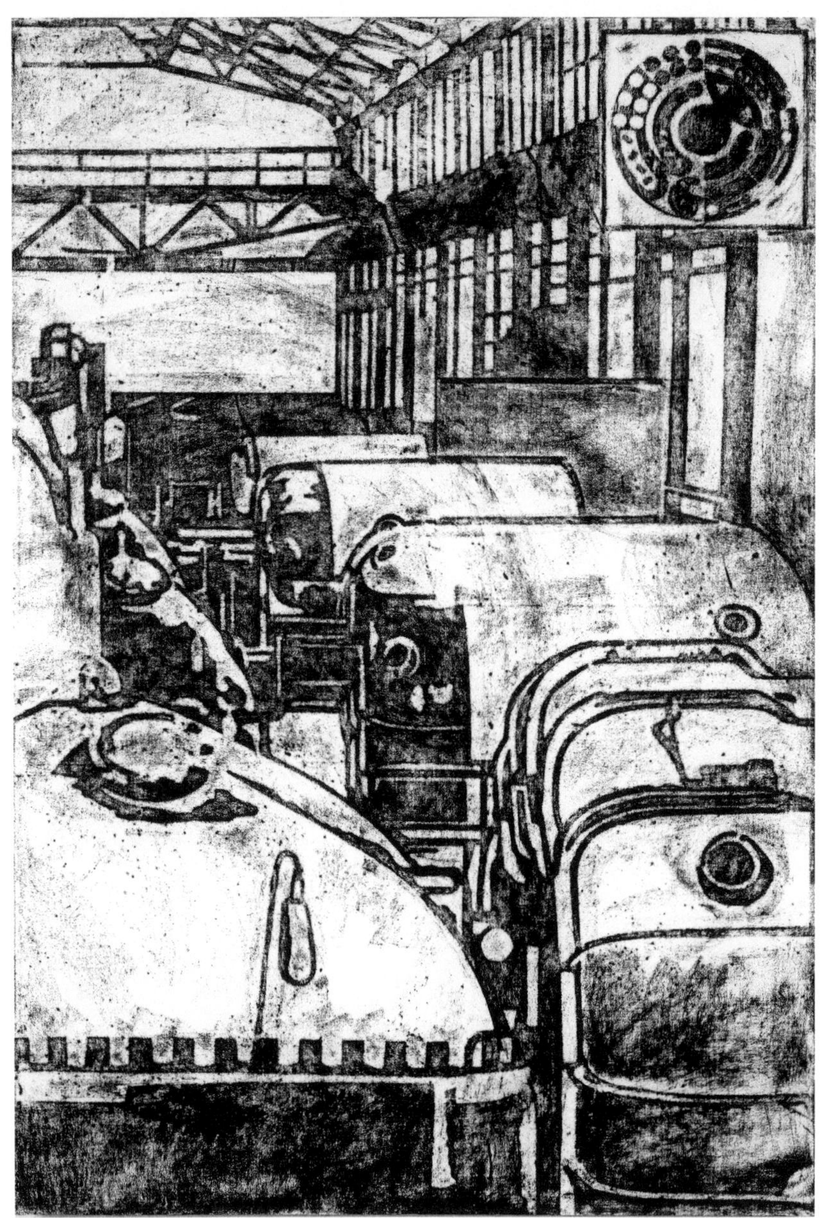

1991.1 Untitled (Generator Hall, Detail), 183 × 122 cm

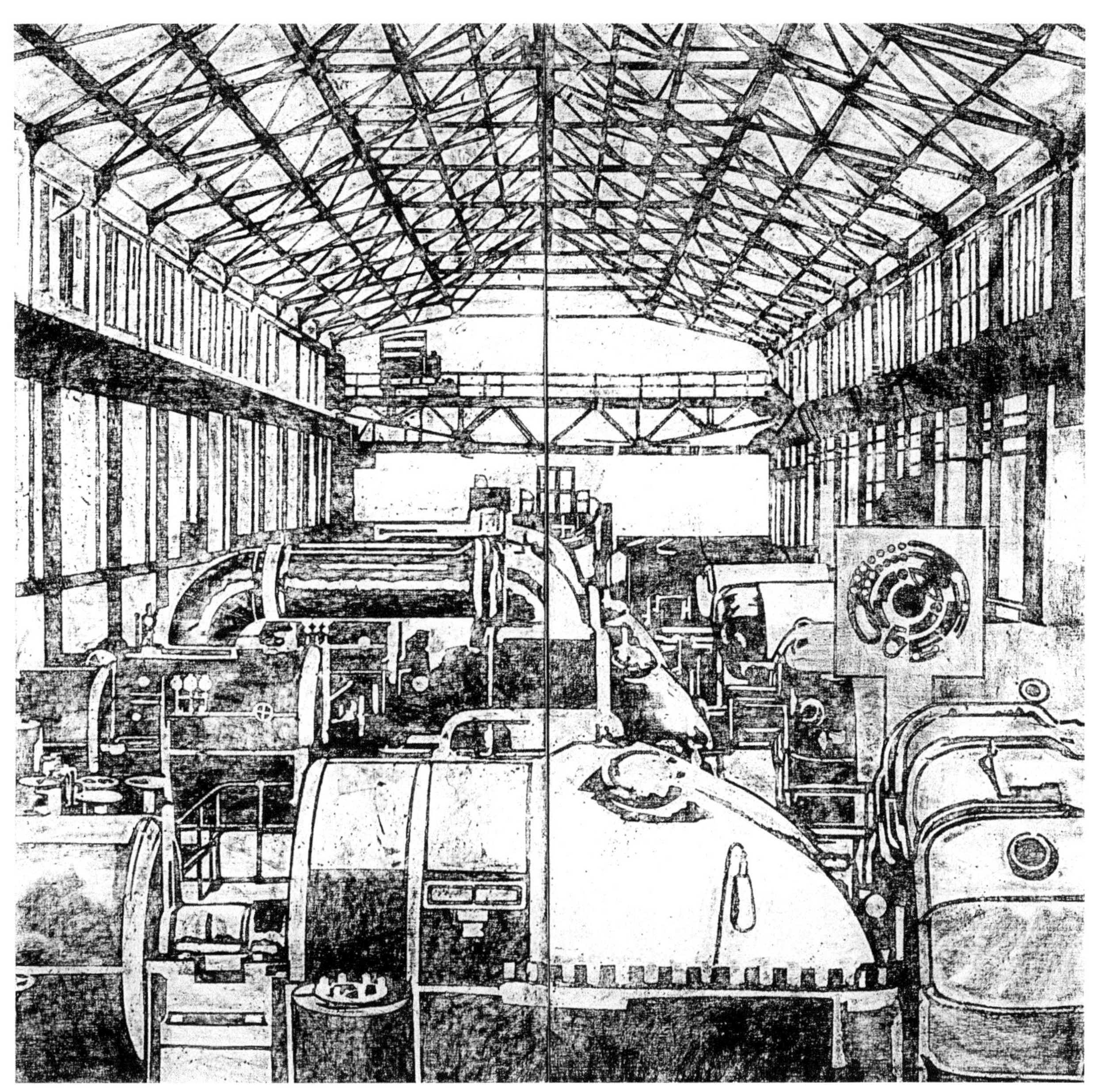

1991.2 Untitled (Generator Hall), 244 × 244 cm

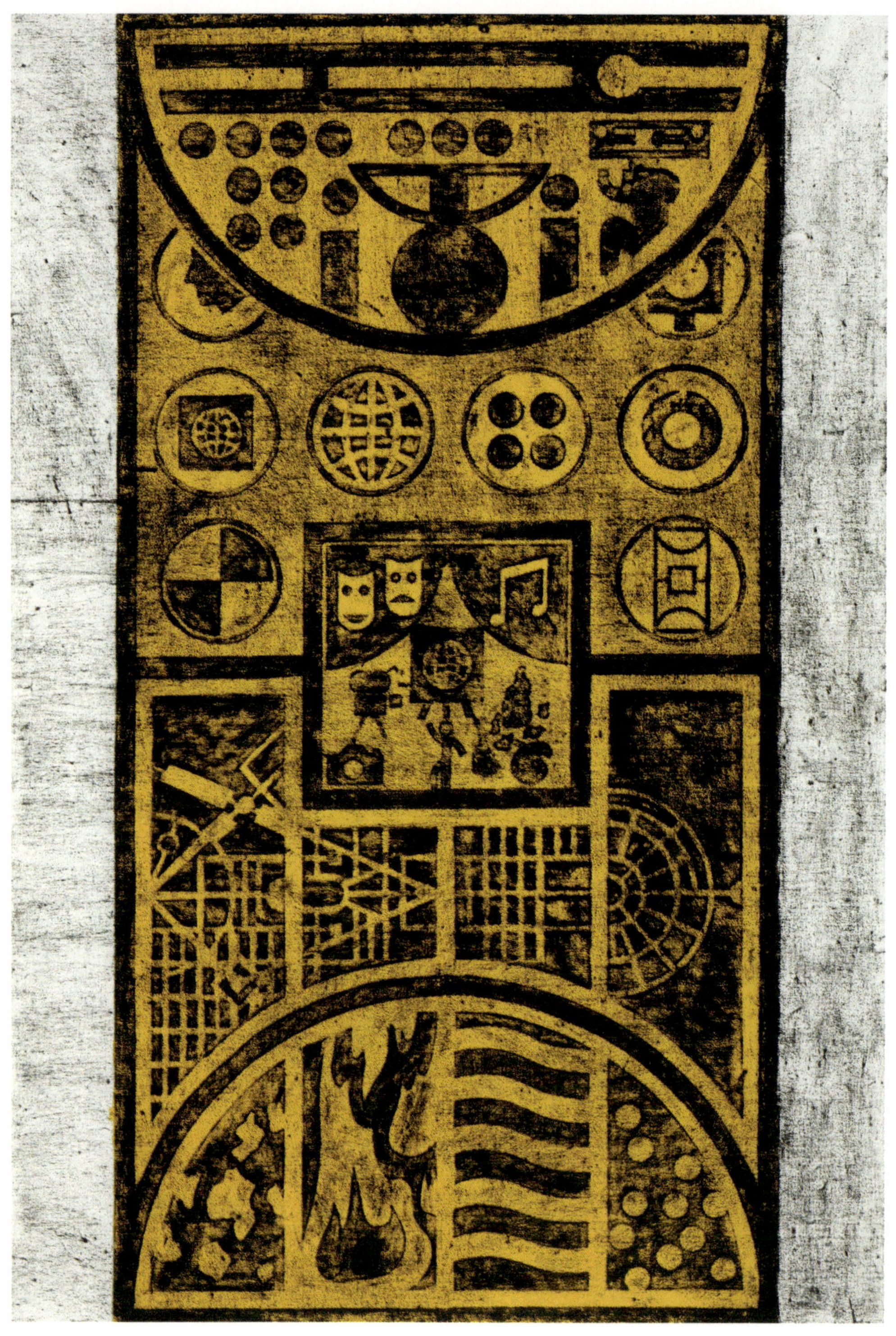

1991.3 City Plan (Overall Chart), 183 × 122 cm

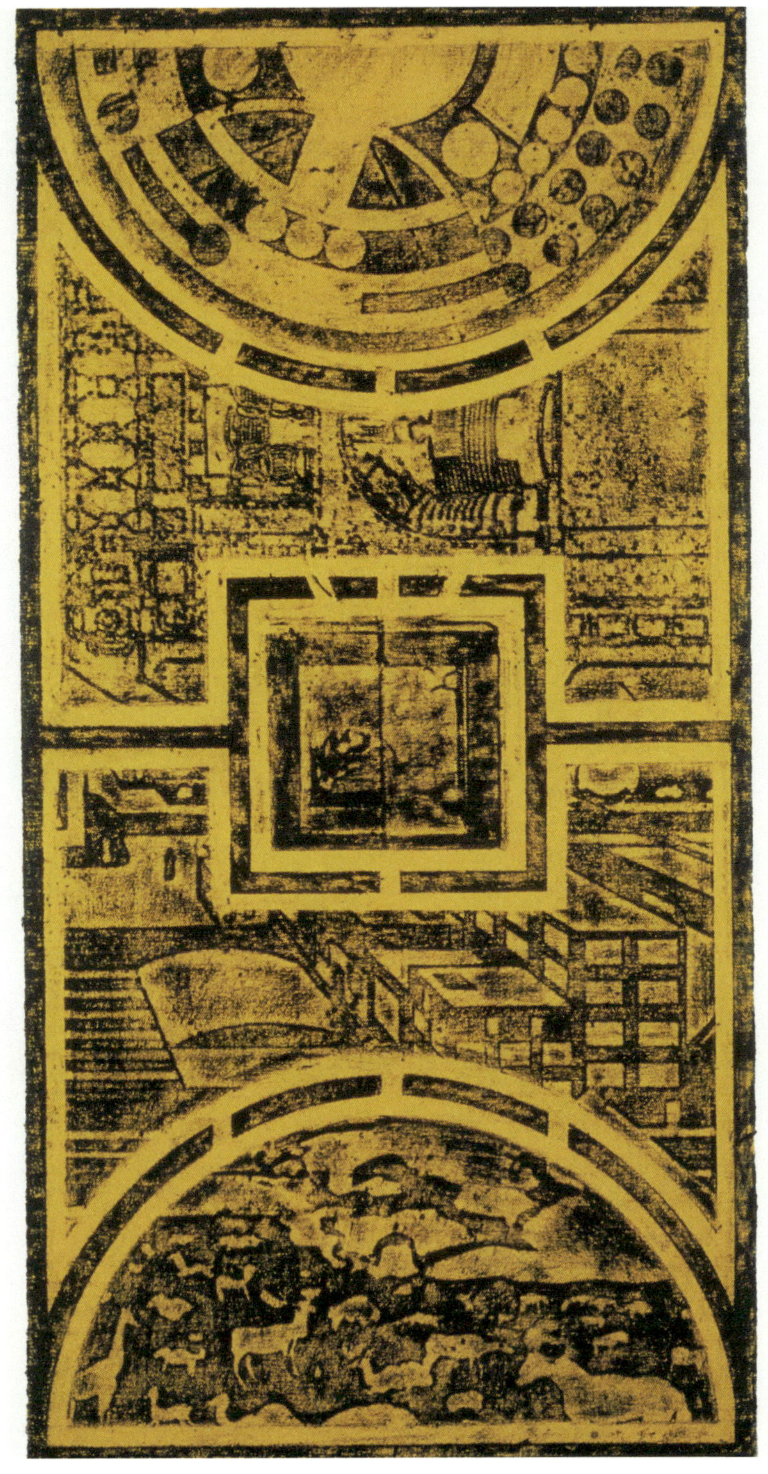

1991.4 City Plan (Overall Chart), 183 × 122 cm

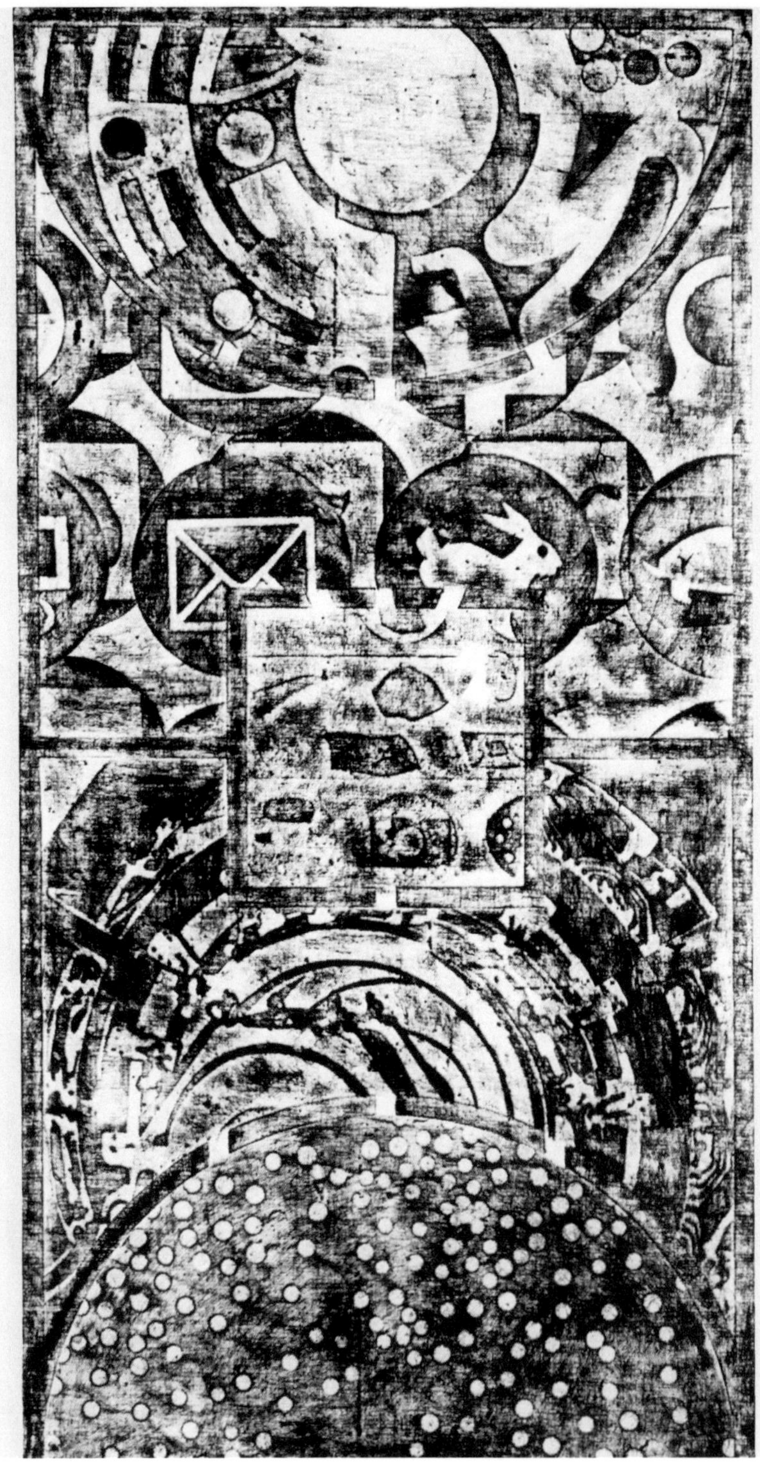

1991.5 City Plan (Overall Chart), 183 × 122 cm

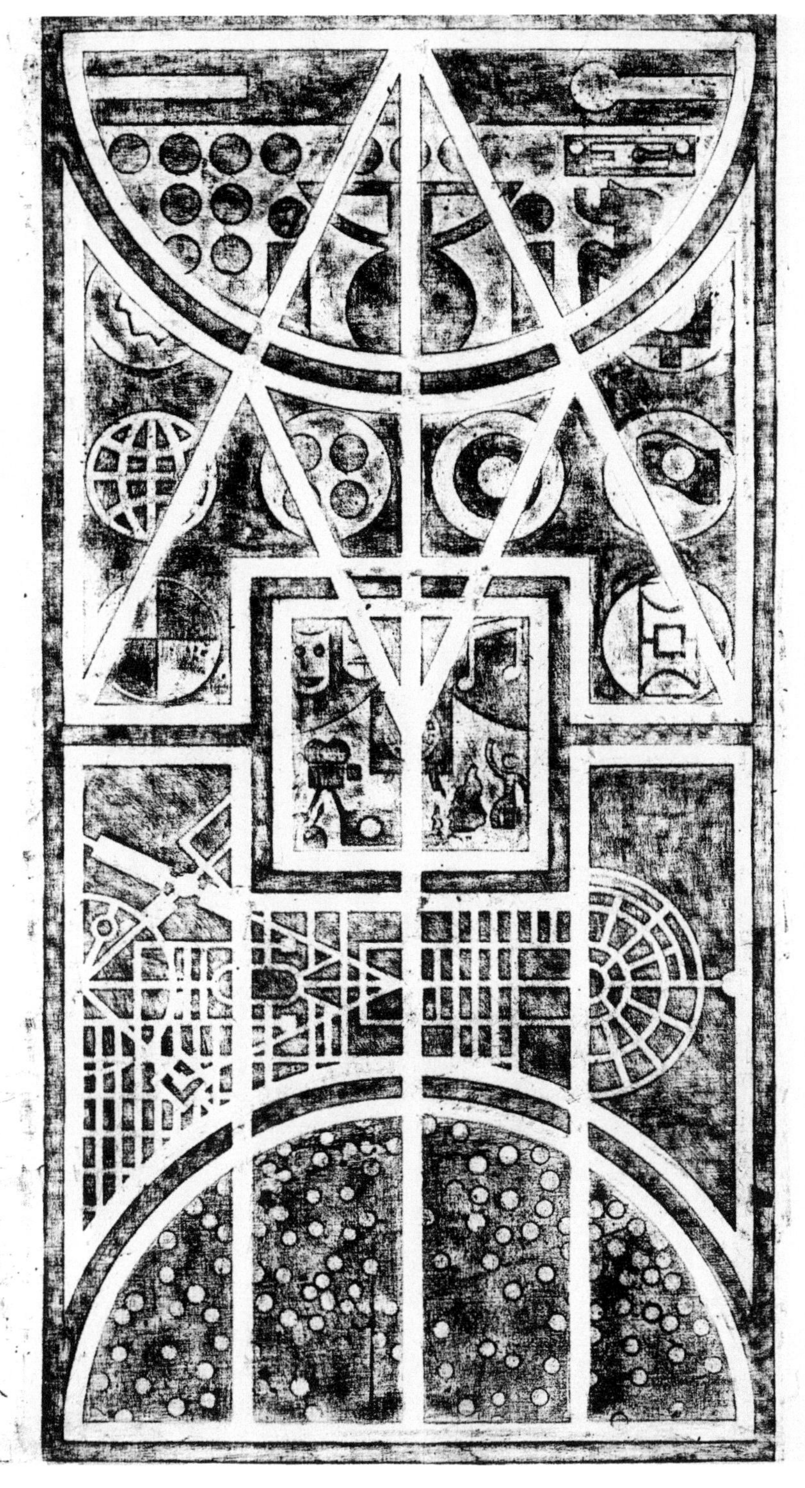

1991.6 City Plan (Overall Chart), 183×122 cm

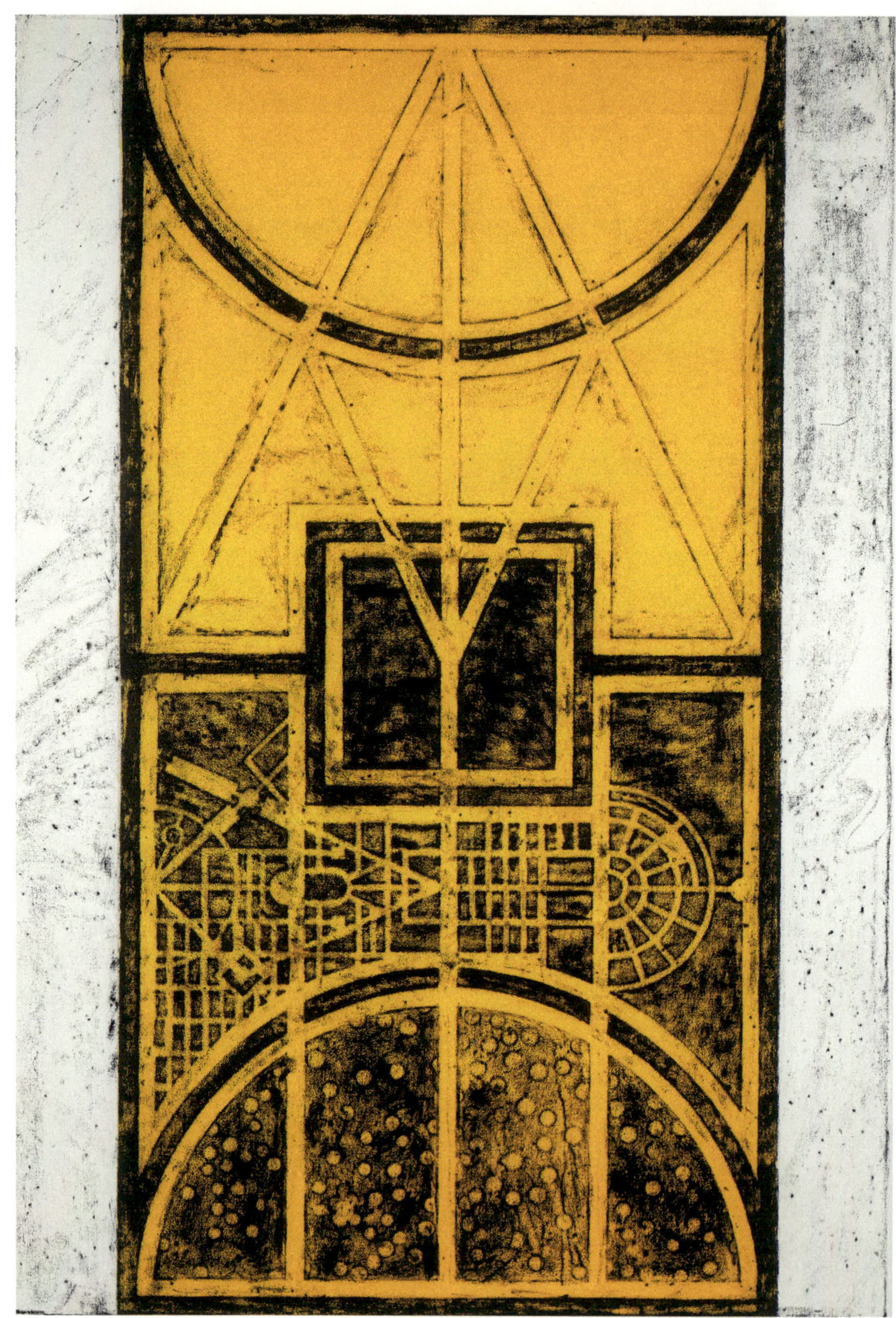

1991.7 Untitled (City Chart), 183 × 122 cm

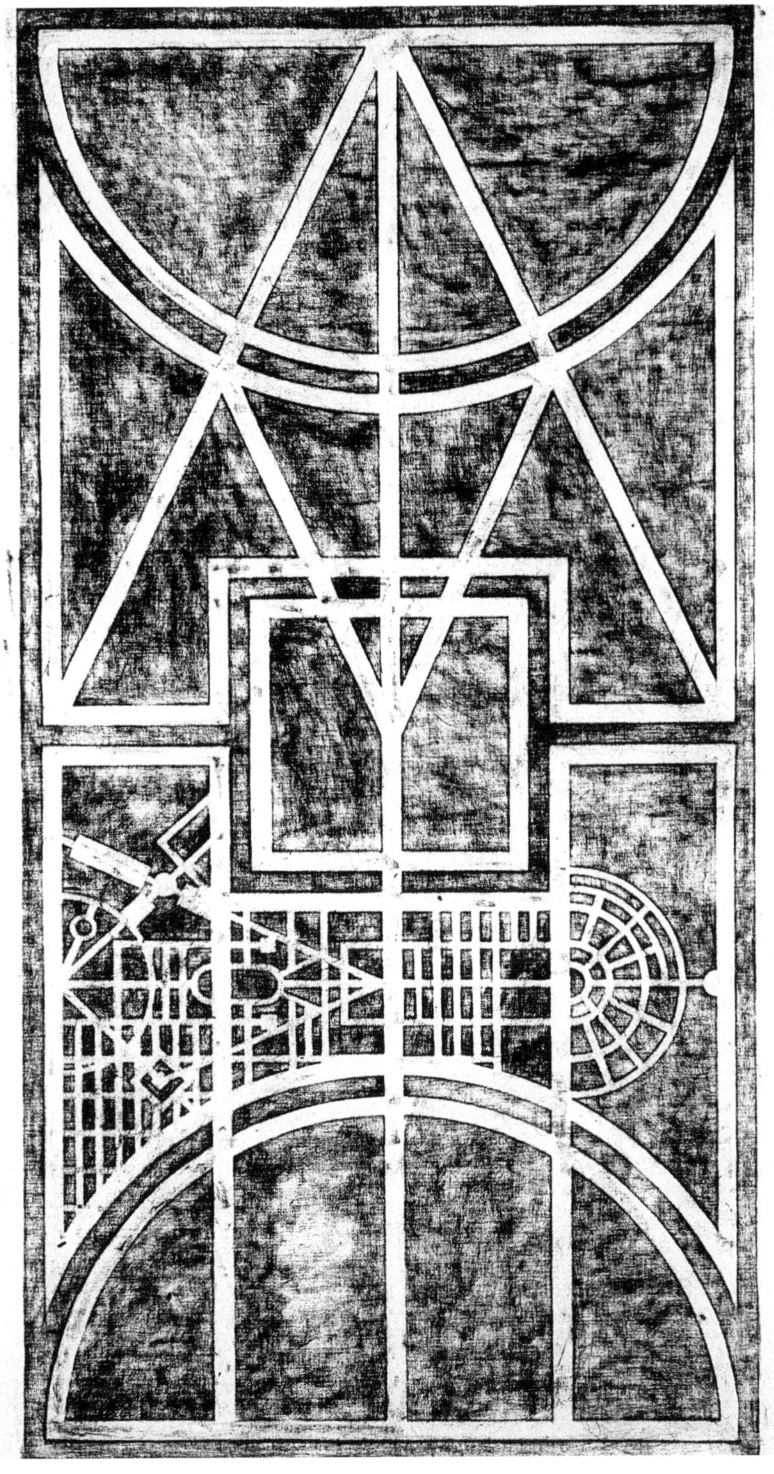

1991.8 Untitled (City Chart Black), 183 × 122 cm

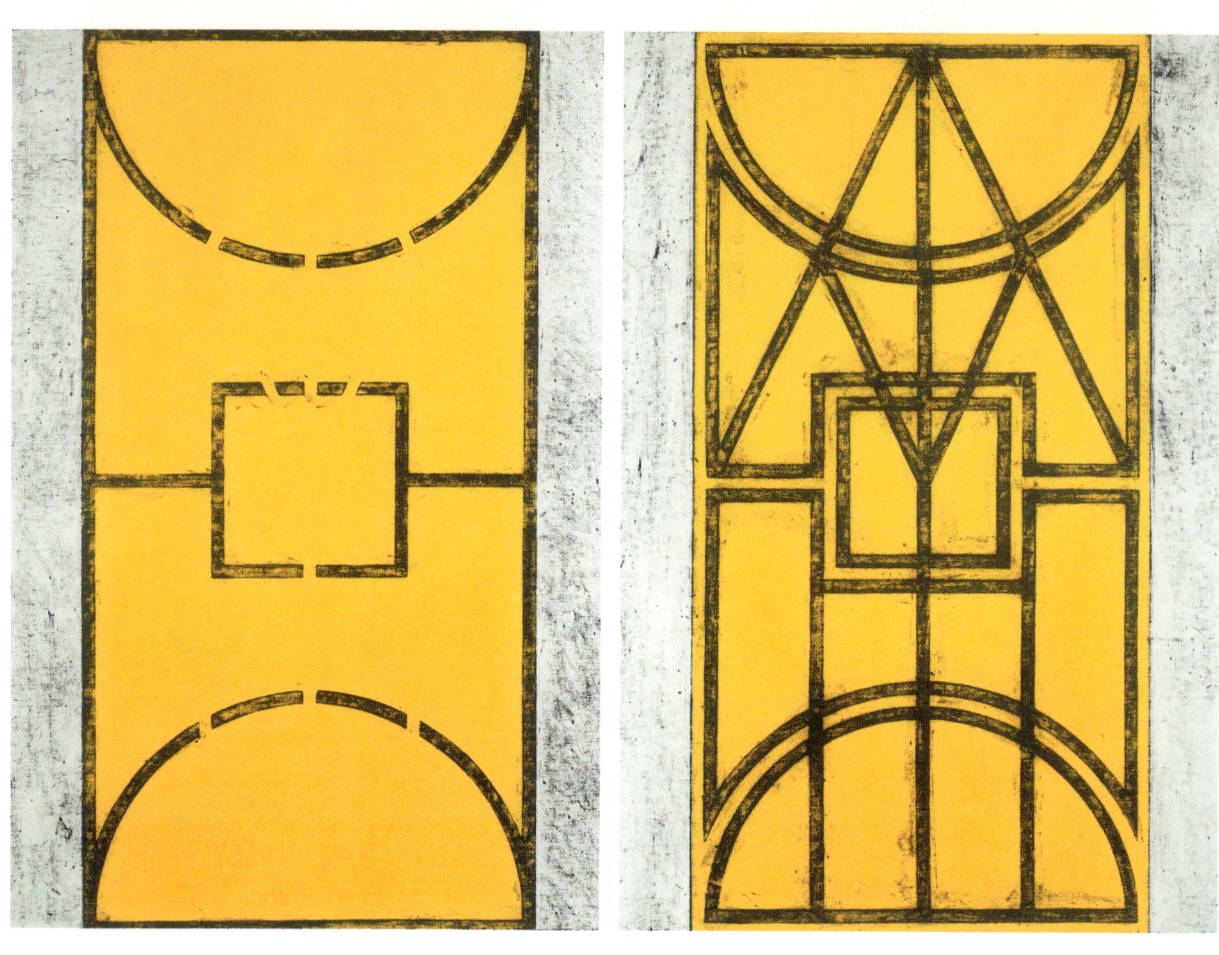

1991.9 Untitled (City Chart), 183 × 122 cm each (diptych)

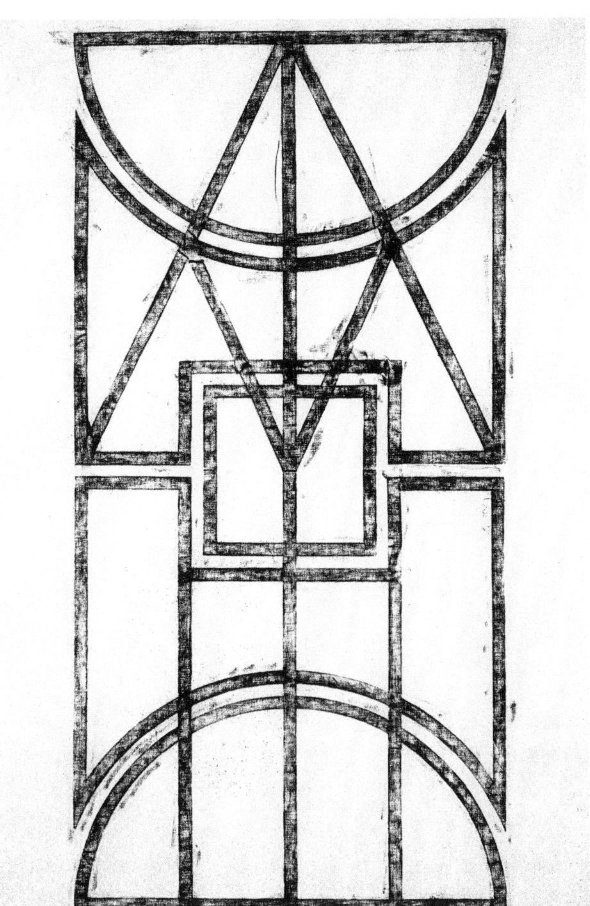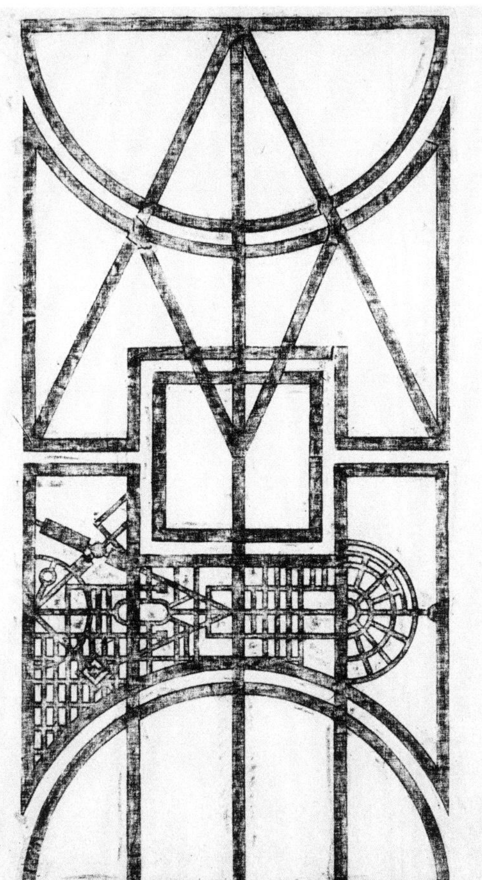

1991.10 Untitled (City Chart), 183 × 122 cm each (diptych)

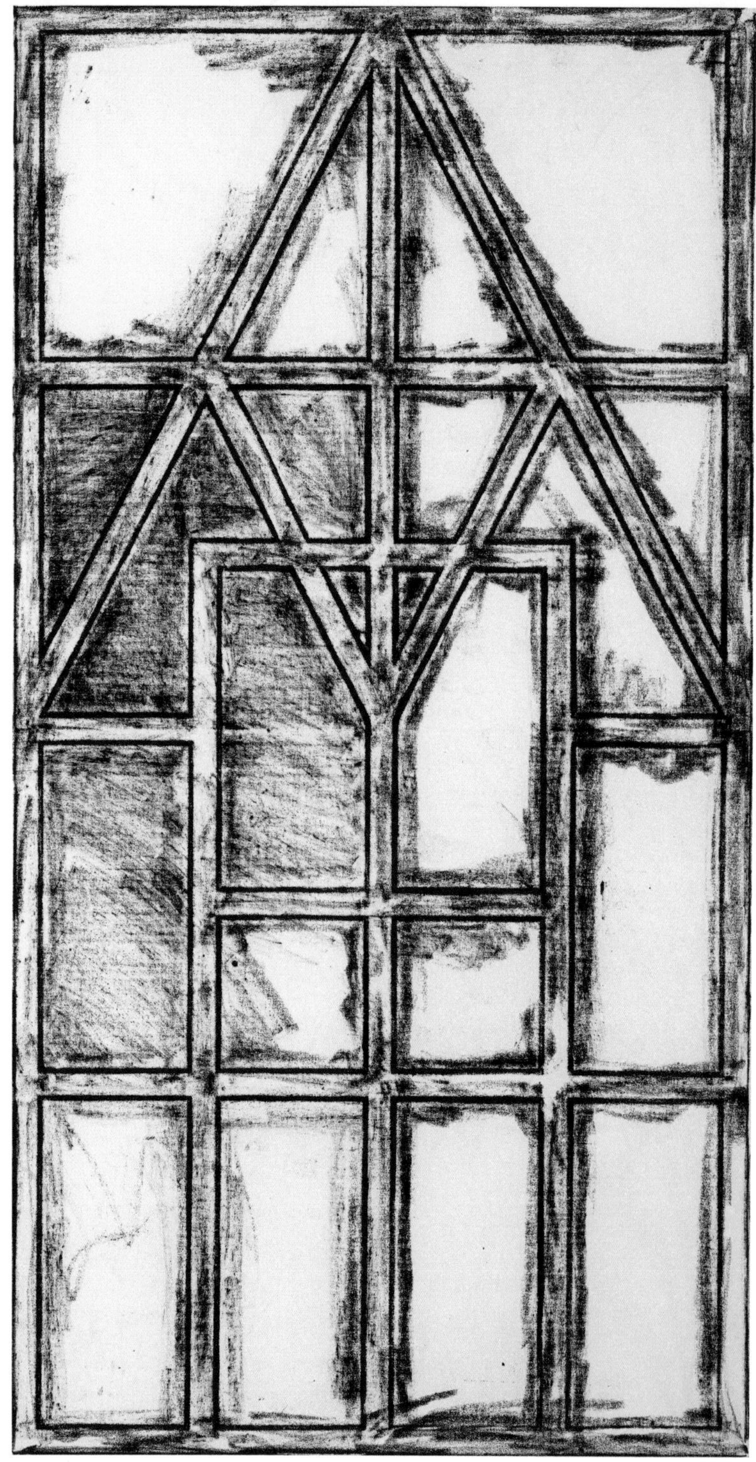

1991.11 Untitled (City Chart #1), 237.5 × 119.5 cm

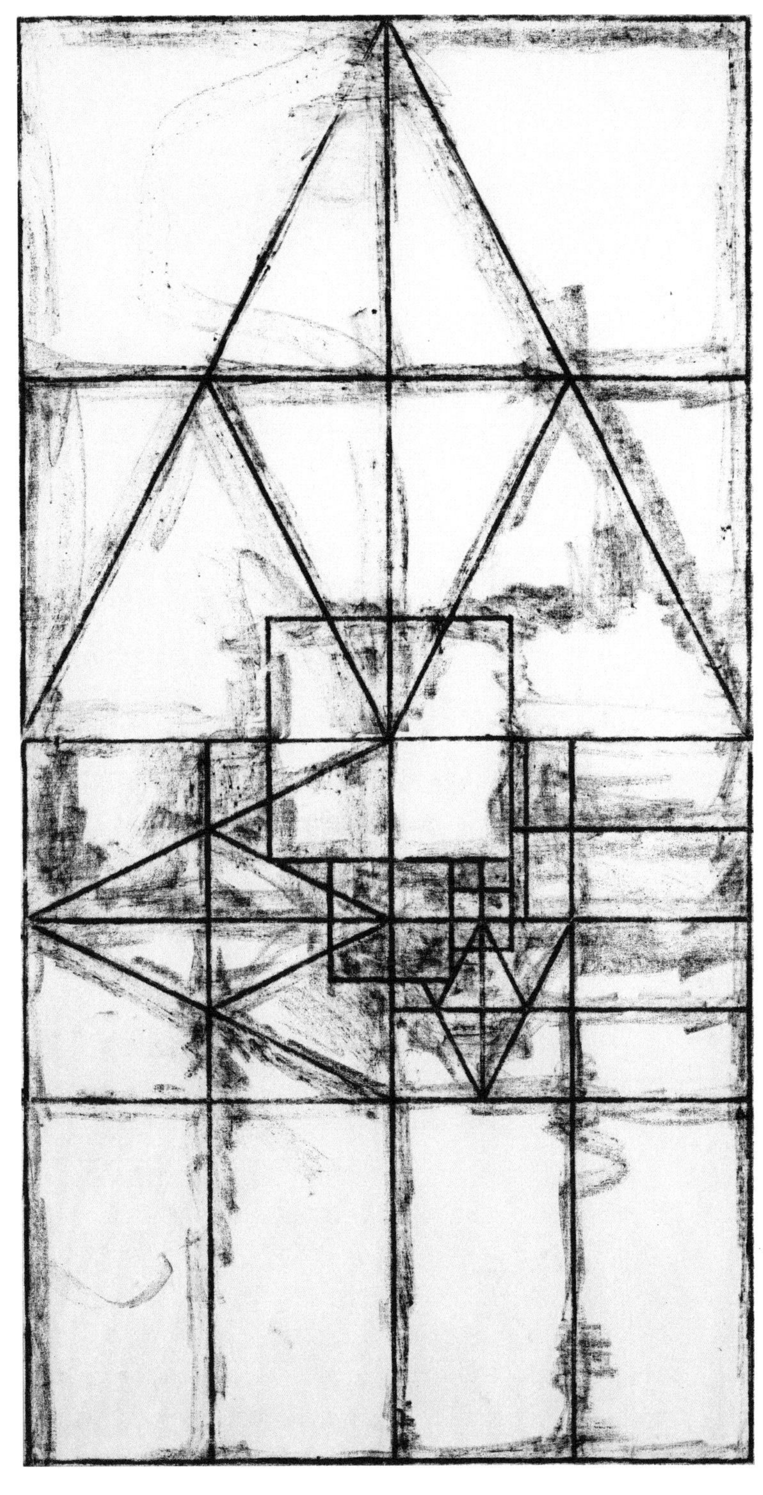

1991.12 Untitled (City Chart #2), 237.5 × 119.5 cm

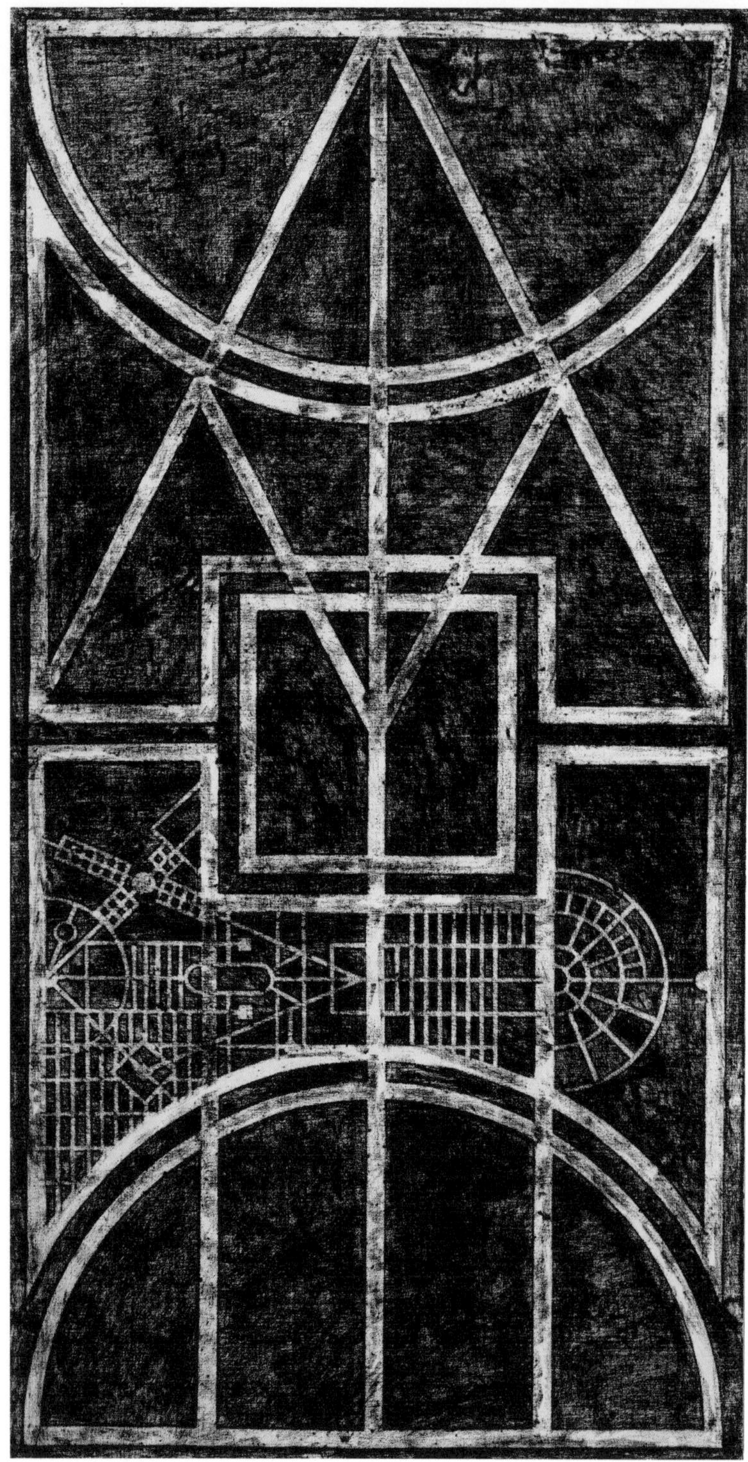

1991.13 Untitled (City Chart Black), 244 × 122 cm

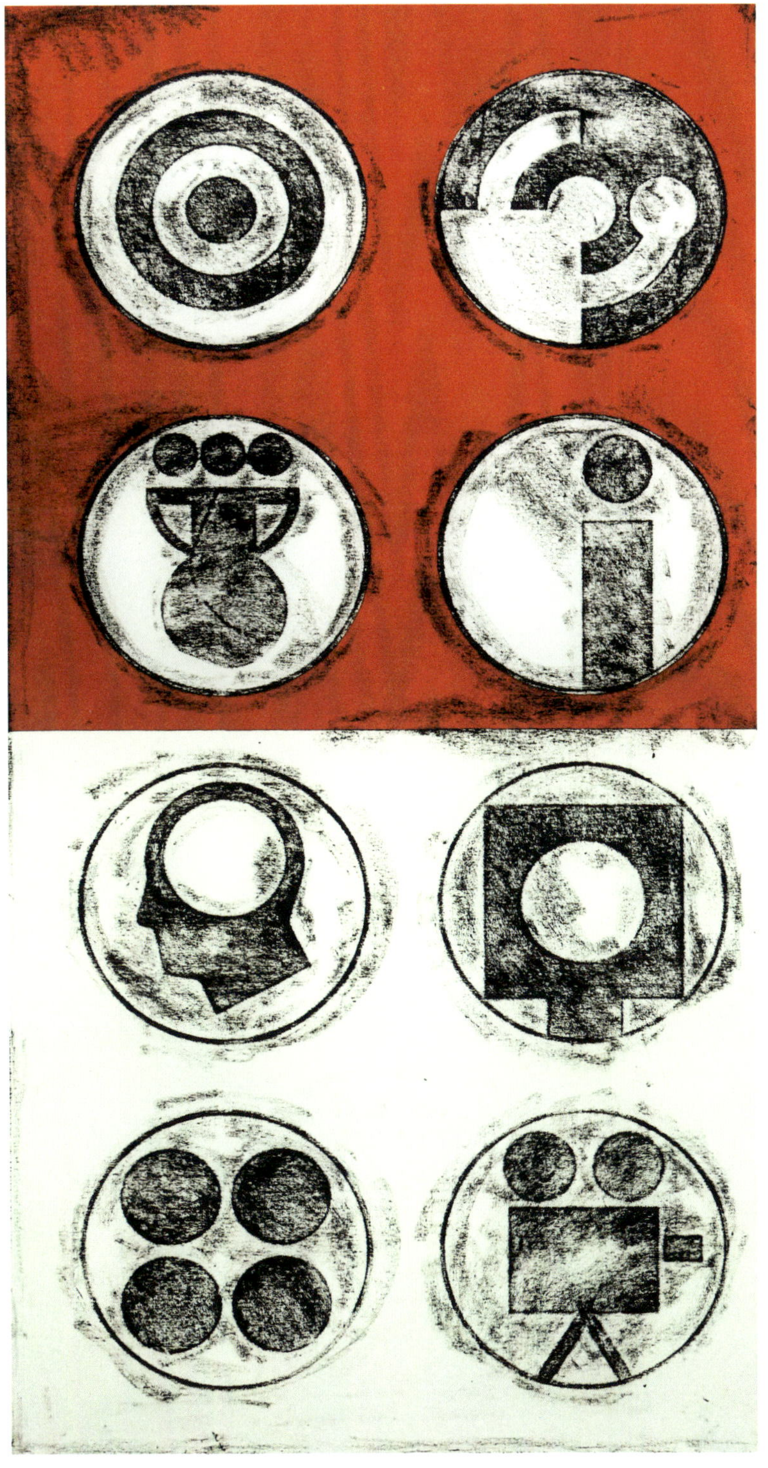

1991.14 Untitled (Cosmology, Signs), 244 × 122 cm

1992

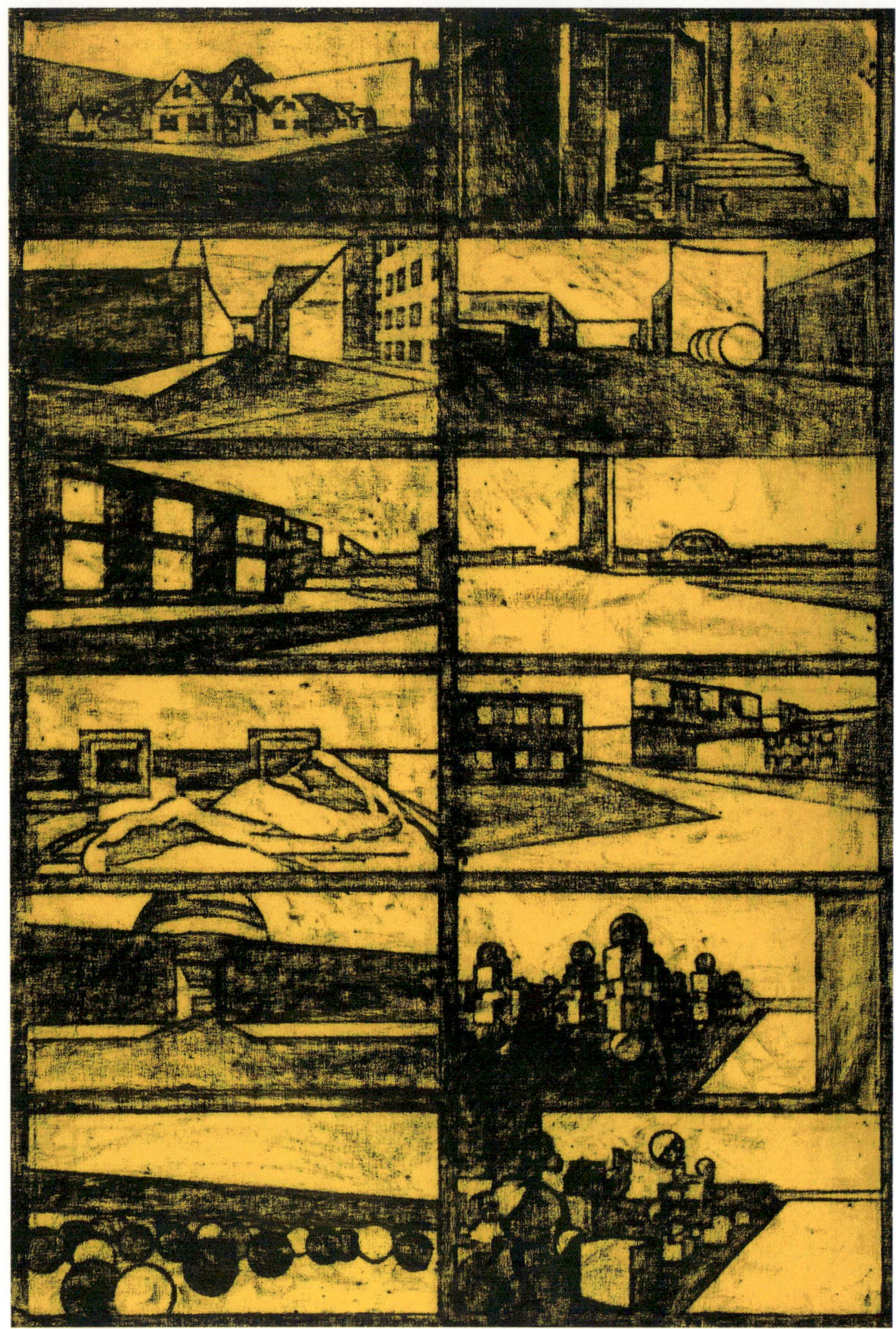

1992.1 Untitled (Computer City), 183 × 122 cm

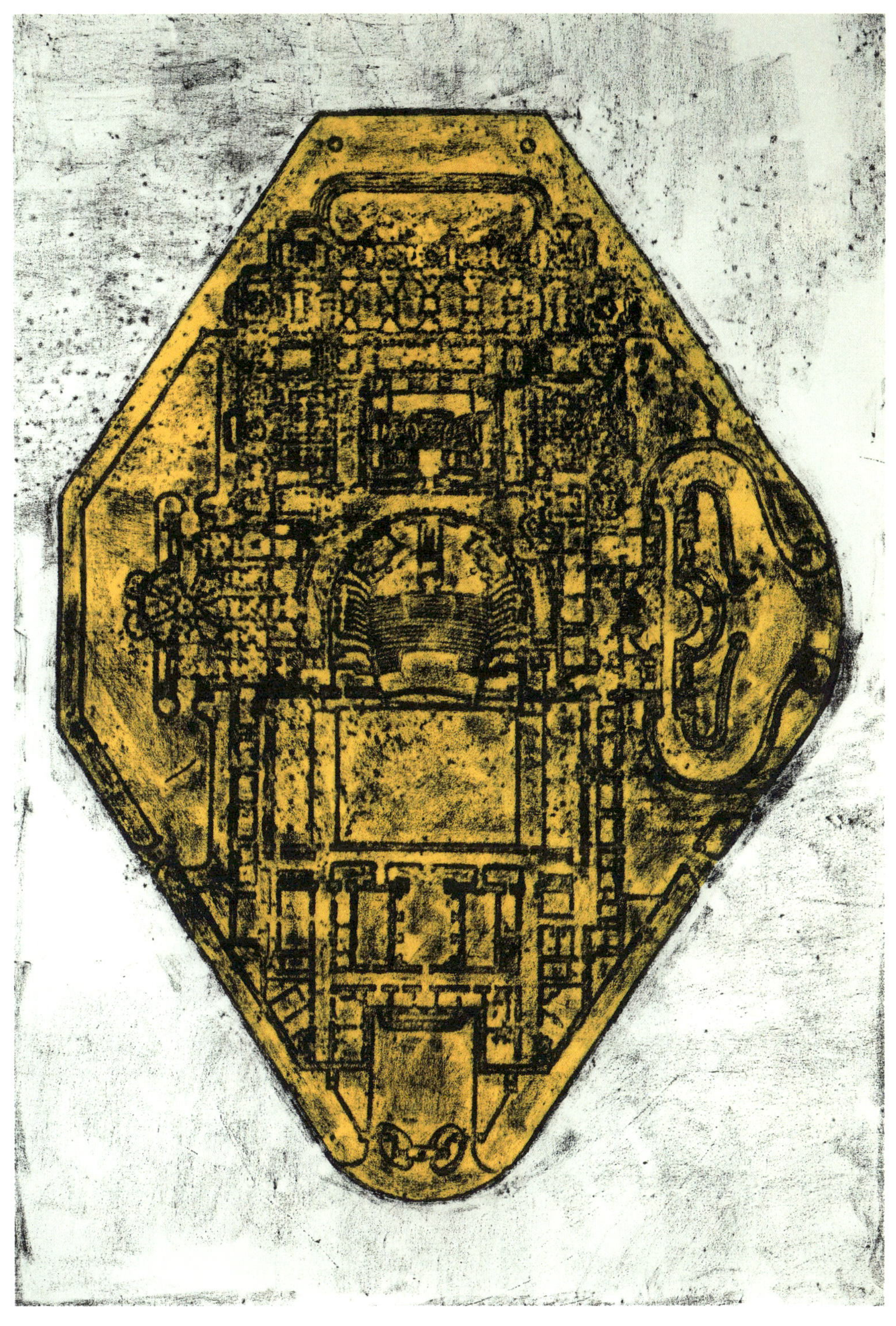

1992.2 Untitled (Paris Opera House), 183 × 122 cm

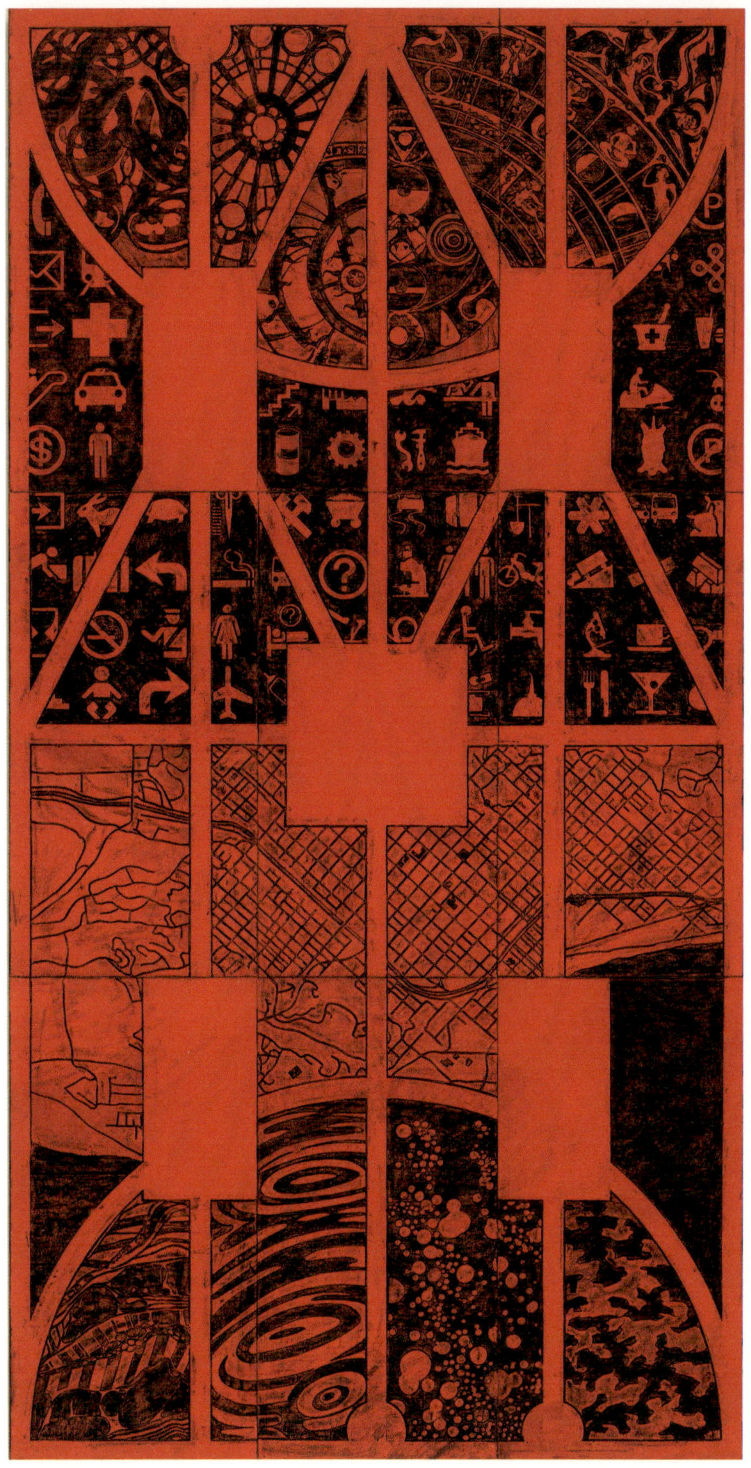

1992.3 Untitled (Five into One City Chart), 731.5 × 366 cm

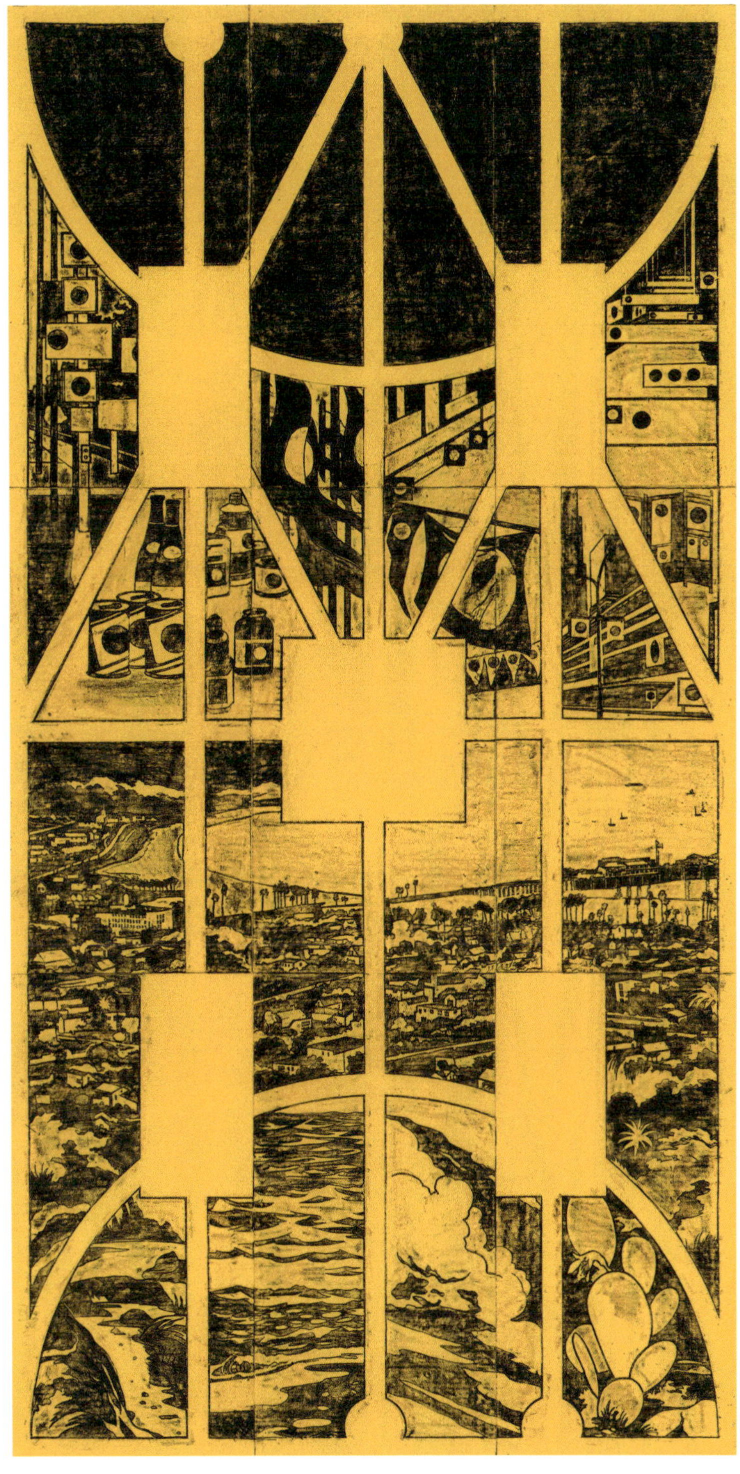

1992.4 Untitled (Five into One City Chart), 731.5 × 366 cm

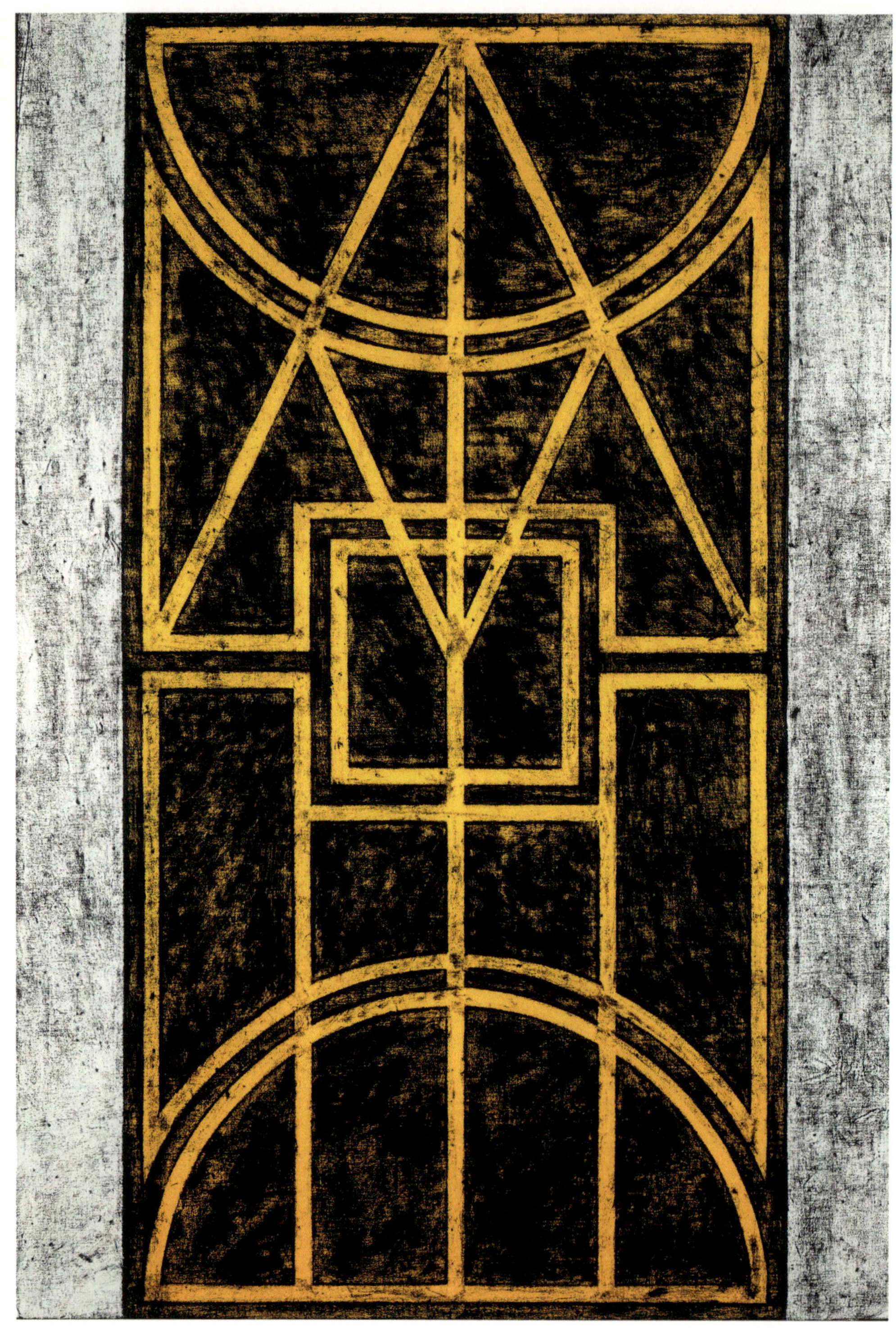

1992.5 Untitled (City Plan), 183 × 122 cm

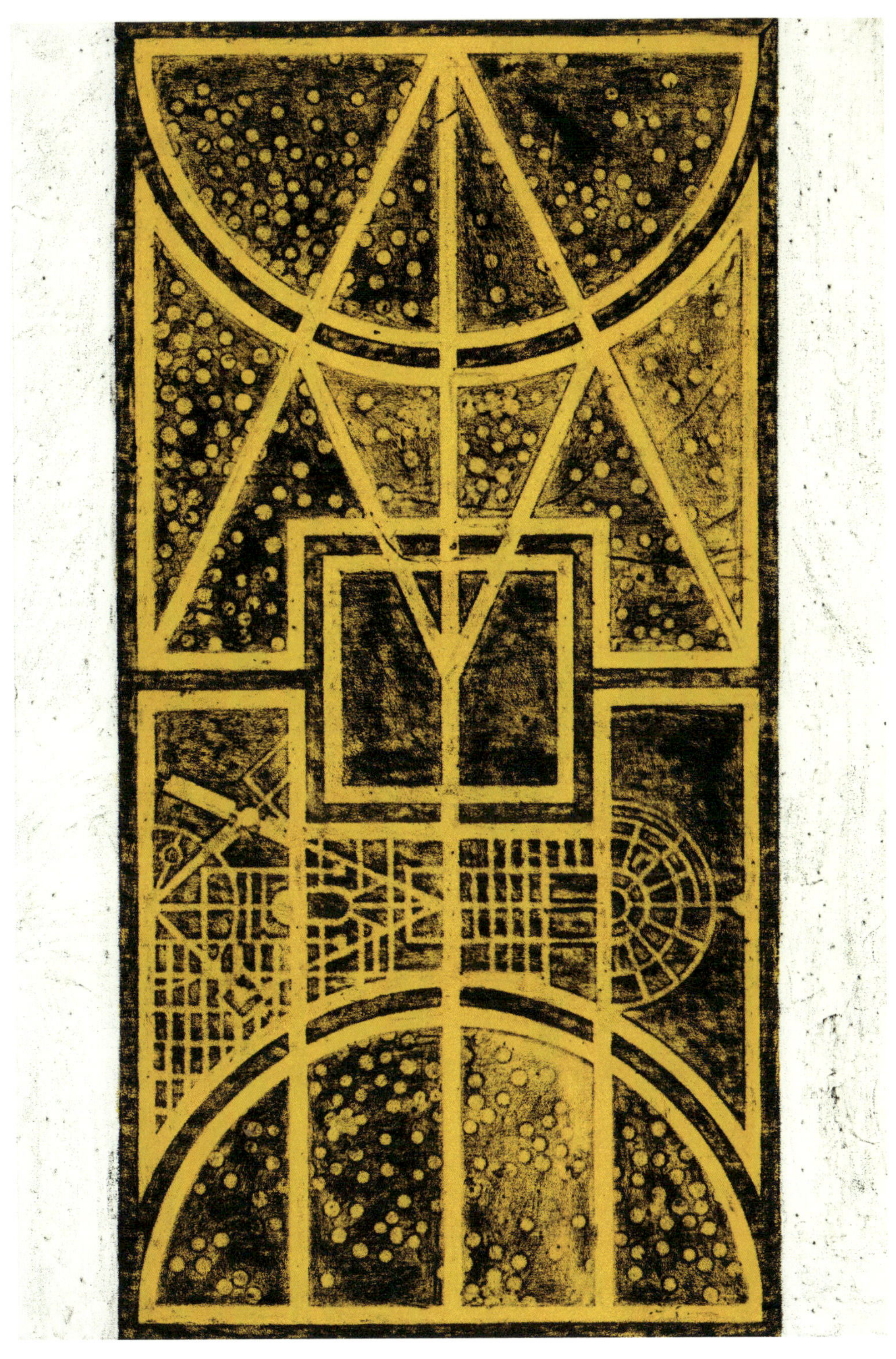

1992.6 Untitled (City Chart: Elements around World Unframed), 183 × 122 cm

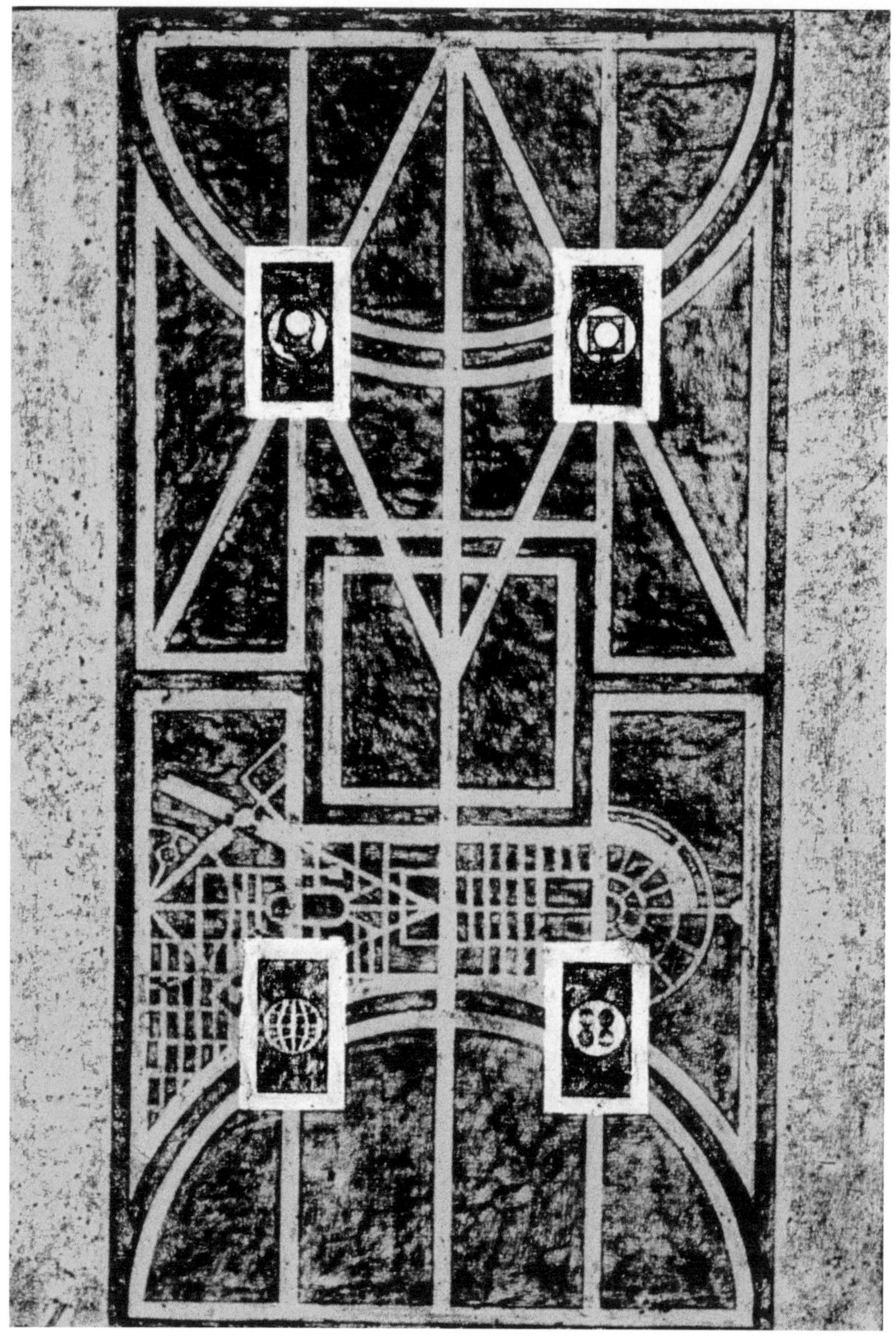

1992.7 Untitled (City Plan), 183 × 122 cm

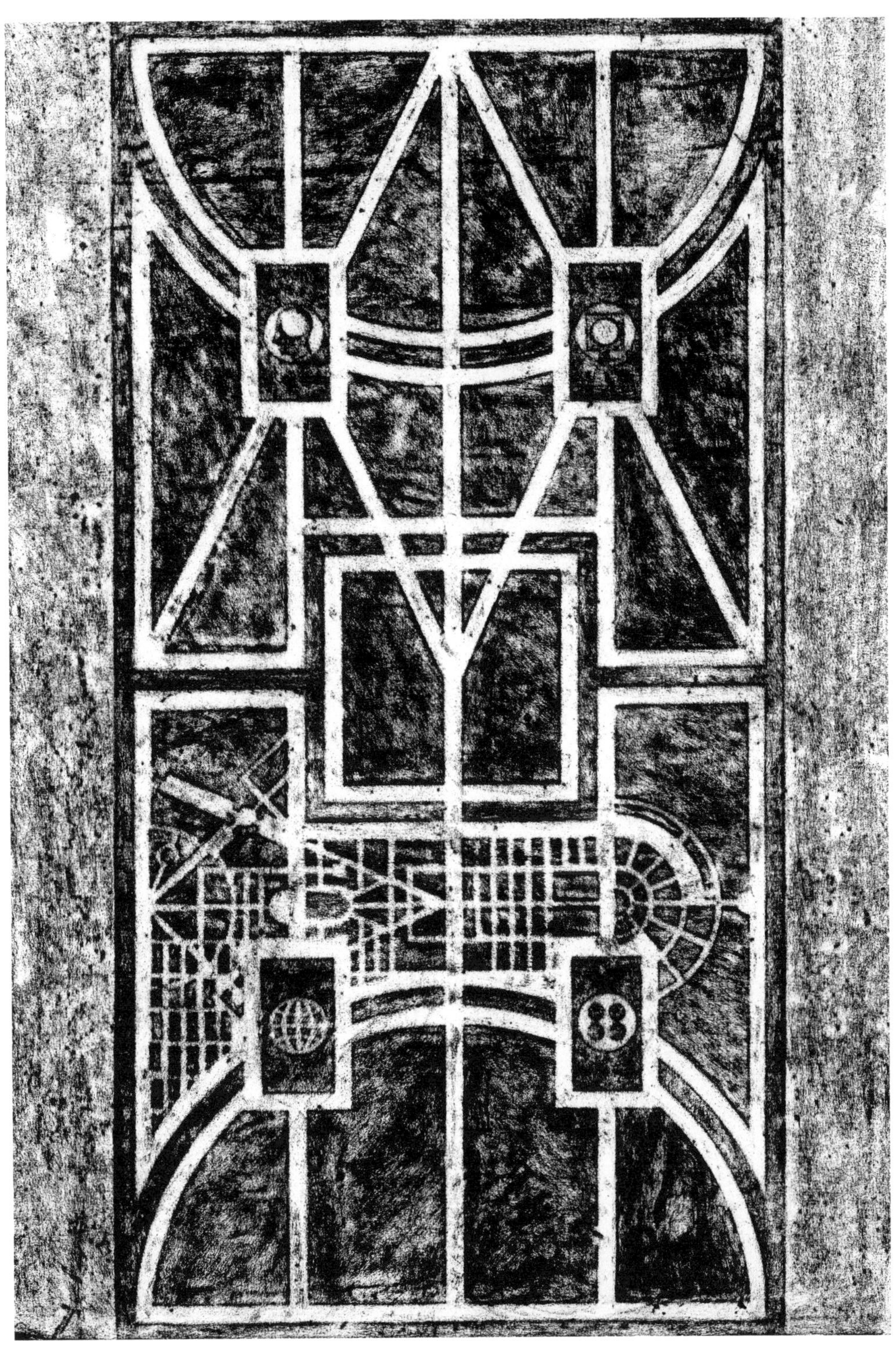

1992.8 Untitled (City Plan), 183 × 122 cm

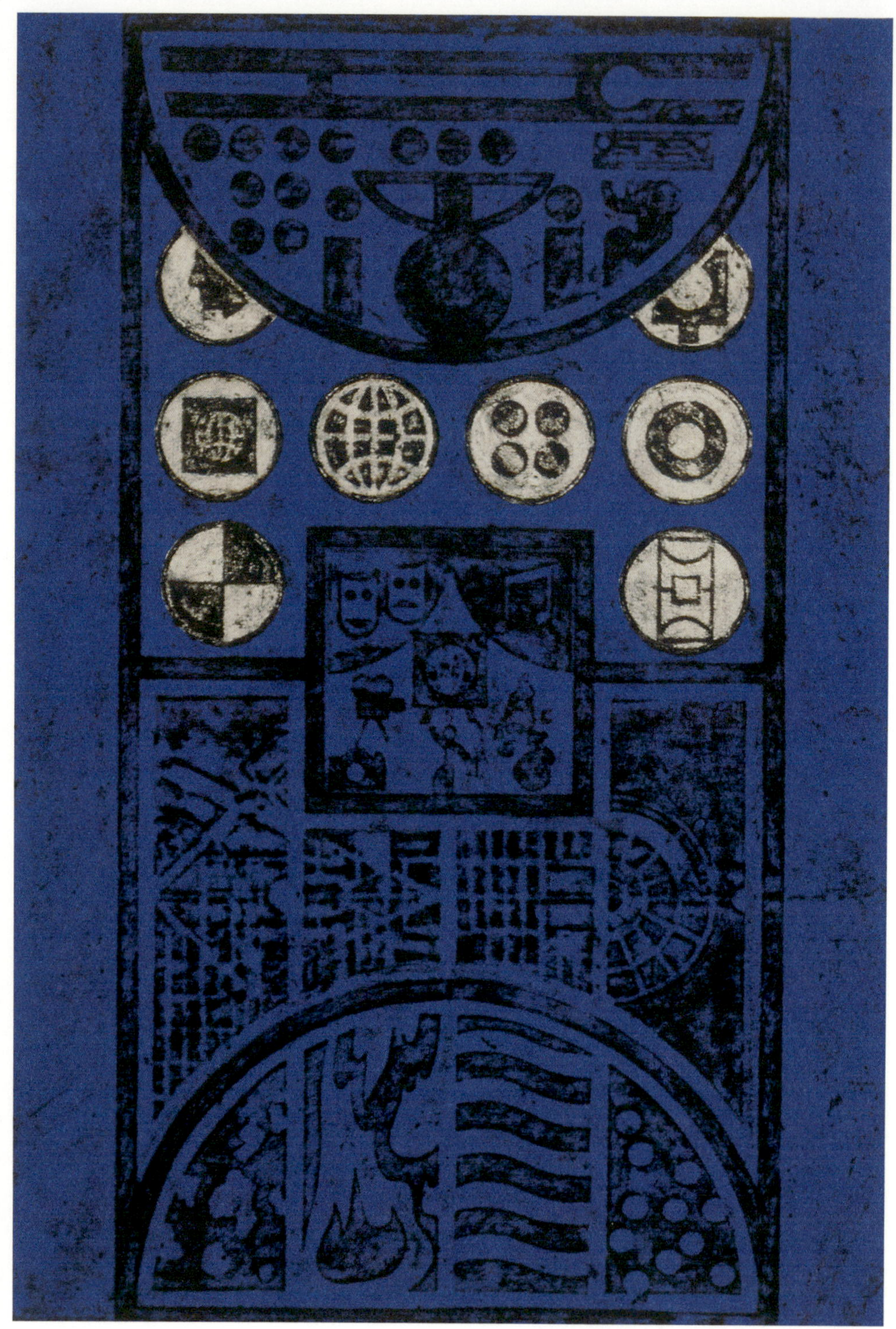

1992.9 Untitled (City Chart with Signs), 183 × 122 cm

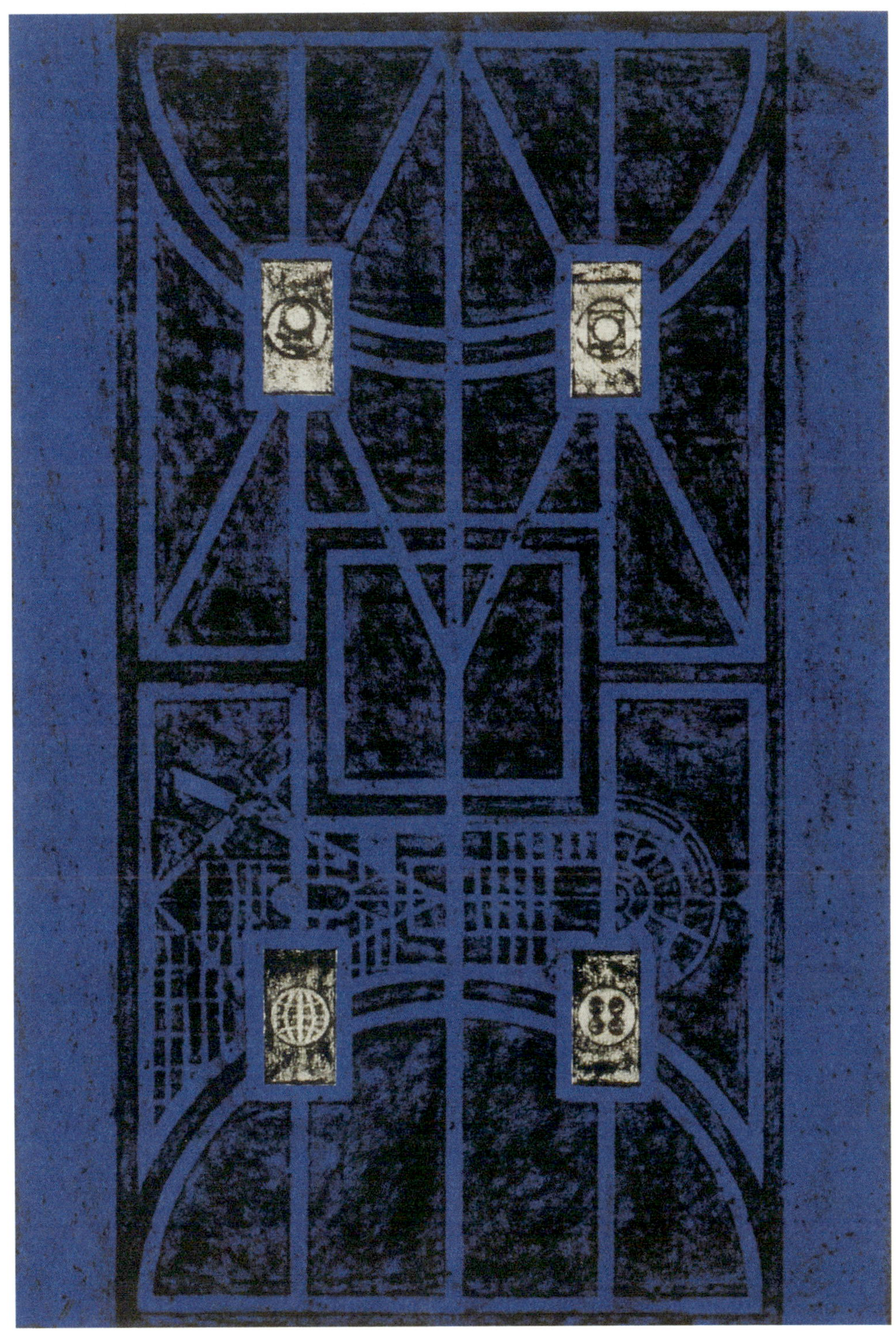

1992.10 Untitled (Five into One City Chart), 183 × 122 cm

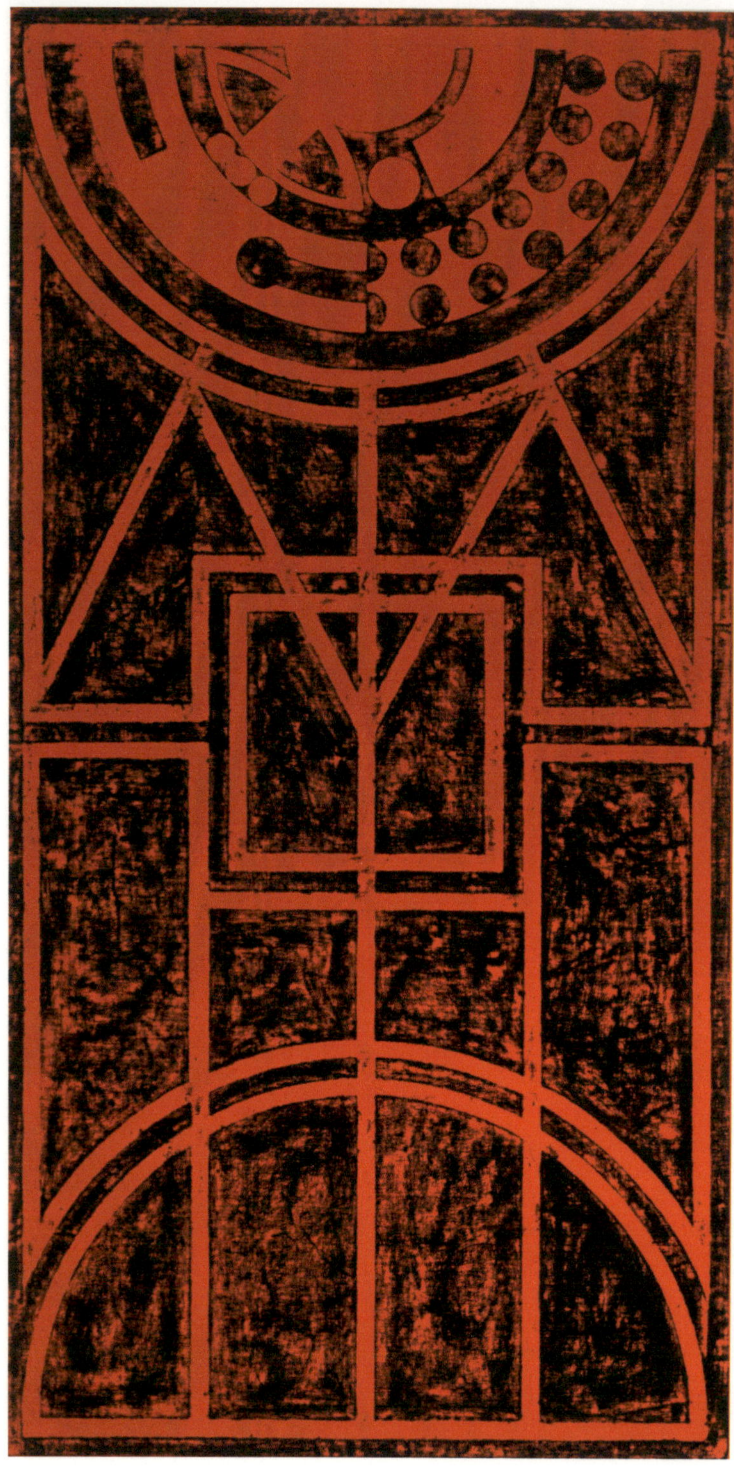

1992.11 Untitled (Red City Chart with Cosmology), 244 × 122 cm

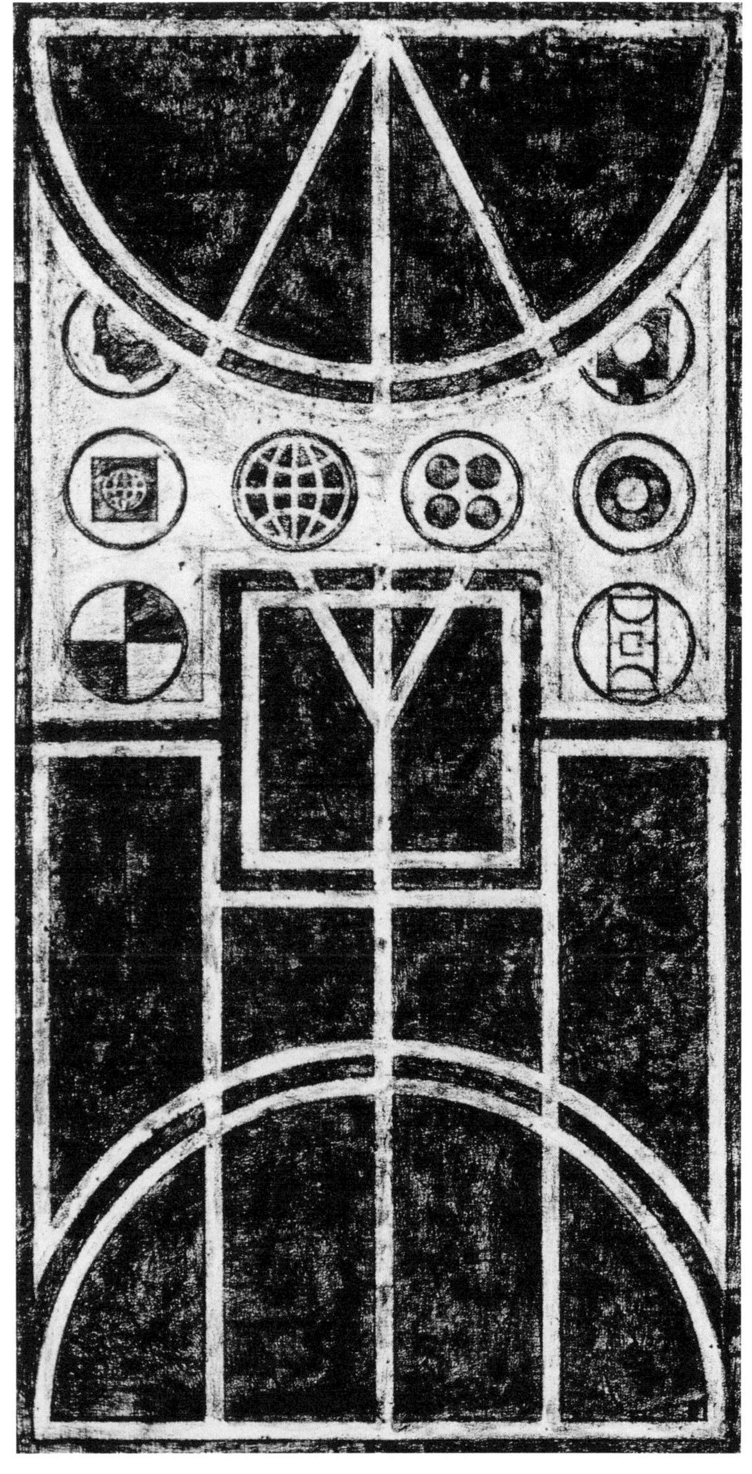

1992.12 Untitled (City Chart with Signs), 244 × 122 cm

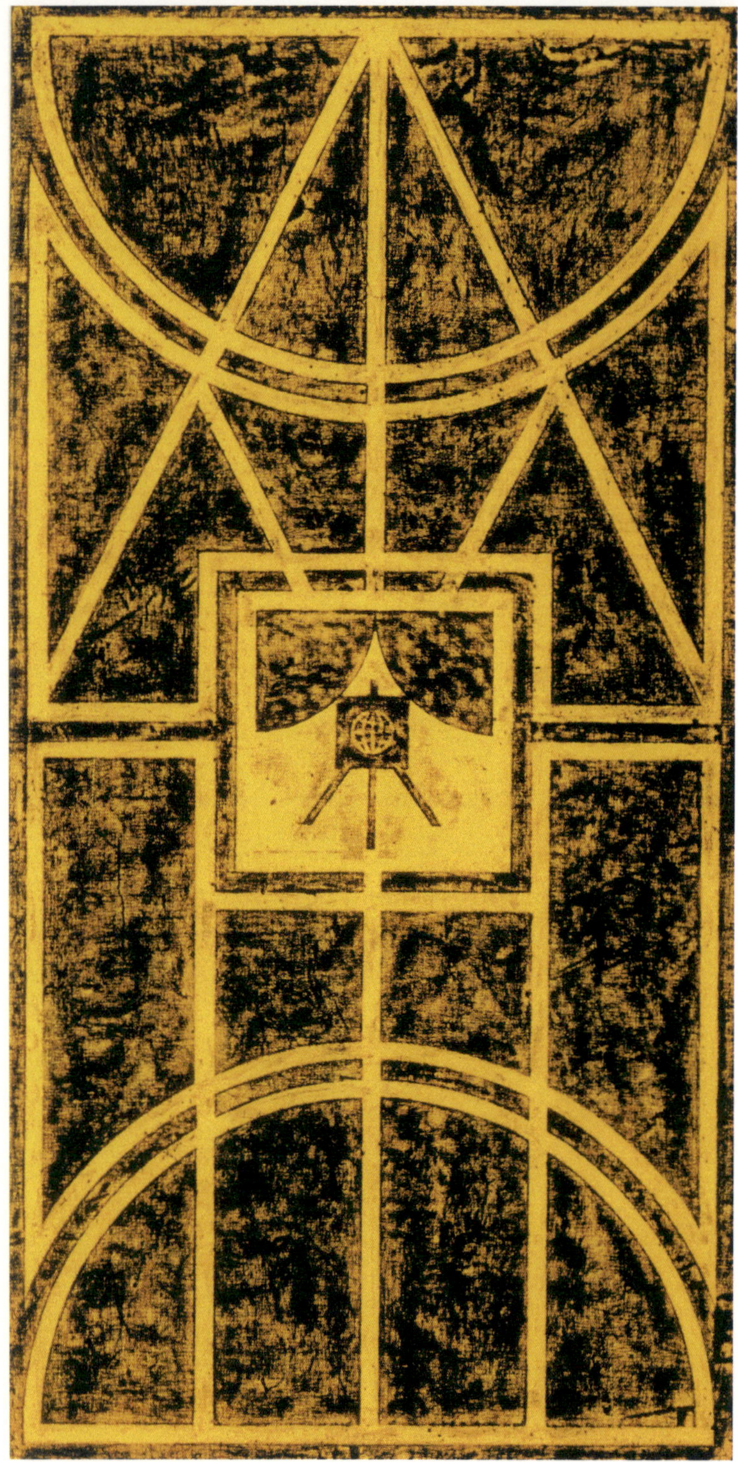

1992.13 Untitled (City Chart with World Framed), 244 × 122 cm

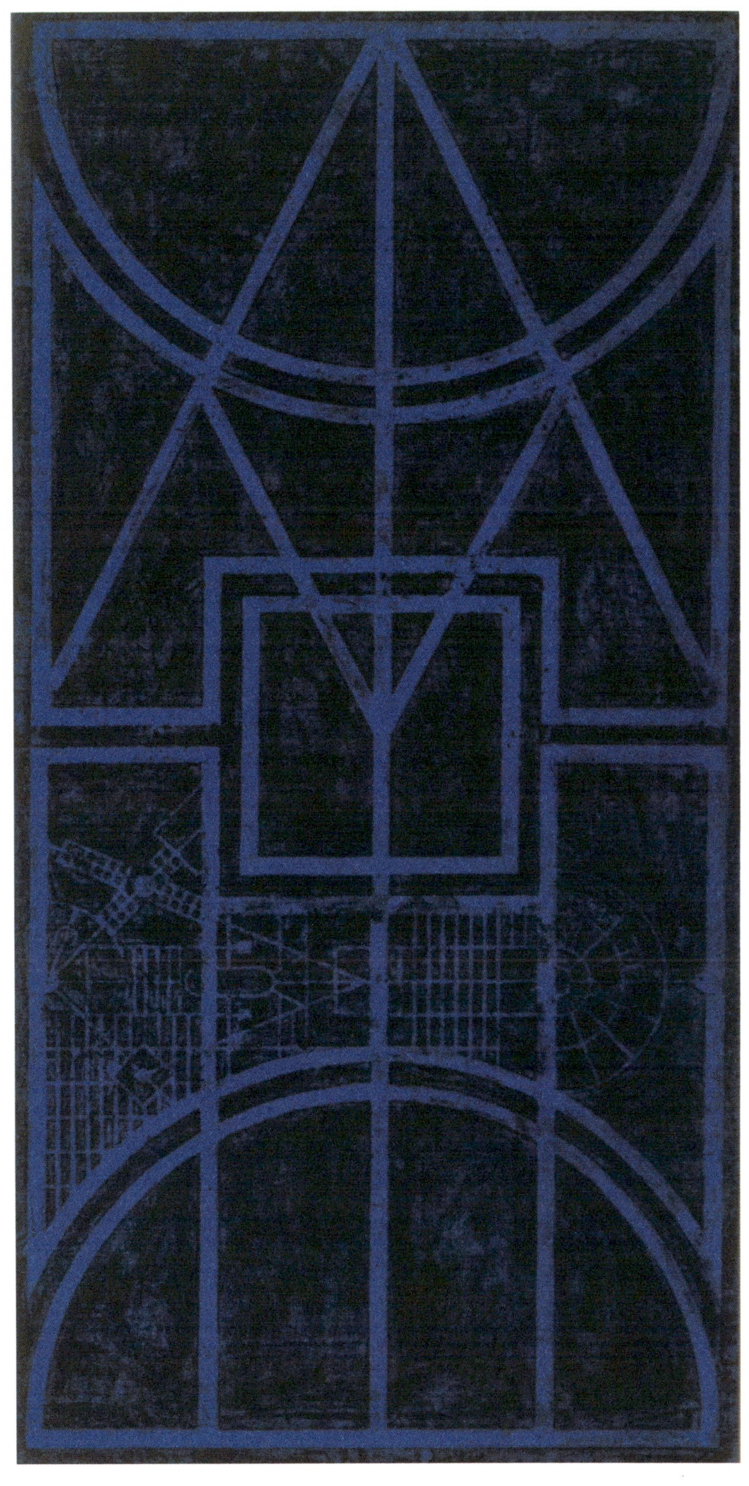

1992.14 Untitled (City Chart with City), 244 × 122 cm

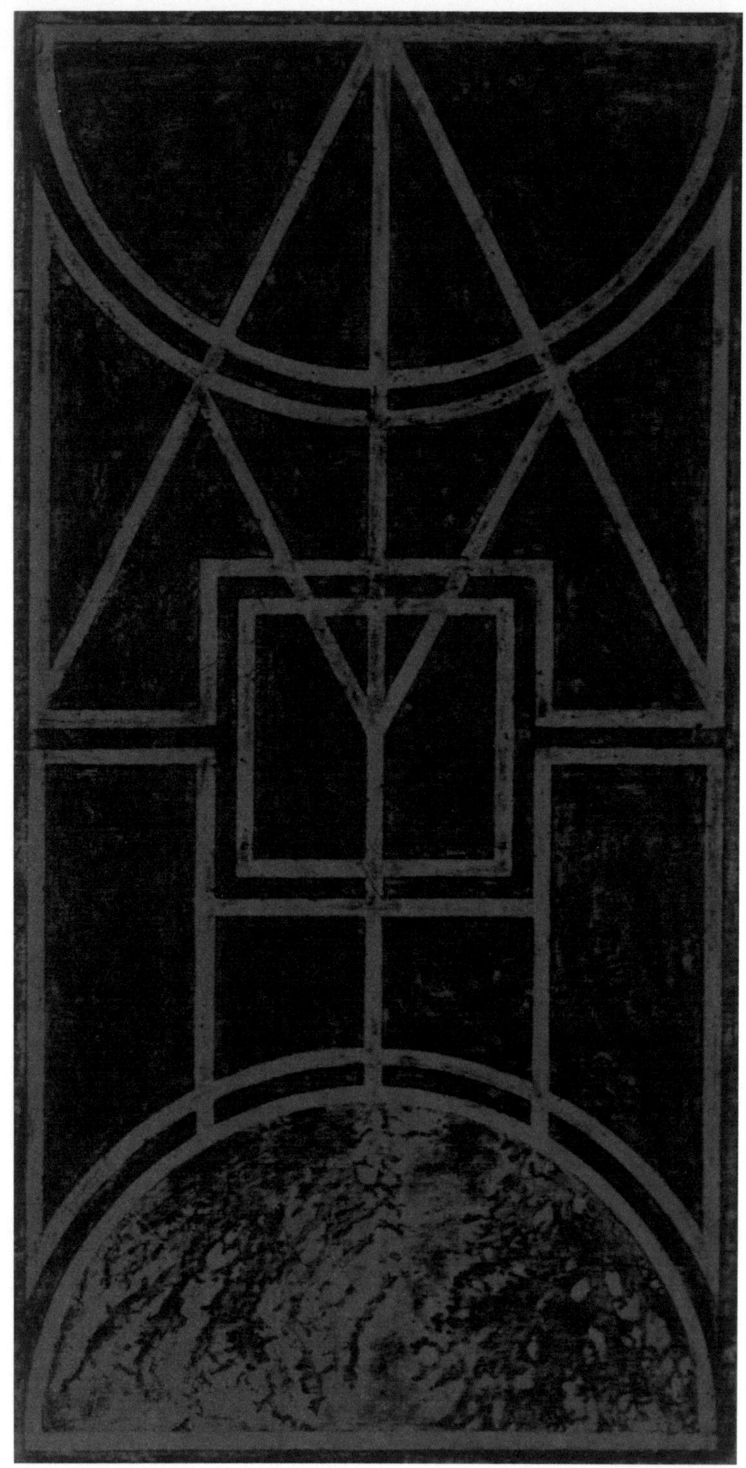

1992.15 Untitled (Green City Chart with Lungs), 244 × 122 cm

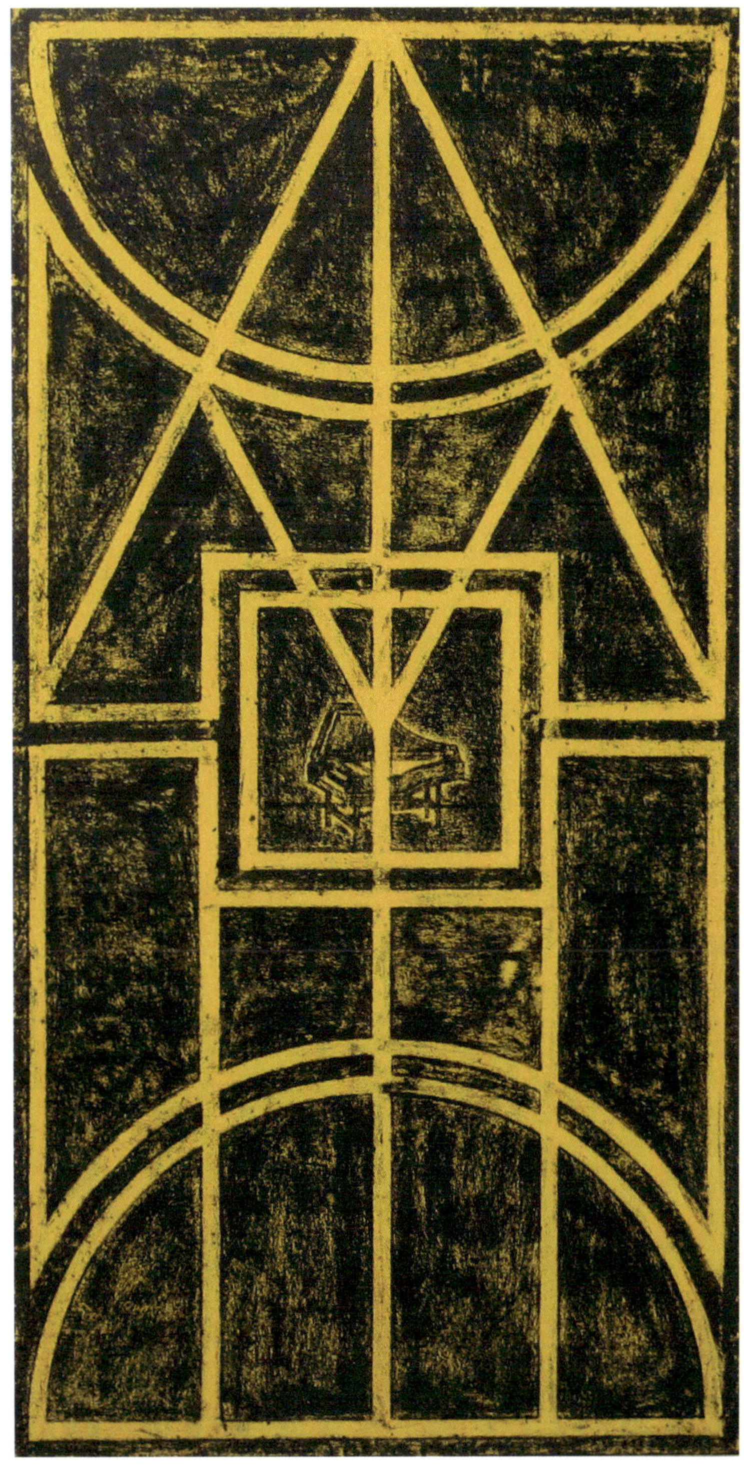

1992.16 Untitled (City Chart with World Framed), 244 × 122 cm

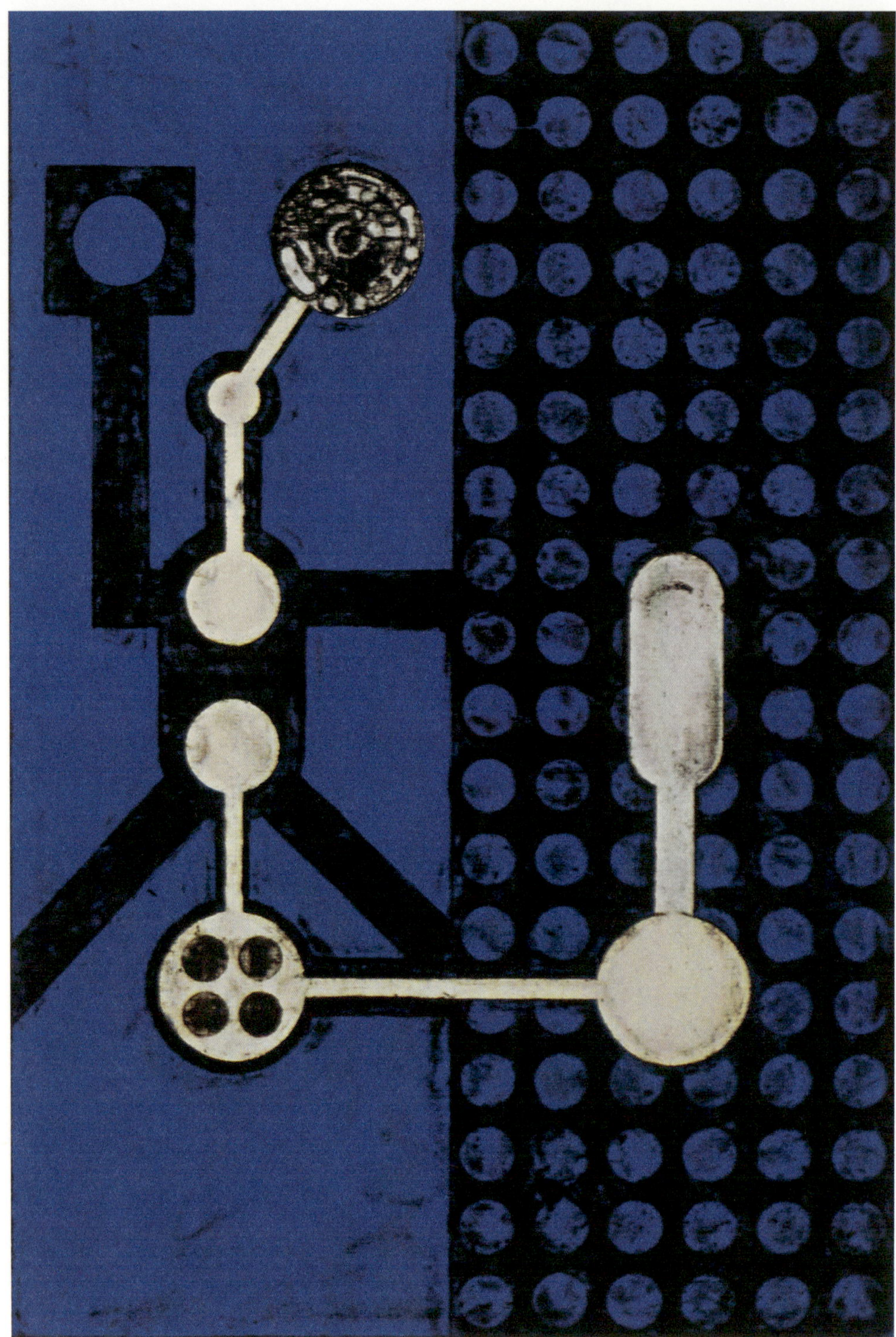

1992.17 Untitled (Anatomy with Boiler and Elements), 183 × 122 cm

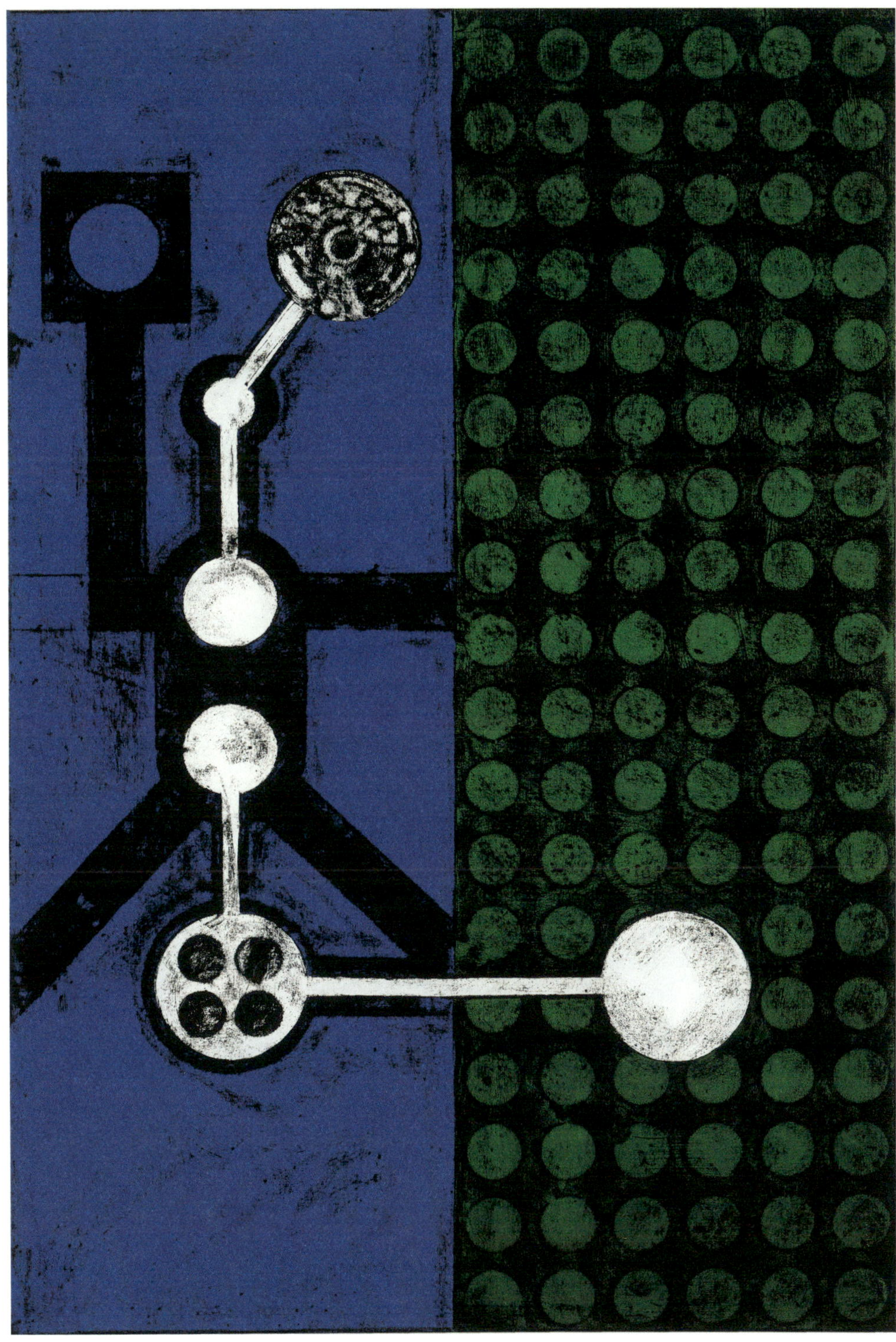

1992.18 Untitled (Anatomy and Elements), 183 × 122 cm

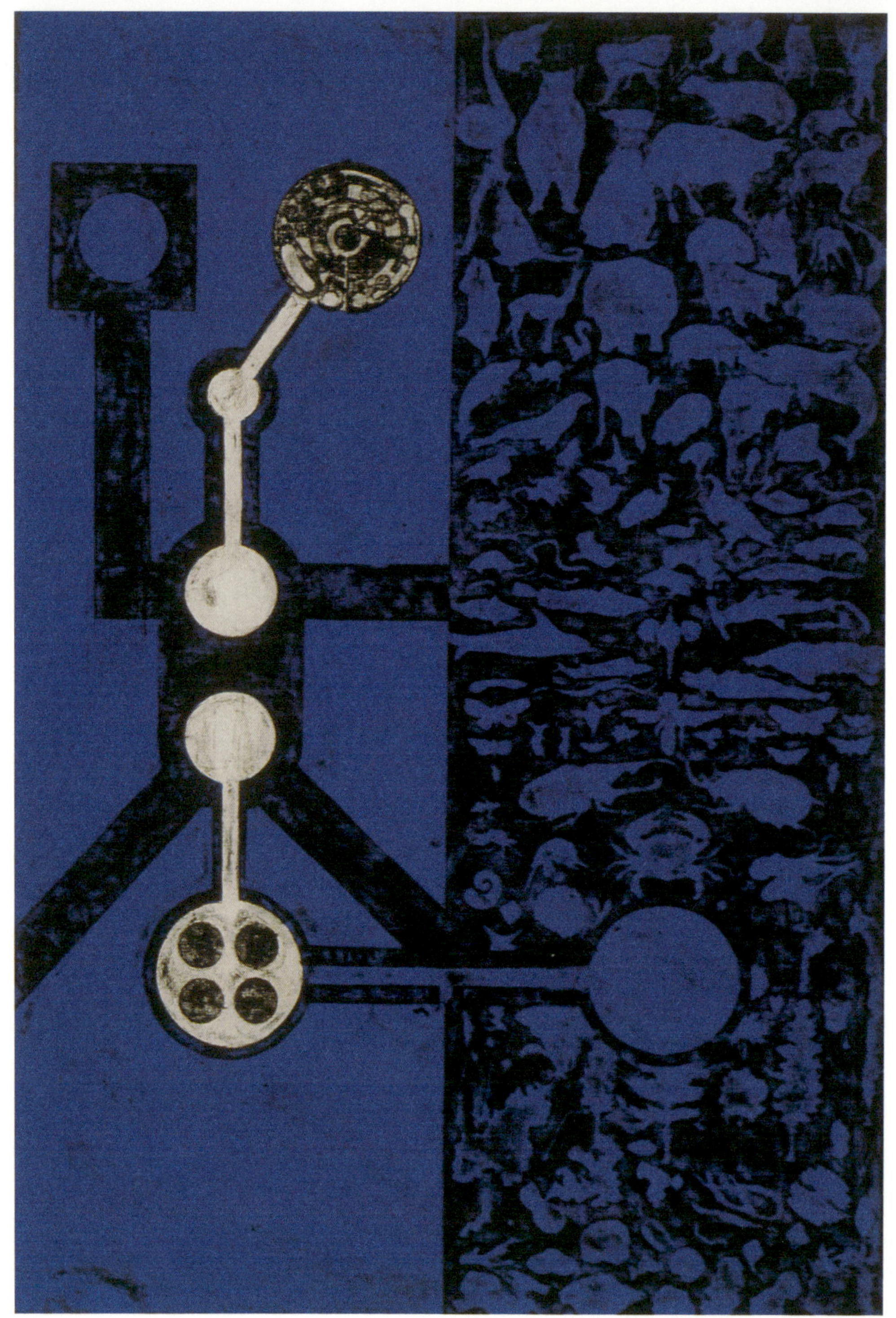

1992.19 Untitled (Anatomy and Evolution), 183 × 122 cm

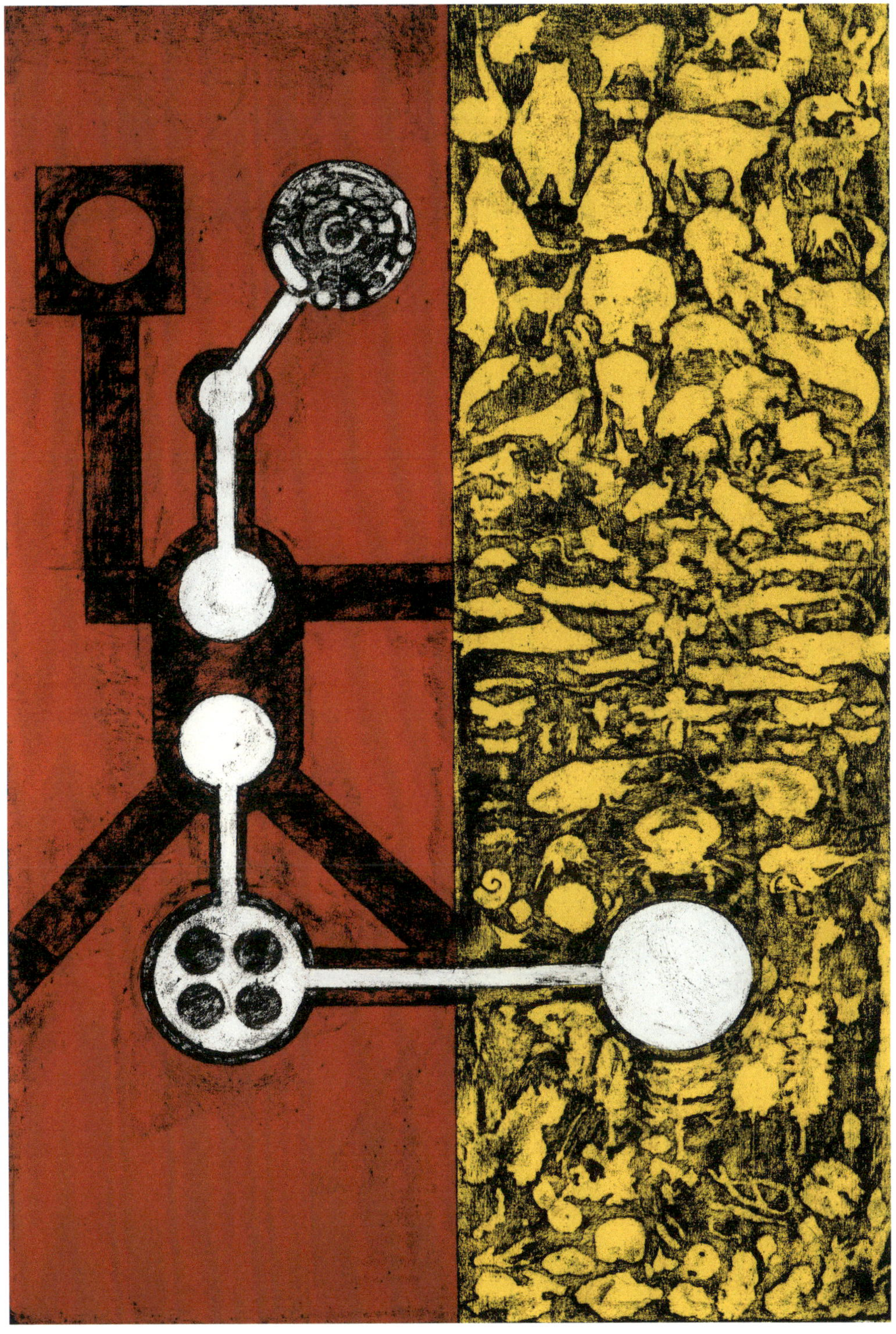

1992.20 Untitled (Anatomy and Evolution), 183 × 122 cm

1995

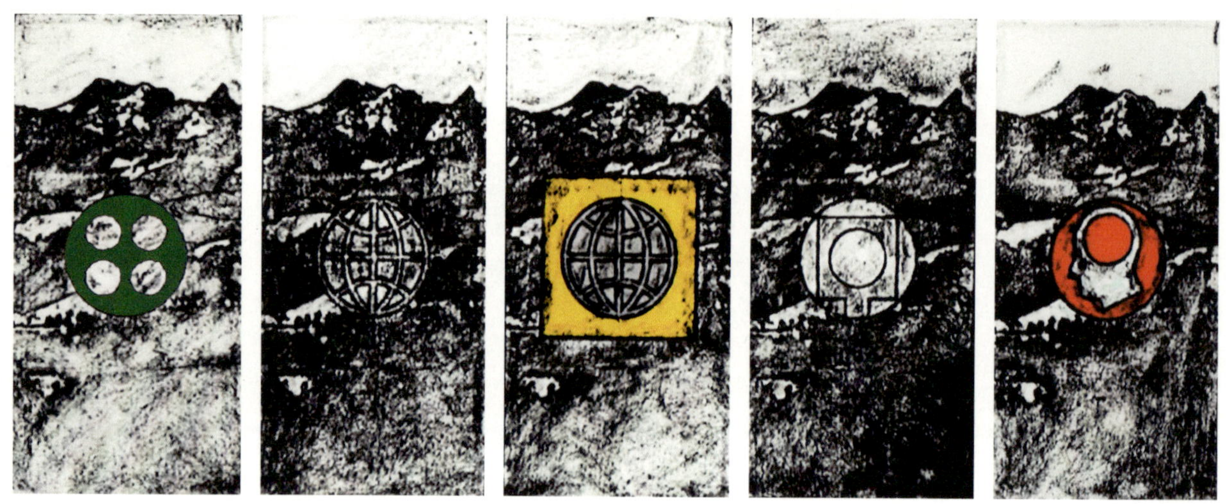

1995.1 Untitled (Landscape with Signs), 120 × 300 cm (5 parts)

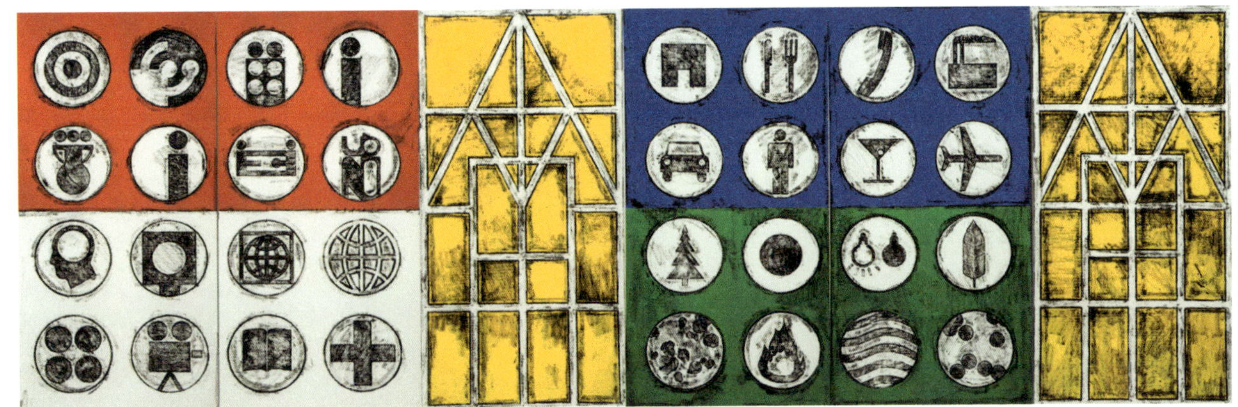

1995.2 Untitled (City and Signs), 240 × 720 cm (6 parts)

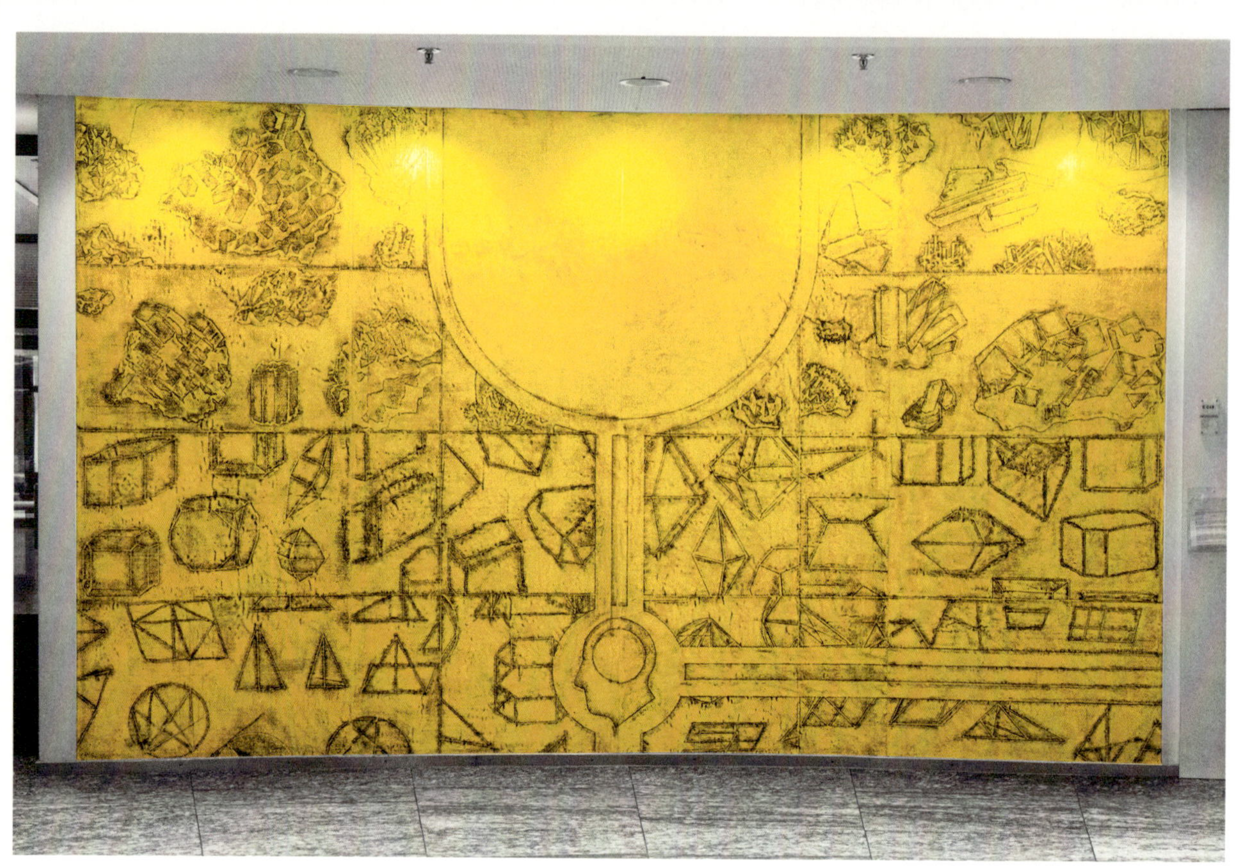

1995.3 Untitled (Öffentliche Versicherung, Braunschweig) (7 parts and 24 small canvases)

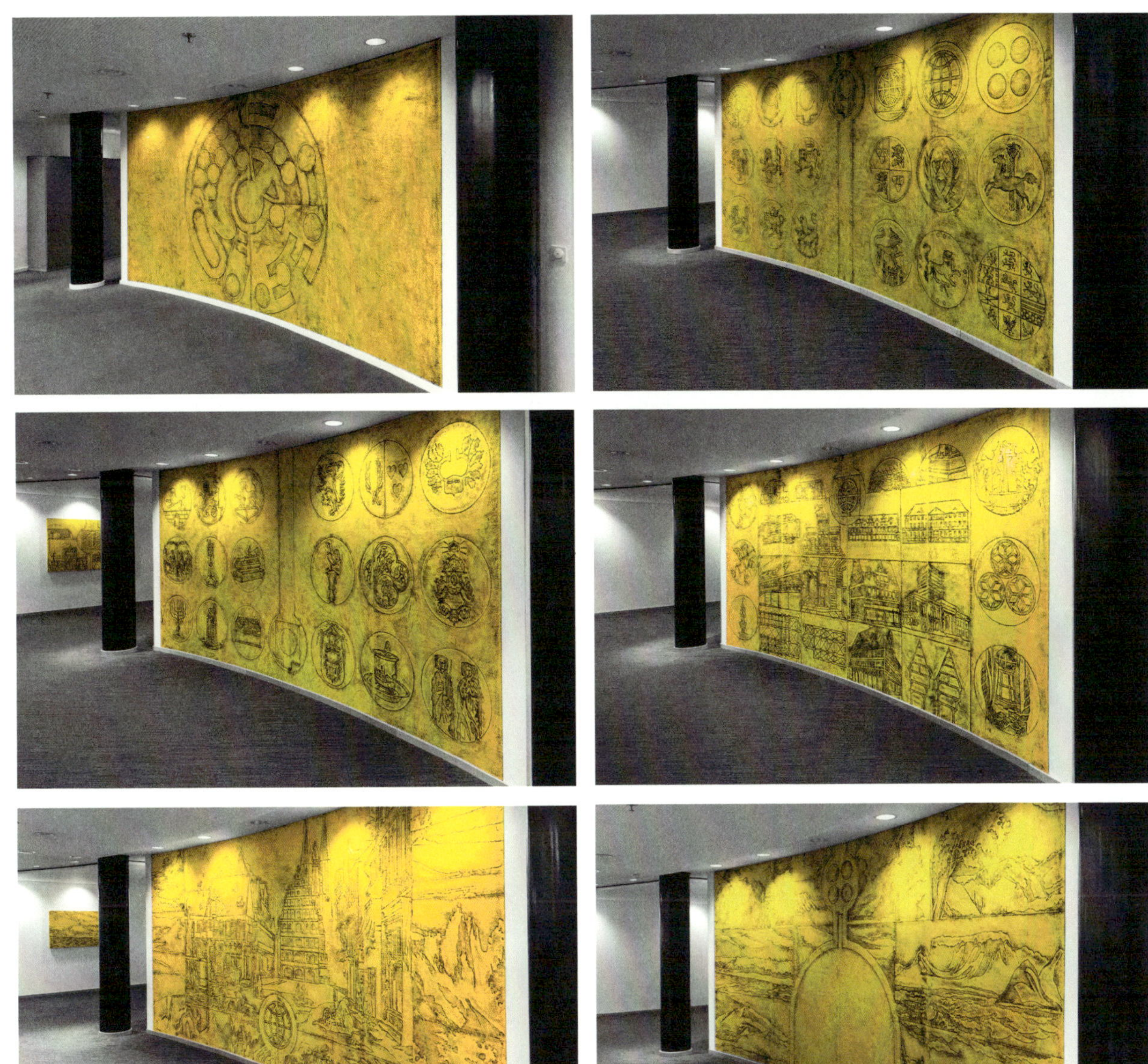

1996

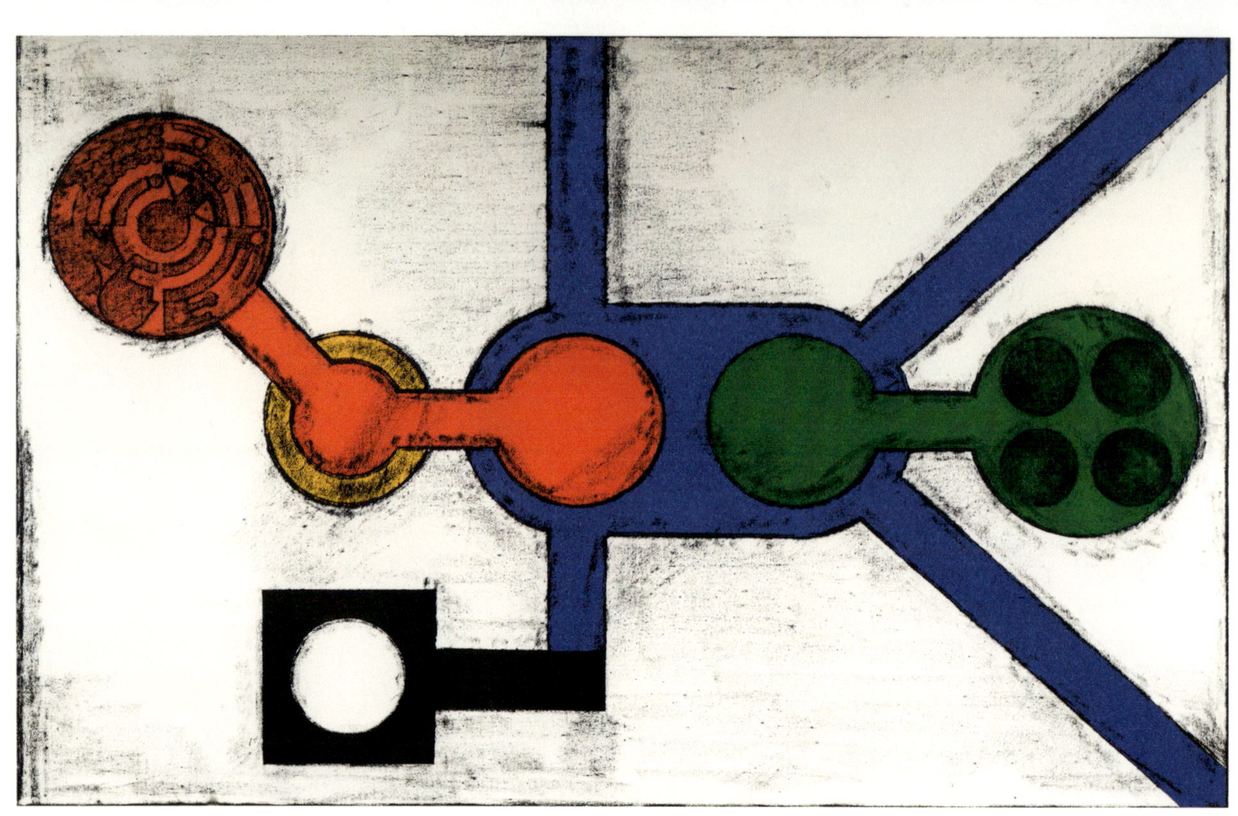

1996.1 Untitled (Anatomy), 122 × 244 cm

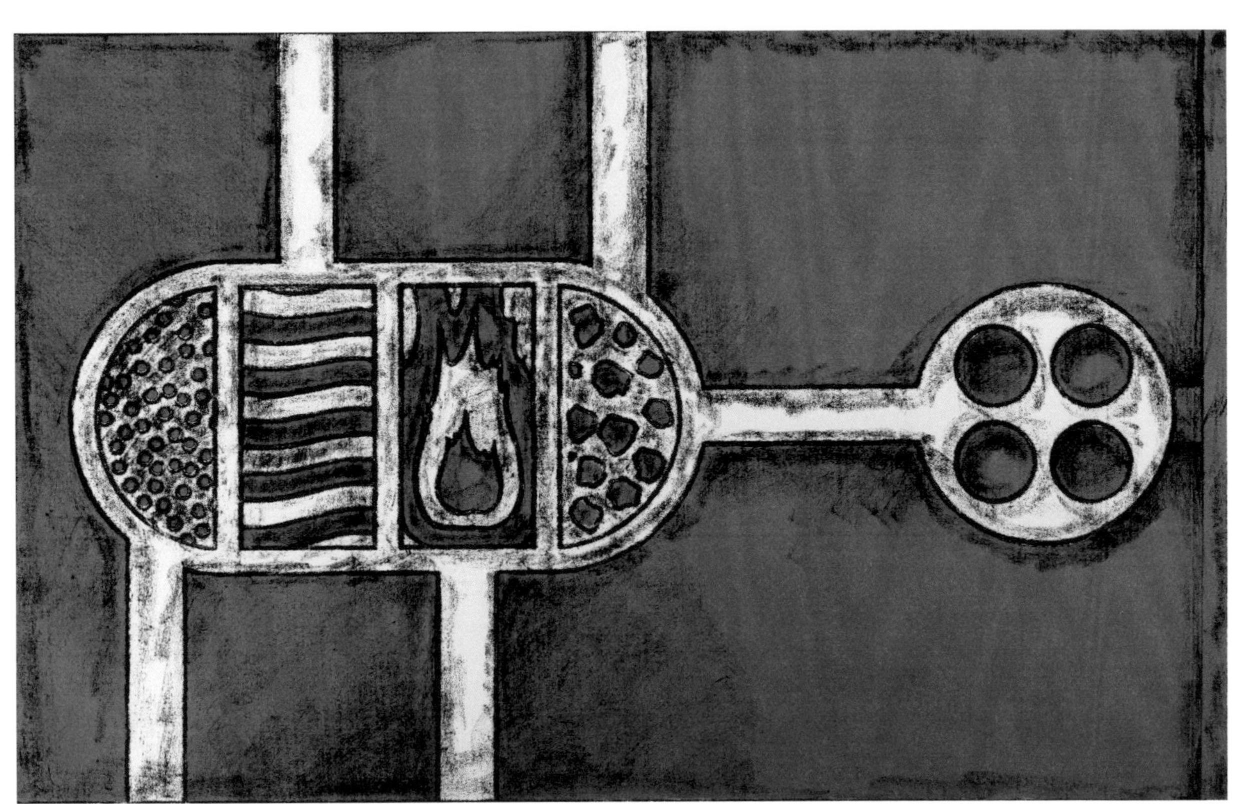

1996.2 Untitled (Boiler), 122 × 244 cm

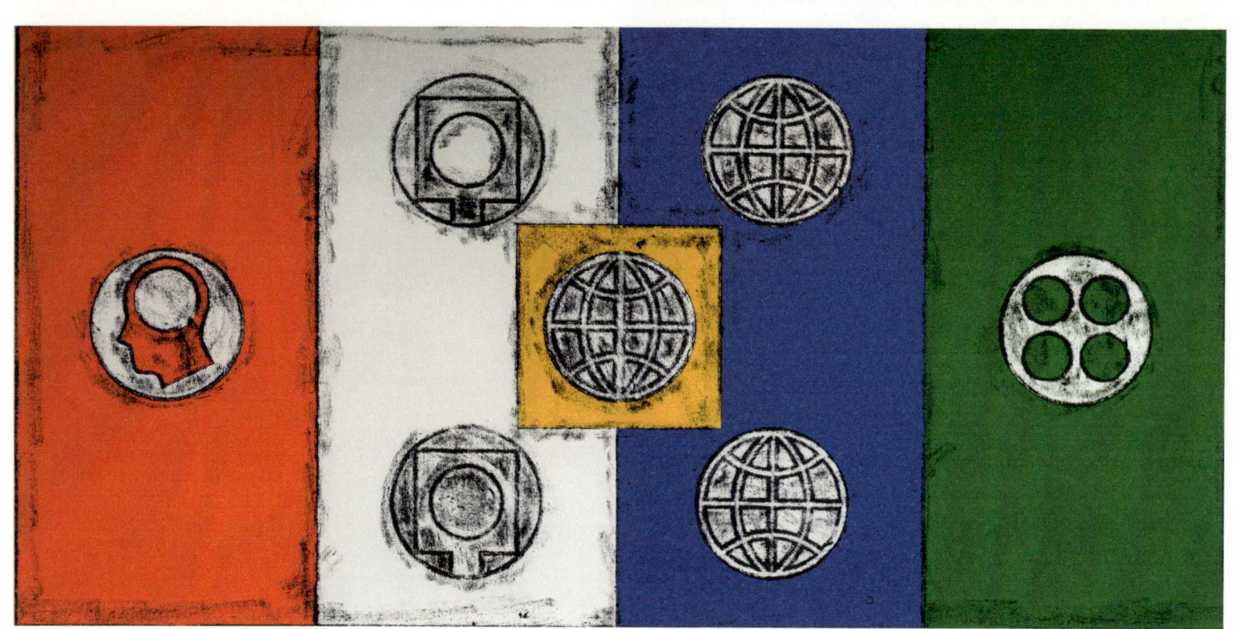

1996.3 Untitled (Chart), 122 × 244 cm

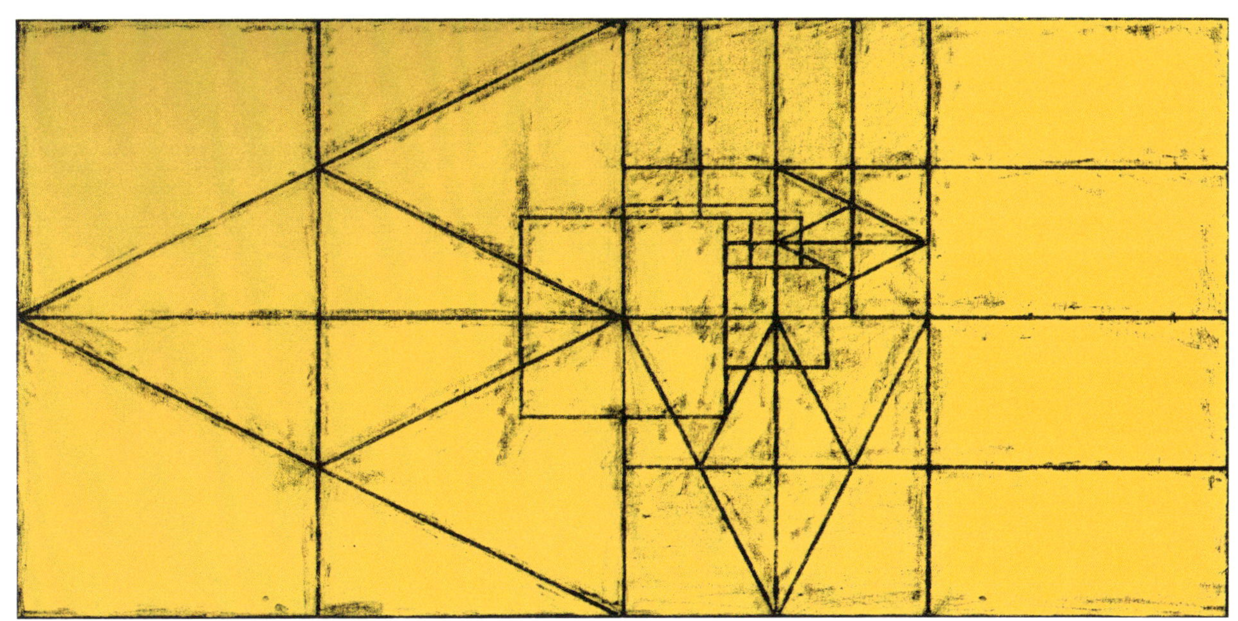

1996.4 Untitled (City Chart), 122 × 244 cm

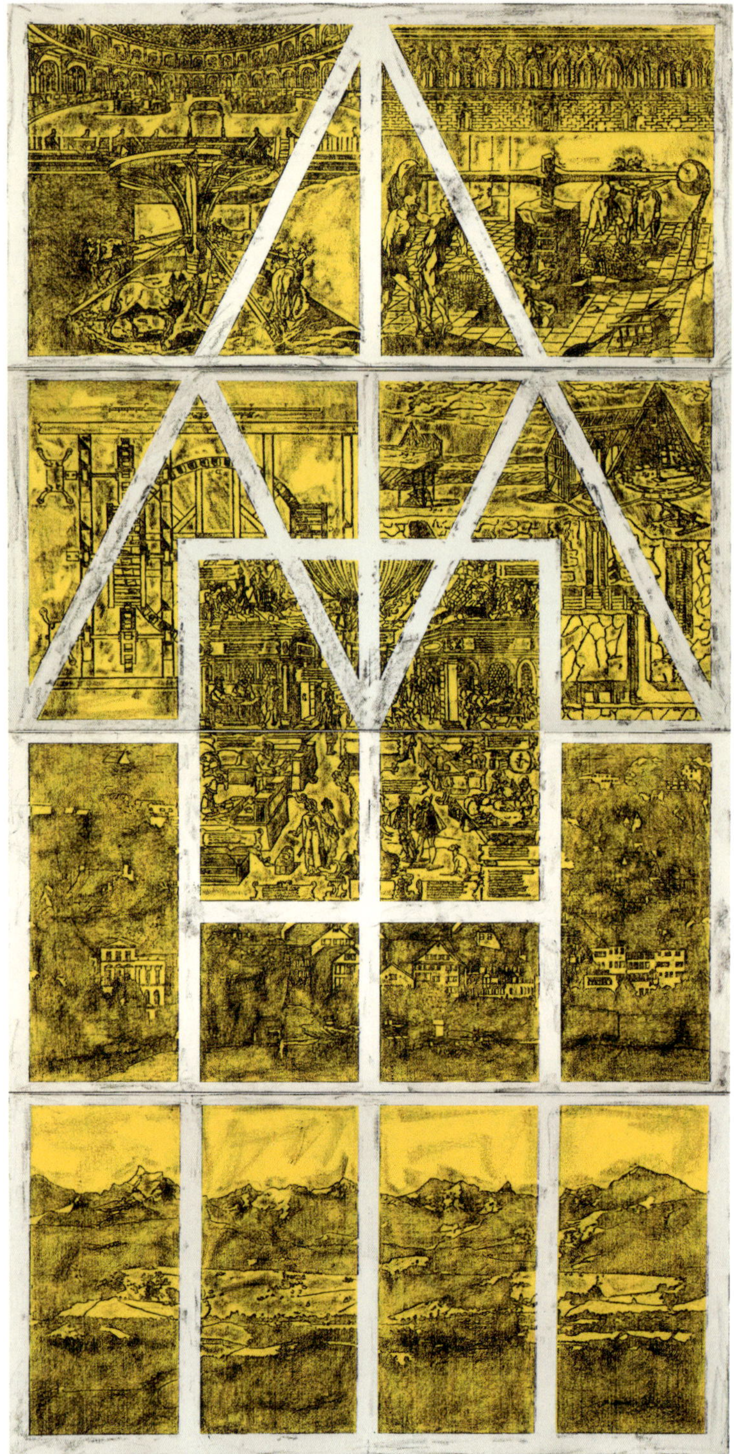

1996.5 Untitled (City Chart), 300 × 150 cm

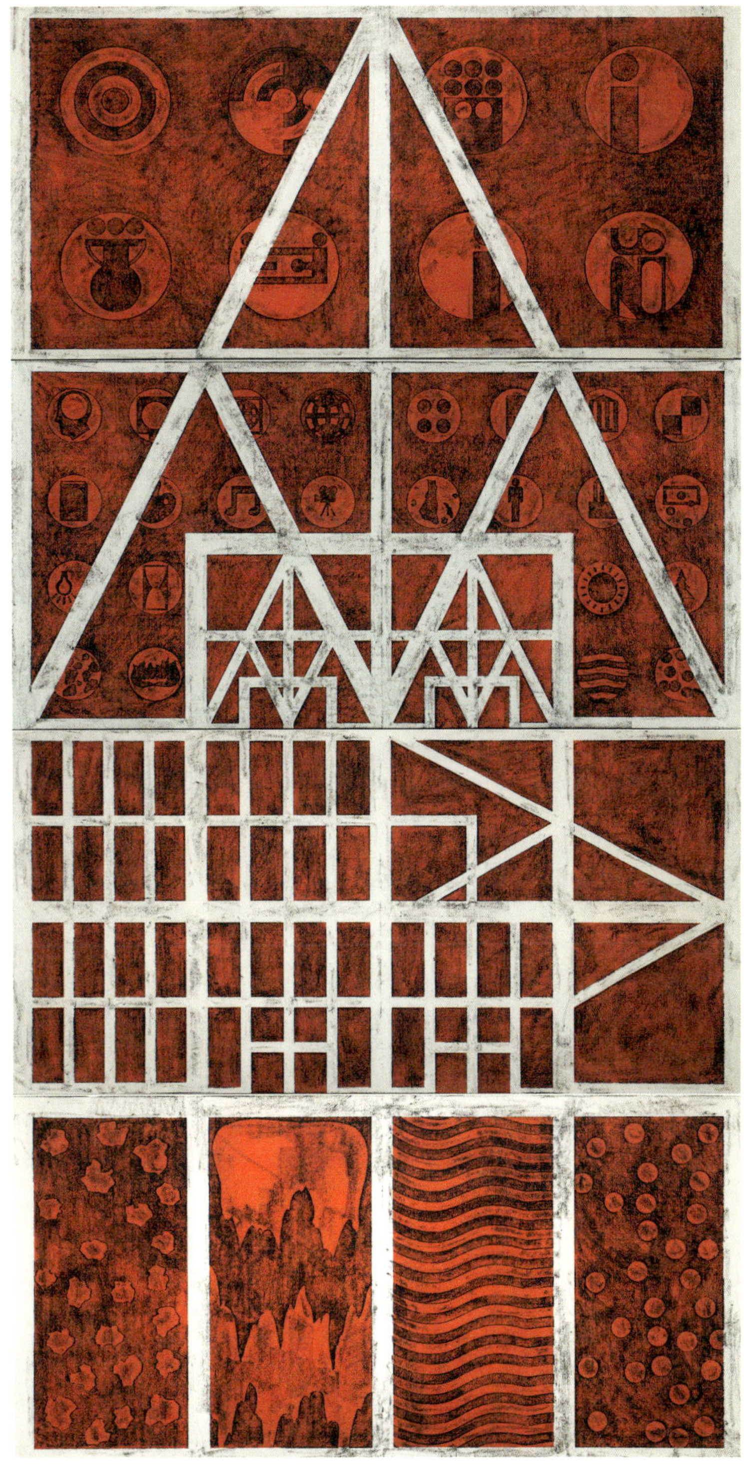

1996.6 Untitled (City Chart), 300 × 150 cm

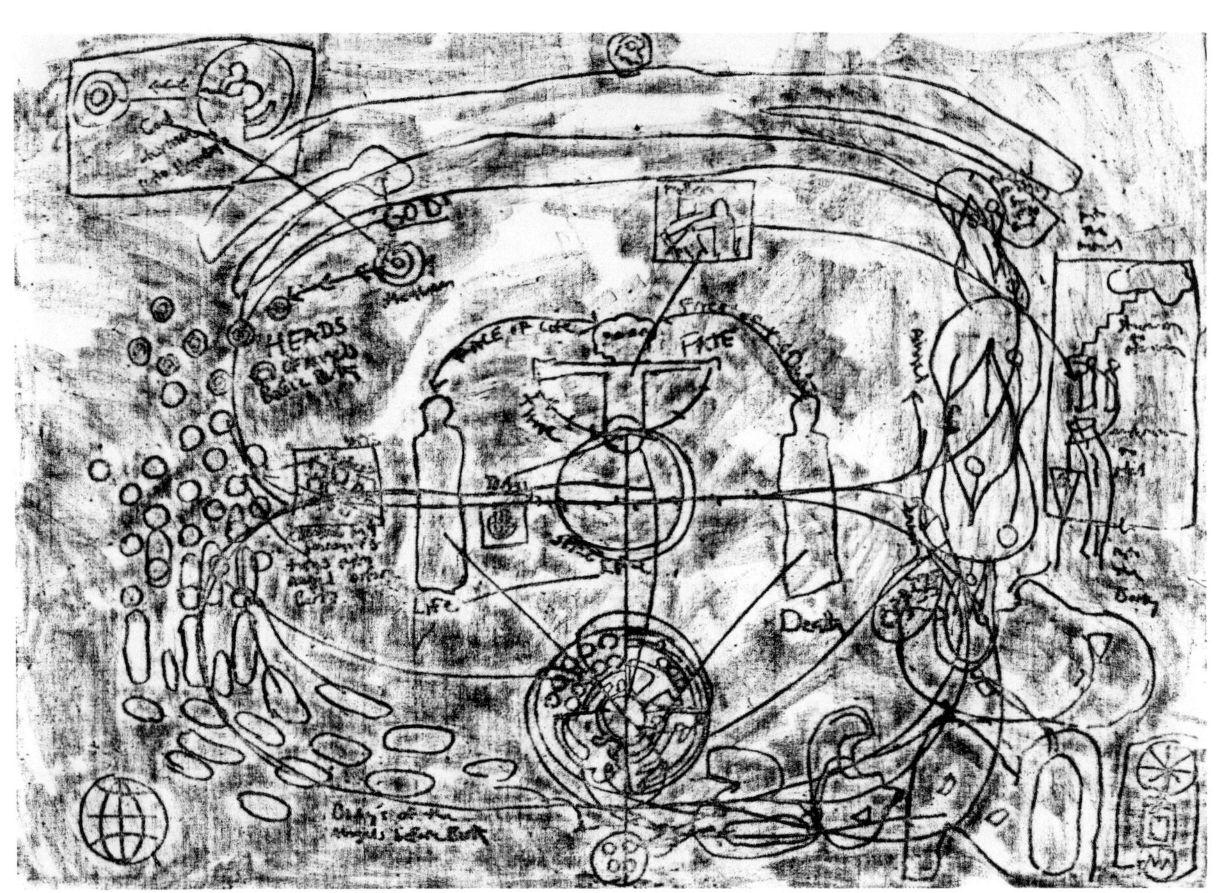

1996.7 Untitled (Cosmology), 142 × 213 cm

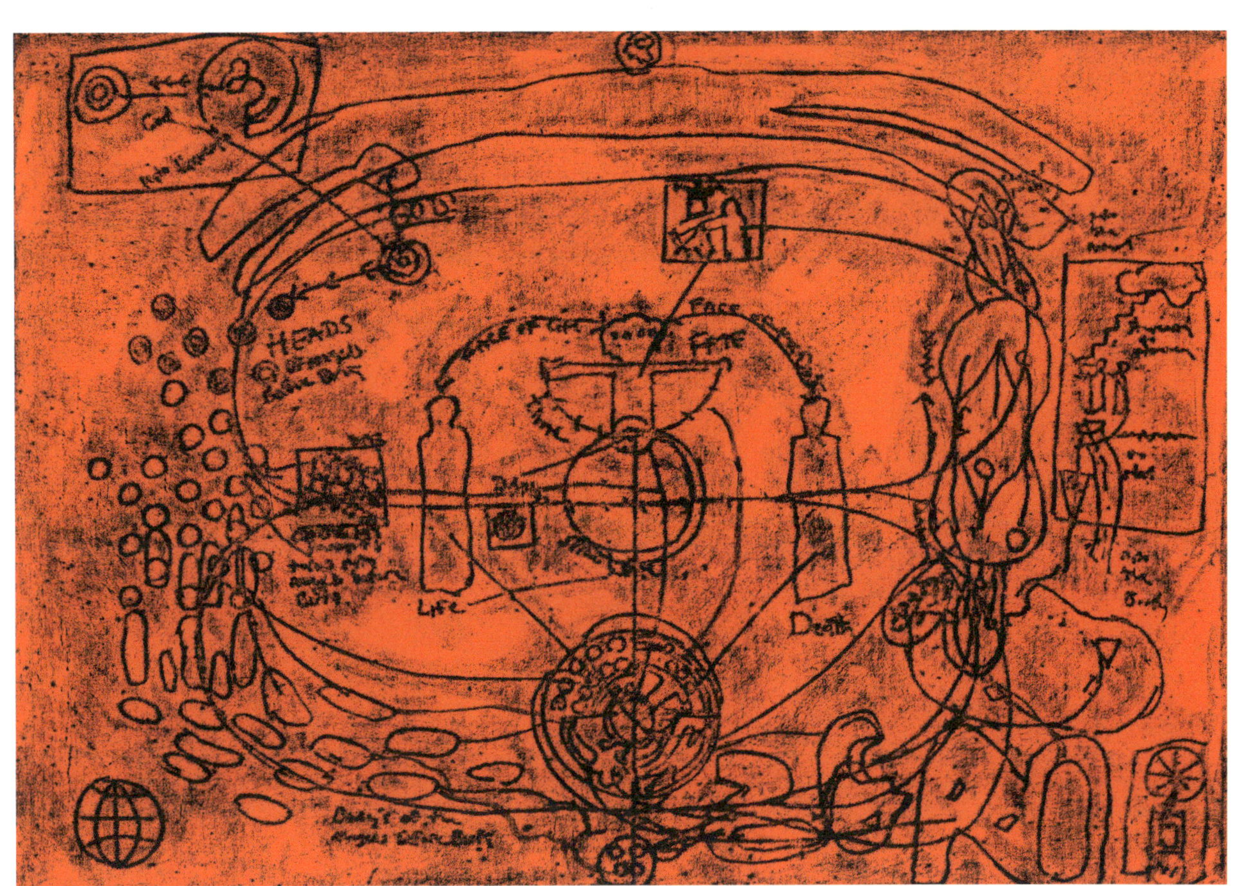

1996.8 Untitled (Cosmology), 142×213 cm

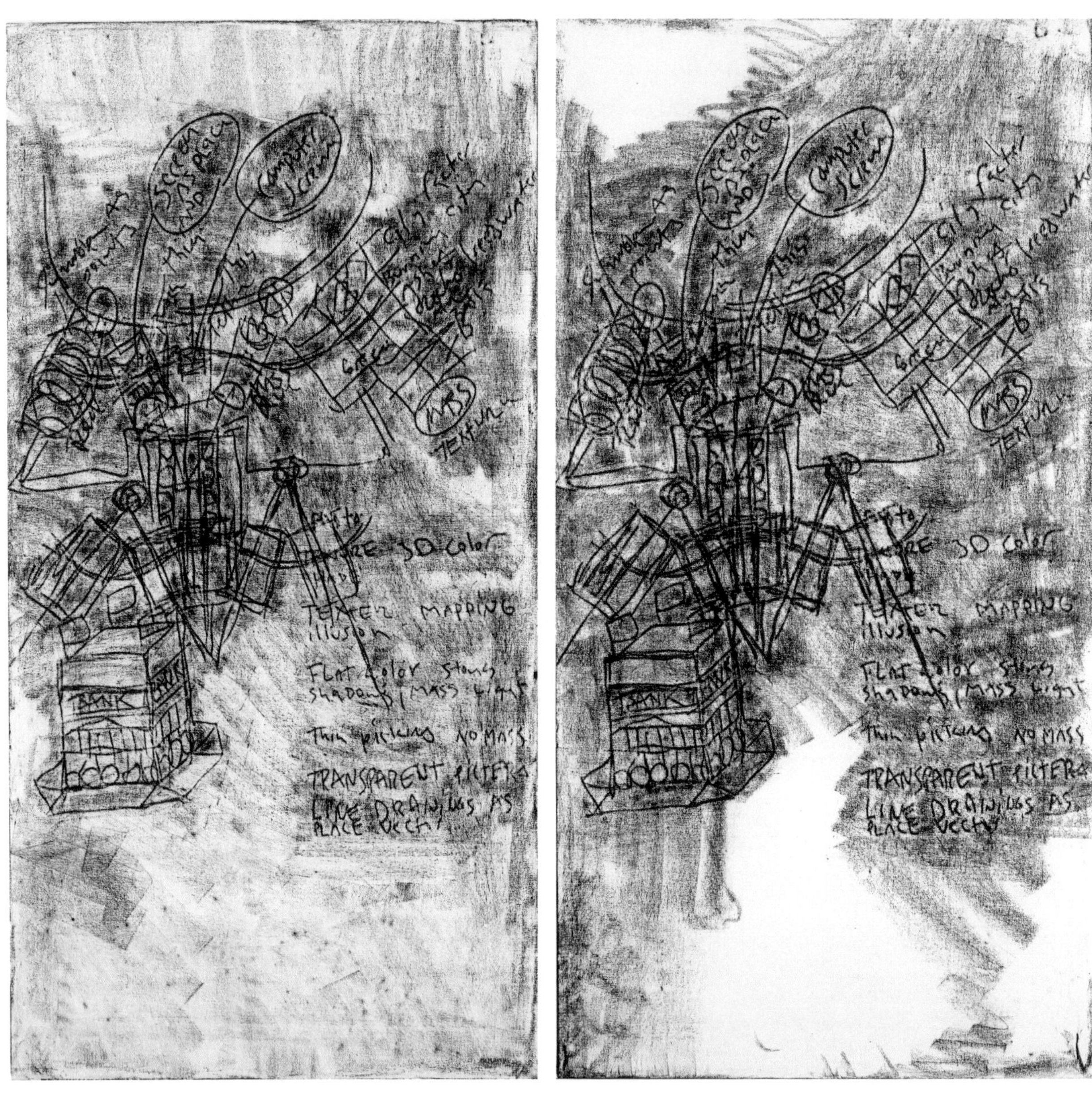

1996.9 Untitled (Notebook), 244 × 122 cm each (diptych)

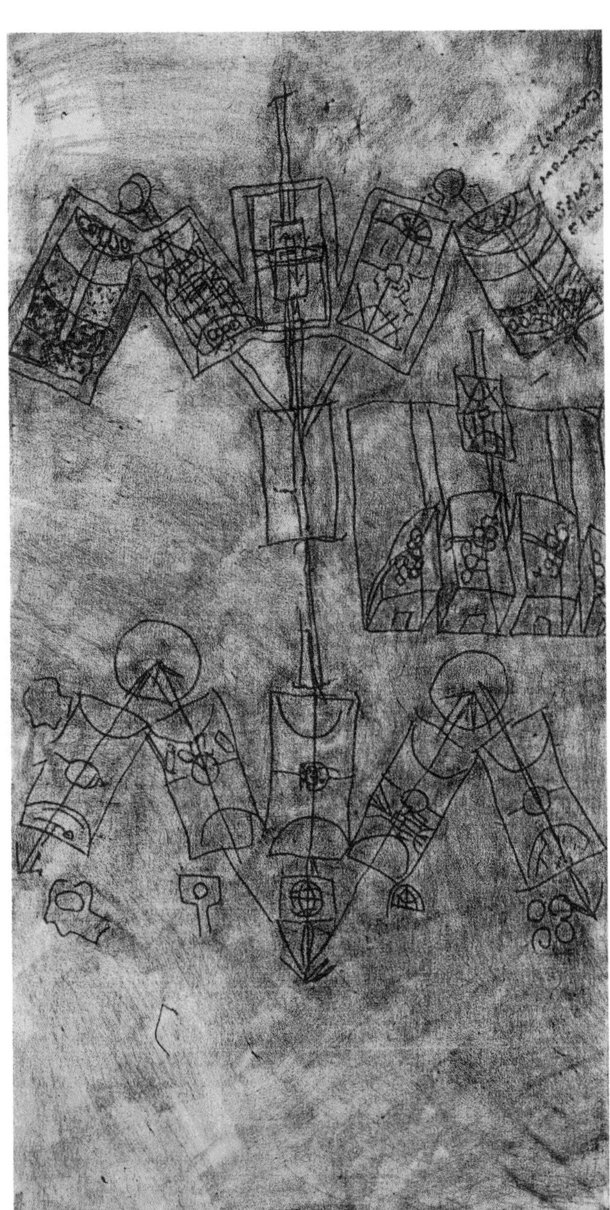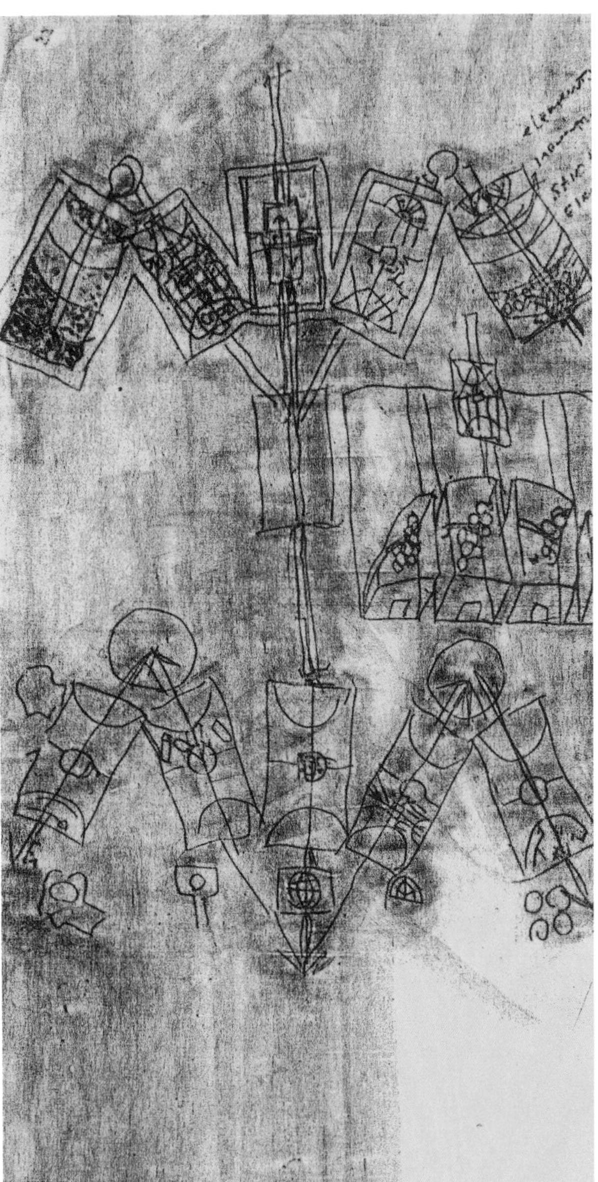

1996.10 Untitled (Notebook), 244 × 122 cm each (diptych)

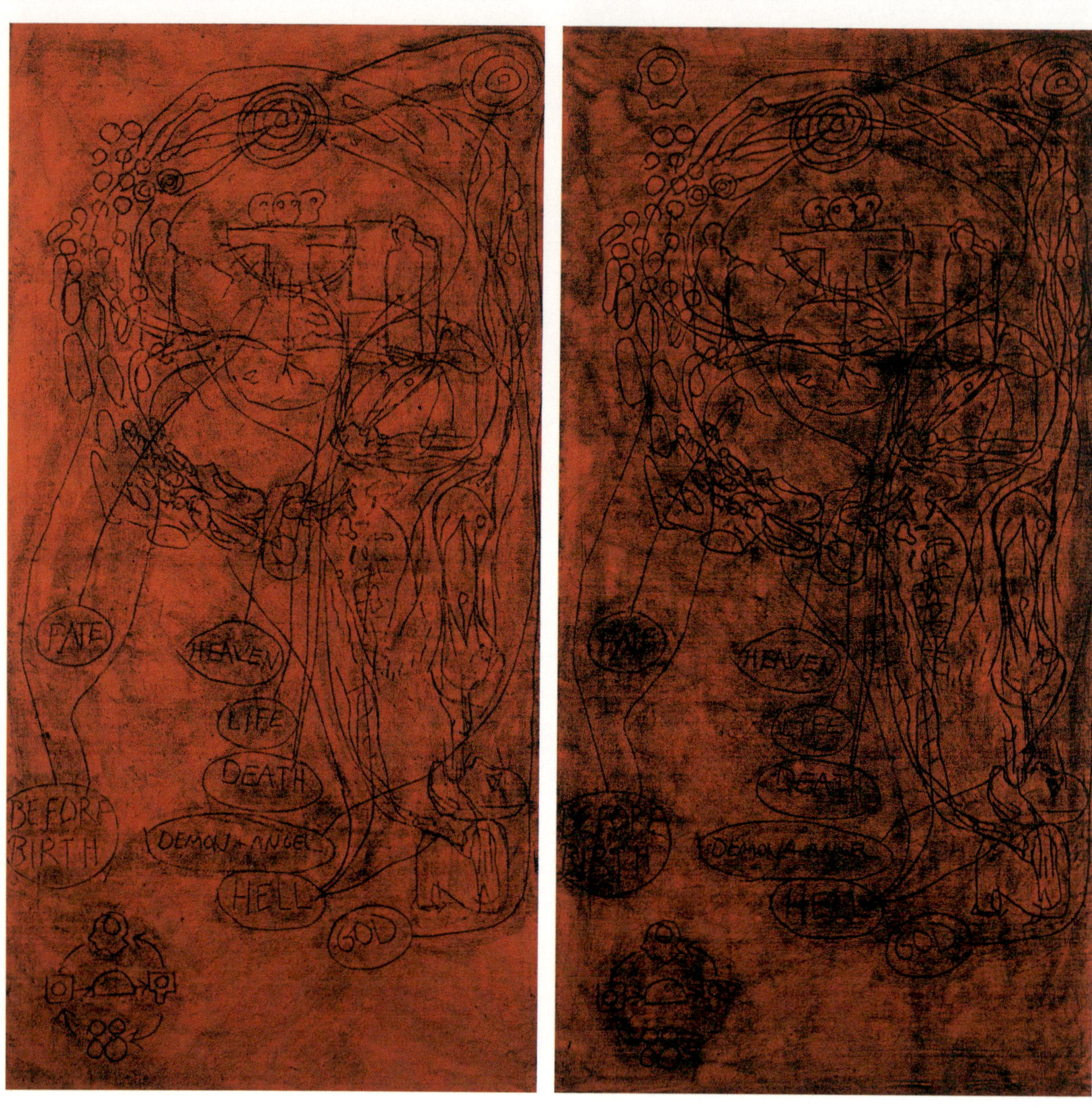

1996.11 Untitled (Notebook), 244 × 122 cm each (diptych)

1997

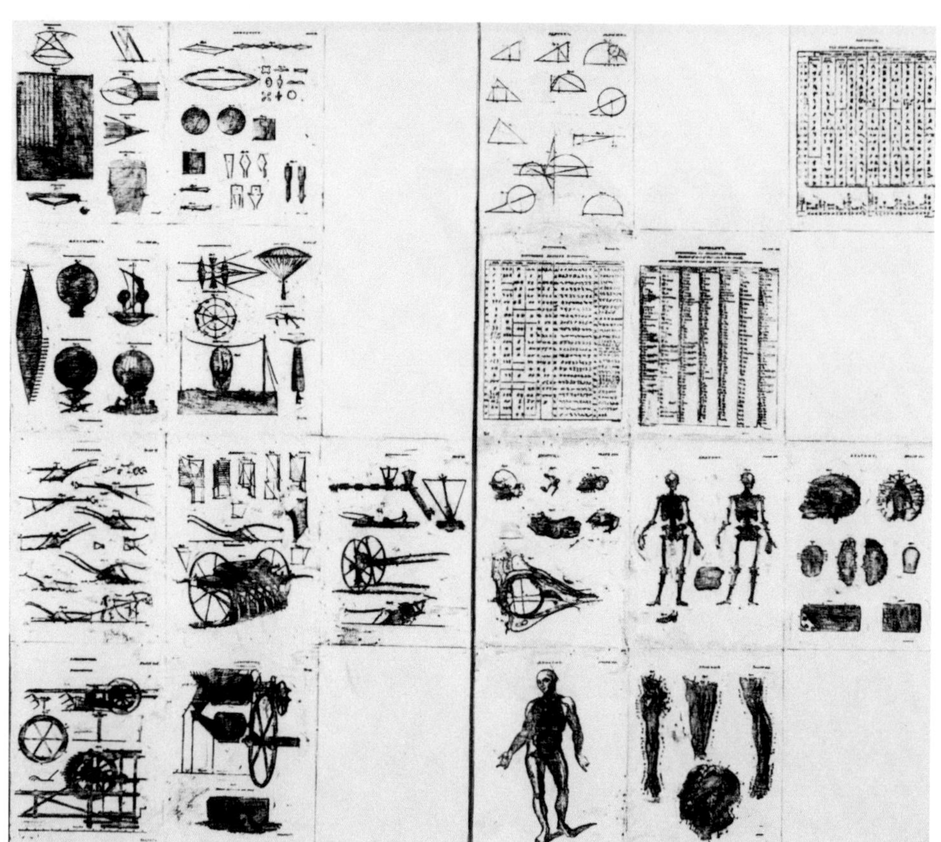

1997.1 Untitled (Vol. I B&W), 1991/1997, 228.5 × 254 cm (2 parts)

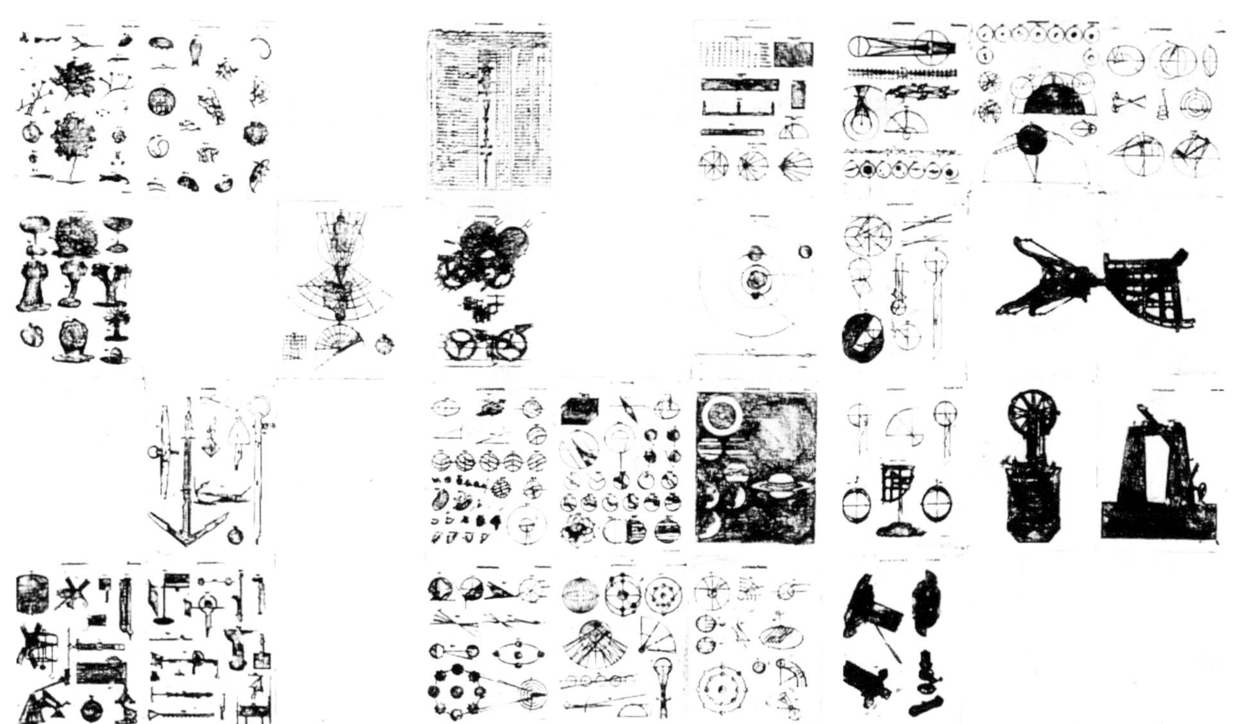

1997.2 Untitled (Vol. II B&W), 1991/1997, 228.5 × 381 cm (3 parts)

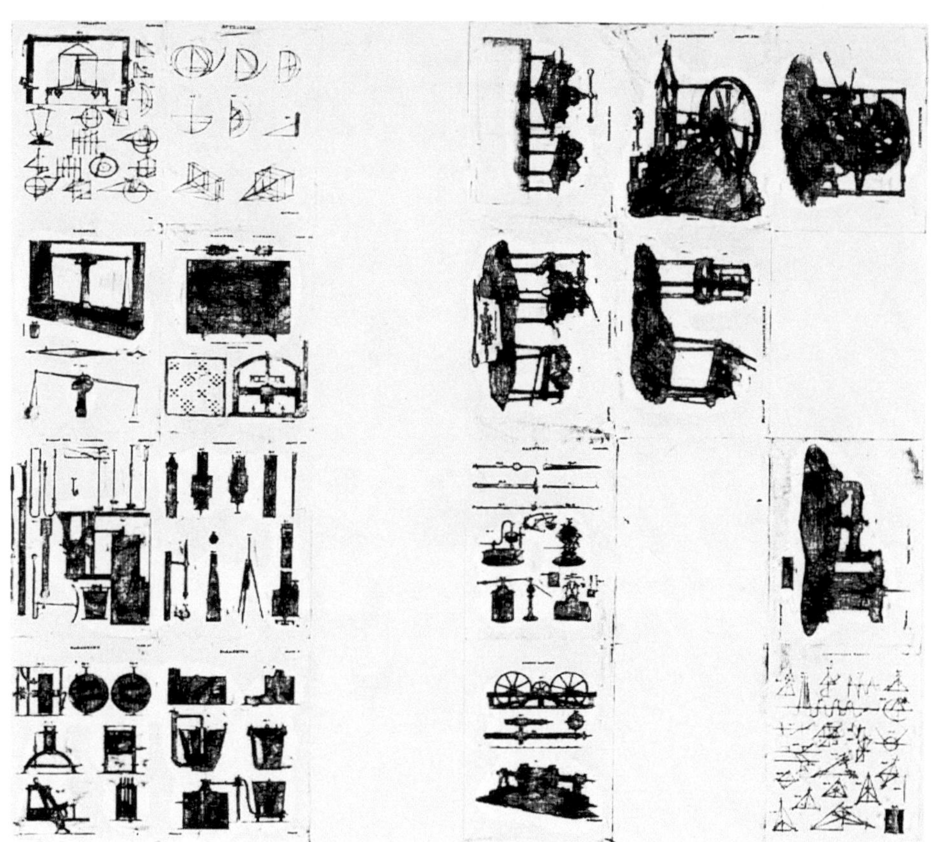

1997.3 Untitled (Vol. III B&W), 1991/1997, 228.5×254 cm (2 parts)

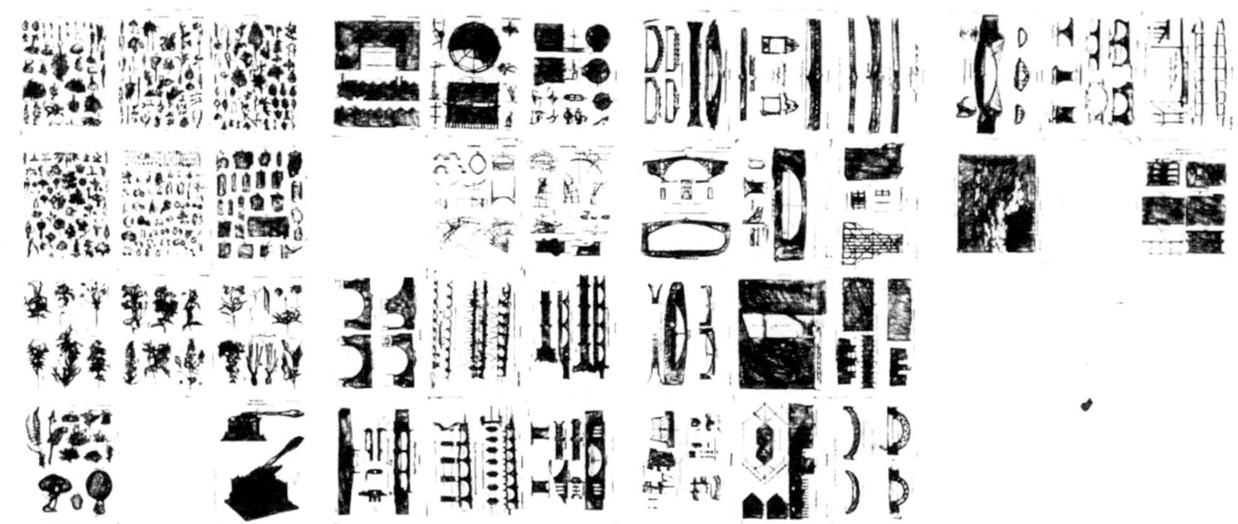

1997.4 Untitled (Vol. IV B&W), 1991 / 1997, 228.5 × 508 cm (4 parts)

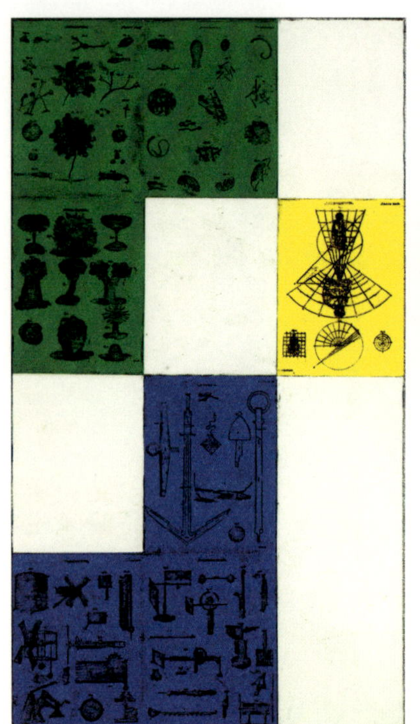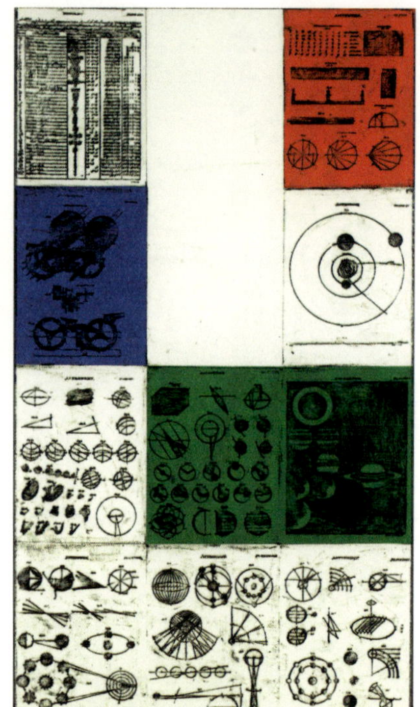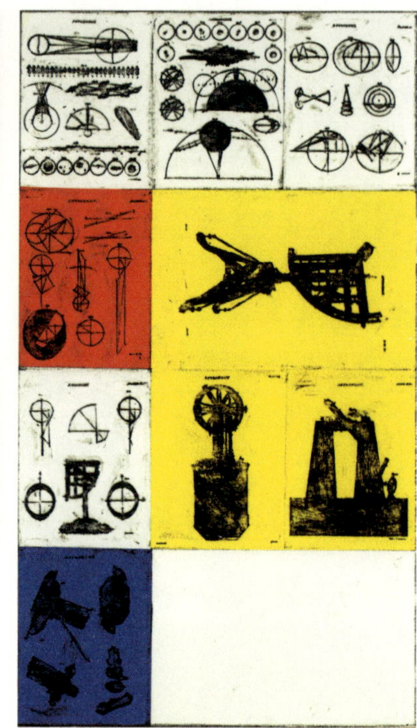

1997.5 Untitled (Vol. II), 1991/1997, 228.5 × 381 cm (3 parts)

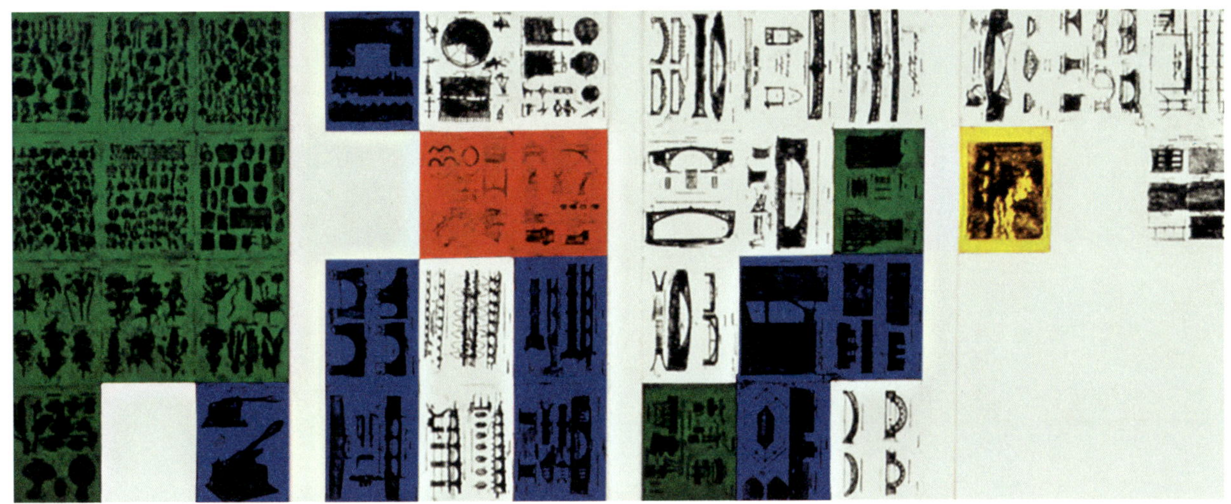

1997.6 Untitled (Vol. IV), 1991 / 1997, 228.5 × 508 cm (4 parts)

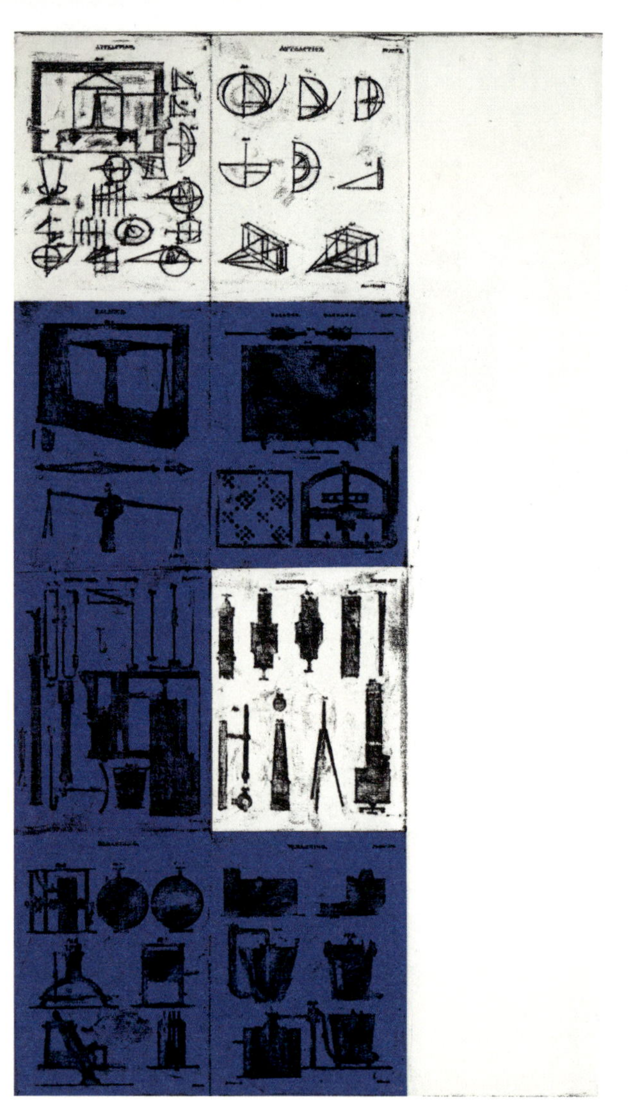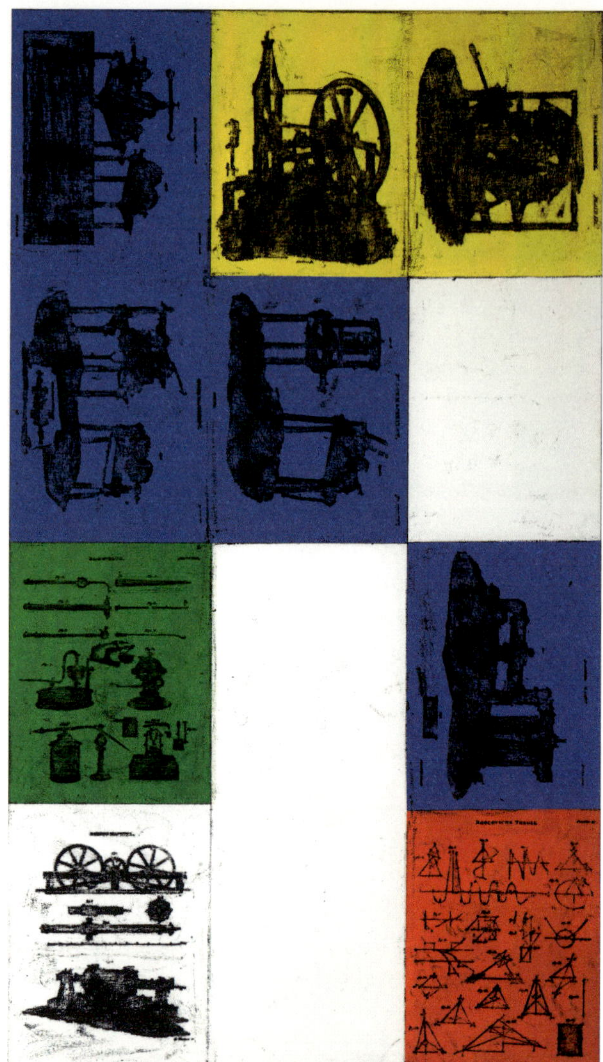

1997.7 Untitled (Vol. …), 228.5 × 254 cm (2 parts)

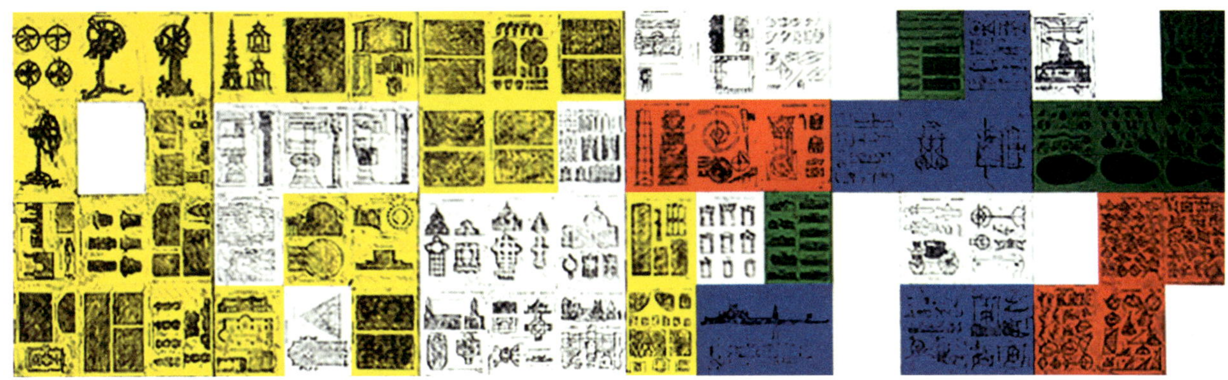

1997.8 Untitled (Vol. VI: Circle to Conic Sections), 1991/1997, 228.5 × 762 cm (6 parts)

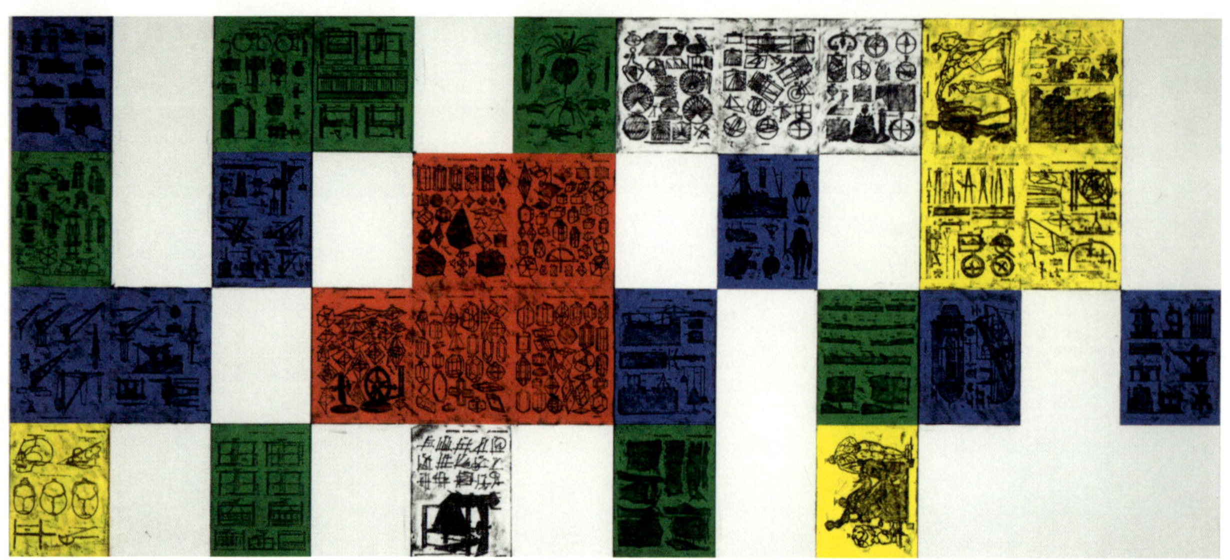

1997.9 Untitled (Vol. VII: Cotton to Drug Mills), 1991/1997, 228.5 × 508 cm (4 parts)

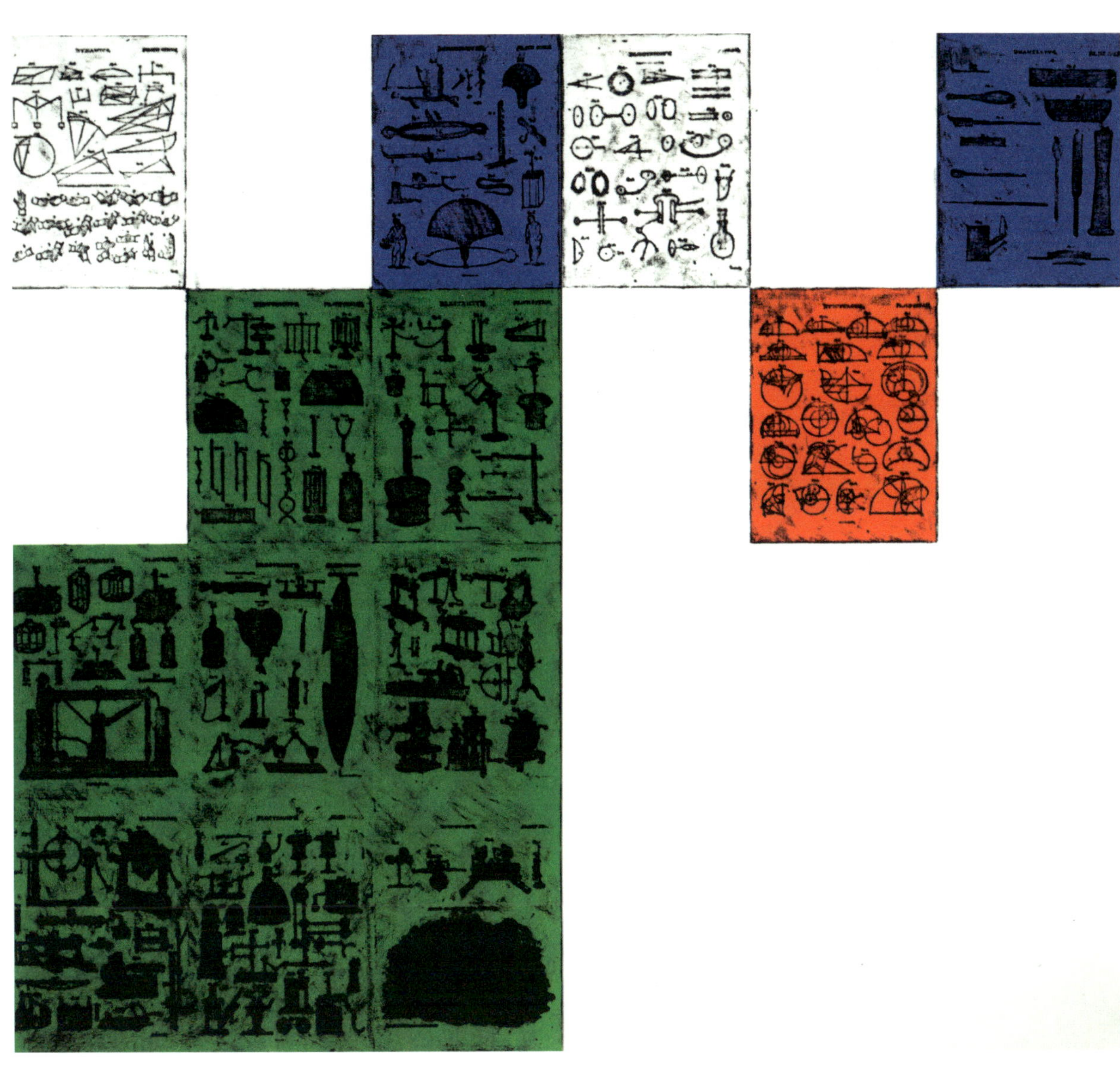

1997.10 Untitled (Vol. VIII: Dynamics to Epicycloid), 1991/1997, 228.5 × 254 cm (2 parts)

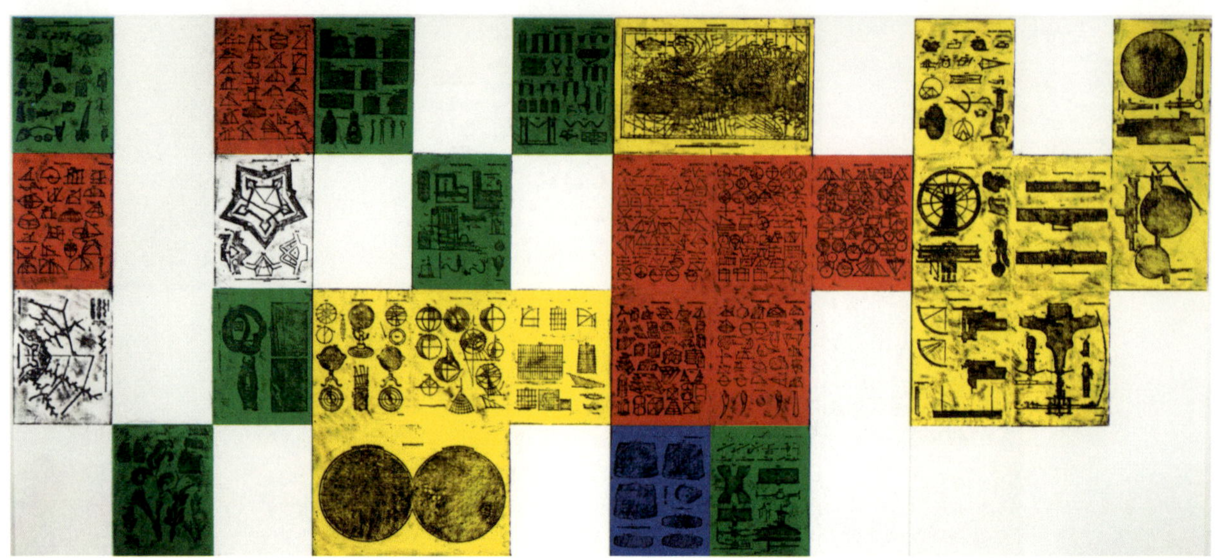

1997.11 Untitled (Vol. IX: …), 1991/1997, 228.5 × 508 cm (4 parts)

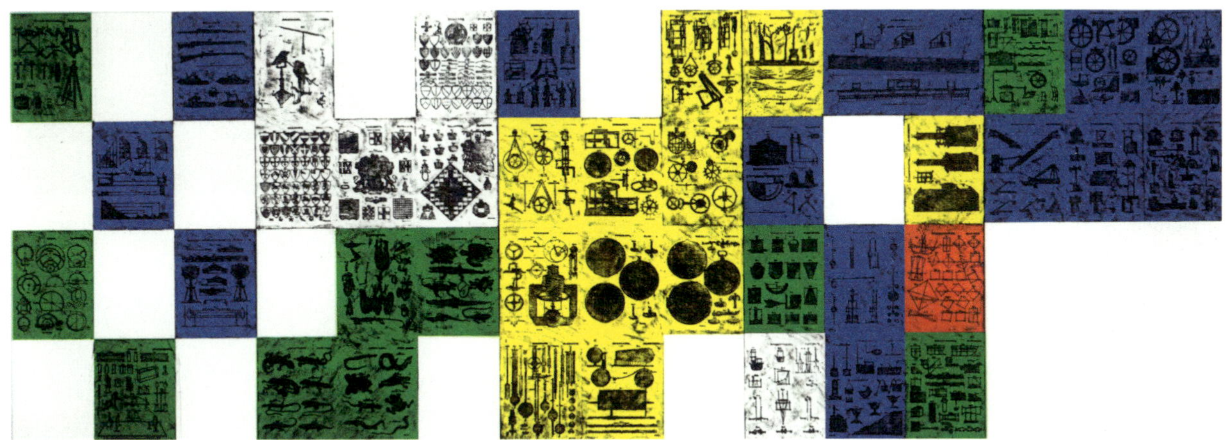

1997.12 Untitled (Vol. X: Groins, Gunflints to Hydrodynamics), 1991/1997, 228.5 × 635 cm (5 parts)

1997.13 Untitled (Vol. XI: Hygrometry to Landscape Gardening), 1991/1997, 228.5 × 381 cm (3 parts)

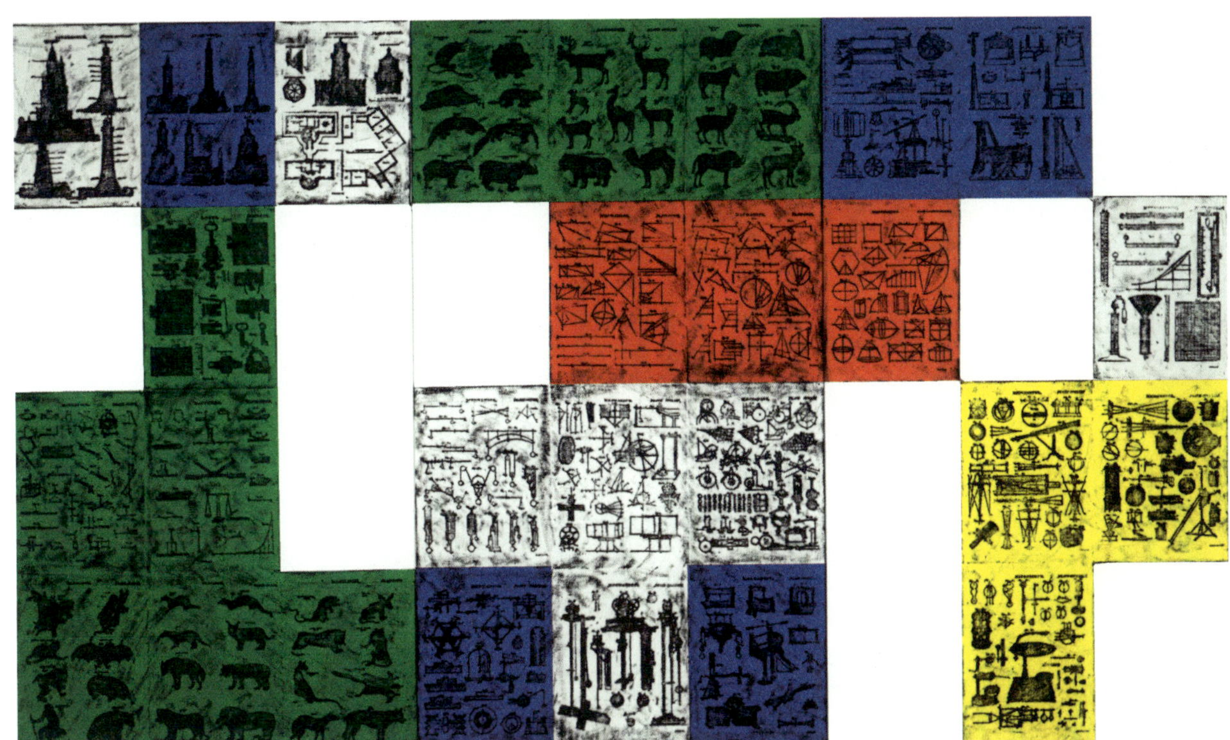

1997.14 Untitled (Vol. XII: …), 1991 / 1997, 228.5 × 508 cm (4 parts)

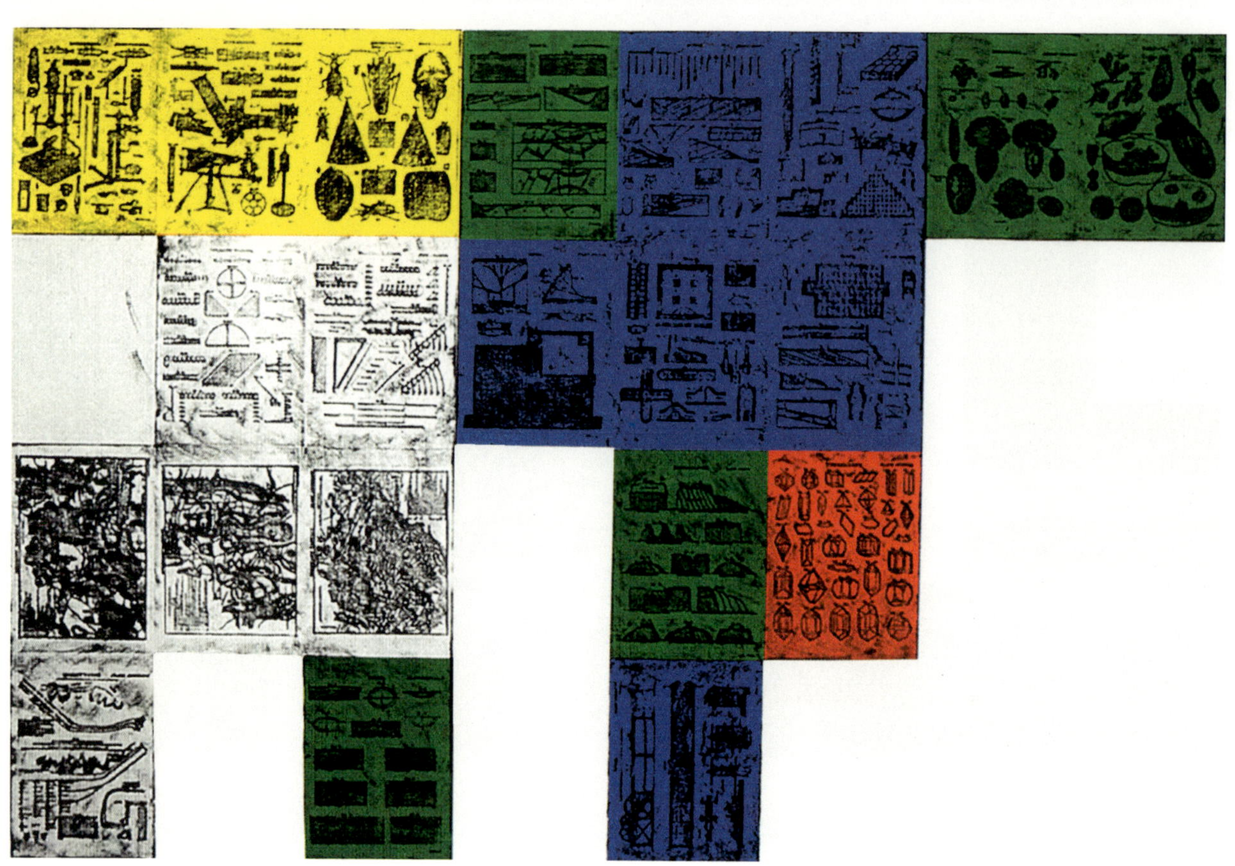

1997.15 Untitled (Vol. XIII: Microscope to Mollusca), 1991/1997, 228.5 × 381 cm (3 parts)

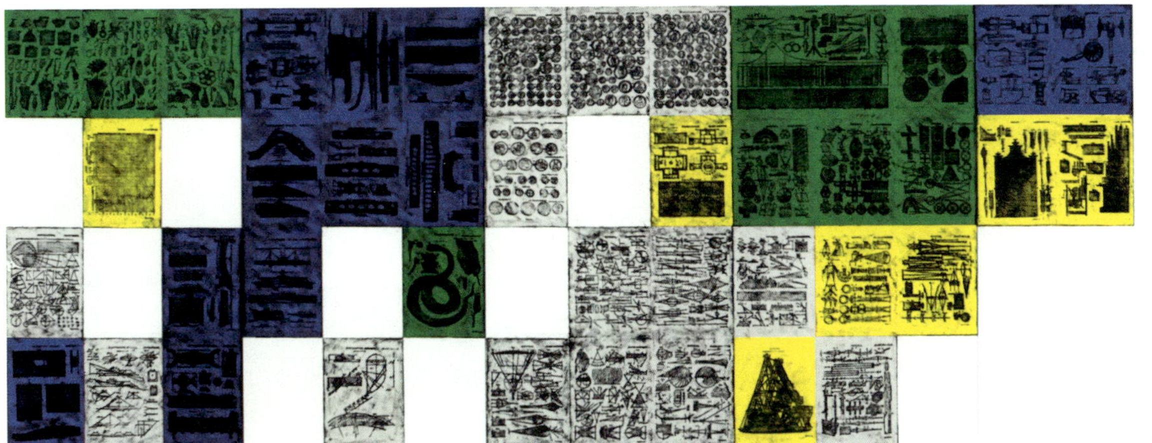

1997.16 Untitled (Vol. XIV: Music to Organ), 1991/1997, 228.5×635 cm (5 parts)

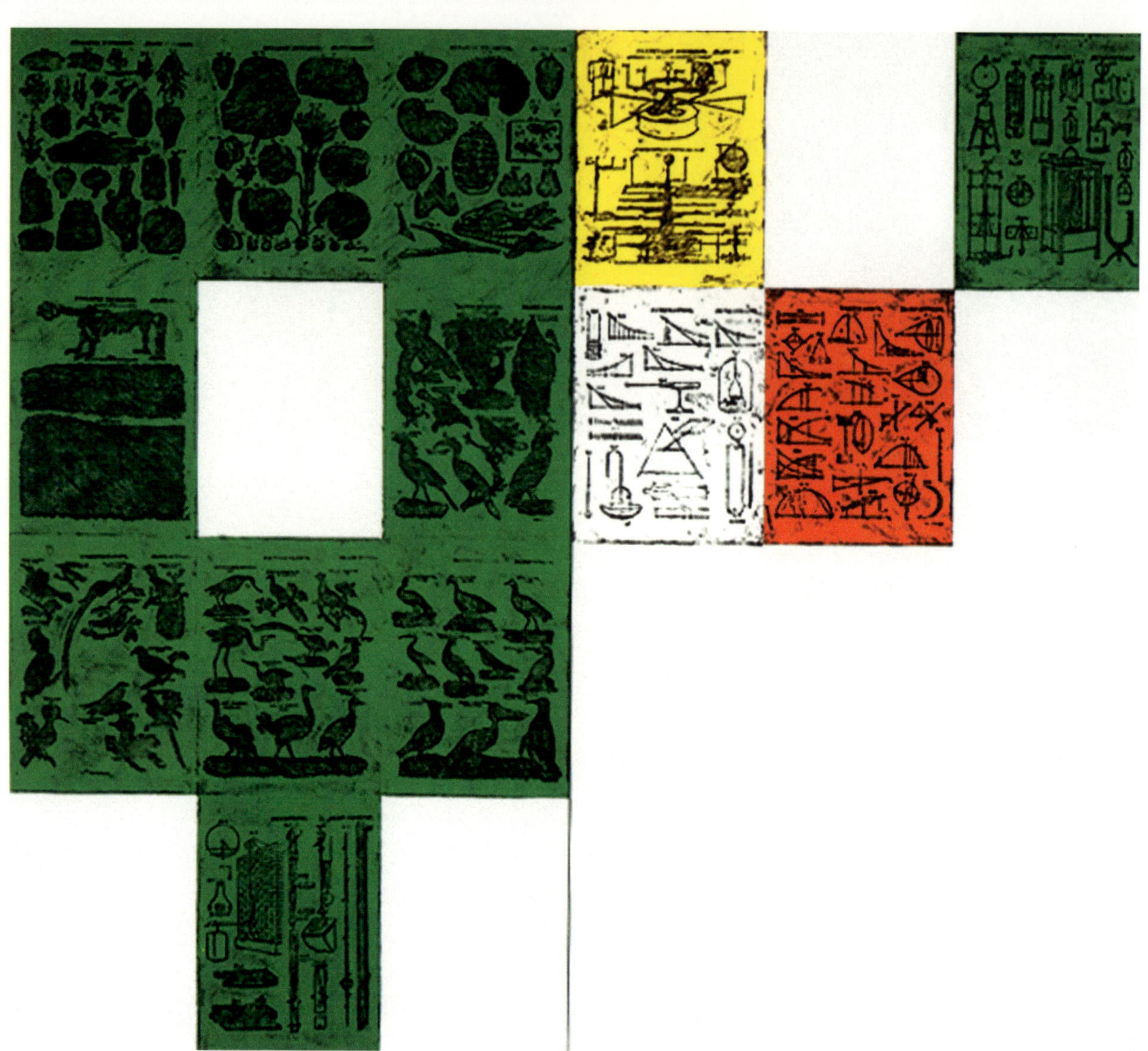

1997.17 Untitled (Vol. XV: Organic Remains to Pneumatic), 1991/1997, 228.5 × 254 cm (2 parts)

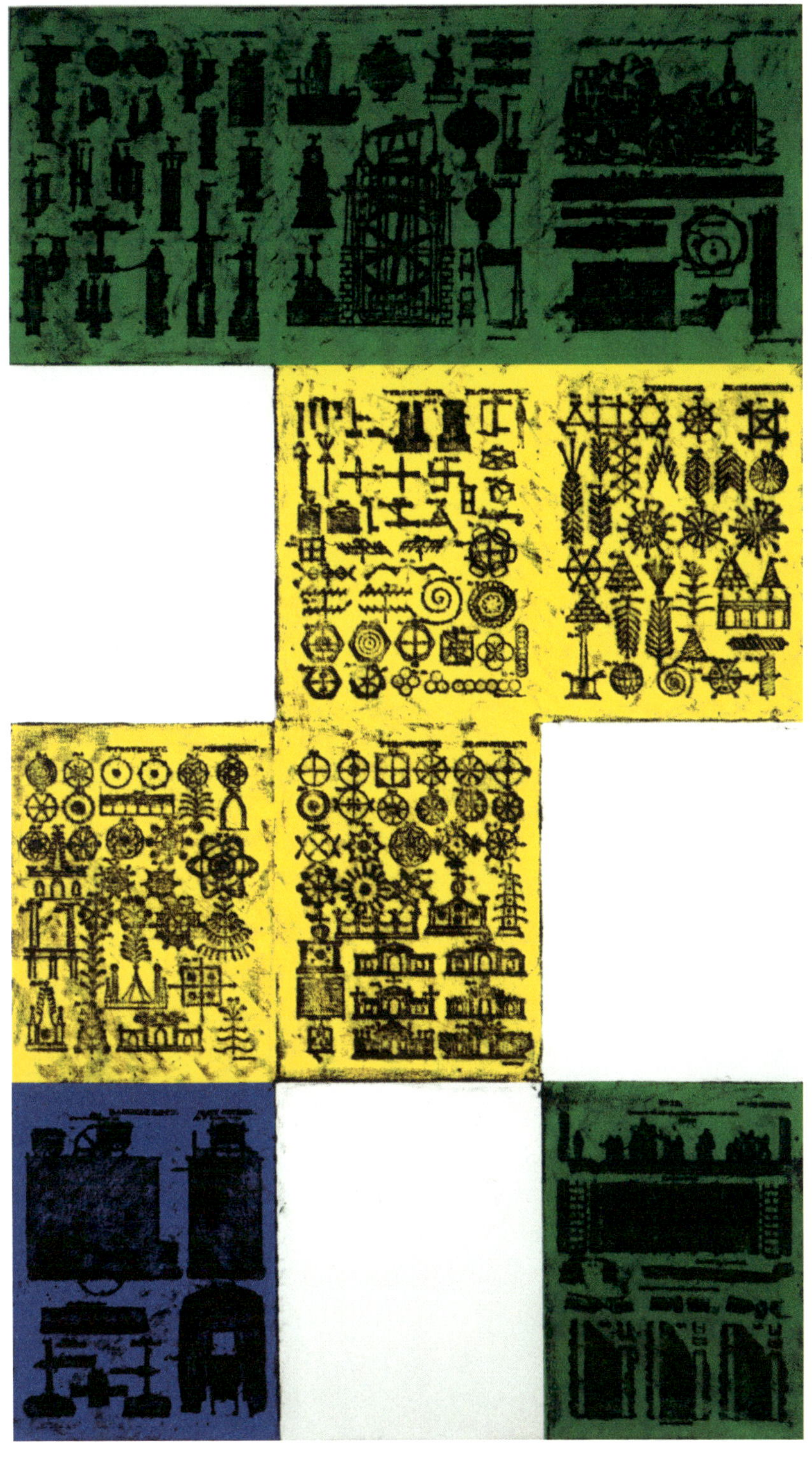

1997.18 Untitled (Vol. XVI: Pump to Road), 1991/1997, 228.5 × 127 cm

2001

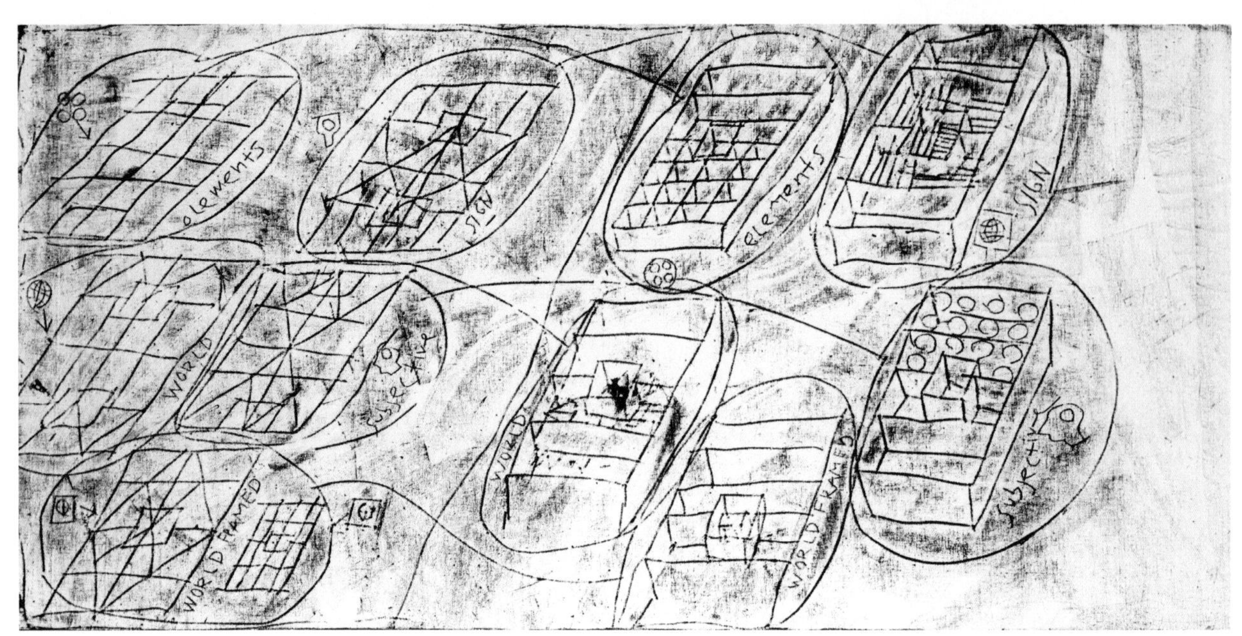

2001.1 Untitled (Notebook), 120.5 × 241 cm

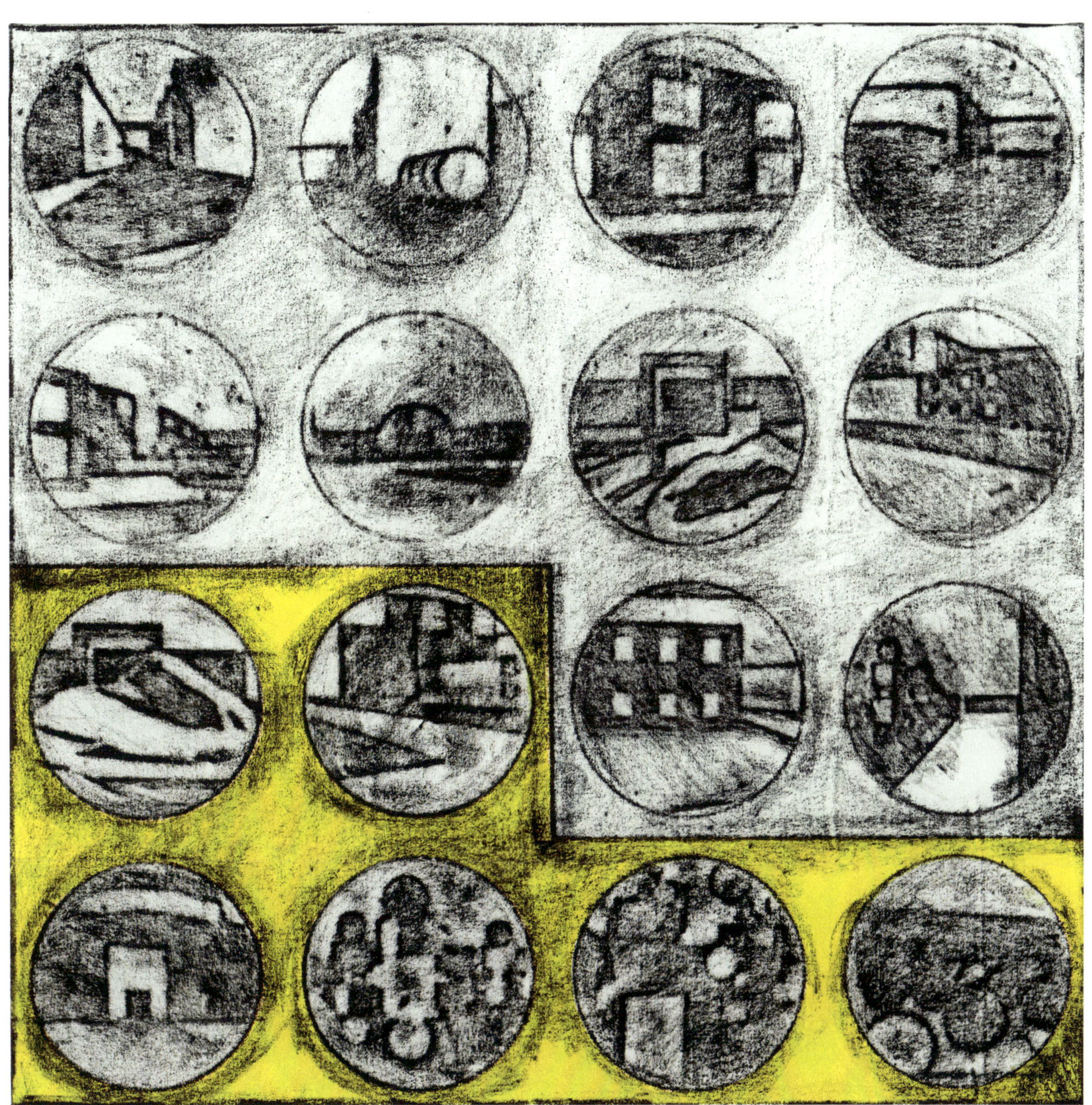

2001.2 Untitled (Details from Computer City), 120.5 × 120.5 cm

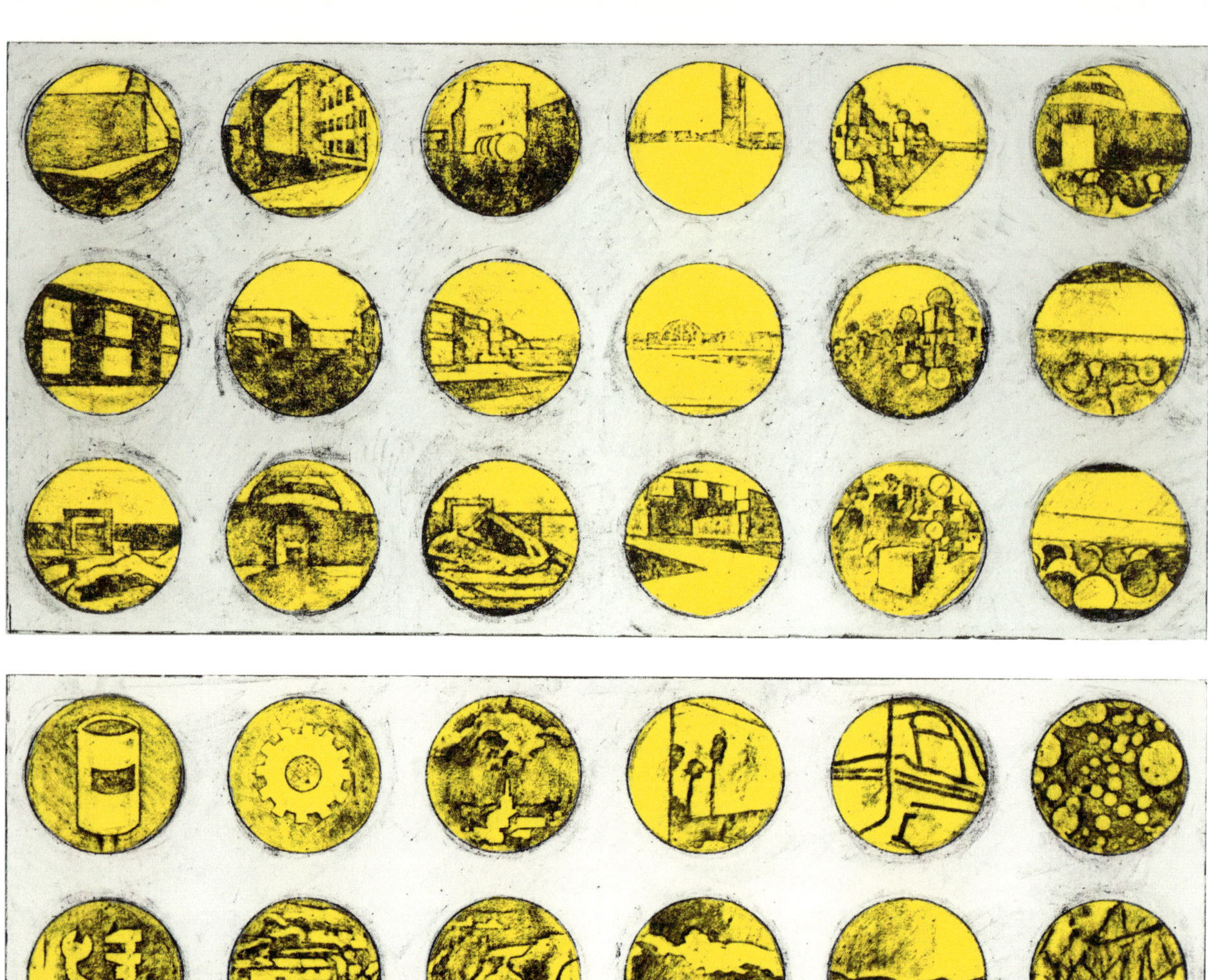

2001.3 Untitled (Details from Computer City), 120.5 × 241 cm
2001.4 Untitled (Details from Computer City), 120.5 × 241 cm

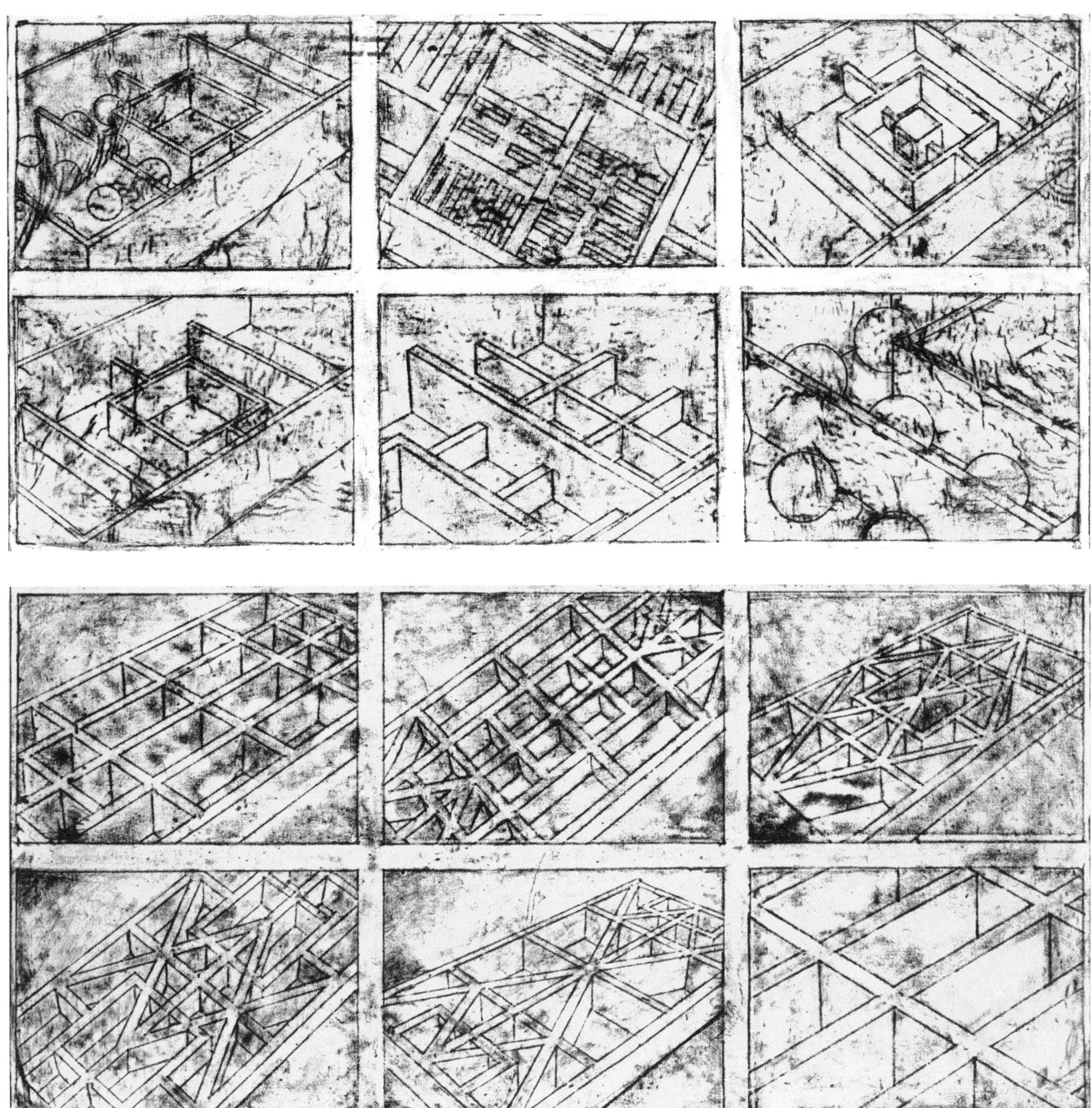

2001.5 Untitled (Details from Computer City), 120.5 × 241 cm
2001.6 Untitled (Details from Computer City), 120.5 × 241 cm

2003

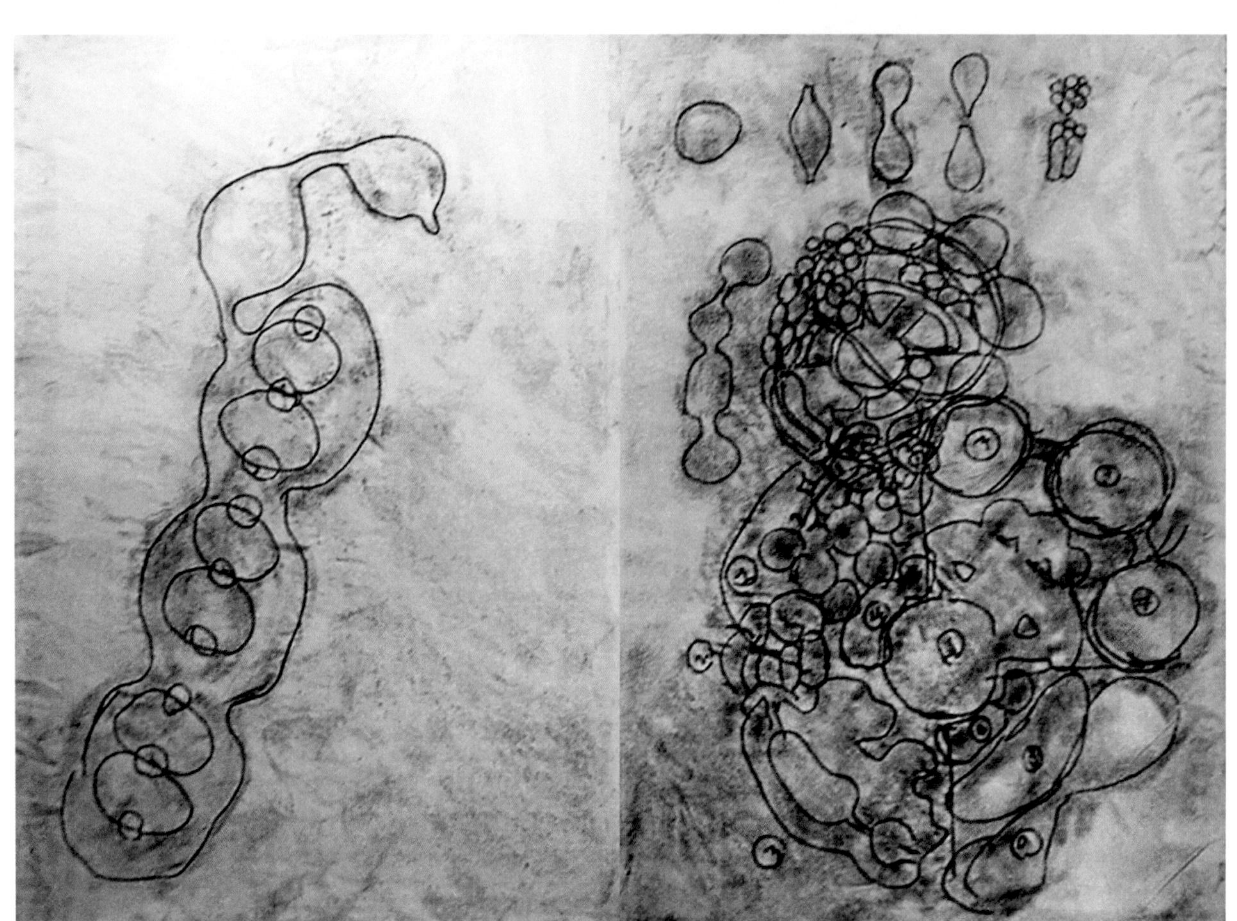

2003.1 Untitled (Notebook), 183 × 244 cm (2 parts)

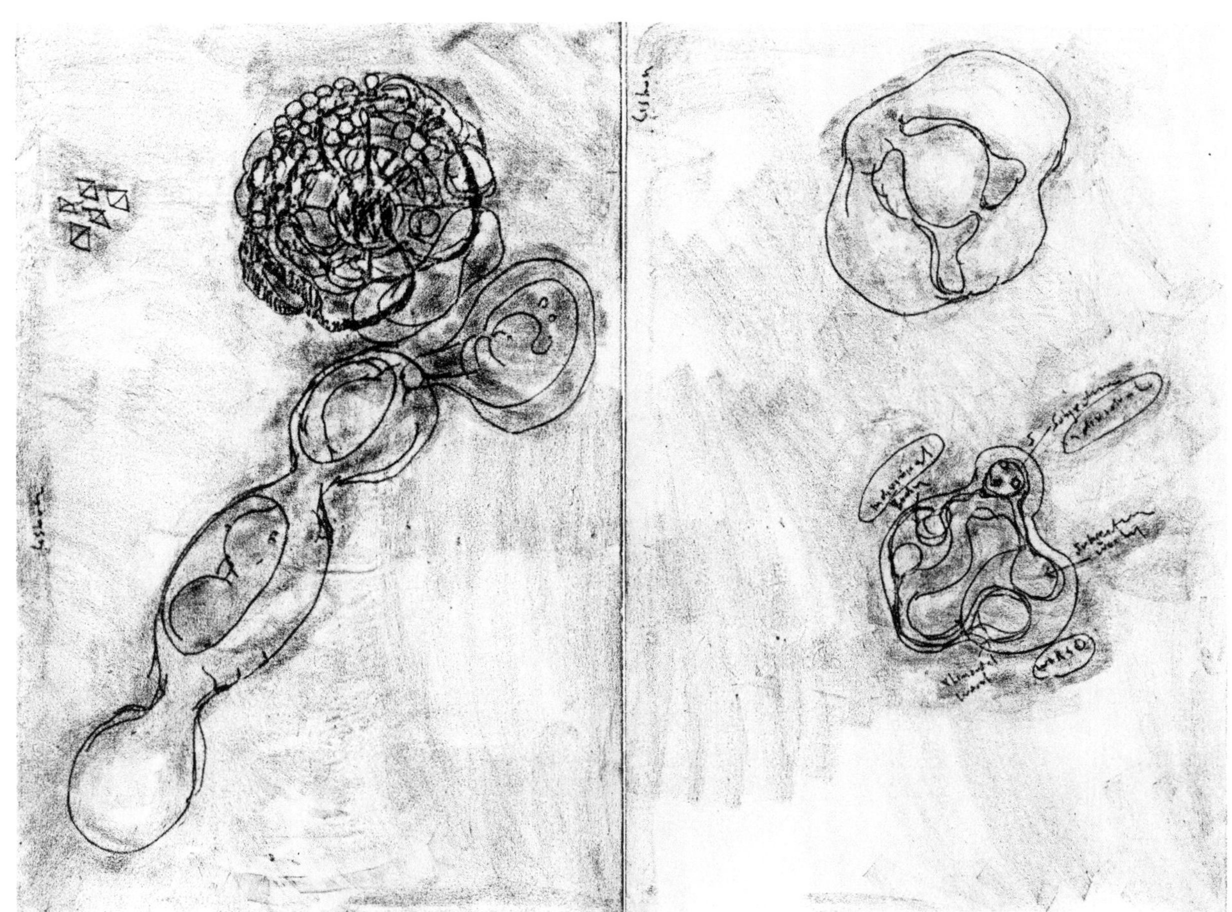

2003.2 Untitled (Notebook), 183×244 cm (2 parts)

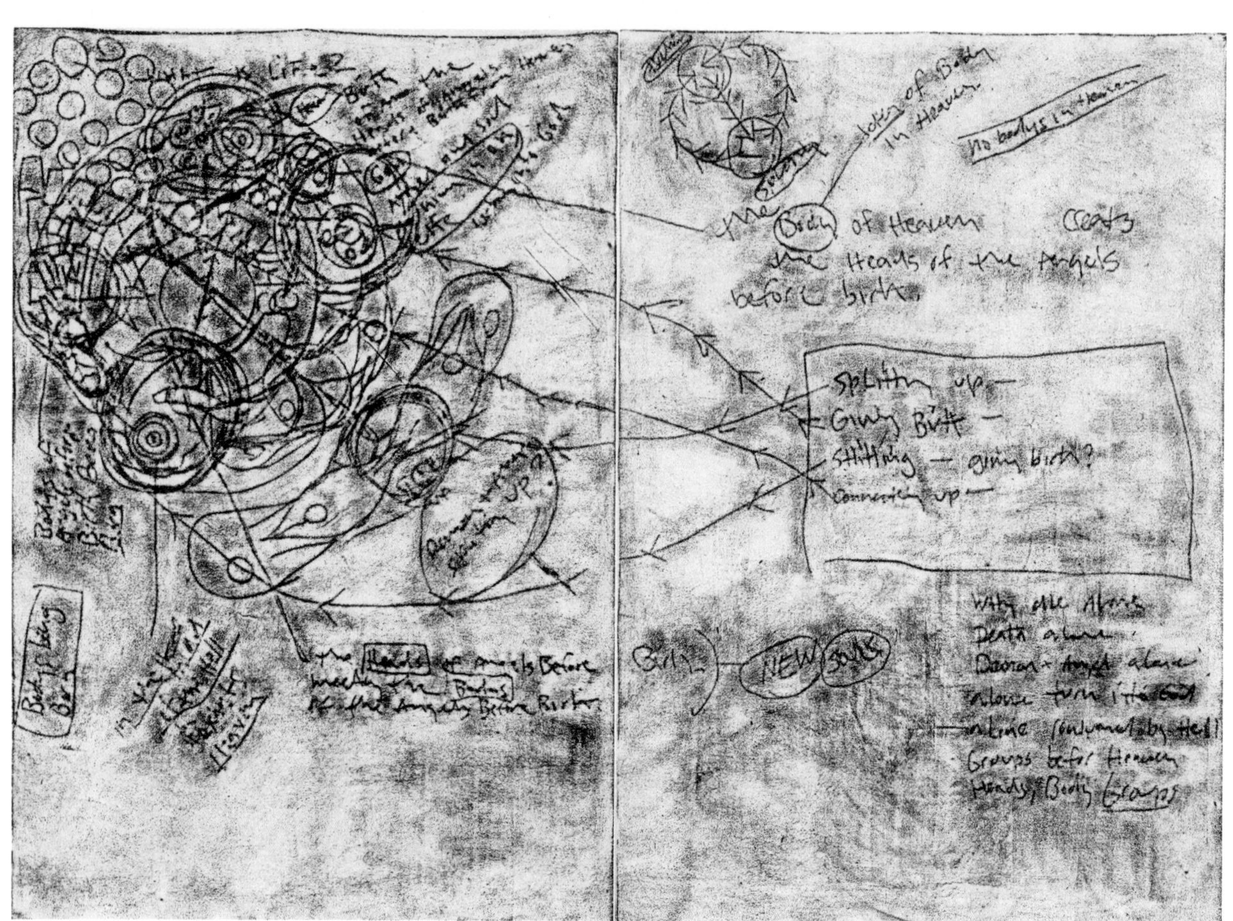

2003.3 Untitled (Notebook), 183 × 244 cm (2 parts)

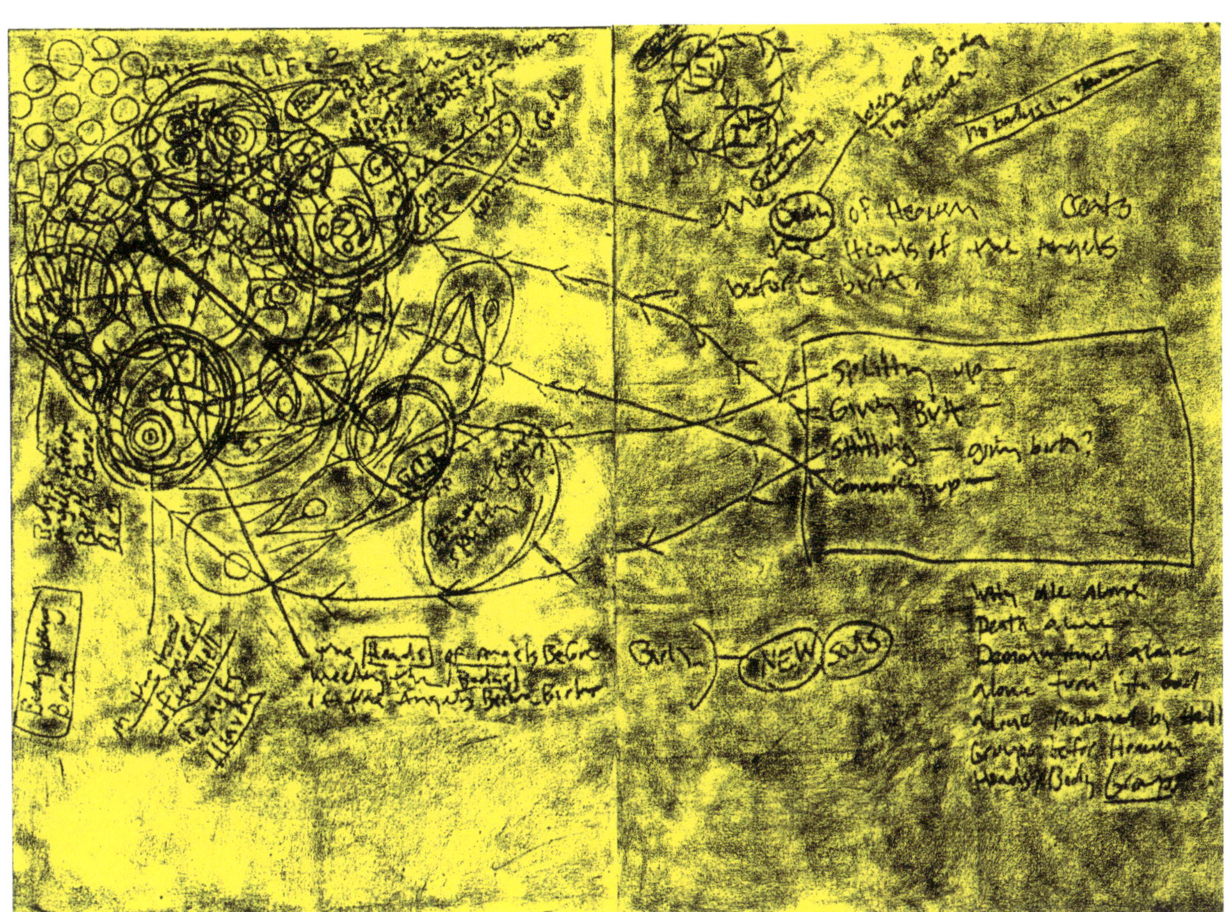

2003.4 Untitled (Notebook), 183 × 244 cm (2 parts)

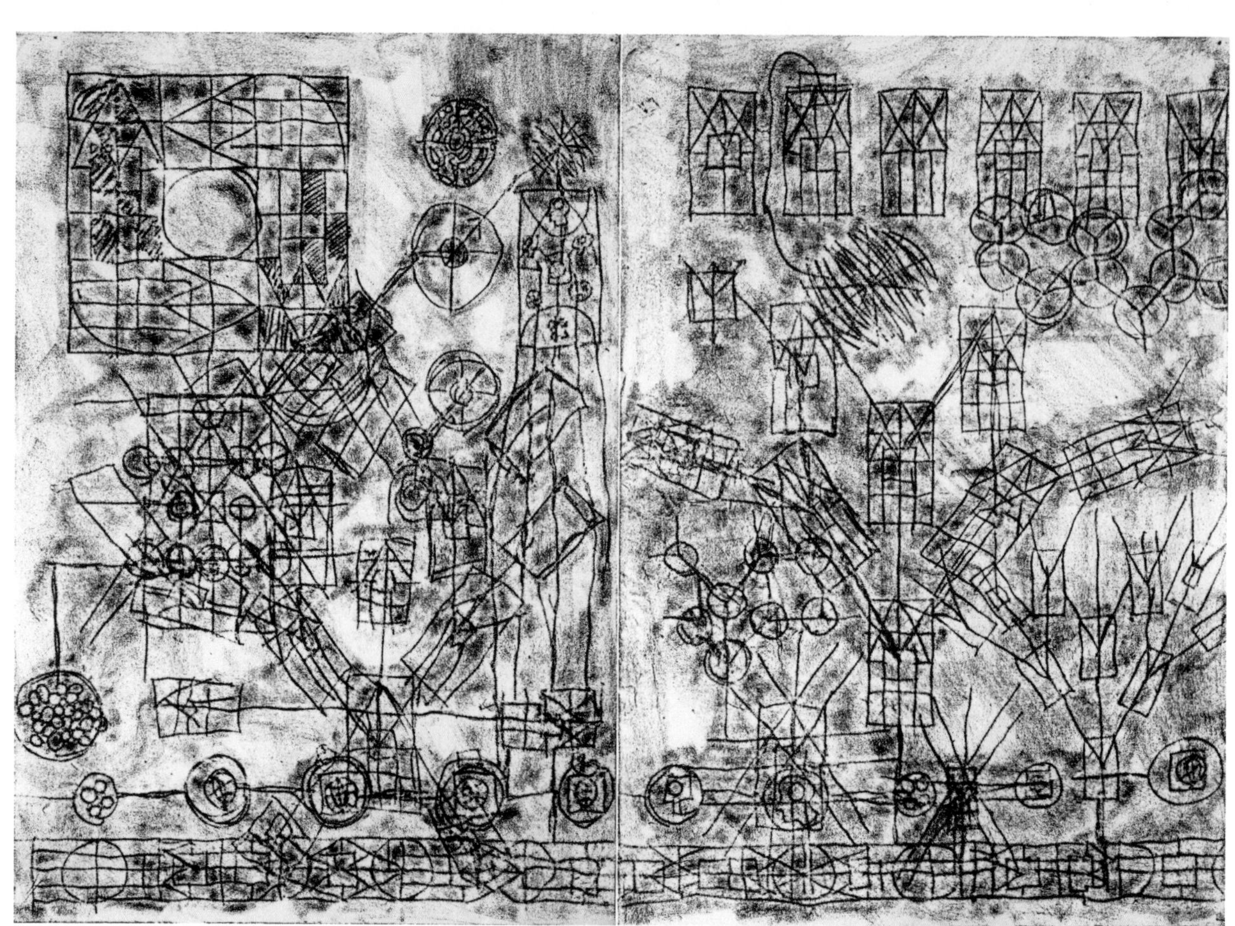

2003.5 Untitled (Notebook), 183 × 244 cm (2 parts)

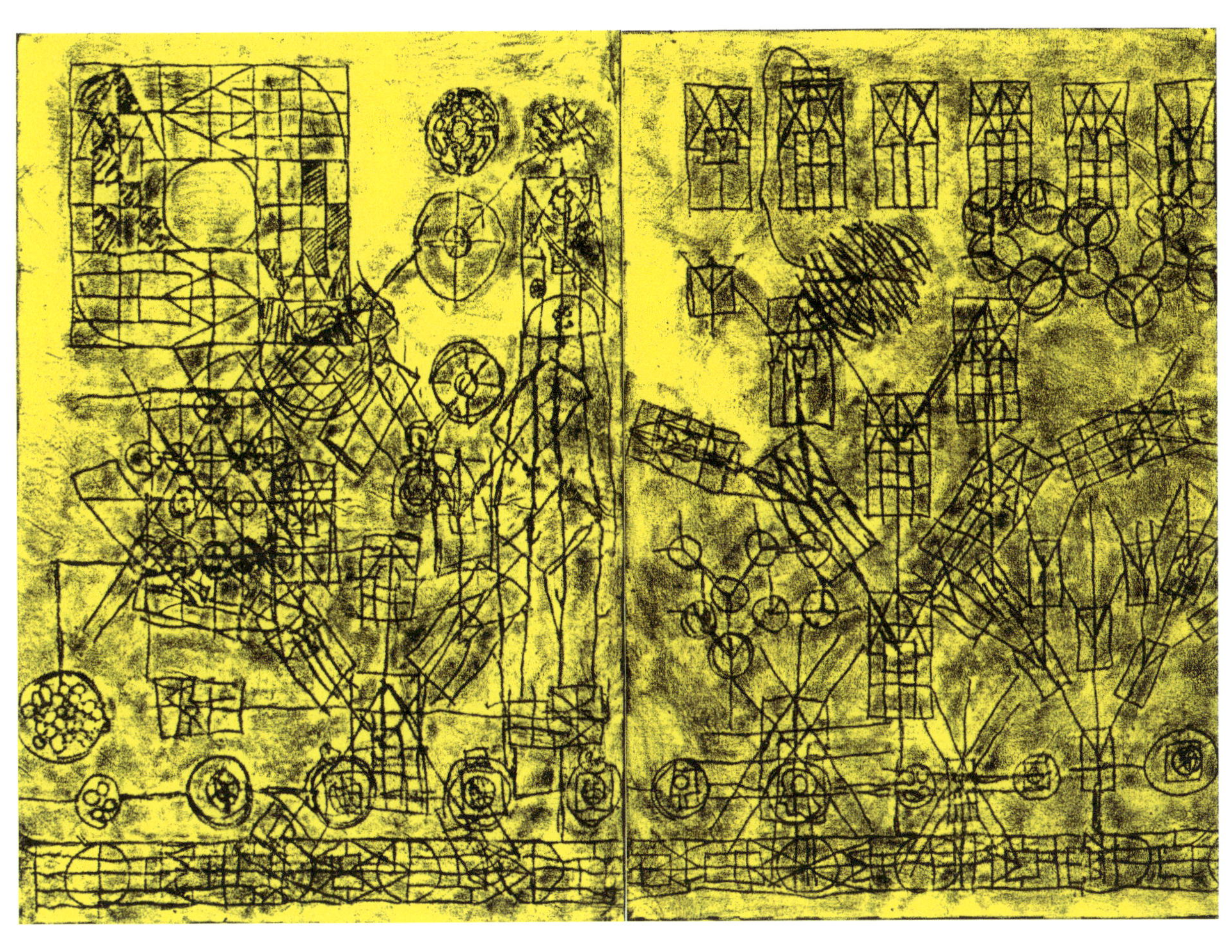

2003.6 Untitled (Notebook), 183×244 cm (2 parts)

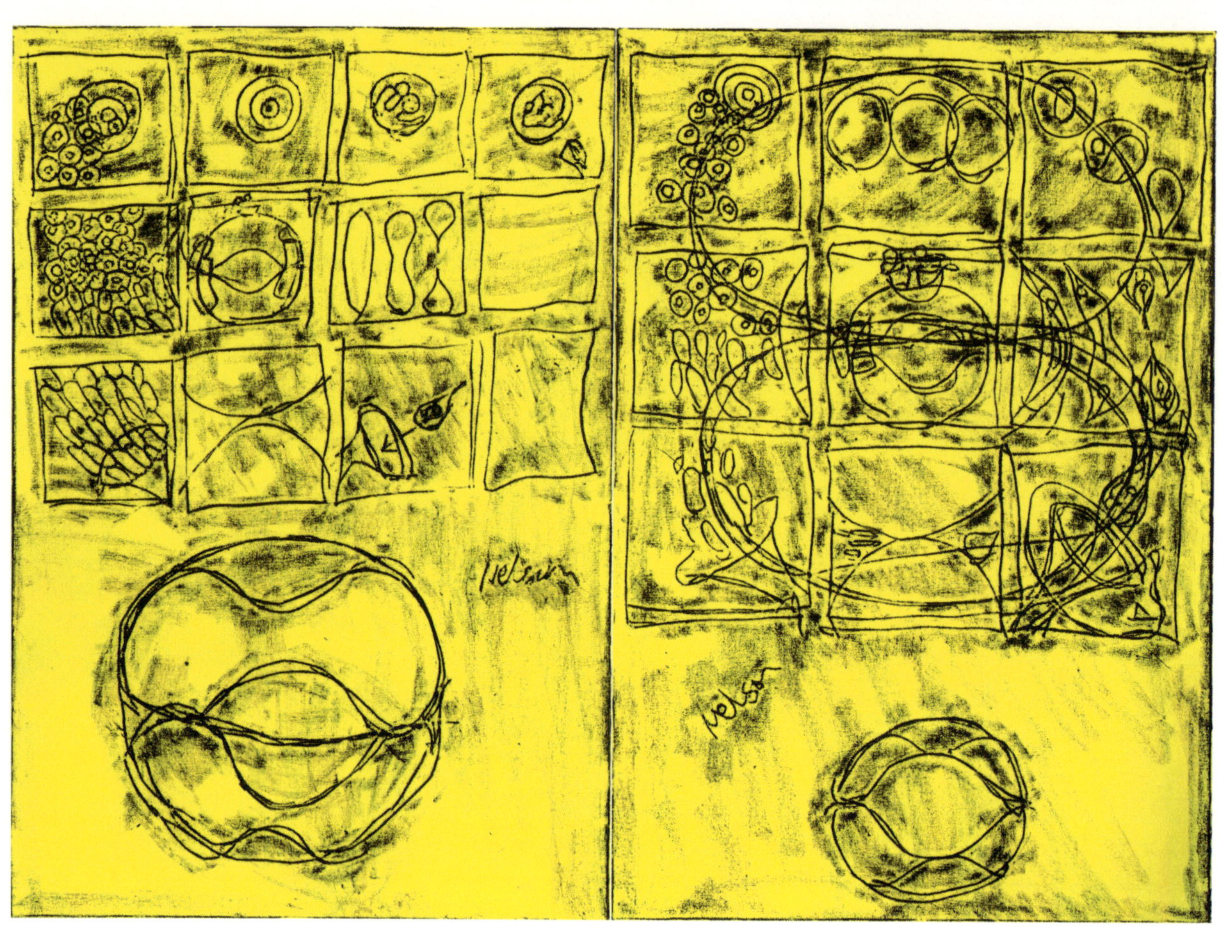

2003.7 Untitled (Notebook), 183 × 244 cm (2 parts)

2005

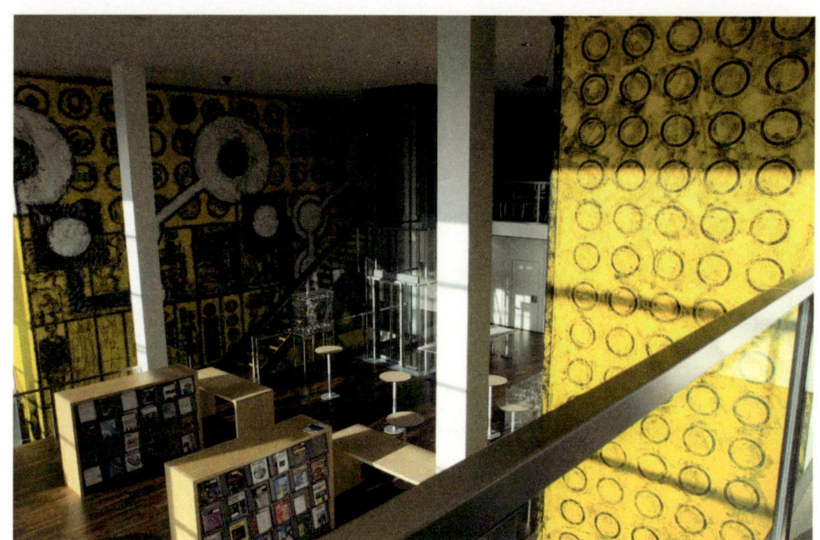

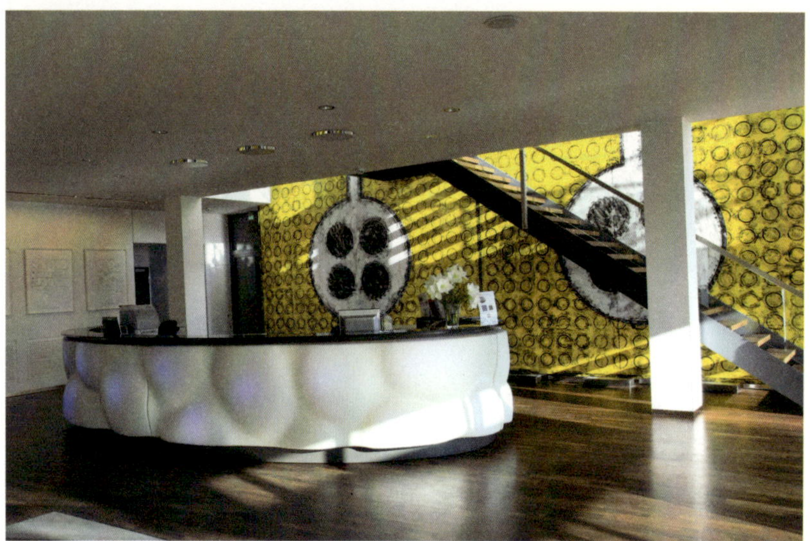

2005.1 Untitled (Actelion), Actelion Research Center, Allschwil

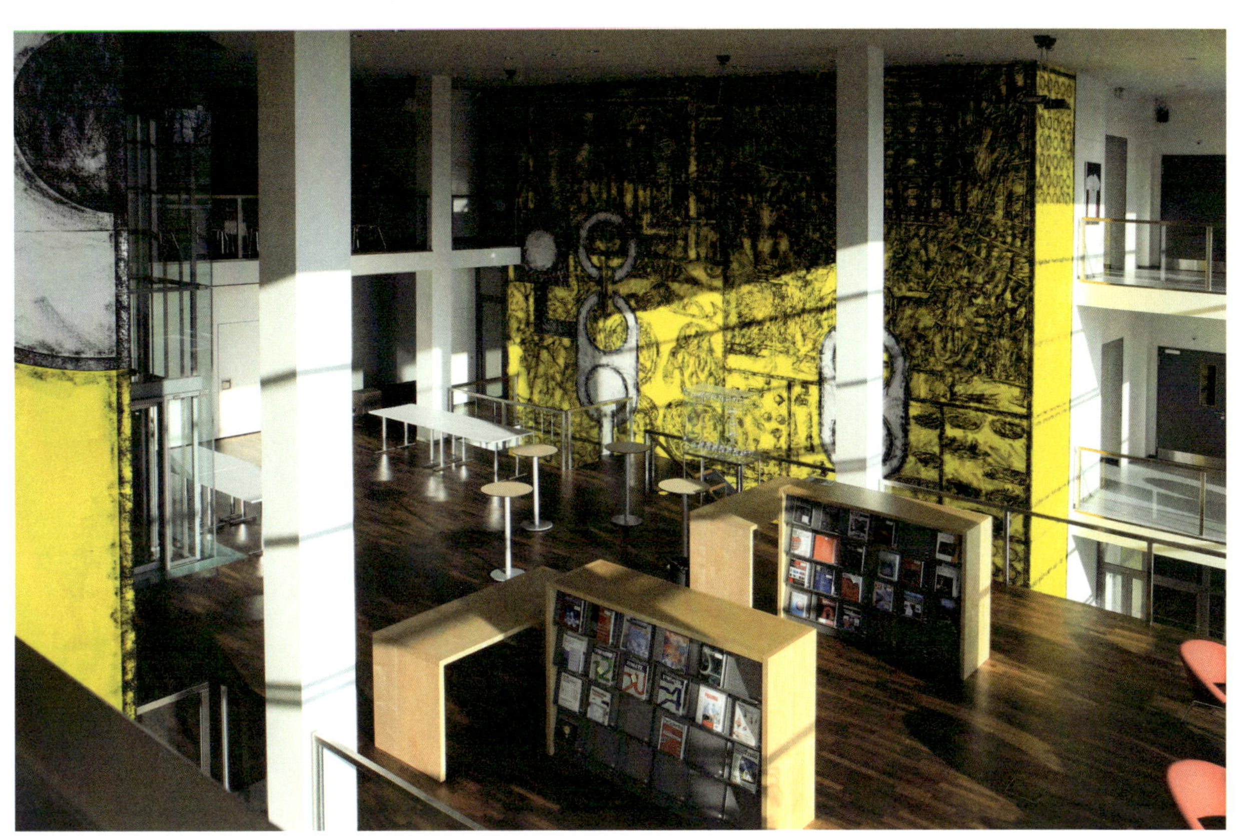

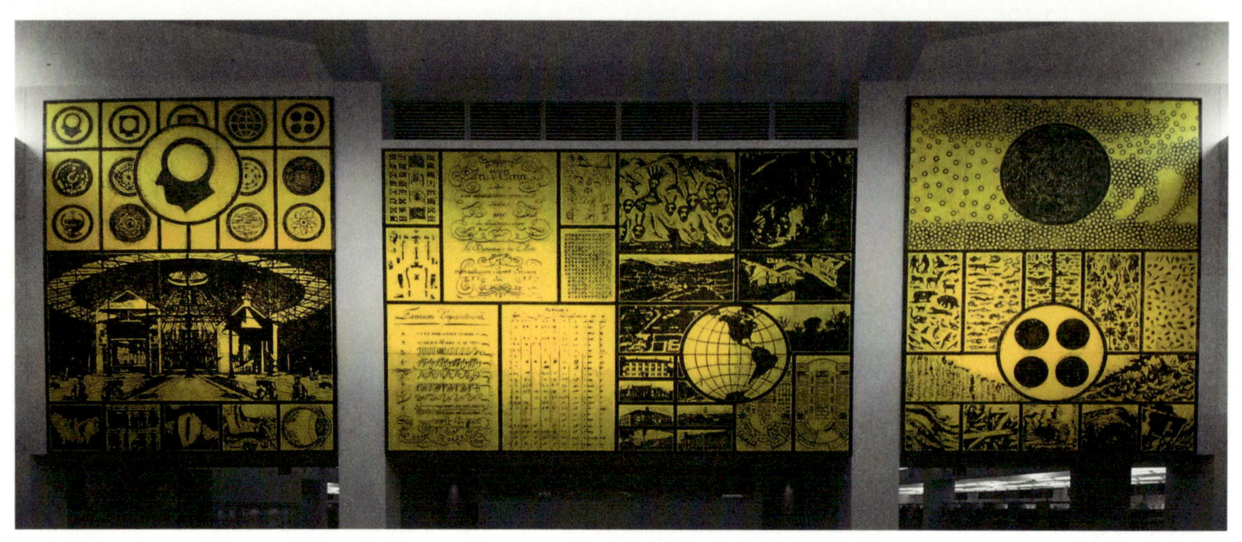

2005.2 Untitled (The Art of Writing), 2004–2005, 762 × 2255.5 cm (64 parts), Middlebury College Museum of Art, Vermont

2007

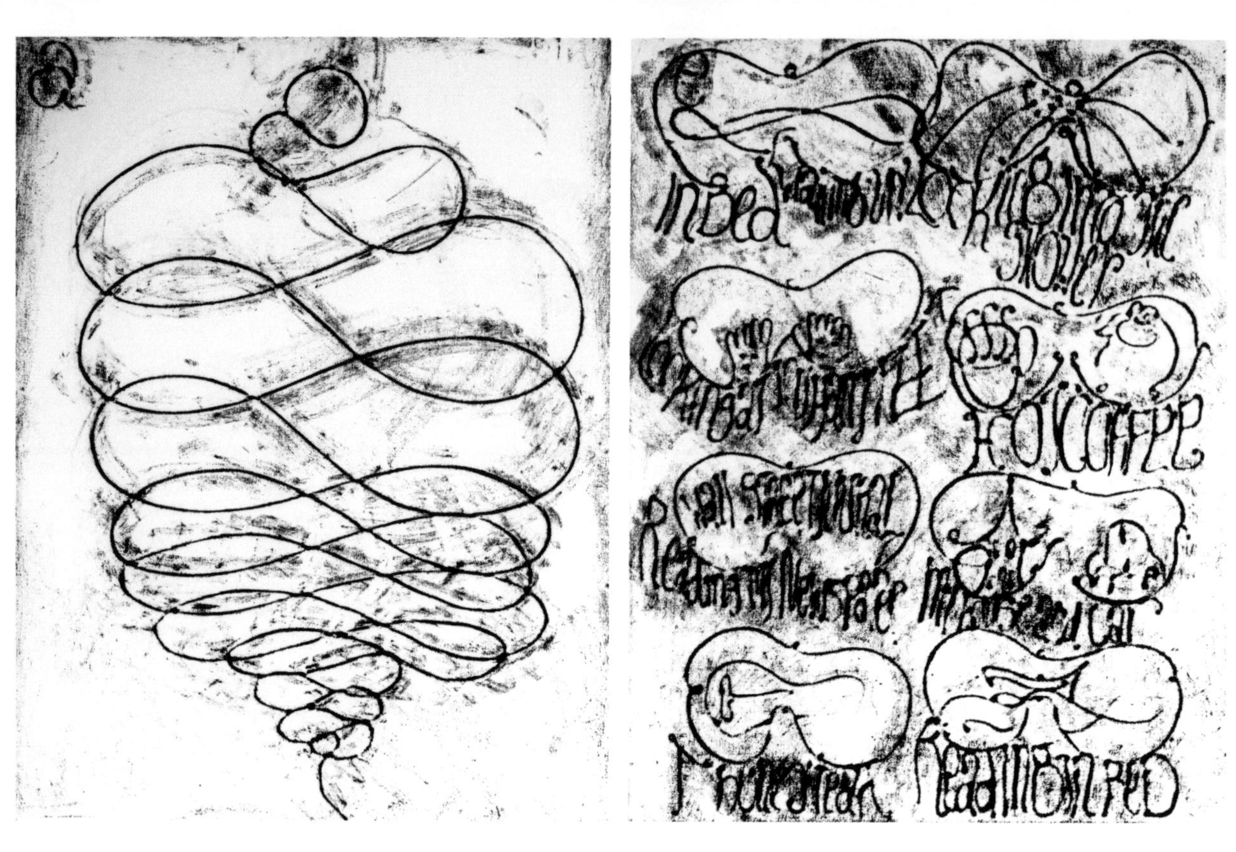

2007.1 Untitled (*Learning from That Person's Work A/E*), 122 × 91.5 each (diptych)

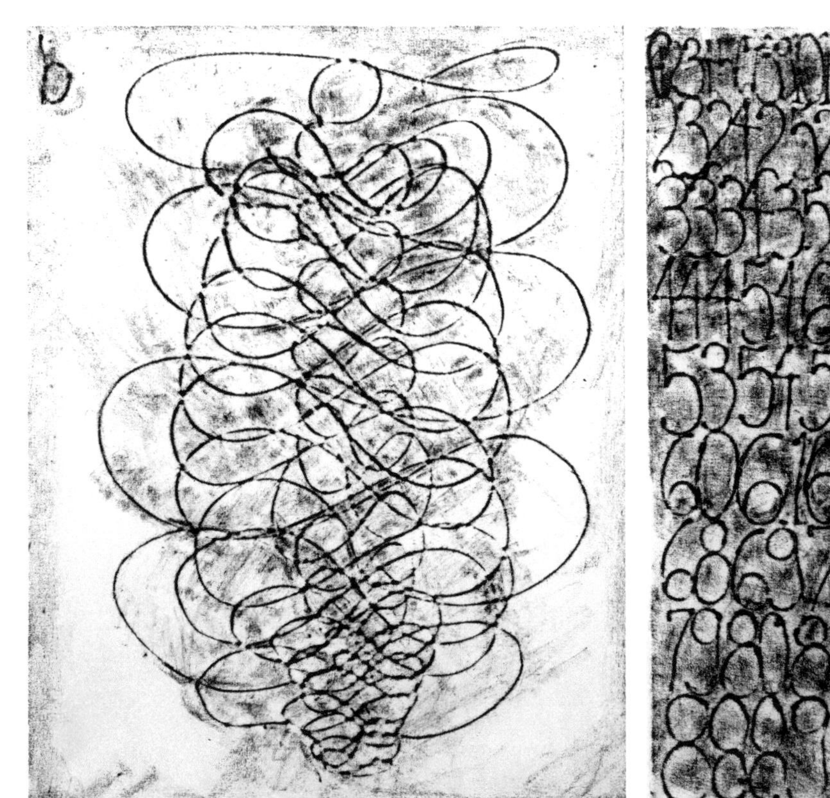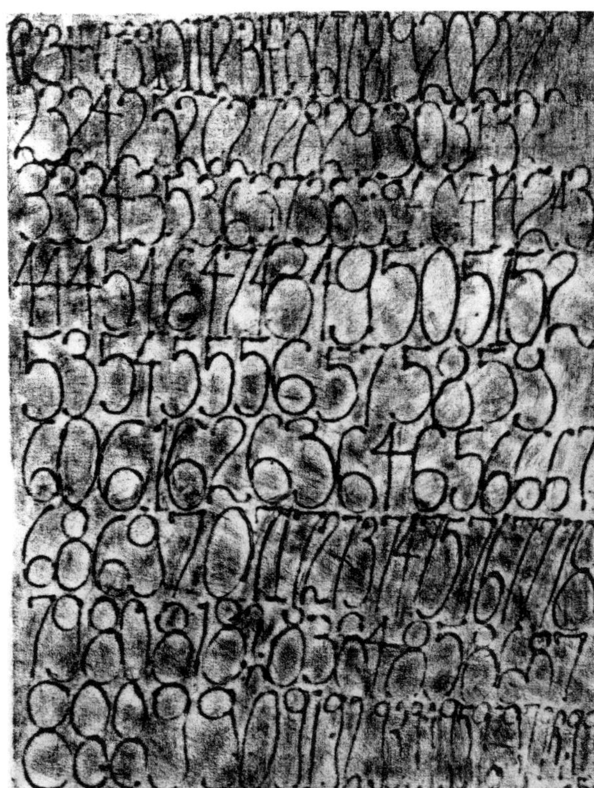

2007.2 Untitled (Learning from That Person's Work B/F), 122 × 91.5 each (diptych)

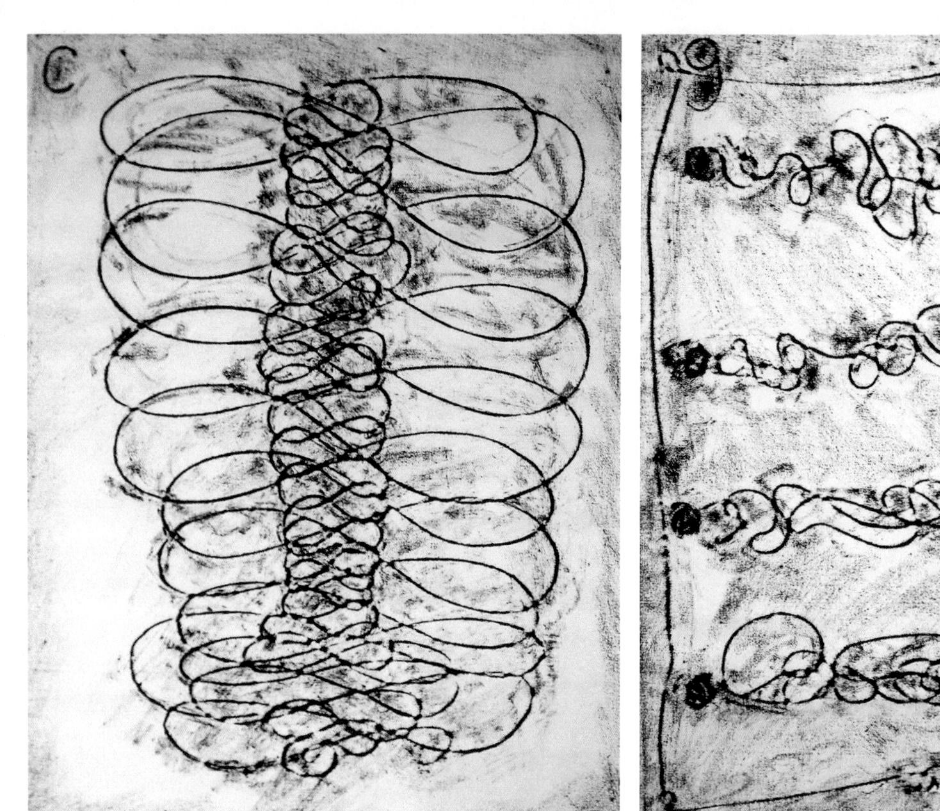
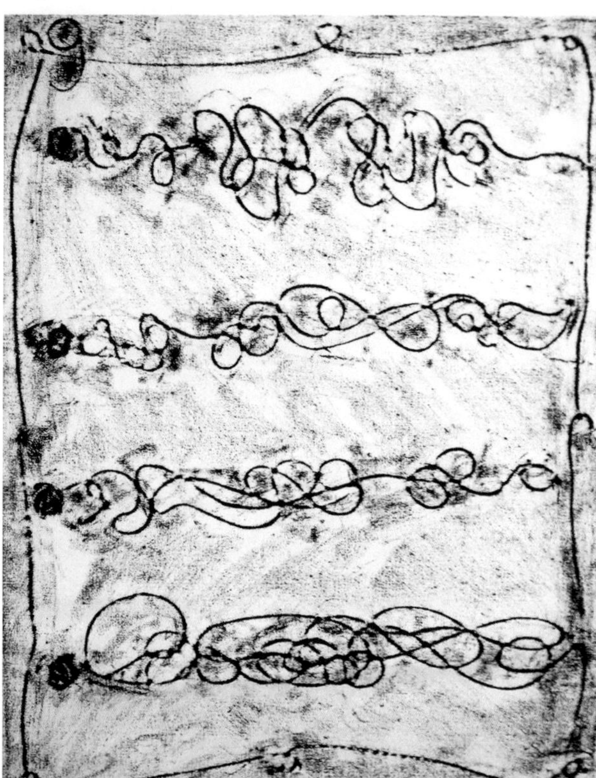

2007.3 Untitled (*Learning from That Person's Work C/G*), 122 × 91.5 each (diptych)

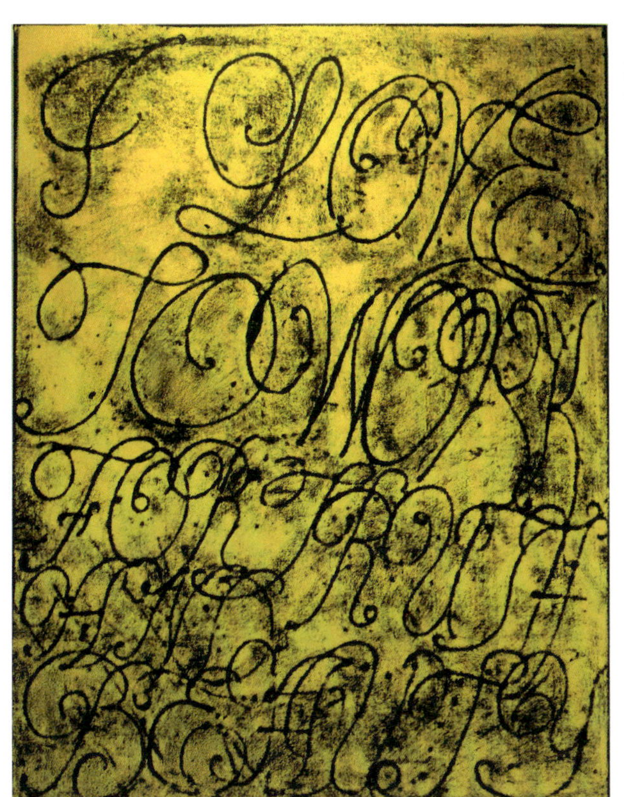

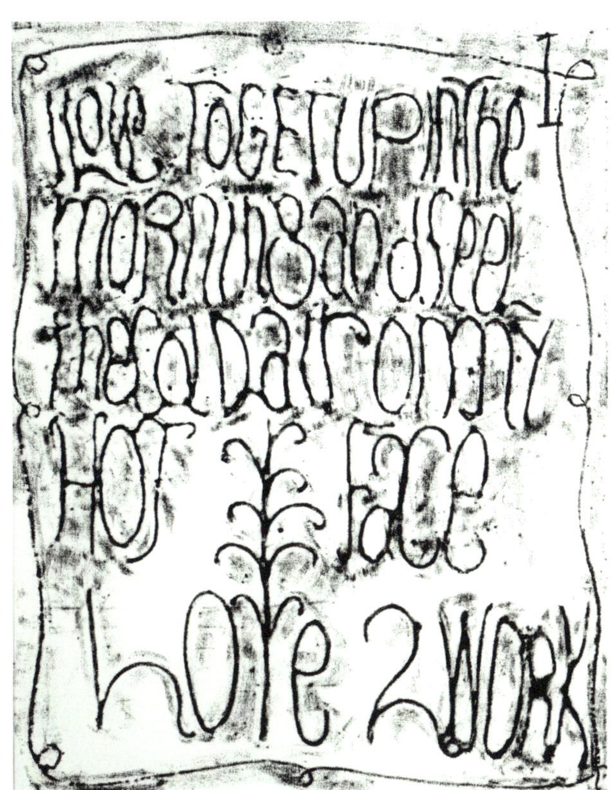

2007.4   Untitled (That Person), 122 × 91.5 cm
2007.5   Untitled (Learning from That Person's Work I), 122 × 91.5 cm

2008

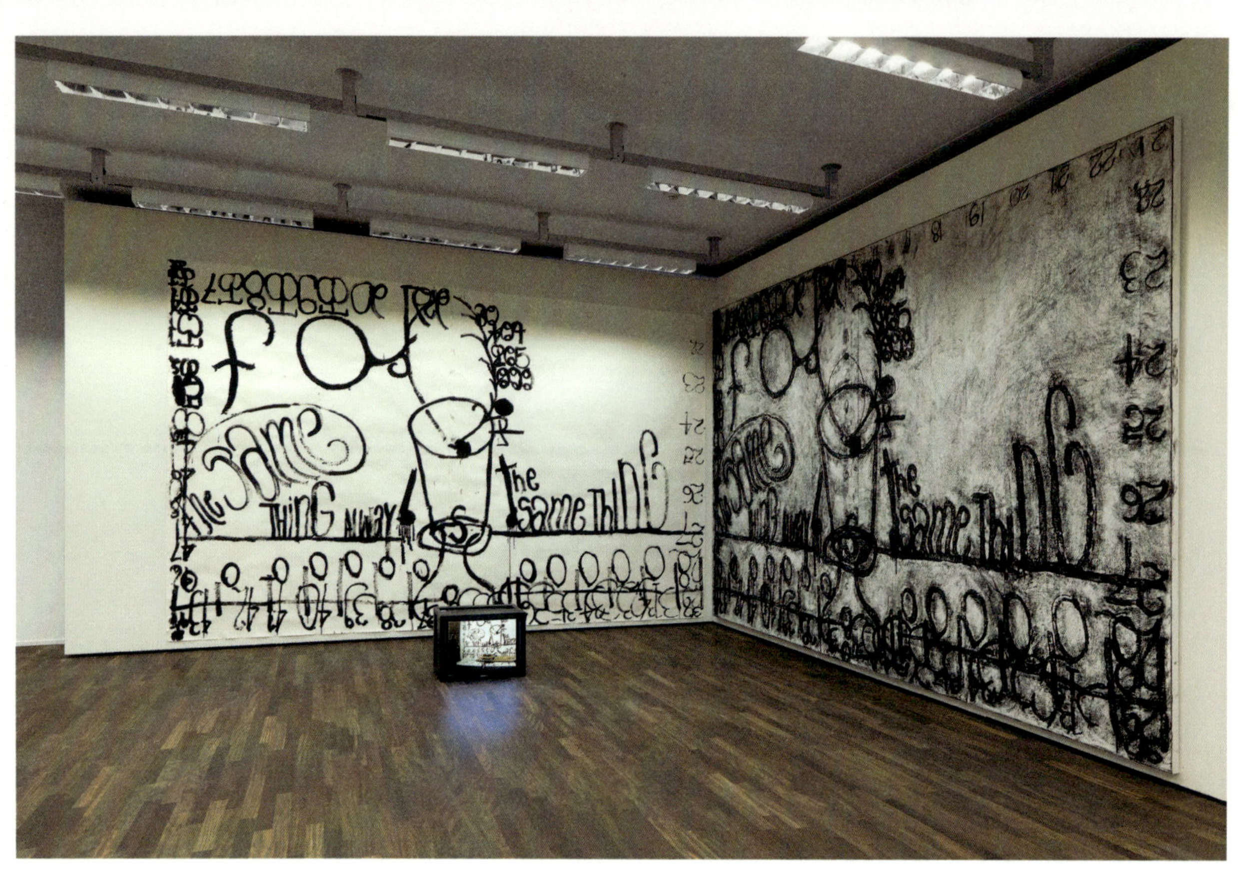

2008.1 Untitled (Combination of the Two, Tang Rubbing A), 332 × 510 cm (2 parts)

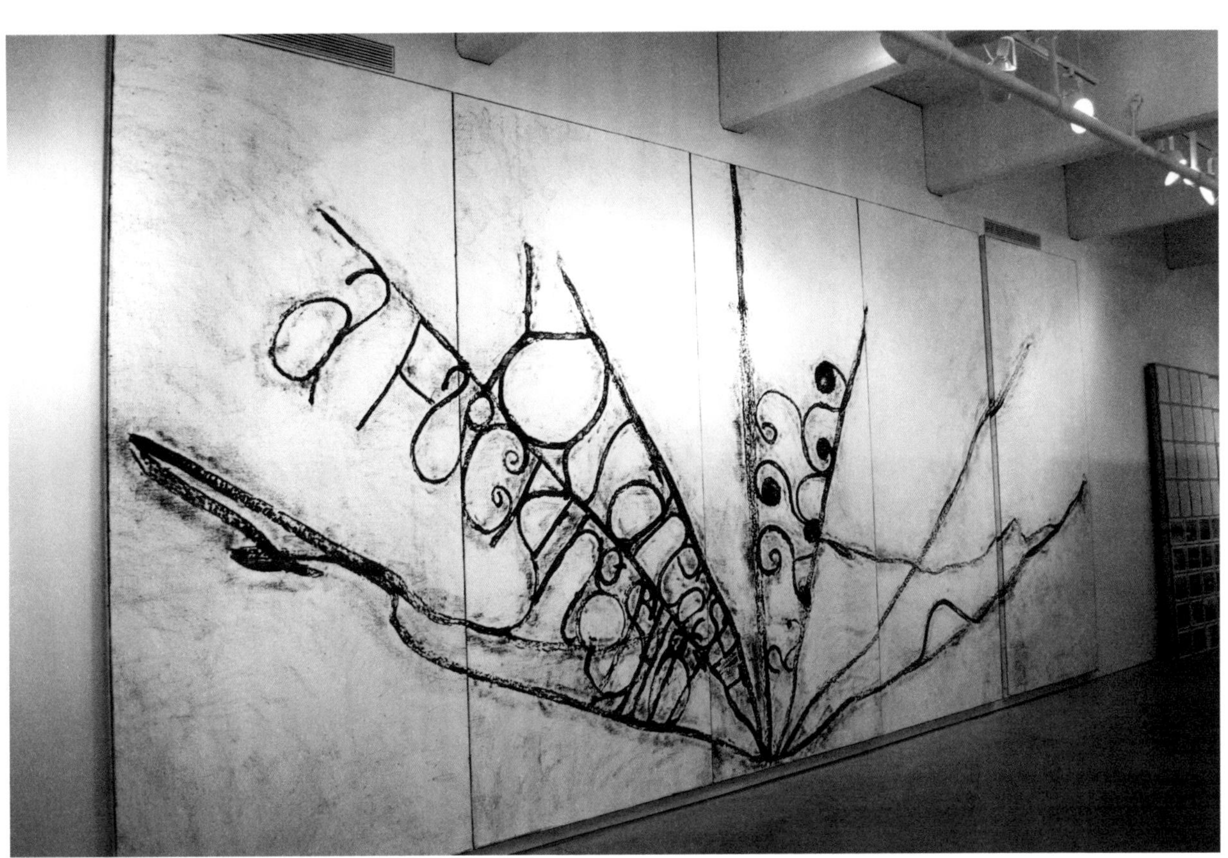

2008.2 Untitled (Combination of the Two, Tate Performance), 244 × 610 cm (2 parts)

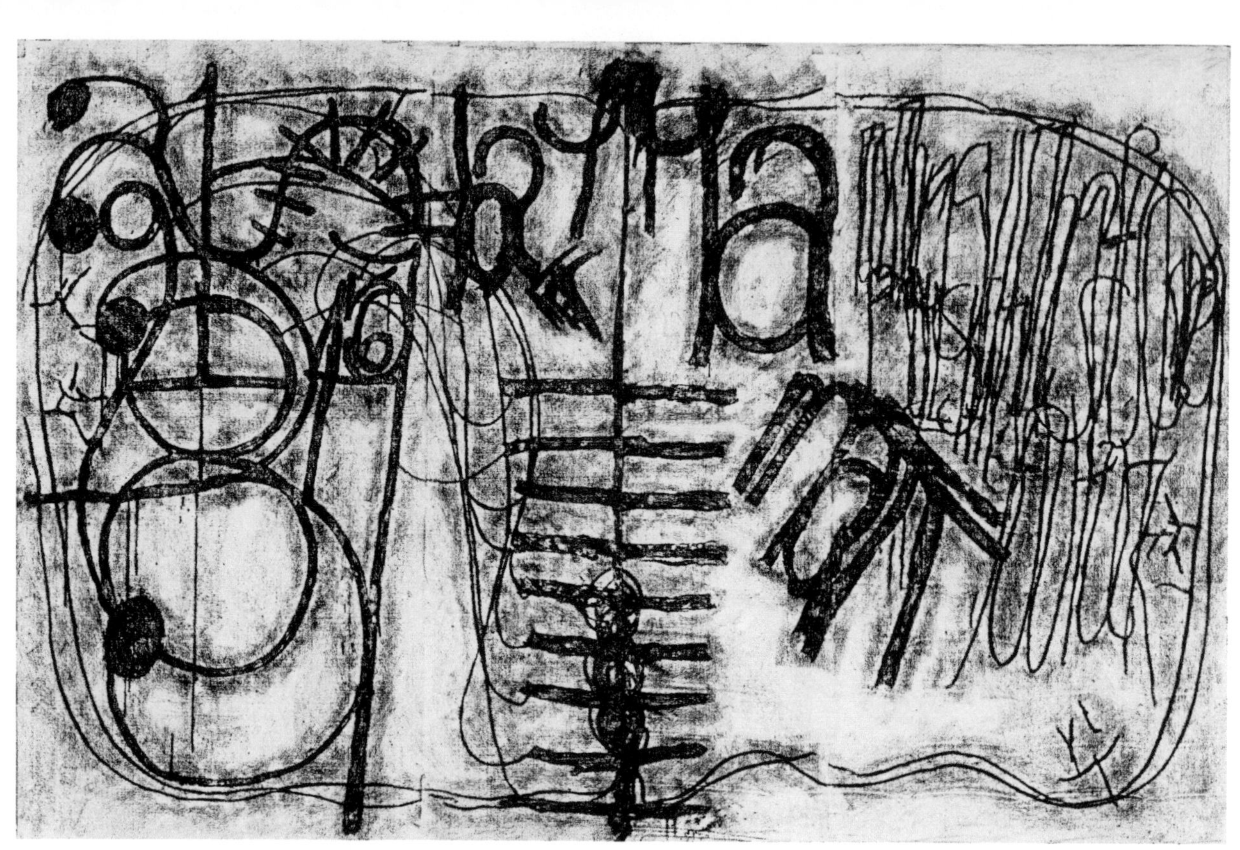

2008.3 Untitled (Combination of the Two, Rubbing A/B), 244 × 366 cm (2 parts)

2009

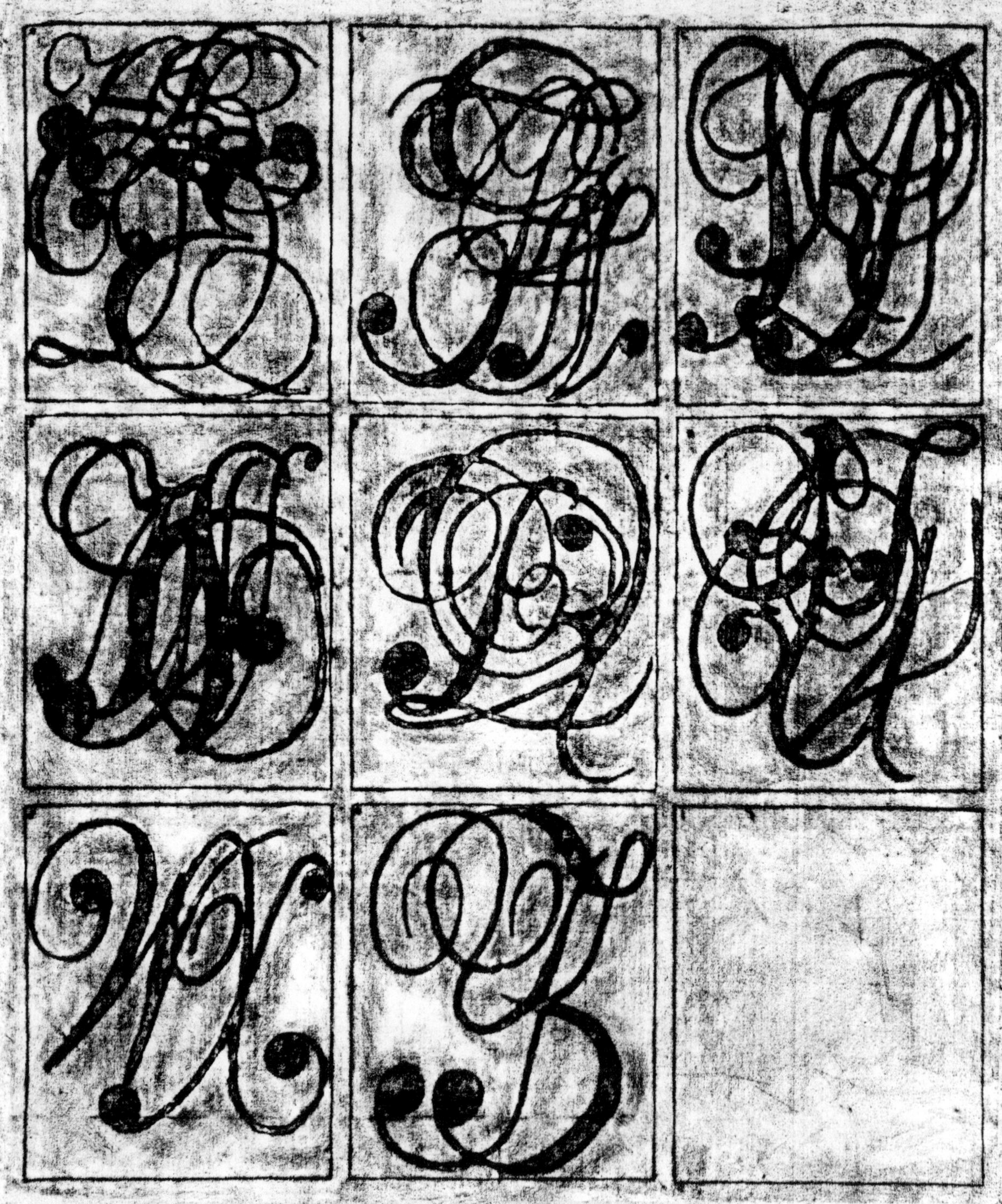

2009.1 Untitled (Learning from That Person's Work), 274 × 228 cm

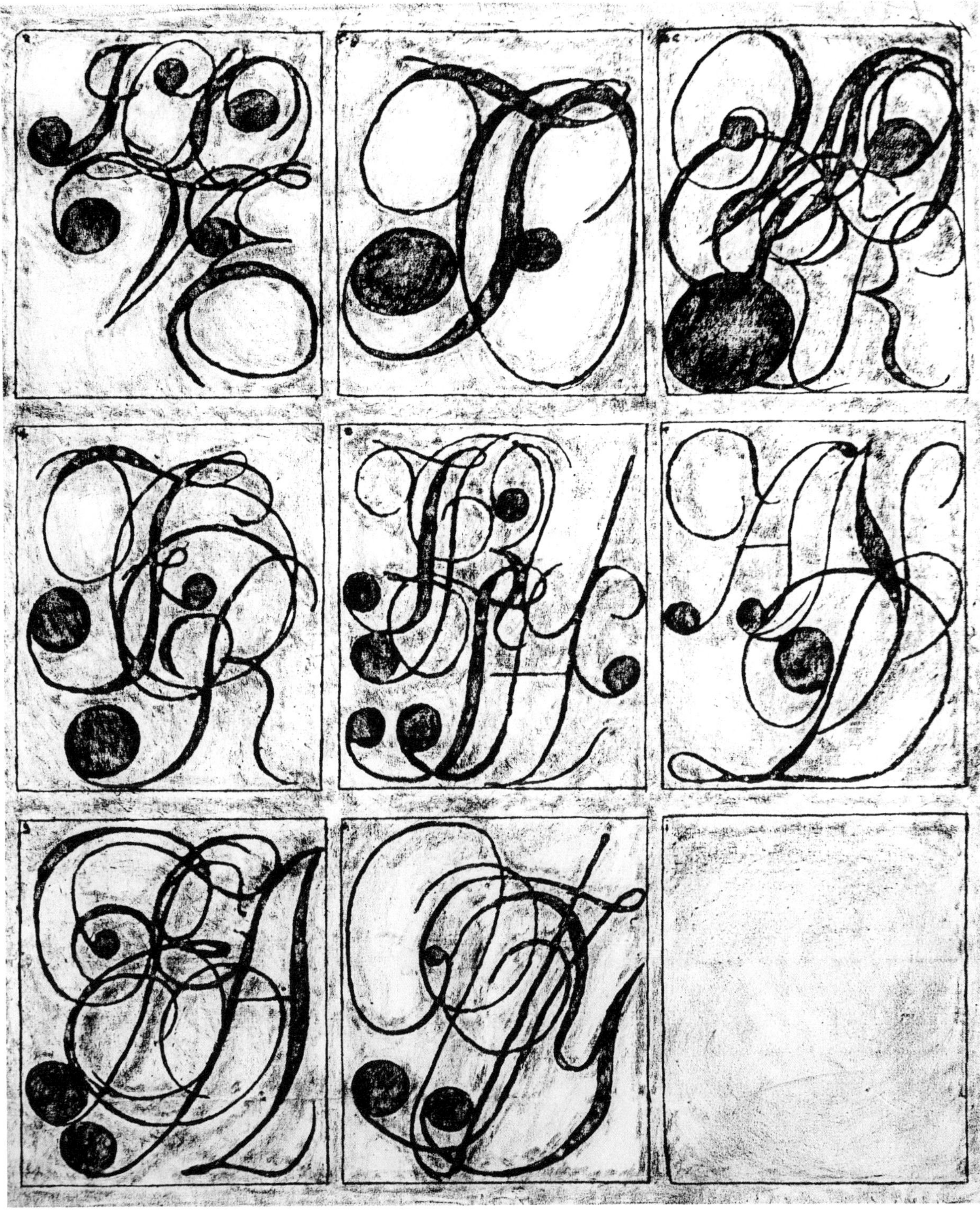

2009.2 Untitled (Learning from That Person's Work), 274 × 228 cm

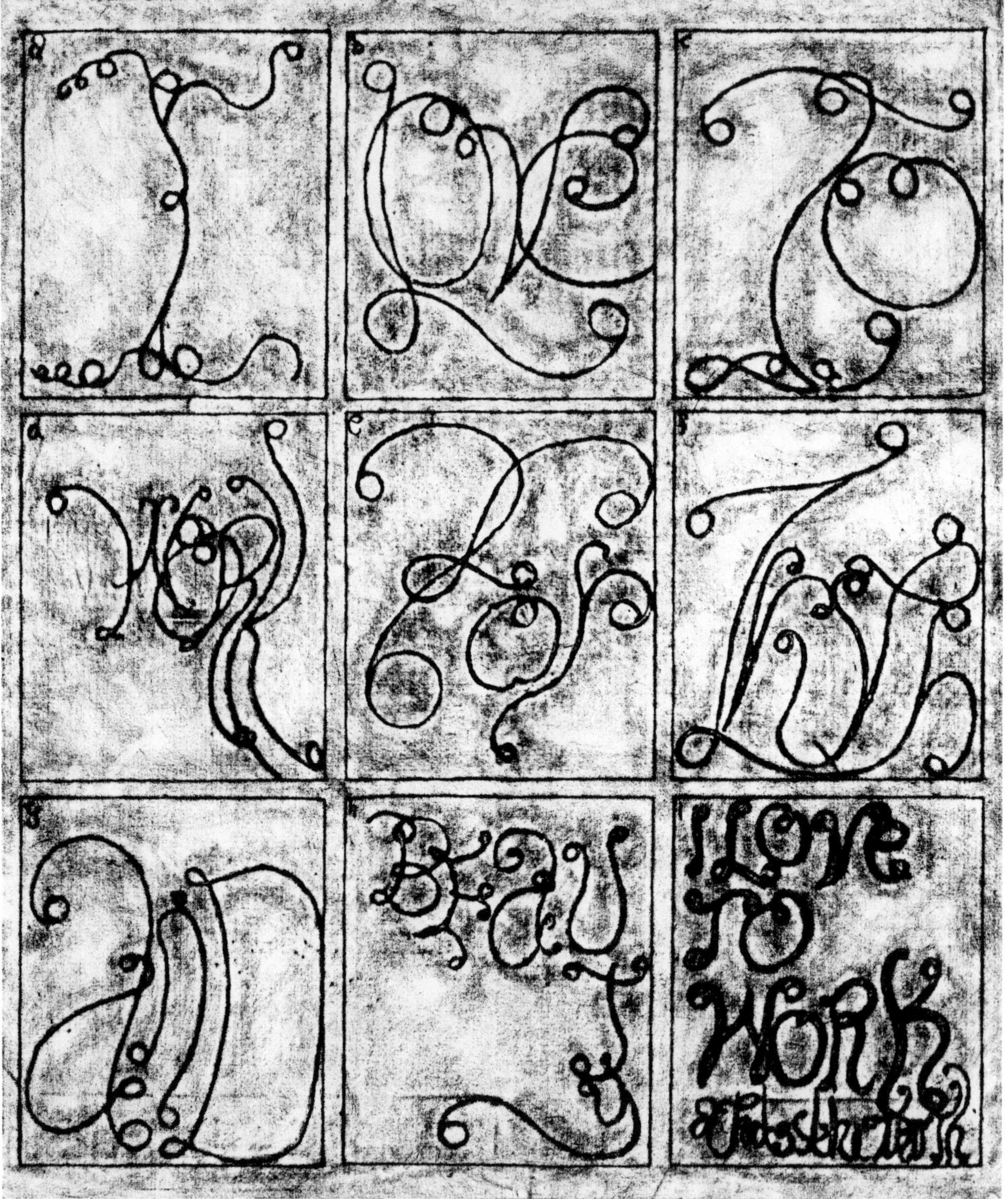

2009.3 Untitled (*Learning from That Person's Work*), 274 × 228 cm

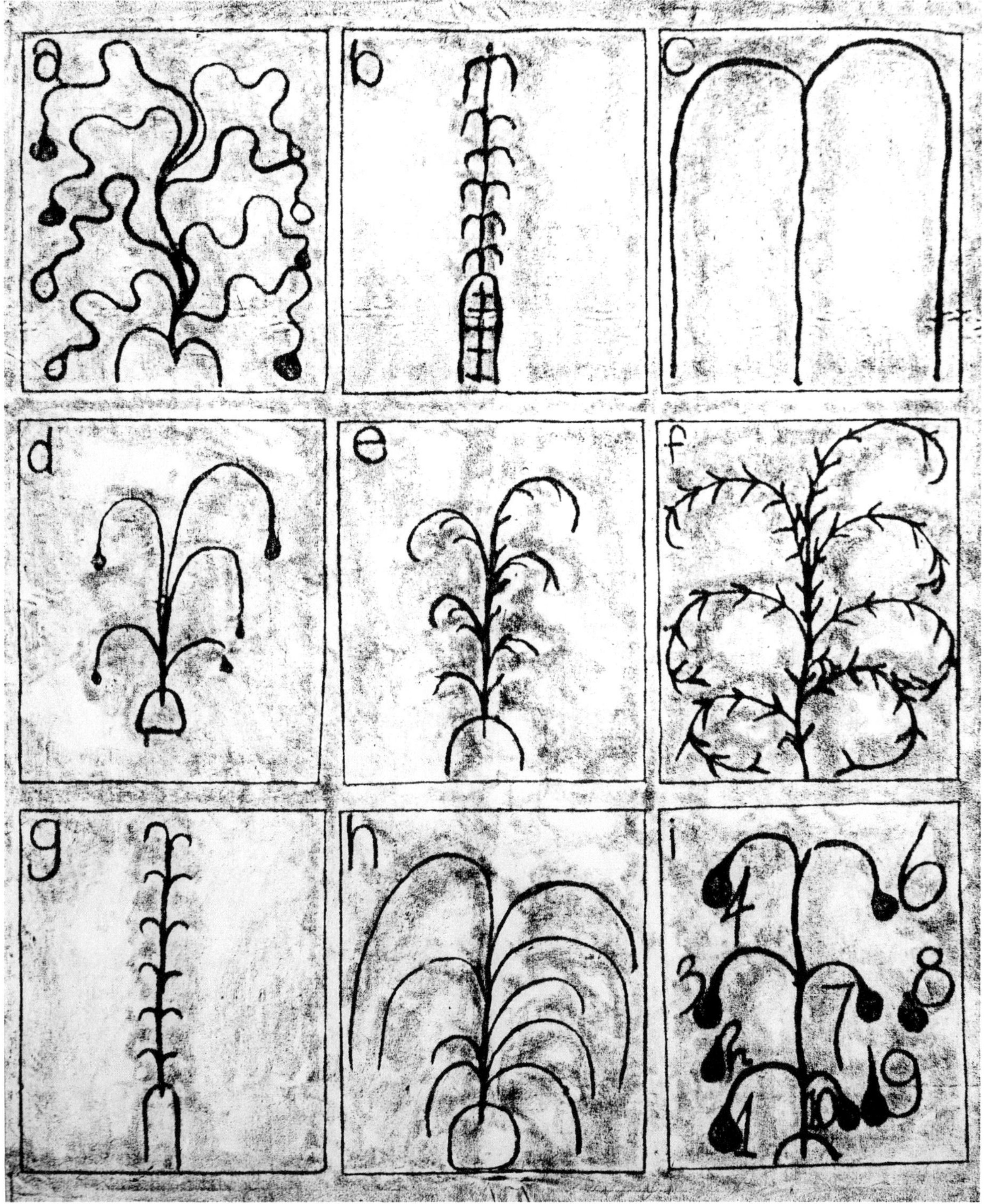

2009.4 Untitled (Learning from That Person's Work), 274 × 228 cm

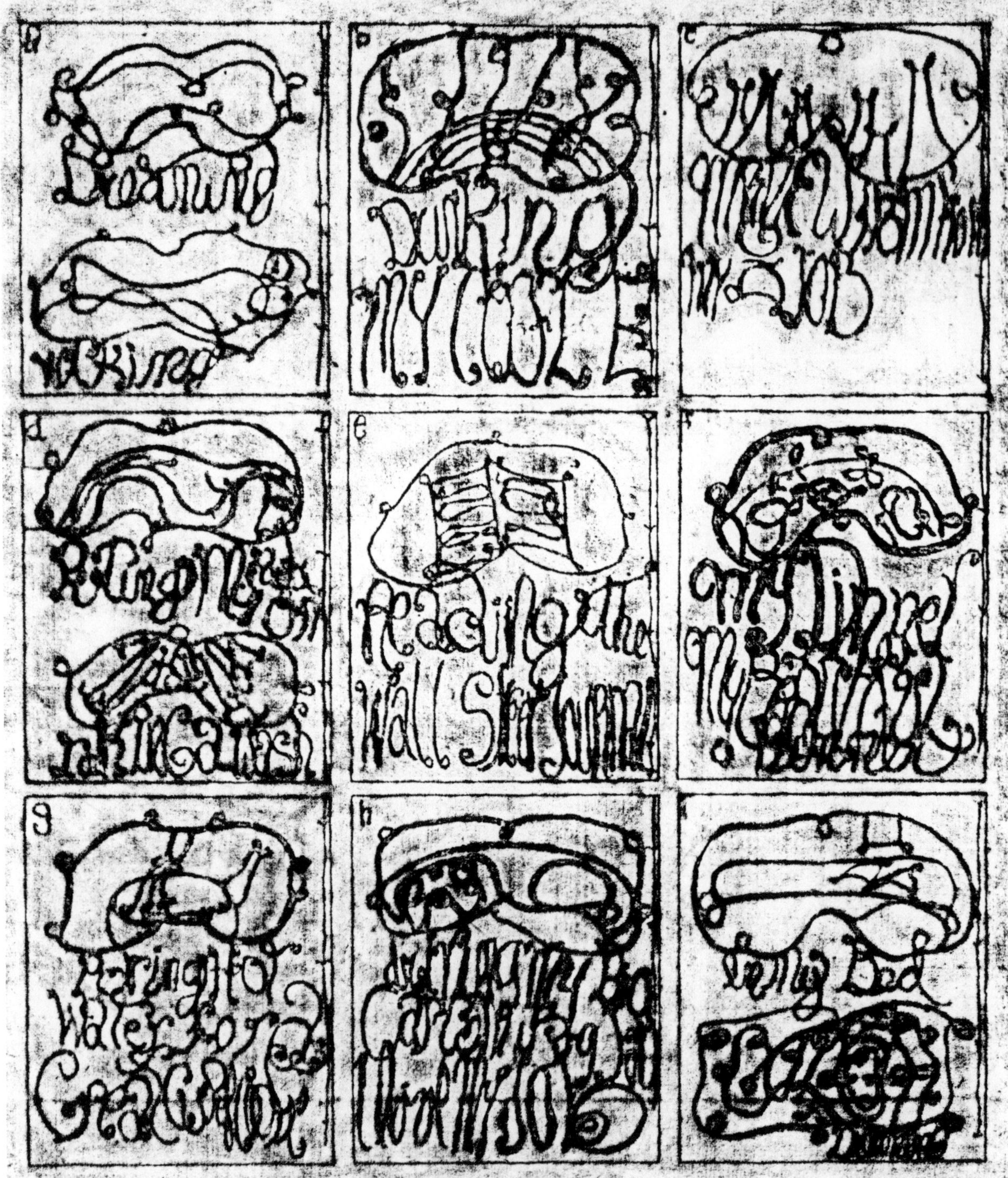

2009.5 Untitled (Learning from That Person's Work), 274 × 228 cm

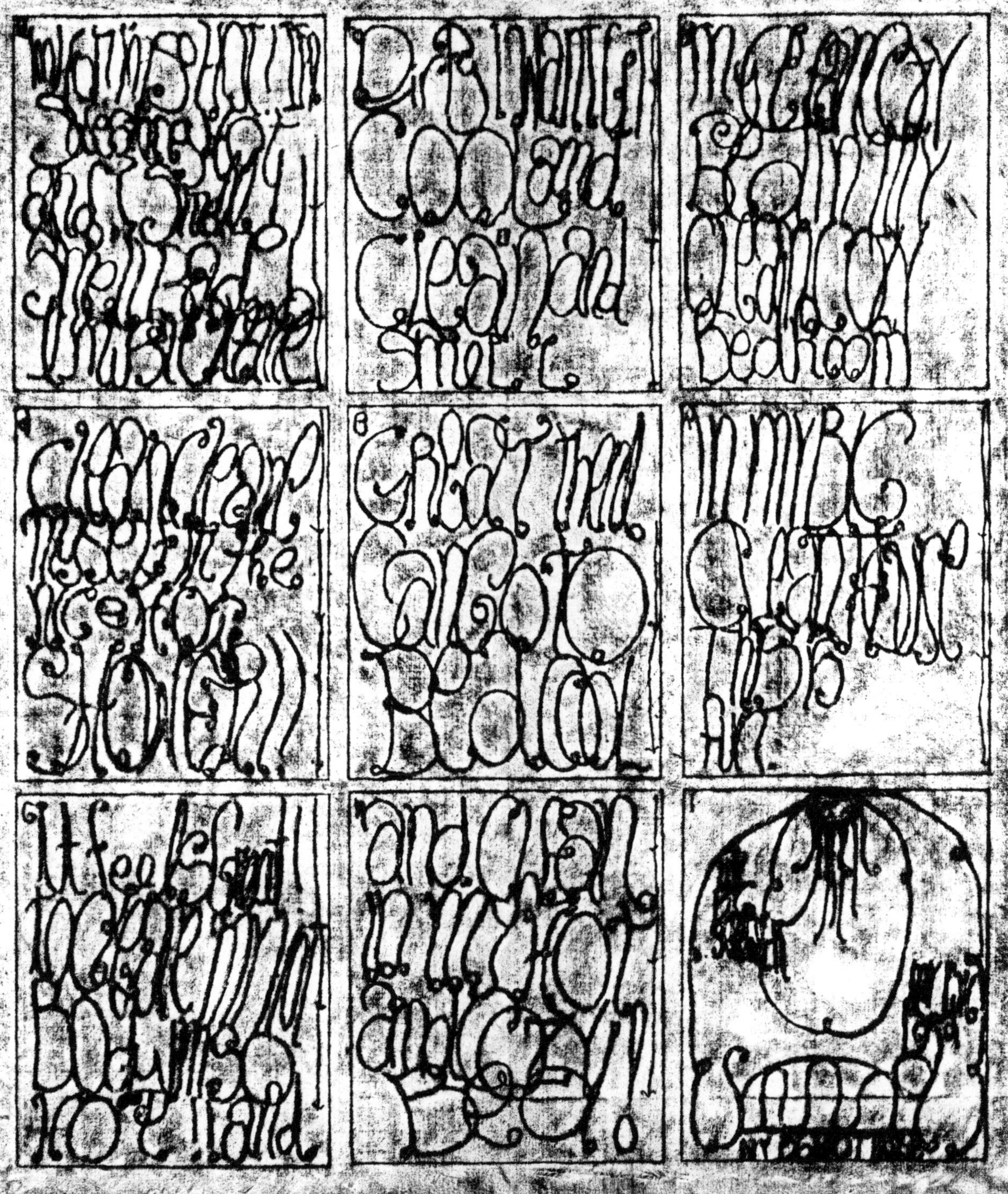

2009.6 Untitled (Learning from That Person's Work), 274 × 228 cm

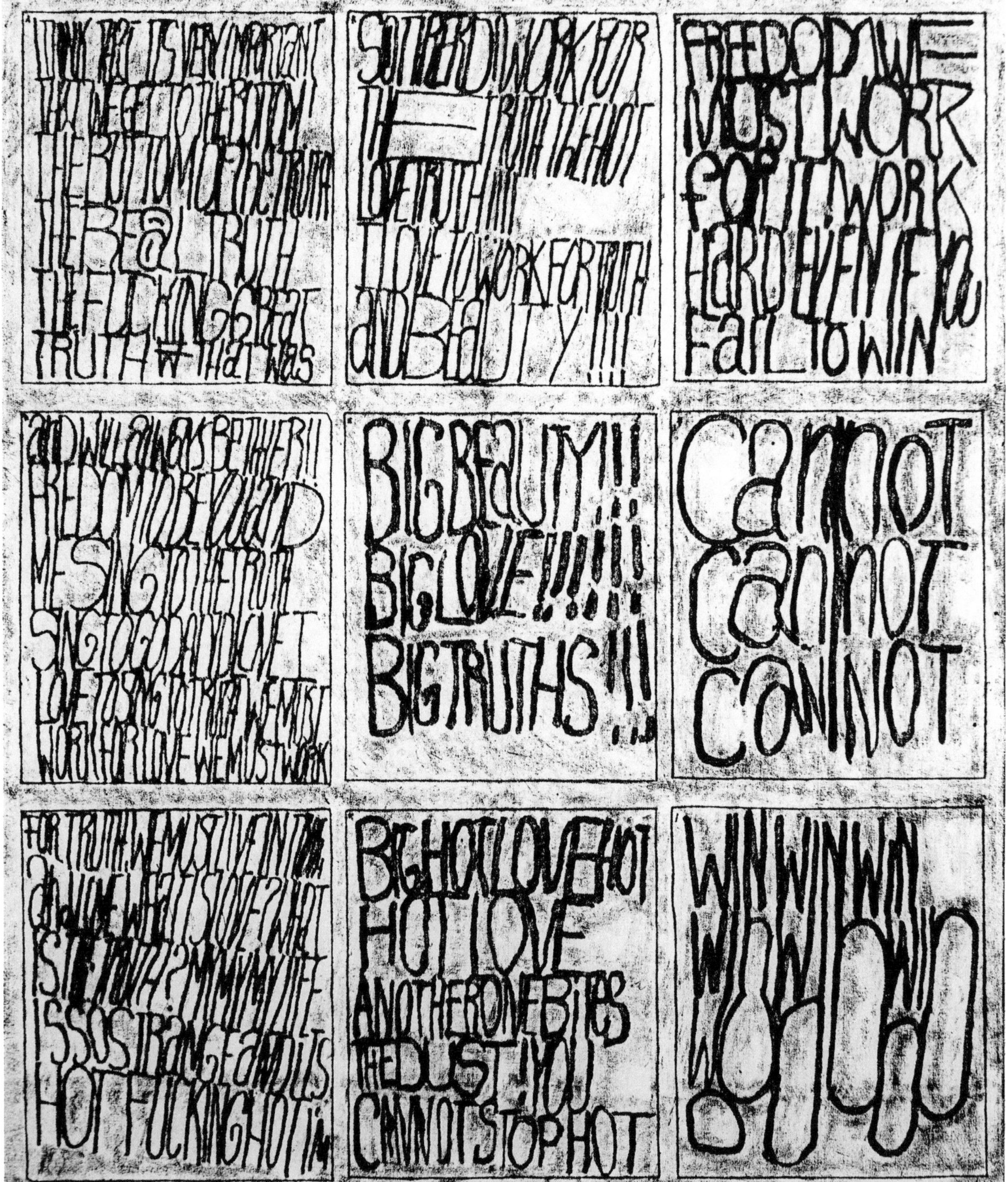

2009.7 Untitled (Learning from That Person's Work), 274 × 228 cm

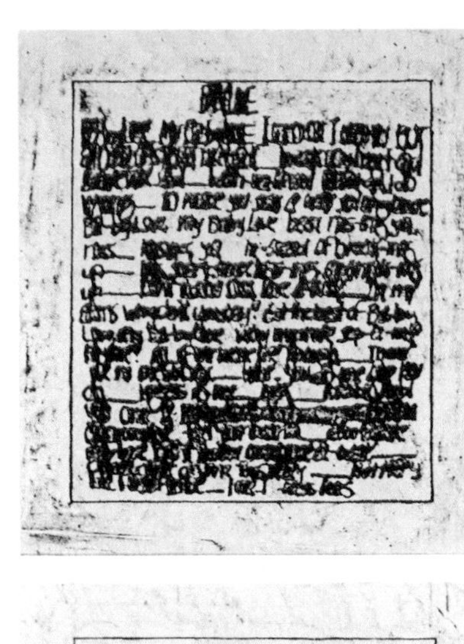
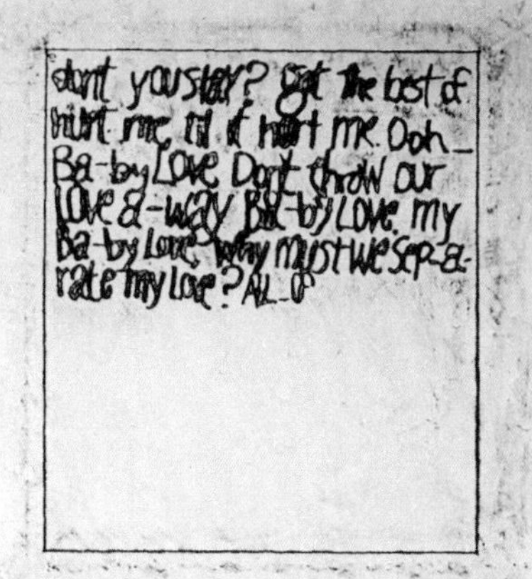
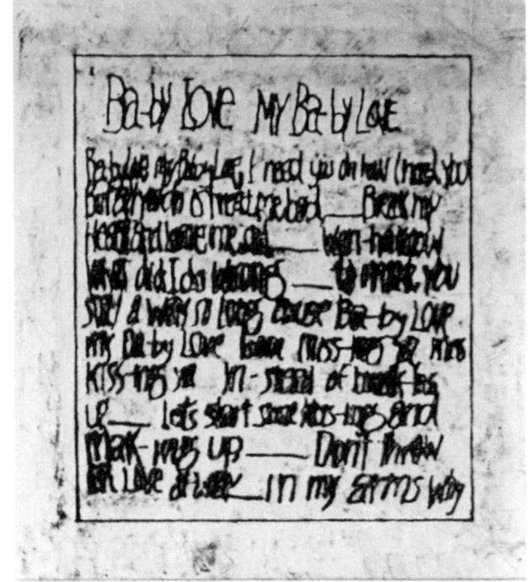
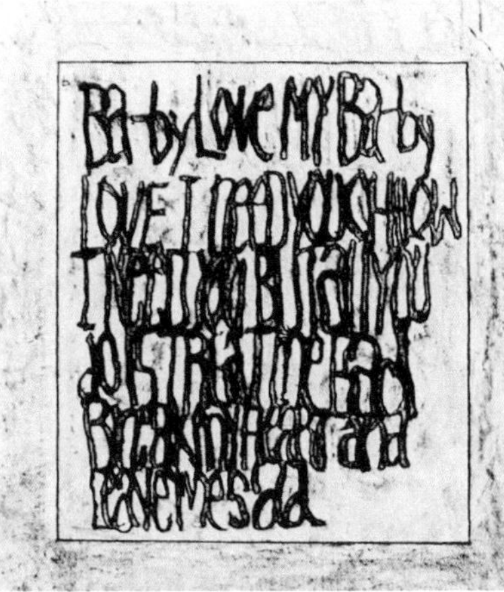
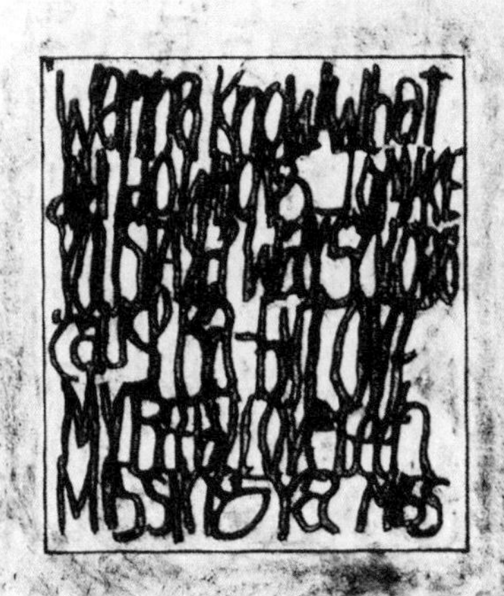
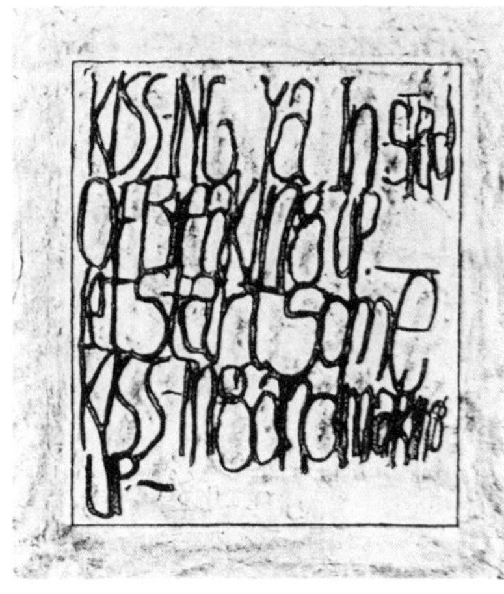
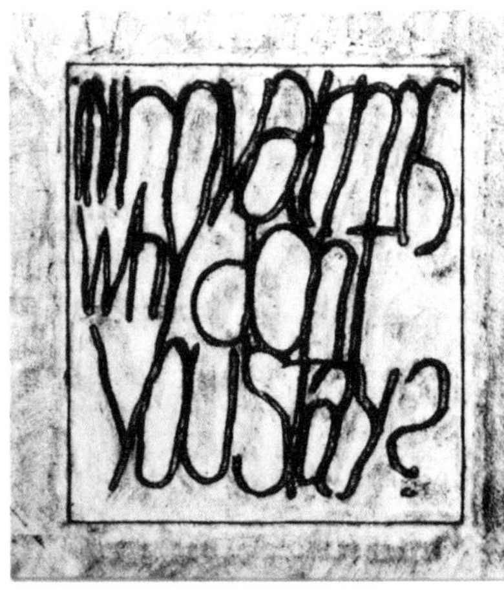
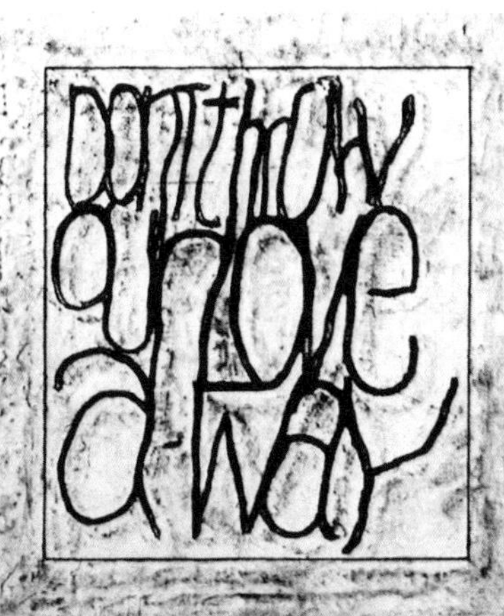

2009.8 Untitled (Learning from That Person's Work), 306 × 267 cm (9 parts)

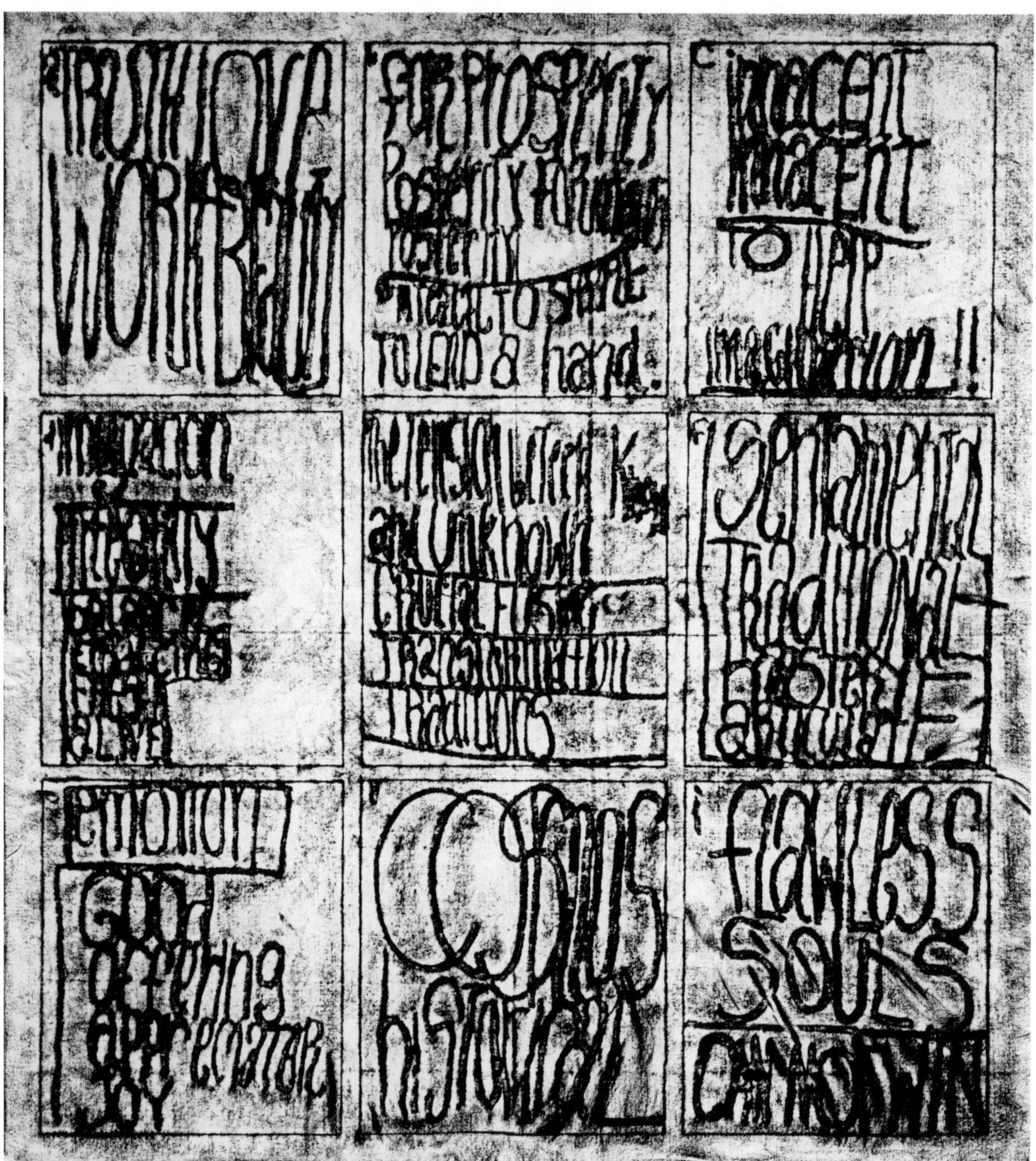

2009.9 Untitled (*Learning from That Person's Work*), 274 × 228 cm each (diptych)

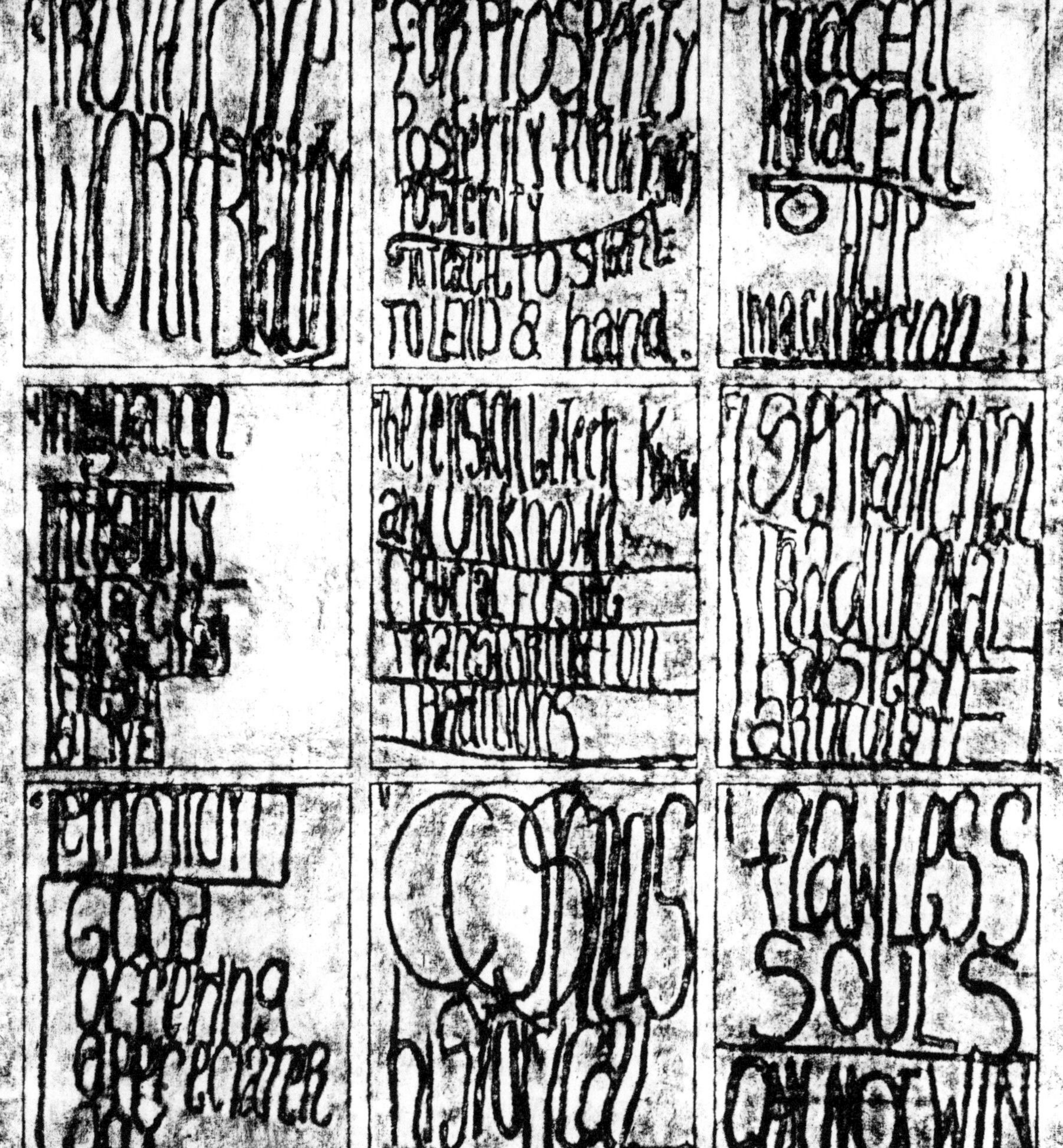

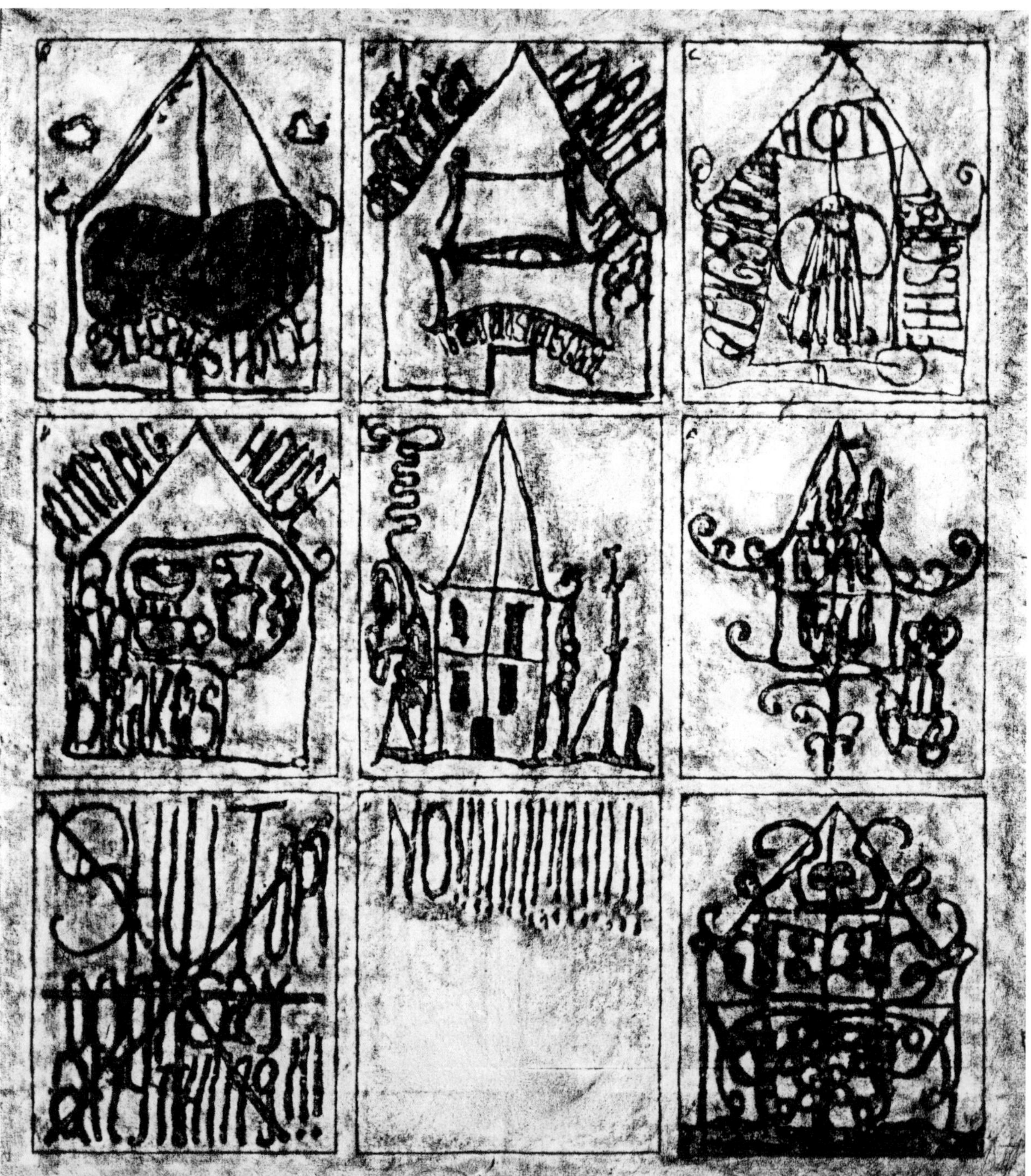

2009.10 Untitled (Learning from That Person's Work), 274 × 228 cm each (diptych)

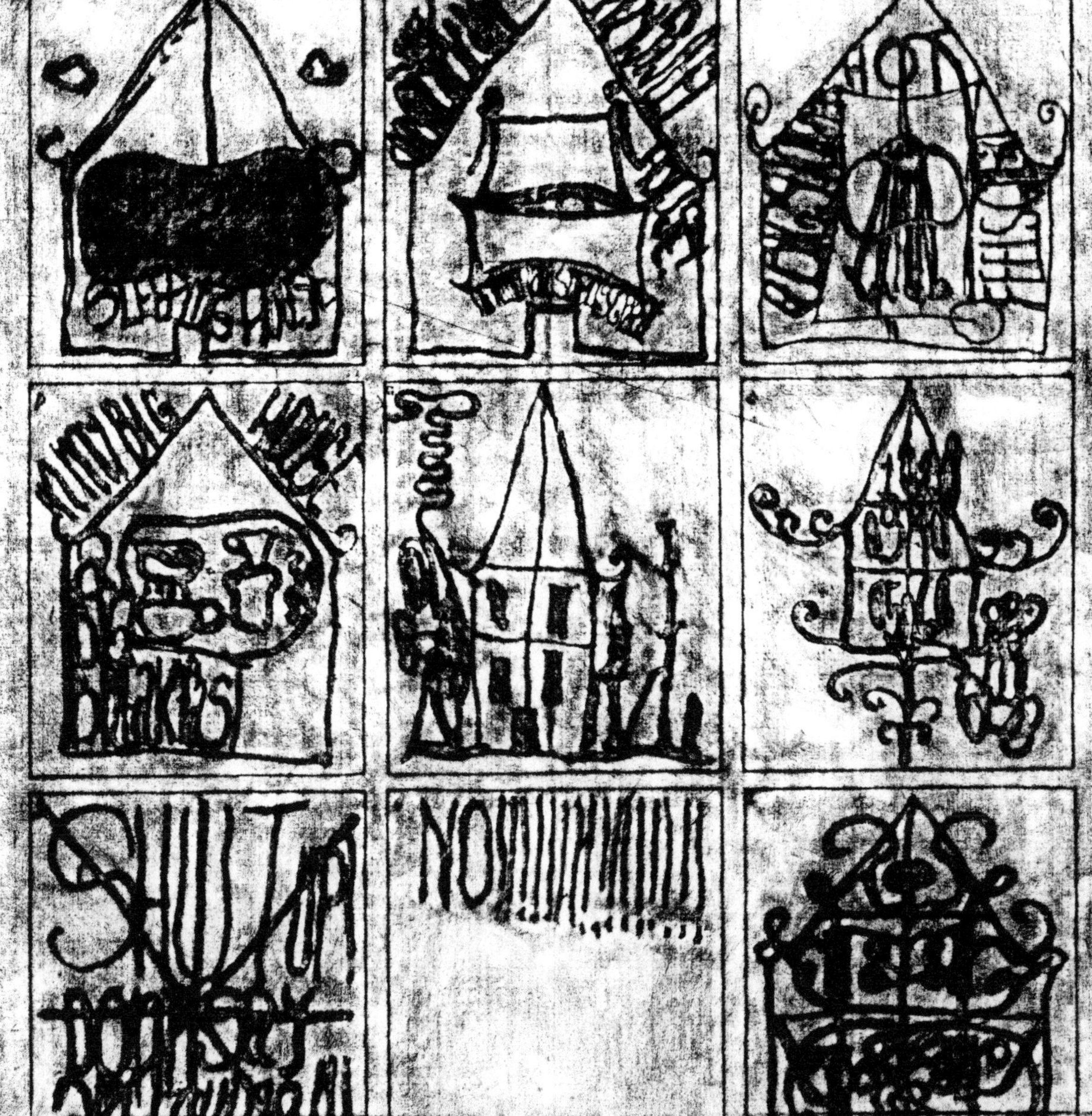

2009.11 Untitled (*Learning from That Person's Work*), 306 × 534 cm (18 parts)

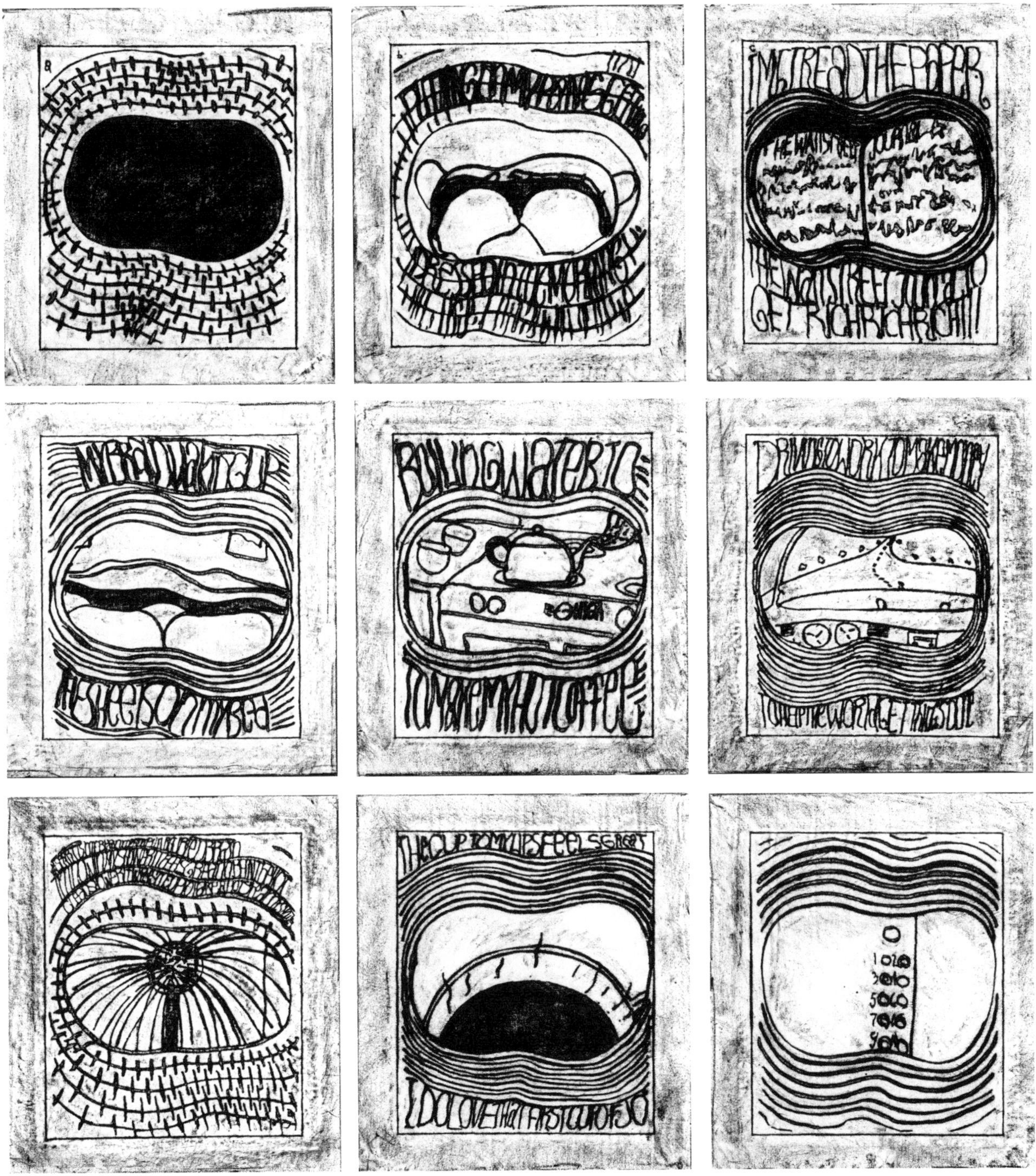

8

TAKING OFF MY PJ'S AND GETTING
DRESSED IN THE MORNING

I'M TIRED THE PAPER
THE WALL STREET JOURNAL
GET RICH RICH RICH!!

MY BED WANTS ME
THE SHEETS ON MY BED

BOILING WATER TO
TO MAKE MY JO COFFEE

DRIVING WORK IN THE CITY
TO KEEP THE WORLD GET THINGS DONE

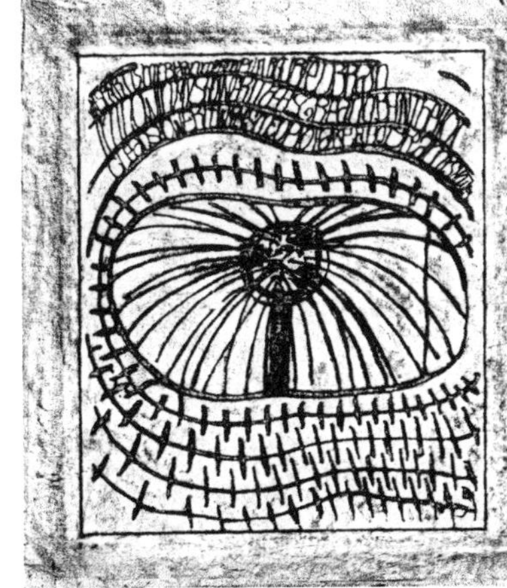

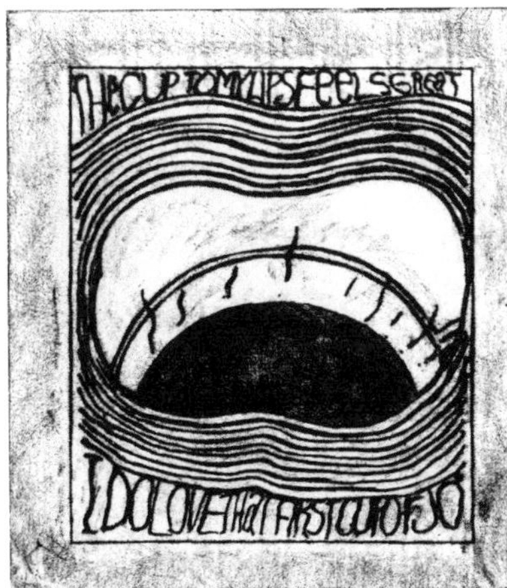

THE CUP TO MY LIPS FEELS GREAT
I DO LOVE THAT FIRST CUP OF JO

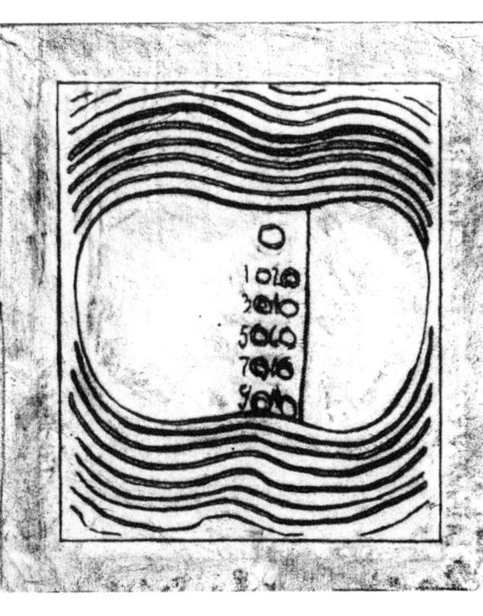

0
10%
30%
50%
70%
90%

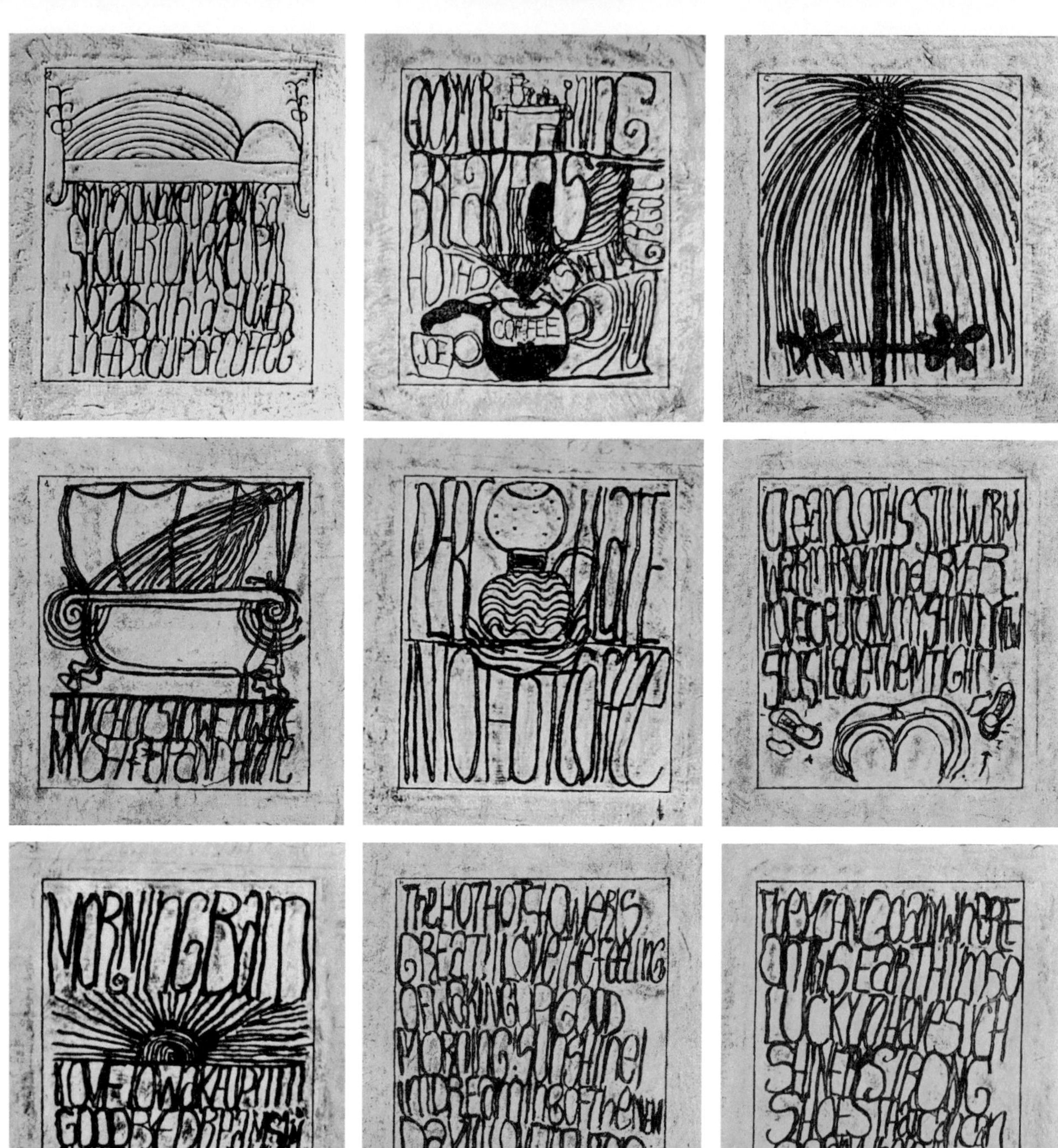

2009.12 Untitled (Learning from That Person's Work), 306 × 267 cm (9 parts)

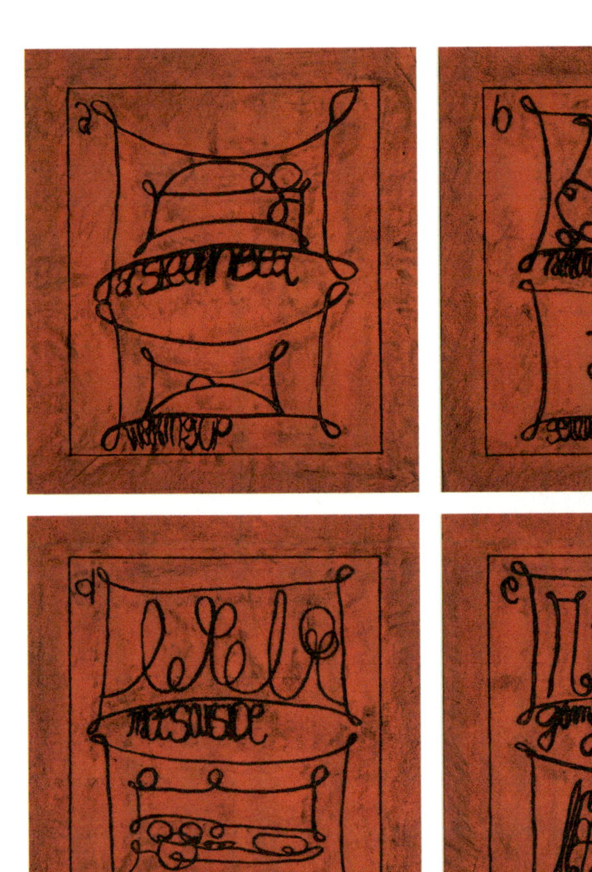
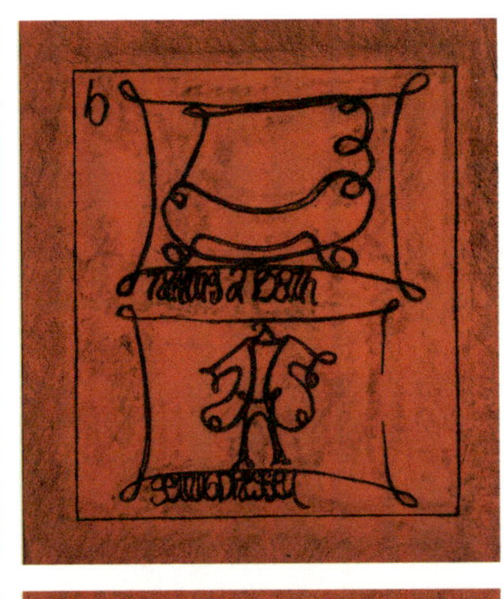
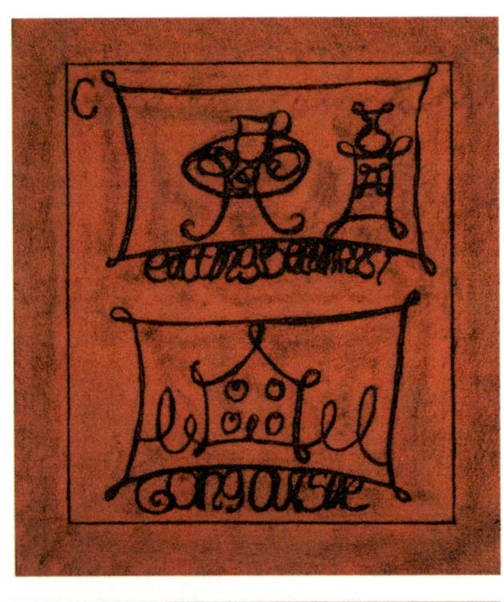
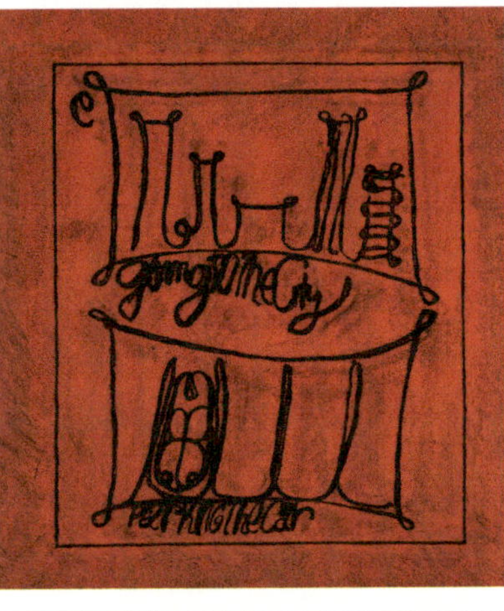
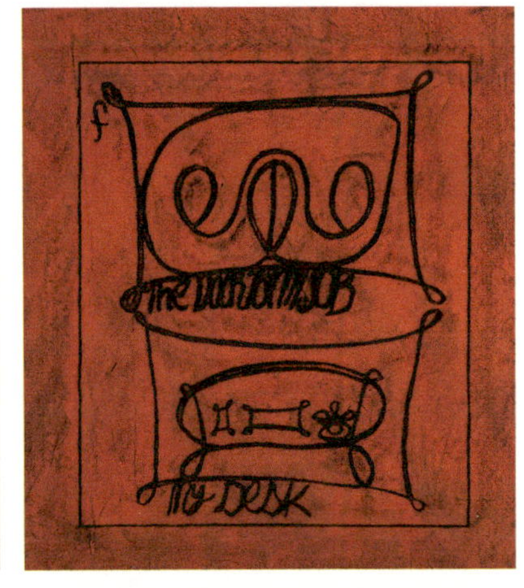
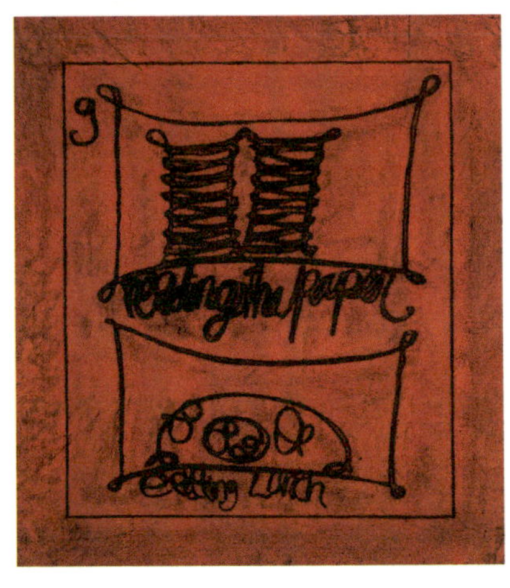
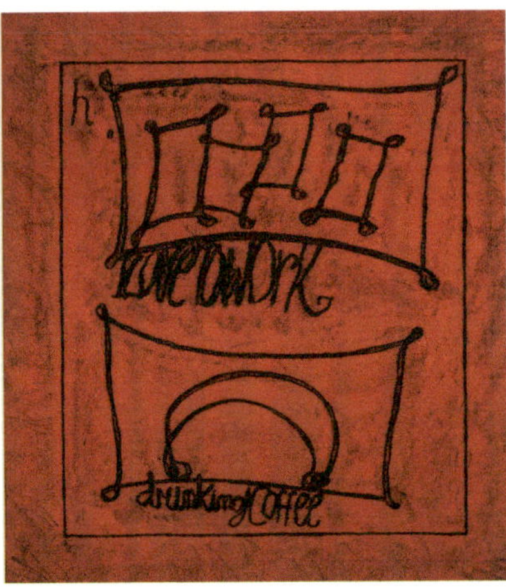
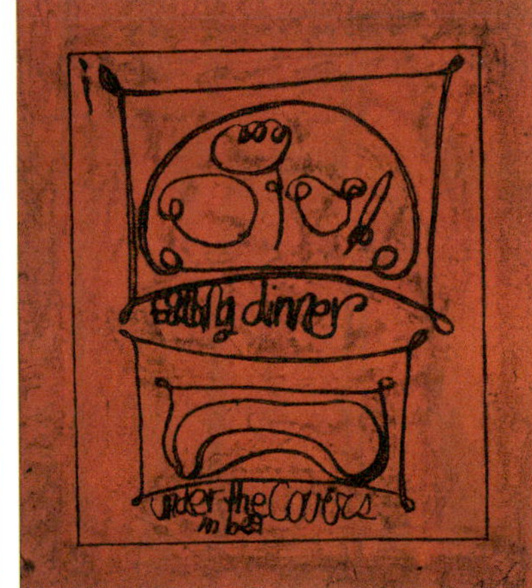

2009.13 Untitled (*Learning from That Person's Work*), 306 × 267 cm (9 parts)

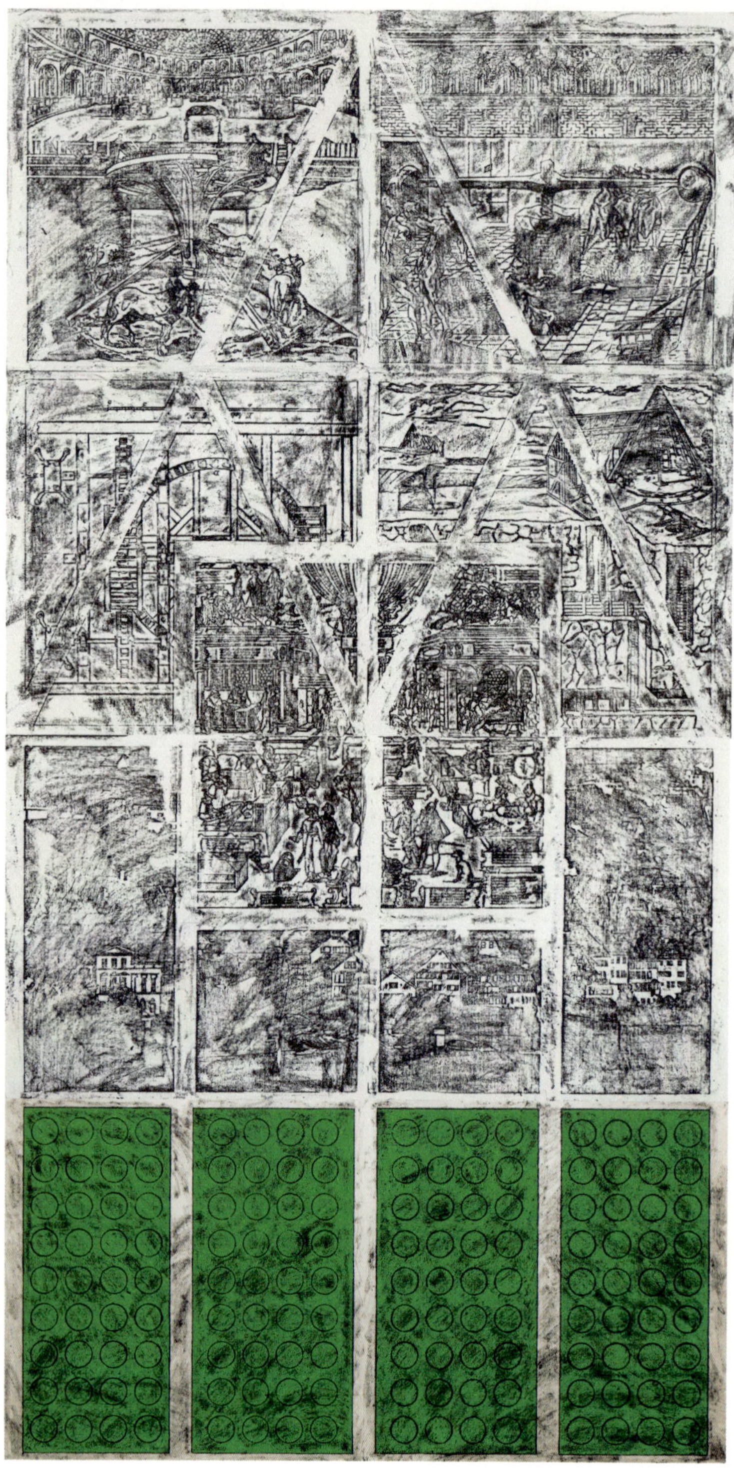

2009.14 Untitled (City Chart), 1996/2009, 600 × 298 cm (4 parts)

2010

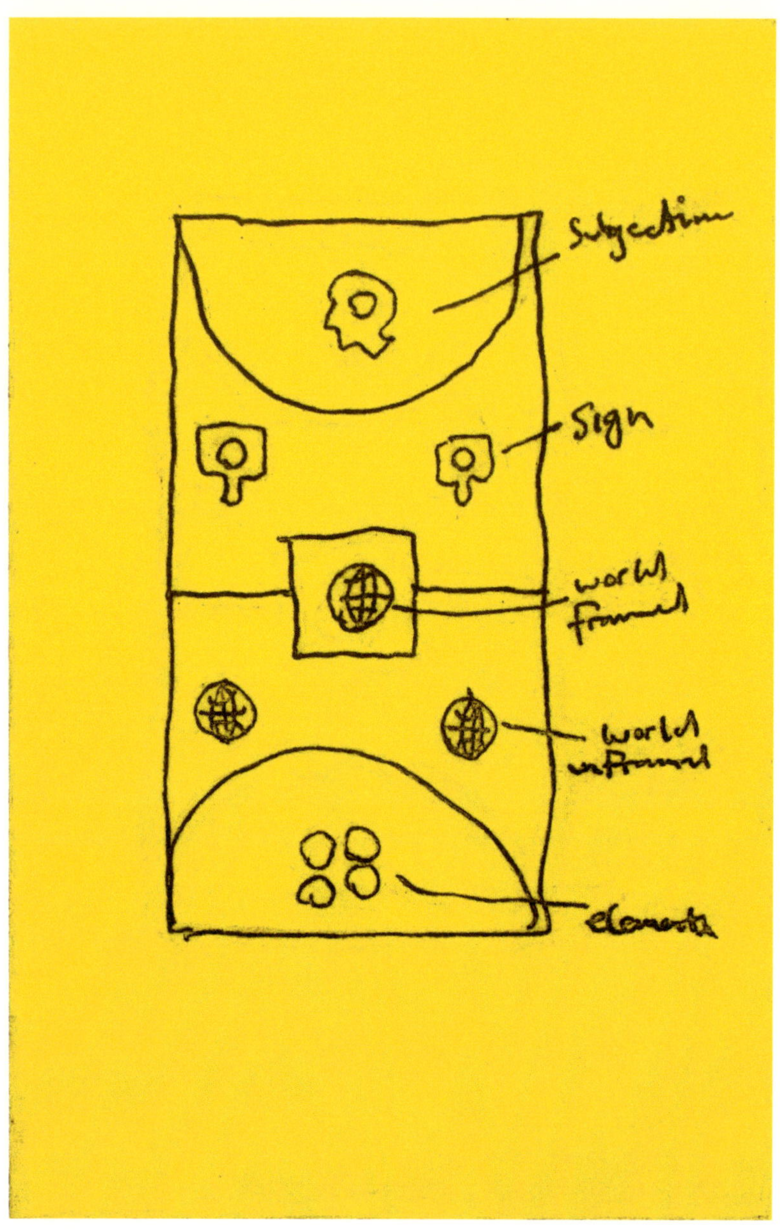

2010.1 Untitled (Notating the Cosmology 1), 169 × 107 cm

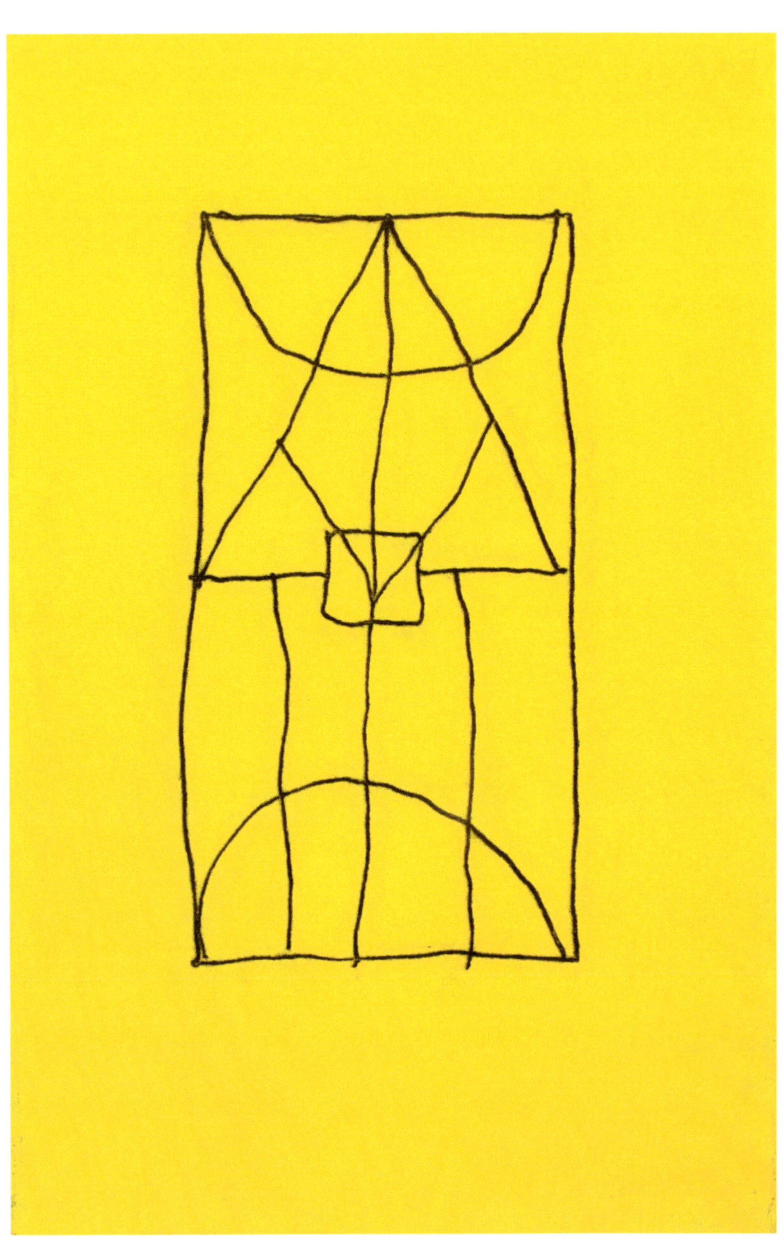

2010.2 Untitled (Notating the Cosmology 2), 169 × 107 cm

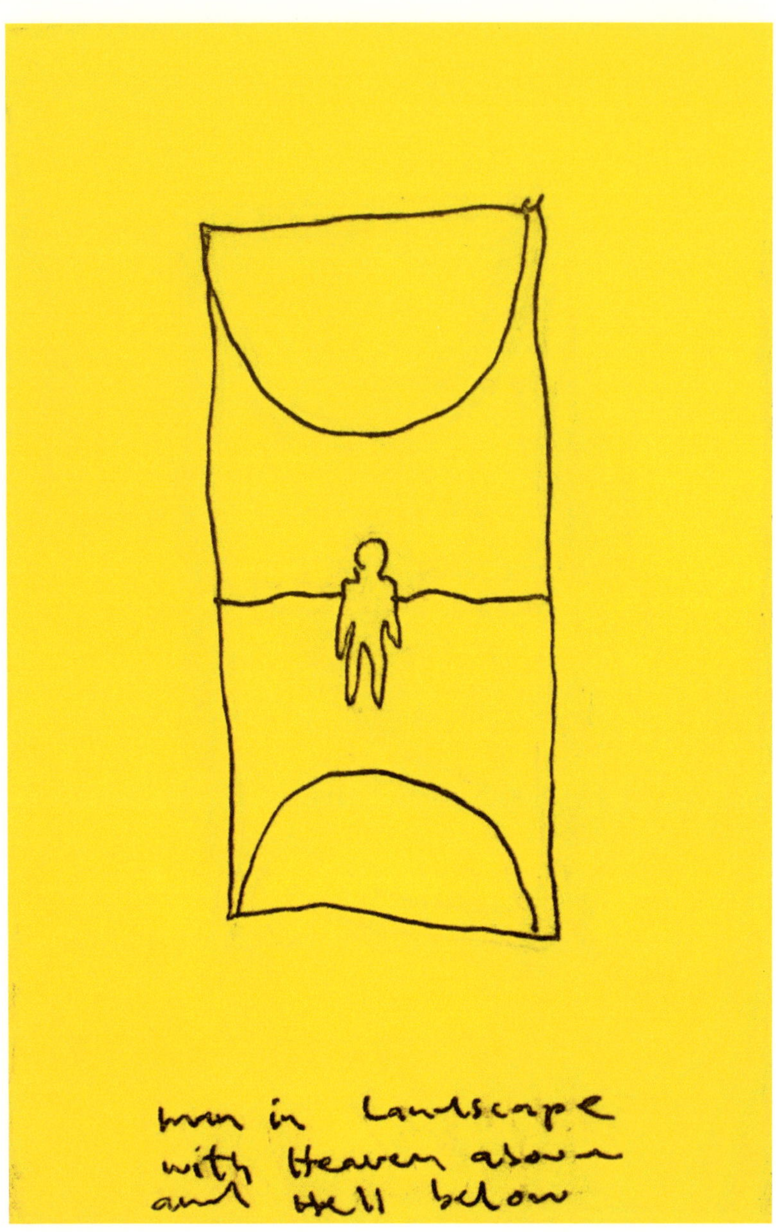

2010.3 Untitled (Notating the Cosmology 3), 169 × 107 cm

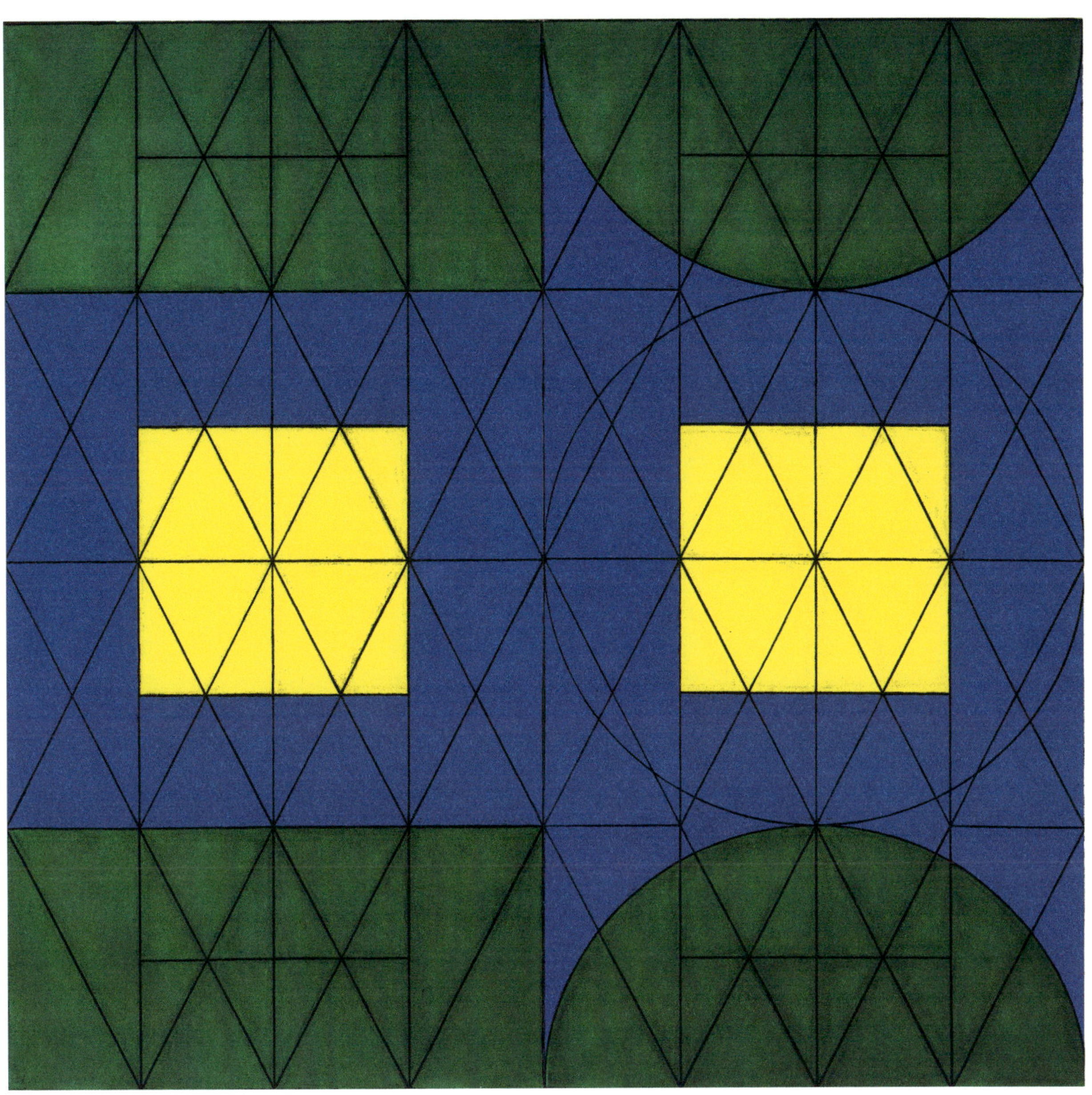

2010.4 Untitled (Overall Chart: Frame Centered Elements), 244 × 244 cm (2 parts)

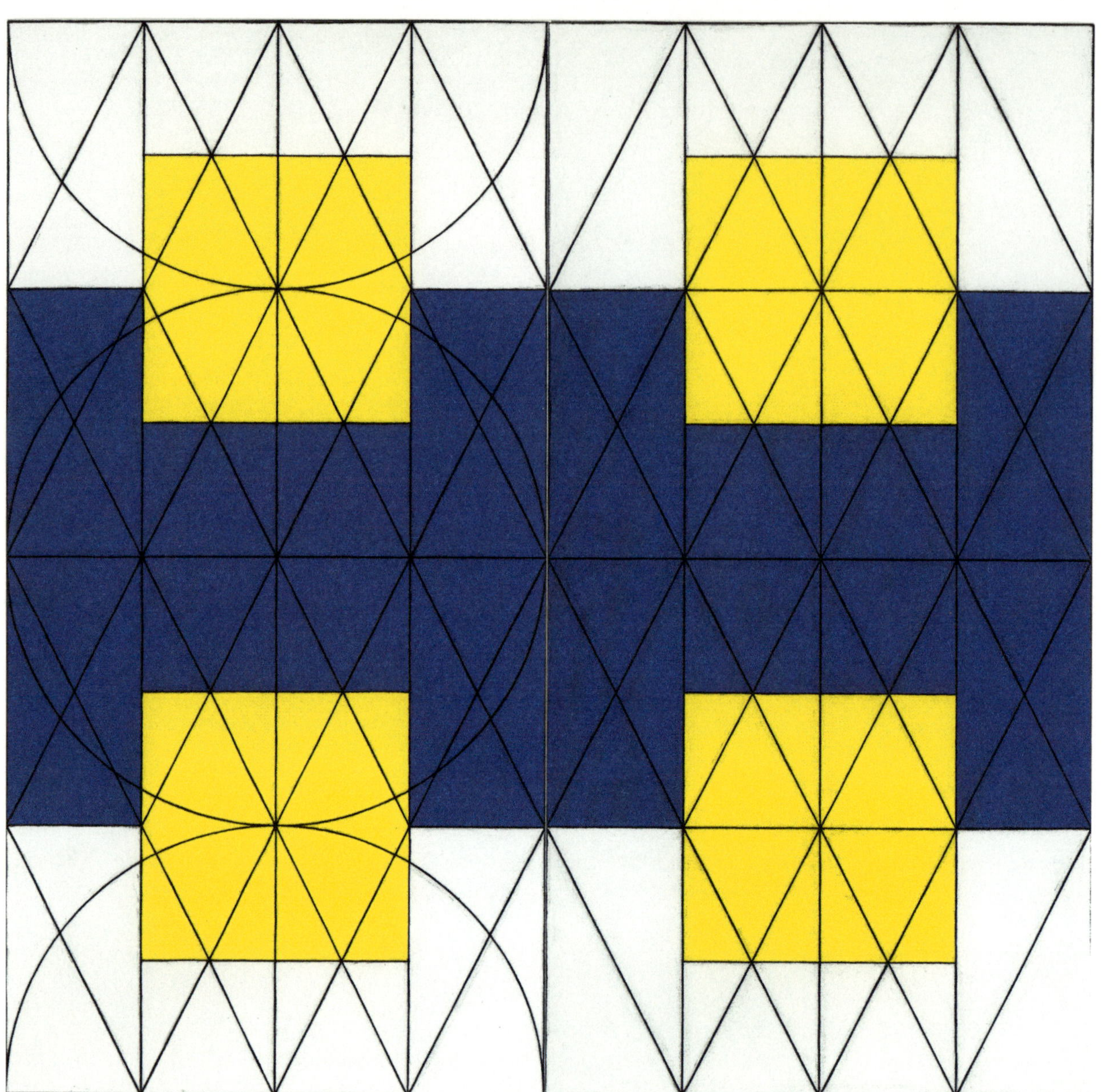

2010.5 Untitled (World Unframed Centered), 244 × 244 cm (2 parts)

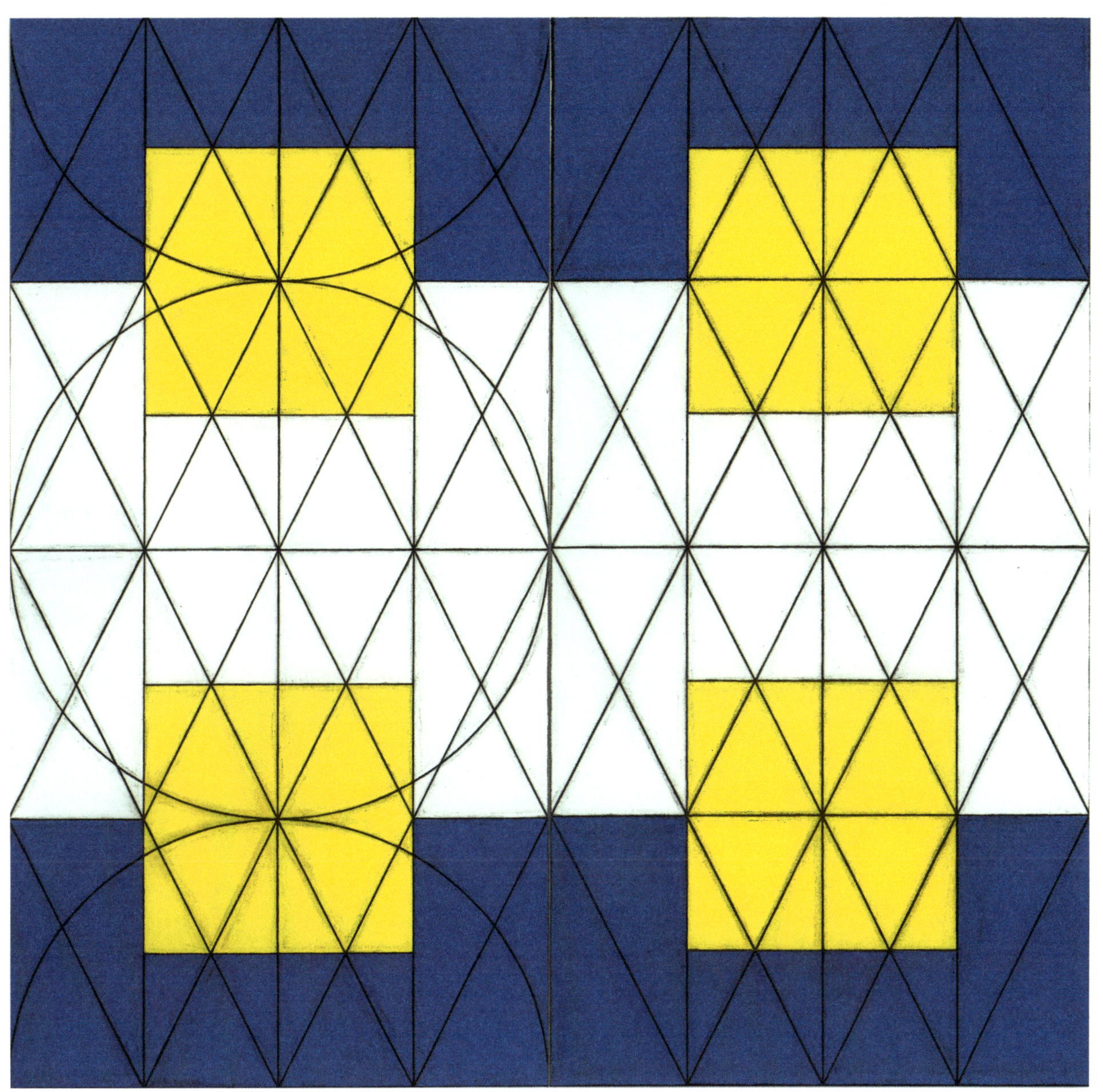

2010.6 Untitled (Centered Language), 244 × 244 cm (2 parts)

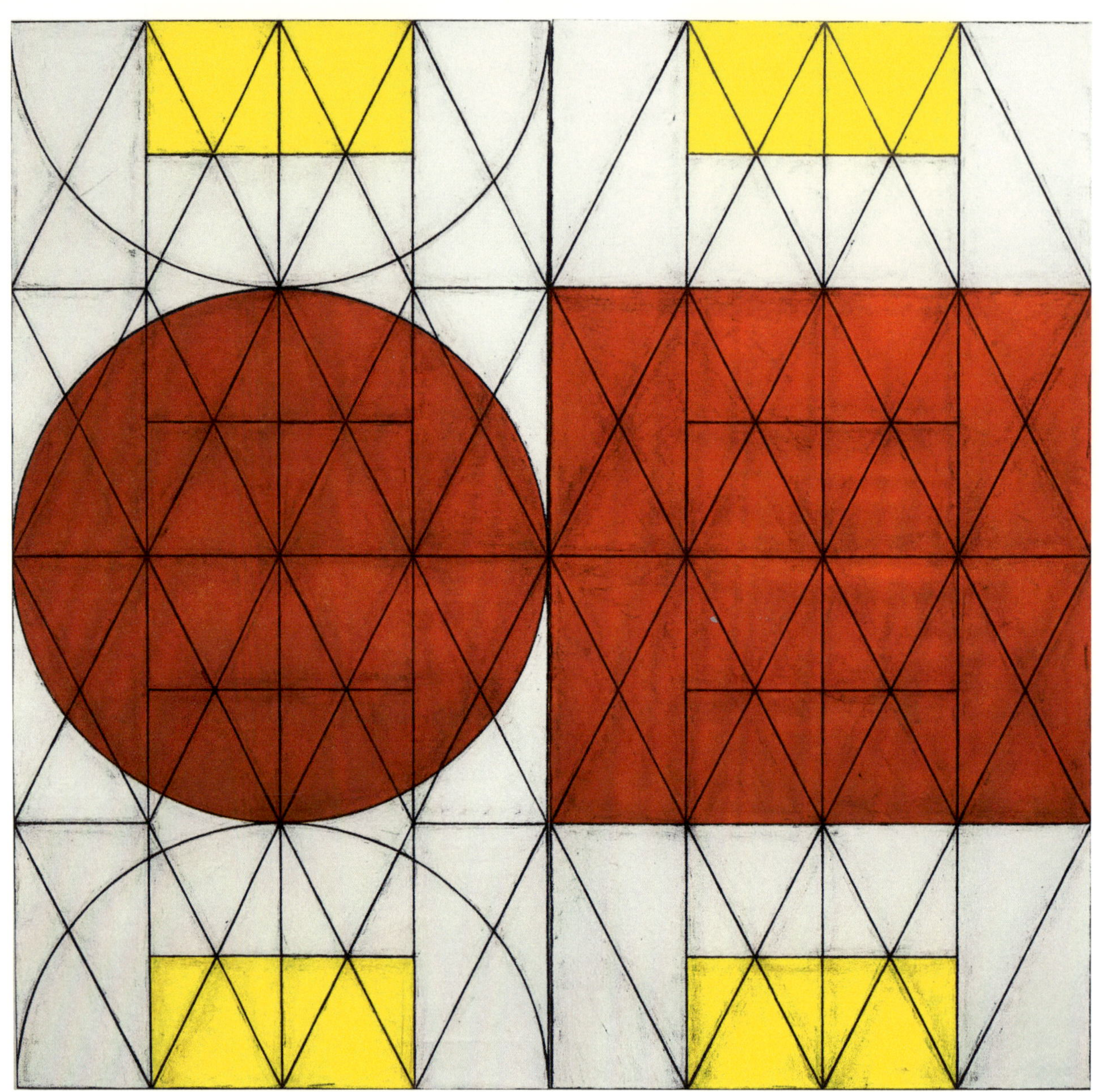

2010.7 Untitled (Subjective Centered), 244×244 cm (2 parts)

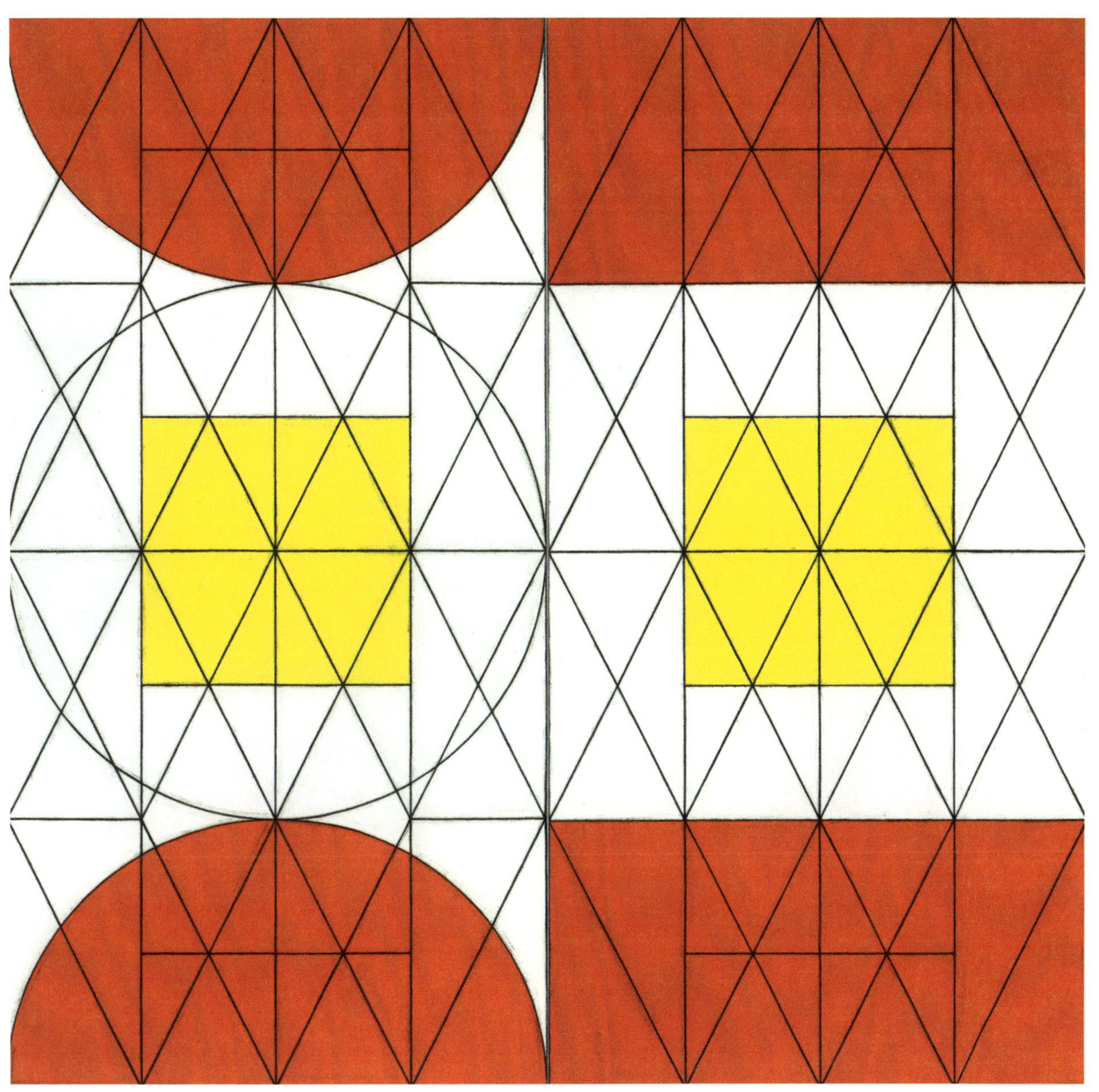

2010.8 Untitled (Centered on the Arts with Subjective), 244 × 244 cm (2 parts)

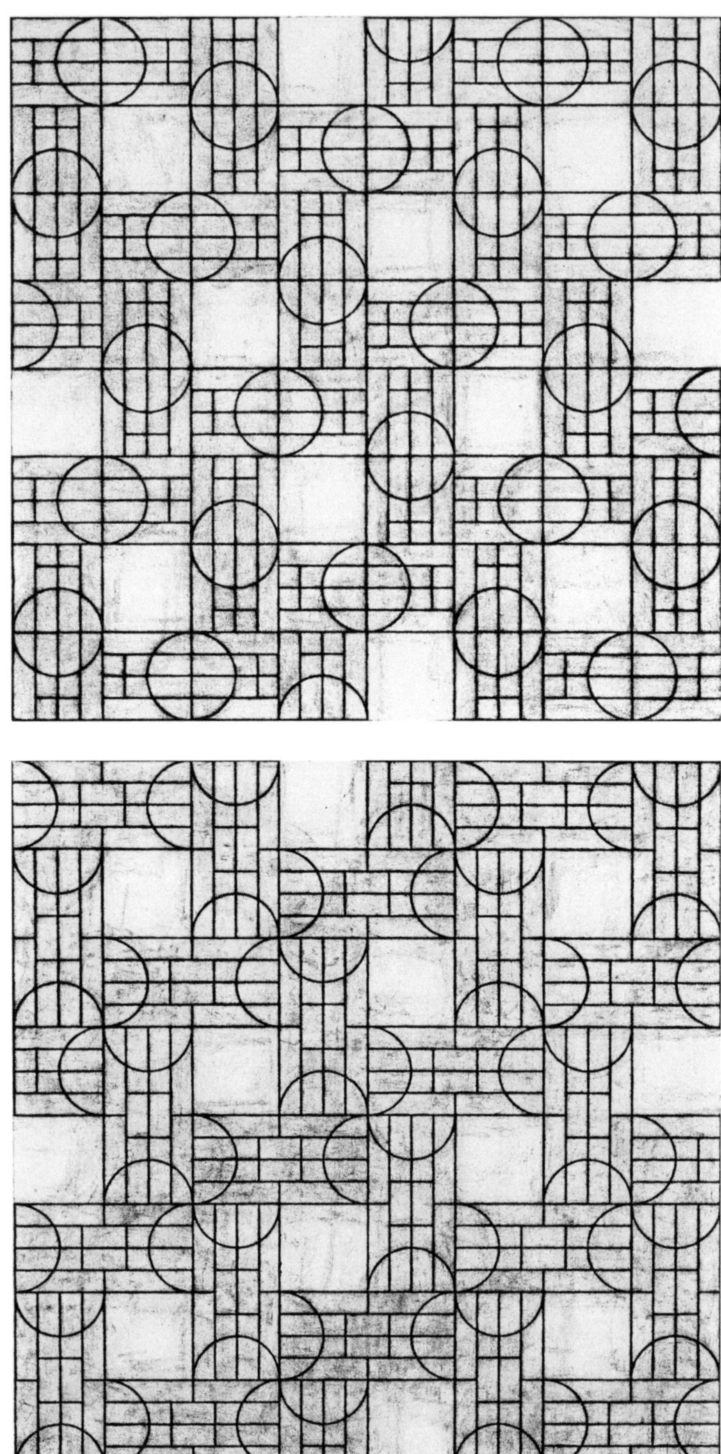

2010.9 Untitled (Field of Cities: Elemental Center), 122 × 122 cm
2010.10 Untitled (Field of Cities: World Framed Center Surrounded by Elements), 122 × 122 cm

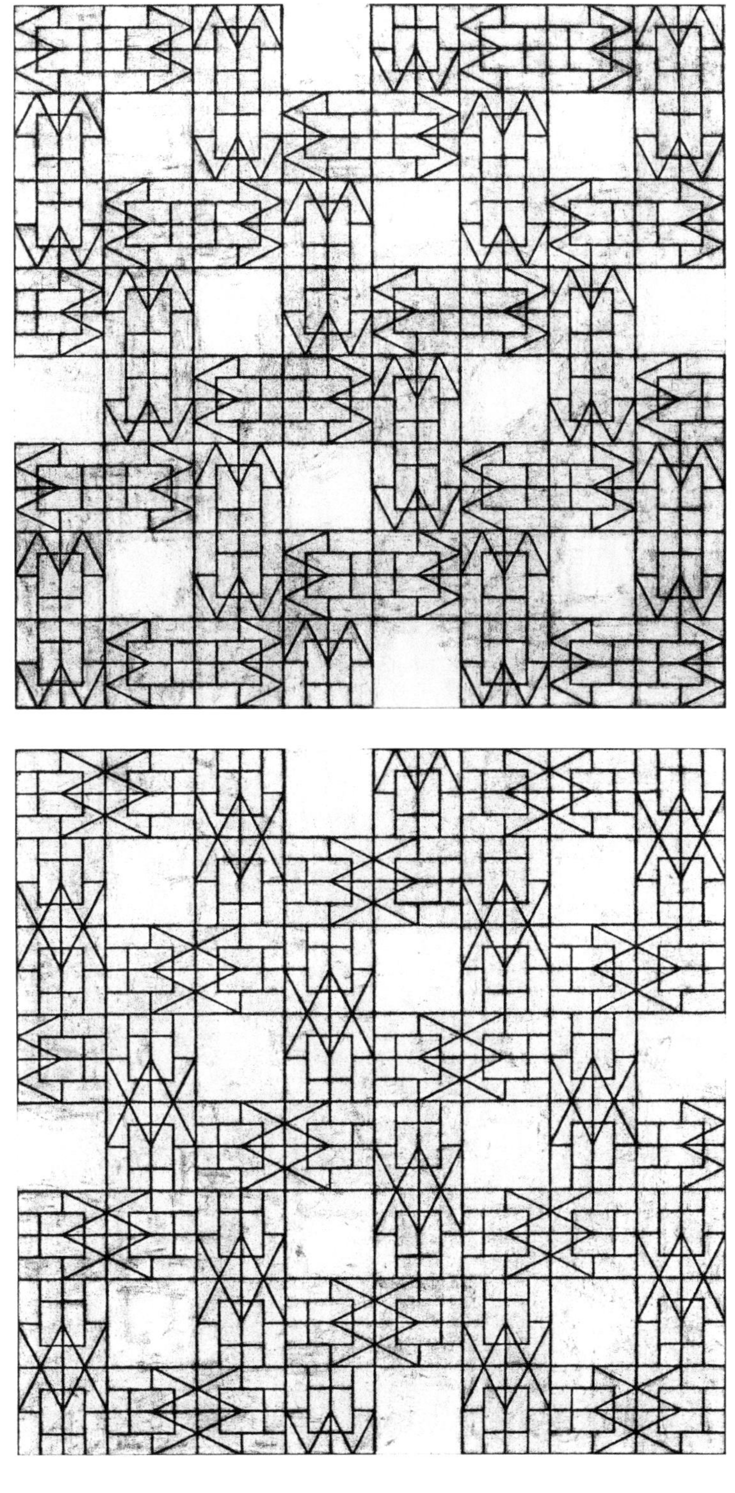

2010.11 Untitled (Field of Cities: World Unframed Center), 122 × 122 cm
2010.12 Untitled (Field of Cities: Language Center), 122 × 122 cm

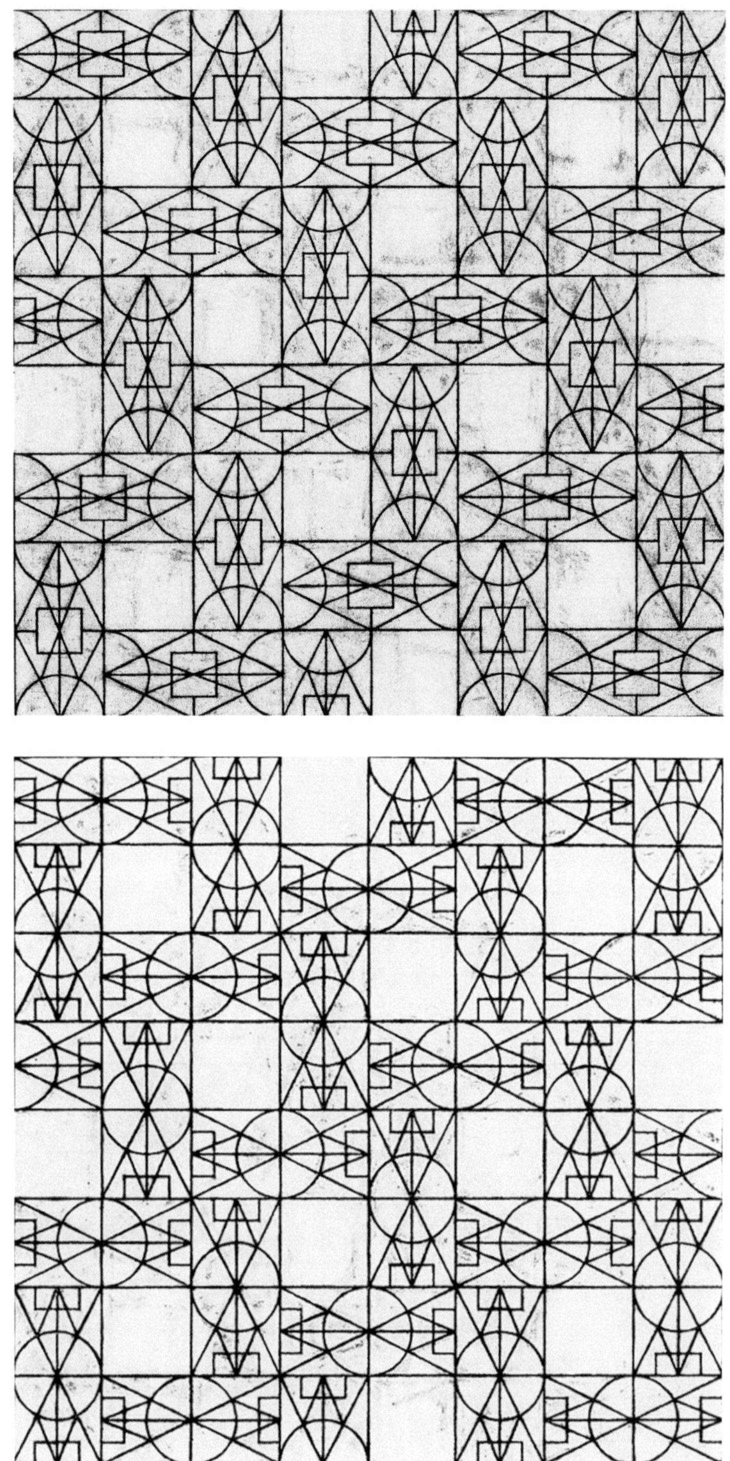

2010.13 Untitled (Field of Cities: World Framed Center Surrounded by Subjective), 122 × 122 cm
2010.14 Untitled (Field of Cities: Subjective Center), 122 × 122 cm

2011

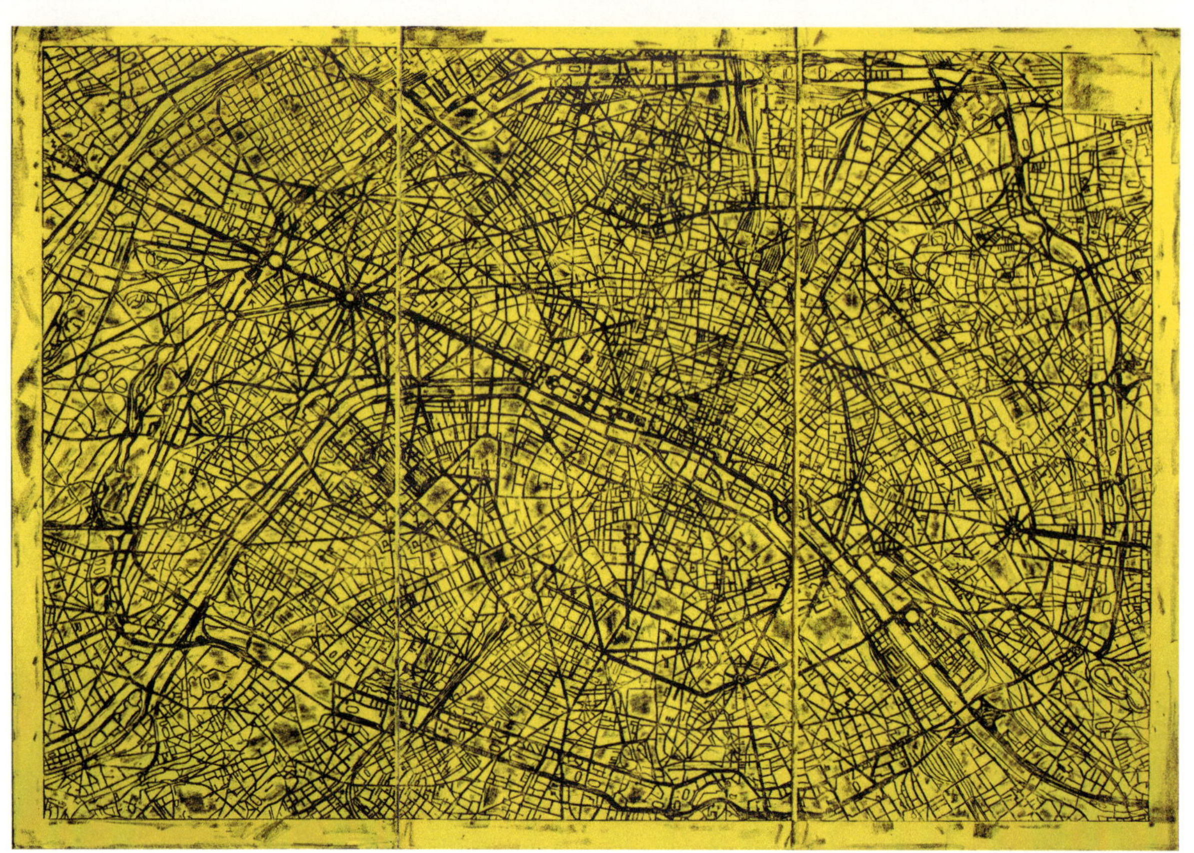

2011.1 Untitled (Paris Street Map I), 305 × 399 cm (3 parts)

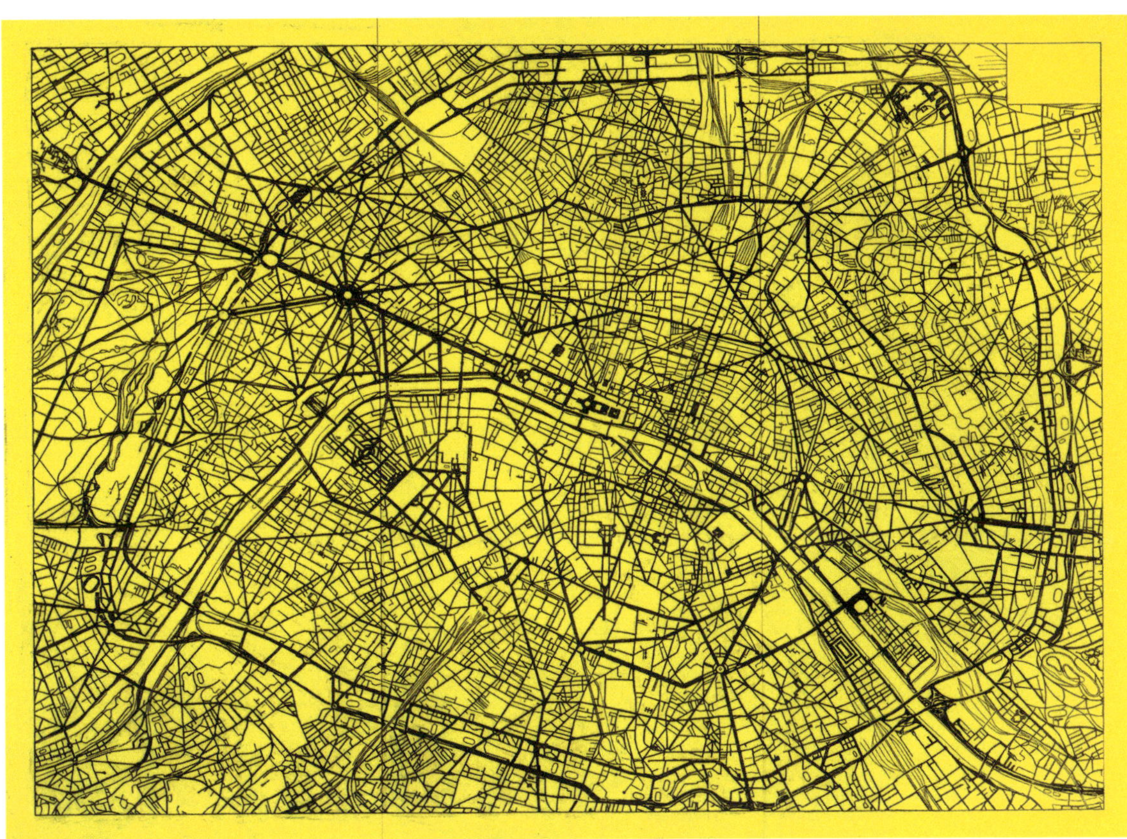

2011.2 Untitled (Paris Street Map II), 305 × 399 cm (3 parts)

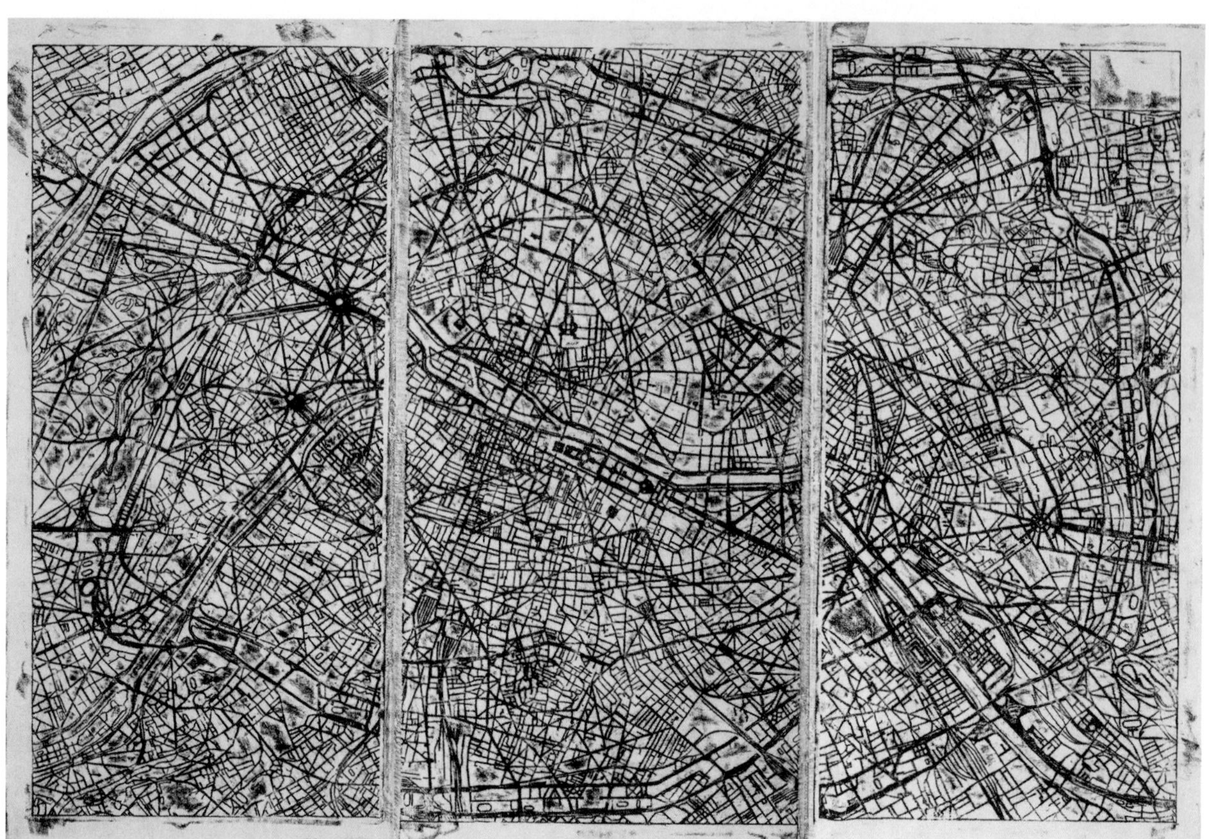

2011.3 Untitled (Paris Street Map), 305 × 399 cm (3 parts)

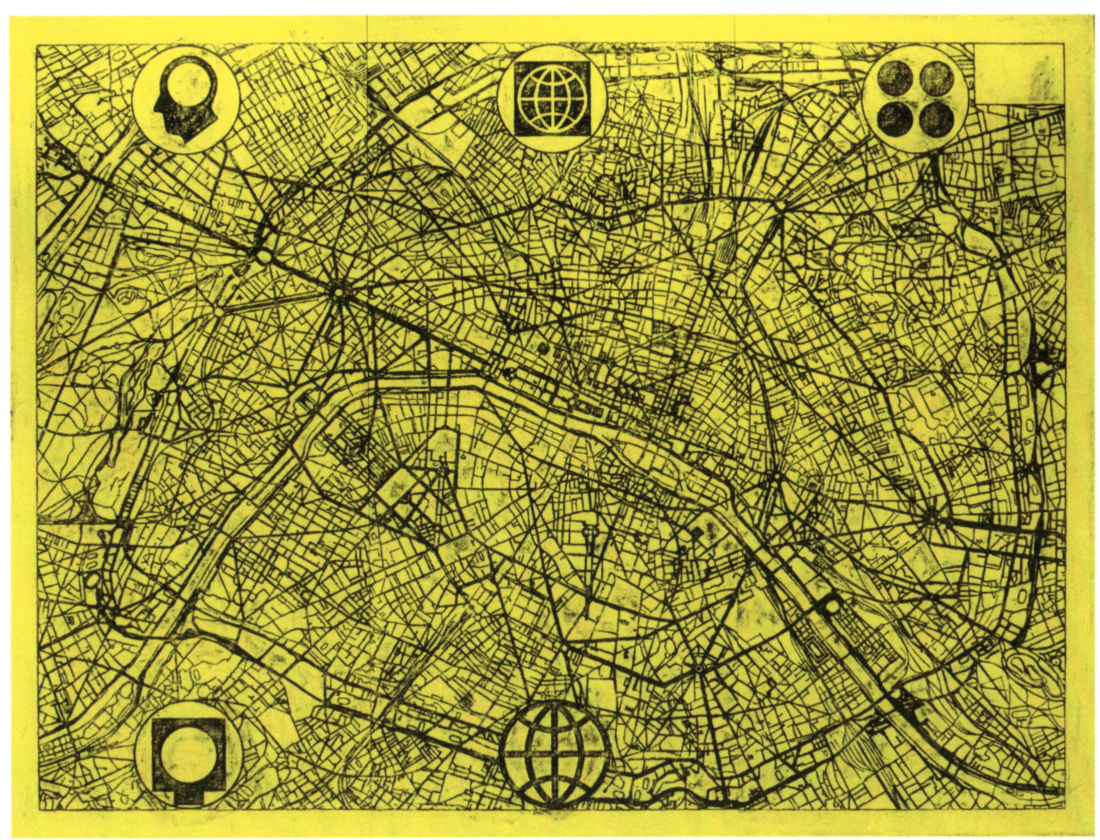

2011.4 Untitled (Paris Street Map with Symbols), 305 × 399 cm (3 parts)

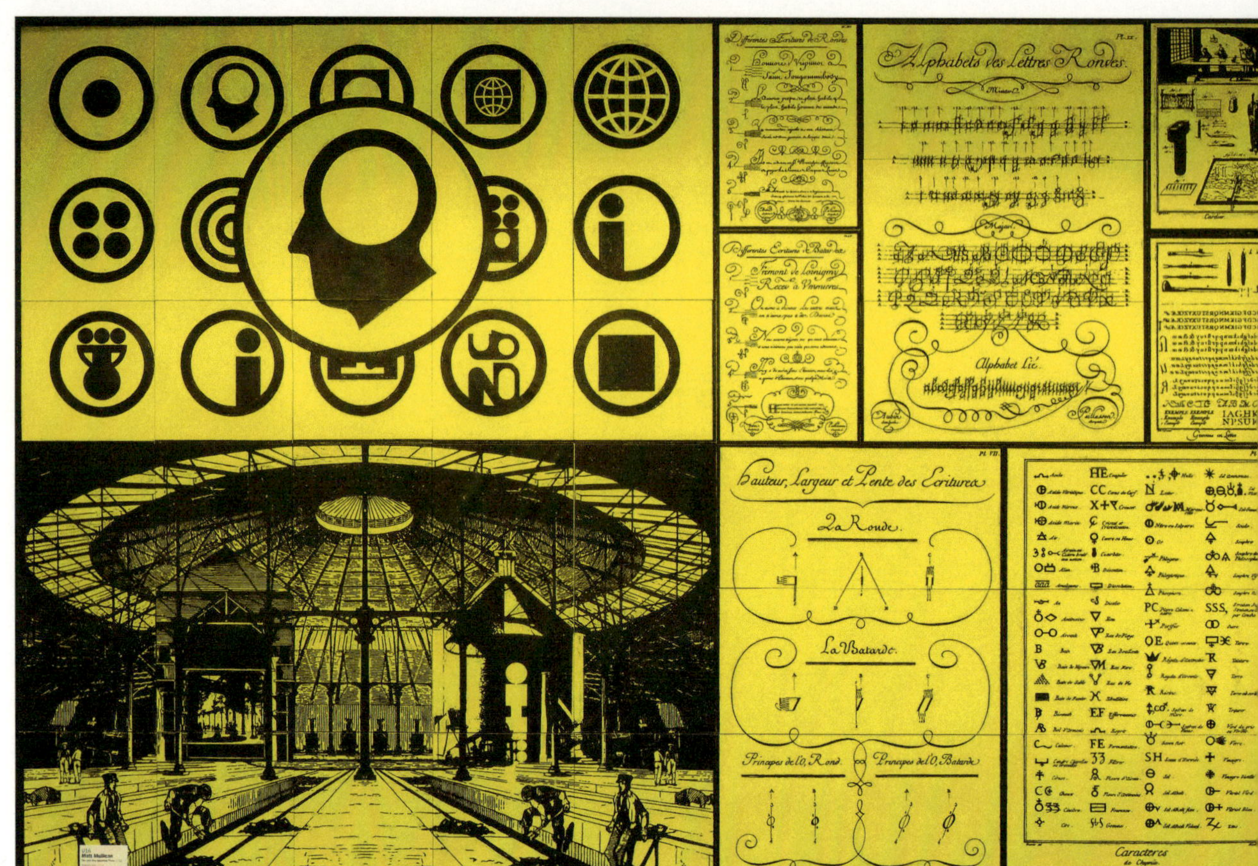

2011.5 Untitled (Two into One Becomes Three), 731.5×2196 cm (70 parts)

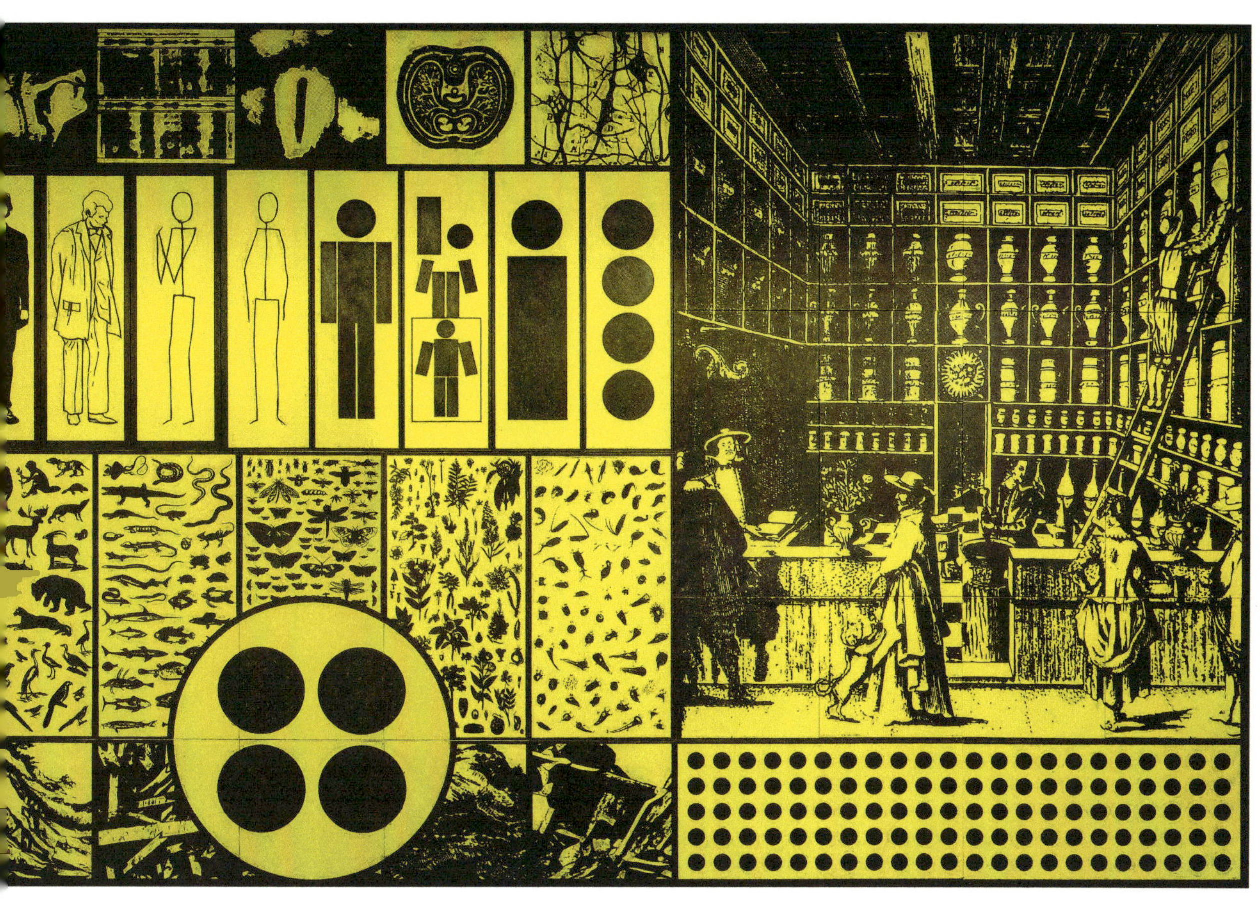

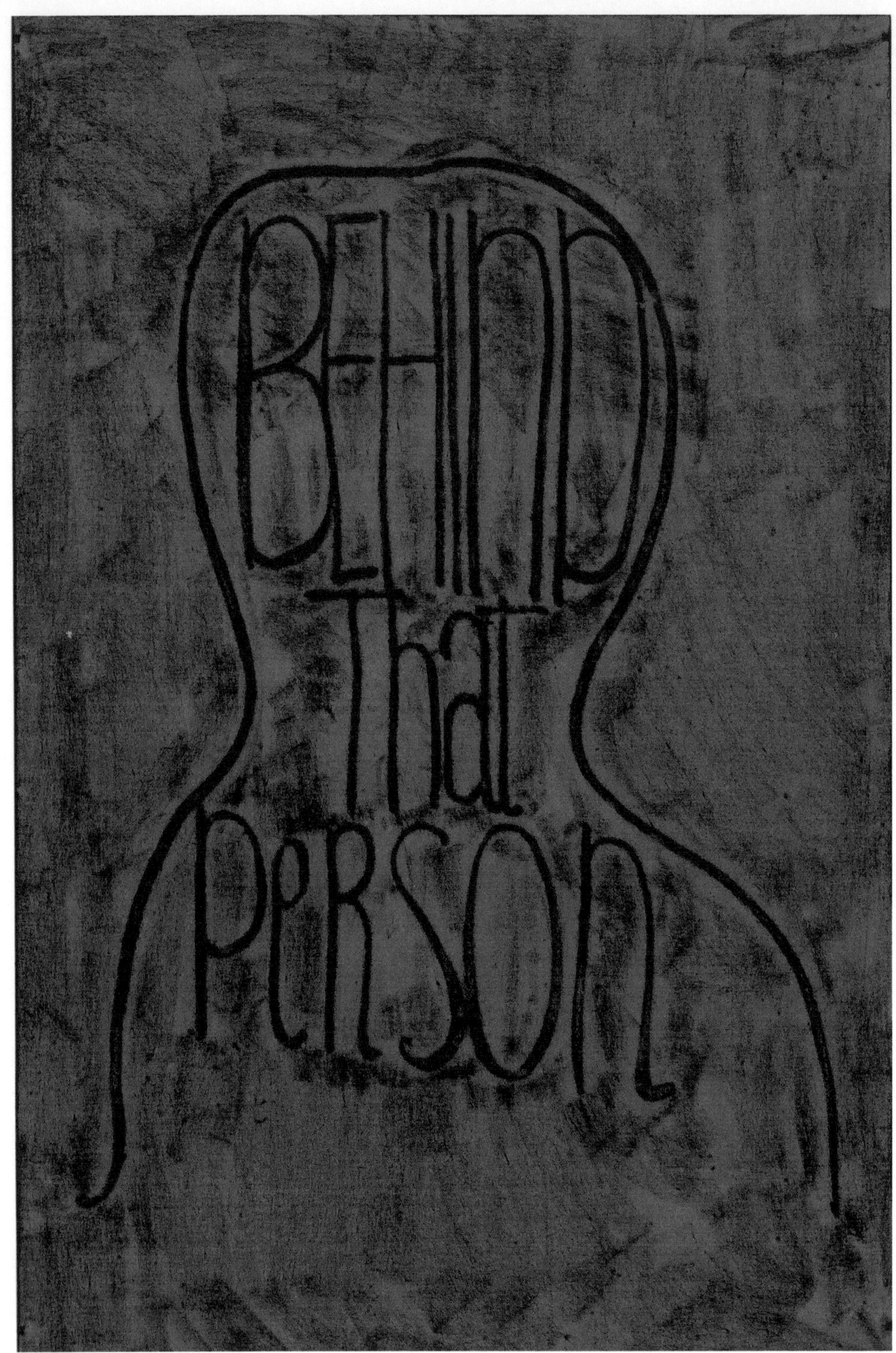

2011.6 Untitled (Behind That Person), 191 × 125 cm

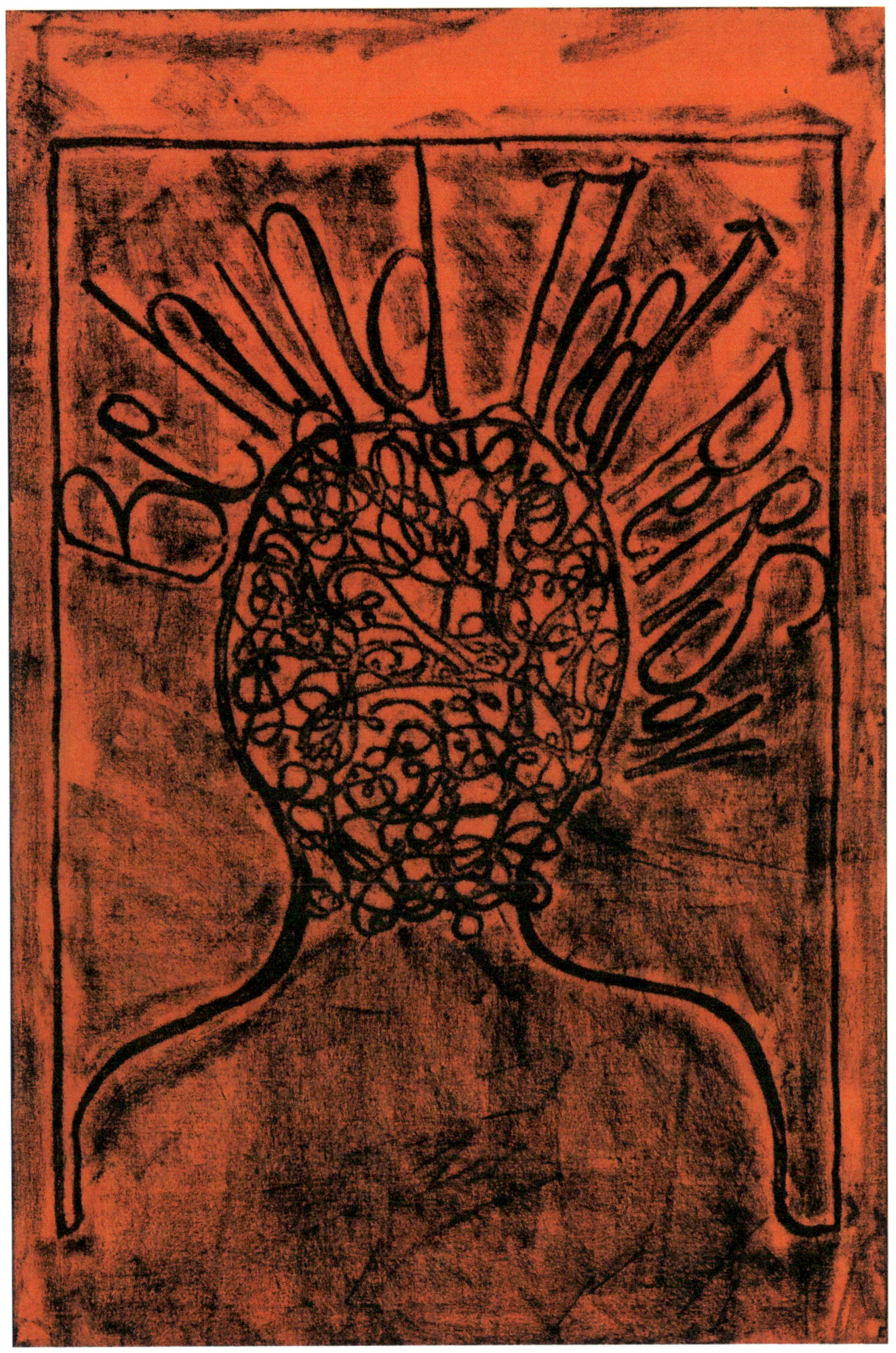

2011.7 Untitled (Behind That Person), 191 × 125 cm

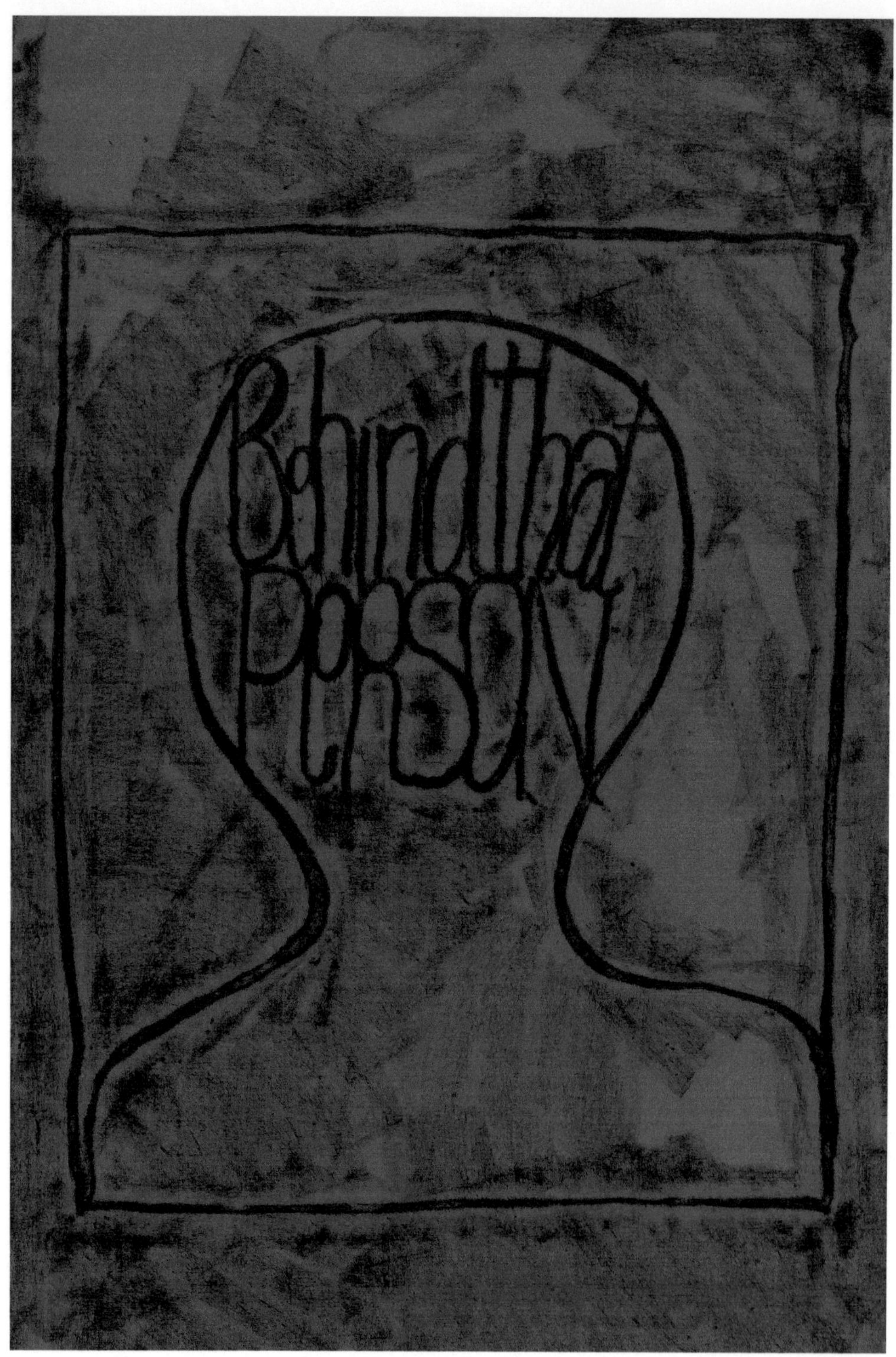

2011.8 Untitled (Behind That Person), 191 × 125 cm

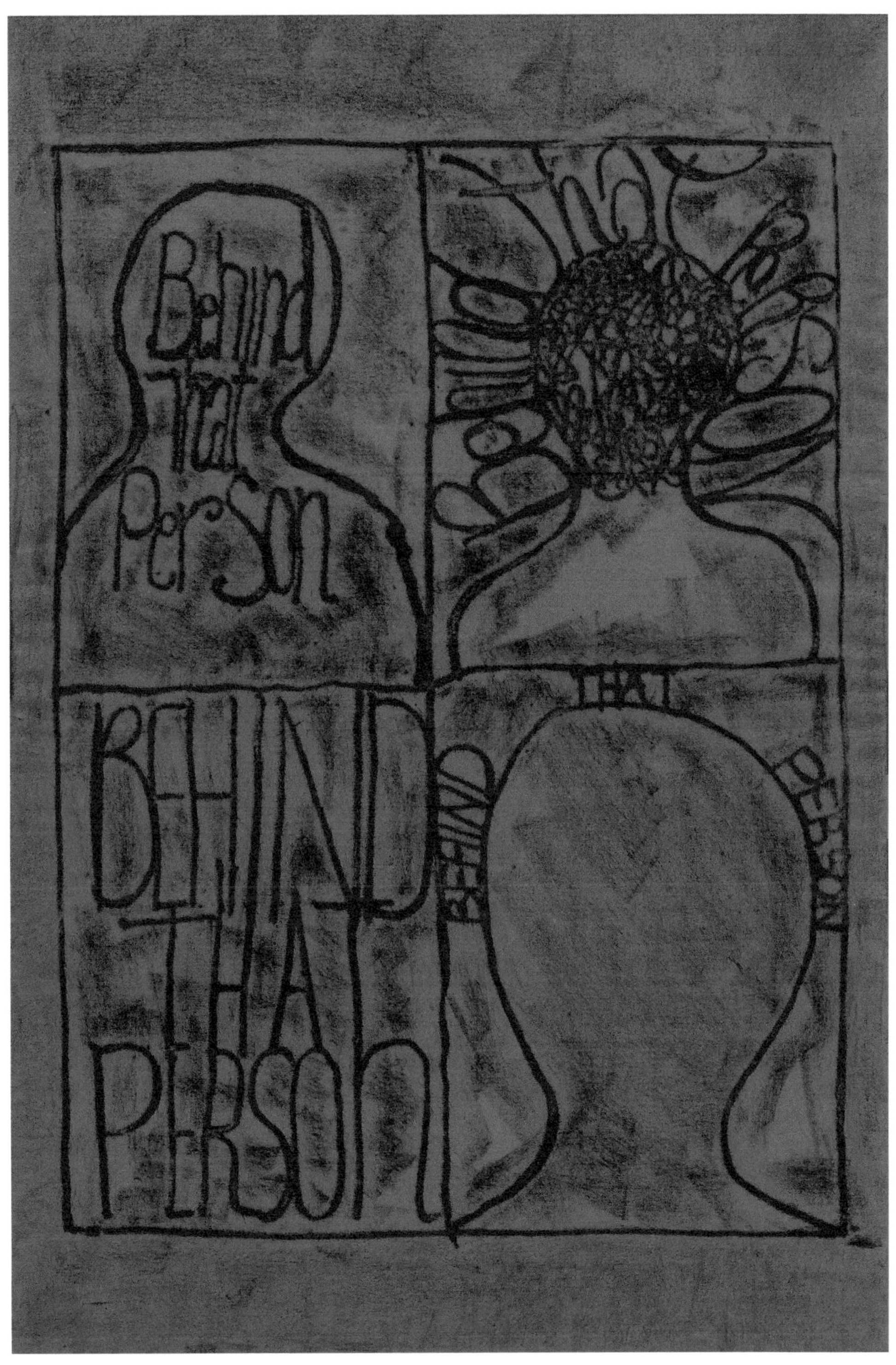

2011.9 Untitled (Behind That Person), 191 × 125 cm

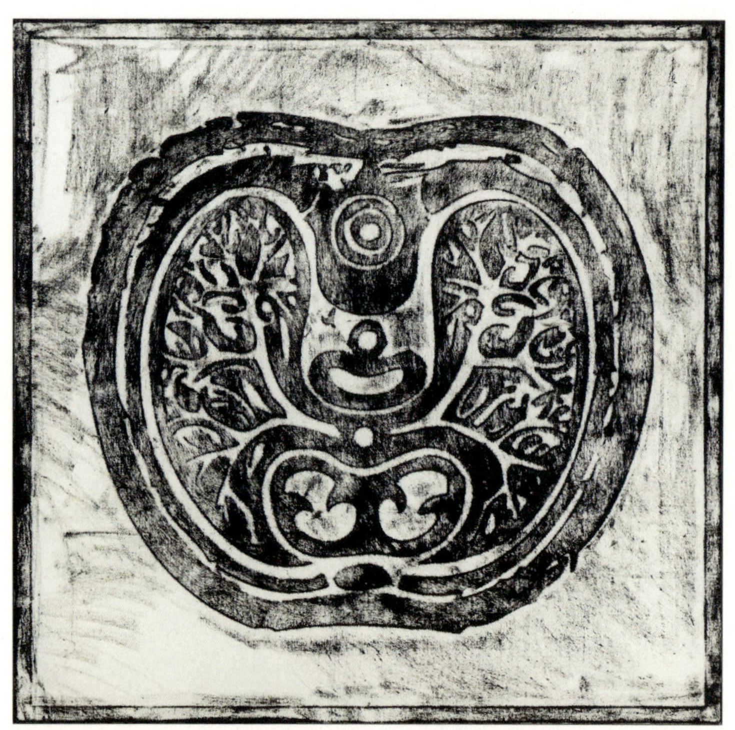

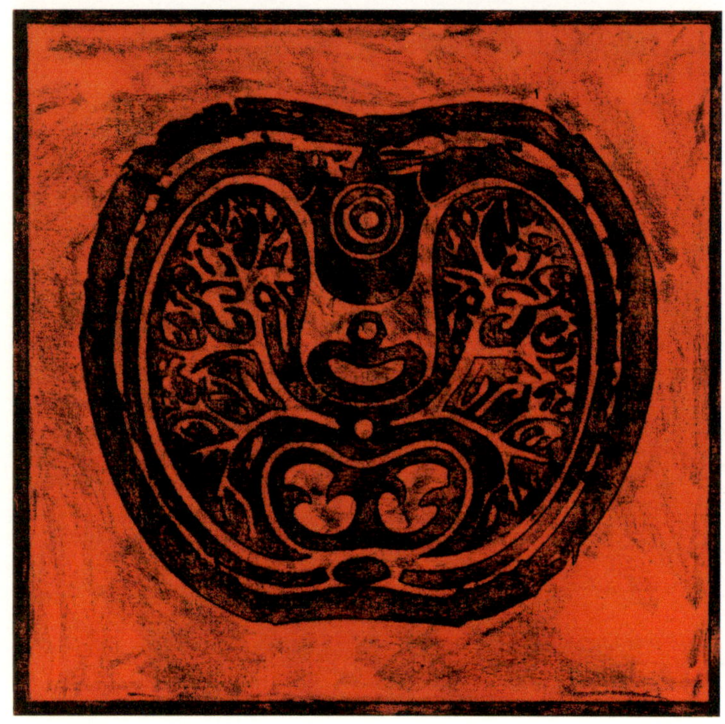

2011.10 Untitled (Brain), 122 × 122 cm
2011.11 Untitled (Brain), 122 × 122 cm

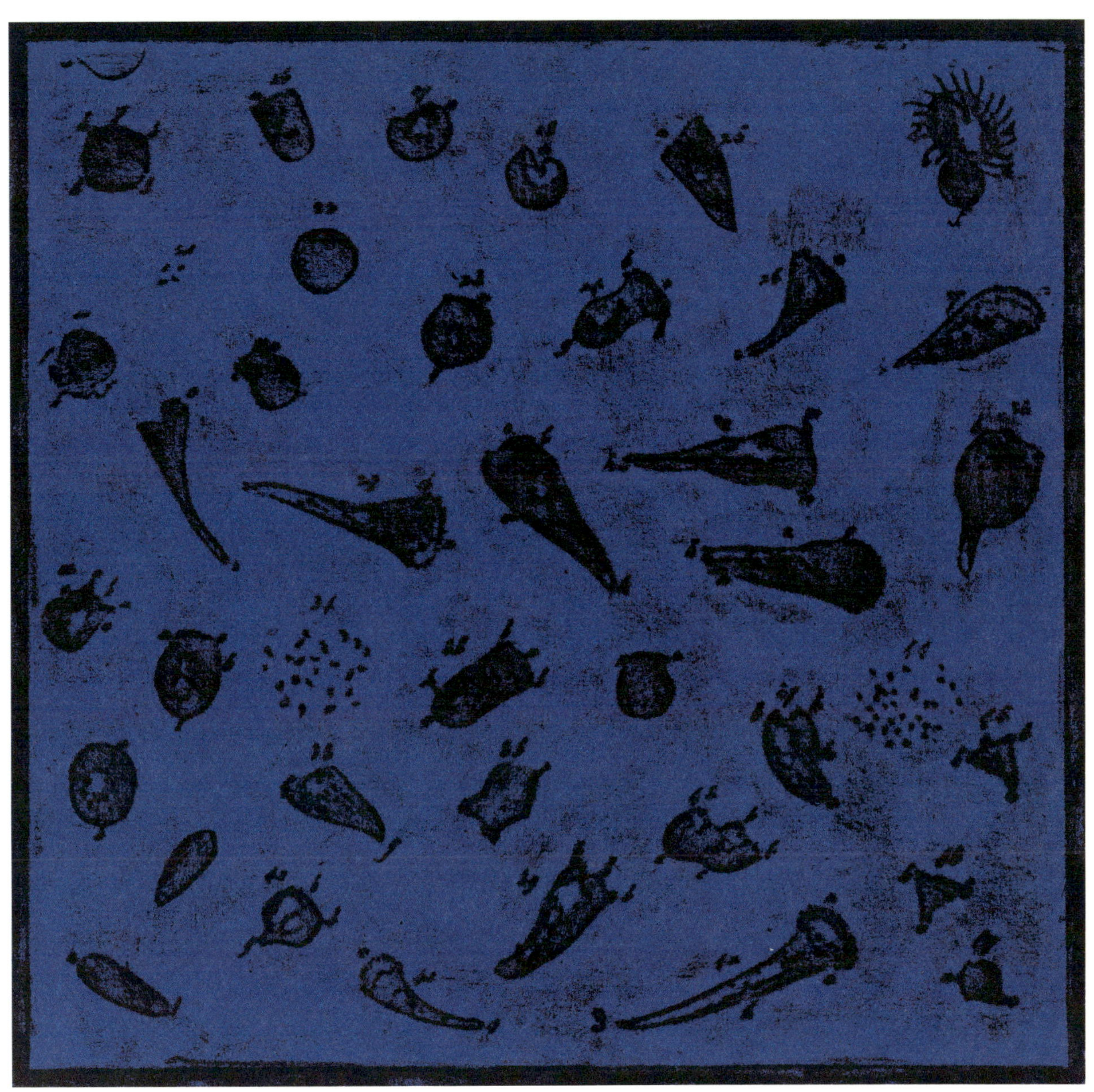

2011.12 Untitled (Simple Life Forms), 122 × 122 cm

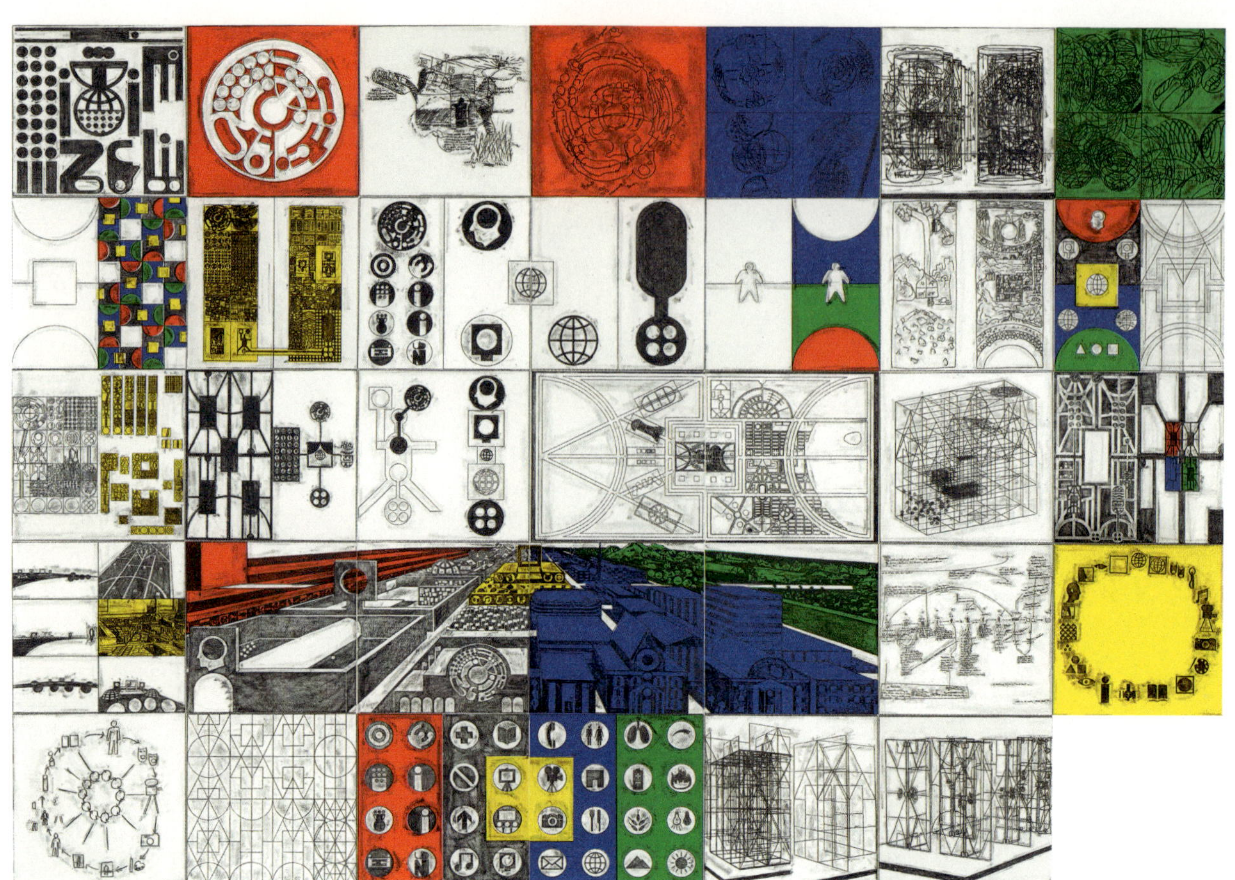

2011.13 Untitled (88 Maps Color), 62×62 cm each (34 parts)

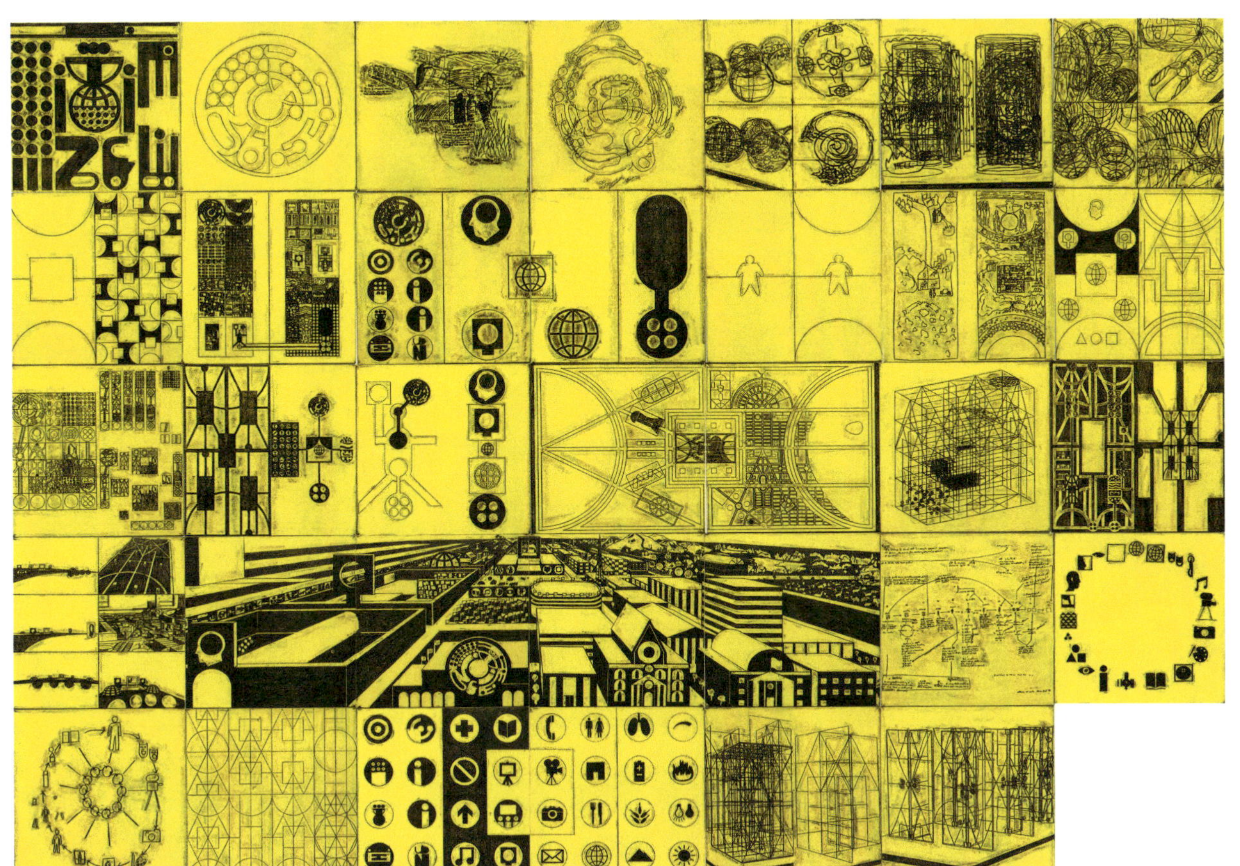

2011.14 Untitled (88 Maps Yellow), 62 × 62 each (34 parts)

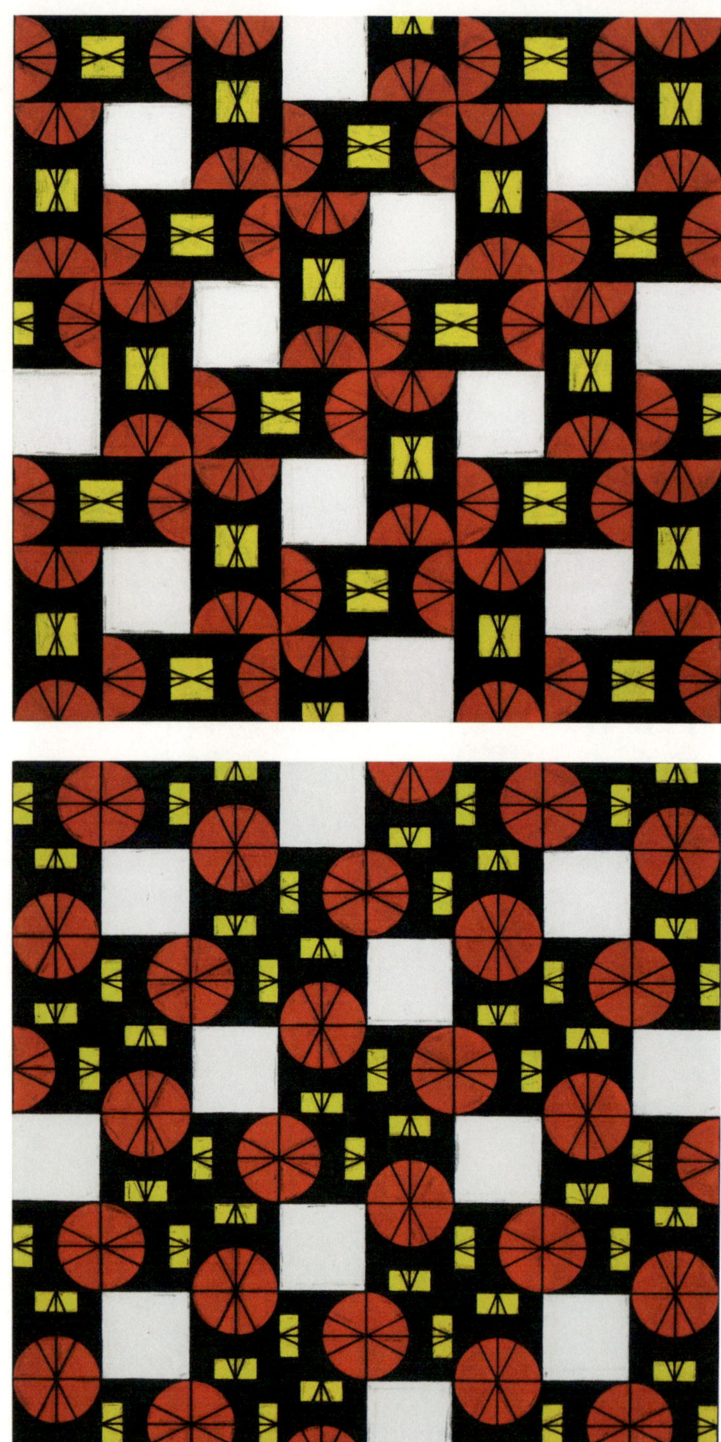

2011.15 Untitled (World Framed with Subject on the Outside), 122 × 122 cm
2011.16 Untitled (World Framed Subjective Centered), 122 × 122 cm

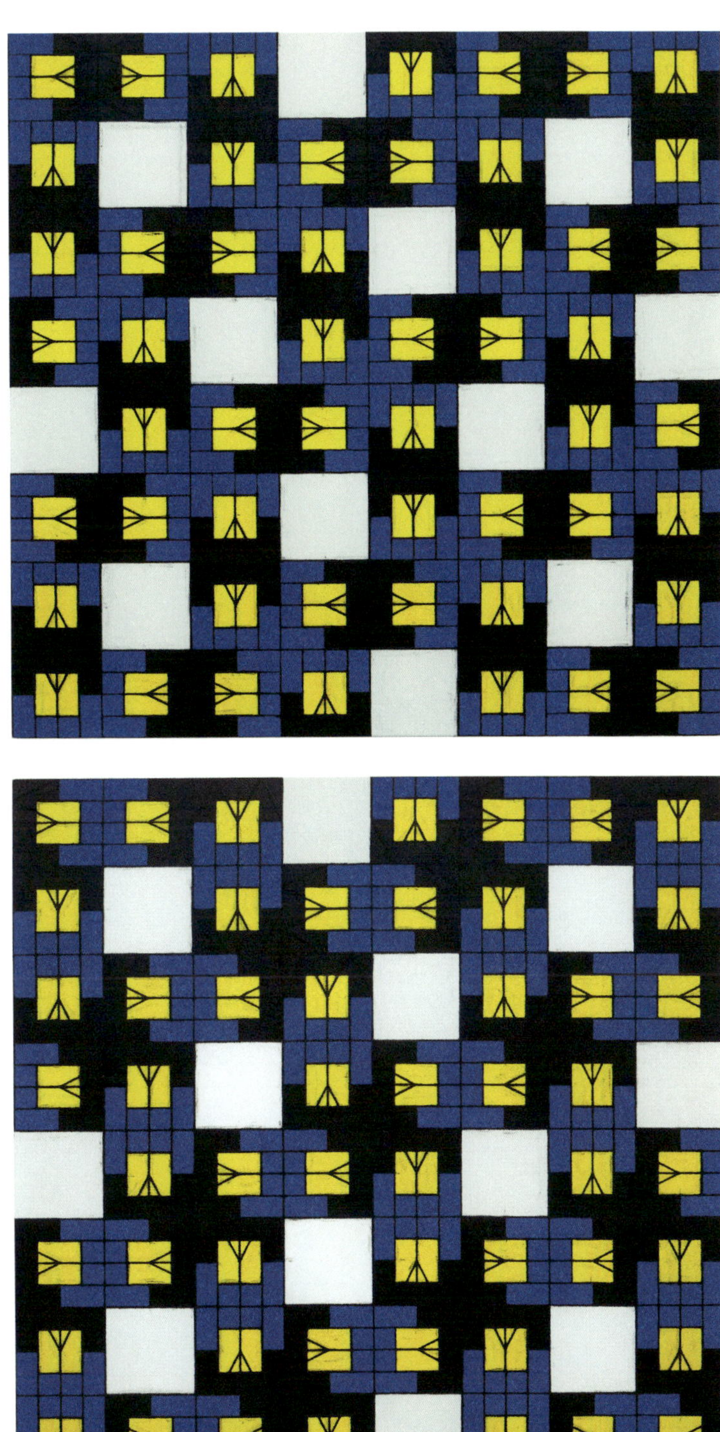

2011.17 Untitled (World Framed with Sign), 122 × 122 cm
2011.18 Untitled (World Framed), 122 × 122 cm

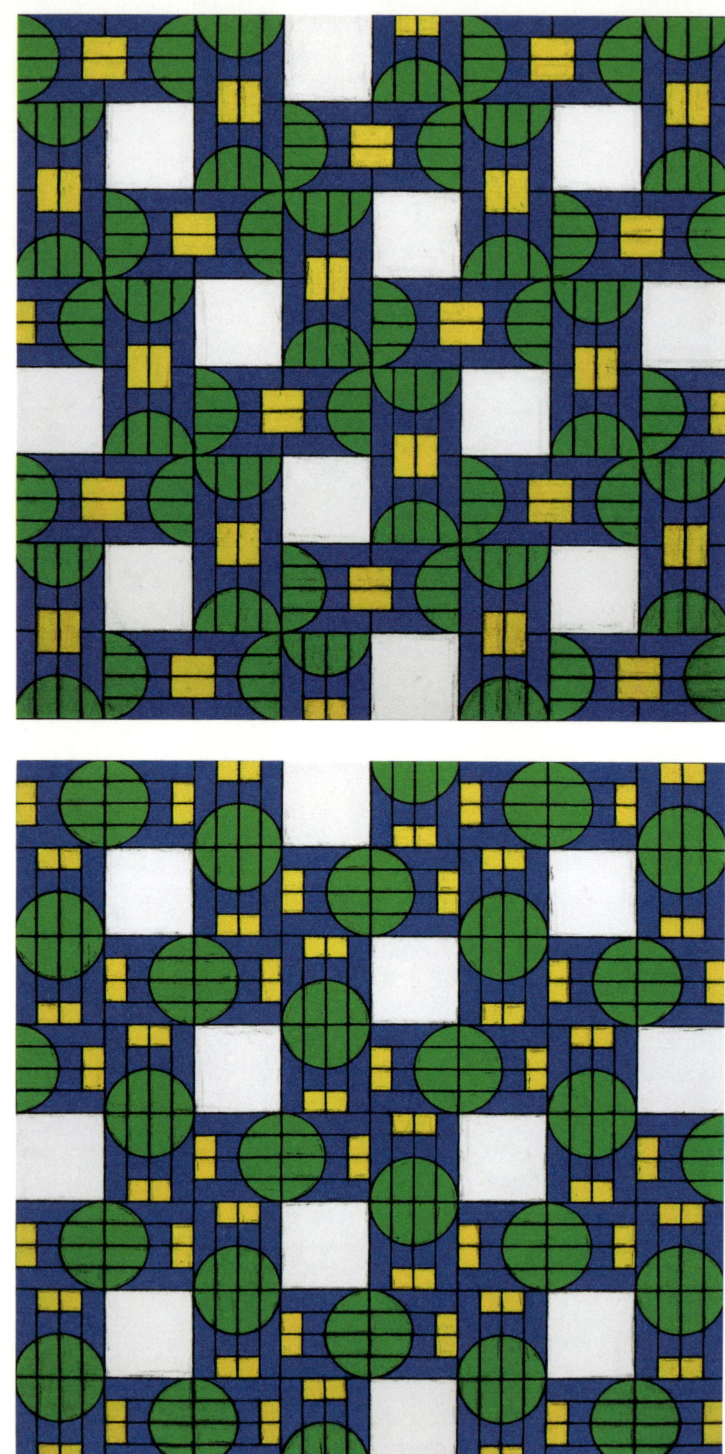

2011.19 Untitled (World Framed with Elements on the Outside), 122 × 122 cm
2011.20 Untitled (World Framed with Elements), 122 × 122 cm

2012

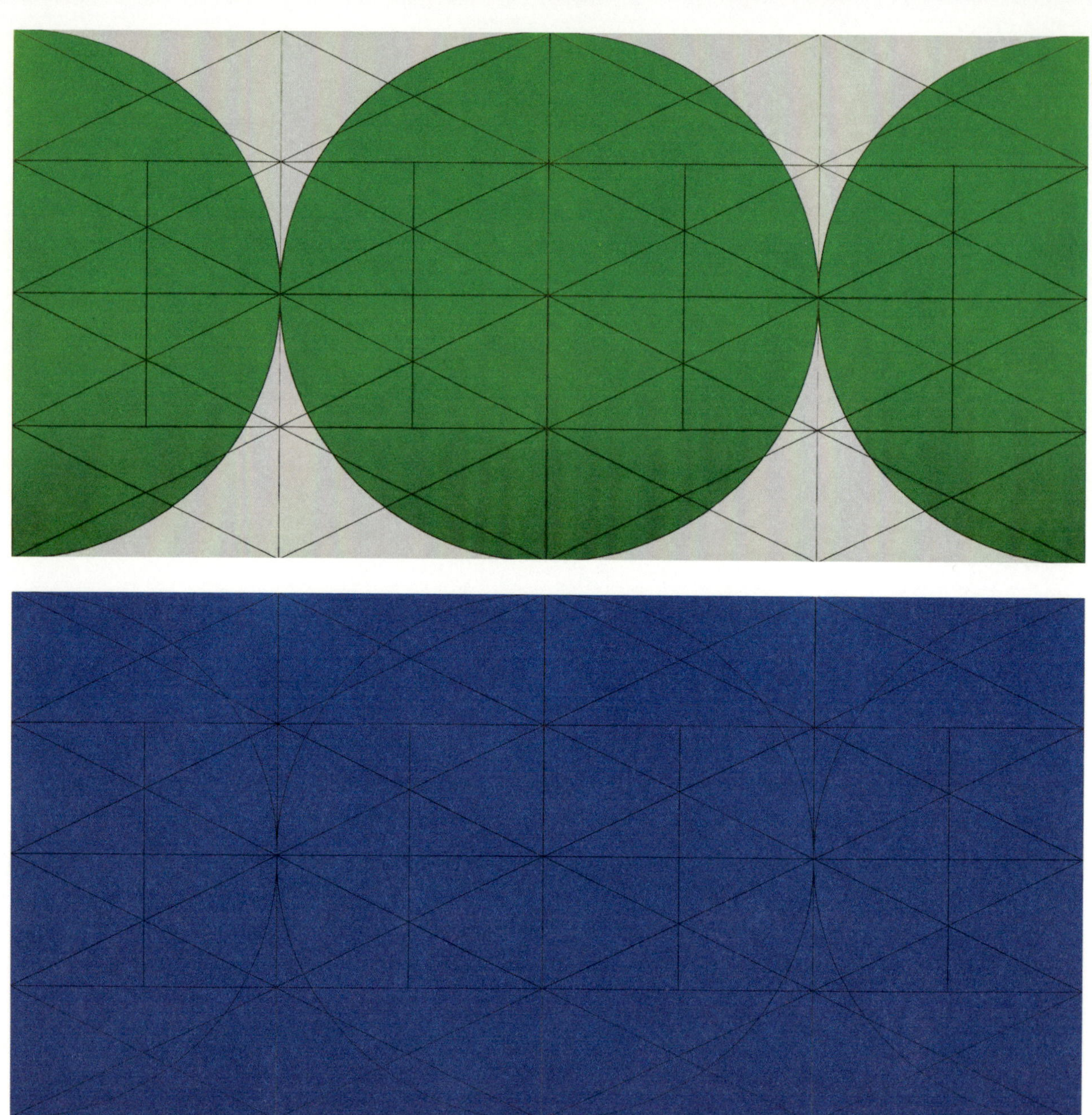

2012.1 Untitled (Elements Property), 244 × 488 cm (4 parts)
2012.2 Untitled (World Unframed Property), 244 × 488 cm (4 parts)

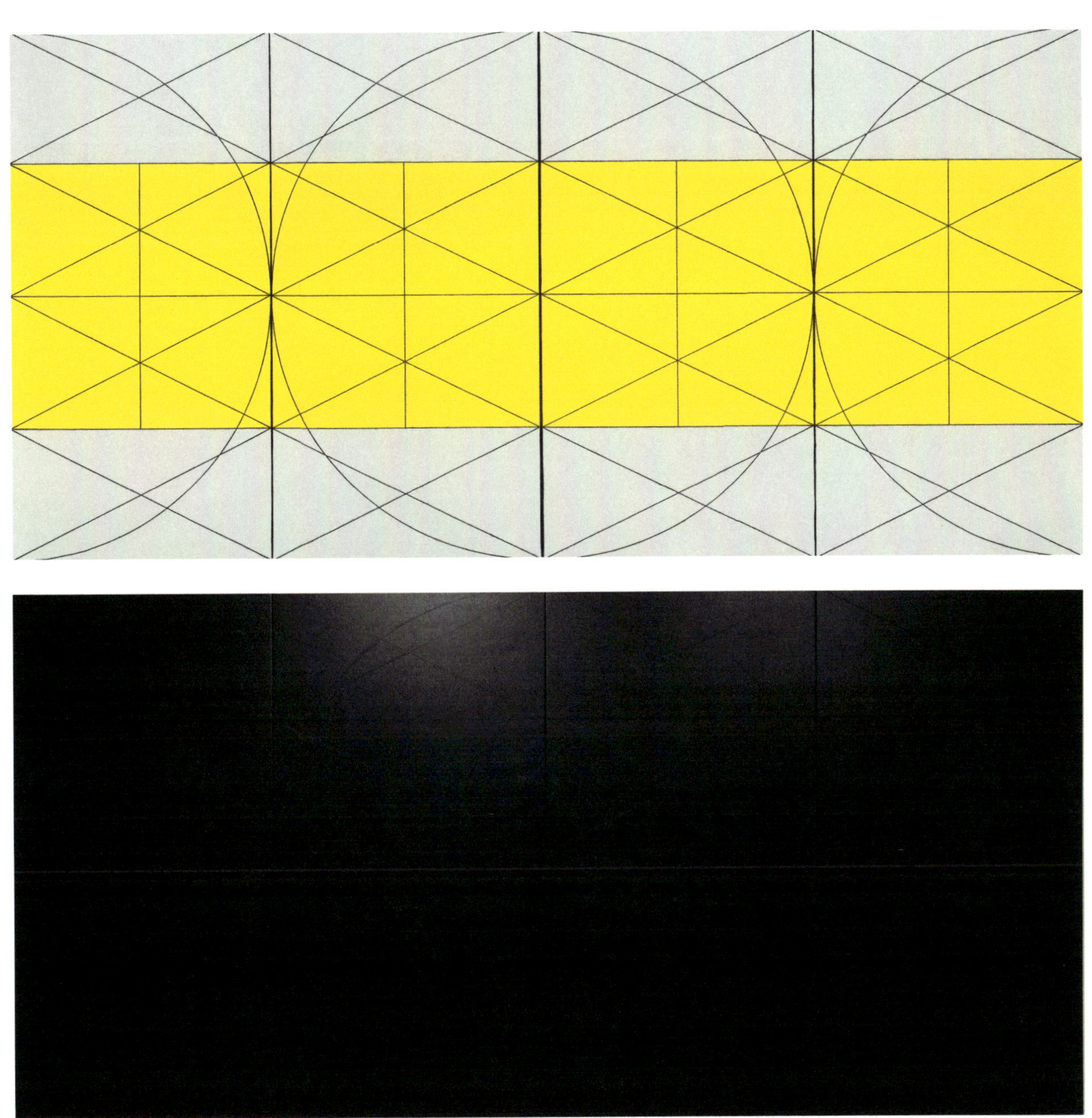

2012.3 Untitled (World Framed Property), 244 × 488 cm (4 parts)
2012.4 Untitled (World Unframed Property), 244 × 488 cm (4 parts)

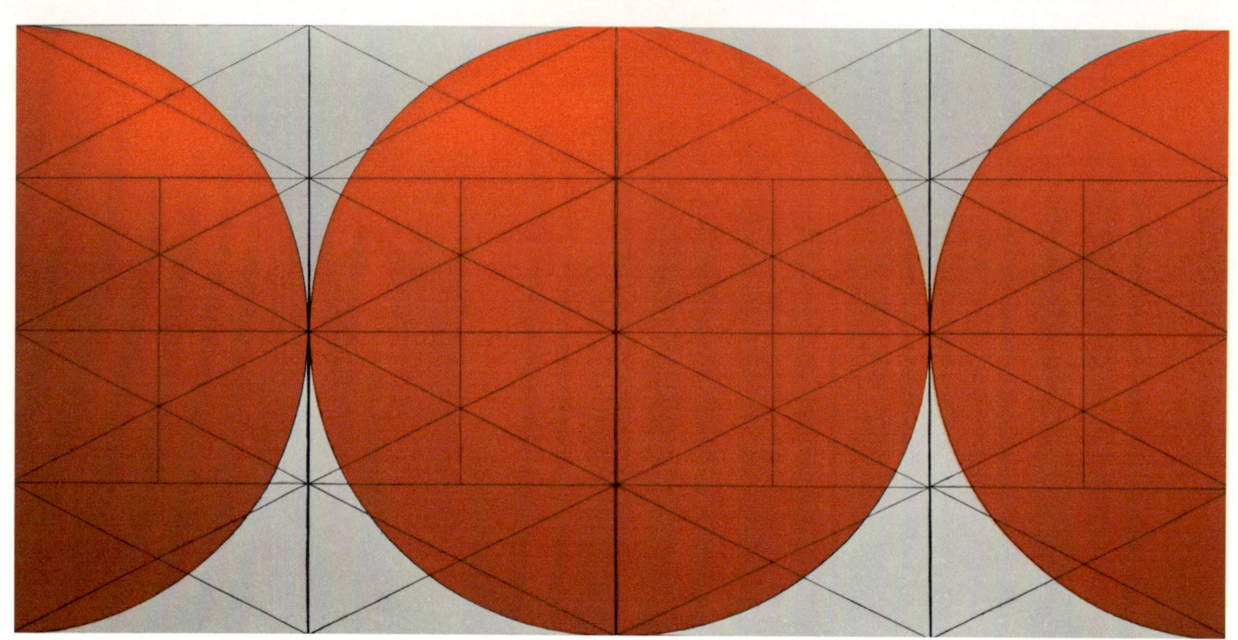

2012.5 Untitled (Subjective Property), 244 × 488 cm (4 parts)

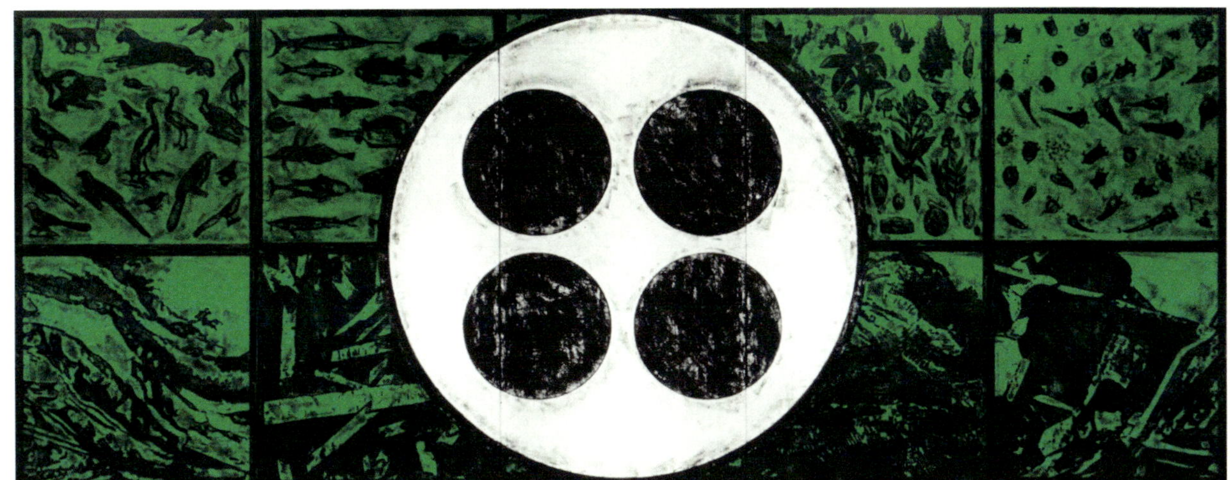

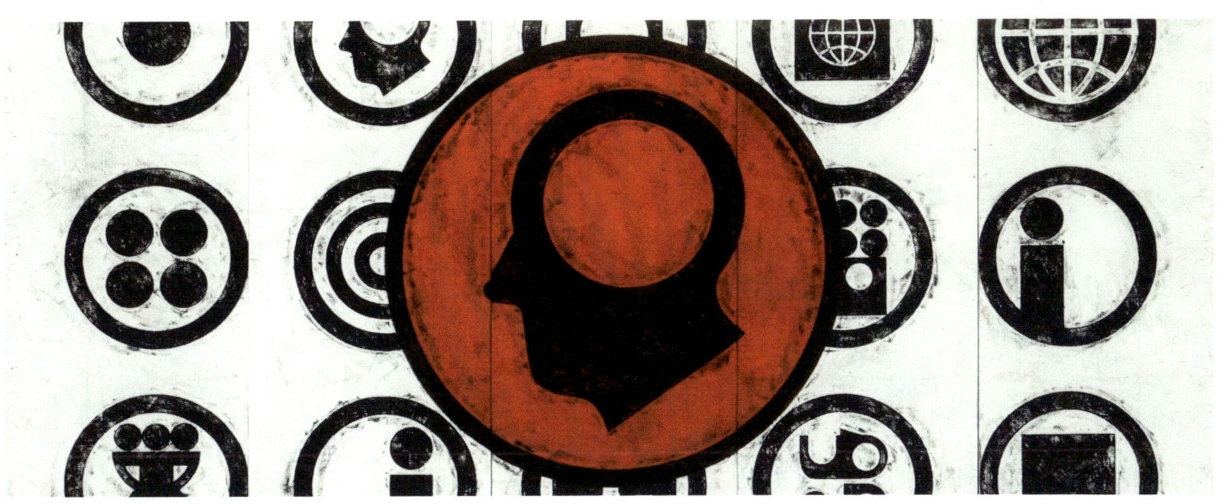

2012.6 Untitled (Elements), 335×610 cm (5 parts)
2012.7 Untitled (Subjective), 335×610 cm (5 parts)

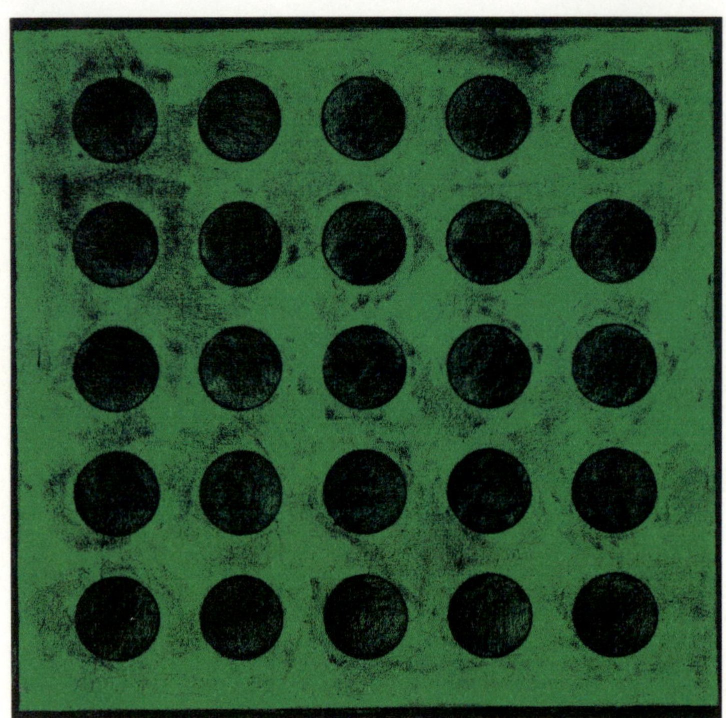

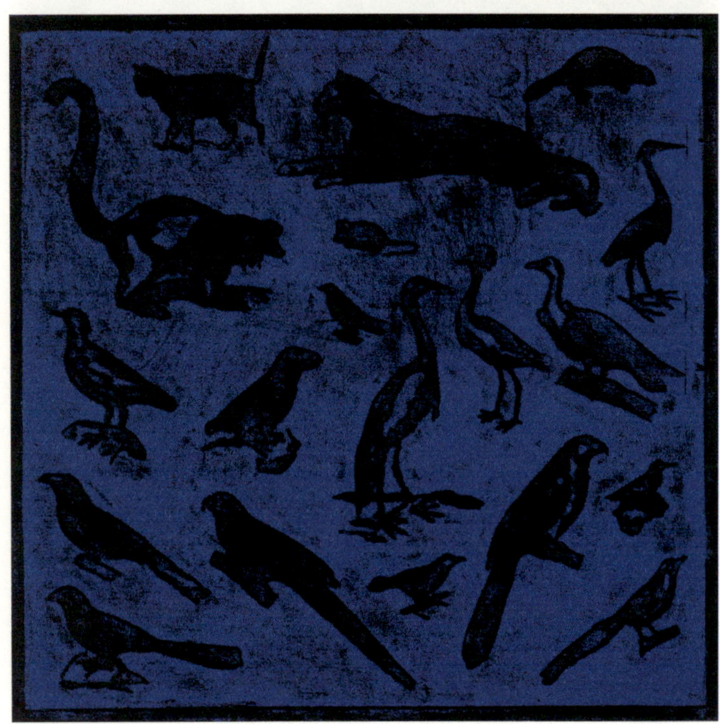

2012.8 Untitled (Elements), 122 × 122 cm
2012.9 Untitled (Mammals and Birds), 122 × 122 cm

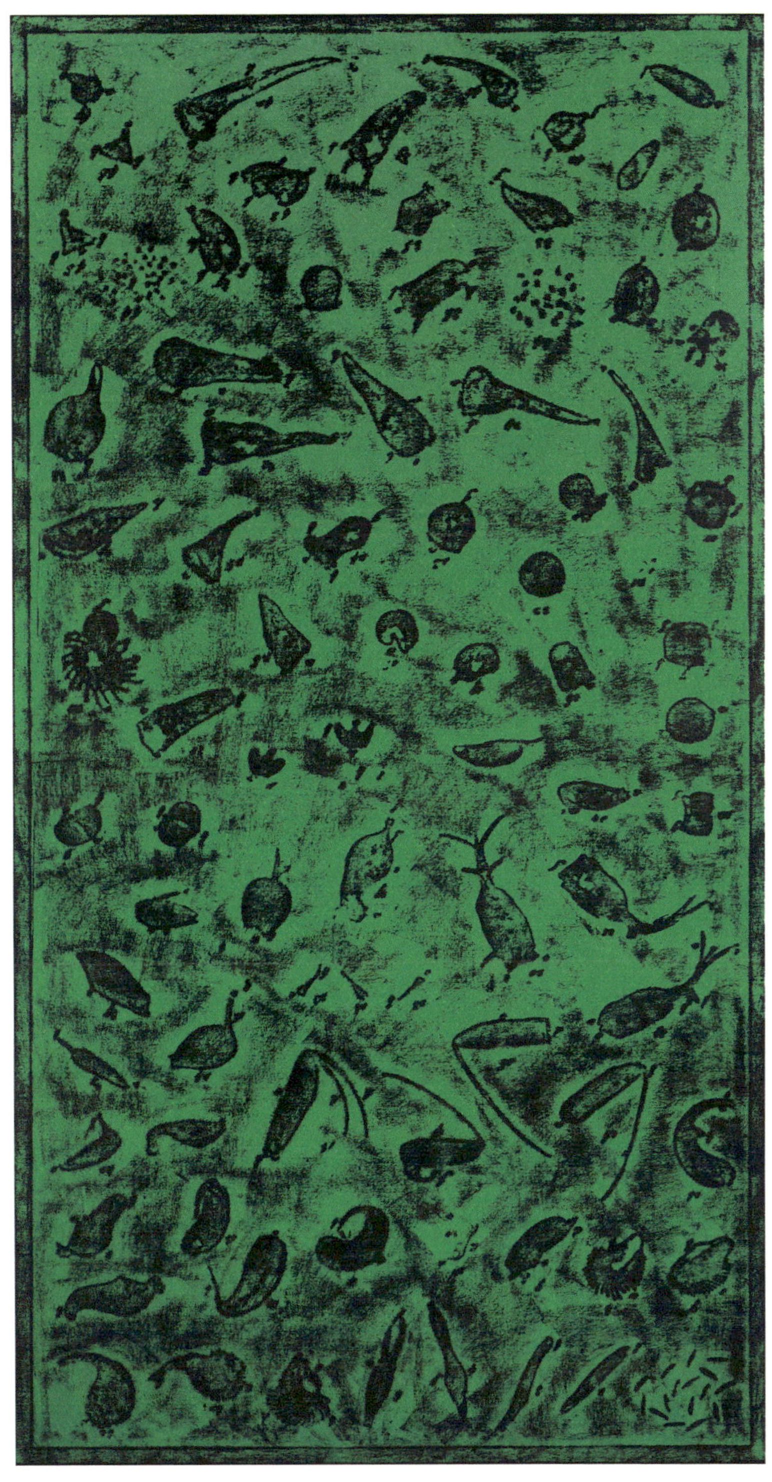

2012.10 Untitled (Lower Life Forms), 244 × 122 cm

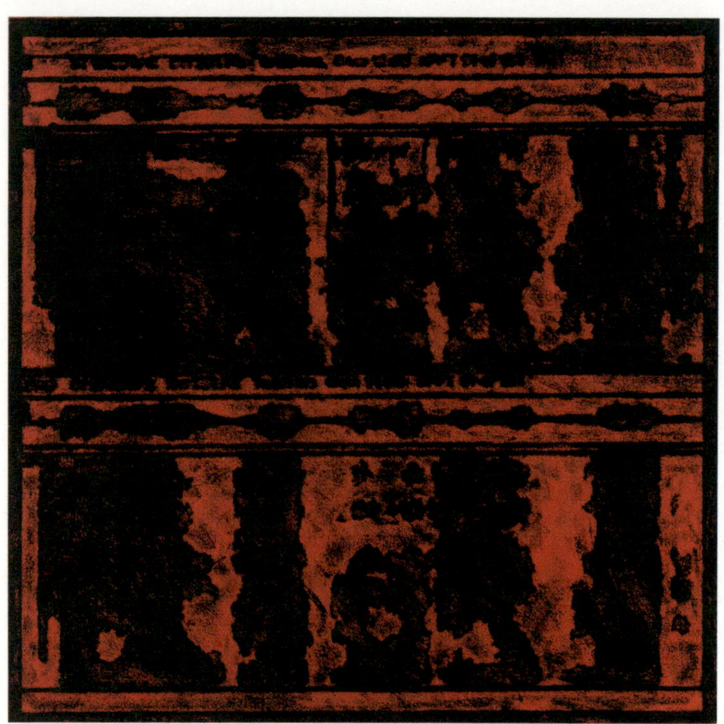
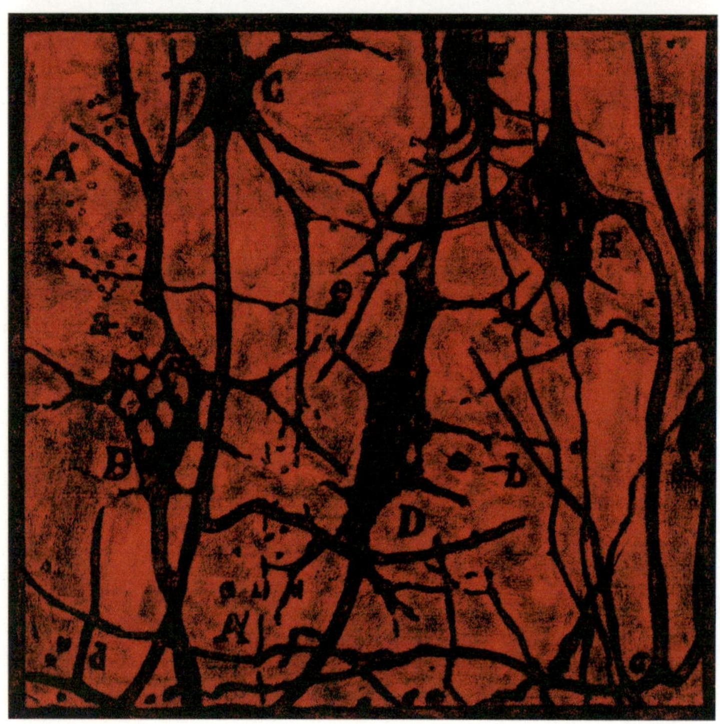

2012.11 Untitled (Sound Waves Speech), 122 × 122 cm
2012.12 Untitled (Neuro System), 122 × 122 cm

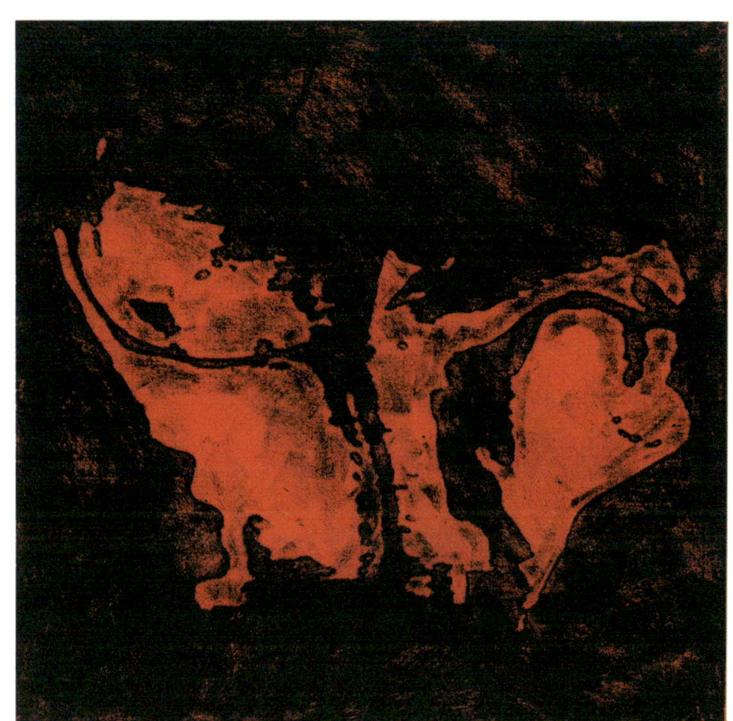

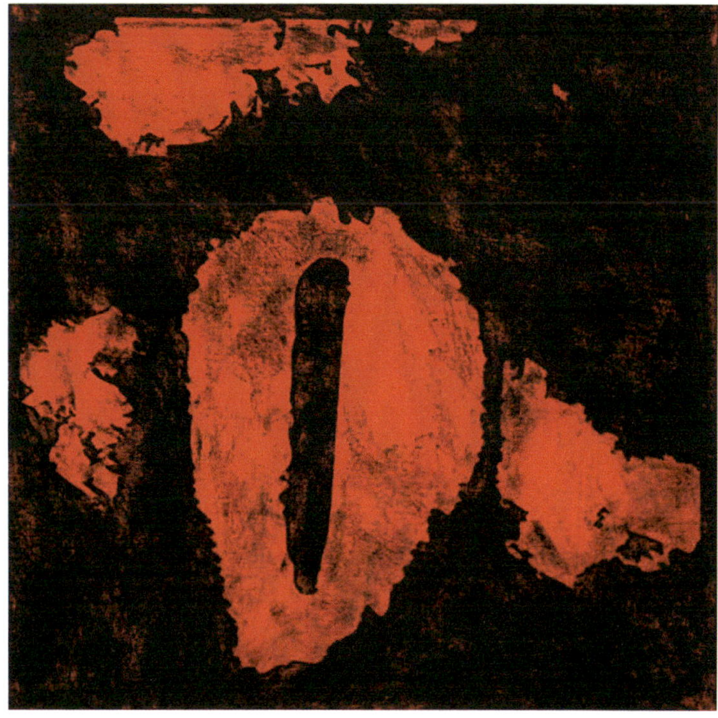

2012.13 Untitled (Face Cutaway Speech), 122 × 122 cm
2012.14 Untitled (Vocal Cords), 122 × 122 cm

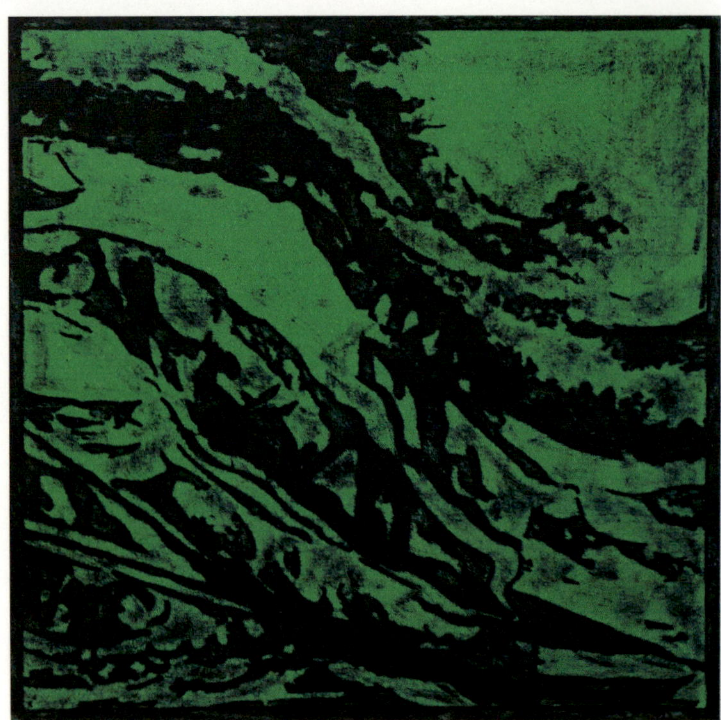

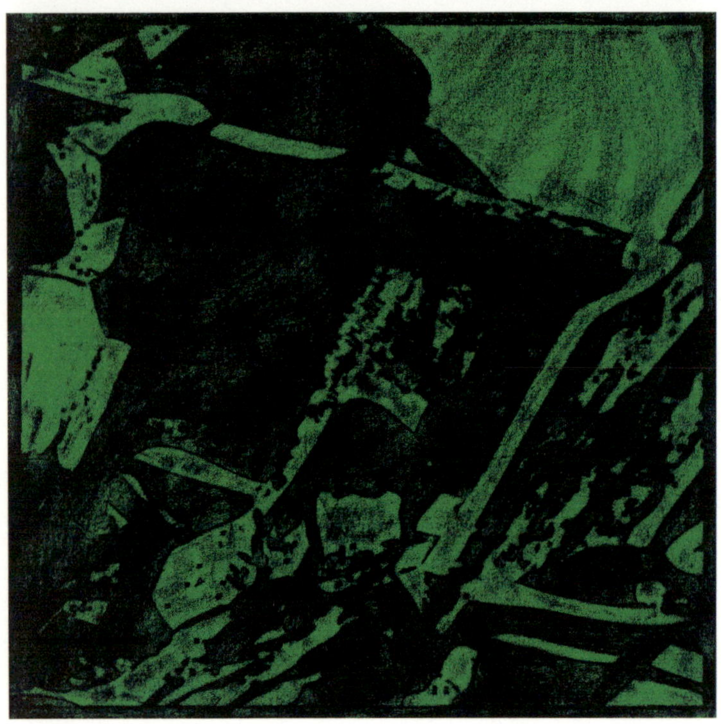

2012.15 Untitled (Geology I), 122 × 122 cm
2012.16 Untitled (Geology II), 122 × 122 cm

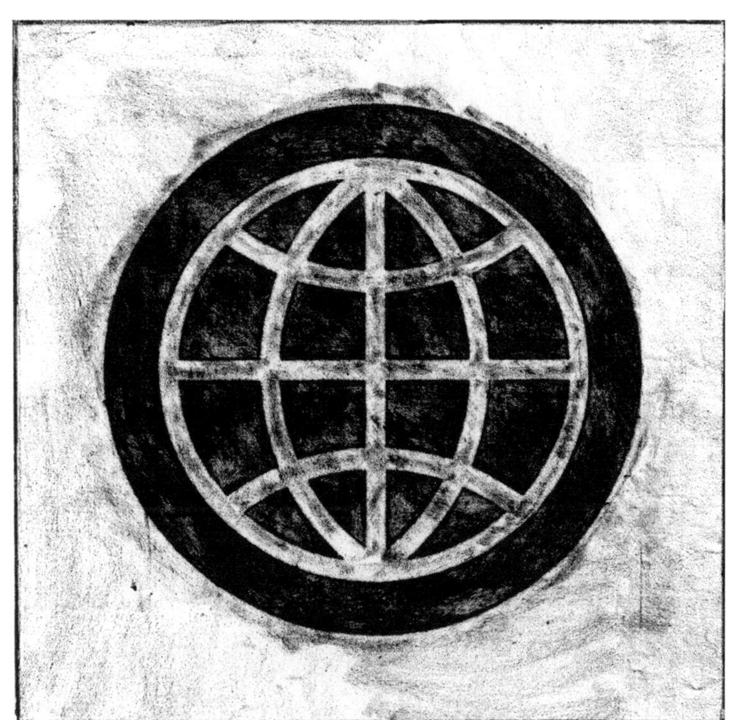

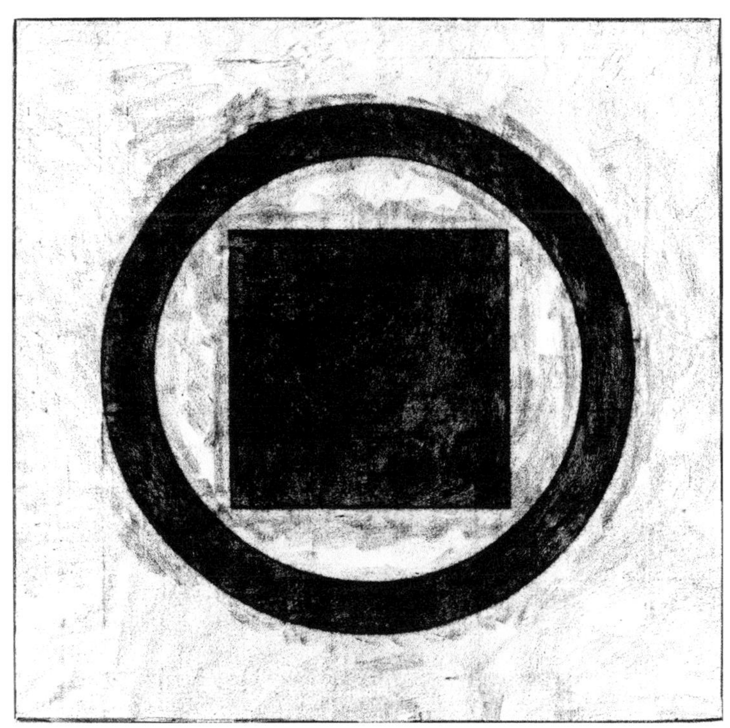

2012.17 Untitled (World Unframed), 122 × 122 cm
2012.18 Untitled (Frame), 122 × 122 cm

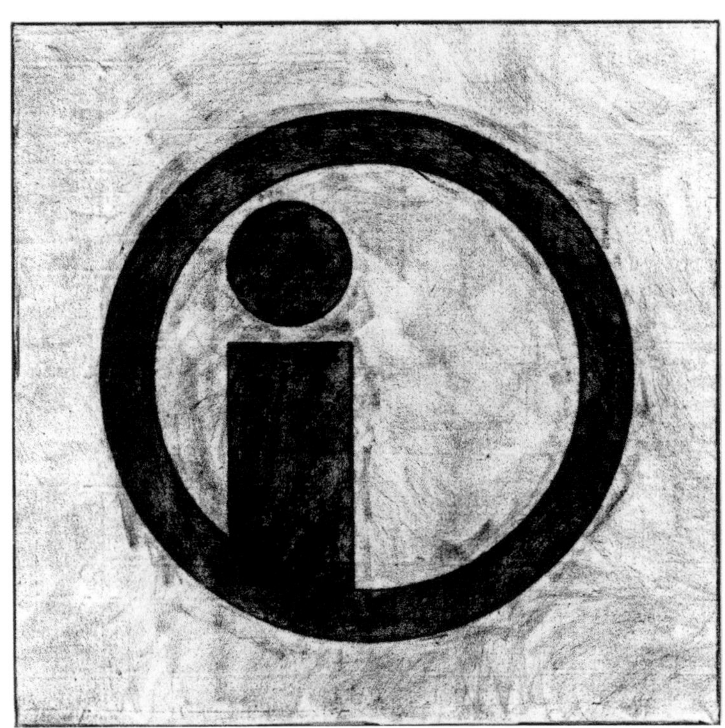

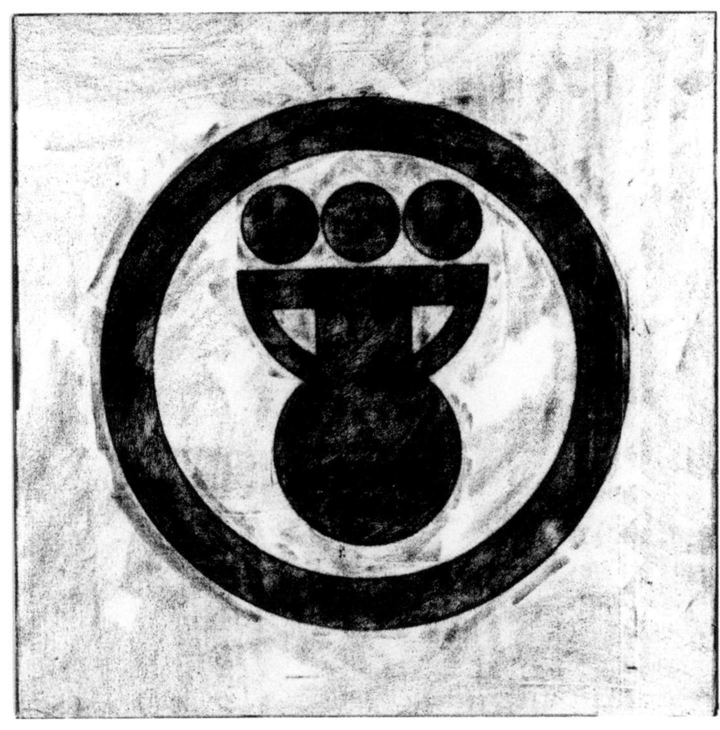

2012.19 Untitled (Life), 122 × 122 cm
2012.20 Untitled (Fate), 122 × 122 cm

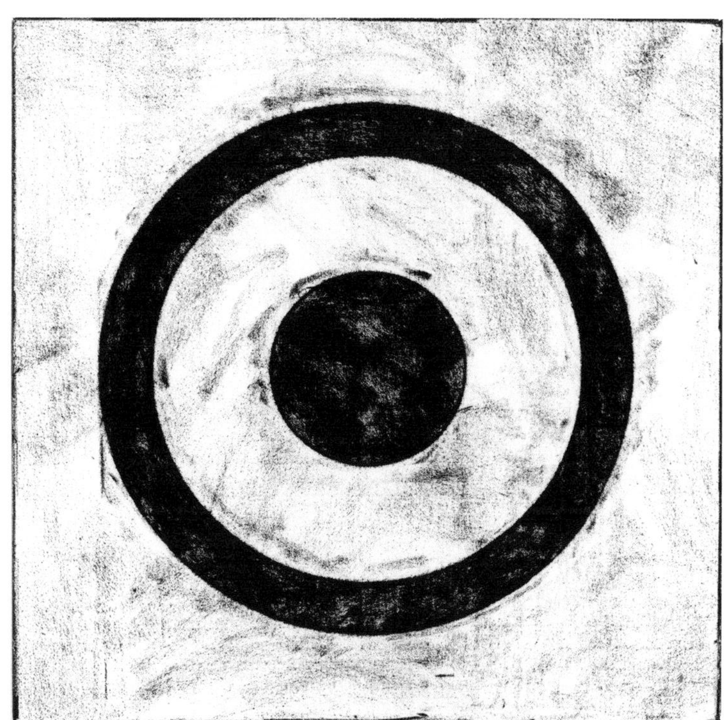

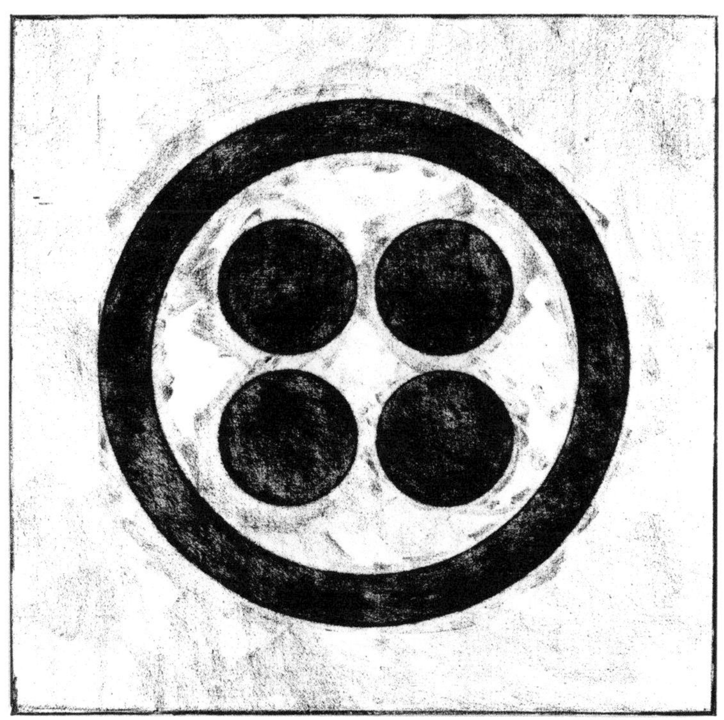

2012.21 Untitled (Sign), 122 × 122 cm
2012.22 Untitled (Elements), 122 × 122 cm

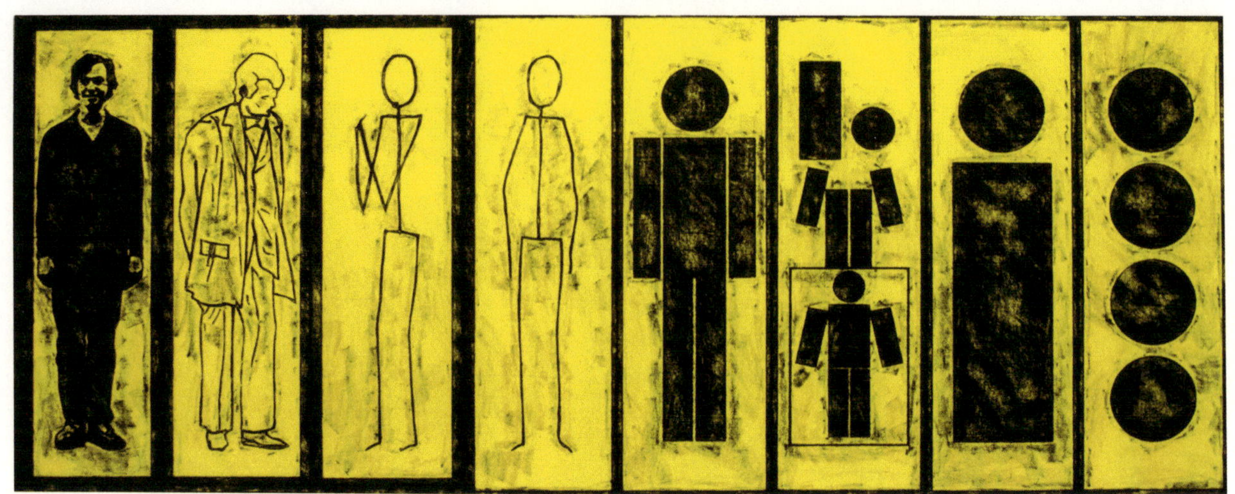

2012.23 Untitled (Who Feels the Most Pain?), 244 × 610 cm (8 parts)

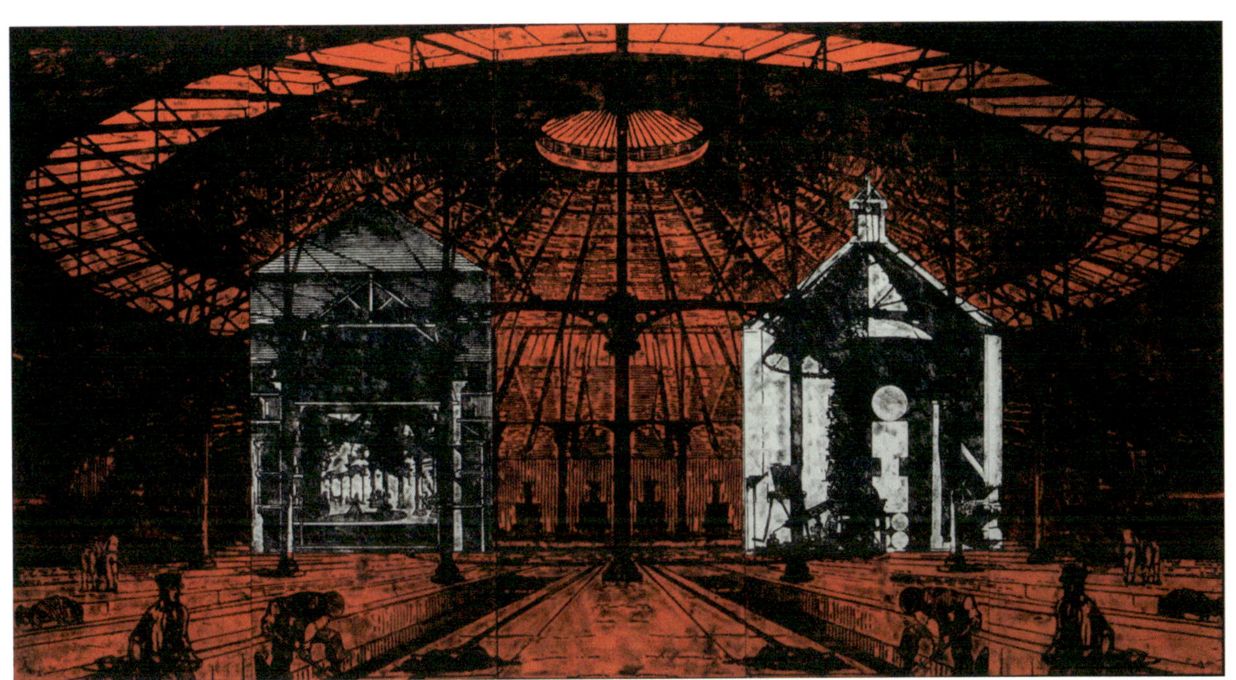

2012.24 Untitled (Roundhouse), 244 × 610 cm (10 parts)

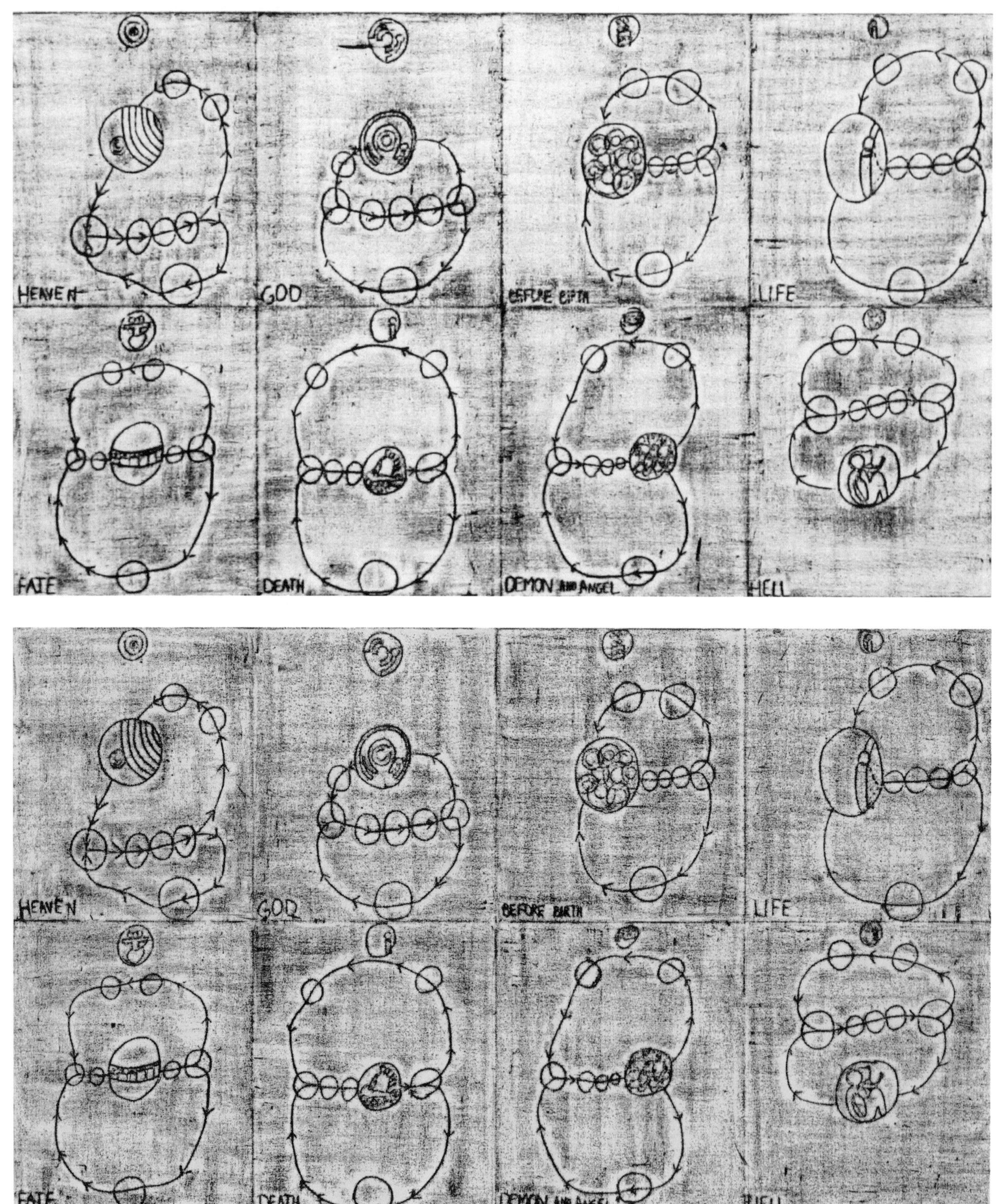

2012.25 Untitled (Cosmological Sequence), 120 × 200 cm
2012.26 Untitled (Cosmological Sequence Yellow), 120 × 200 cm

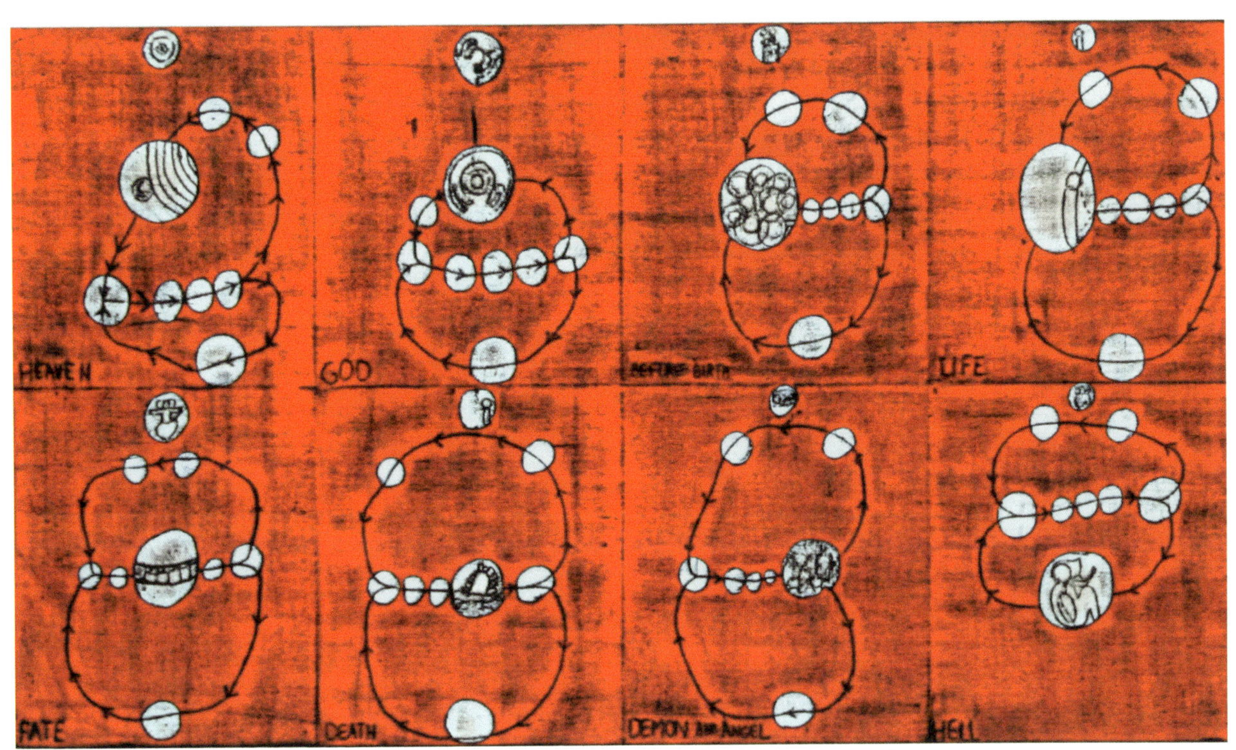

2012.27 Untitled (Cosmological Sequence), 120 × 200 cm

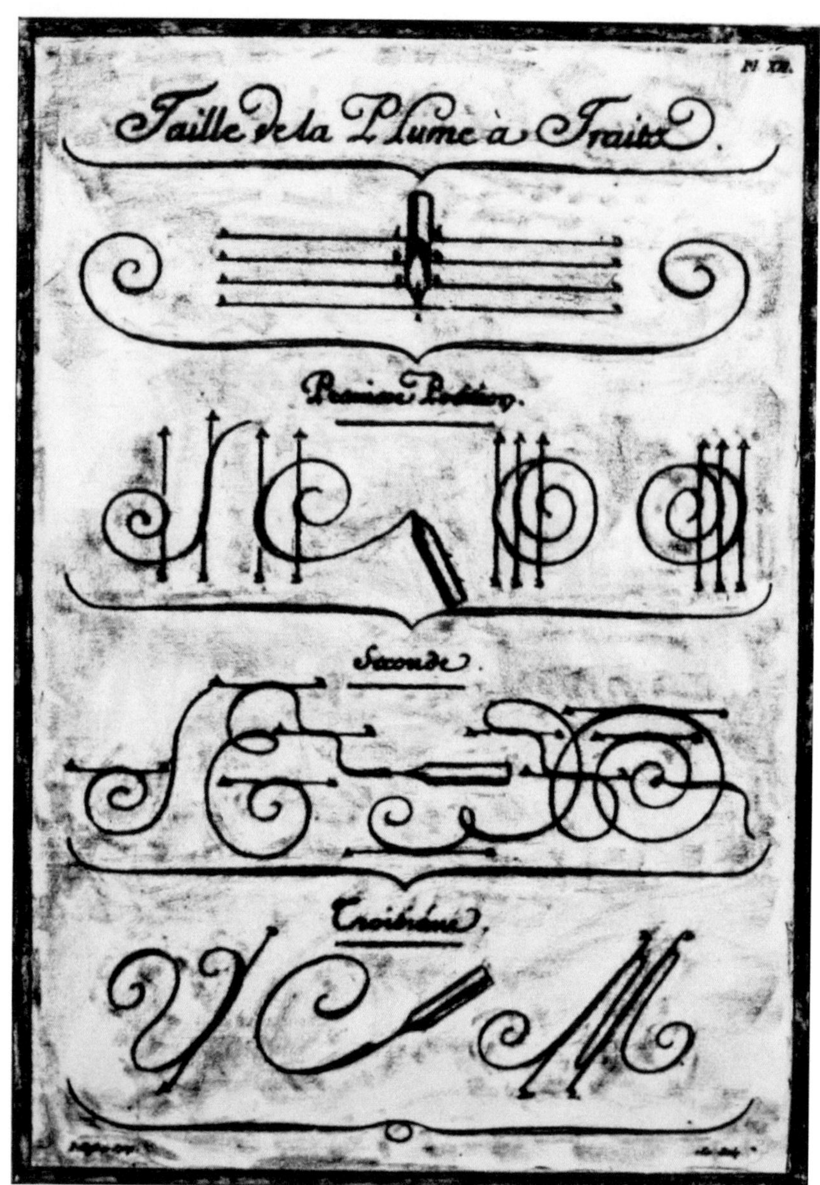

2012.28 Untitled (Diderot: Taille de la Plume à Traiter), 183 × 122 cm

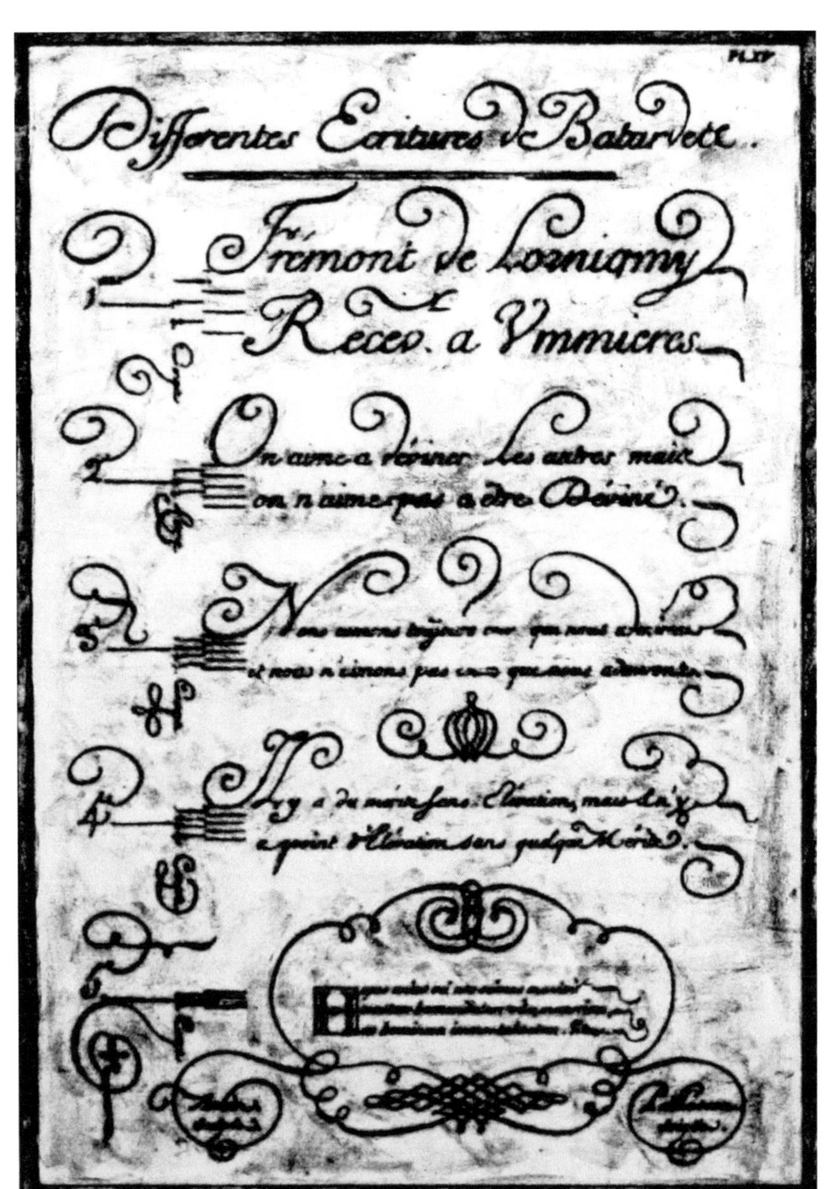

2012.29 Untitled (Diderot: Différentes Écritures de Bâtardes), 183 × 122 cm

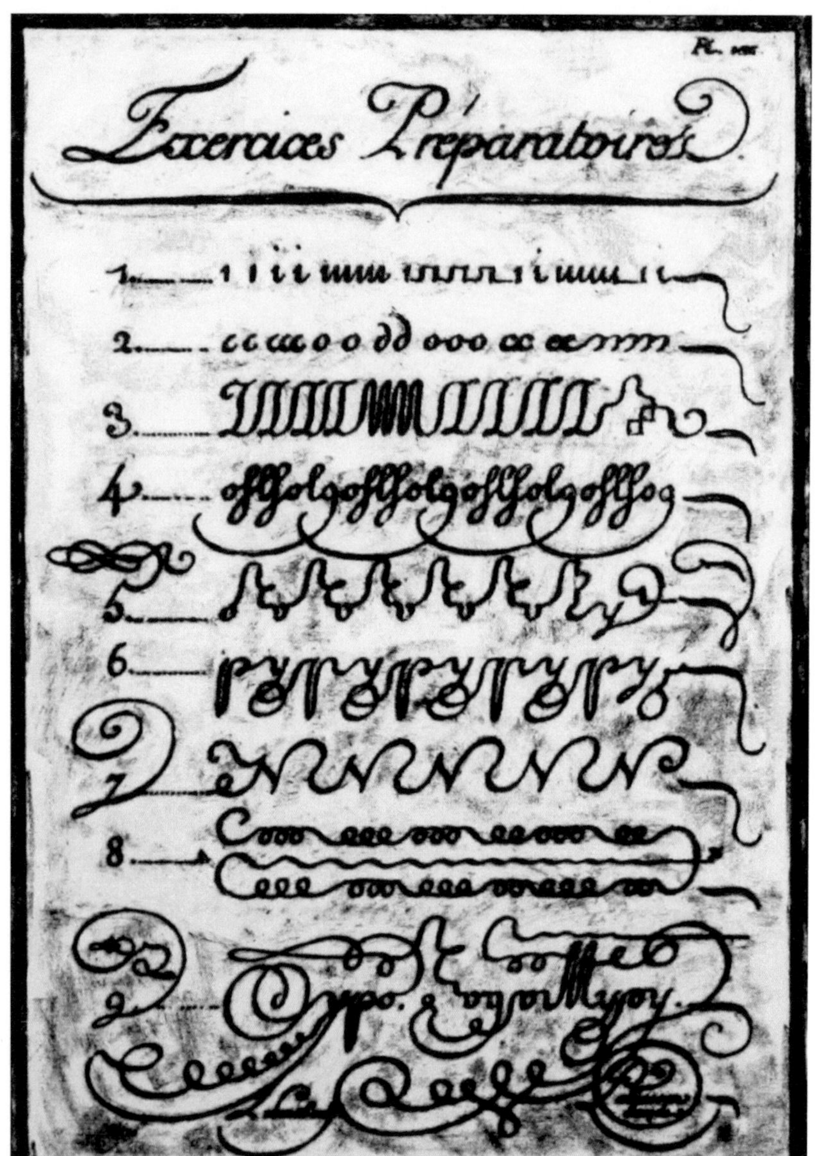

2012.30 Untitled (Diderot: Exercices Préparatoires), 183 × 122 cm

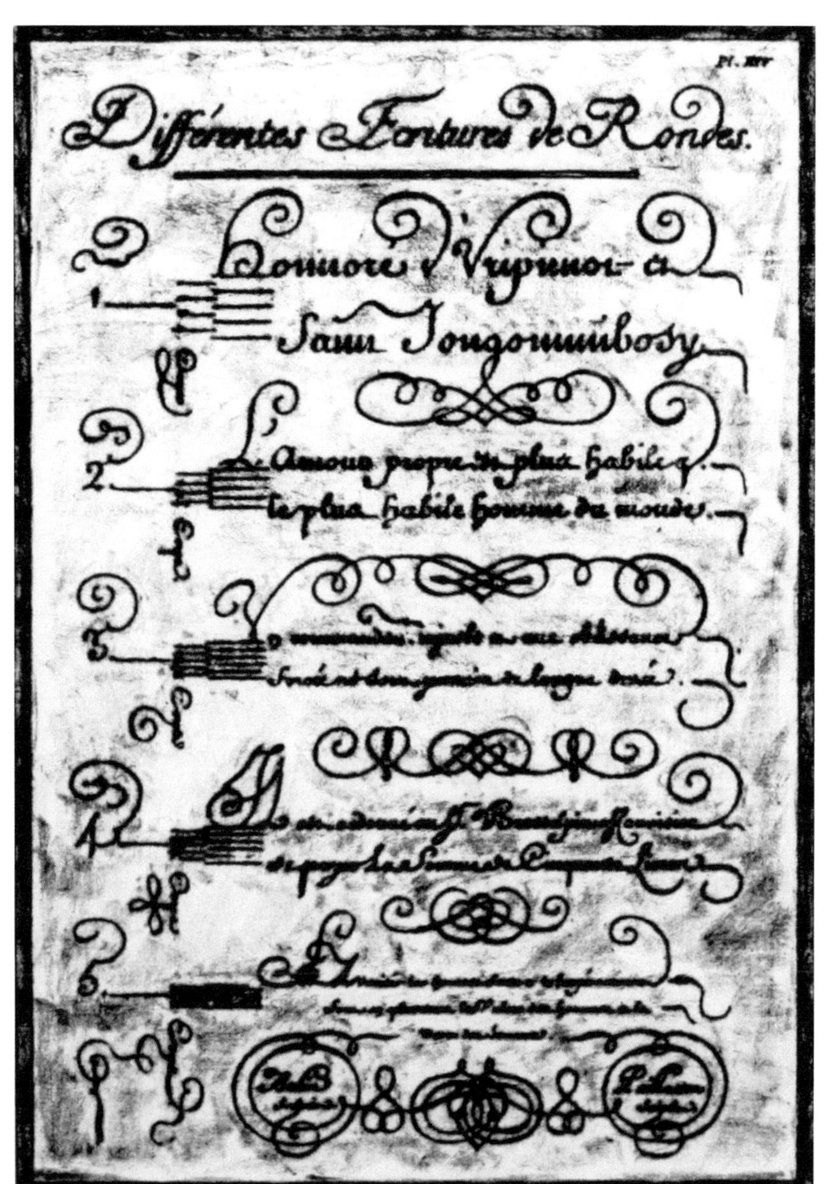

2012.31 Untitled (Diderot: Différentes Écritures de Rondes), 183 × 122 cm

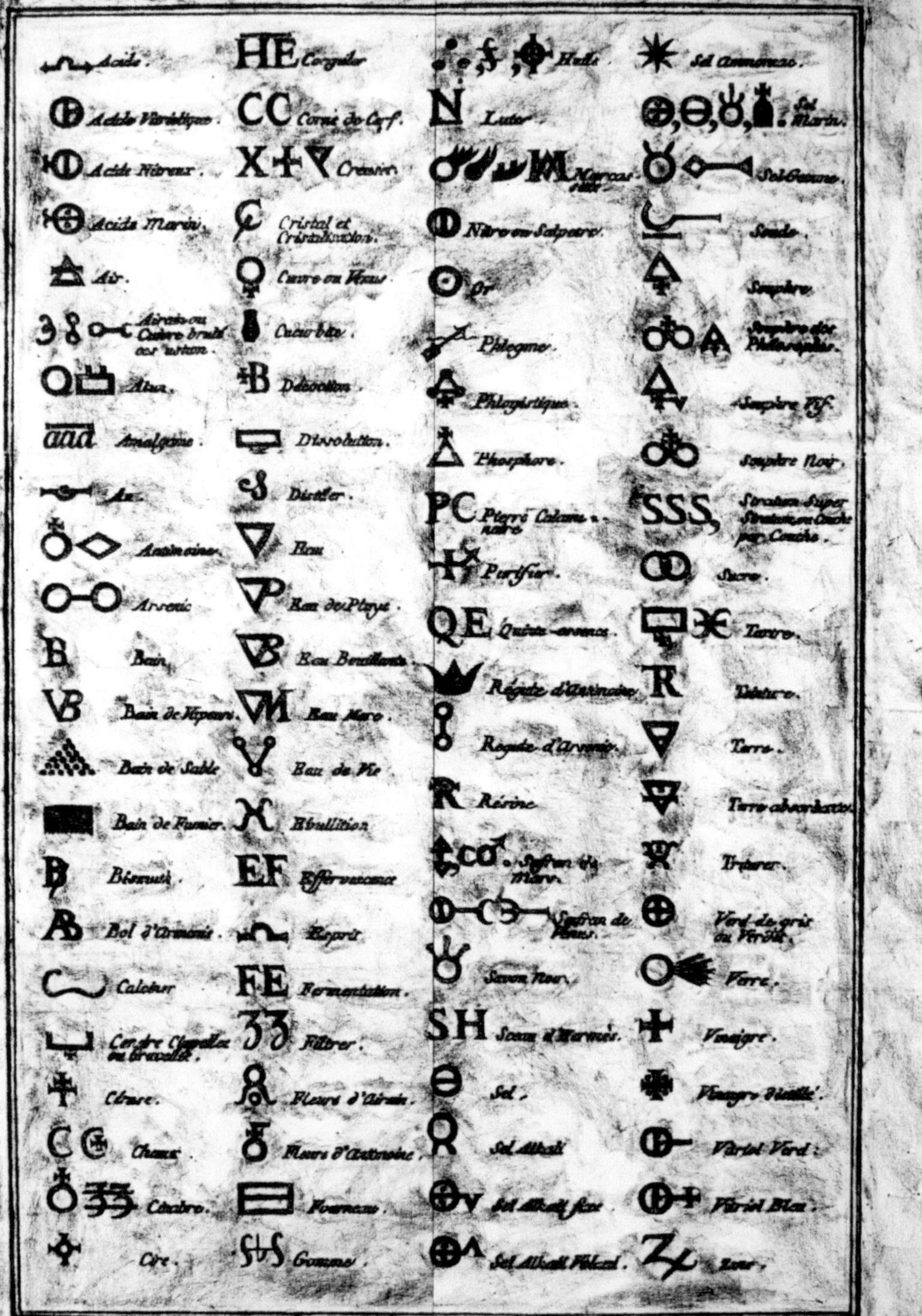

2012.32 Untitled (Diderot: Symbolis), 335×244 cm

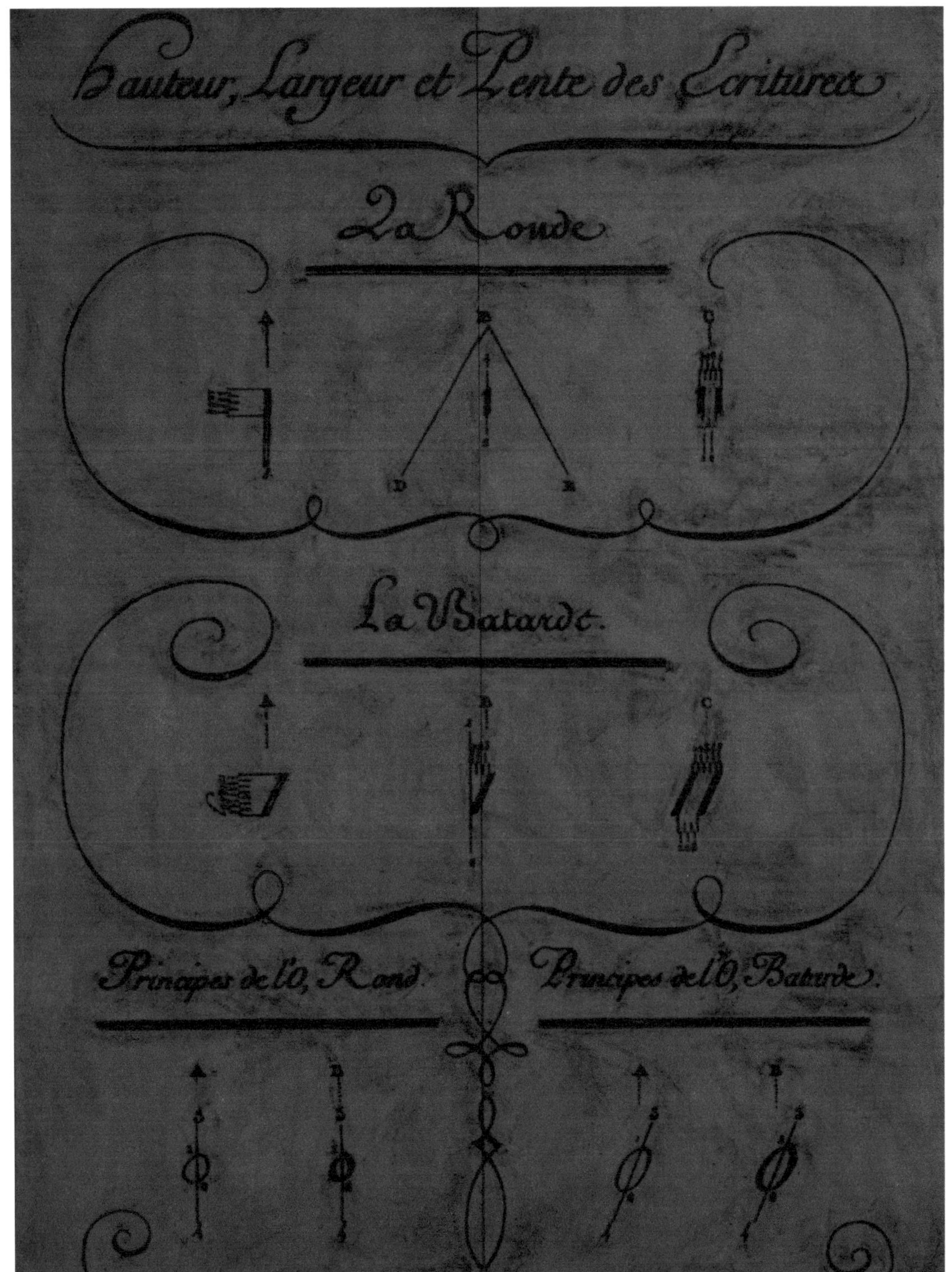

2012.33 Untitled (Diderot: Hauteur, Largeur et Lente des Écritures), 335 × 244 cm

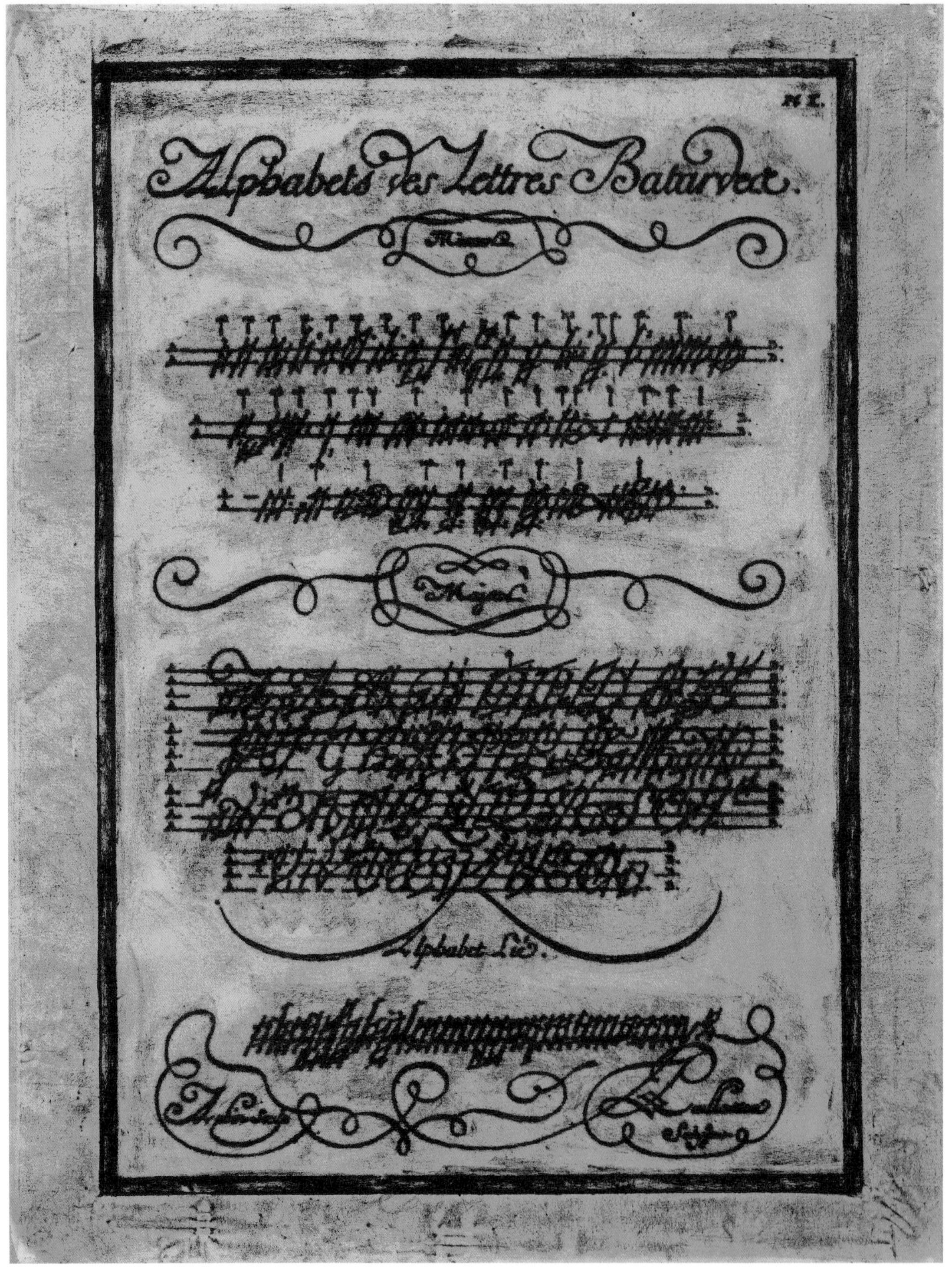

2012.34 Untitled (Diderot: Alphabets des Lettres de Bâtardes), 183 × 122 cm

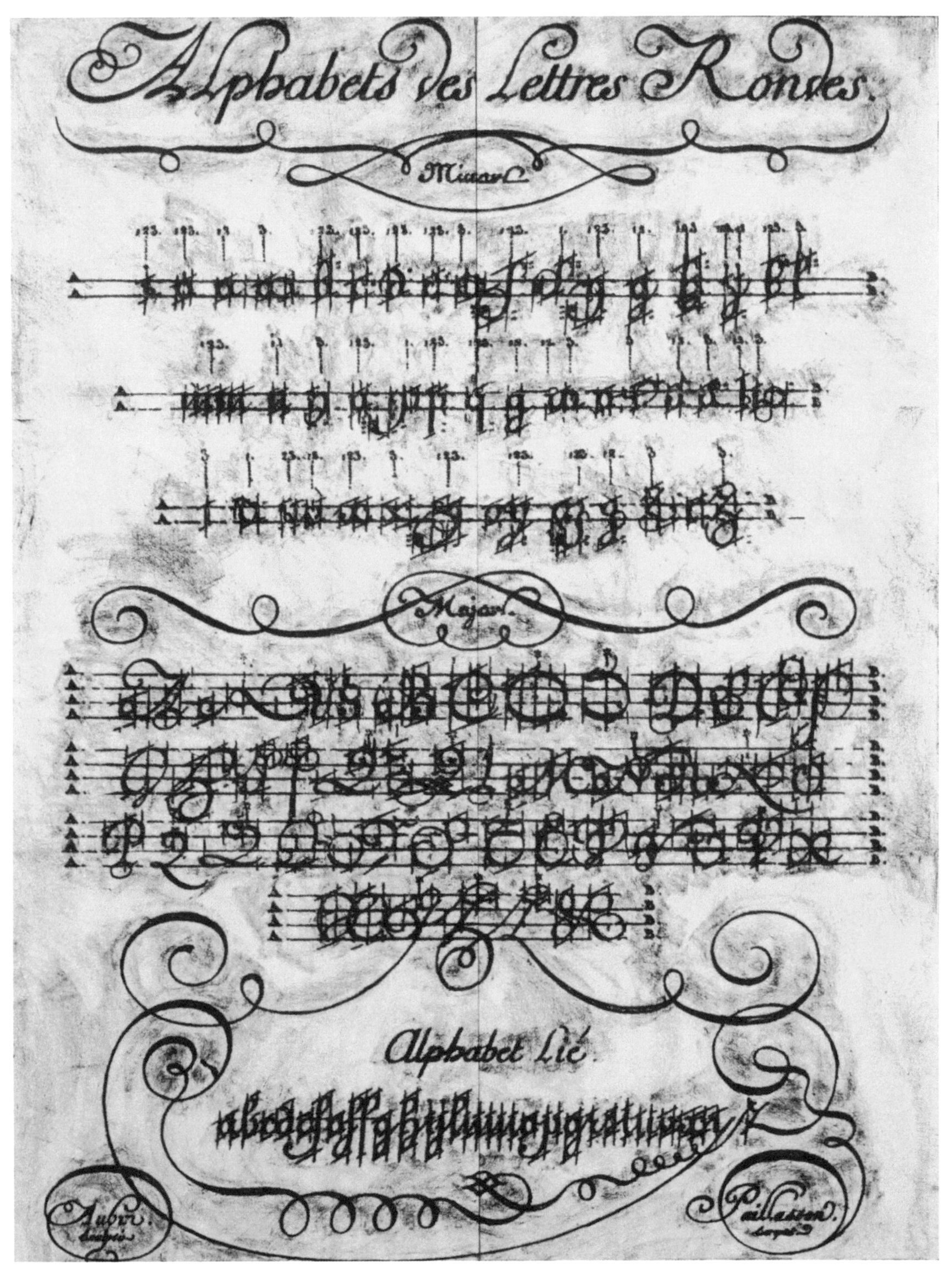

2012.35 Untitled (Diderot: Alphabets des Lettres Rondes), 335 × 122 cm

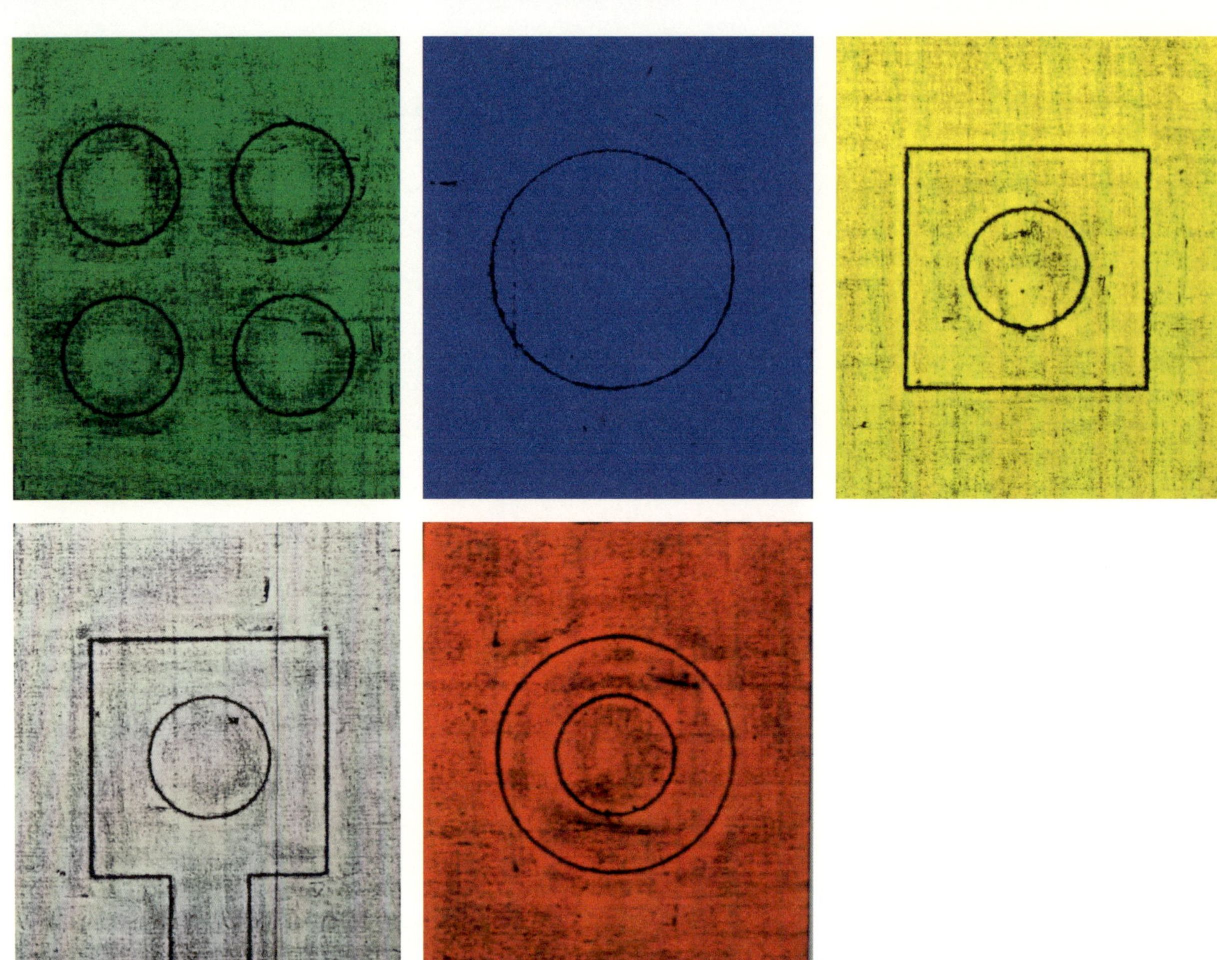

2012.36 Untitled (5 Signs Outline), 60 × 50 cm each (5 parts)

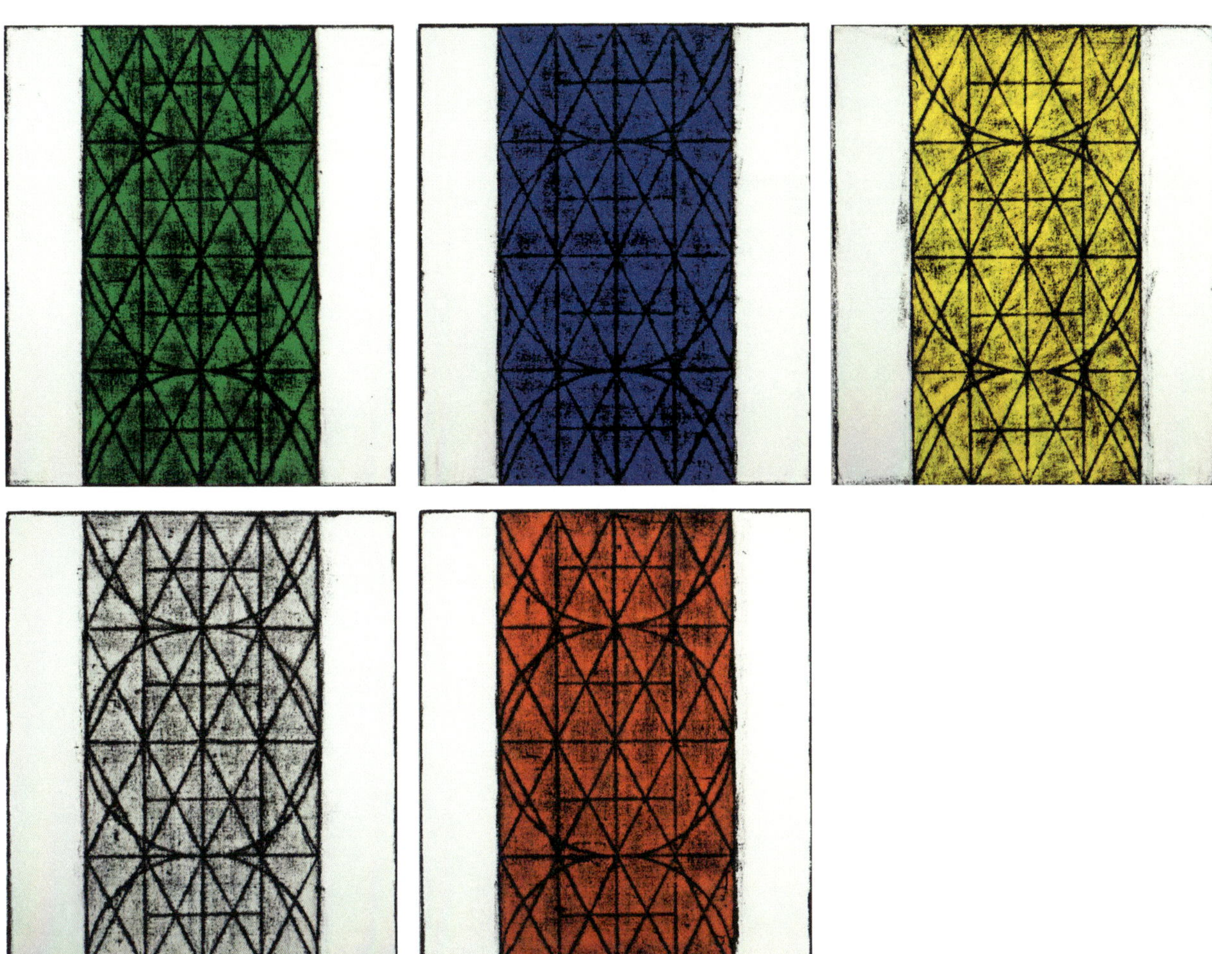

2012.37   Untitled (Cosmology: Property), 60 × 50 cm each (5 parts)

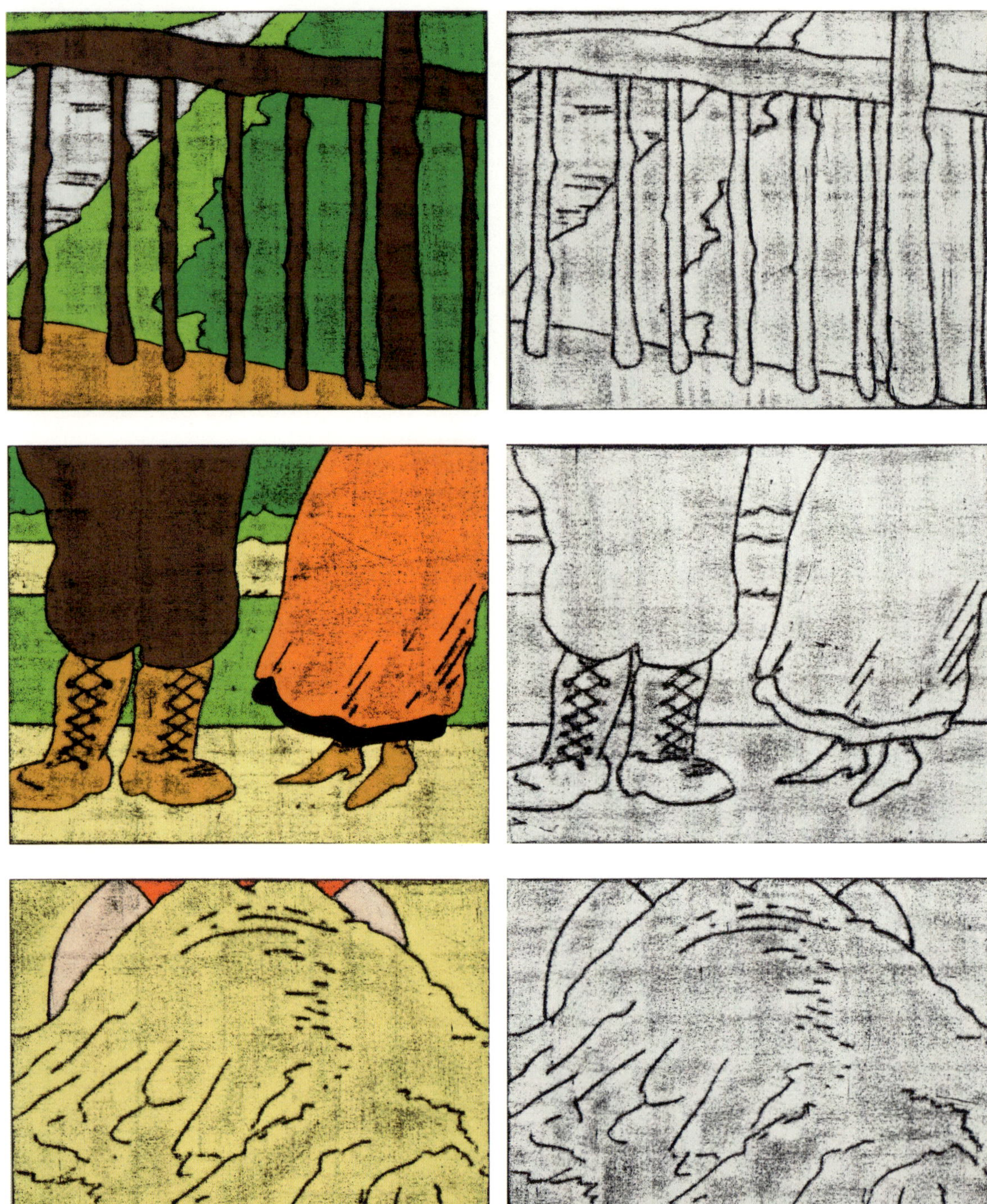

2012.38 Untitled (Elements), 50 × 60 cm each (diptych)
2012.39 Untitled (Elements), 50 × 60 cm each (diptych)
2012.40 Untitled (Elements), 50 × 60 cm each (diptych)

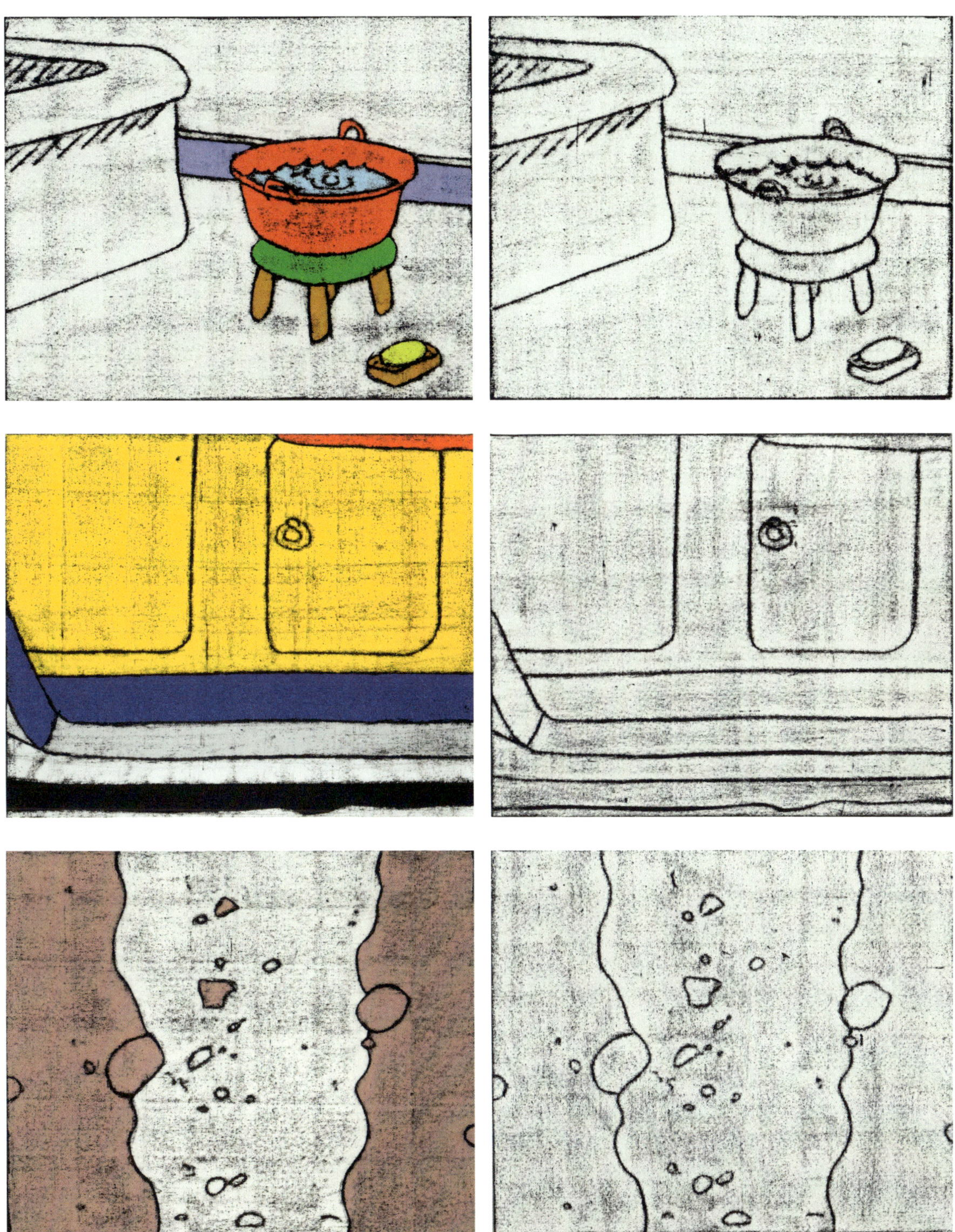

2012.41 Untitled (Elements), 50 × 60 cm each (diptych)
2012.42 Untitled (Elements), 50 × 60 cm each (diptych)
2012.43 Untitled (Elements), 50 × 60 cm each (diptych)

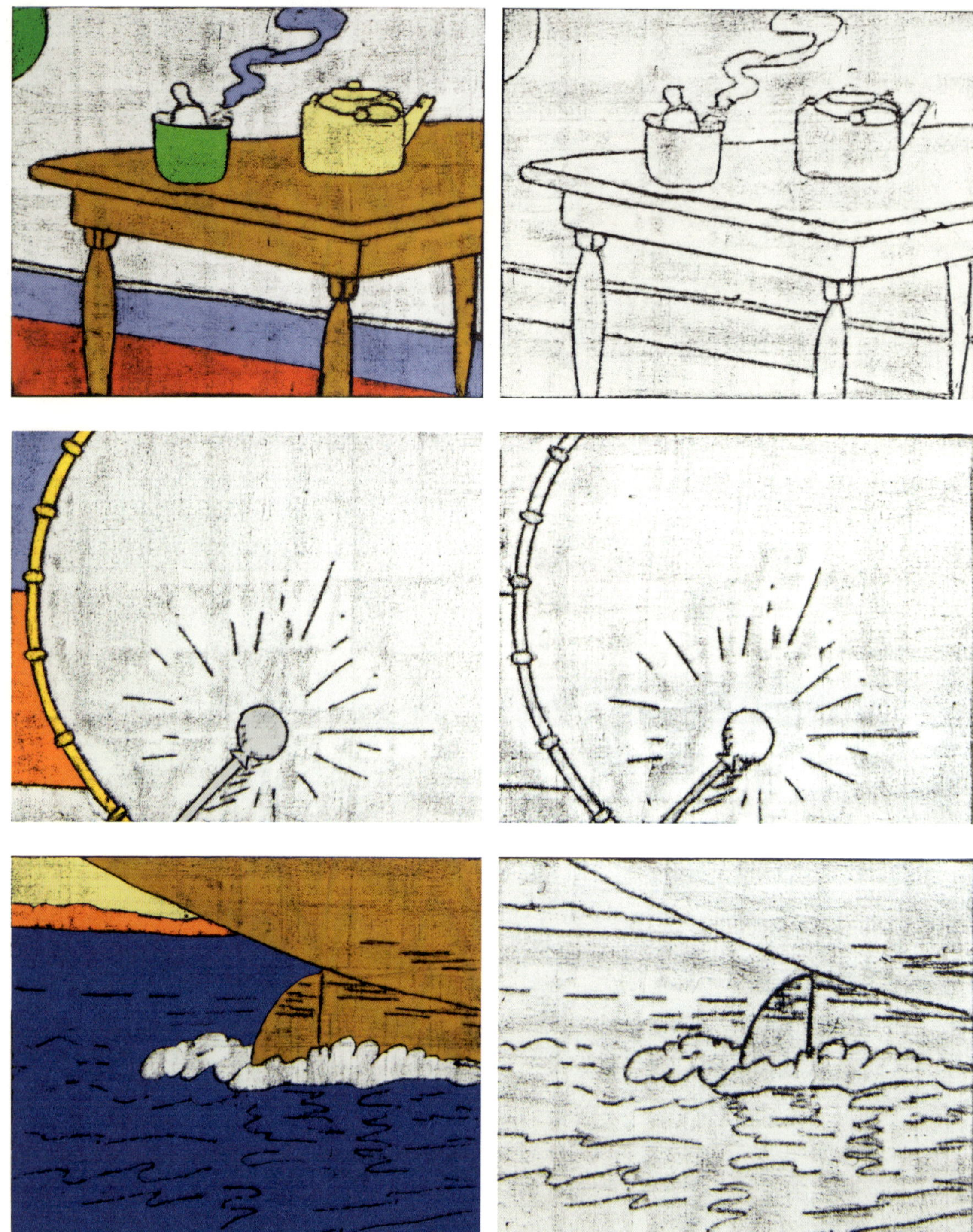

2012.44 Untitled (Elements), 50×60 cm each (diptych)
2012.45 Untitled (Elements), 50×60 cm each (diptych)
2012.46 Untitled (Elements), 50×60 cm each (diptych)

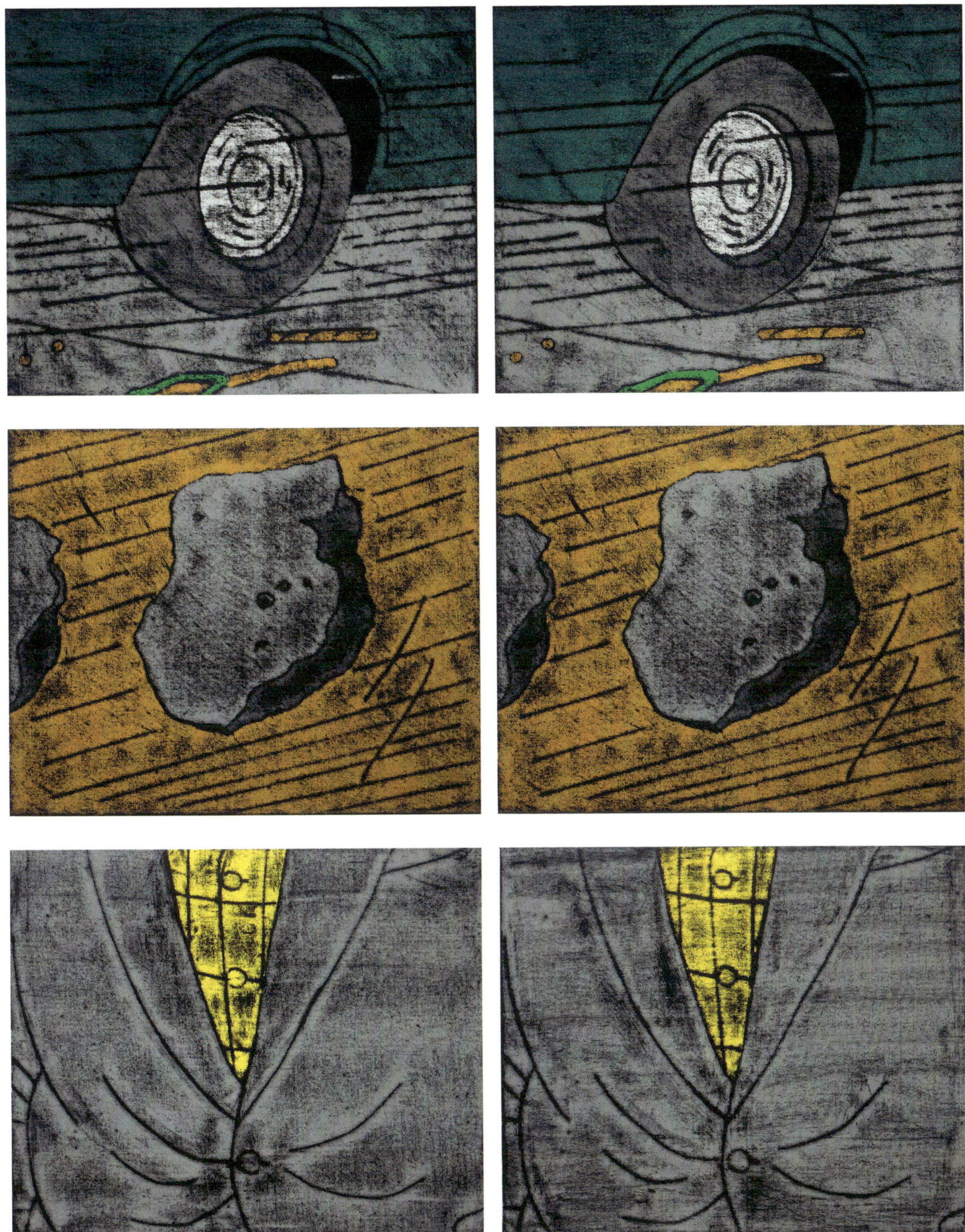

2012.47 Untitled (Elements), 50 × 60 cm each (diptych)
2012.48 Untitled (Elements), 50 × 60 cm each (diptych)
2012.49 Untitled (Elements), 50 × 60 cm each (diptych)

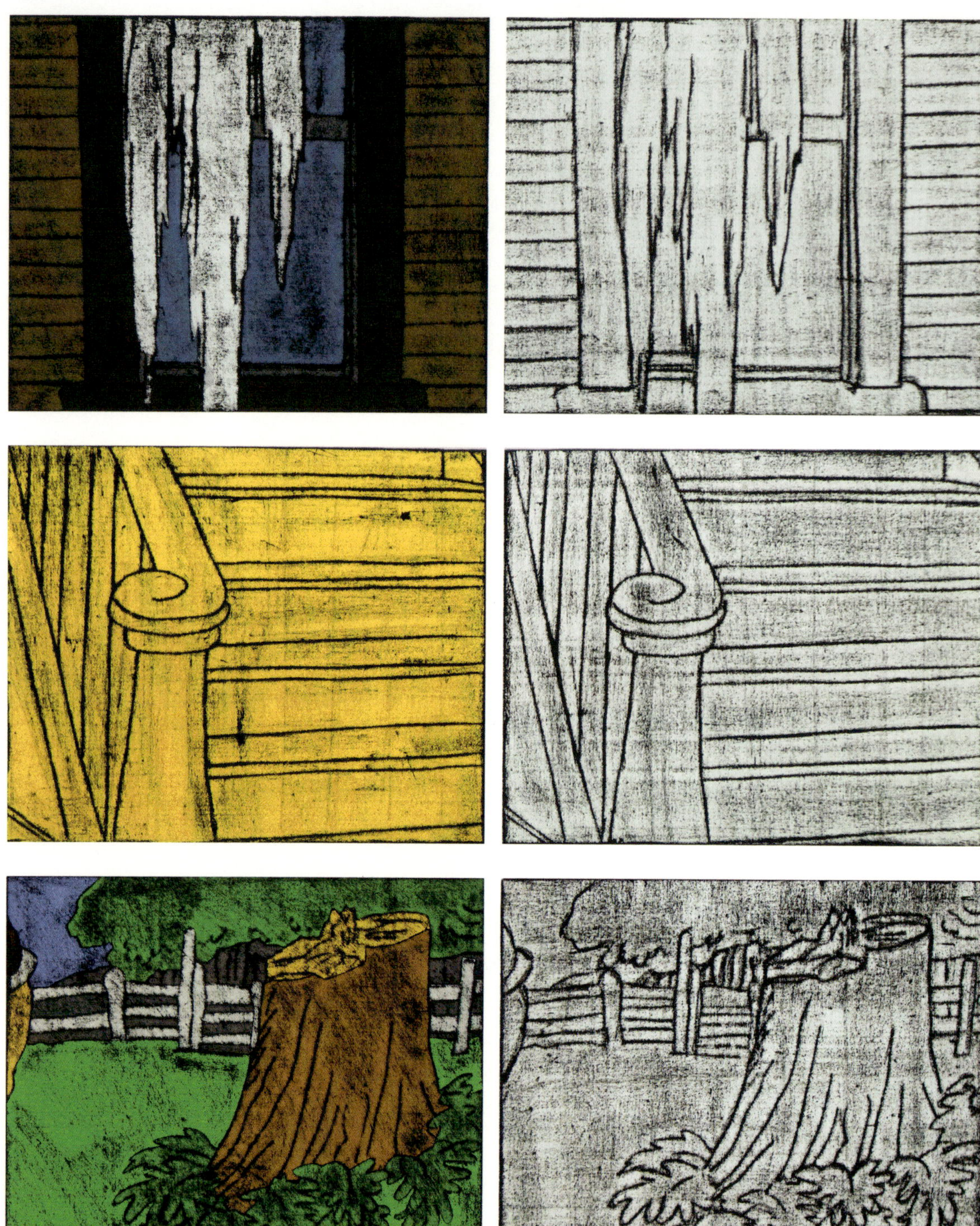

2012.50 Untitled (Elements), 50 × 60 cm each (diptych)
2012.51 Untitled (Elements), 50 × 60 cm each (diptych)
2012.52 Untitled (Elements), 50 × 60 cm each (diptych)

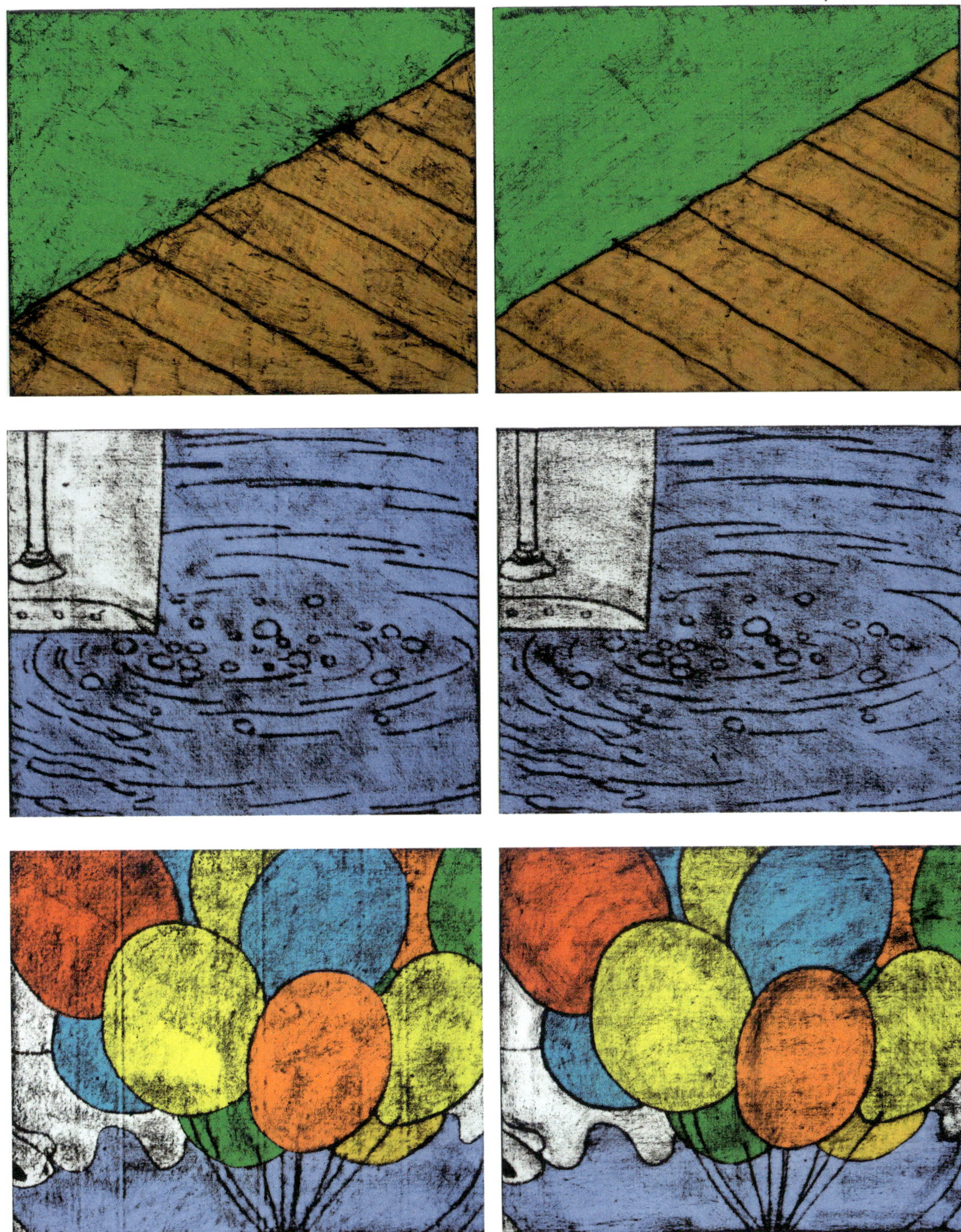

2012.53 Untitled (Elements), 50 × 60 cm each (diptych)
2012.54 Untitled (Elements), 50 × 60 cm each (diptych)
2012.55 Untitled (Elements), 50 × 60 cm each (diptych)

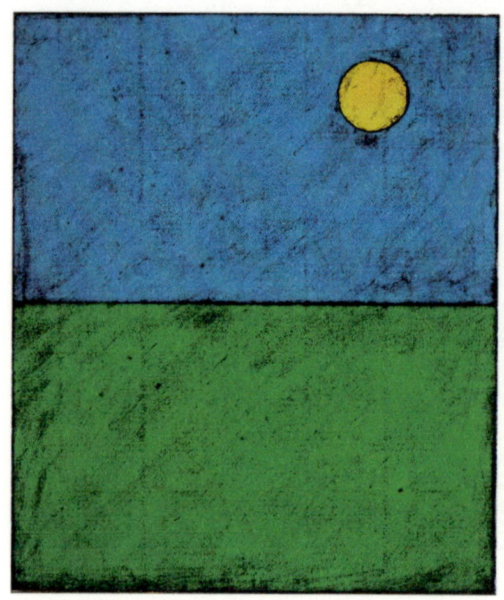
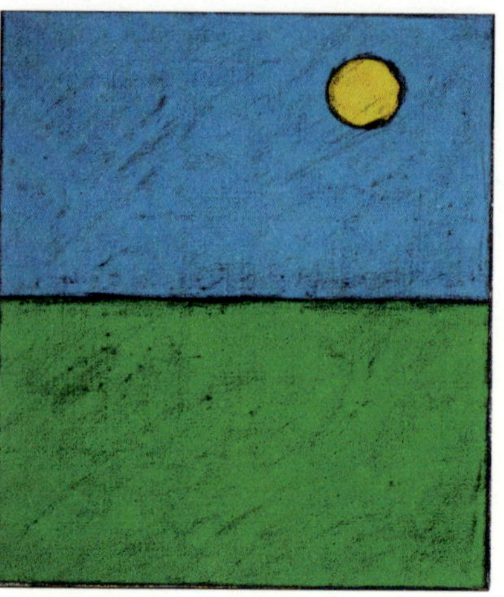
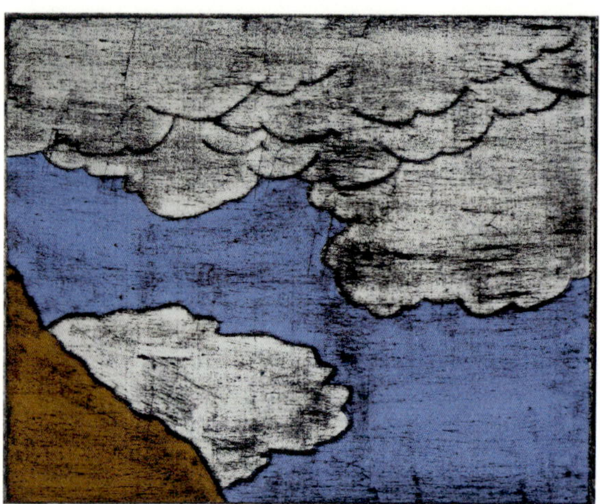
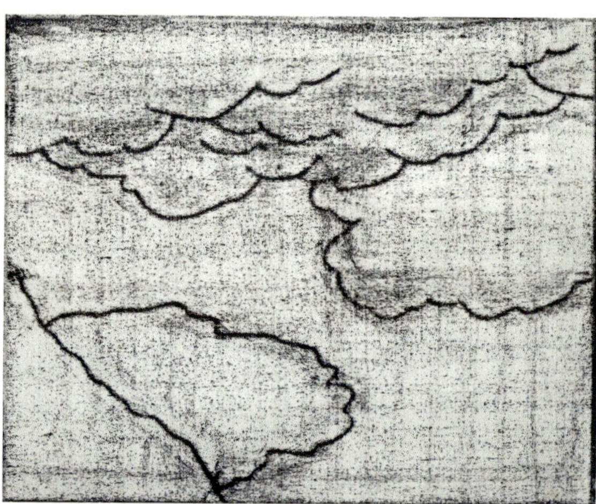
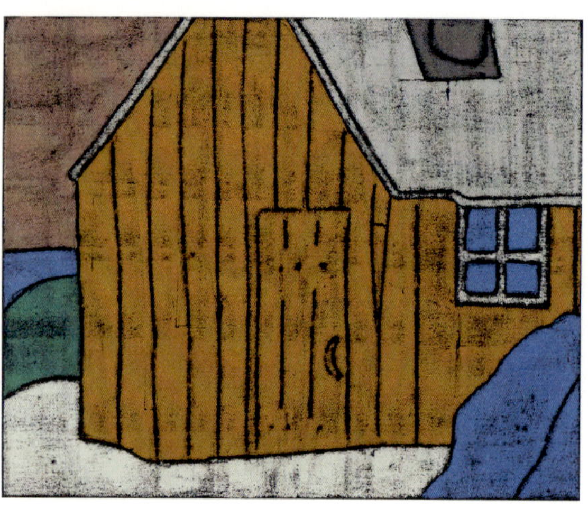
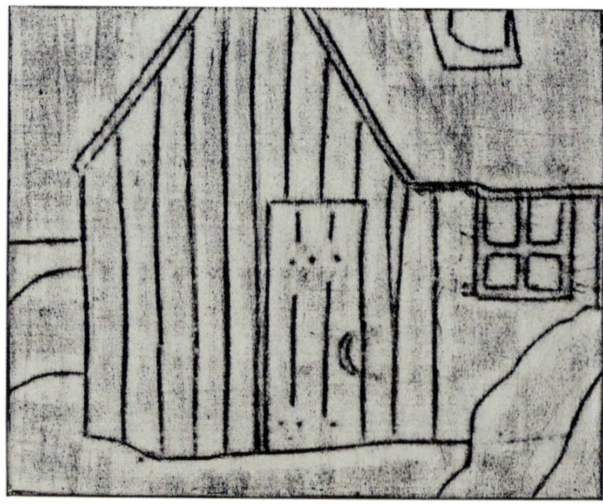

2012.56 Untitled (Elements), 60×50 cm each (diptych)
2012.57 Untitled (Elements), 50×60 cm each (diptych)
2012.58 Untitled (Elements), 50×60 cm each (diptych)

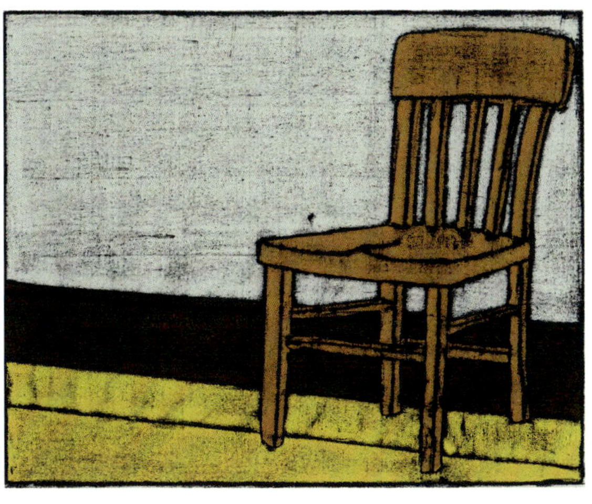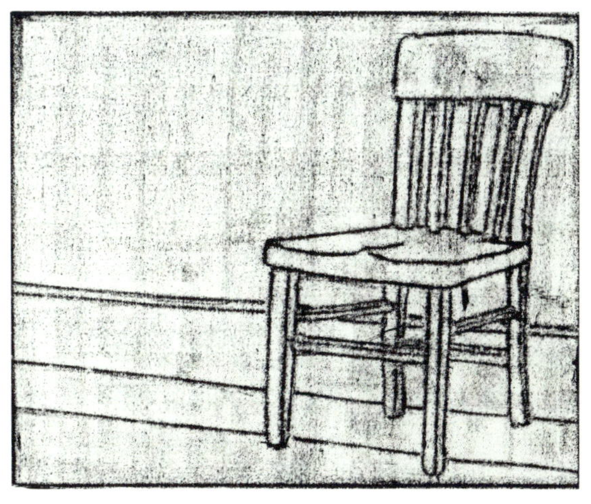
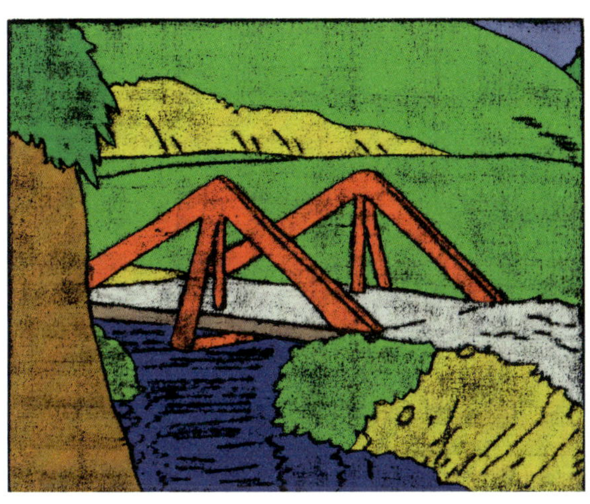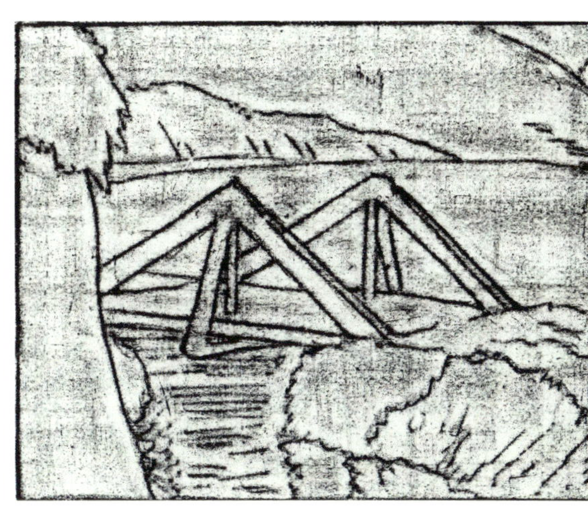
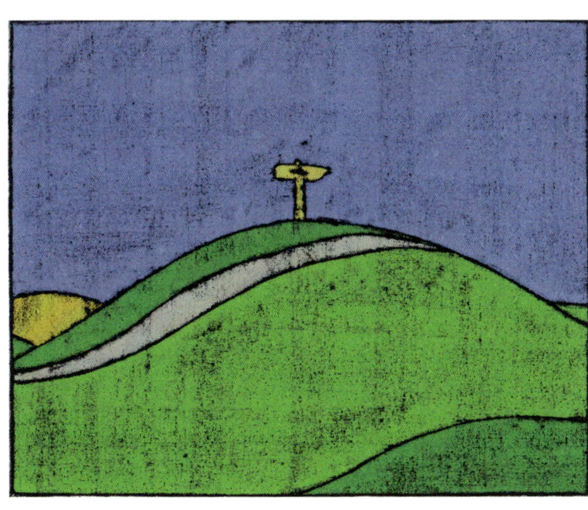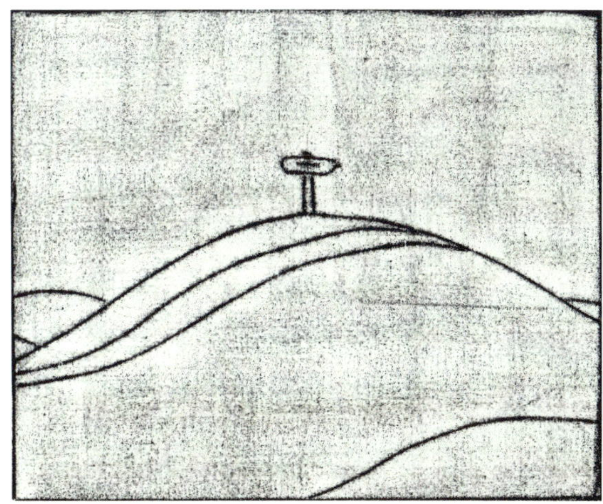

2012.59 Untitled (Elements), 50 × 60 cm each (diptych)
2012.60 Untitled (Elements), 50 × 60 cm each (diptych)
2012.61 Untitled (Elements), 50 × 60 cm each (diptych)

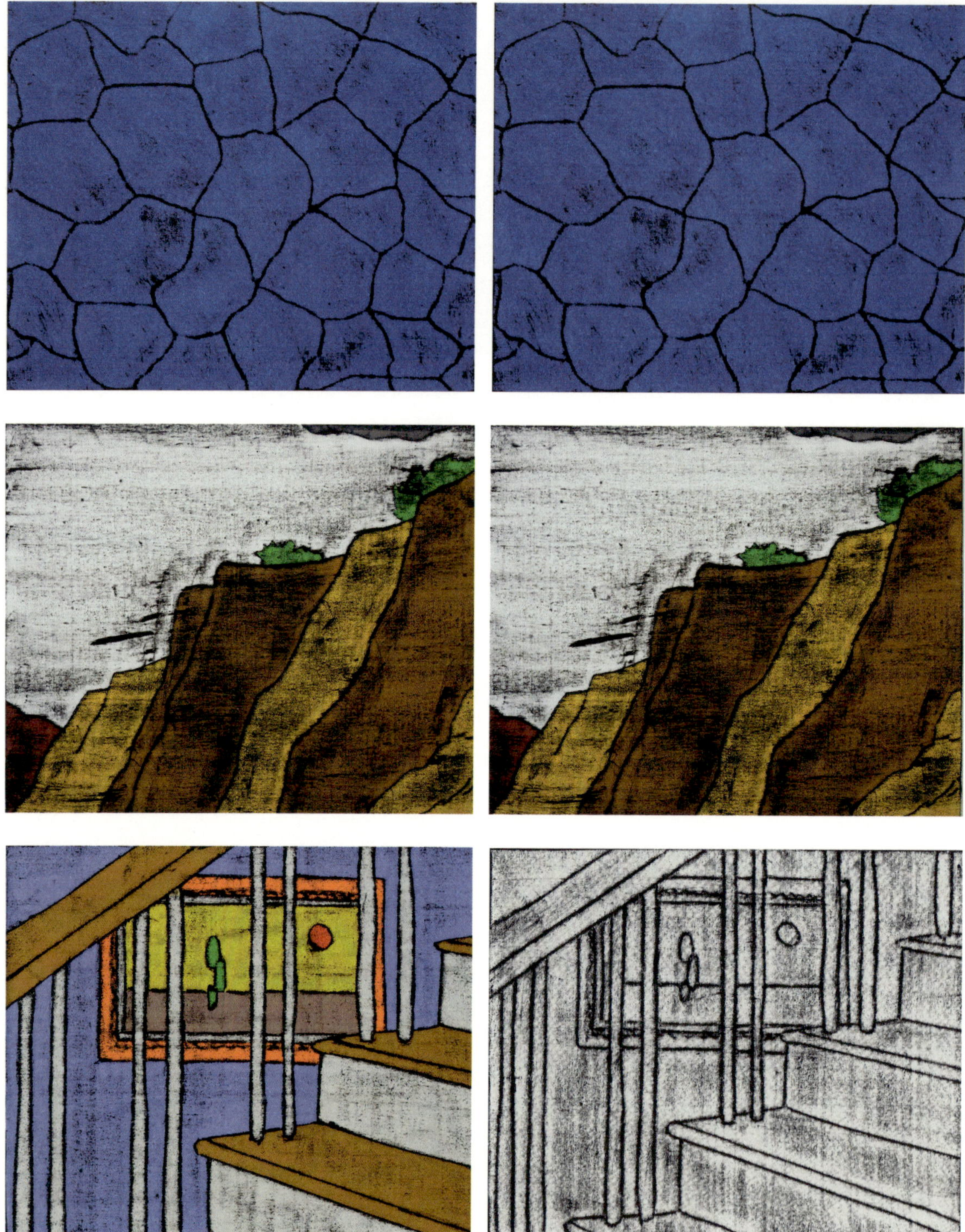

2012.62 Untitled (Elements), 50 × 60 cm each (diptych)
2012.63 Untitled (Elements), 50 × 60 cm each (diptych)
2012.64 Untitled (Elements), 50 × 60 cm each (diptych)

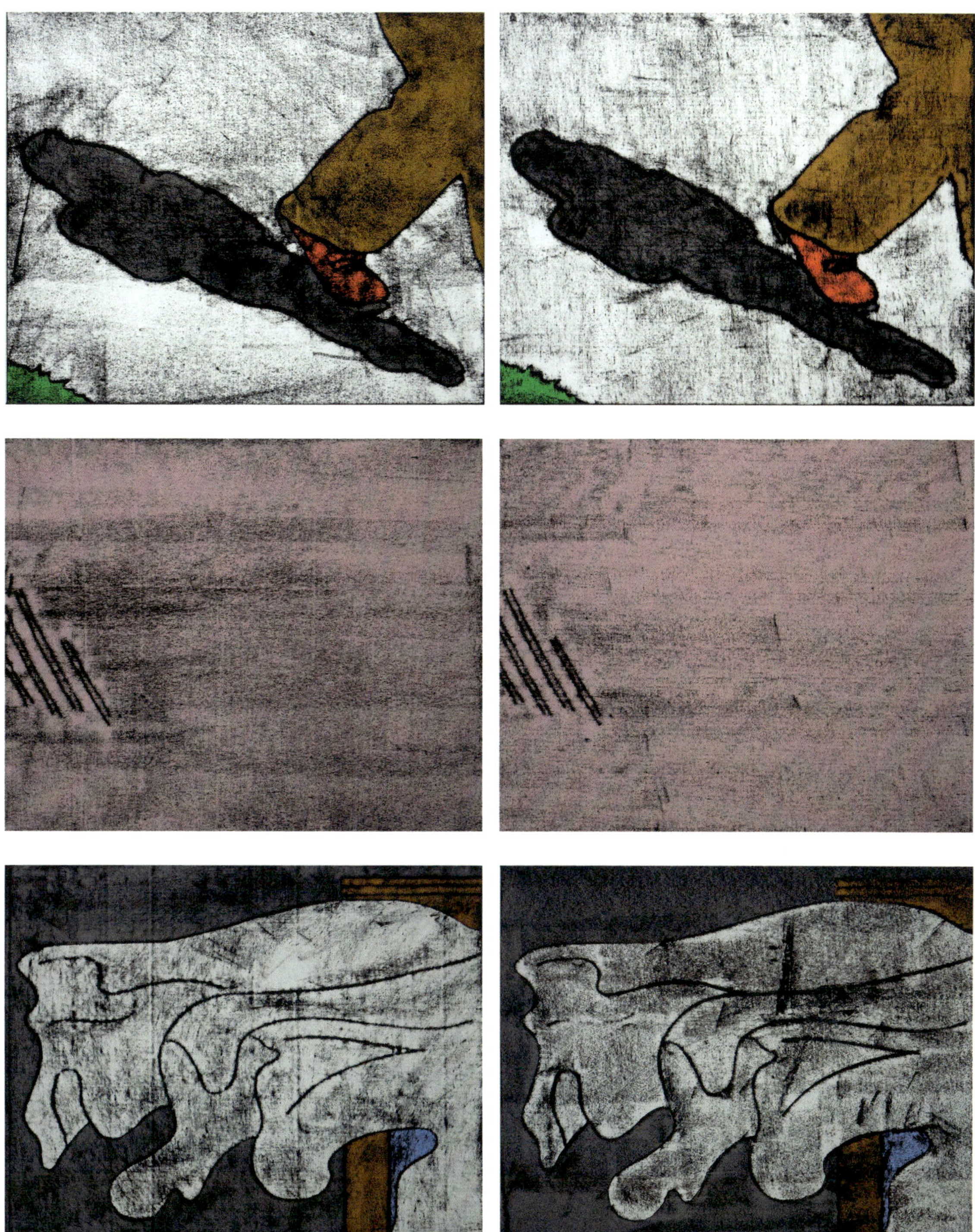

2012.65 Untitled (Elements), 50 × 60 cm each (diptych)
2012.66 Untitled (Elements), 50 × 60 cm each (diptych)
2012.67 Untitled (Elements), 50 × 60 cm each (diptych)

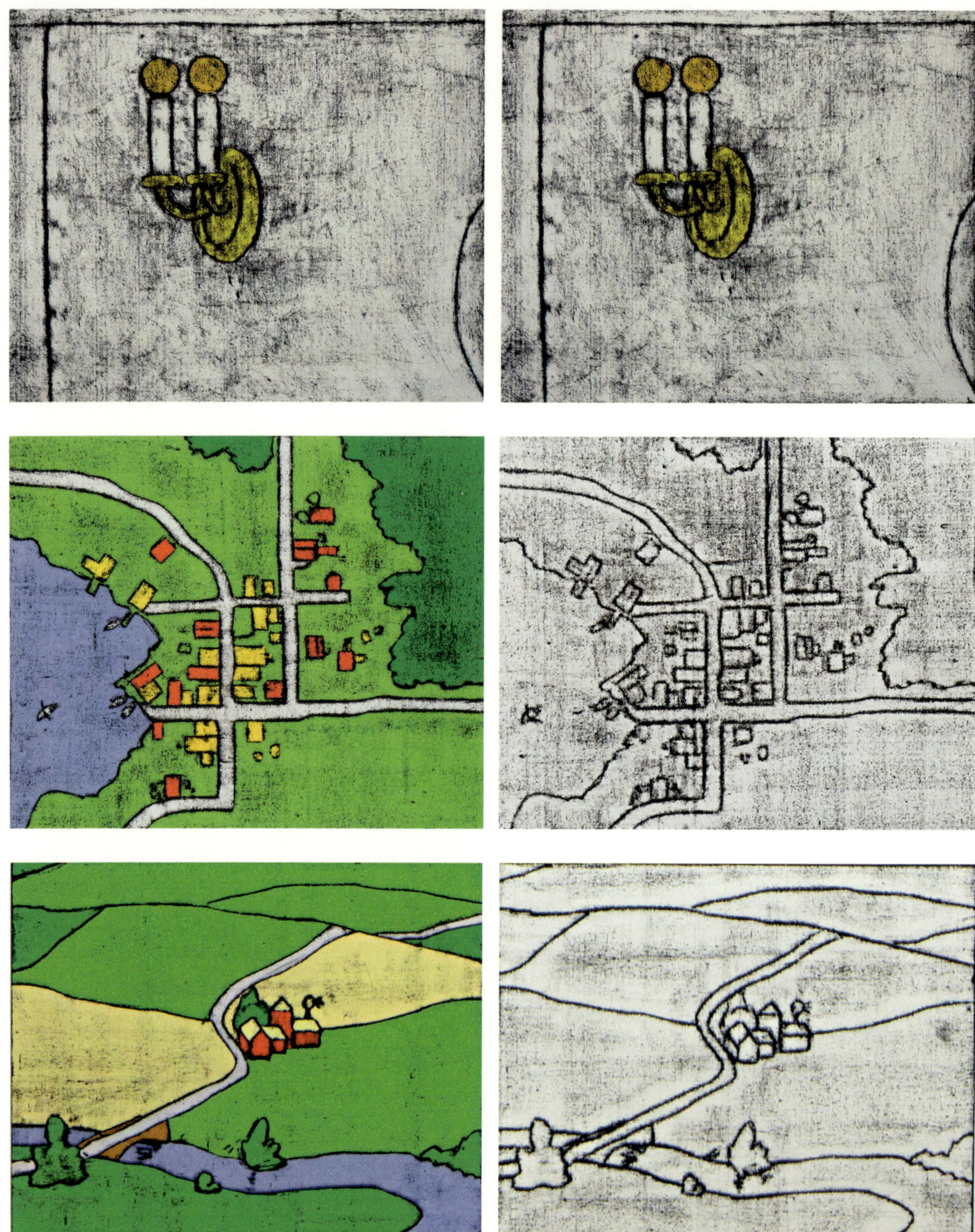

2012.68 Untitled (Elements), 50 × 60 cm each (diptych)
2012.69 Untitled (Elements), 50 × 60 cm each (diptych)
2012.70 Untitled (Elements), 50 × 60 cm each (diptych)

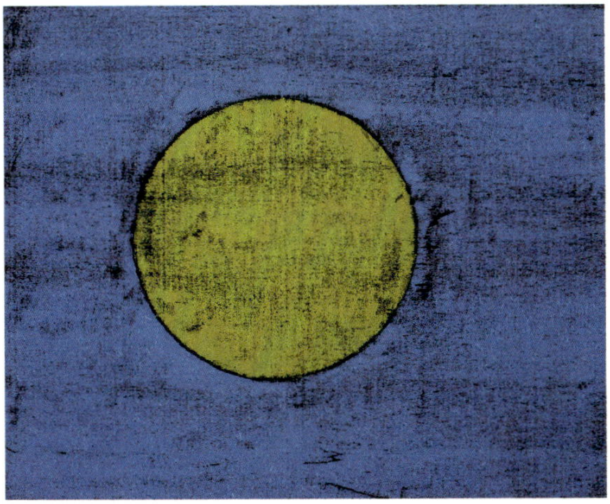

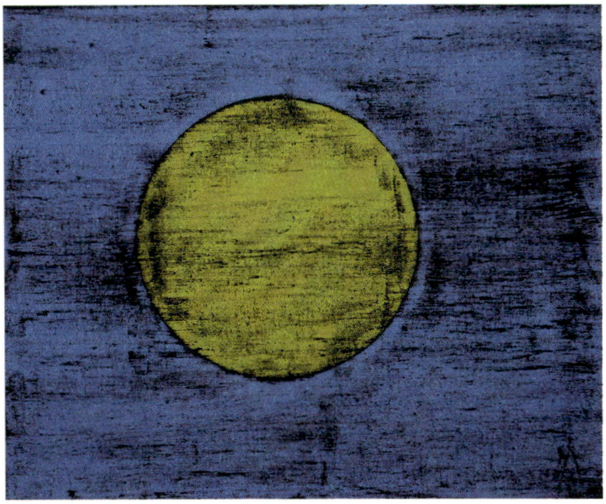

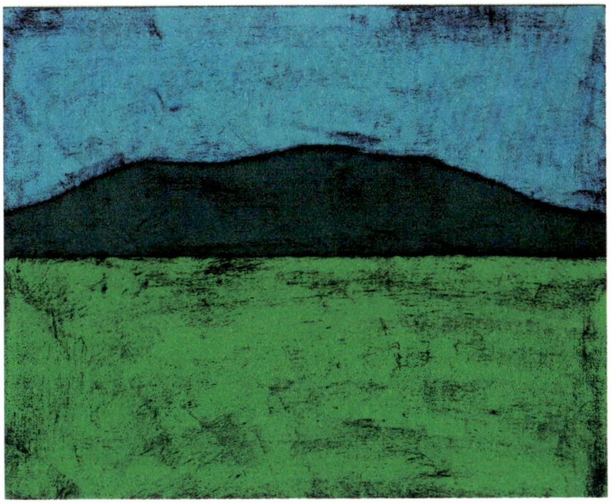

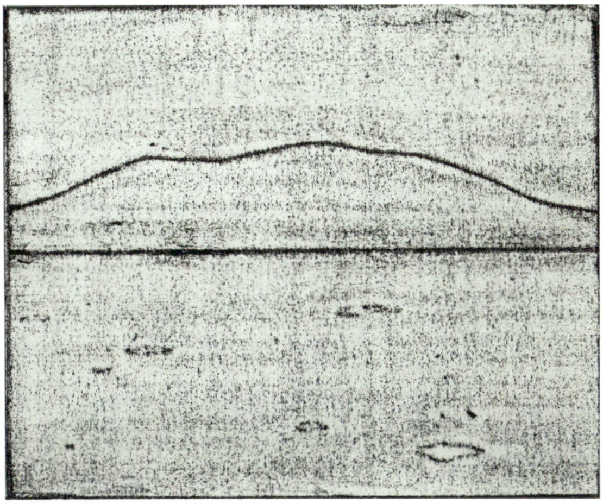

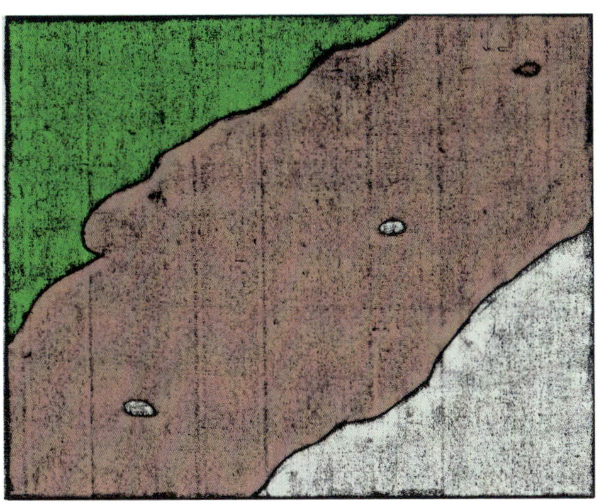

2012.71 Untitled (Elements), 50 × 60 cm each (diptych)
2012.72 Untitled (Elements), 50 × 60 cm each (diptych)
2012.73 Untitled (Elements), 50 × 60 cm

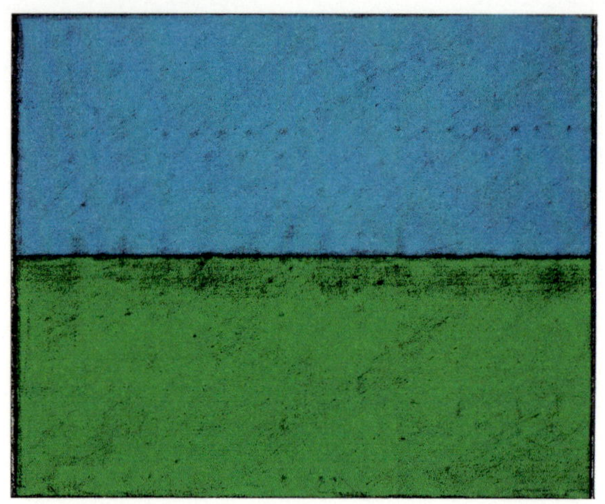

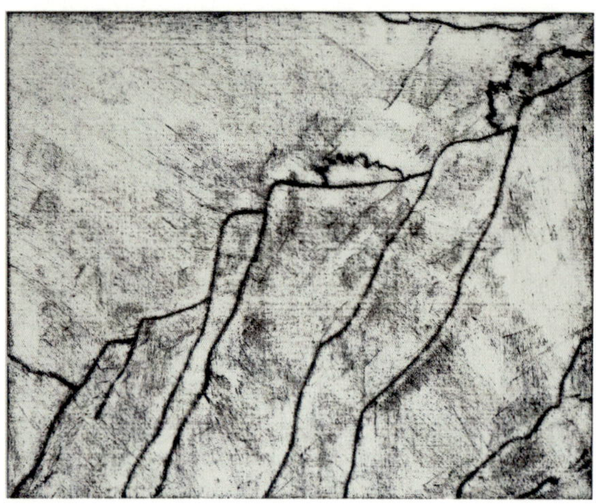

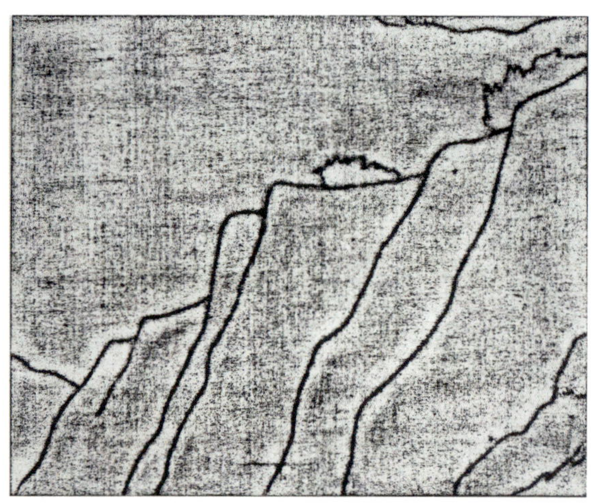

2012.74 Untitled (Elements), 50 × 60 cm
2012.75 Untitled (Elements), 50 × 60 cm
2012.76 Untitled (Elements), 50 × 60 cm

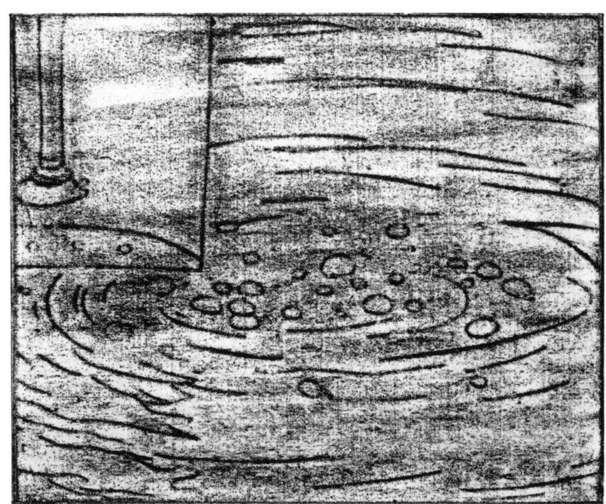

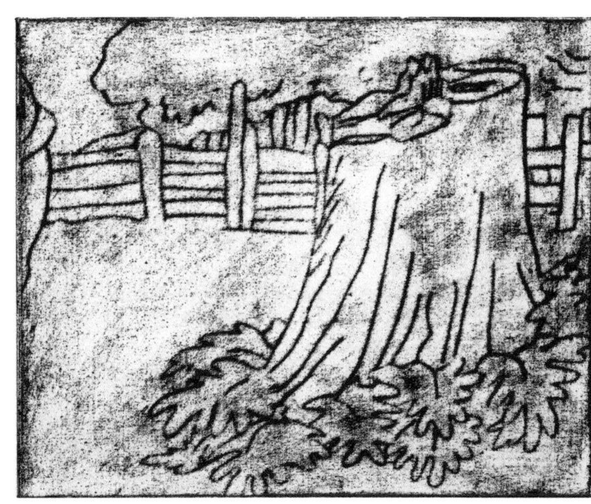

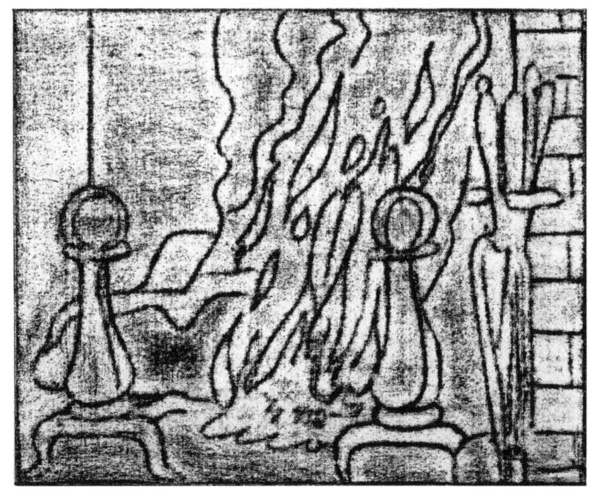

2012.77 Untitled (Elements), 50 × 60 cm
2012.78 Untitled (Elements), 50 × 60 cm
2012.79 Untitled (Elements), 50 × 60 cm

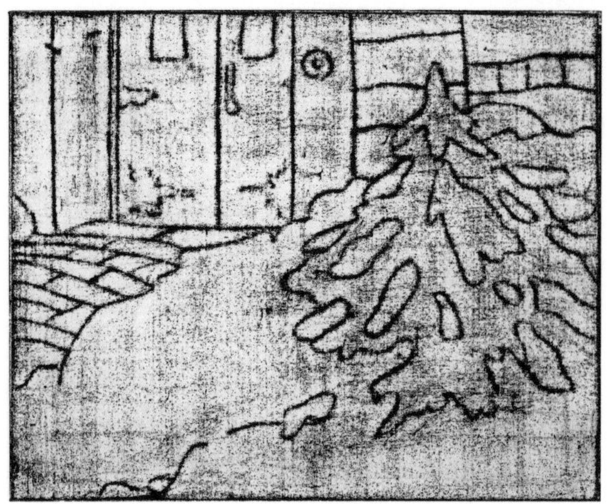

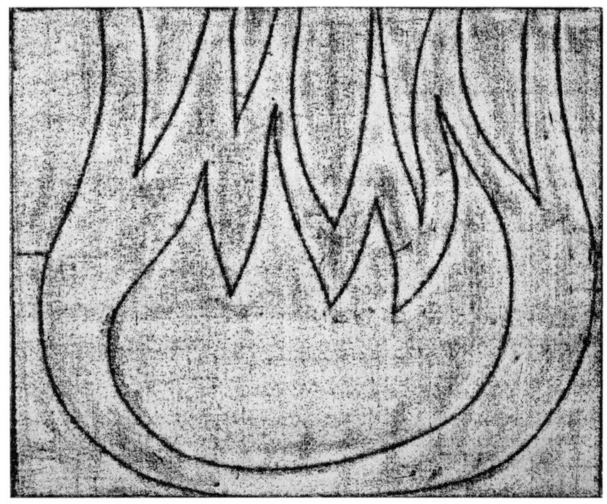

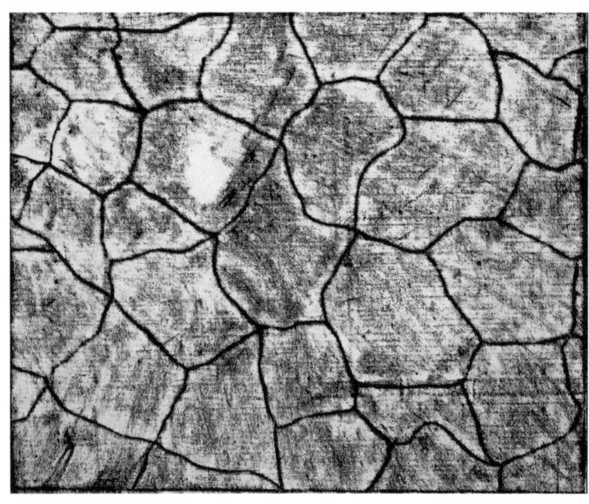

2012.80 Untitled (Elements), 50 × 60 cm
2012.81 Untitled (Elements), 50 × 60 cm
2012.82 Untitled (Elements), 50 × 60 cm

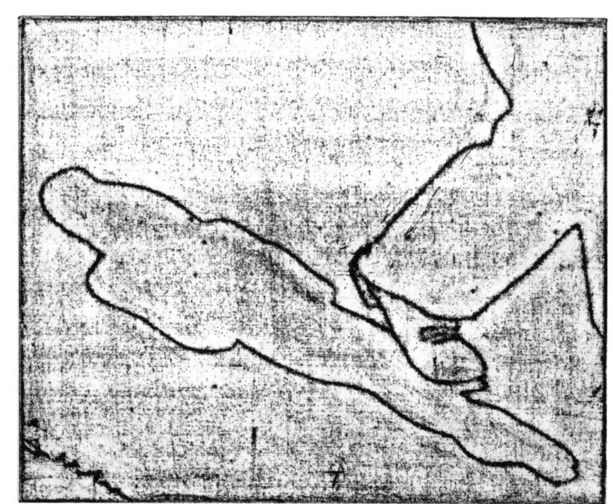

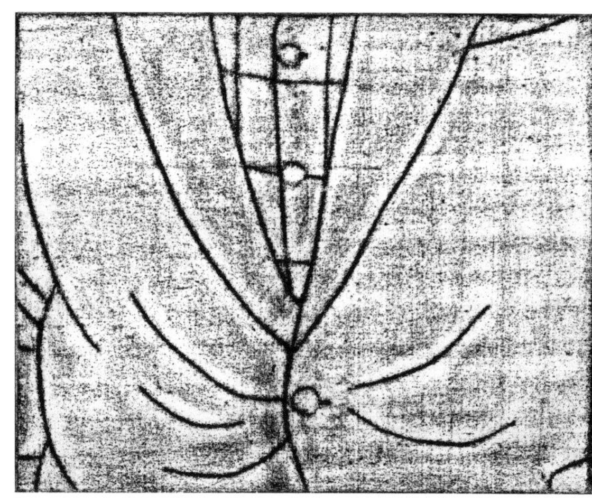

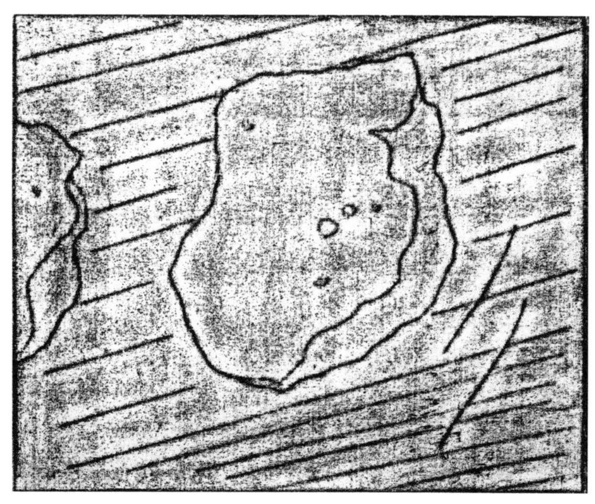

2012.83 Untitled (Elements), 50 × 60 cm
2012.84 Untitled (Elements), 50 × 60 cm
2012.85 Untitled (Elements), 50 × 60 cm

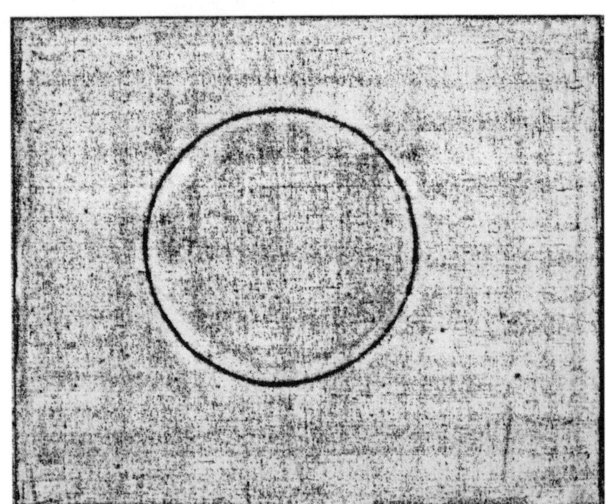

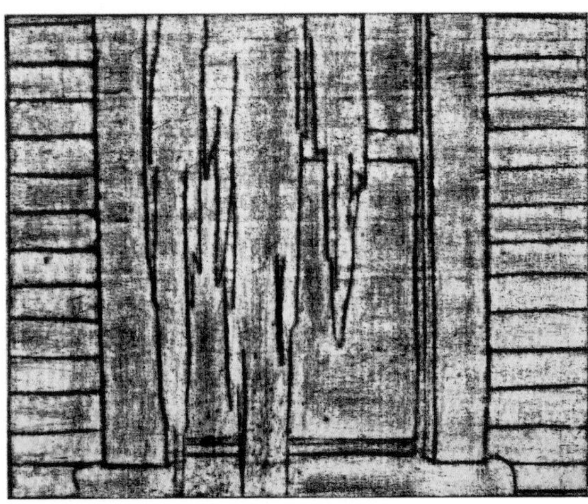

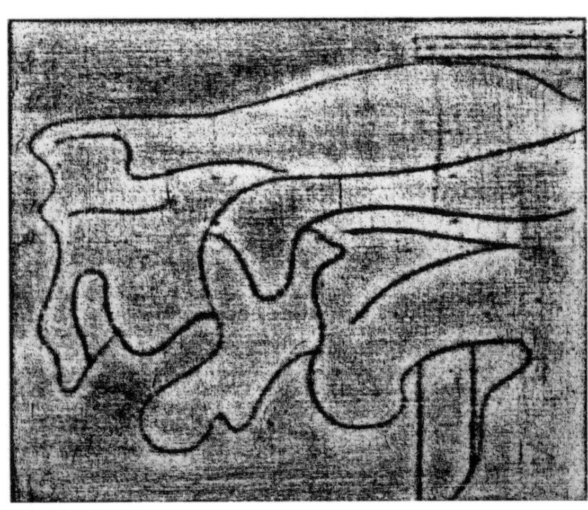

2012.86 Untitled (Elements), 50 × 60 cm
2012.87 Untitled (Elements), 50 × 60 cm
2012.88 Untitled (Elements), 50 × 60 cm

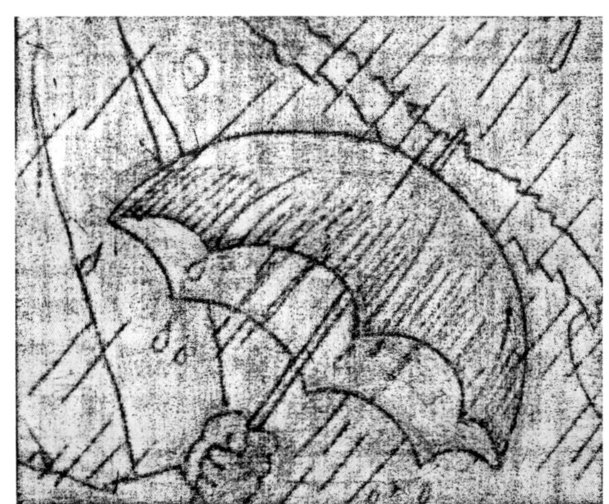

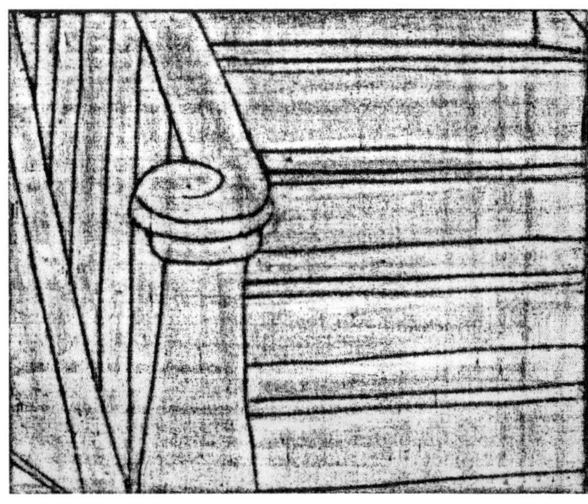

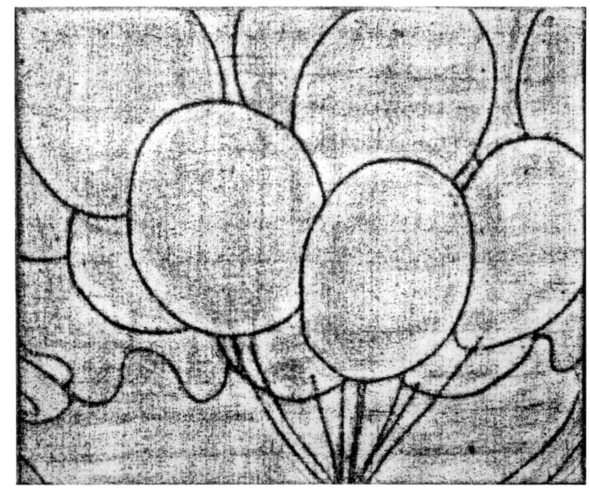

2012.89 Untitled (Elements), 50 × 60 cm
2012.90 Untitled (Elements), 50 × 60 cm
2012.91 Untitled (Elements), 50 × 60 cm

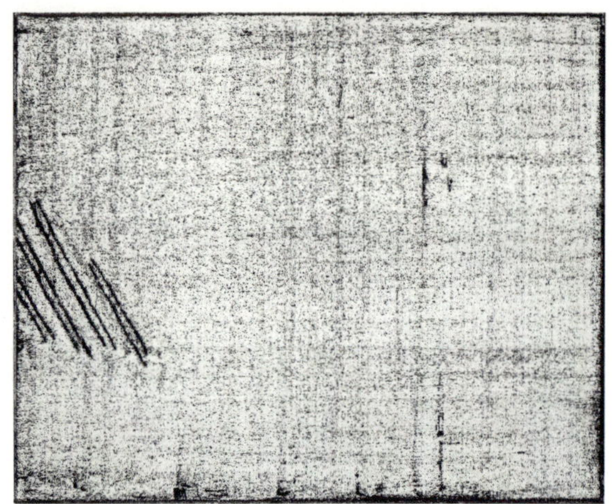

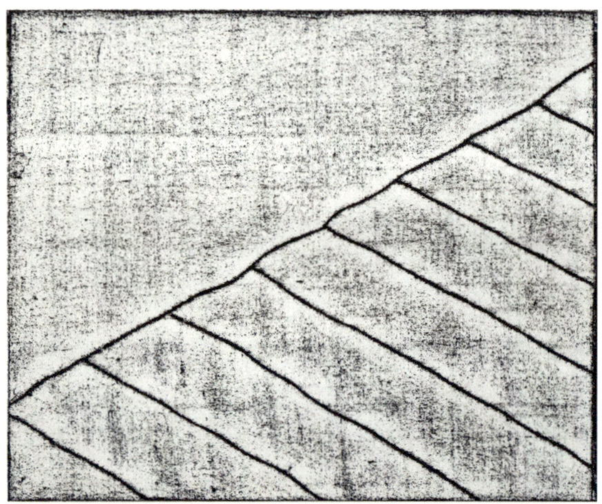

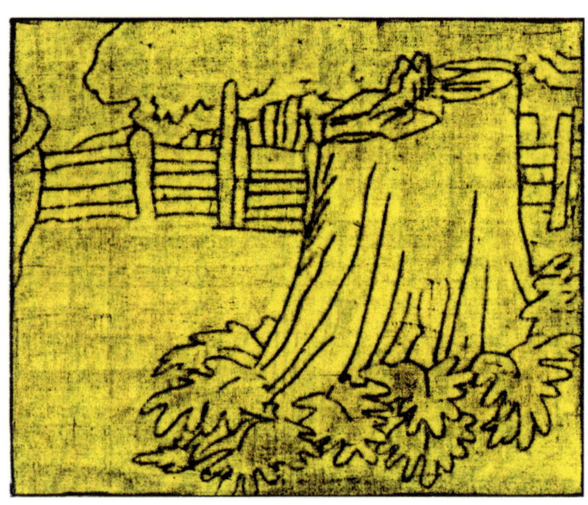

2012.92 Untitled (Elements), 50 × 60 cm
2012.93 Untitled (Elements), 50 × 60 cm
2012.94 Untitled (Elements), 50 × 60 cm

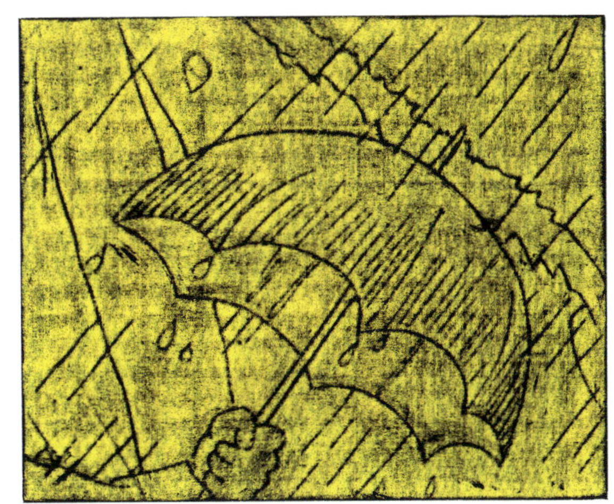

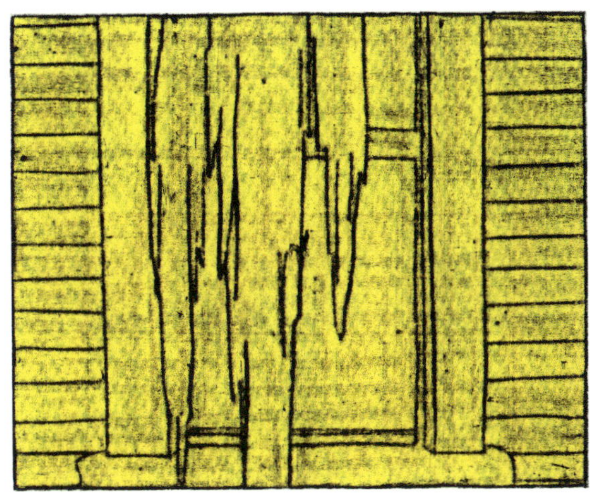

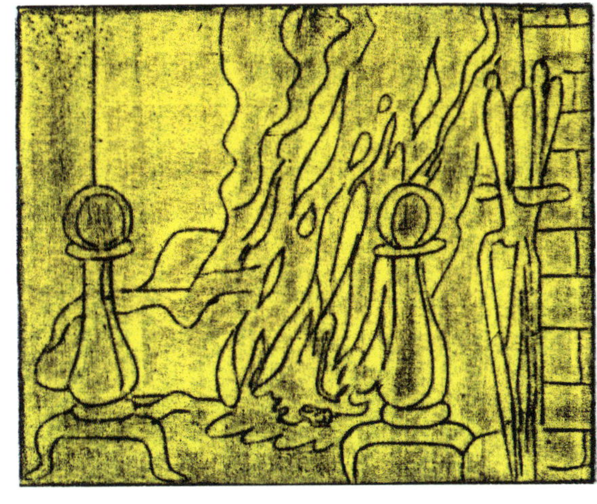

2012.95 Untitled (Elements), 50 × 60 cm
2012.96 Untitled (Elements), 50 × 60 cm
2012.97 Untitled (Elements), 50 × 60 cm

2013

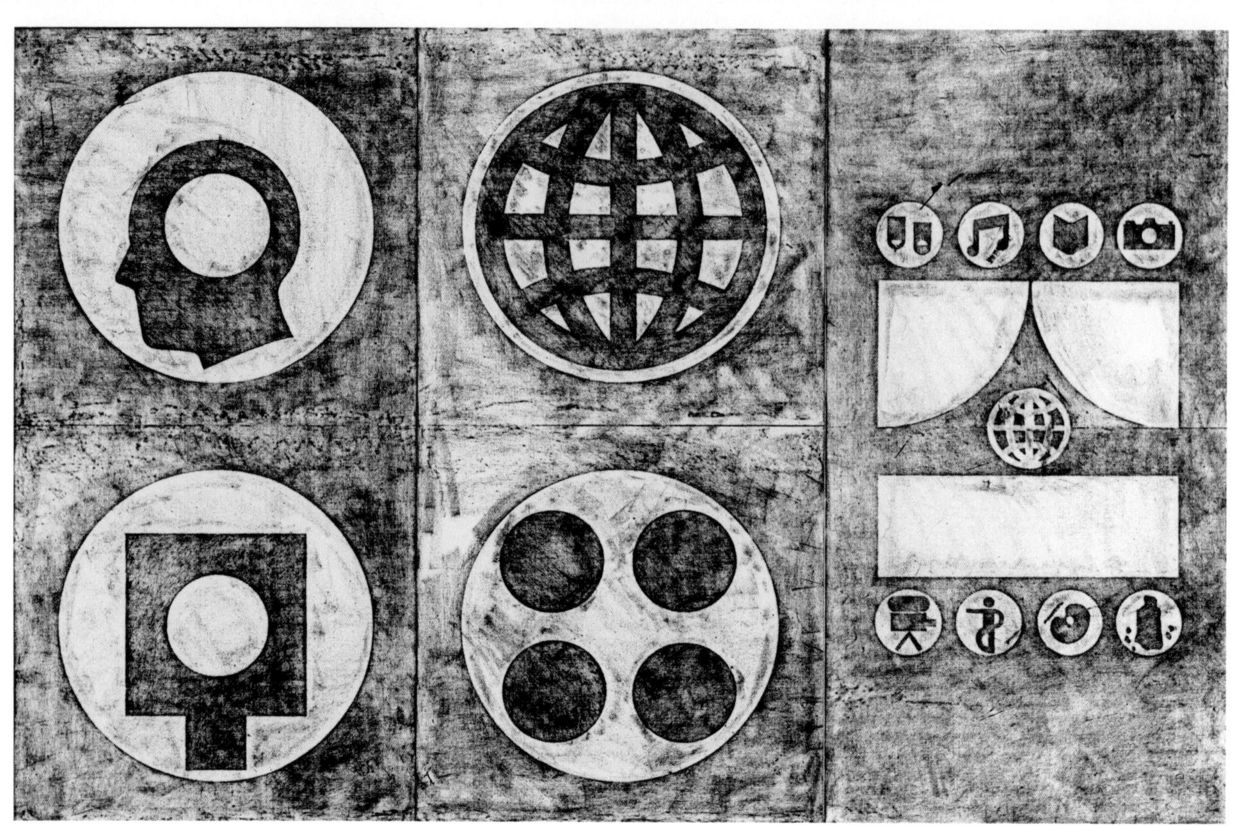

2013.1 Untitled (5 Worlds), 1987/2013, 244 × 366 (3 parts)

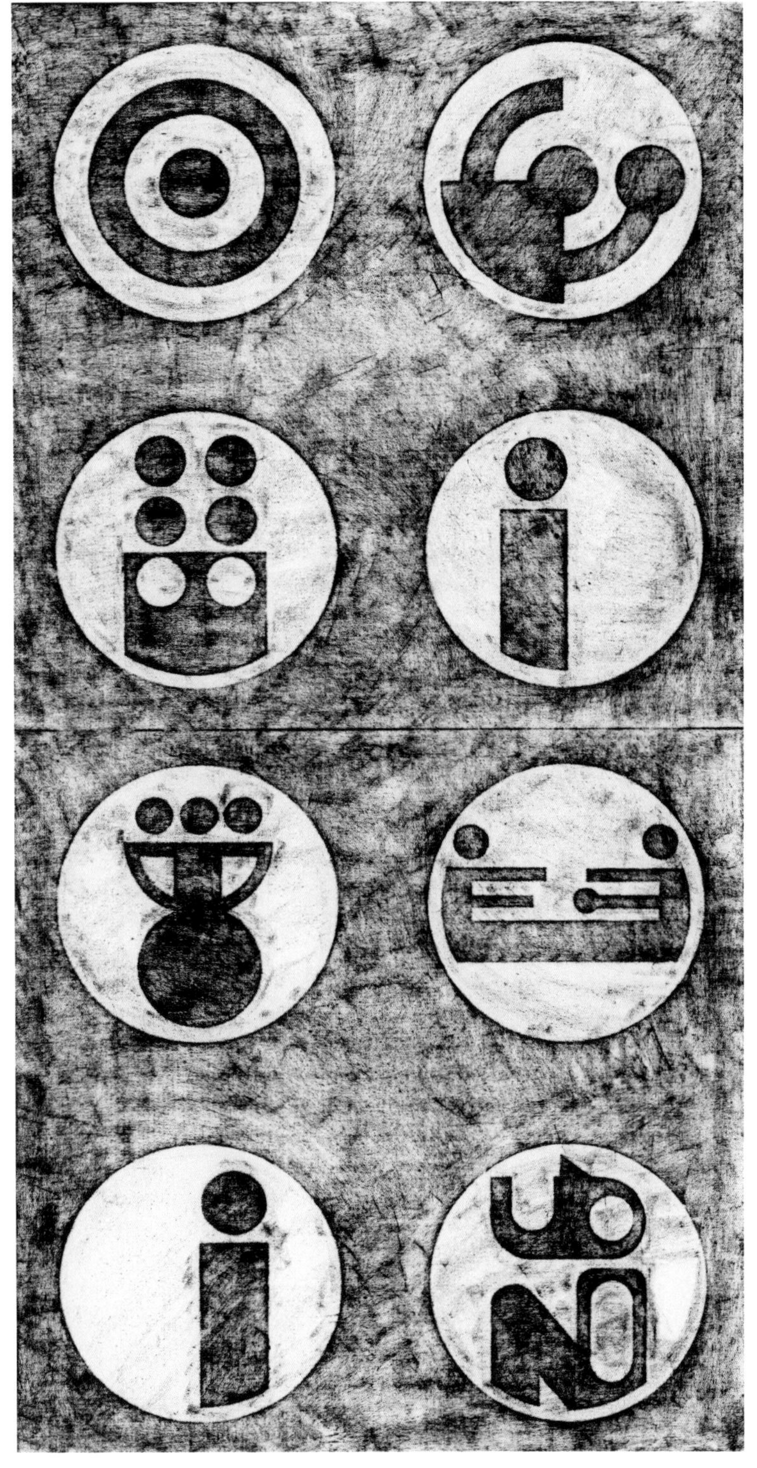

2013.2 Untitled (Cosmology), 1987/2013, 244 × 122 cm

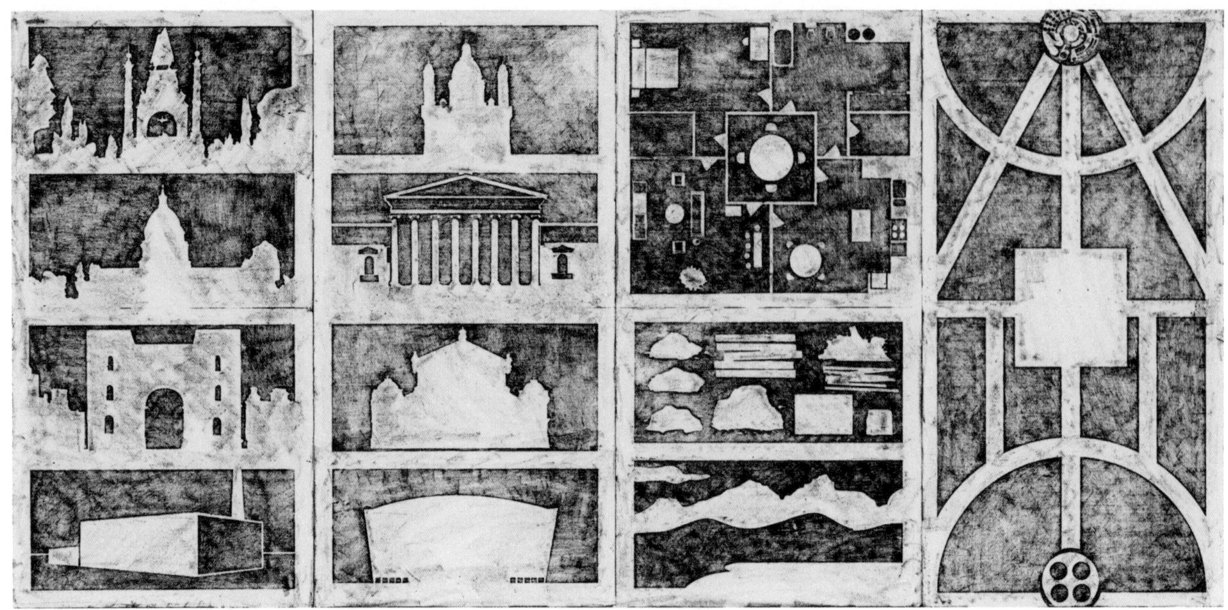

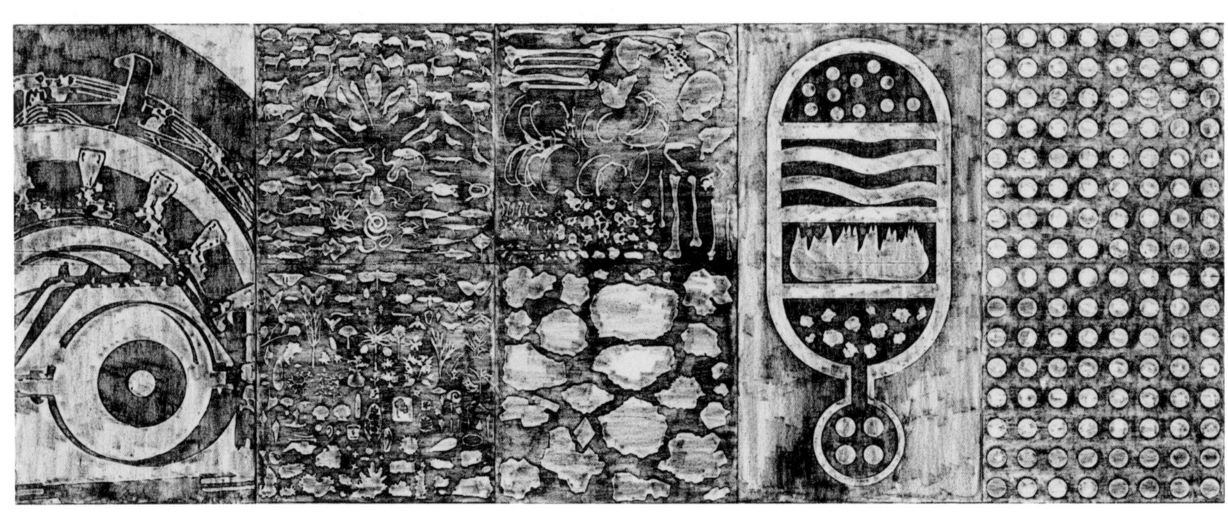

2013.3 Untitled (City), 1987/2013, 244 × 488 cm (4 parts)
2013.4 Untitled (Elements), 1987/2013, 244 × 609.5 cm (5 parts)

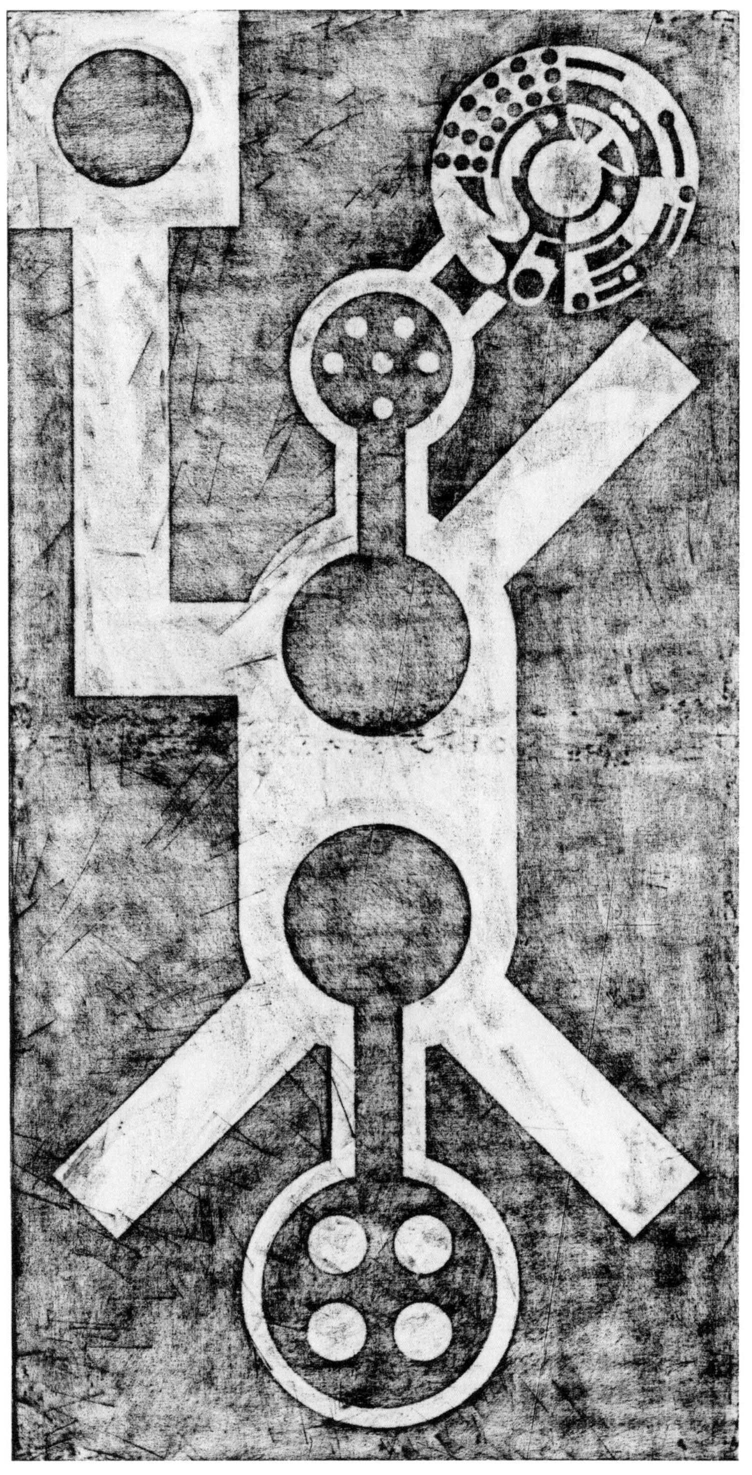

2013.5 Untitled (Anatomy), 1987/2013, 244 × 122 cm

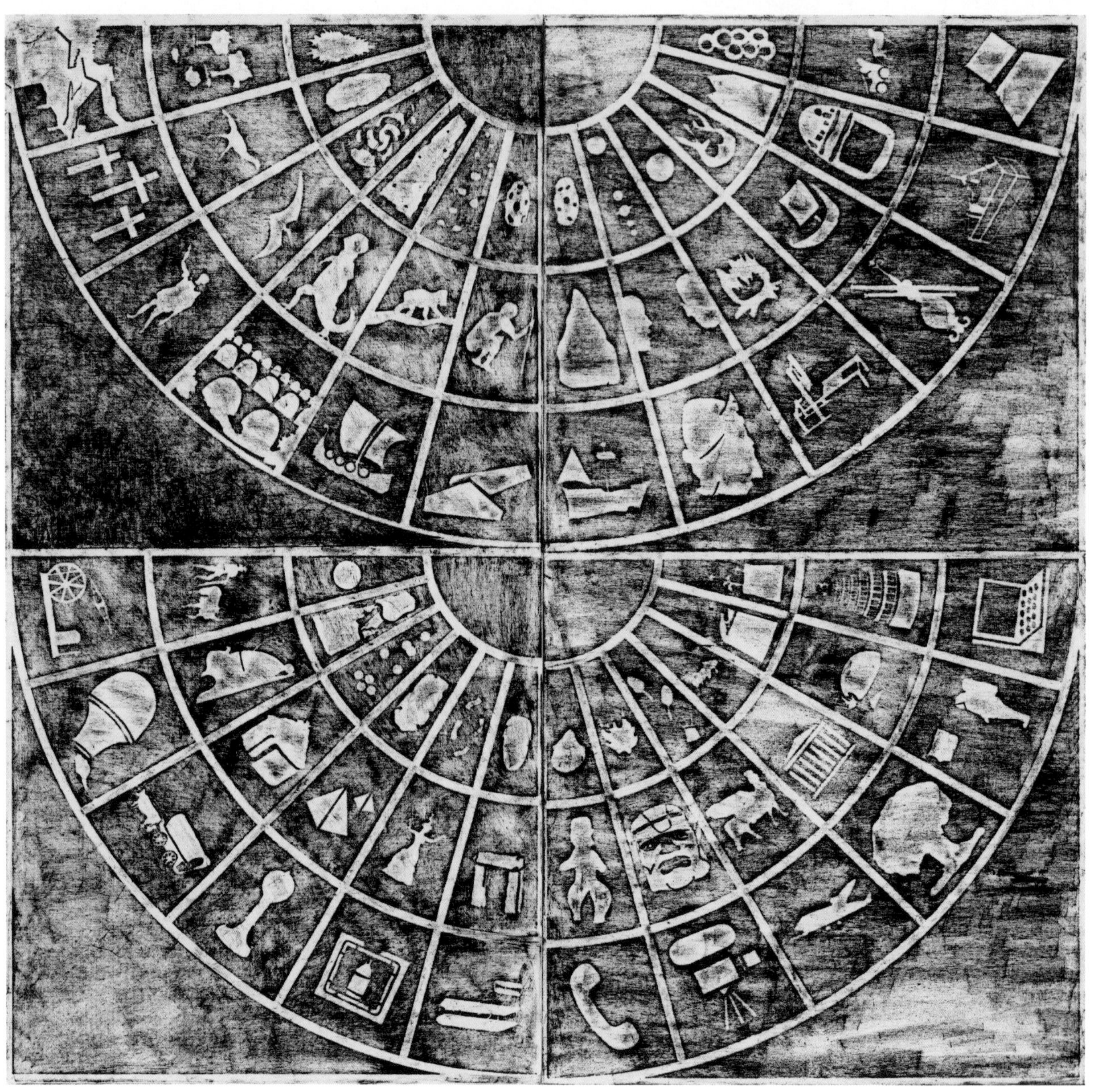

2013.6 Untitled (History), 1987/2013, 244 × 244 cm (2 parts)

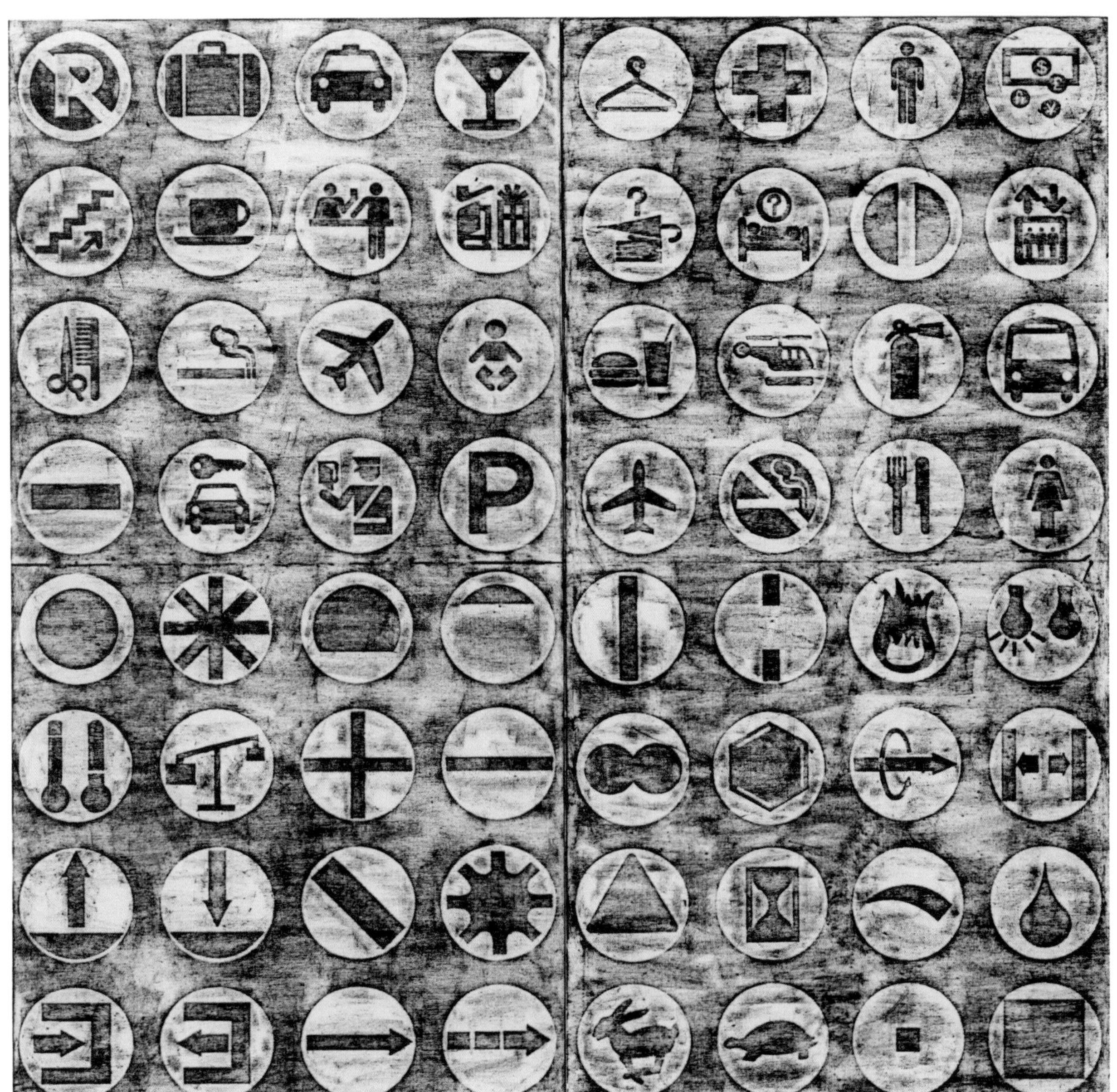

2013.7 Untitled (Signs), 1987/2013, 244 × 244 cm (2 parts)

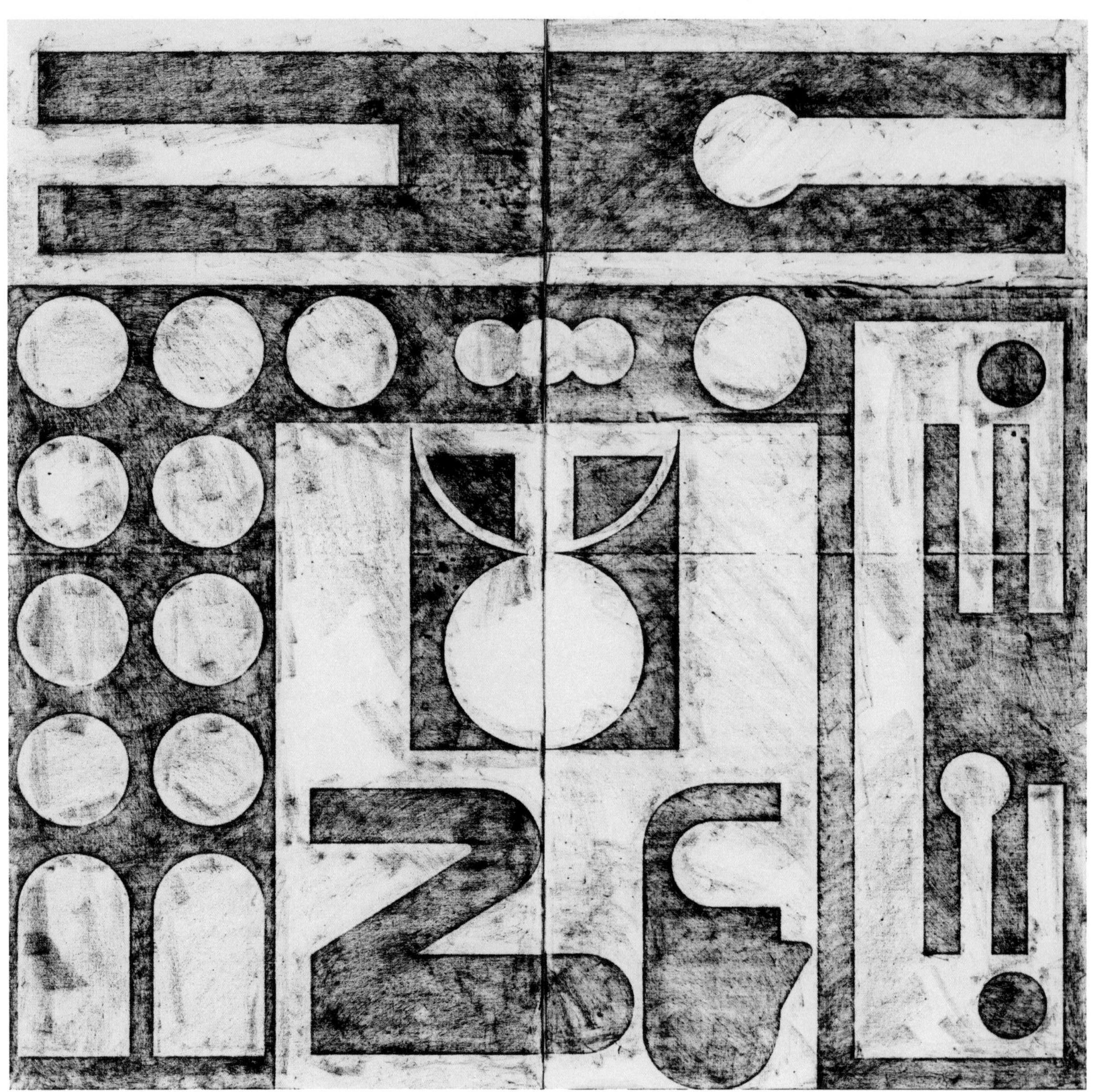

2013.8 Untitled (Integrated Cosmology), 1987/2013, 244 × 244 cm (2 parts)

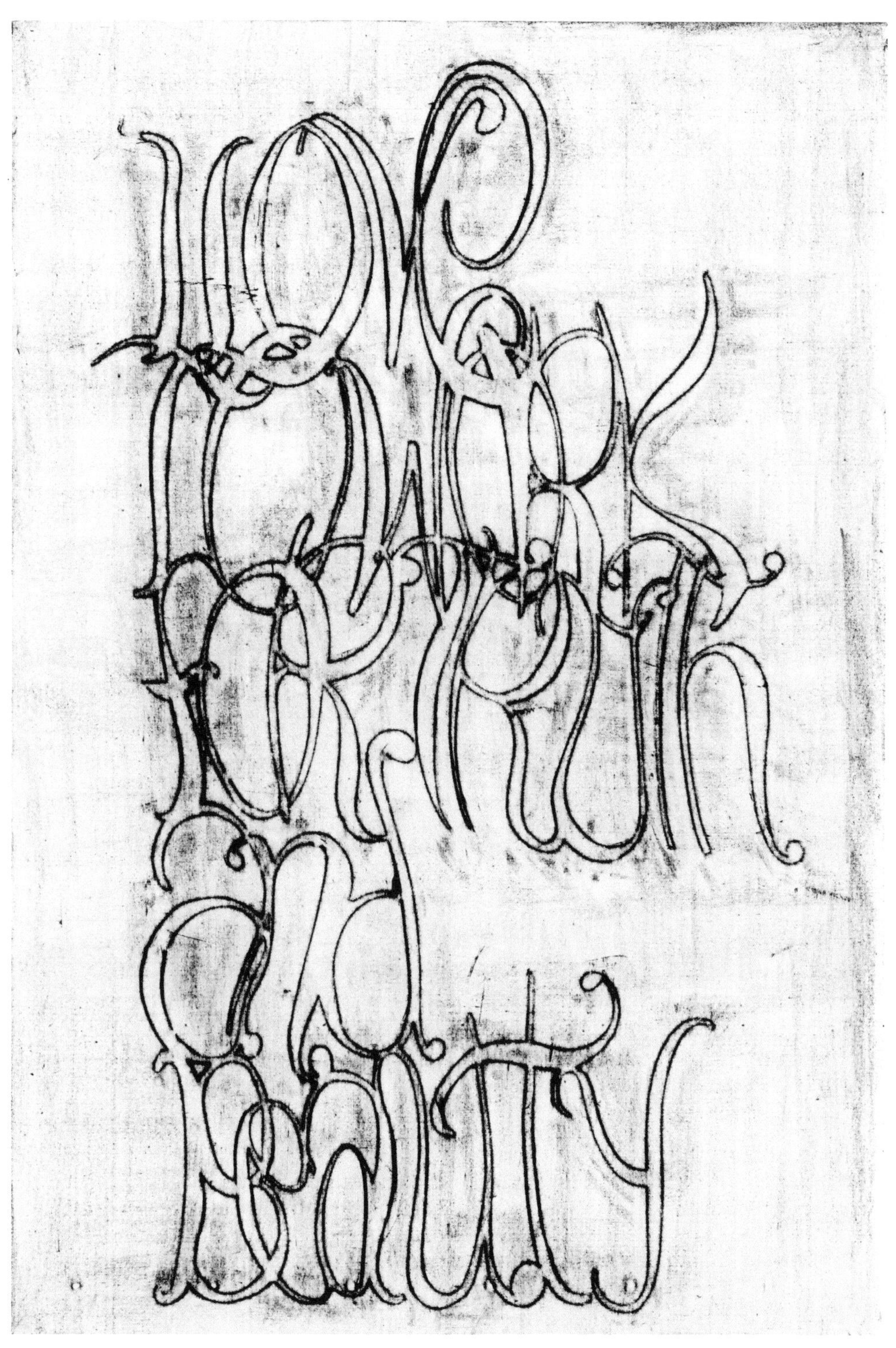

2013.9 Untitled (That Person: I Love to Work for Truth and Beauty), 183 × 122 cm

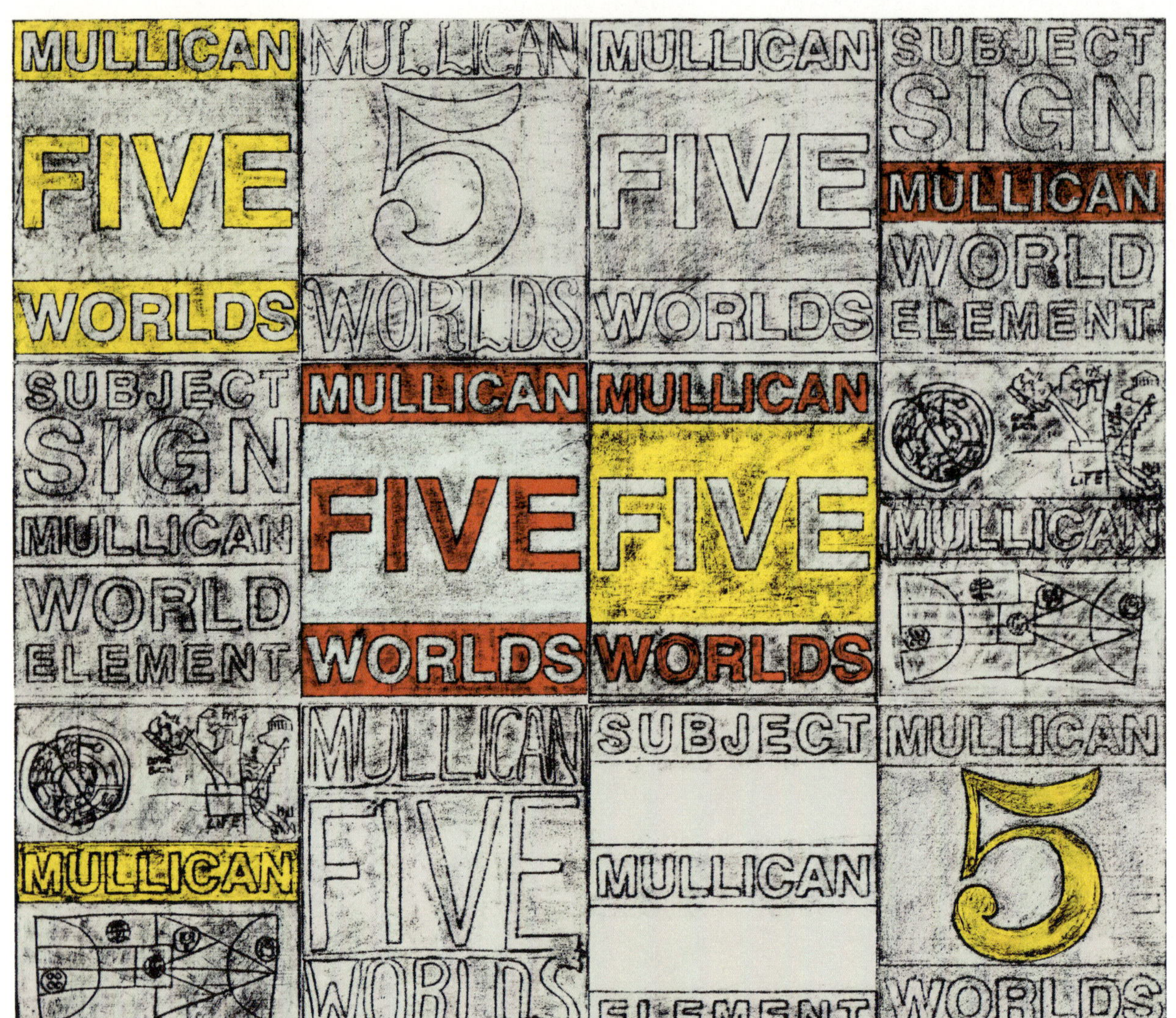

2013.10 Untitled (12 Covers I), 180 × 200 cm (12 parts)

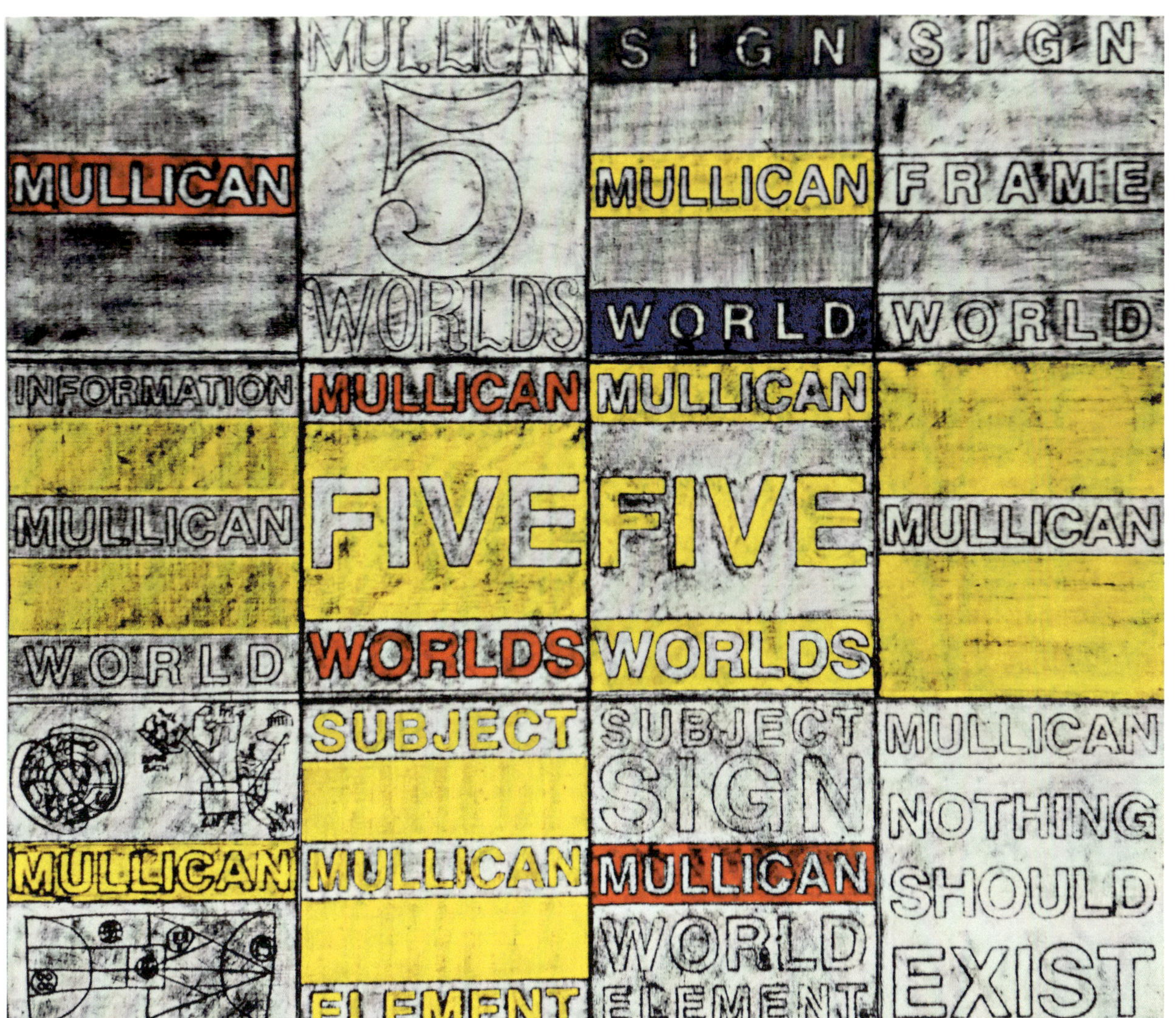

2013.11 Untitled (12 Covers II), 180 × 200 cm (12 parts)

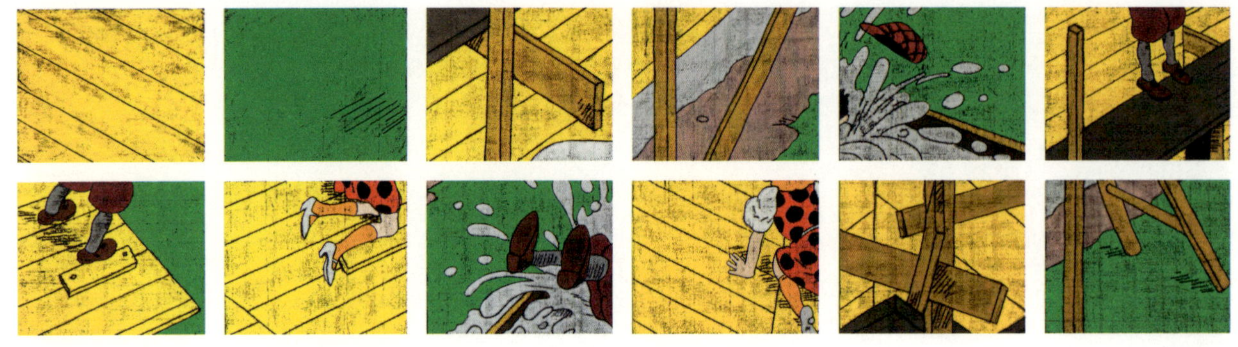

2013.12 Untitled (12 from 1 Picture), 50 × 60 cm each (12 parts)

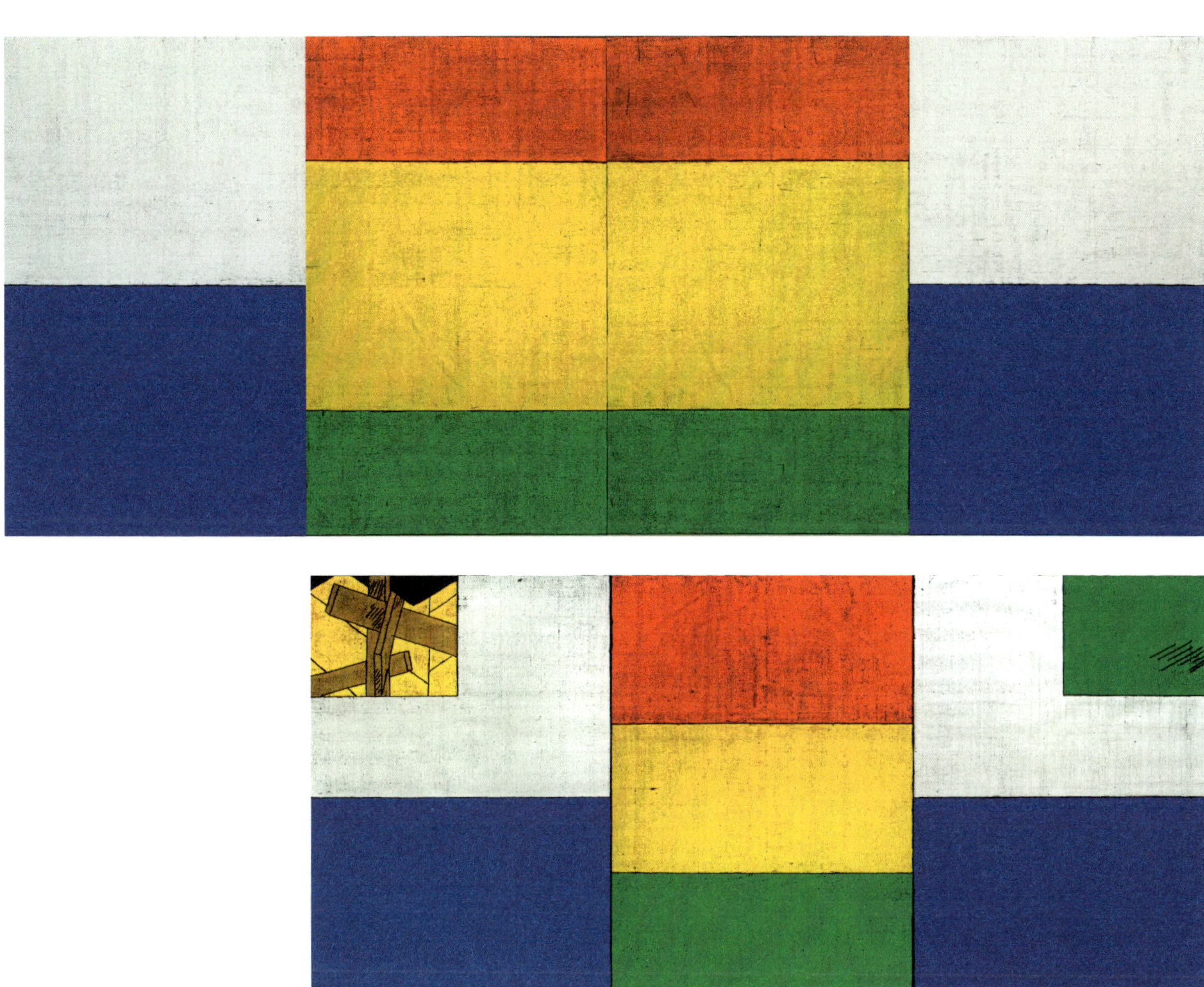

2013.13 Untitled (Overall Chart), 200 × 480 cm (4 parts)
2013.14 Untitled (Overall Chart with Two Details), 183 × 366 cm (3 parts)

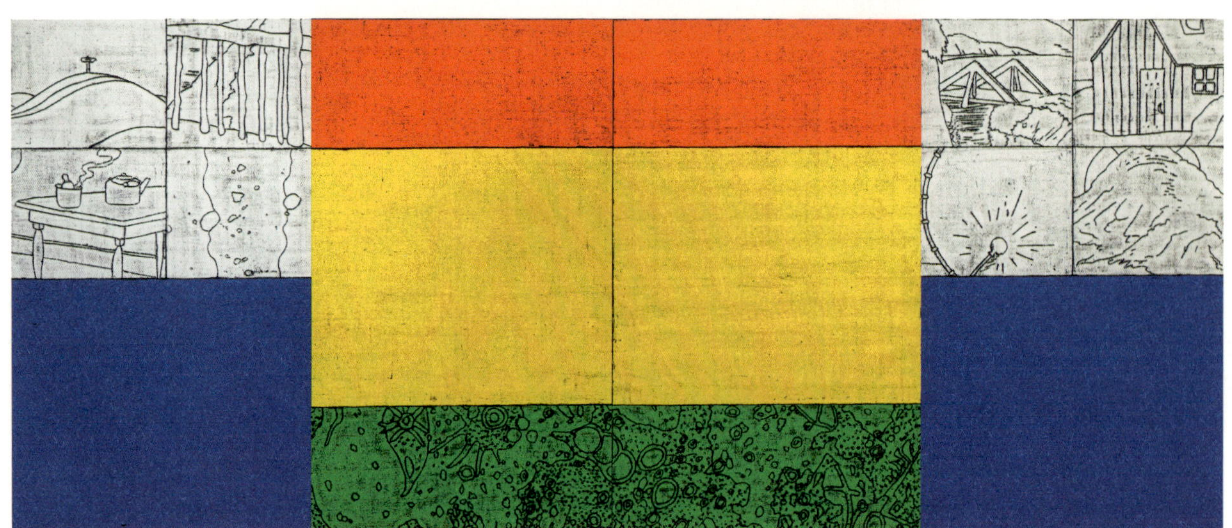

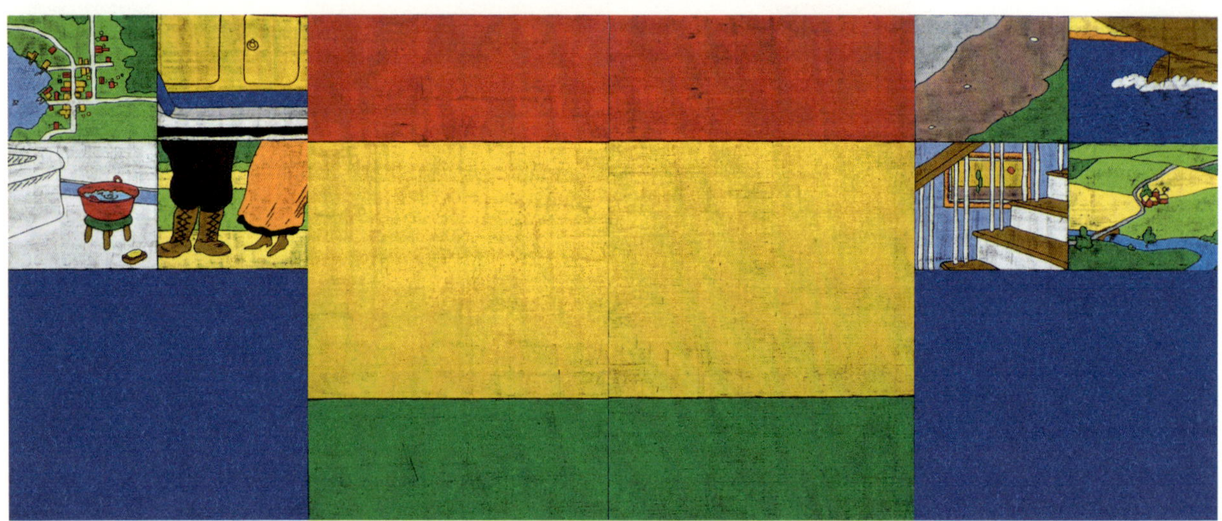

2013.15 Untitled (Overall Chart with Comic Book Details and Detail of the Moon), 200 × 480 cm (4 parts)
2013.16 Untitled (Overall Chart with Comic Book Details), 200 × 480 cm (4 parts)

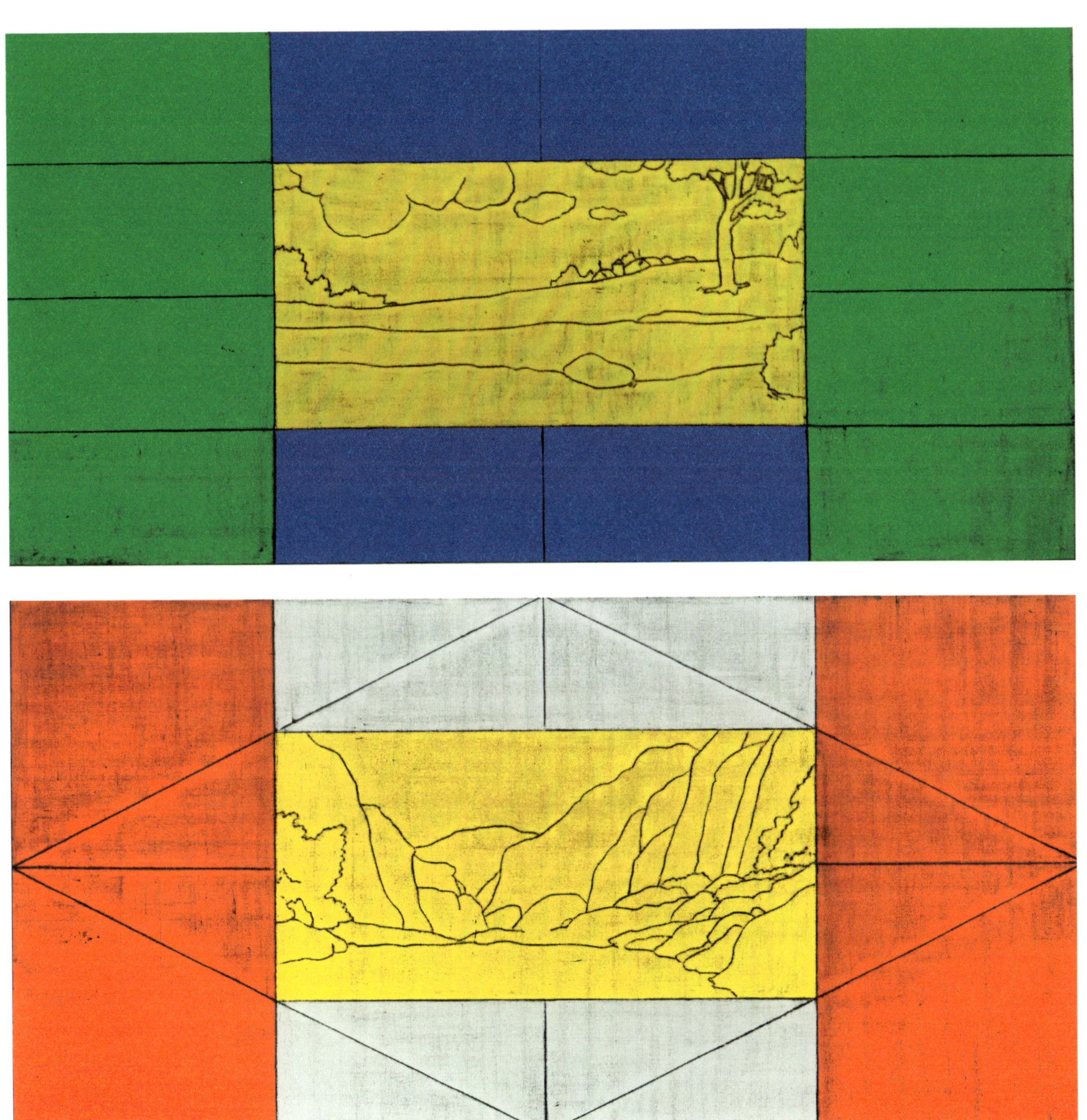

2013.17 Untitled (Frame World Elements), 120 × 240 cm (2 parts)
2013.18 Untitled (Subject Sign Frame), 120 × 240 cm (2 parts)

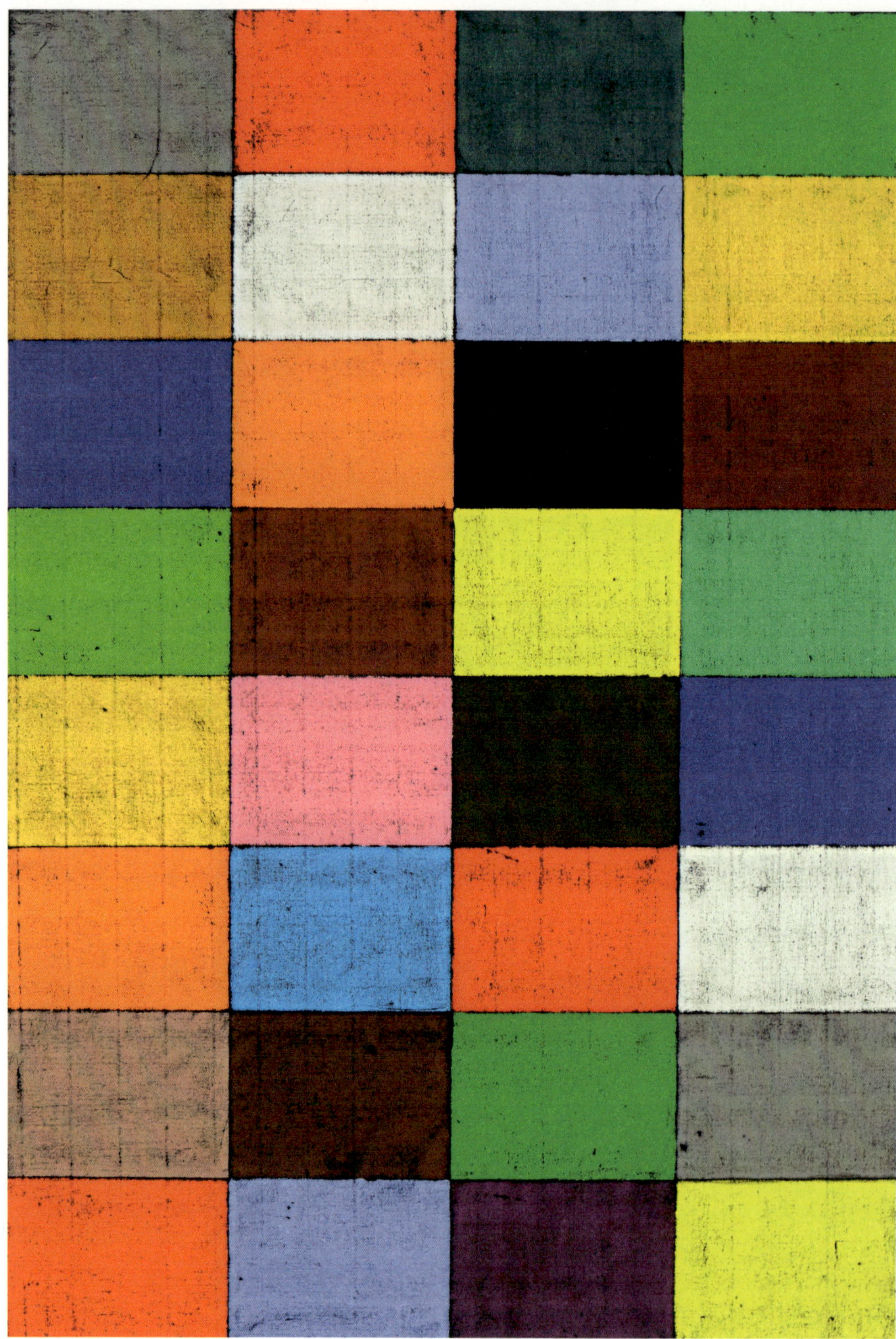

2013.19 Untitled (Light patterns), 183 × 122 cm

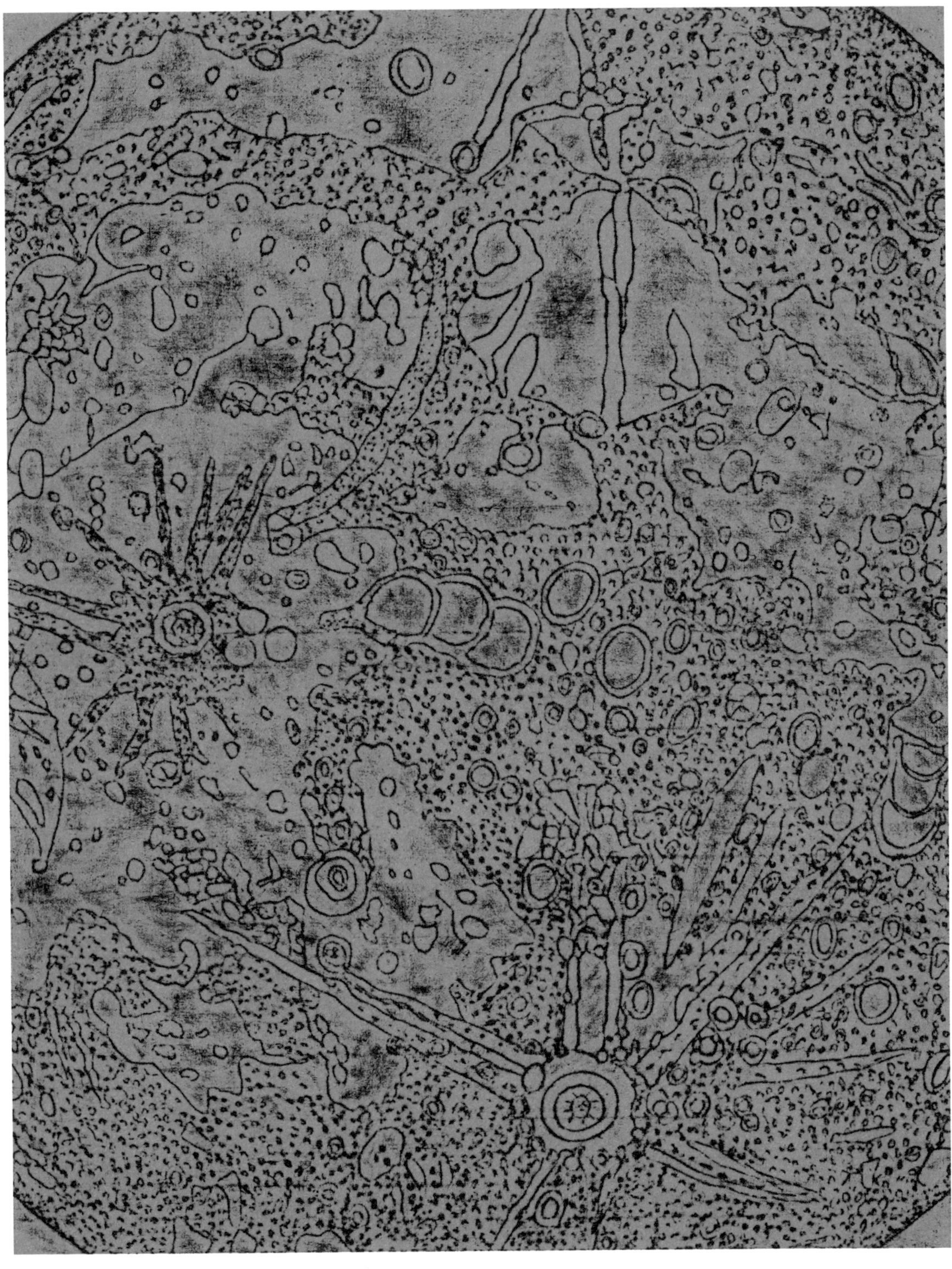

2013.20 Untitled (The Moon in the 17ᵗʰ Century), 244 × 183 cm

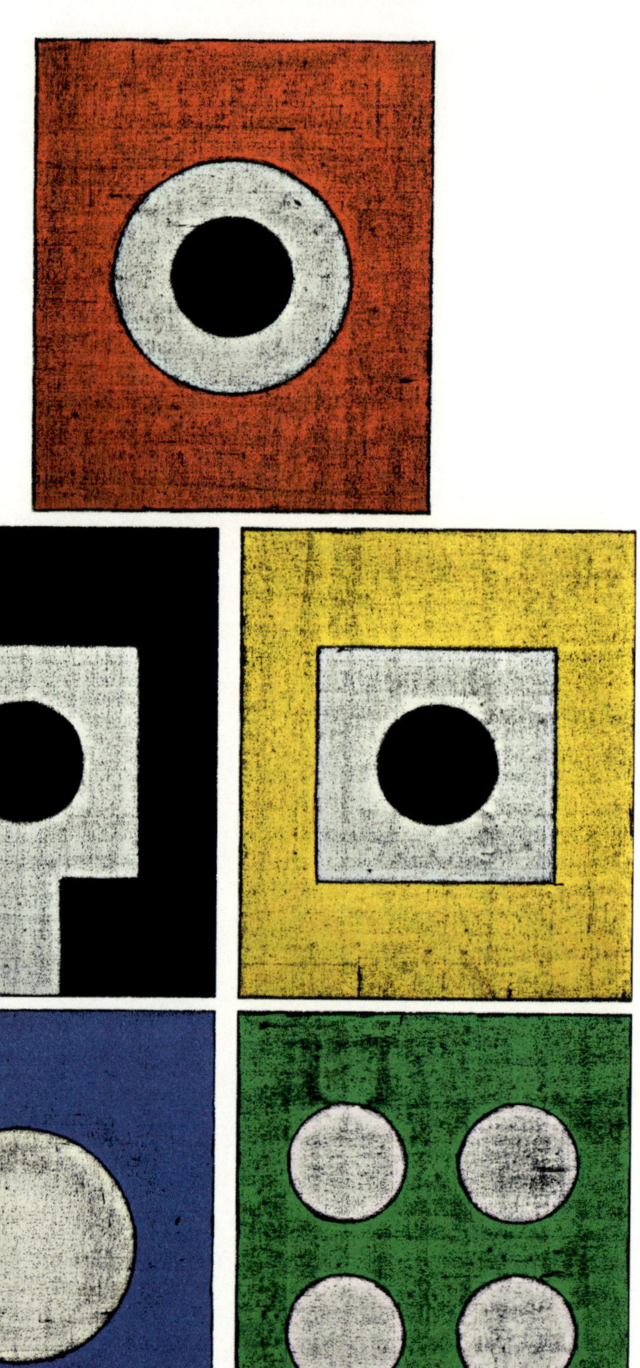

2013.21 Untitled (Cosmology, Signs), 60 × 50 cm each (5 parts)

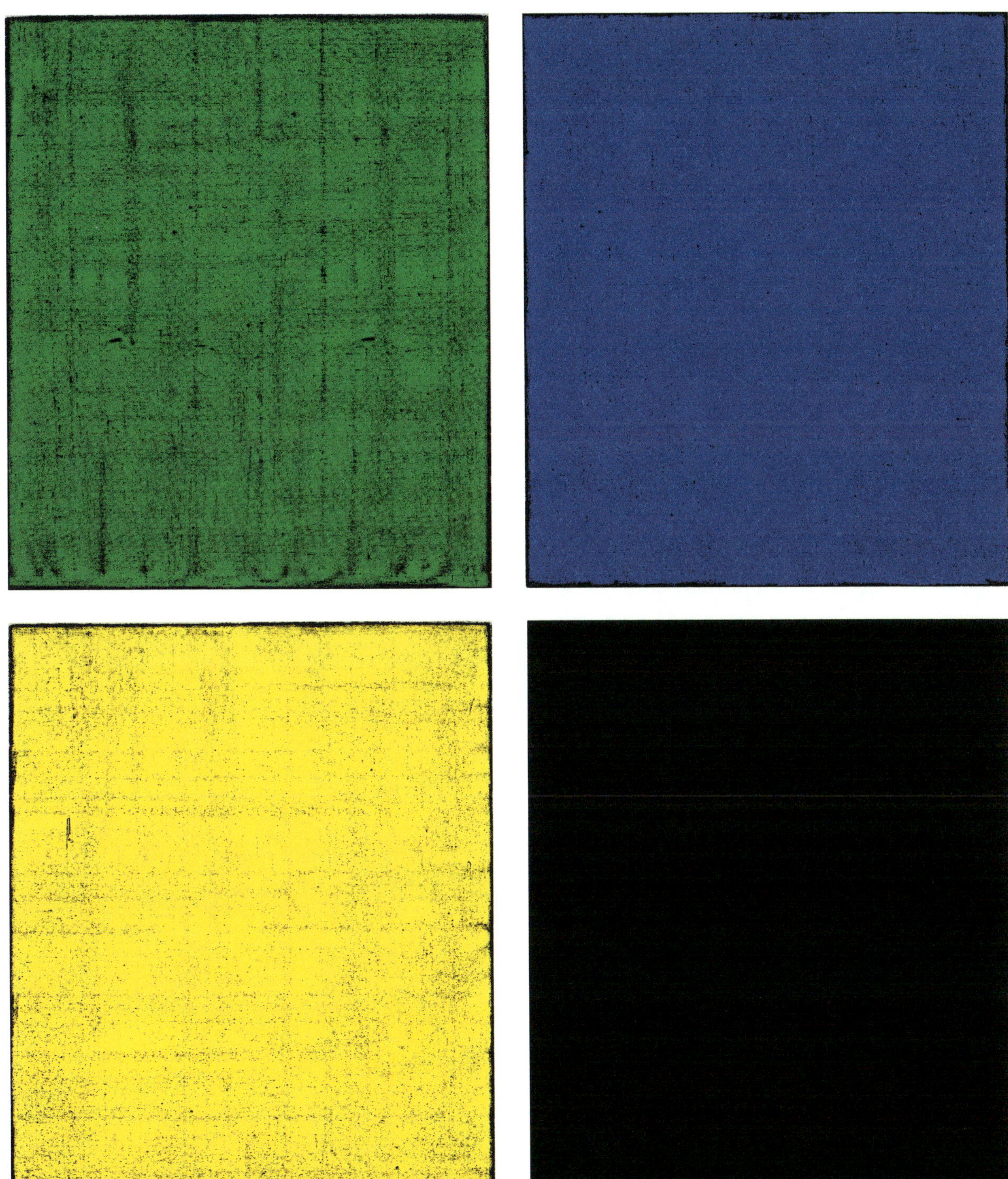

2013.22 Untitled (Elements Color), 60 × 50 cm
2013.23 Untitled (World Color), 60 × 50 cm
2013.24 Untitled (Frame Color), 60 × 50 cm
2013.25 Untitled (Sign Color), 60 × 50 cm

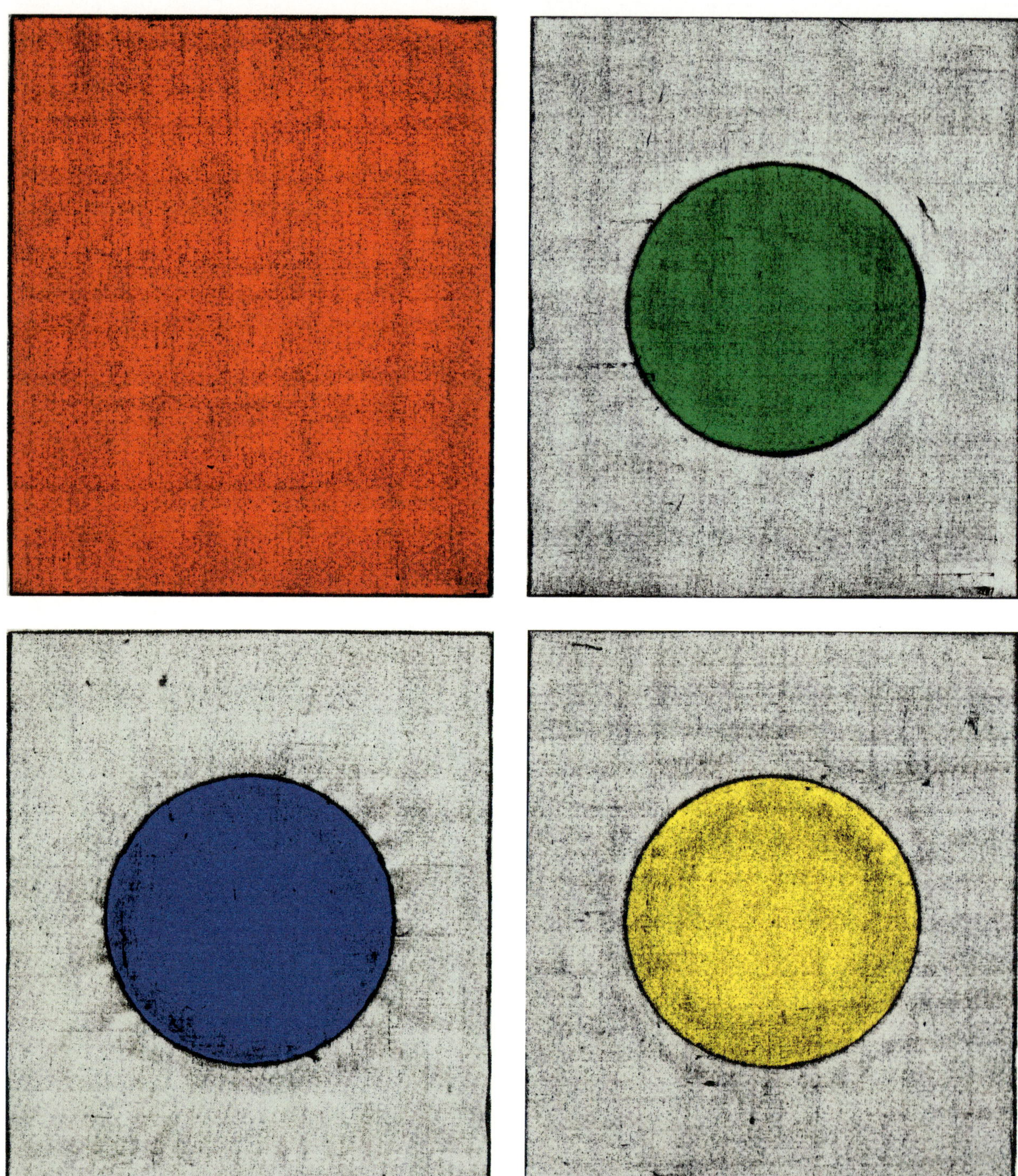

2013.26 Untitled (Subjective Color), 60 × 50 cm
2013.27 Untitled (Elemental Sign), 60 × 50 cm
2013.28 Untitled (World Sign), 60 × 50 cm
2013.29 Untitled (Frame Sign), 60 × 50 cm

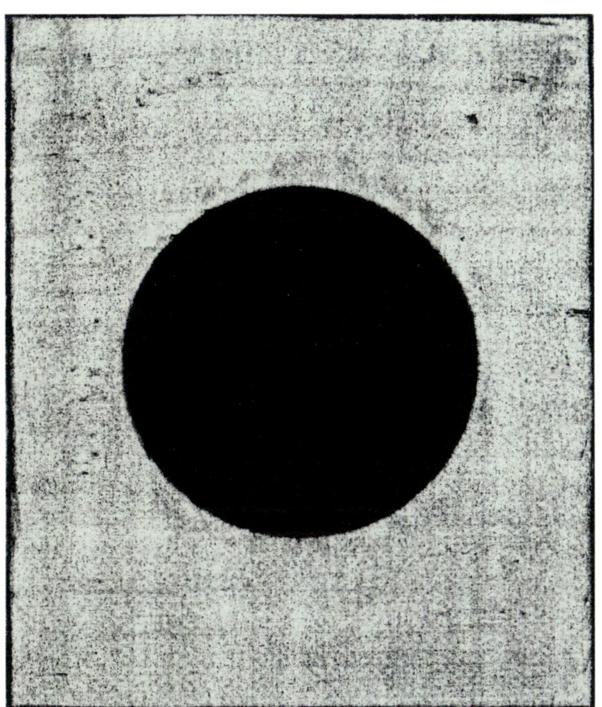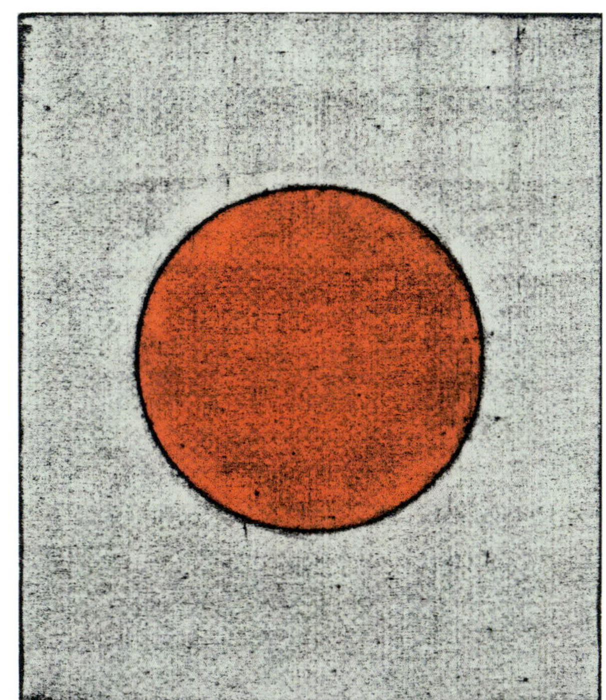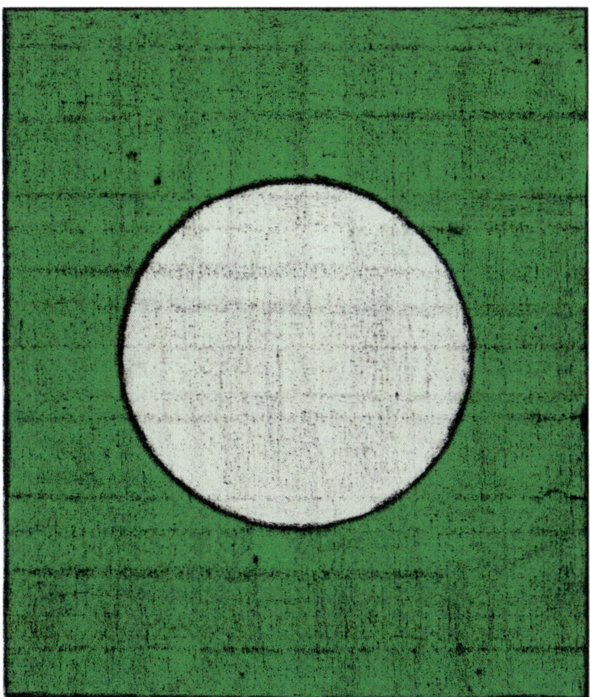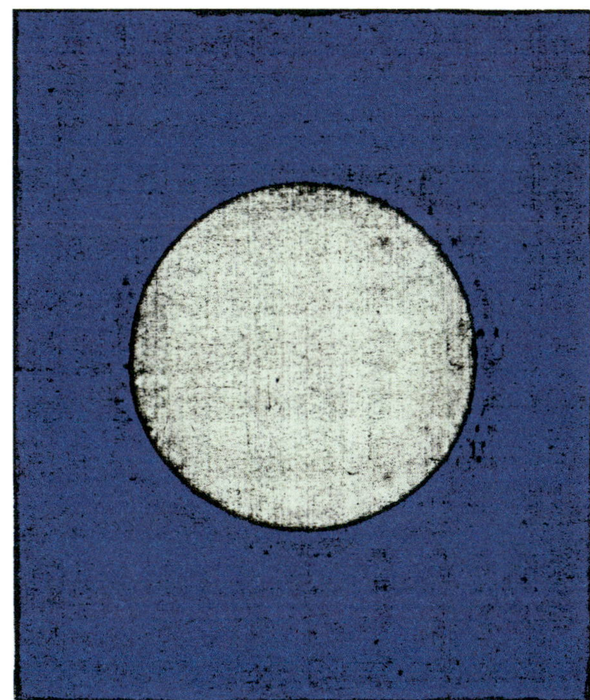

2013.30 Untitled (Sign), 60 × 50 cm
2013.31 Untitled (Subjective Sign), 60 × 50 cm
2013.32 Untitled (Sign in Elements), 60 × 50 cm
2013.33 Untitled (Sign in World), 60 × 50 cm

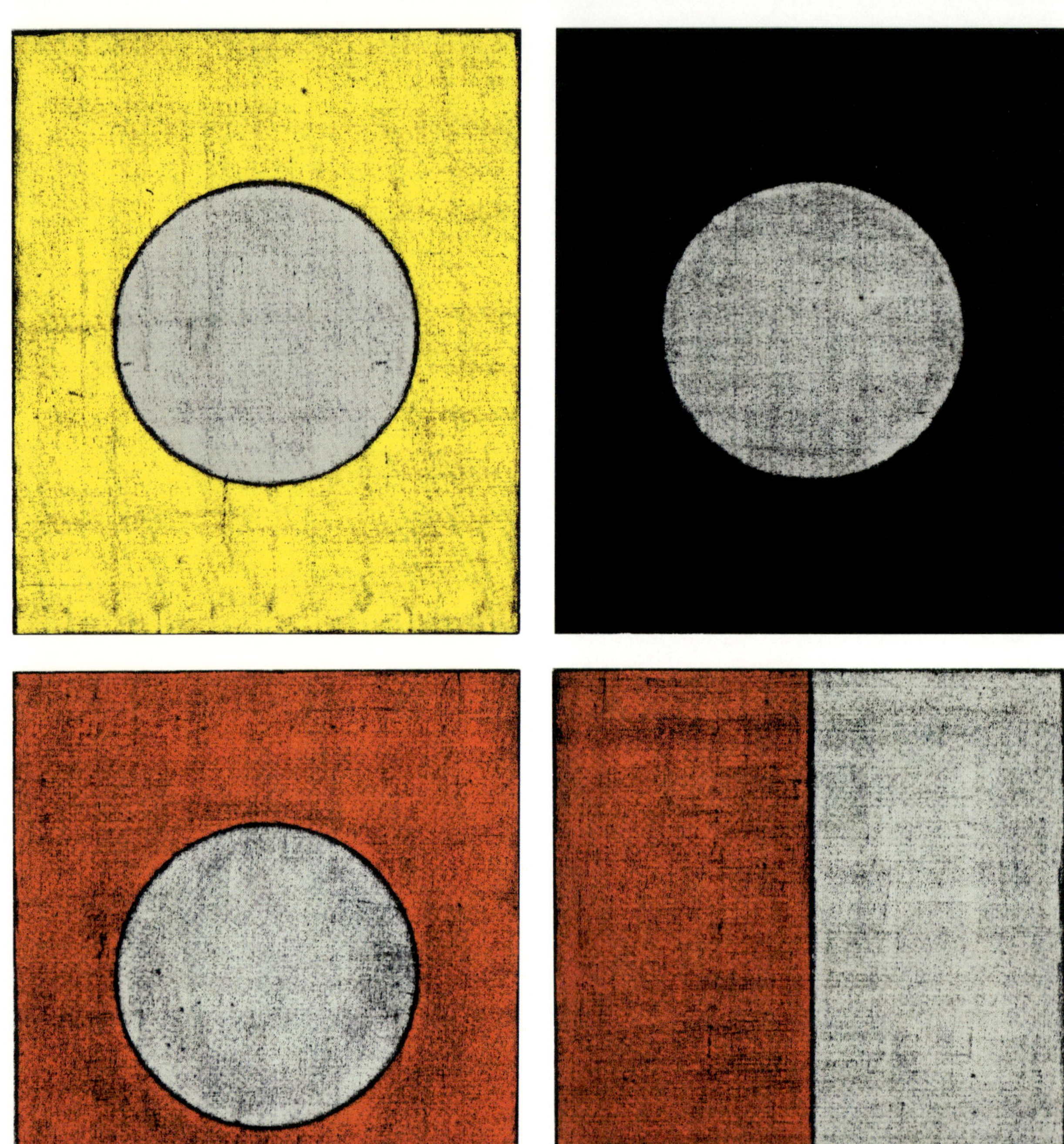

2013.34 Untitled (Sign in Frame), 60 × 50 cm
2013.35 Untitled (Sign in Sign), 60 × 50 cm
2013.36 Untitled (Sign in Subject), 60 × 50 cm
2013.37 Untitled (Colored Borders, Vertical Line I), 60 × 50 cm

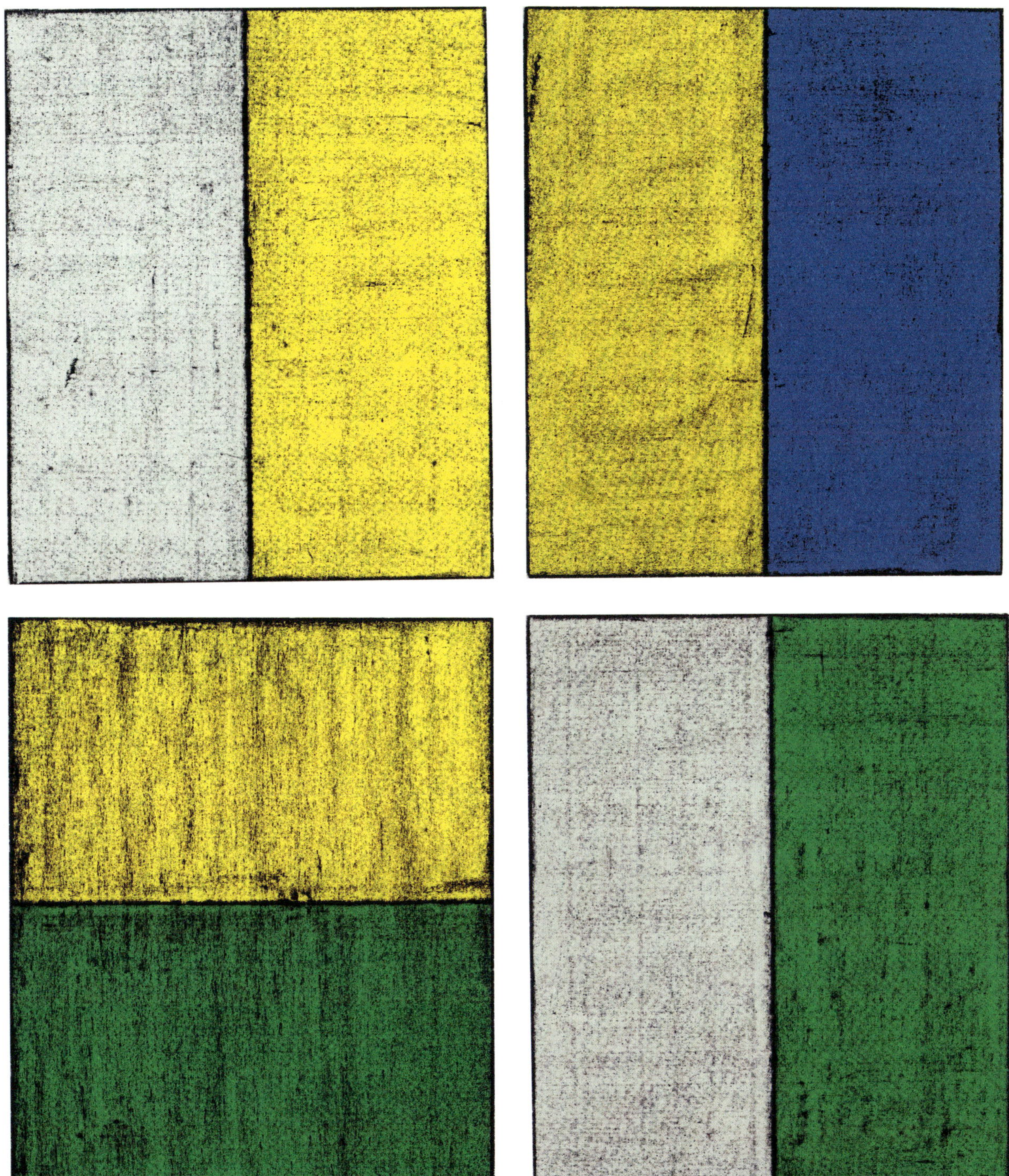

2013.38 Untitled (Colored Borders, Vertical Line II), 60 × 50 cm
2013.39 Untitled (Colored Borders, Vertical Line VI), 60 × 50 cm
2013.40 Untitled (Colored Borders, Horizontal Line II), 60 × 50 cm
2013.41 Untitled (Colored Borders, Vertical Line IV), 60 × 50 cm

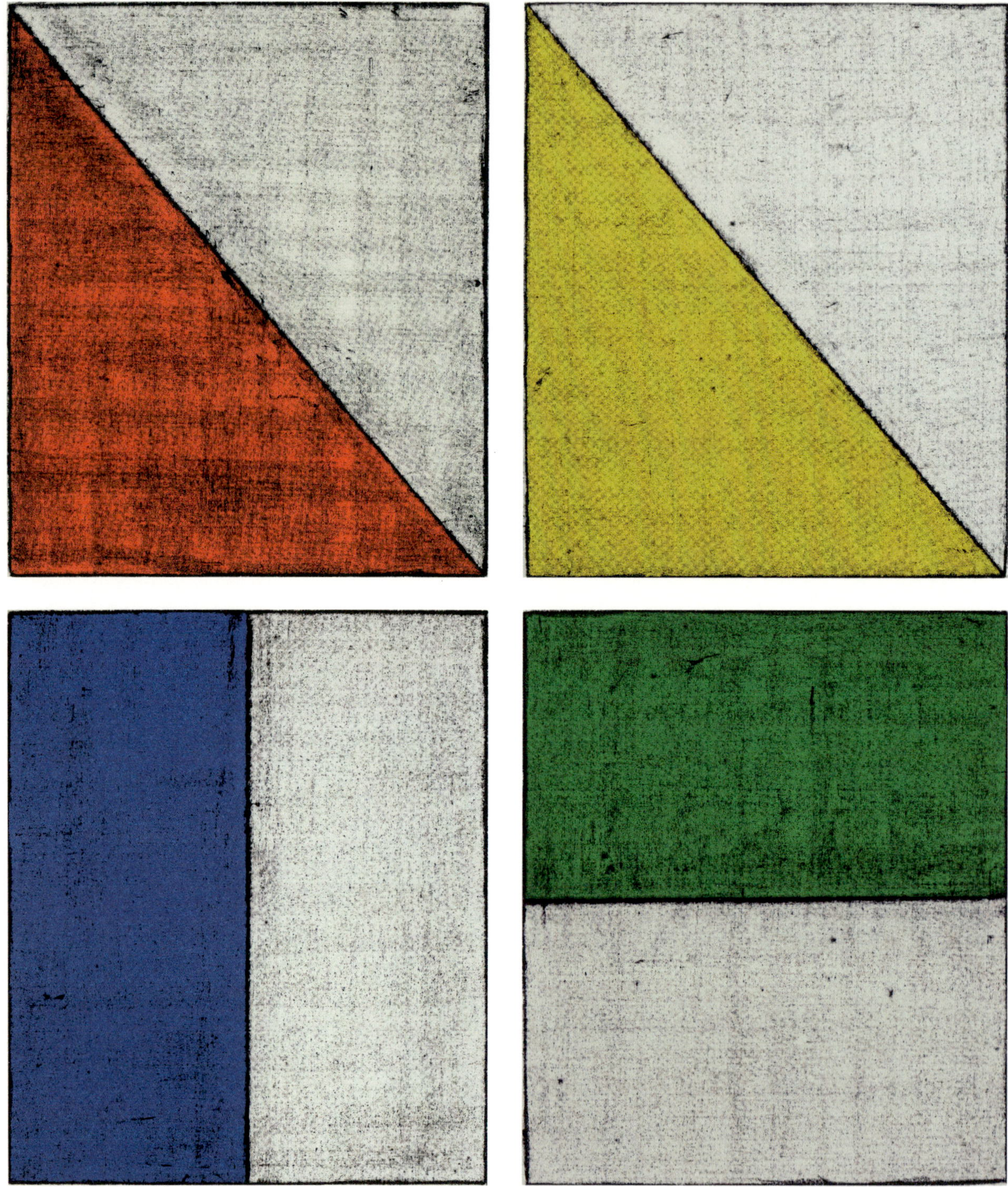

2013.42 Untitled (Colored Borders, Diagonal Line II), 60 × 50 cm
2013.43 Untitled (Colored Borders, Diagonal Line II), 60 × 50 cm
2013.44 Untitled (Colored Borders, Vertical Line III), 60 × 50 cm
2013.45 Untitled (Colored Borders, Horizontal Line III), 60 × 50 cm

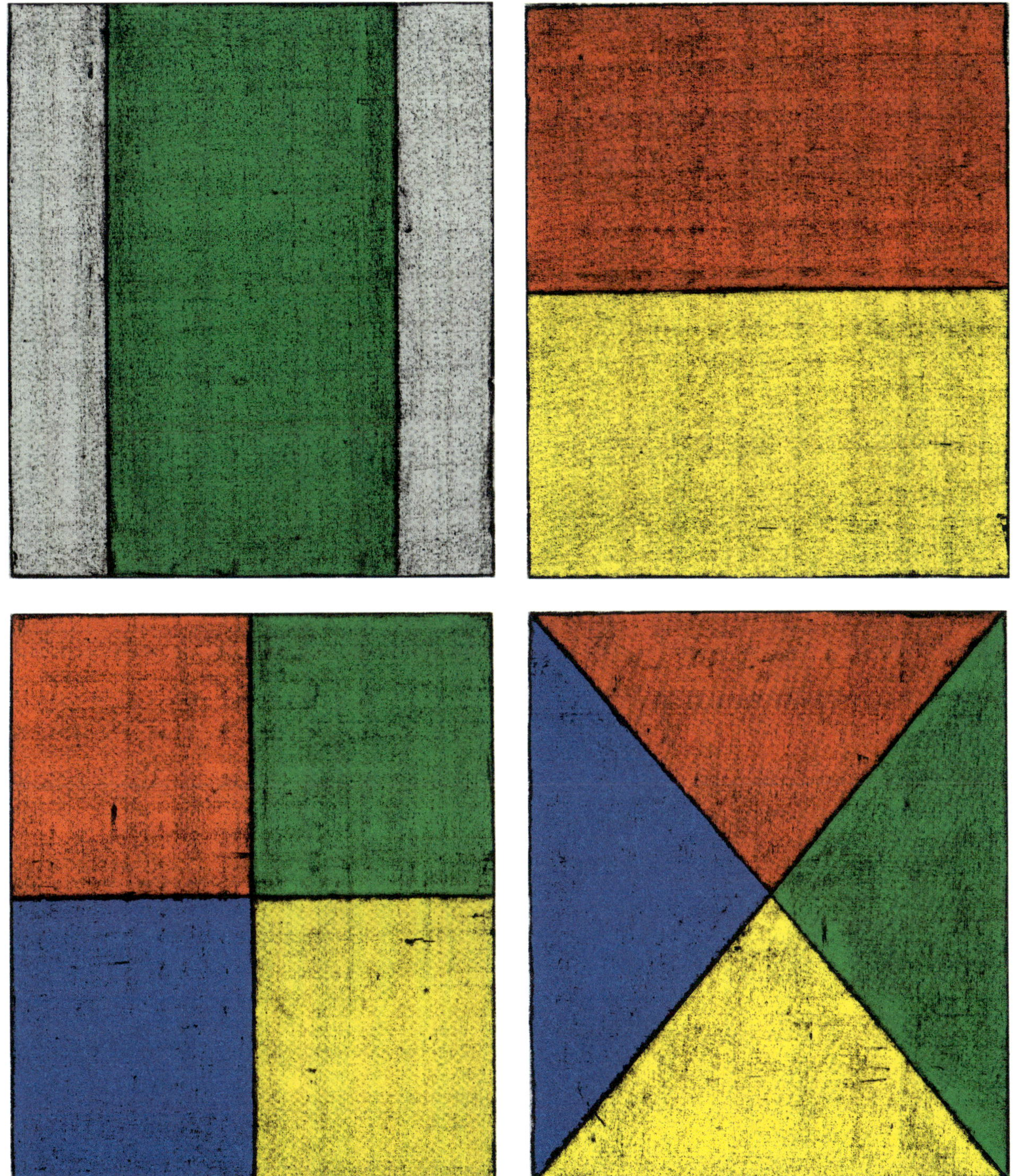

2013.46 Untitled (Colored Borders, Vertical Line V), 60 × 50 cm
2013.47 Untitled (Colored Borders, Horizontal Line I), 60 × 50 cm
2013.48 Untitled (Colored Borders Quartered II), 60 × 50 cm
2013.49 Untitled (Colored Borders Quartered I), 60 × 50 cm

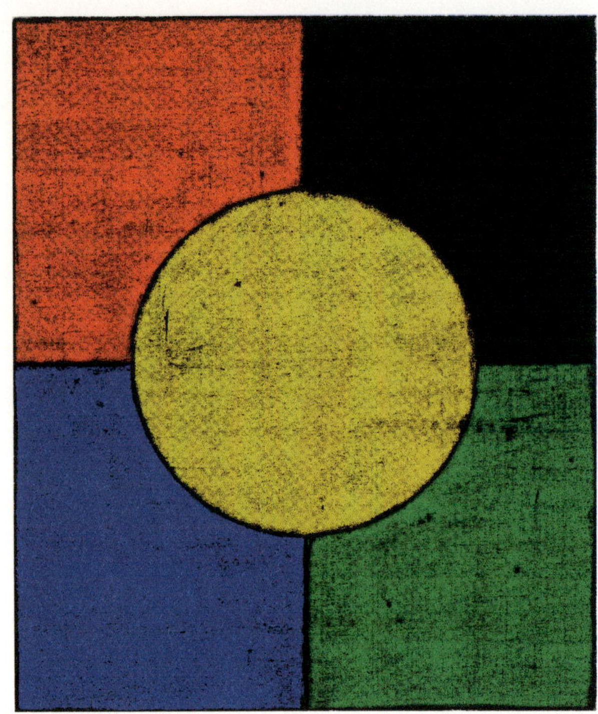

2013.50 Untitled (5 Worlds Chart), 60 × 50 cm

2014

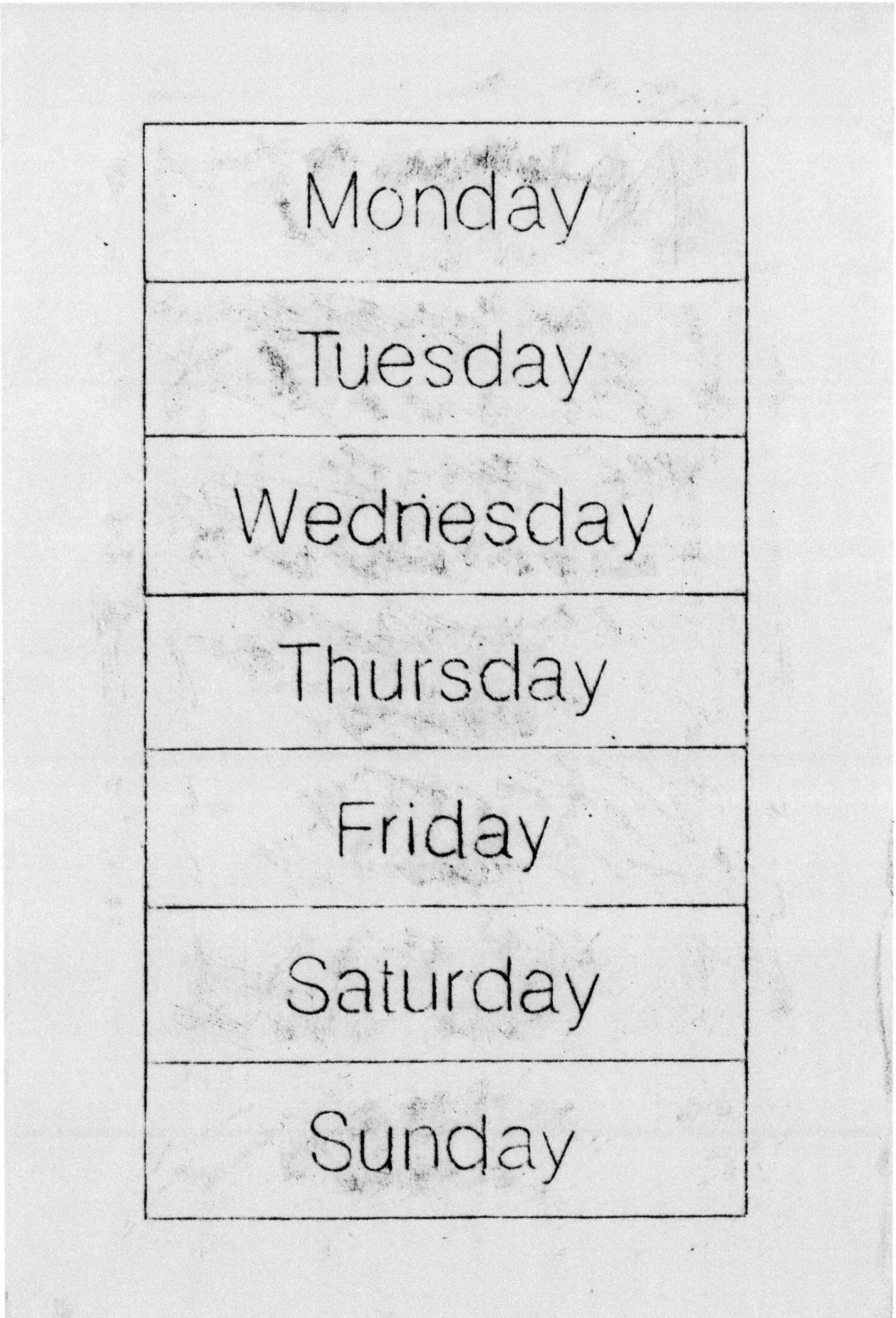

| Monday |
| Tuesday |
| Wednesday |
| Thursday |
| Friday |
| Saturday |
| Sunday |

2014.1 Untitled (Days of the Week), 183 × 122 cm

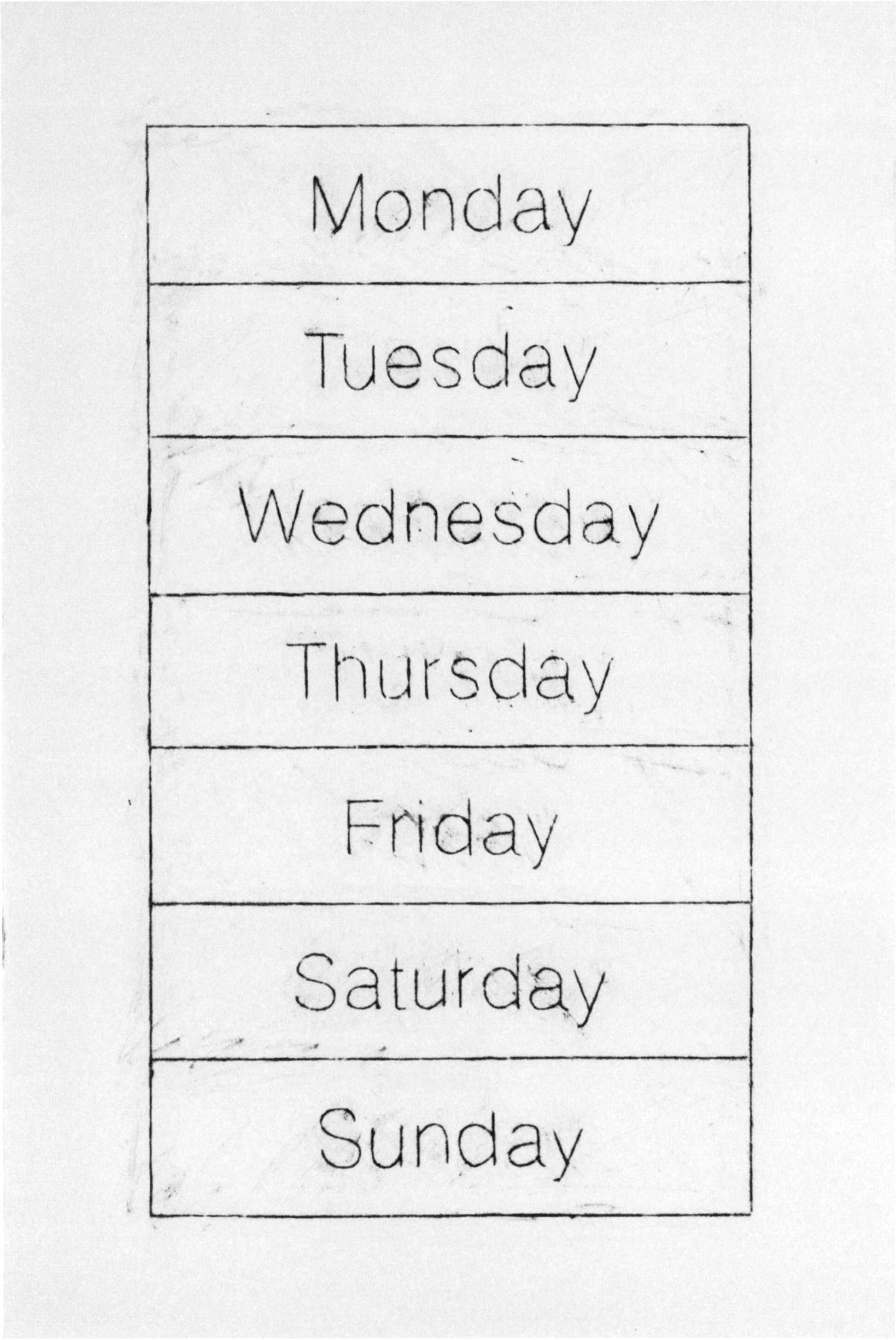

Monday

Tuesday

Wednesday

Thursday

Friday

Saturday

Sunday

2014.2 Untitled (Days of the Week), 183 × 122 cm

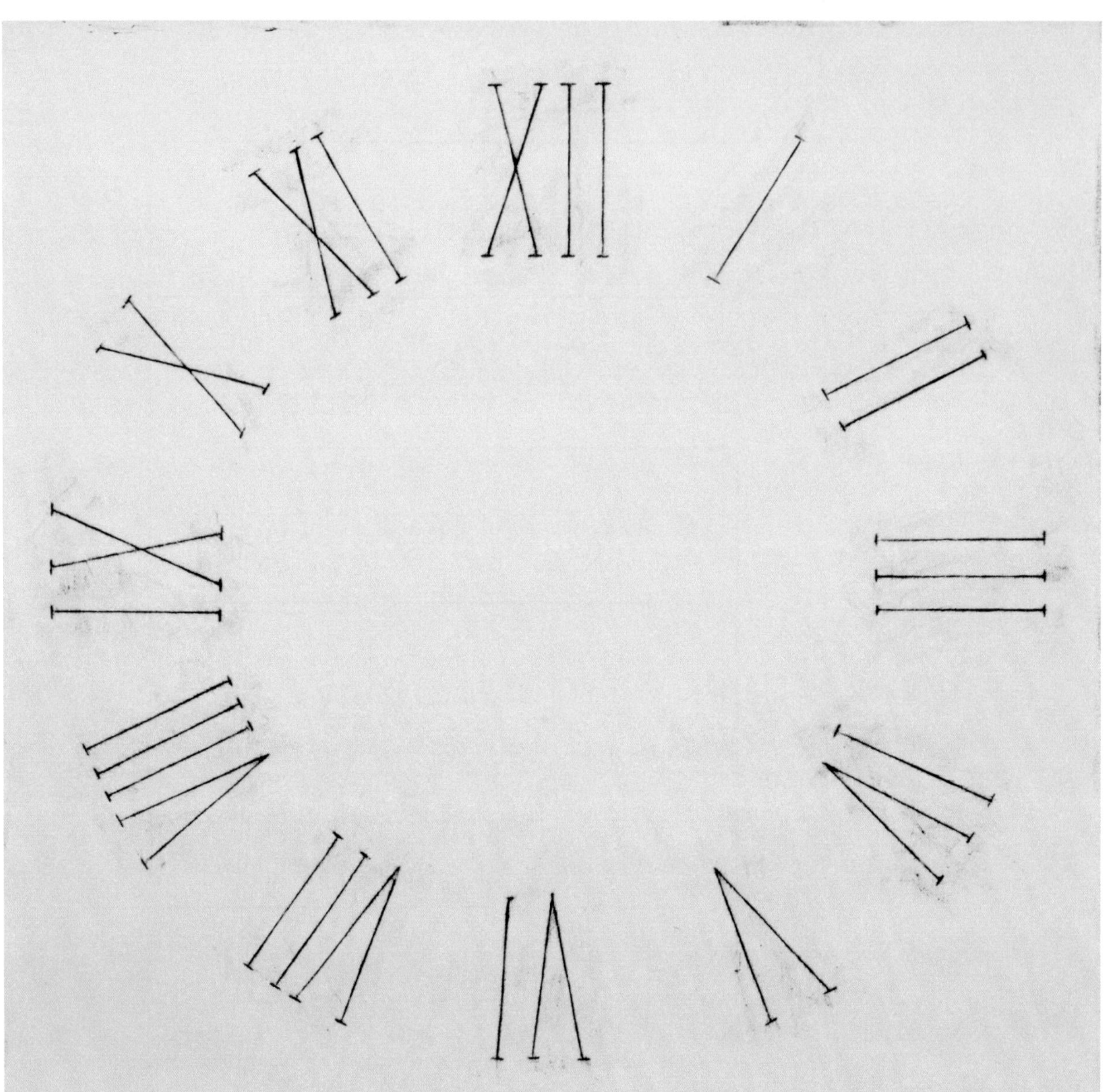

2014.3 Untitled (12 Hours), 150 × 150 cm

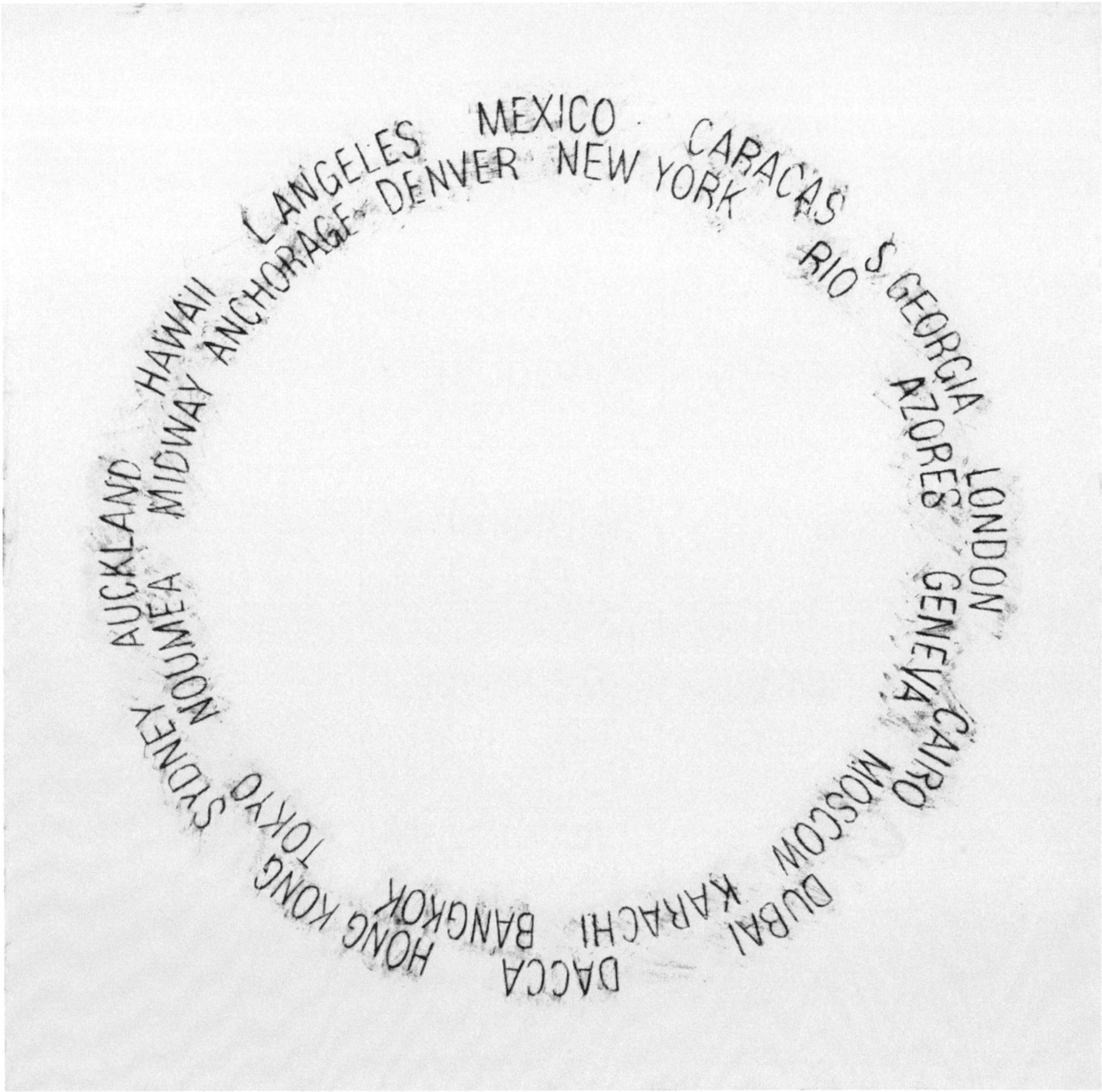

2014.4 Untitled (Time Zones), 150 × 150 cm

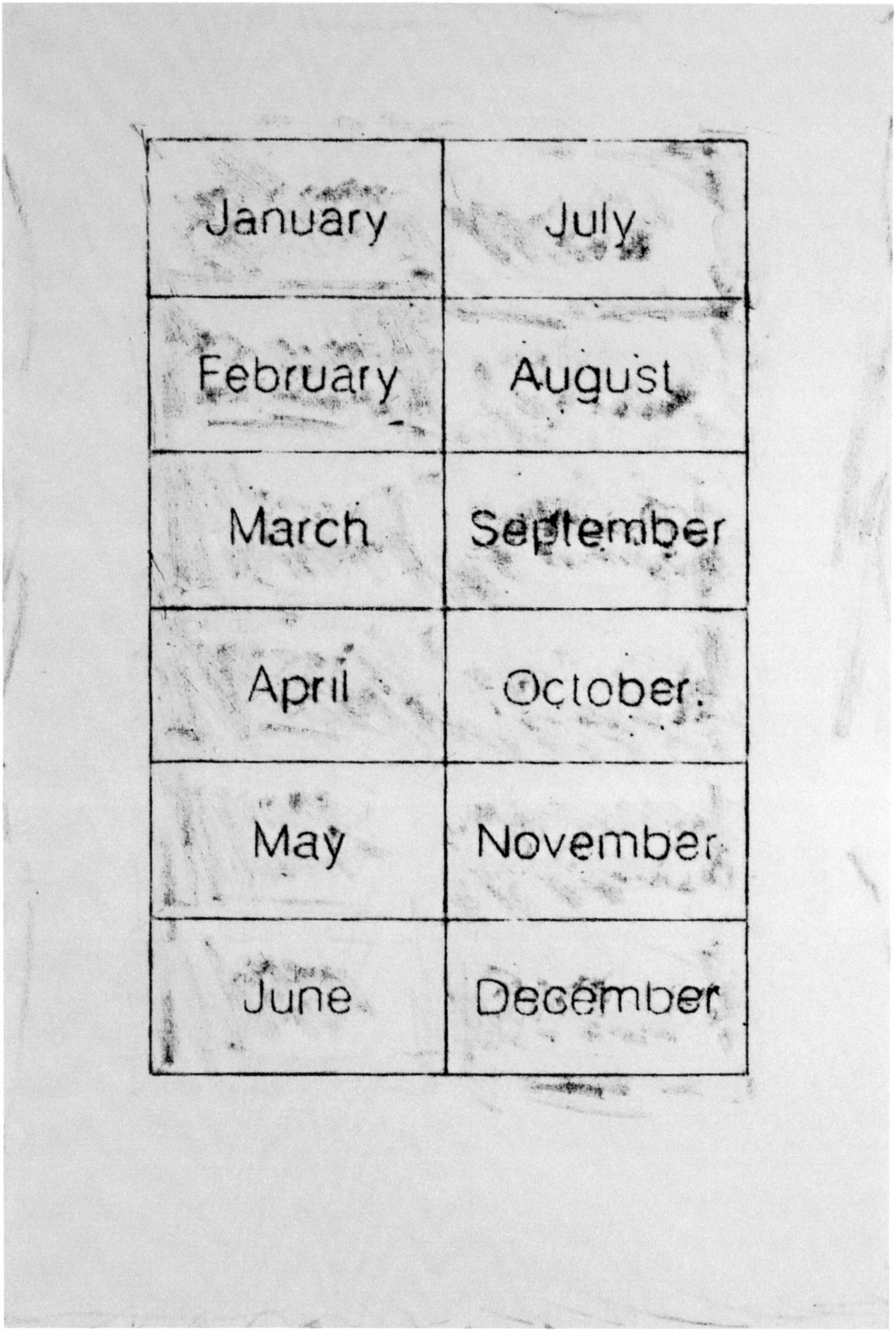

January	July
February	August
March	September
April	October
May	November
June	December

2014.5 Untitled (Months of the Year), 183 × 122 cm

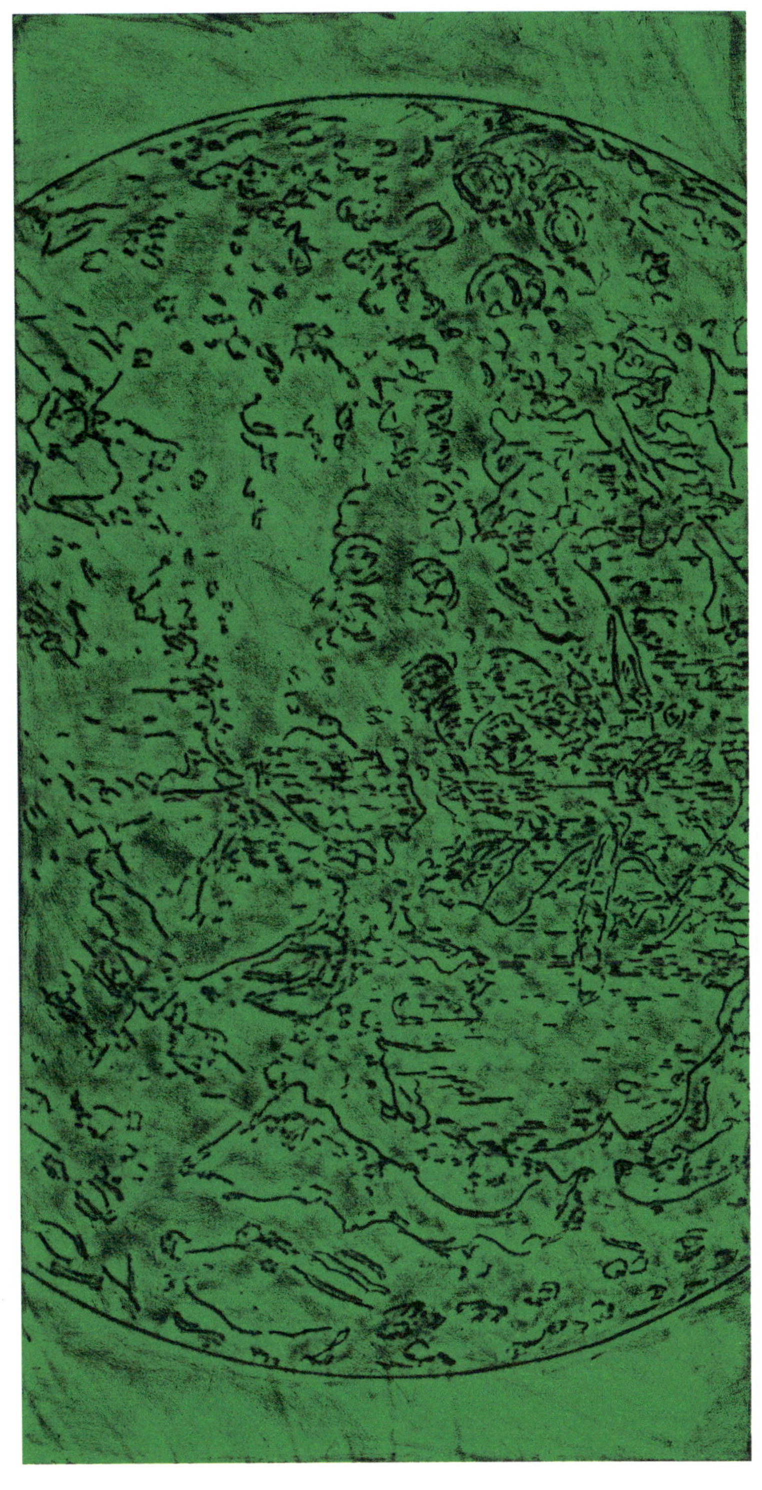

2014.6 Untitled (Moon), 240 × 120 cm

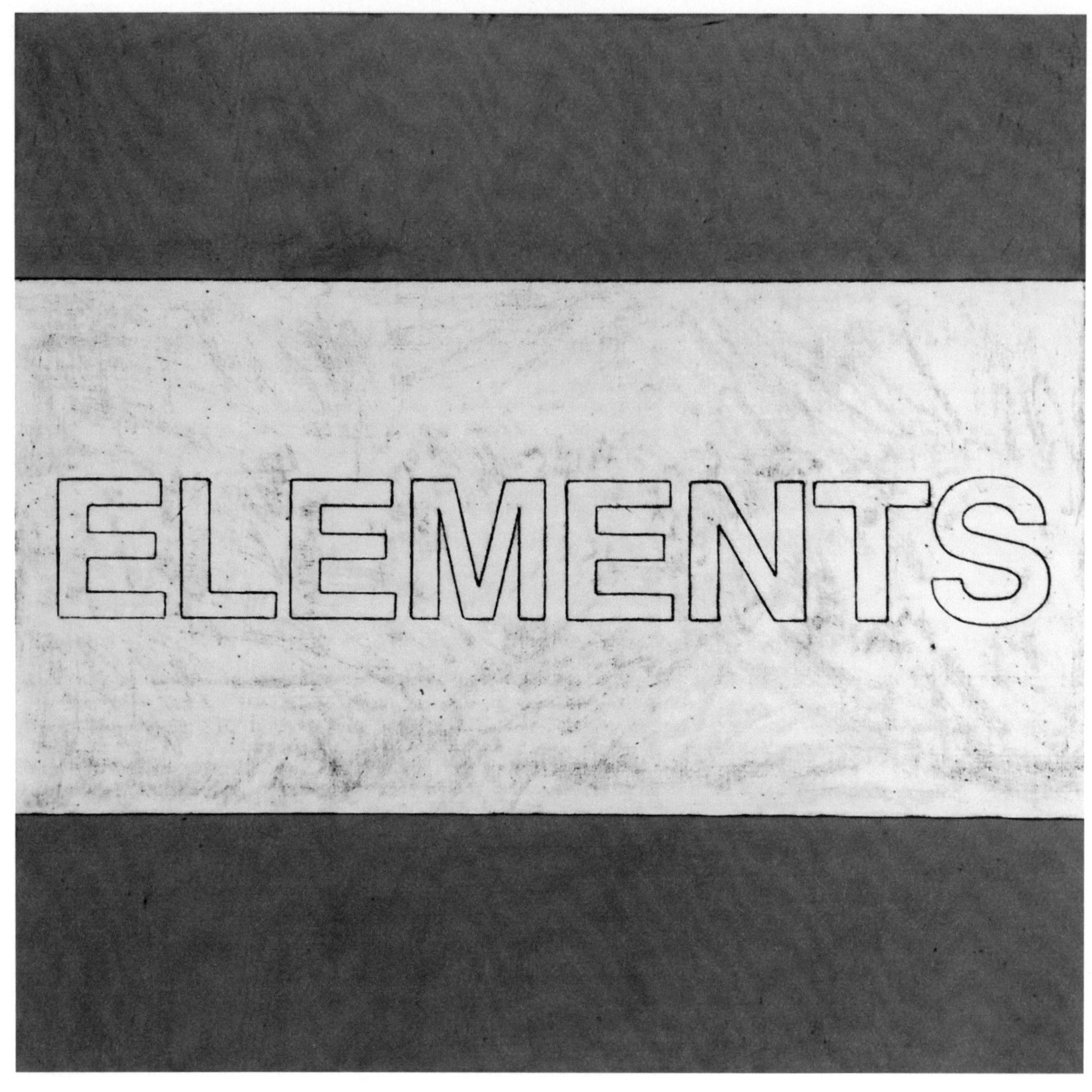

2014.7 Untitled (Elements), 200×200 cm

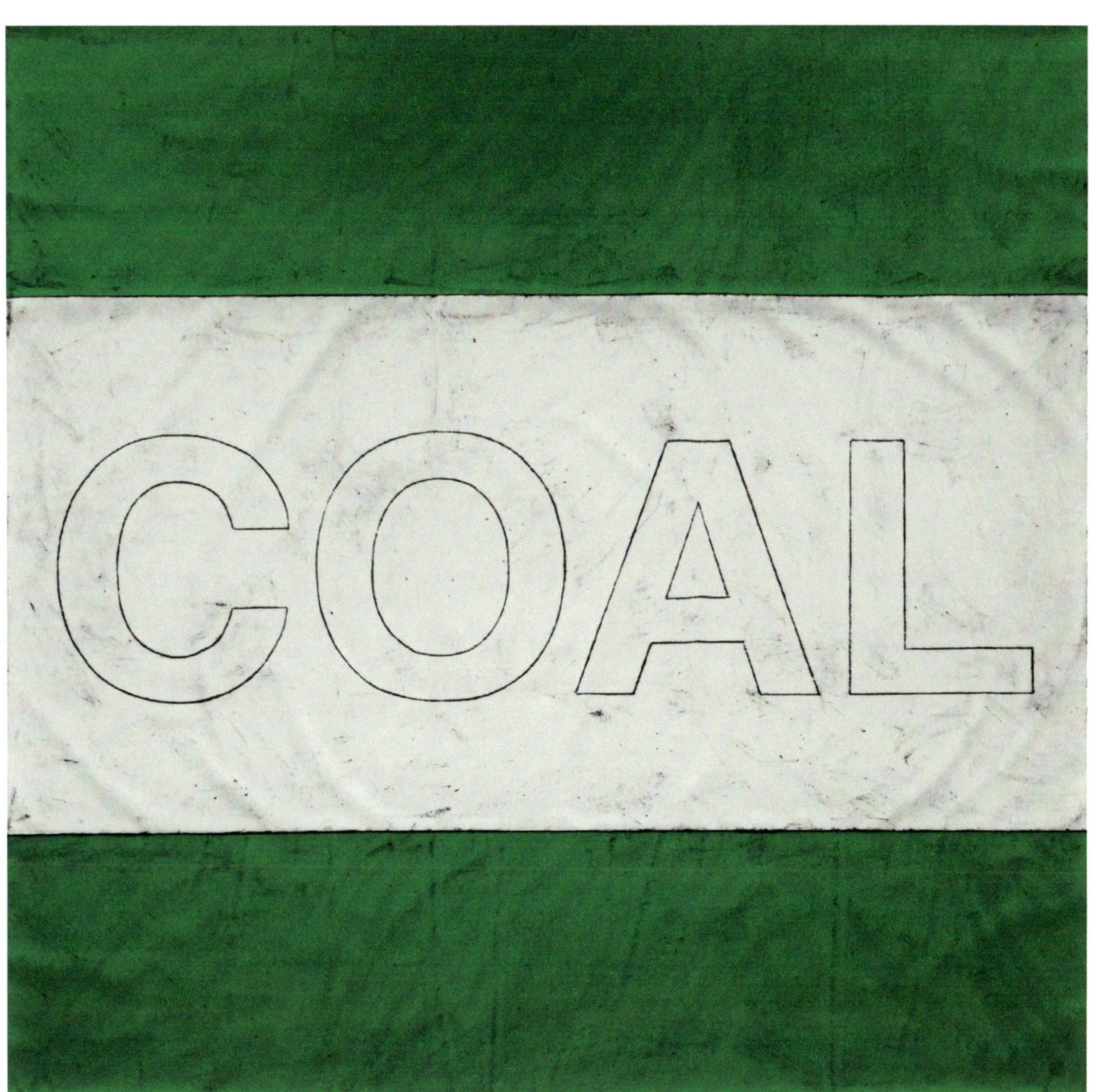

2014.8 Untitled (Coal), 200 × 200 cm

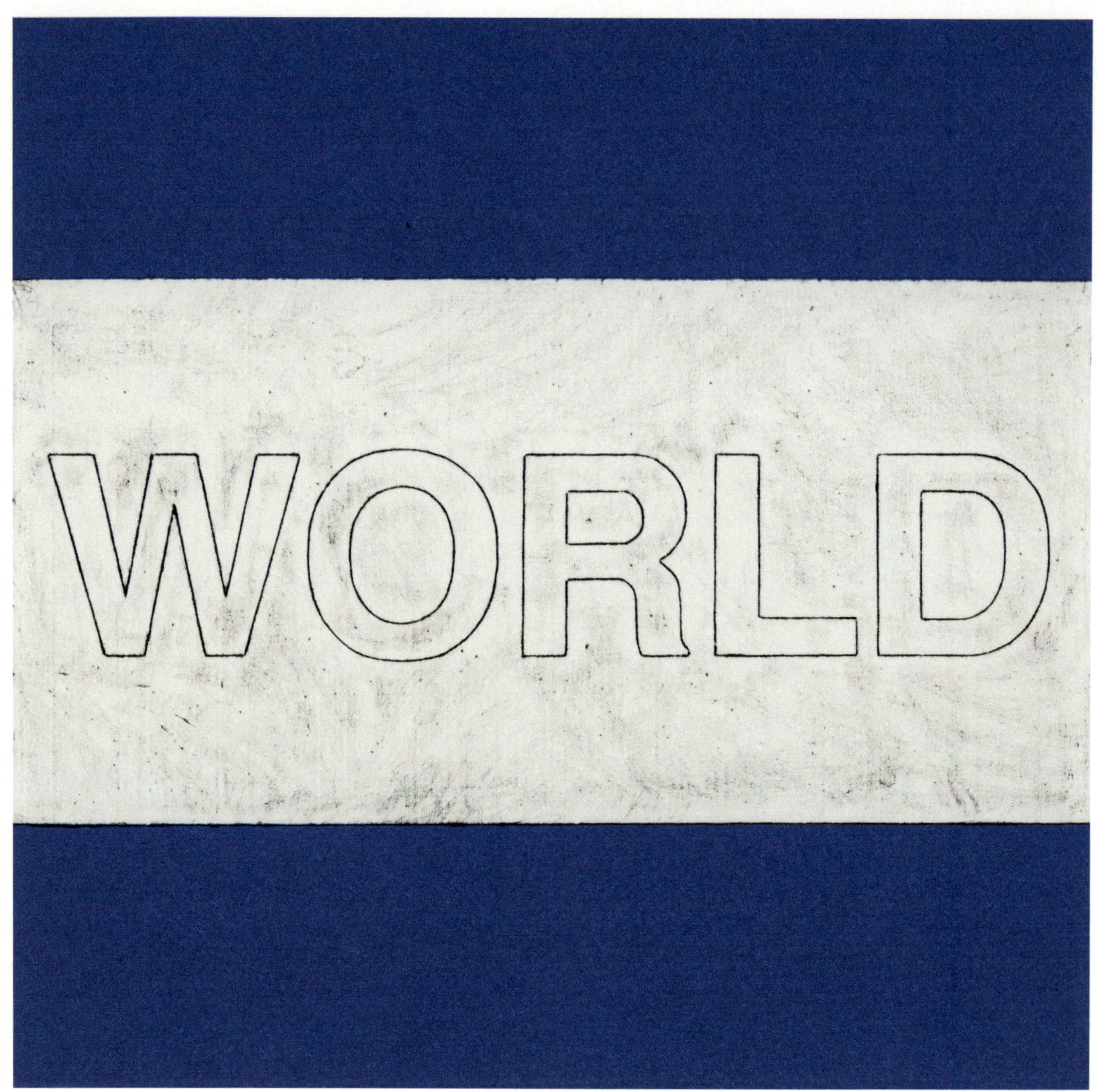

2014.9 Untitled (World), 200×200 cm

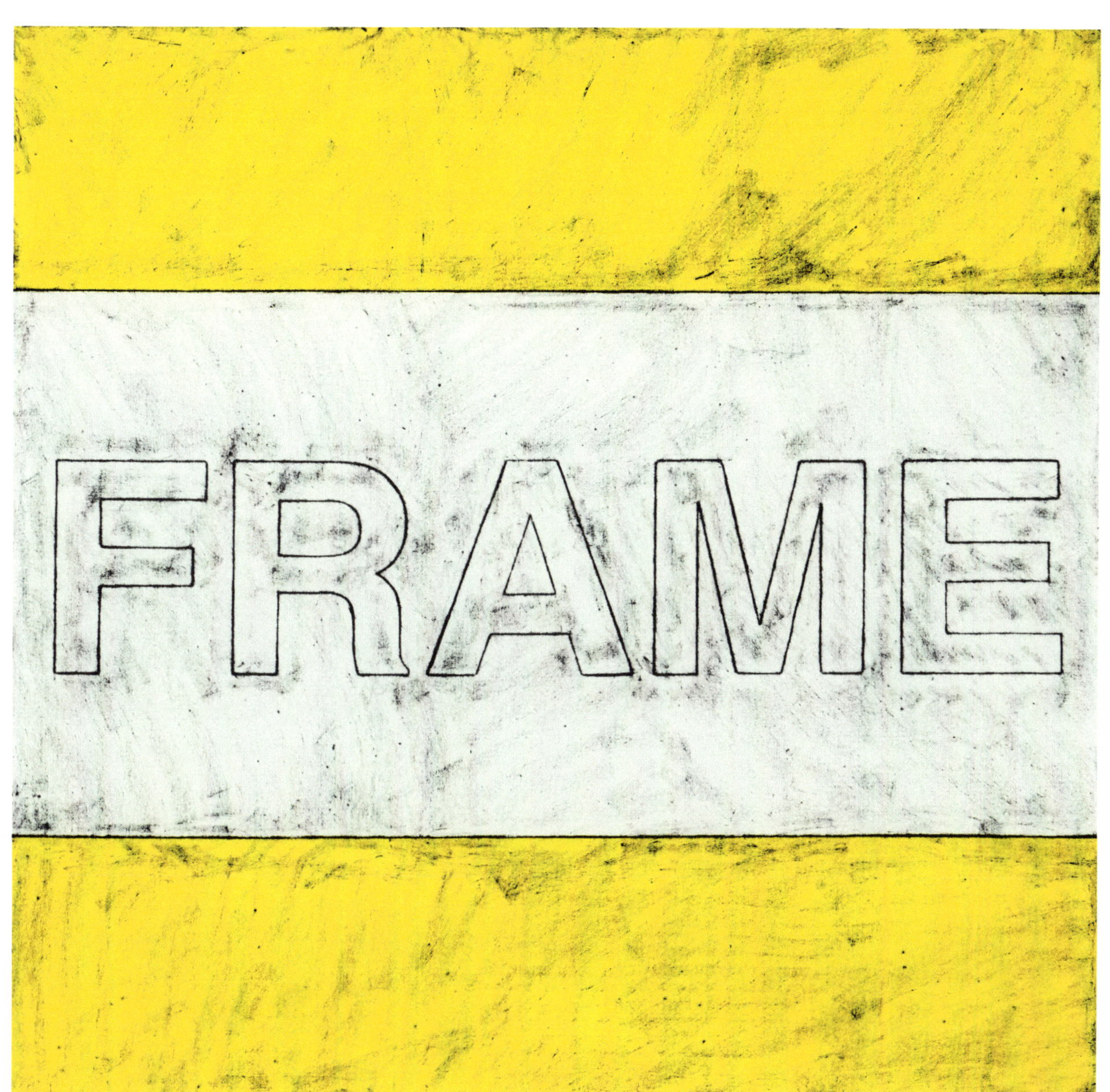

2014.10 Untitled (World Framed), 200 × 200 cm

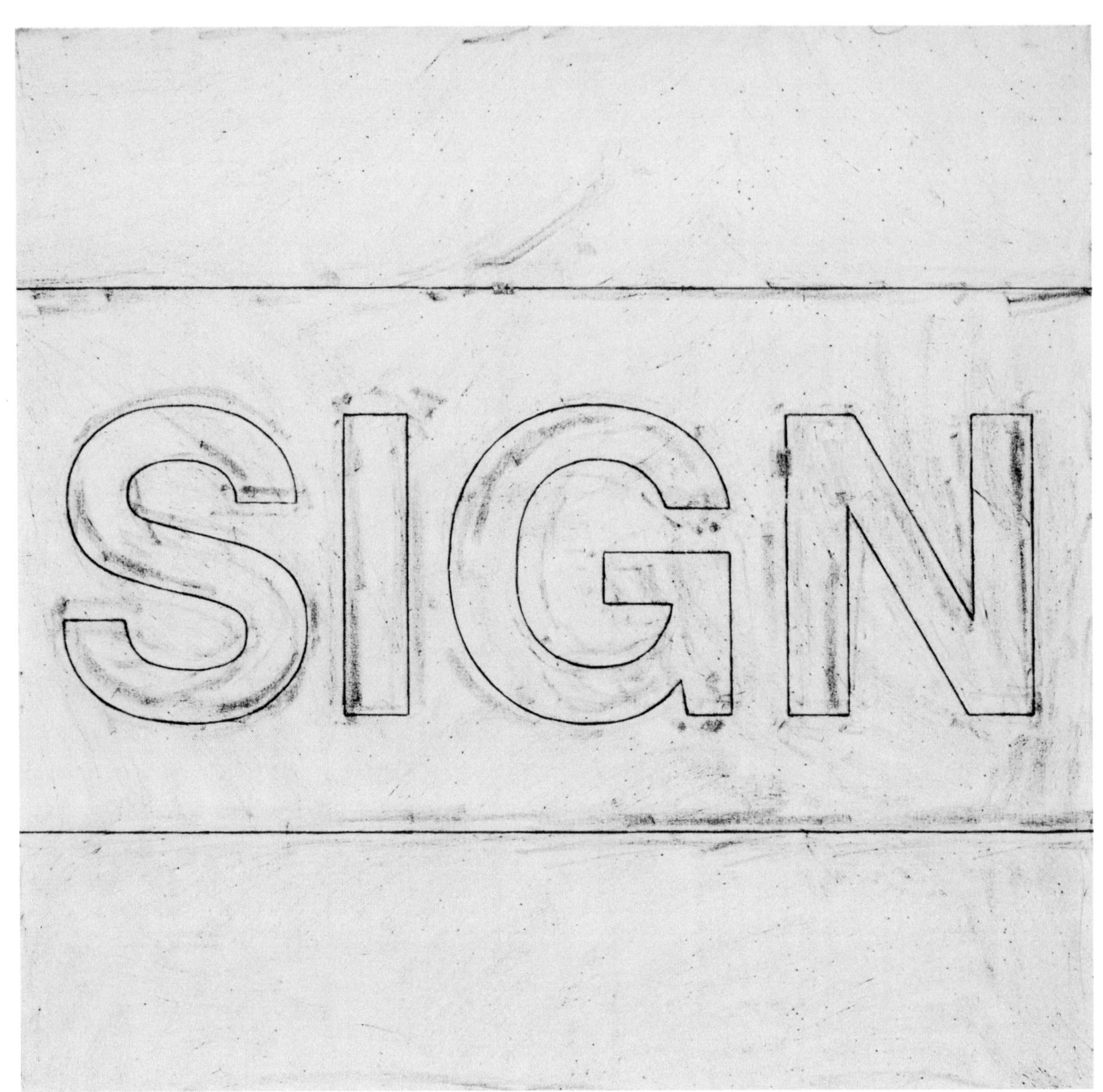

2014.11 Untitled (Sign), 200×200 cm

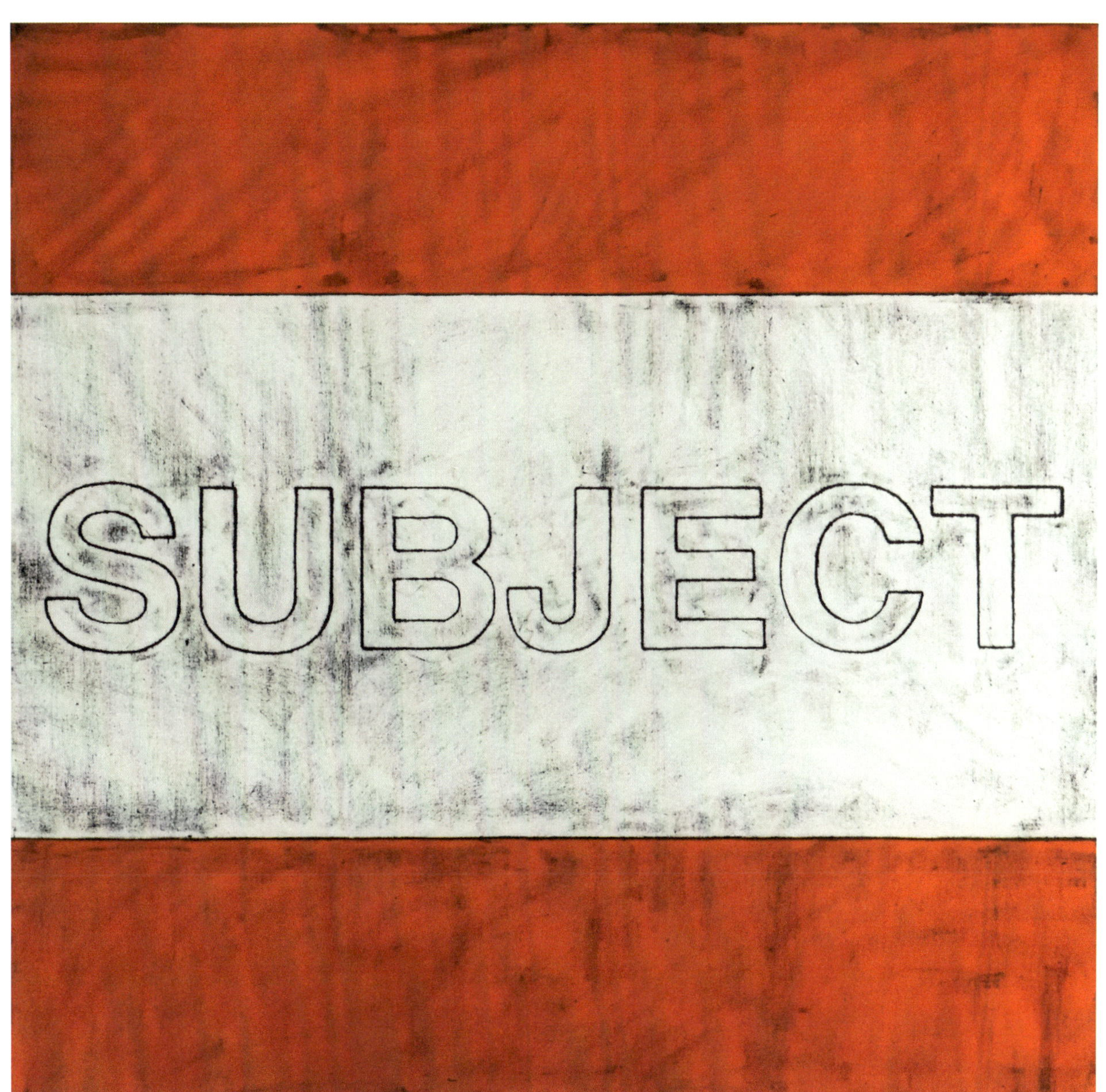

2014.12 Untitled (Subject), 200×200 cm

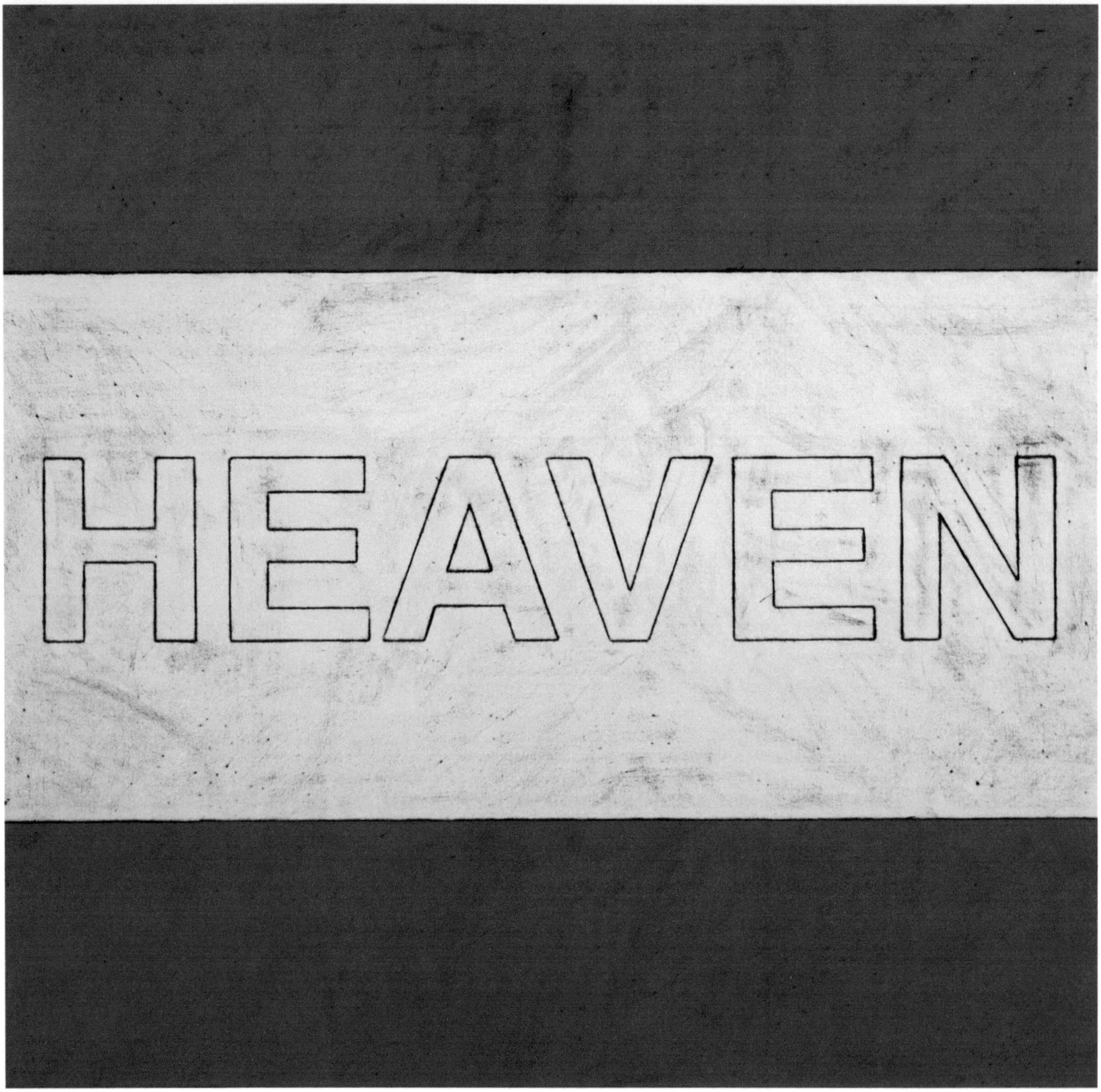

2014.13 Untitled (Heaven), 200 × 200 cm

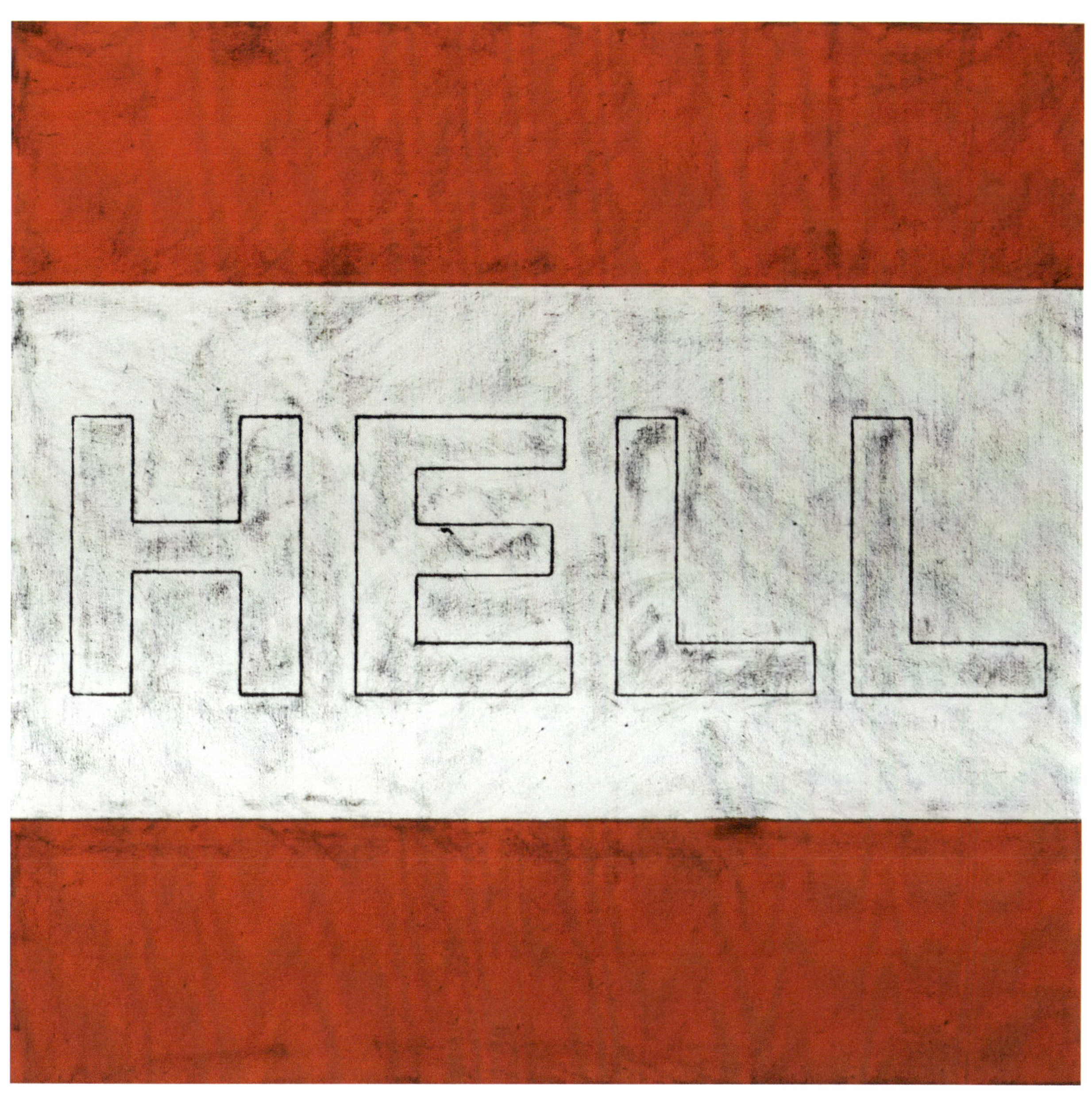

2014.14 Untitled (Hell), 200 × 200 cm

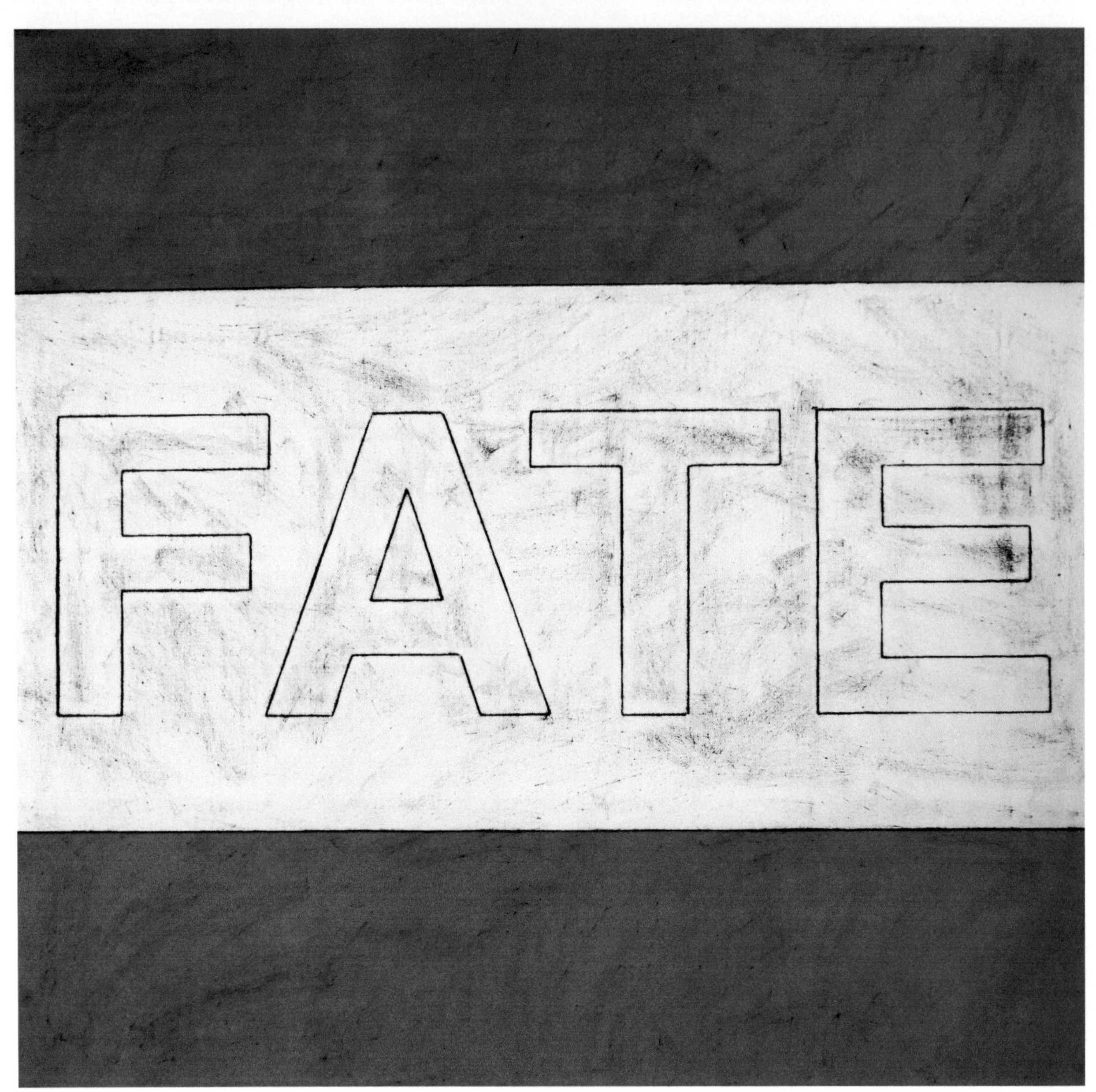

2014.15 Untitled (Fate), 200 × 200 cm

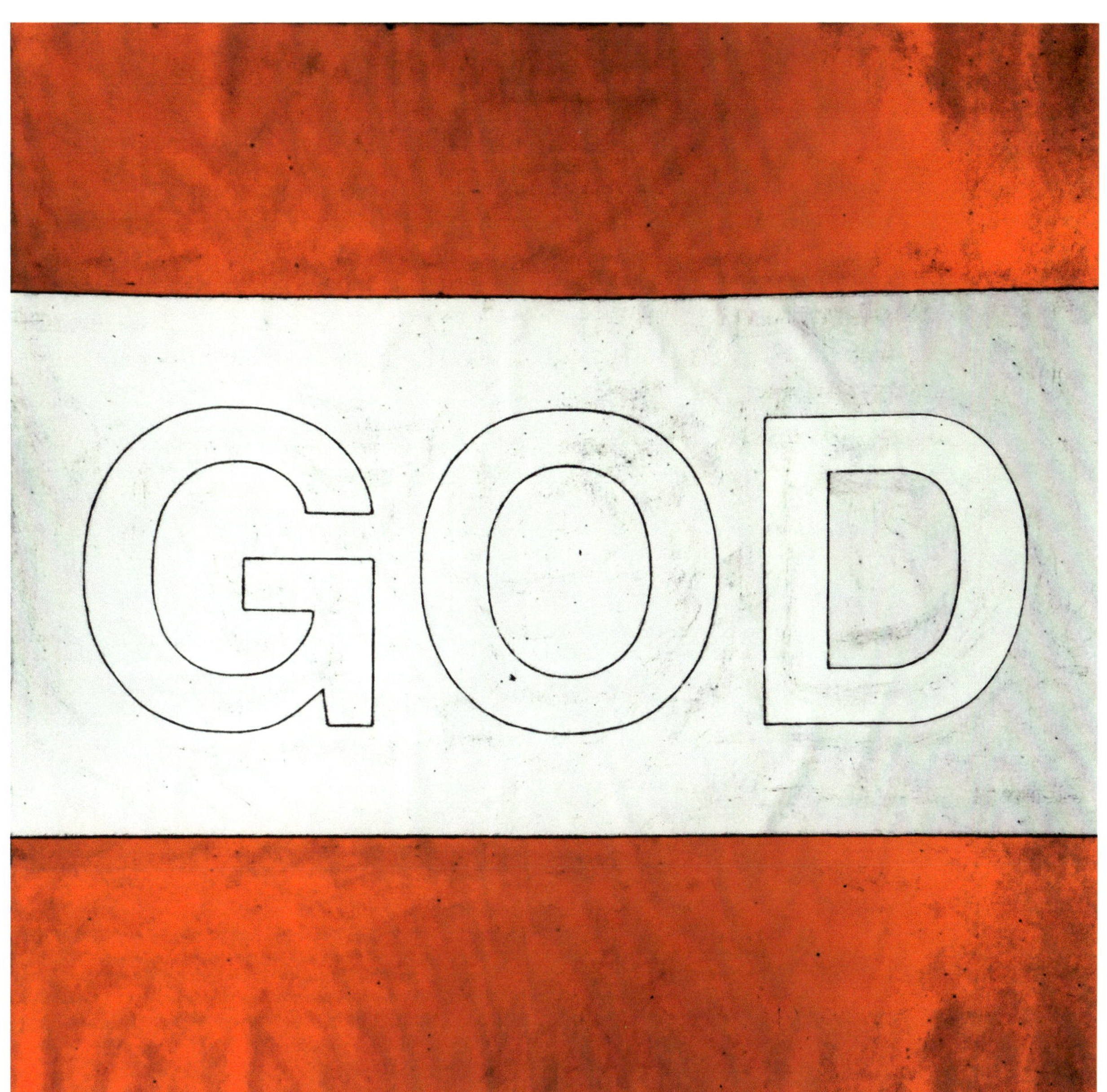

2014.16 Untitled (God), 200×200 cm

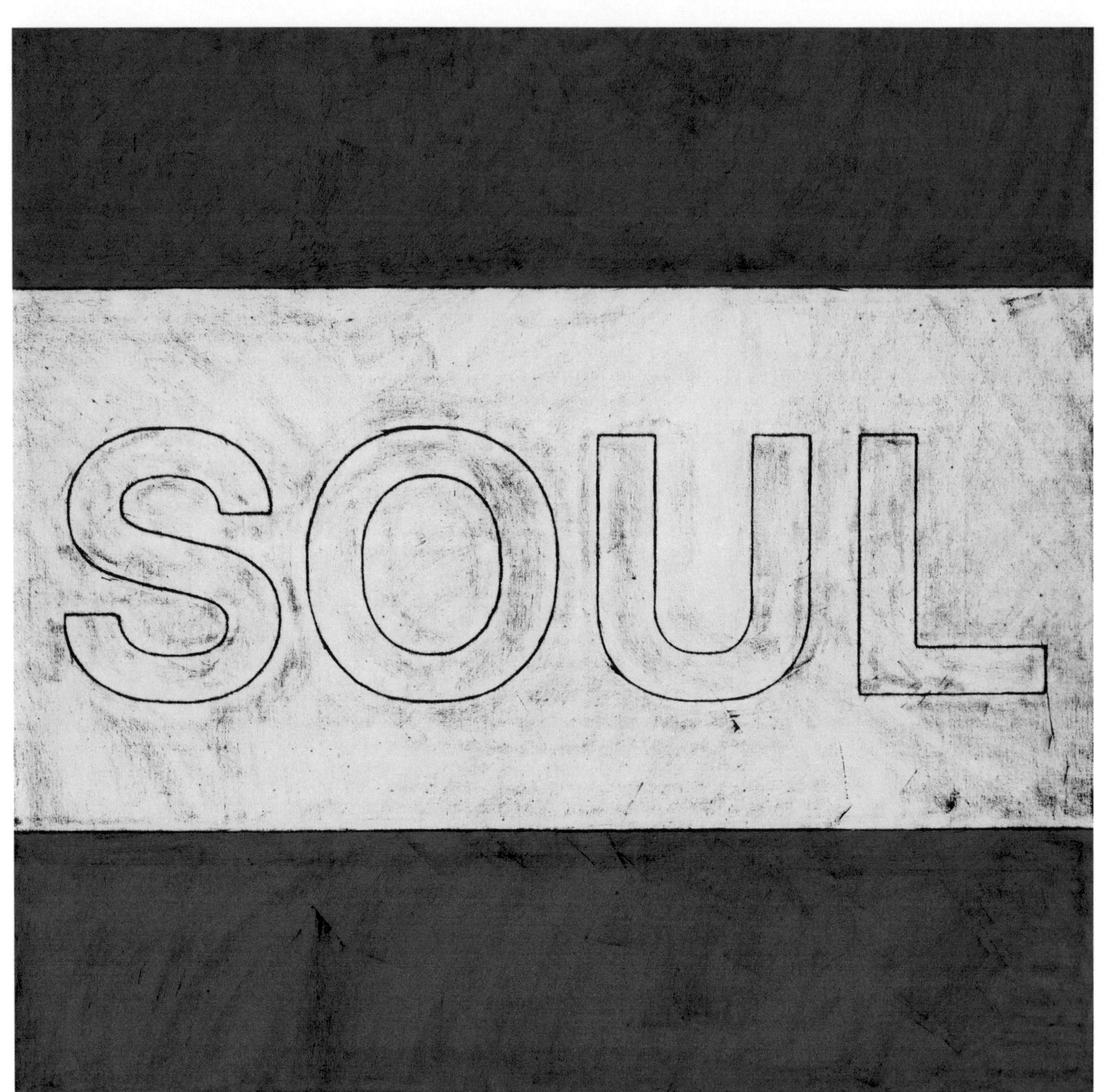

2014.17 Untitled (Soul), 200×200 cm

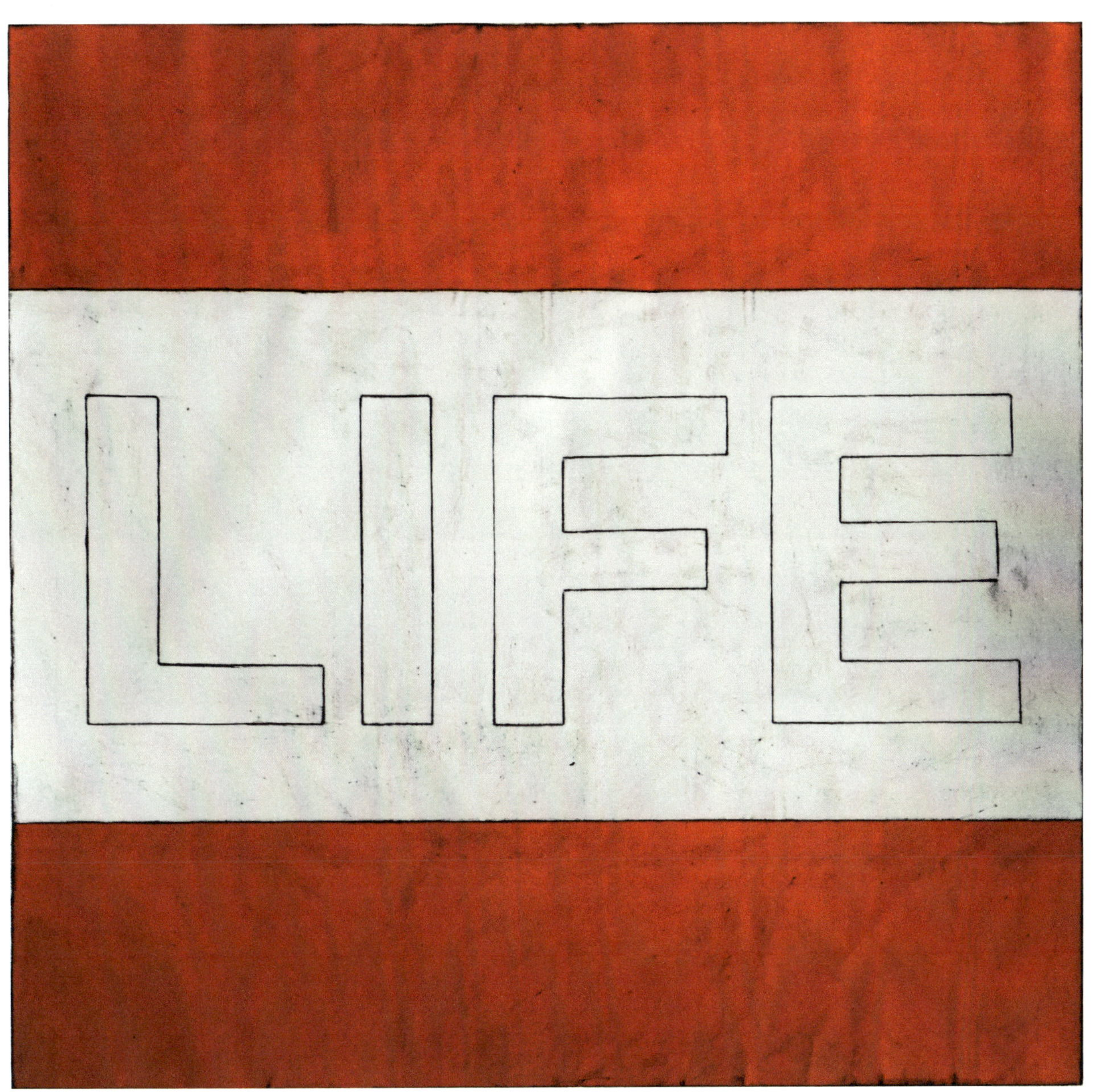

2014.18 Untitled (Life), 200 × 200 cm

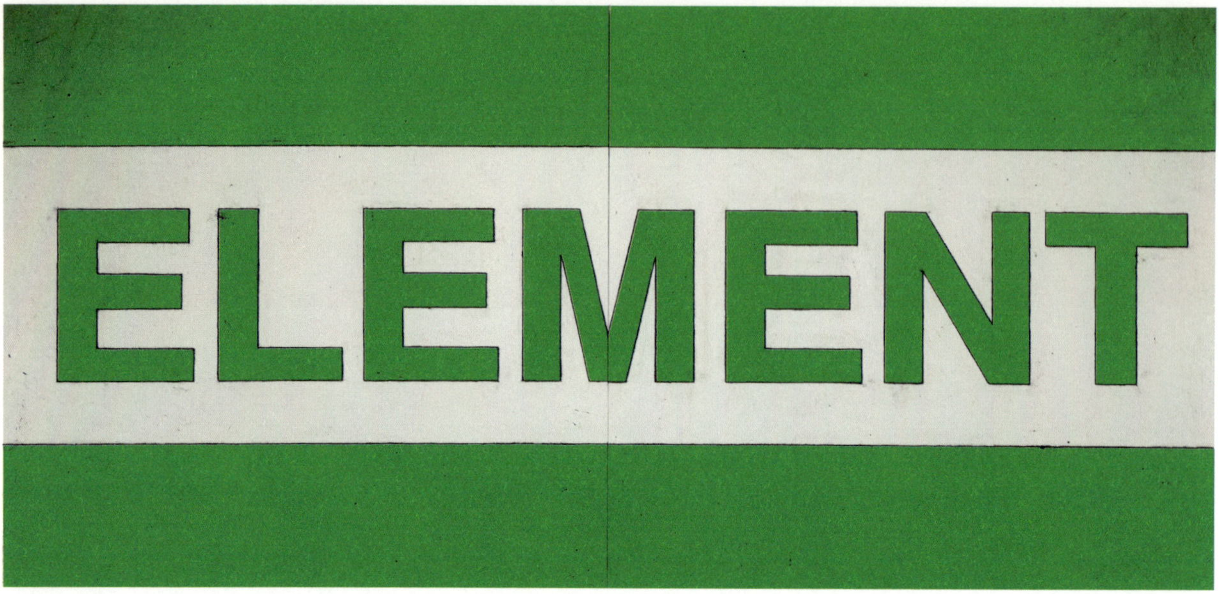

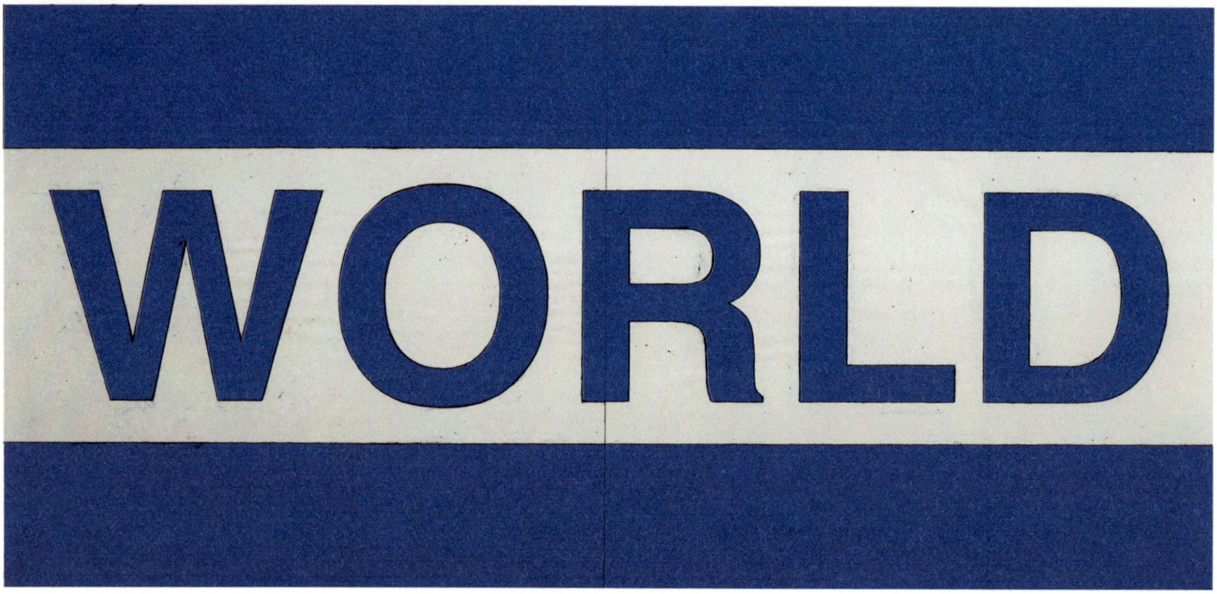

2014.19 Untitled (Element), 200 × 400 cm (2 parts)
2014.20 Untitled (World), 200 × 400 cm (2 parts)

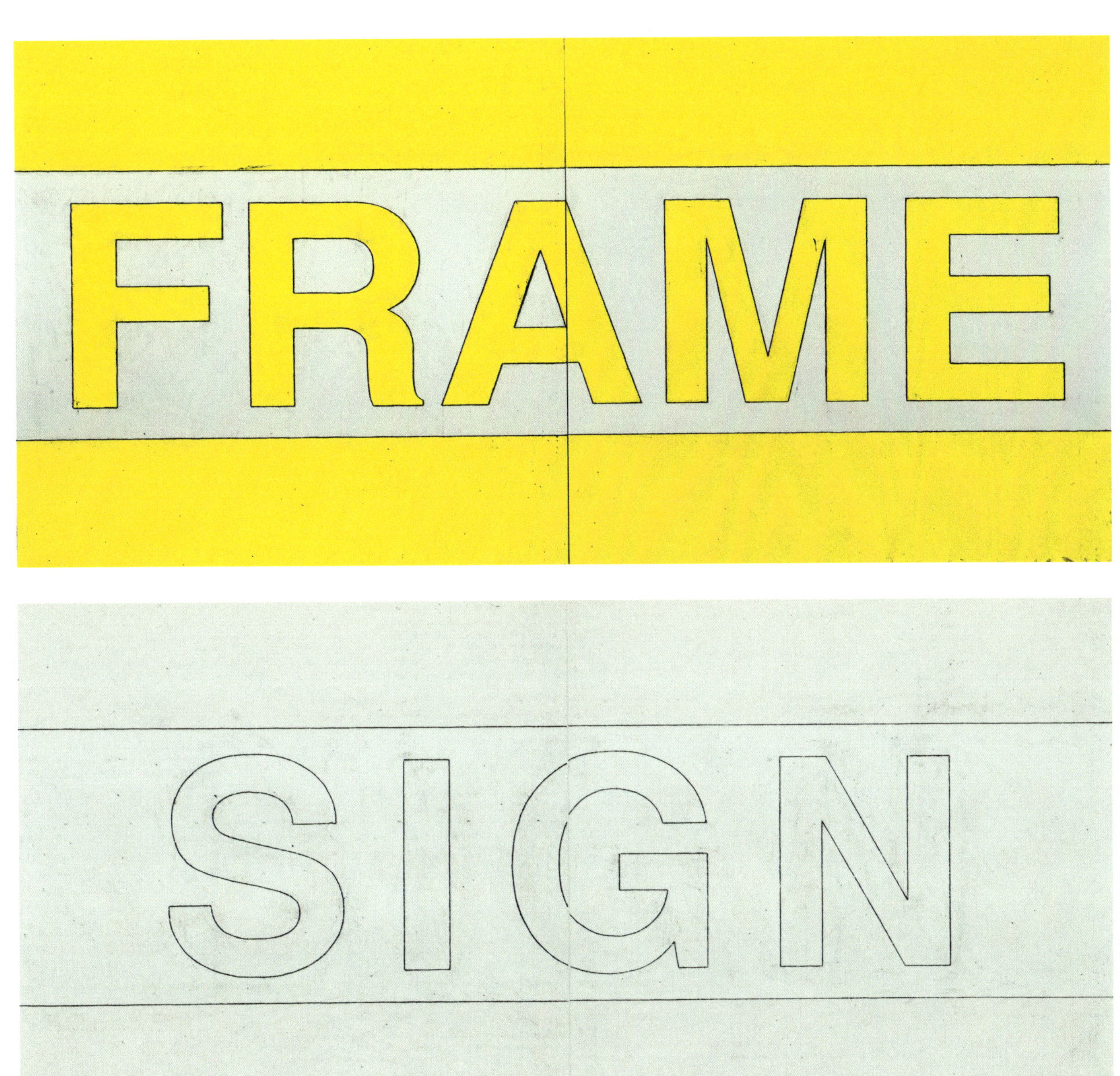

2014.21 Untitled (Frame), 200 × 400 cm (2 parts)
2014.22 Untitled (Sign), 200 × 400 cm (2 parts)

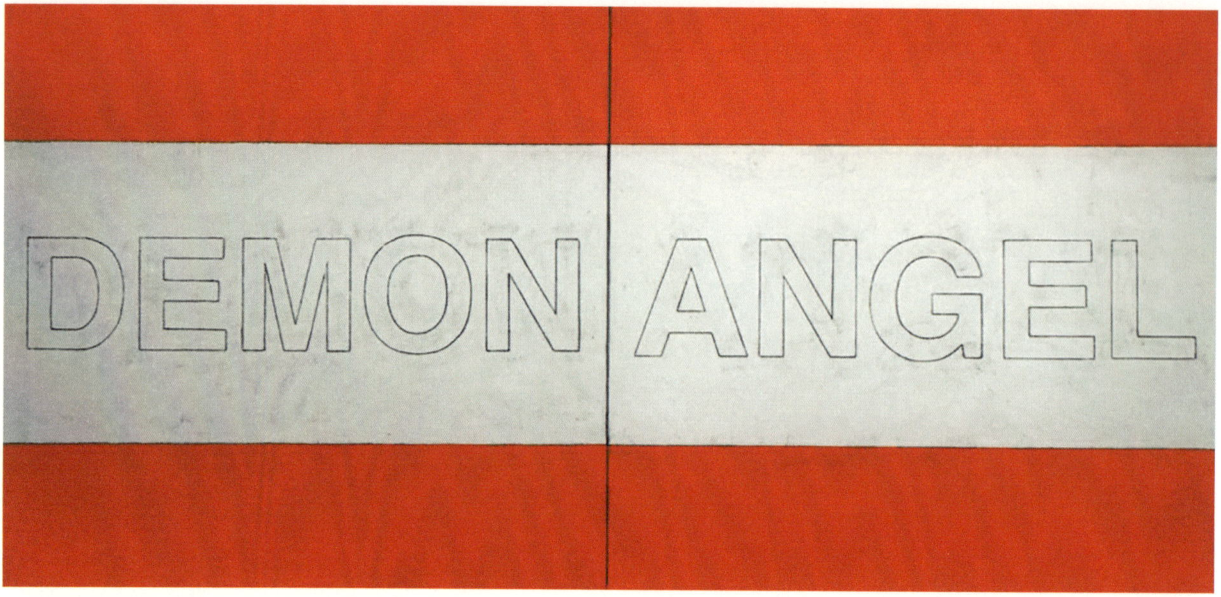

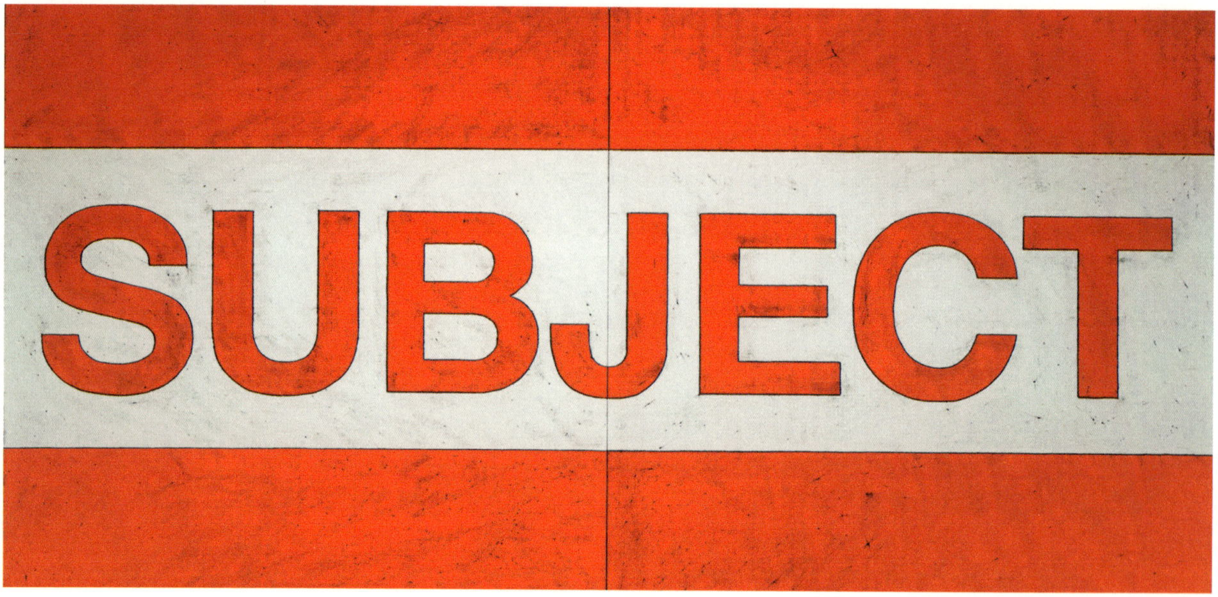

2014.23 Untitled (Demon Angel), 200 × 400 cm (2 parts)
2014.24 Untitled (Subject), 200 × 400 cm (2 parts)

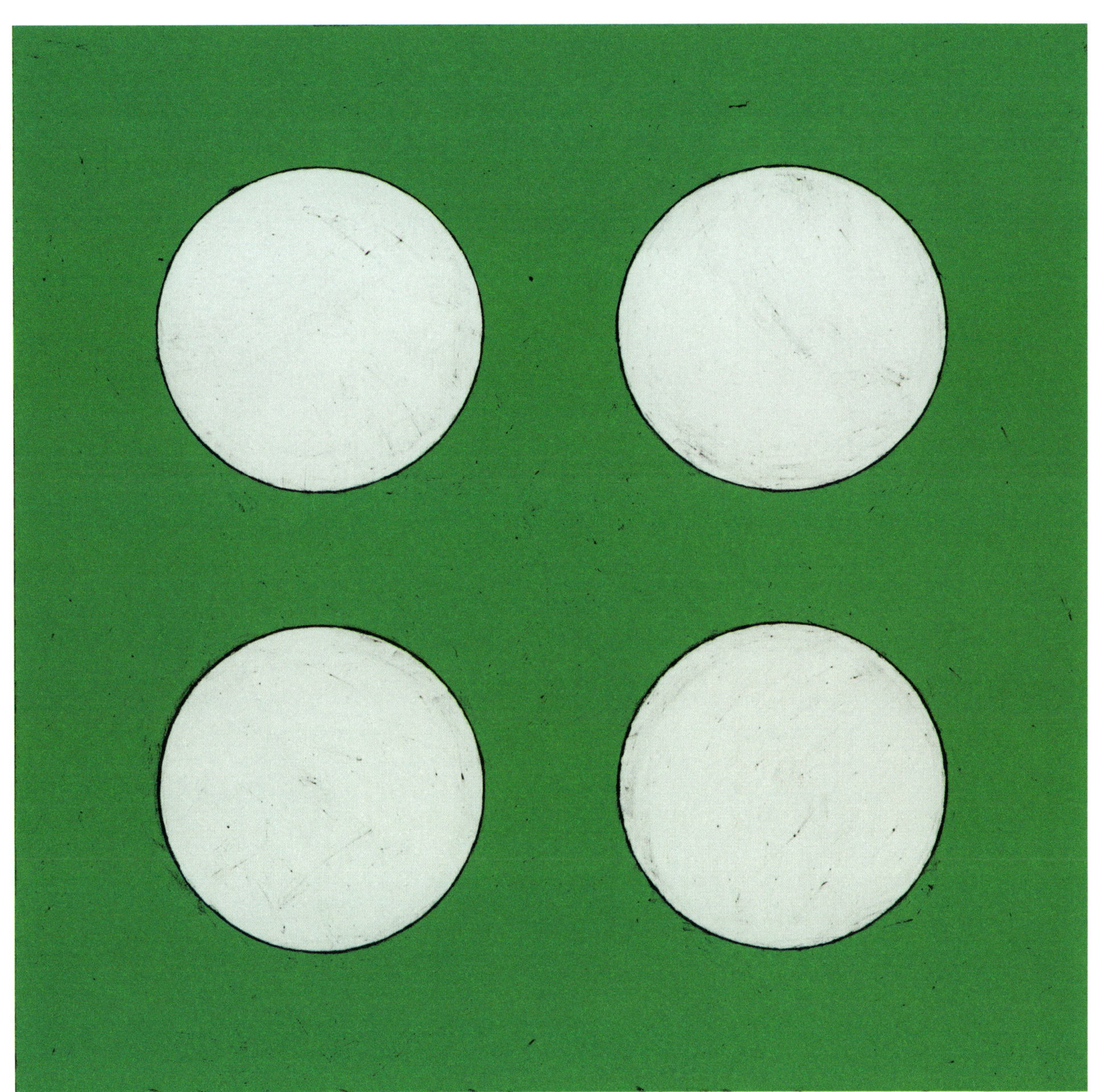

2014.25 Untitled (Elements), 200×200 cm

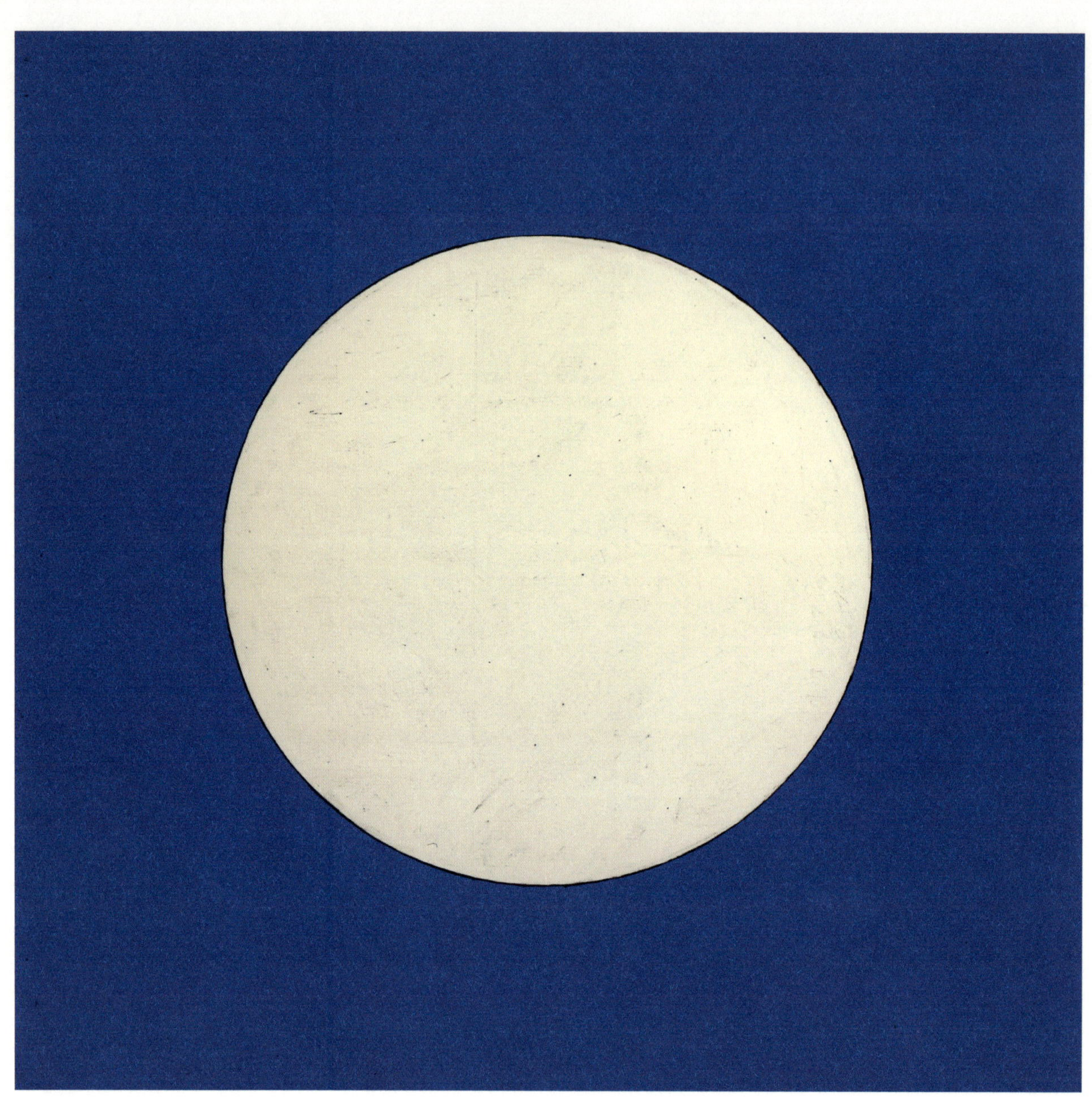

2014.26 Untitled (World Unframed), 200 × 200 cm

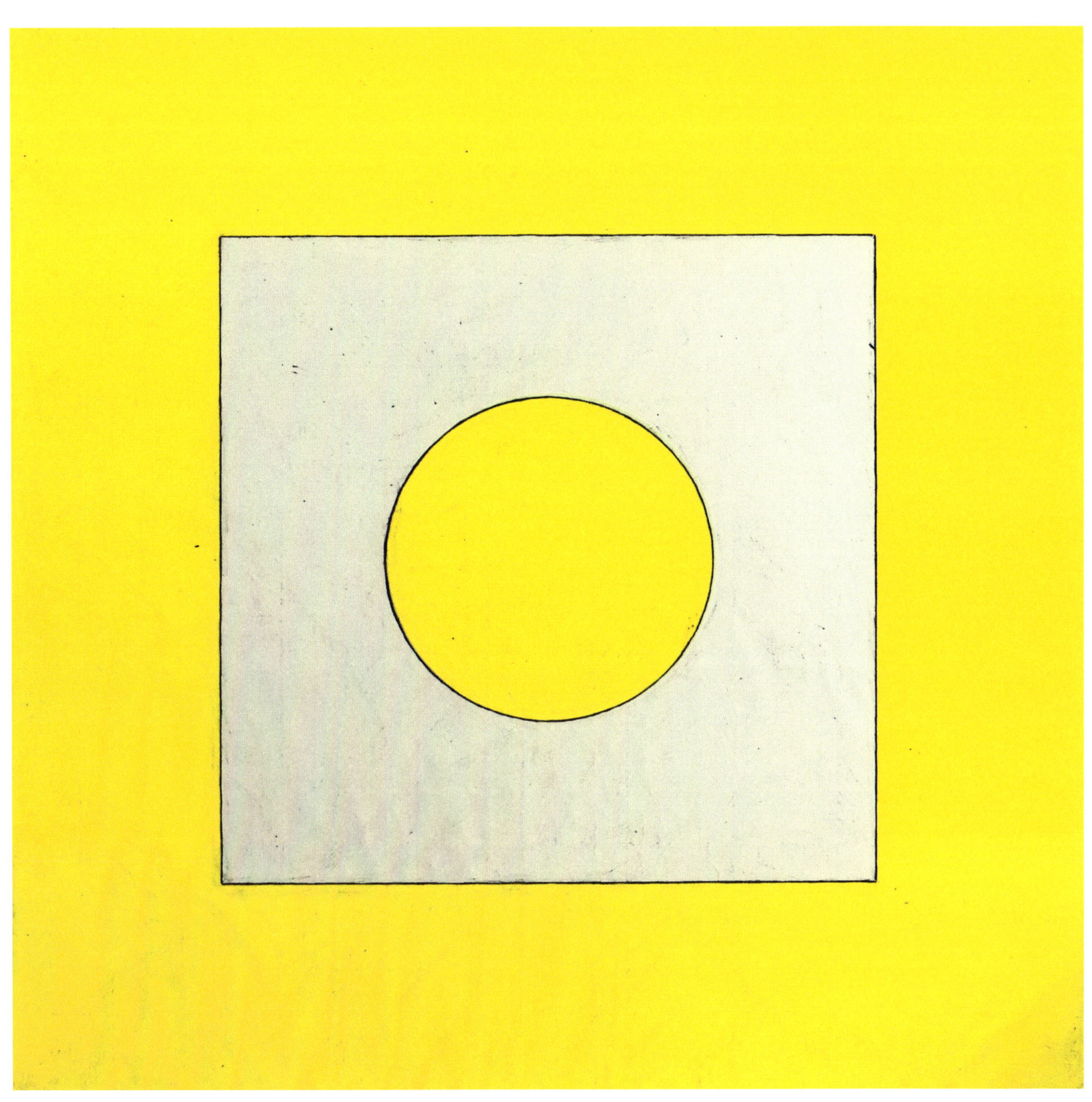

2014.27 Untitled (Frame), 200 × 200 cm

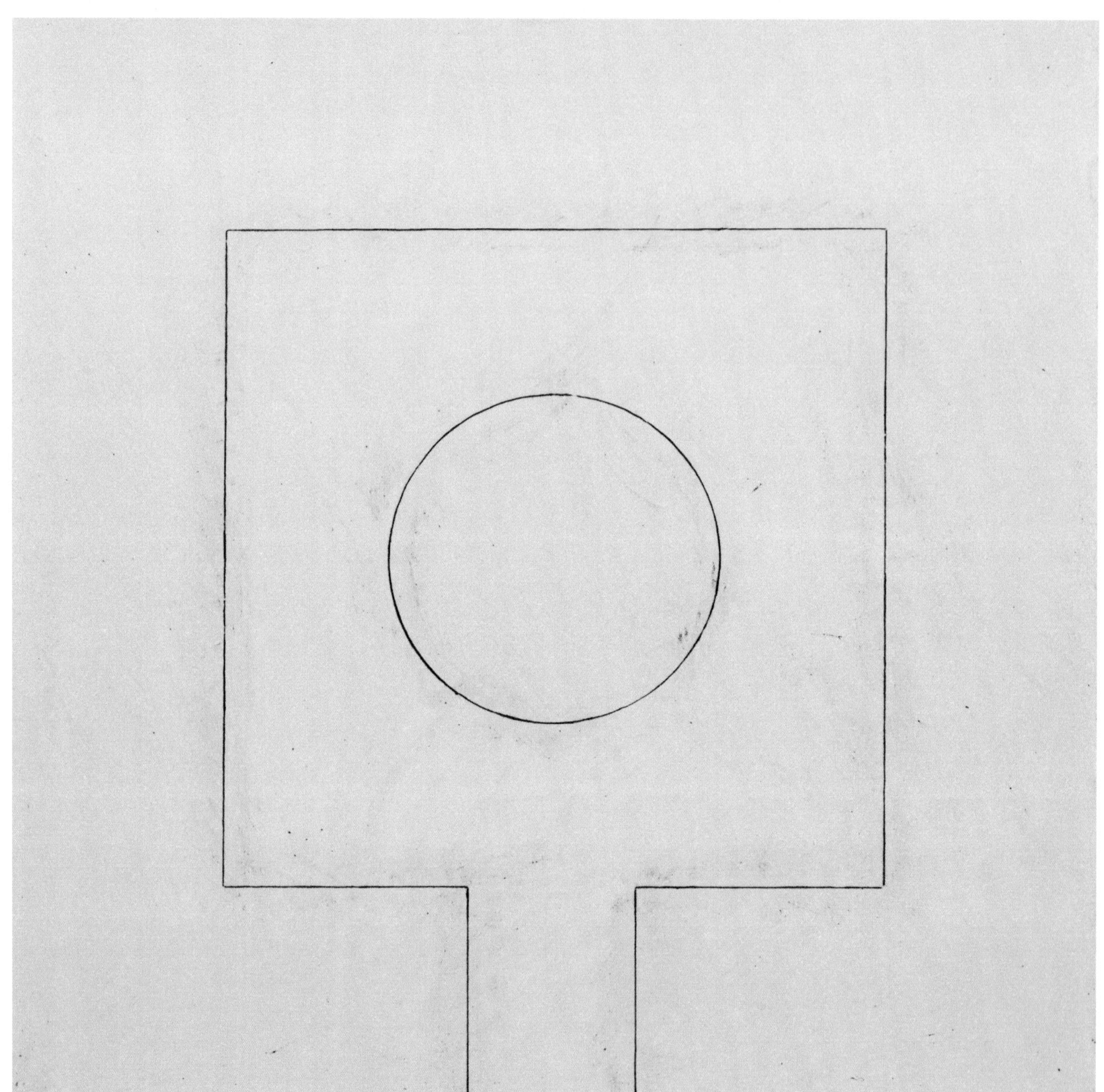

2014.28 Untitled (Sign), 200×200 cm

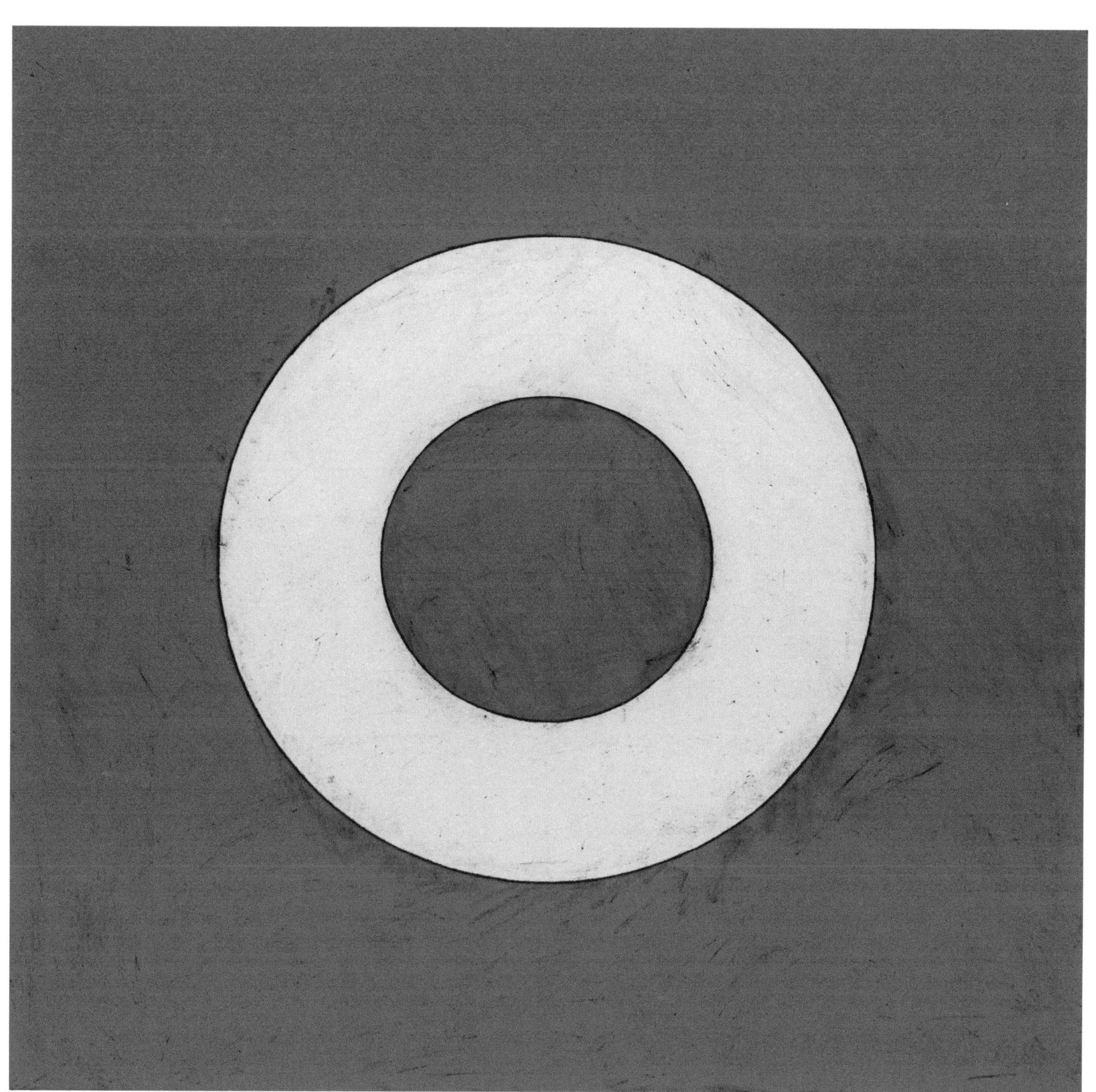

2014.29 Untitled (Subjective), 200 × 200 cm

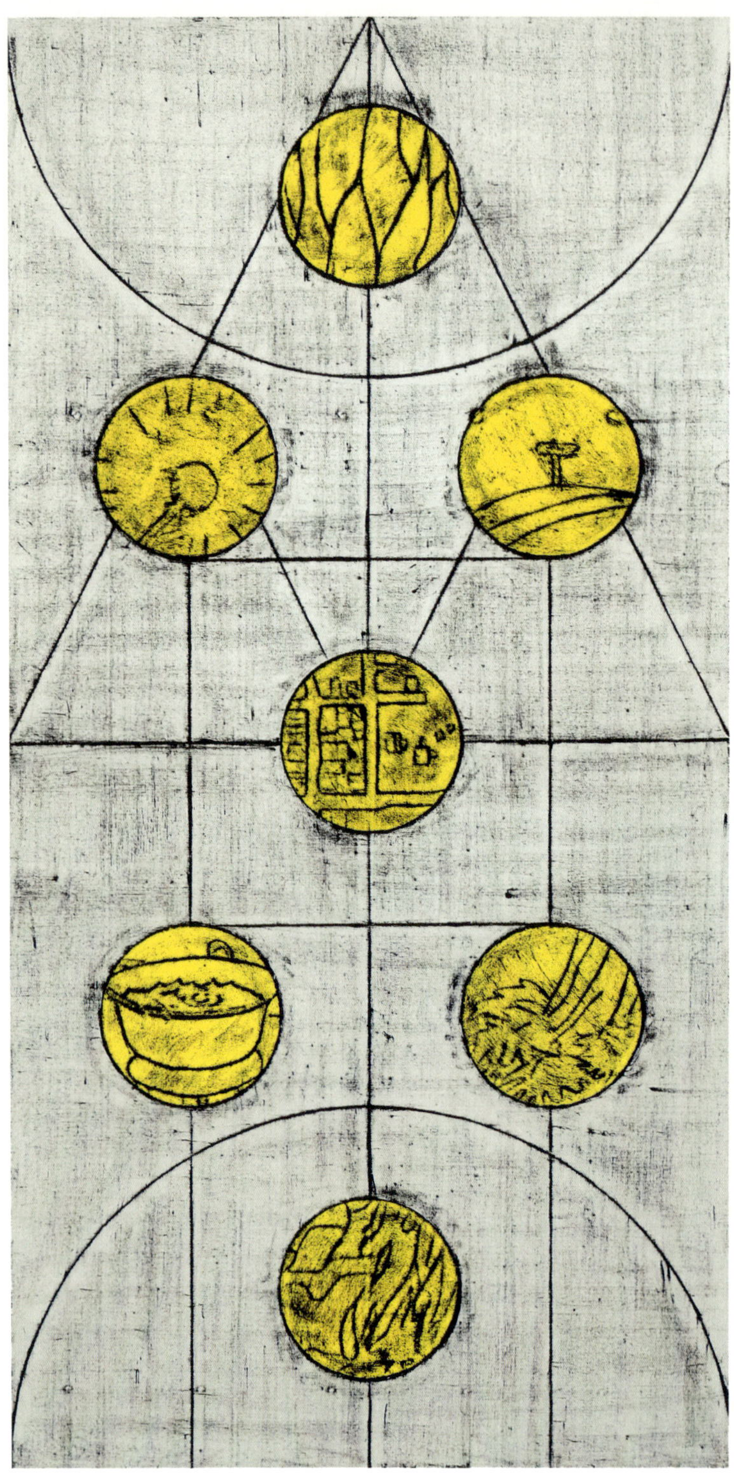

2014.30 Untitled (7 Details), 200 × 100 cm

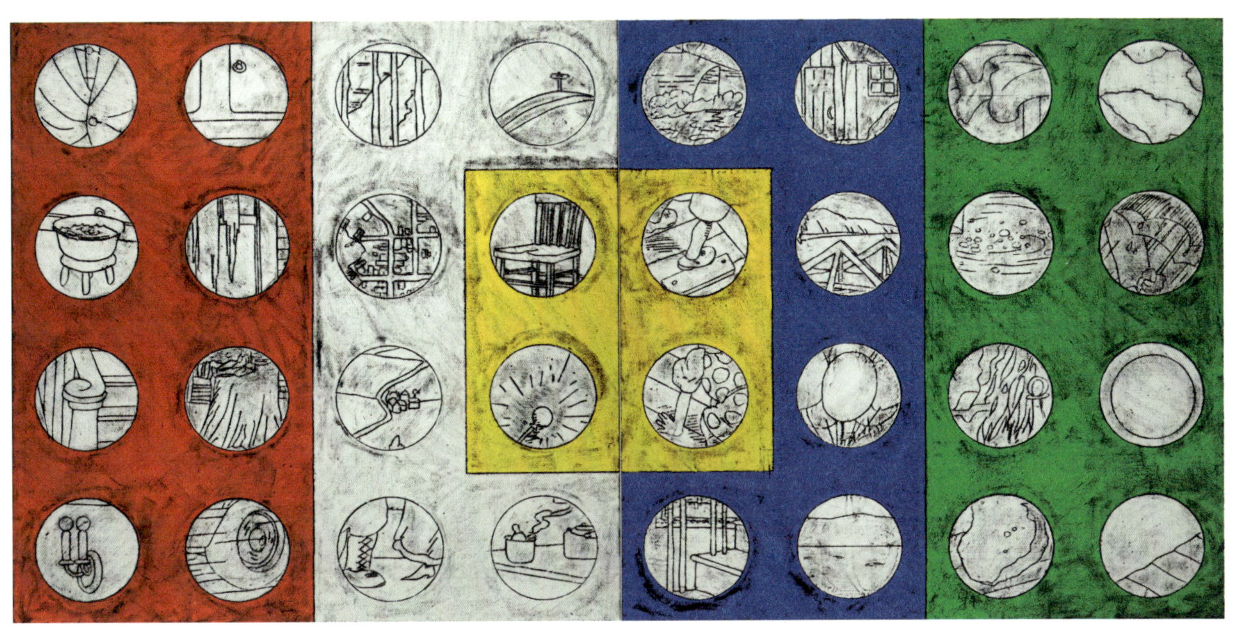

2014.31 Untitled (32 Details), 200 × 400 cm (2 parts)

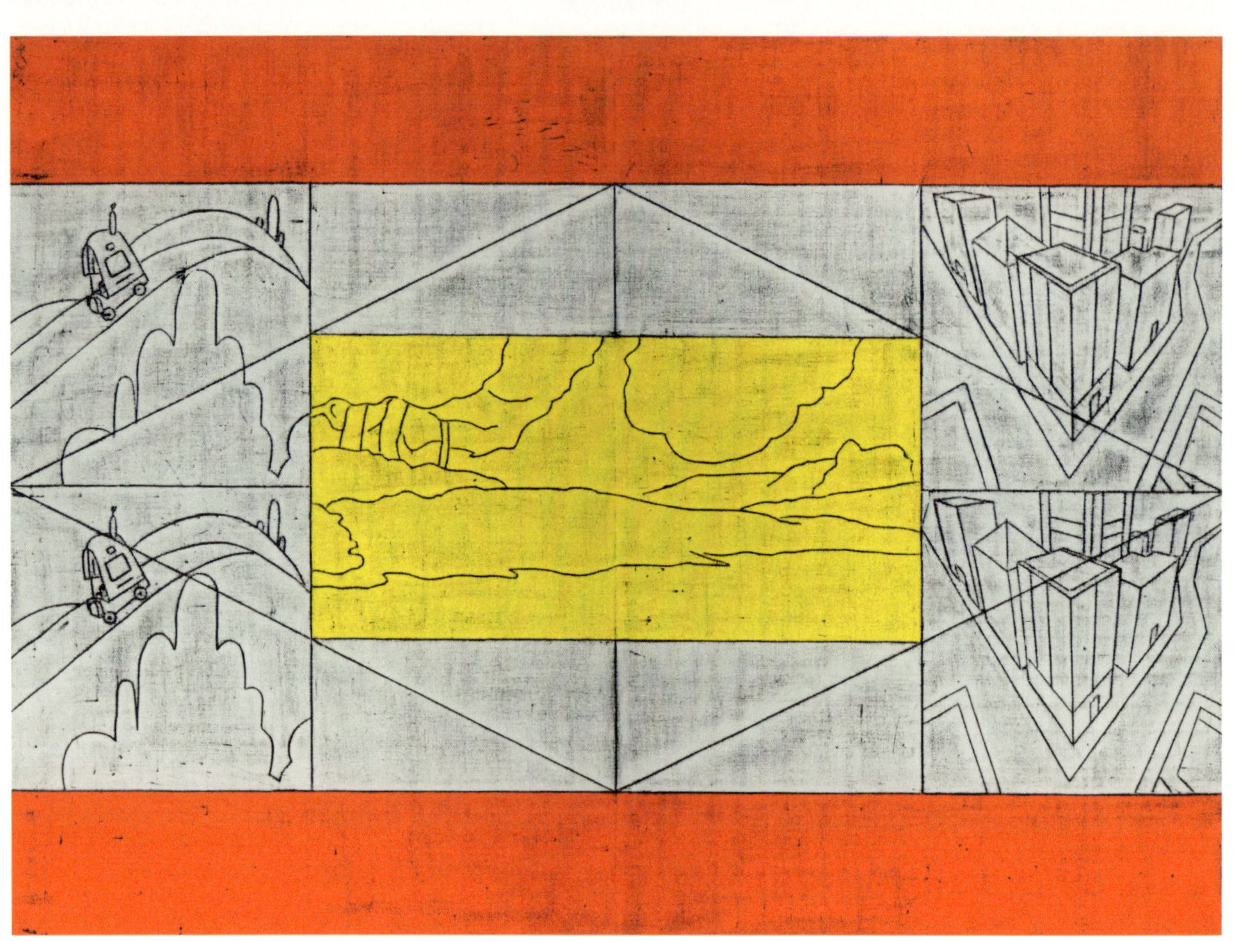

2014.32 Untitled (Animated), 183 × 244 (2 parts)

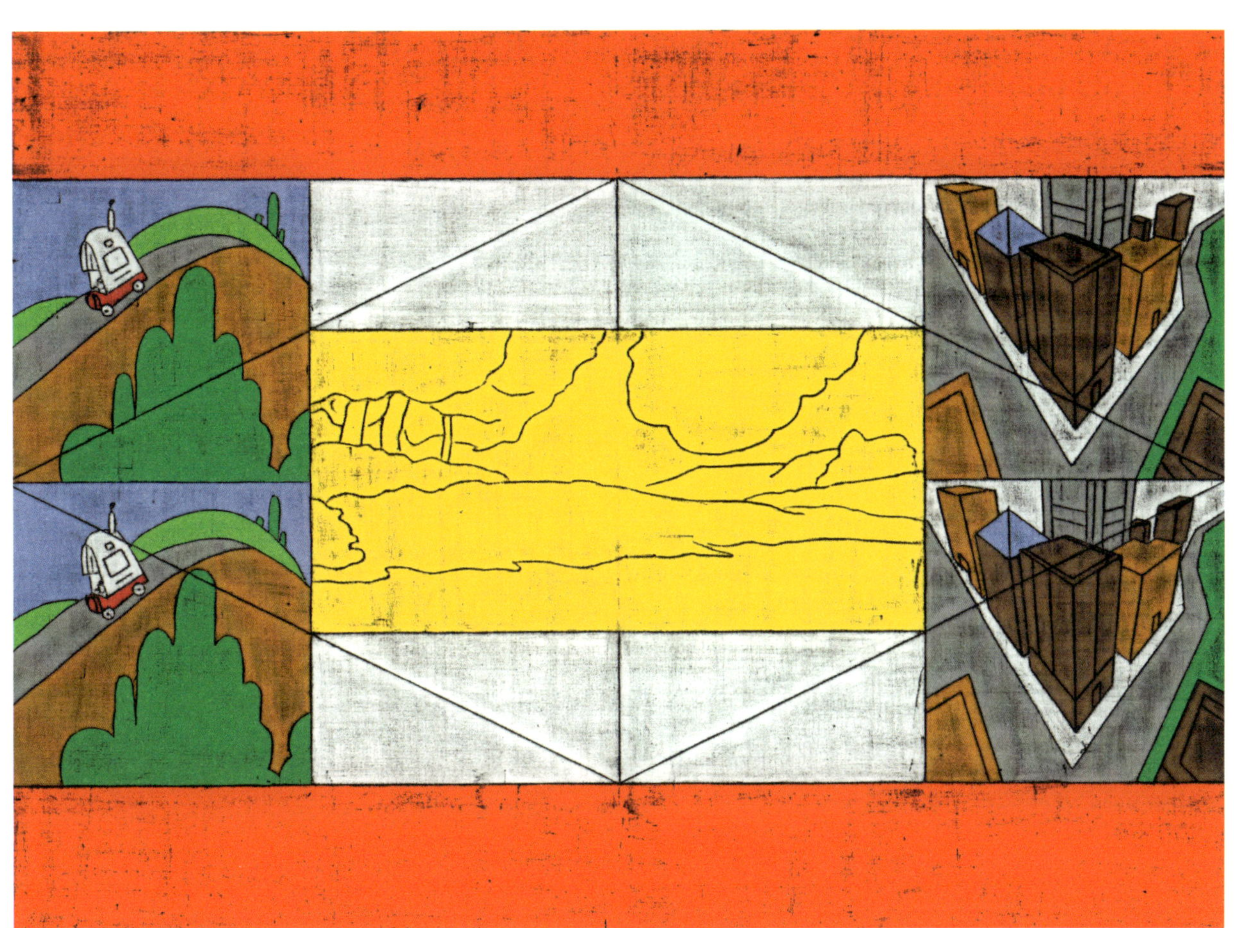

2014.33 Untitled (Animated), 183 × 244 (2 parts)

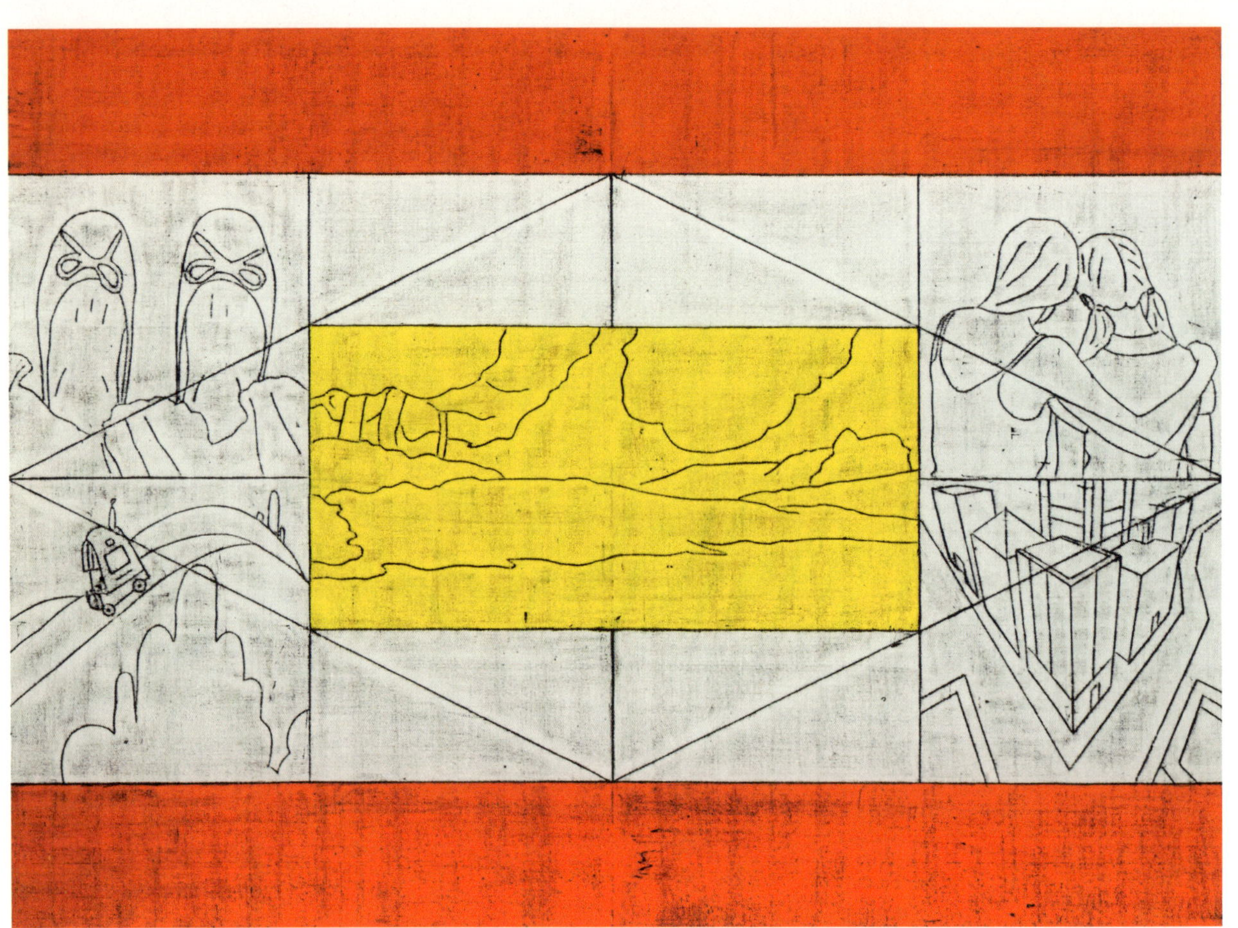

2014.34 Untitled (Animated), 183 × 244 (2 parts)

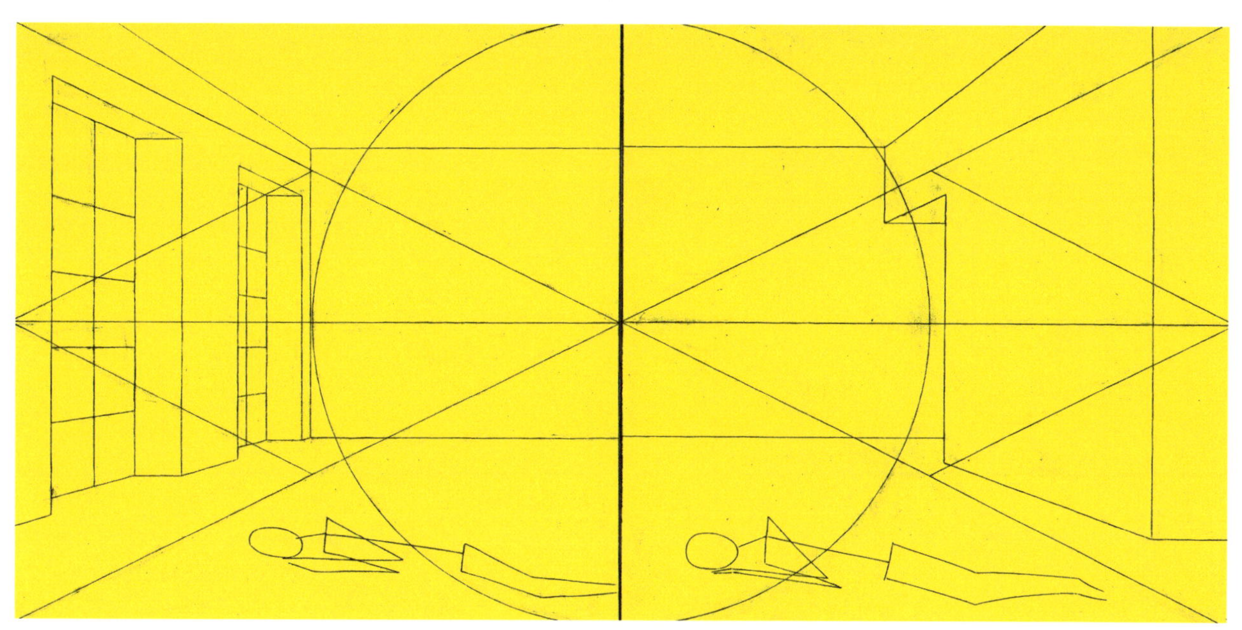

2014.35 Untitled (Two People in the Subject), 200 × 400 cm (2 parts)

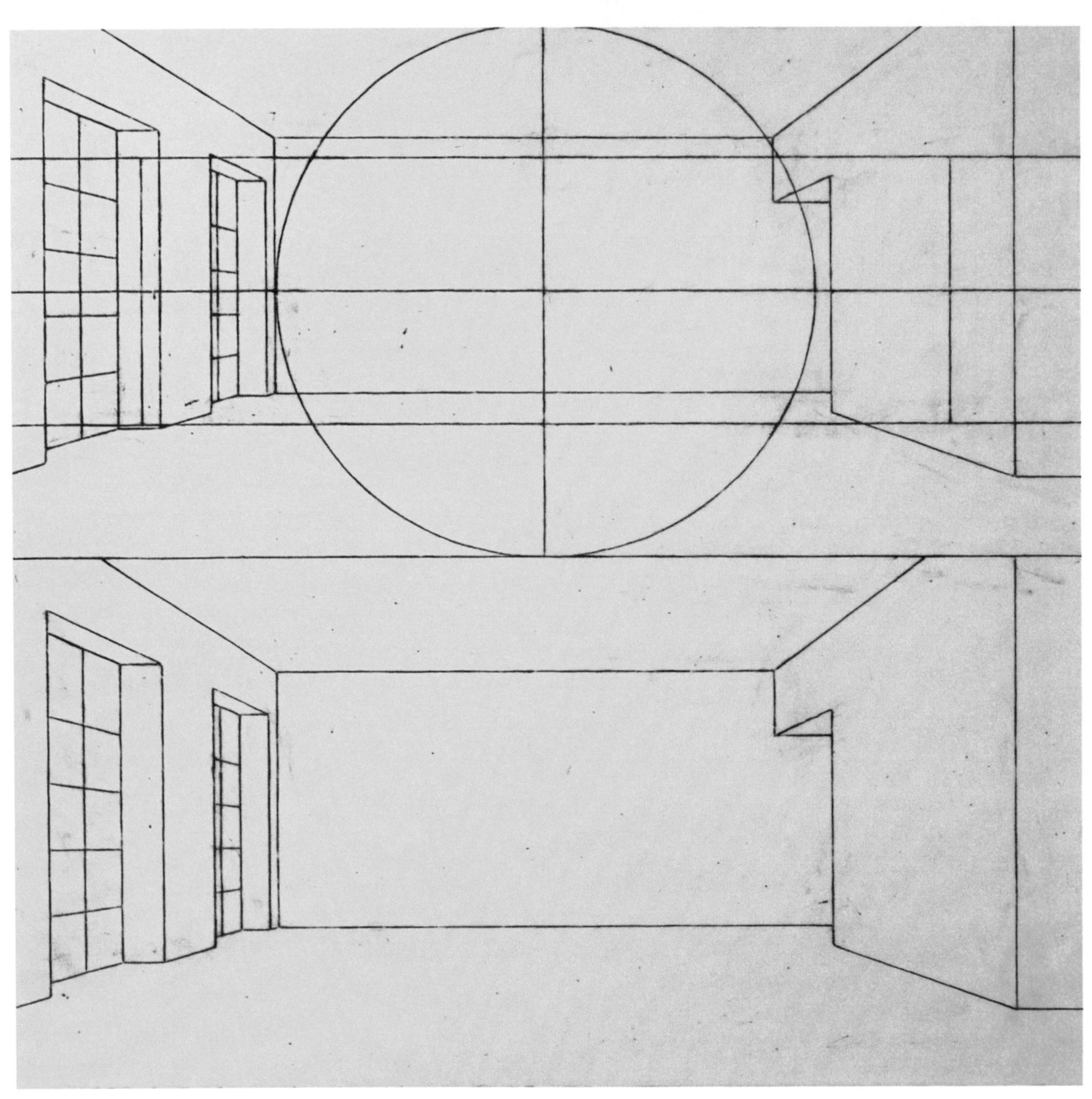

2014.36 Untitled (Element and Empty Interior), 200 × 200 cm

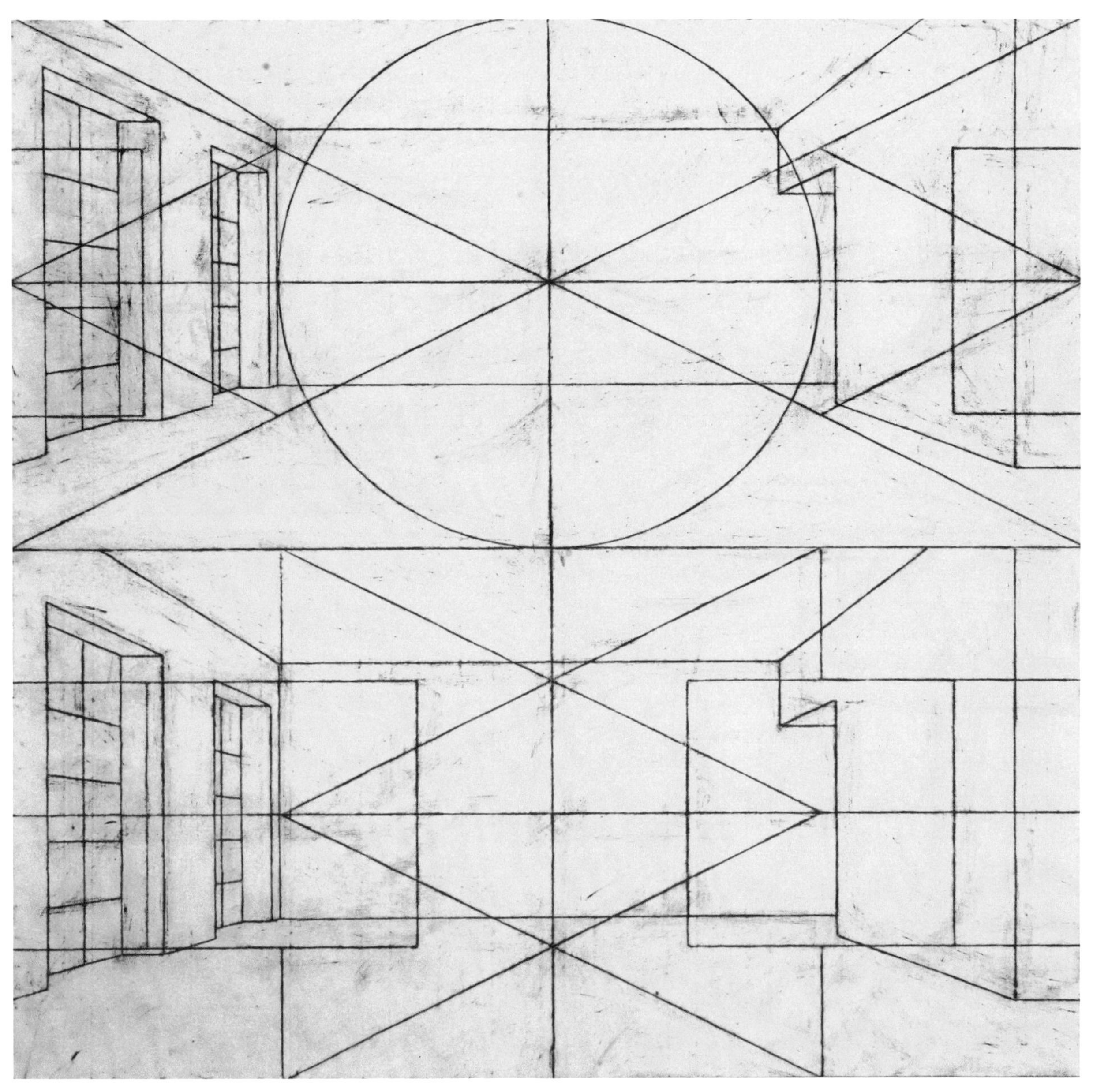

2014.37 Untitled (Subject and Sign Interior), 200 × 200 cm

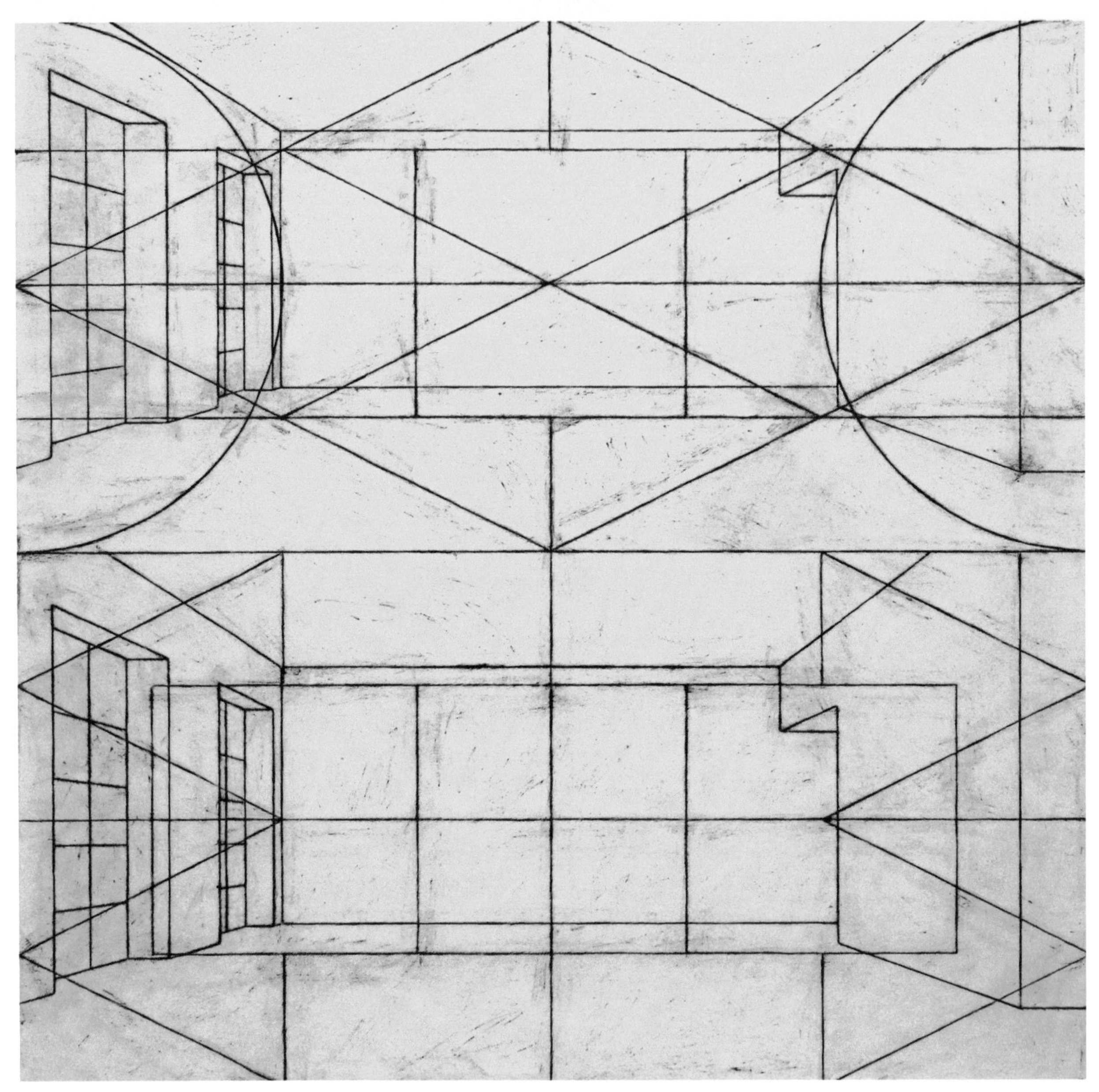

2014.38 Untitled (Frame and World Interior), 200 × 200 cm

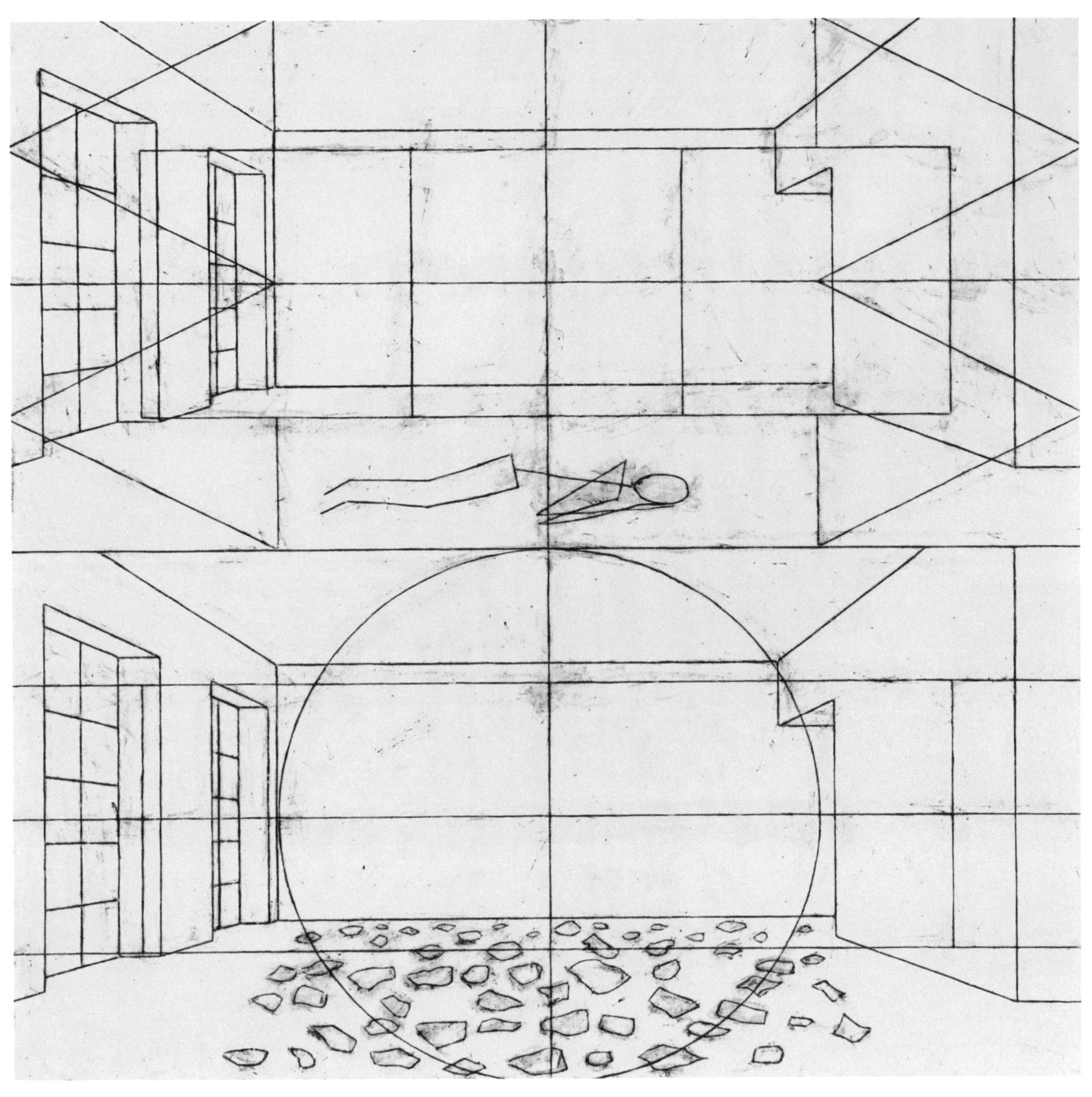

2014.39 Untitled (World Interior with Figure/Elemental Interior with Pieces), 200 × 200 cm

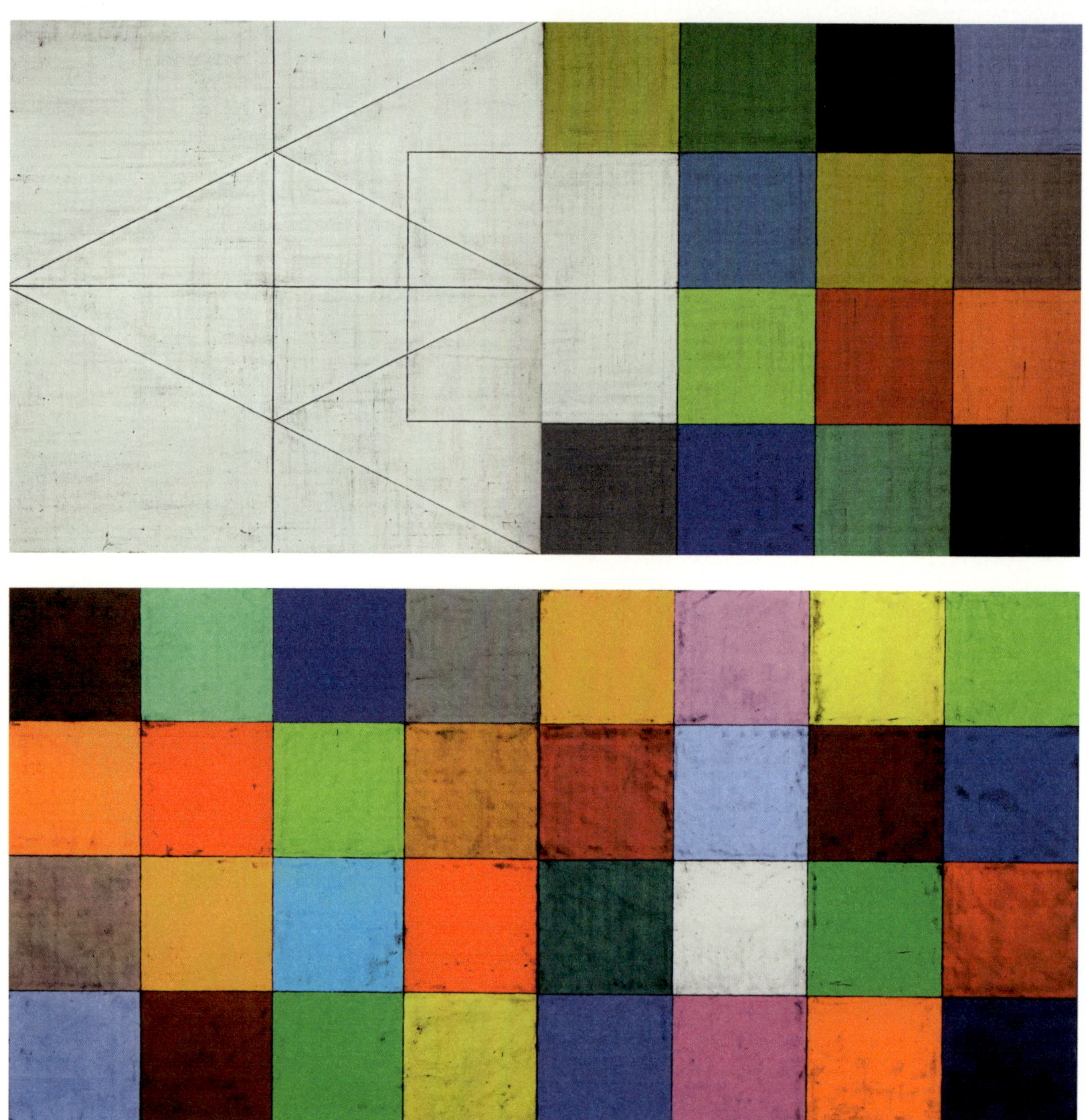

2014.40 Untitled (City and Light Patterns), 200 × 400 cm (2 parts)
2014.41 Untitled (Light Patterns), 200 × 400 cm (2 parts)

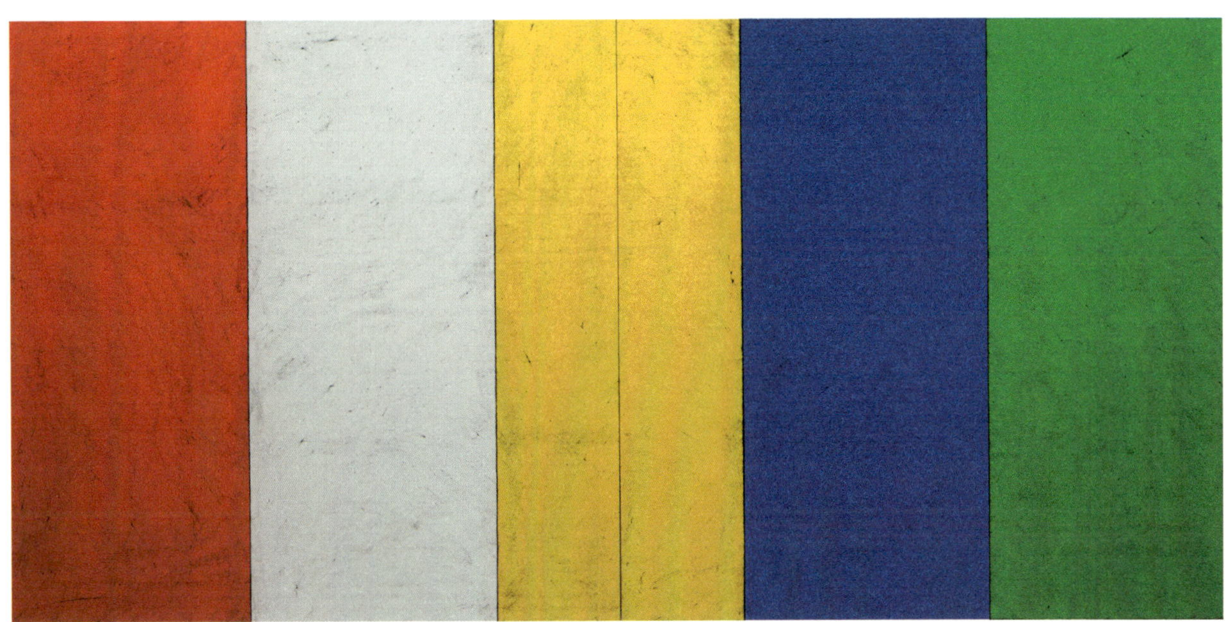

2014.42 Untitled (Overall Chart), 200 × 400 cm (2 parts)

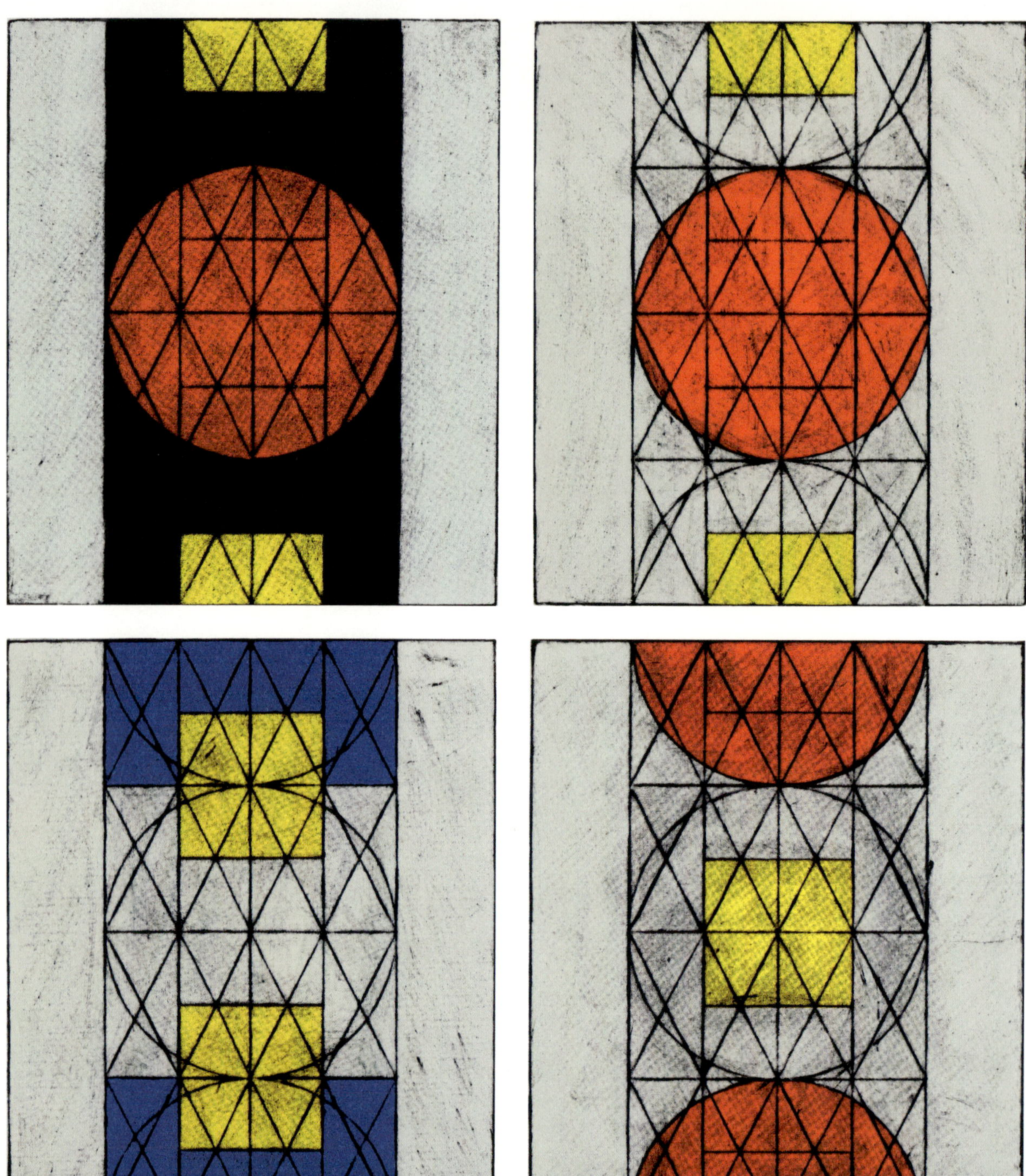

2014.43 Untitled (Centering on the Subjective with Black), 60 × 50 cm
2014.44 Untitled (Centering on the Subjective), 60 × 50 cm
2014.45 Untitled (Centering on Signs), 60 × 50 cm
2014.46 Untitled (Centering on the Frame with Subjective), 60 × 50 cm

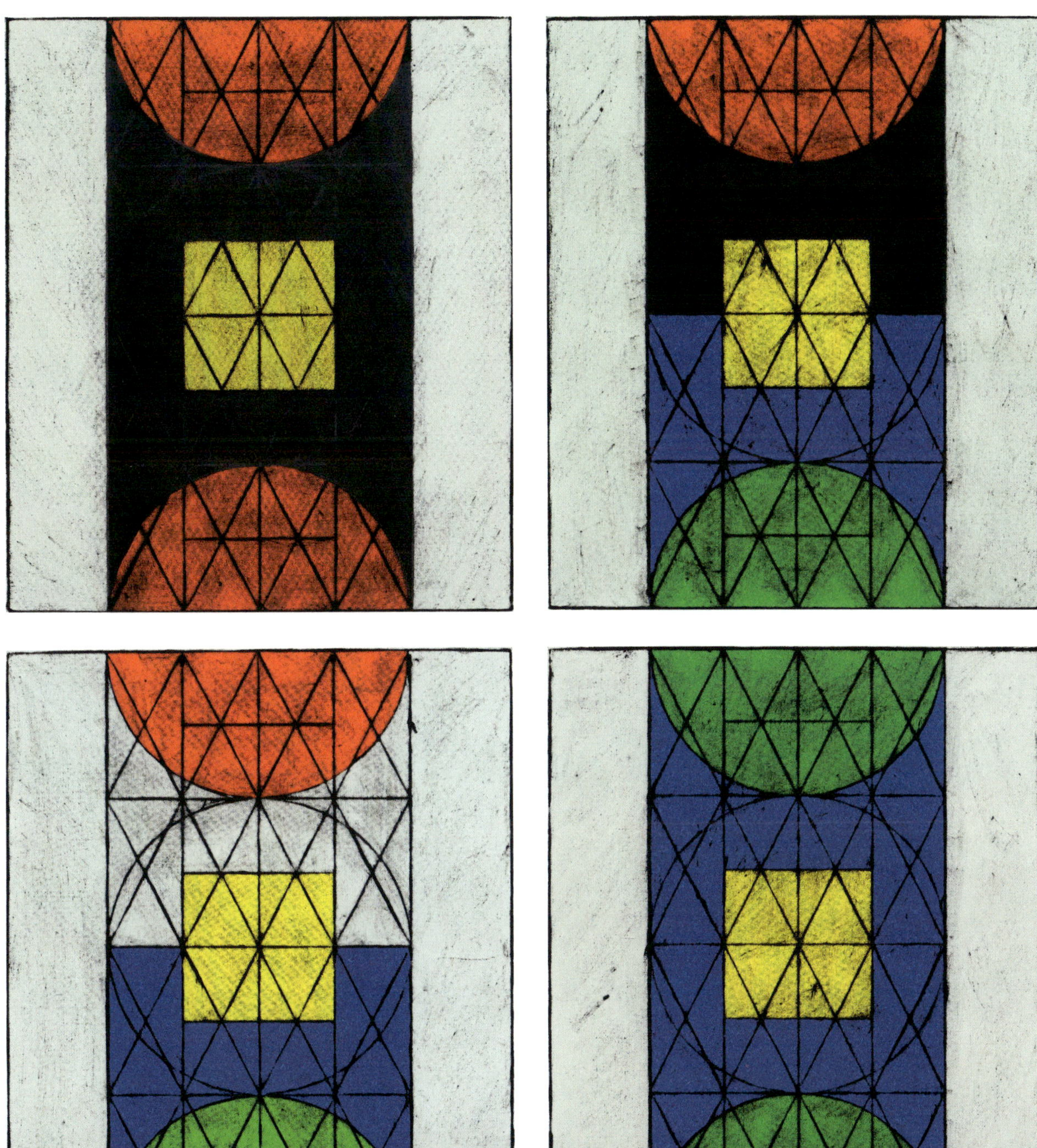

2014.47 Untitled (Centering on the World Framed with Subjective), 60 × 50 cm
2014.48 Untitled (Centering on the Frame/Overall Chart with Black), 60 × 50 cm
2014.49 Untitled (Centering on the Frame/Overall Chart with White), 60 × 50 cm
2014.50 Untitled (Centering on the World Framed with Elements), 60 × 50 cm

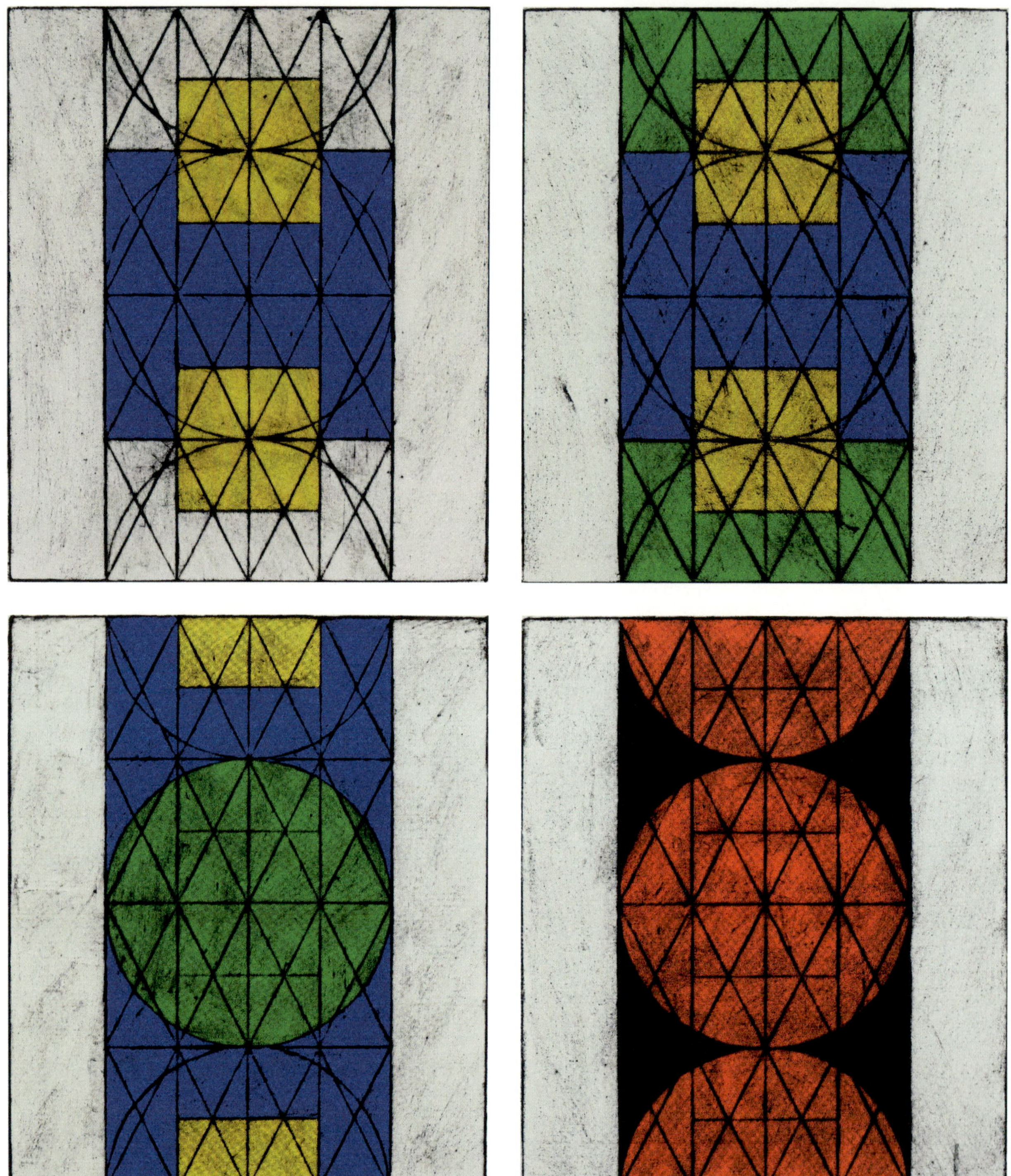

2014.51   Untitled (Centering on the World Unframed), 60 × 50 cm
2014.52   Untitled (Centering on the World), 60 × 50 cm
2014.53   Untitled (Centering on the Elements), 60 × 50 cm
2014.54   Untitled (The Subjective in Overall Pattern), 60 × 50 cm

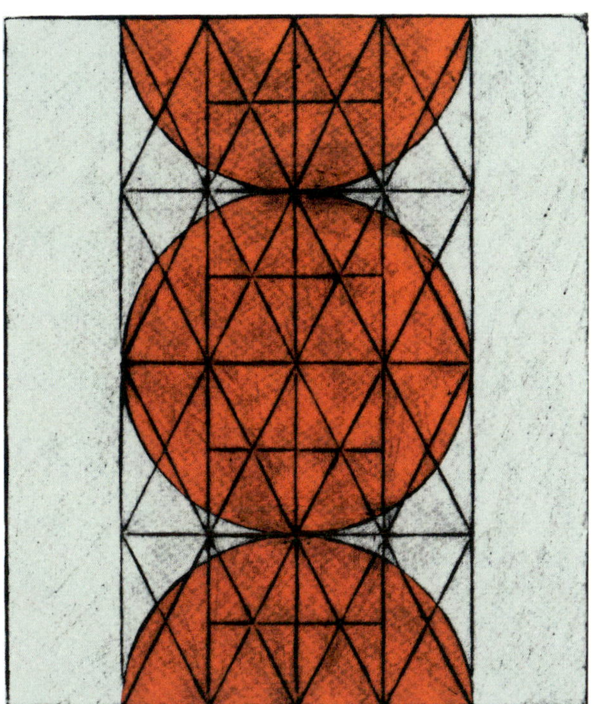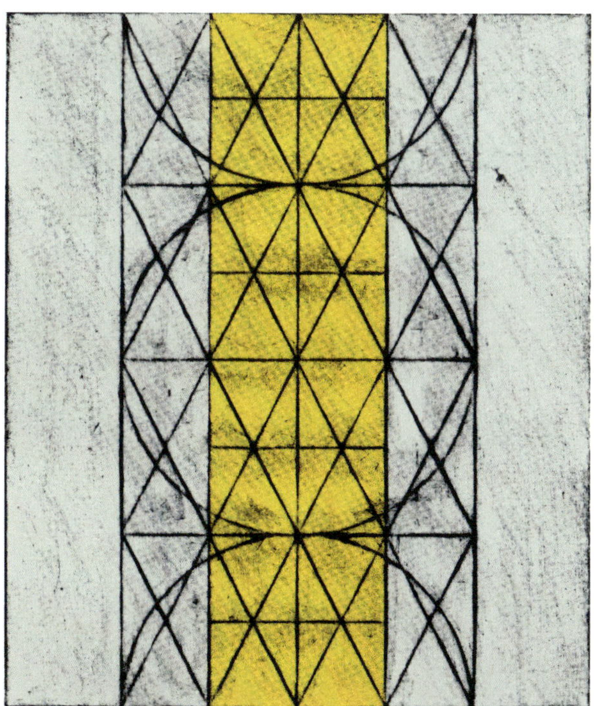

2014.55 Untitled (The Subjective in Overall Pattern), 60 × 50 cm
2014.56 Untitled (The Sign in Overall Pattern), 60 × 50 cm
2014.57 Untitled (The Frame in Overall Pattern), 60 × 50 cm

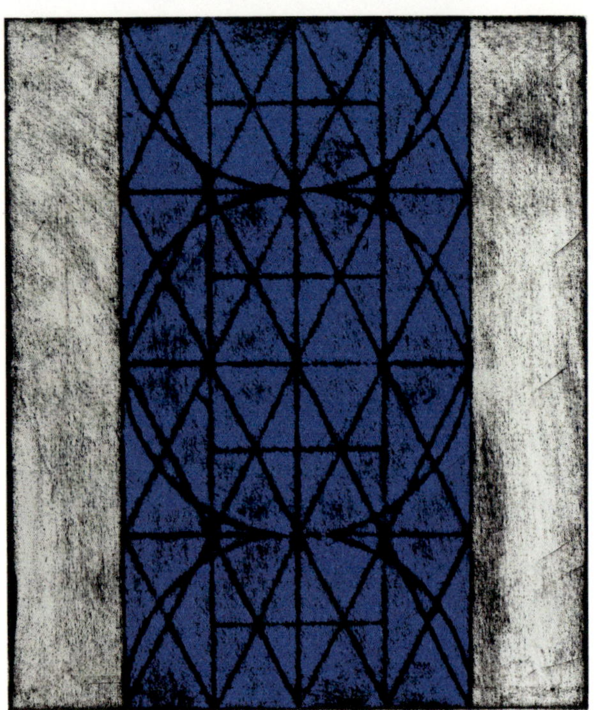

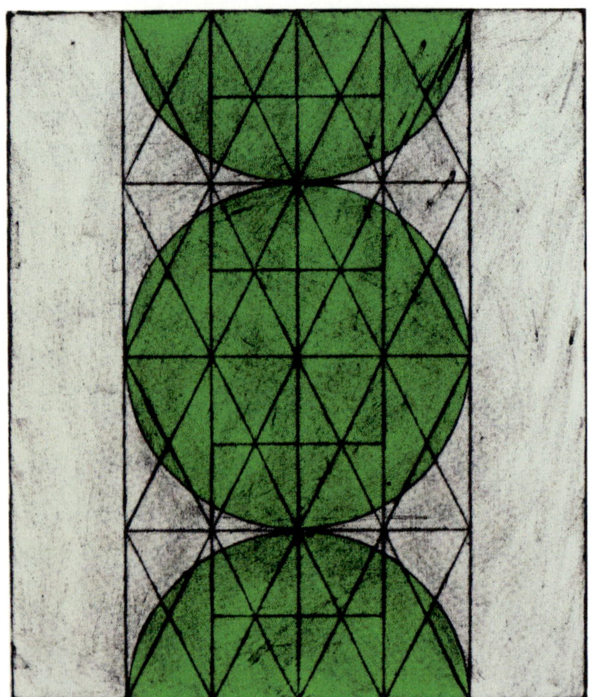

2014.58 Untitled (The World Unframed in Overall Pattern), 60 × 50 cm
2014.59 Untitled (The Elements in Overall Pattern), 60 × 50 cm

2015

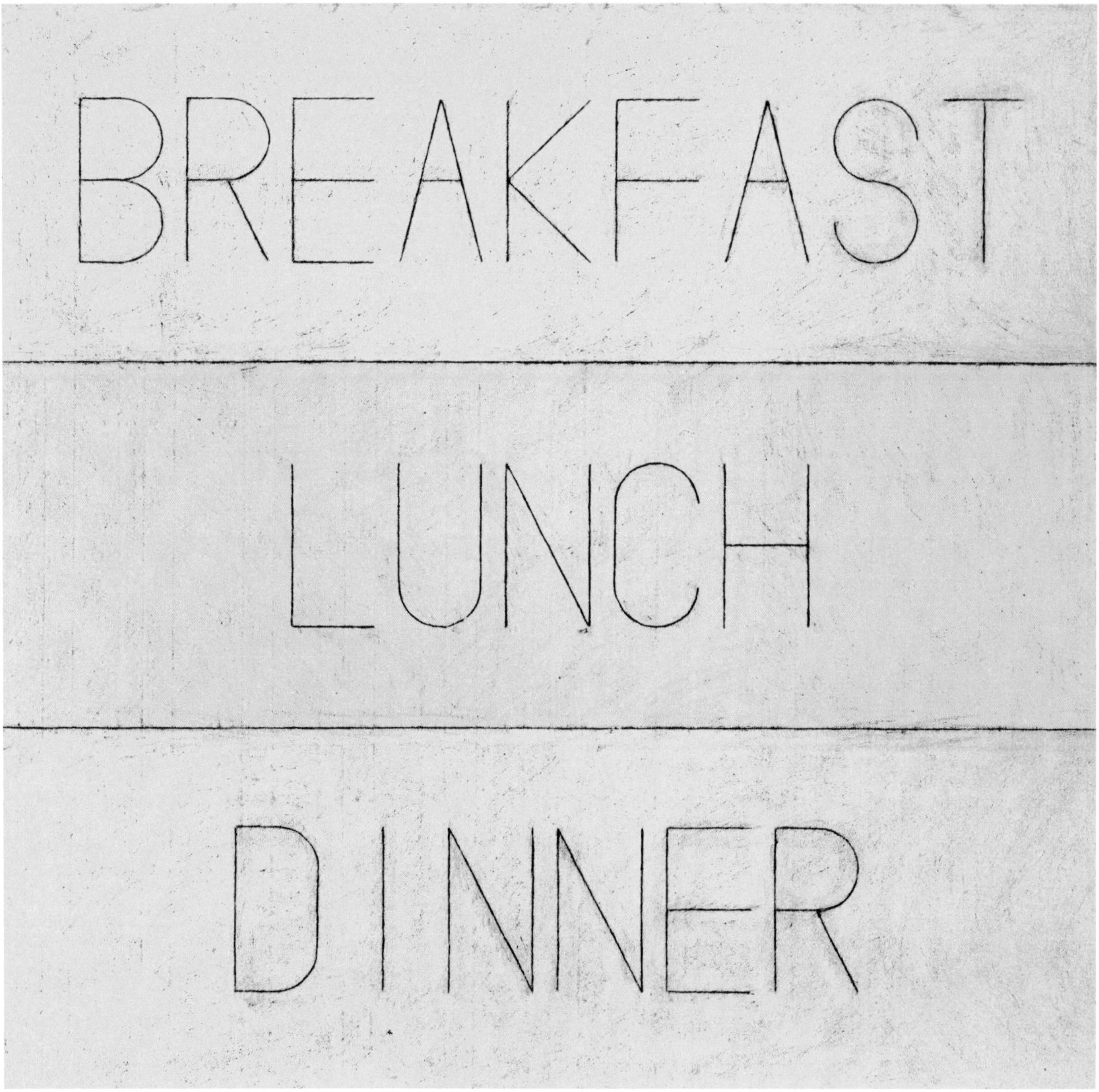

BREAKFAST

LUNCH

DINNER

2015.1 Untitled (Breakfast Lunch Dinner), 200 × 200 cm

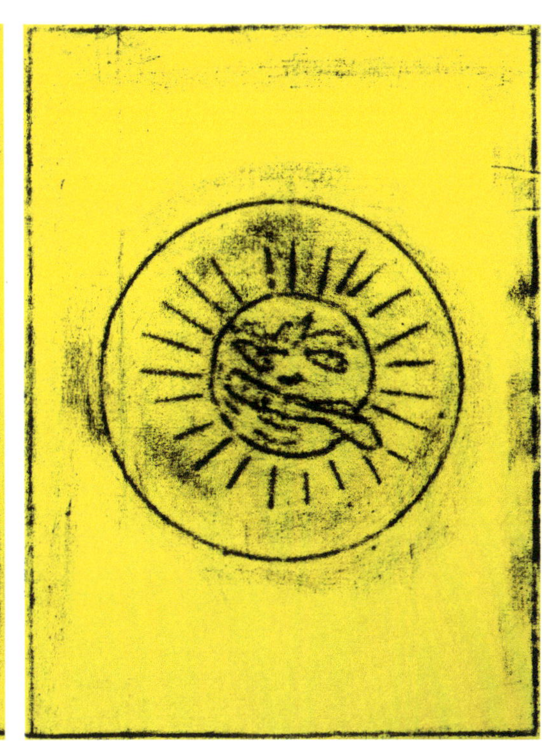

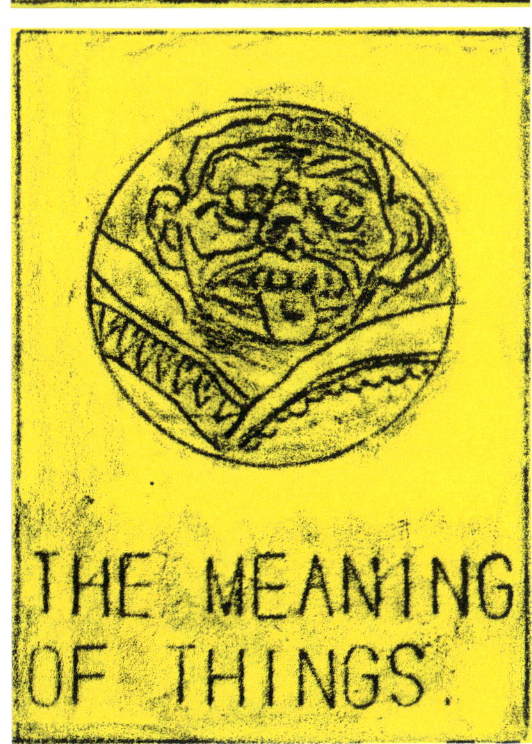

2015.2 Untitled (The Meaning of Things), 59.5 × 42 cm each (diptych)
2015.3 Untitled (The Meaning of Things), 59.5 × 42 cm

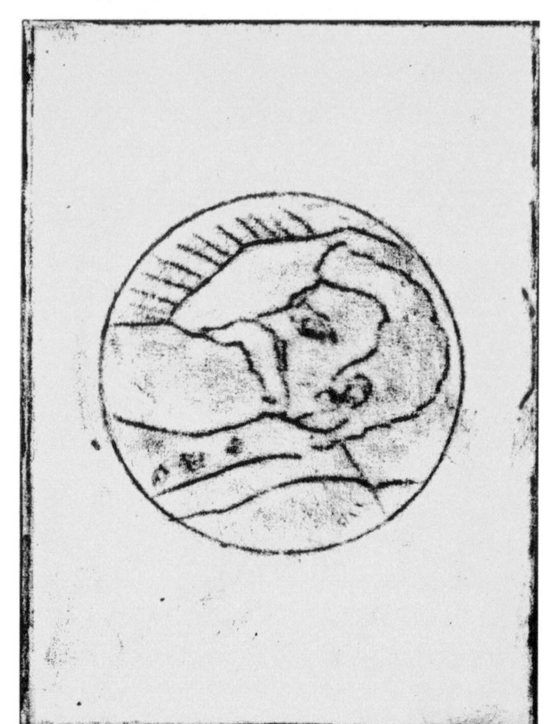

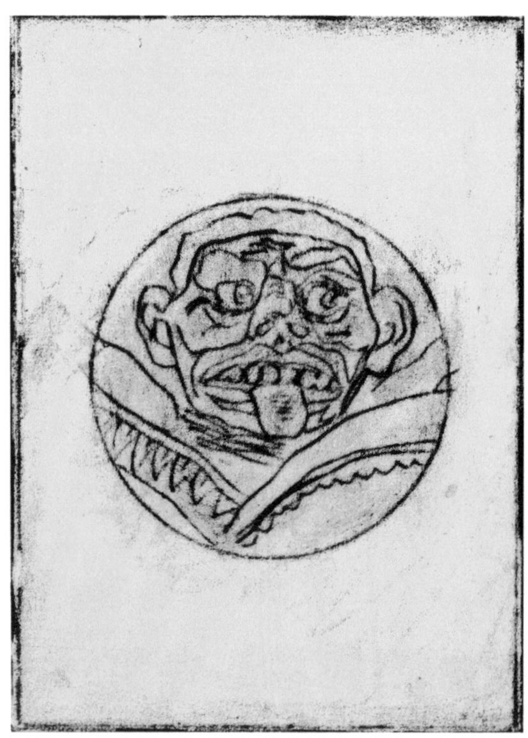

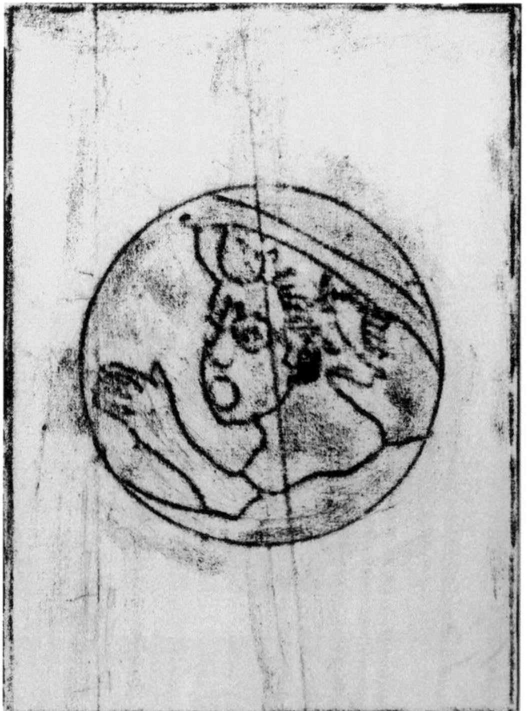

2015.4 Untitled (The Meaning of Things), 59.5 × 42 cm each (quadriptych)

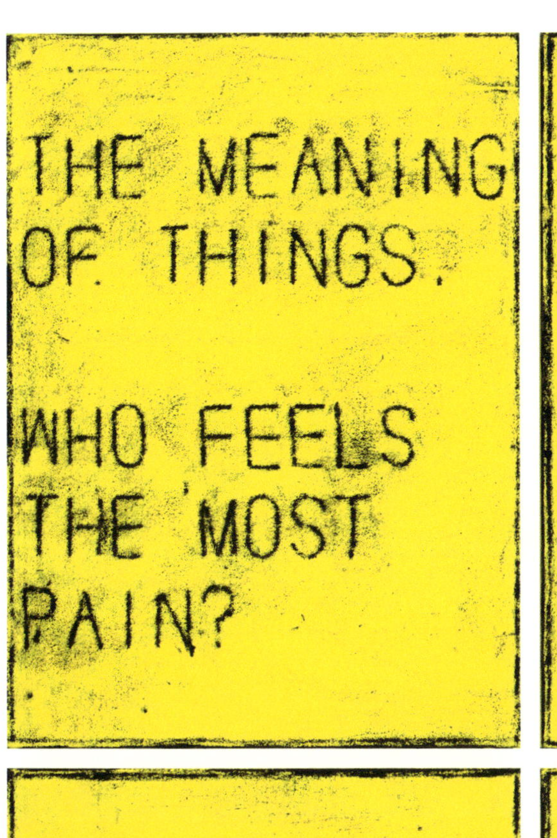

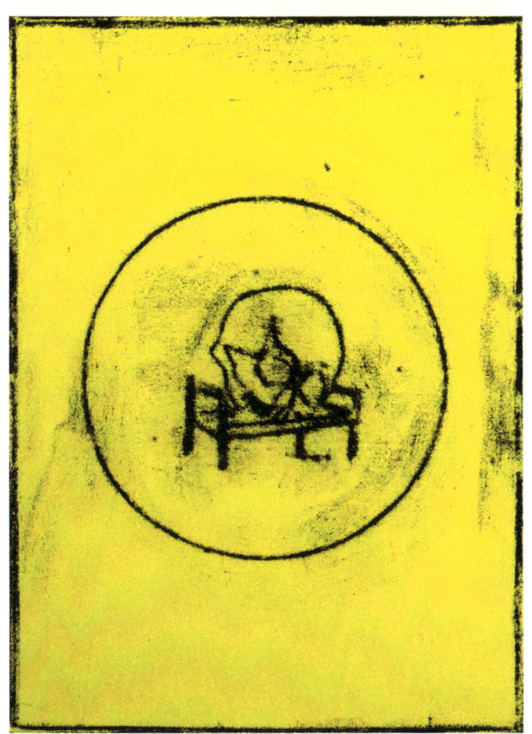
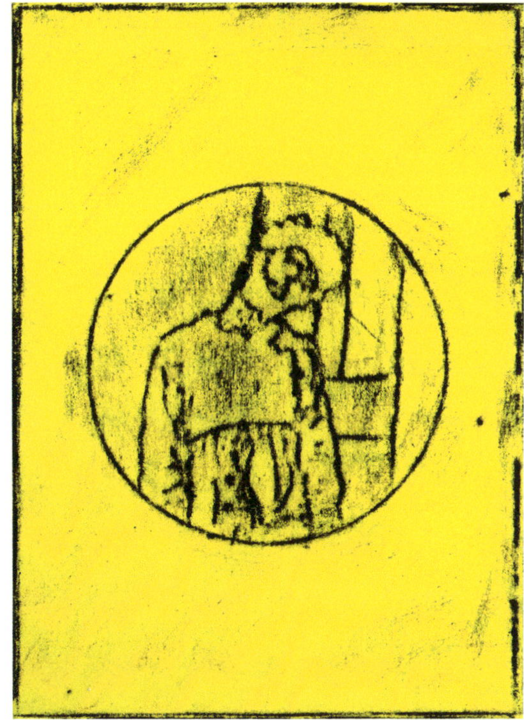

2015.5 Untitled (The Meaning of Things), 59.5 × 42 cm each (quadriptych)

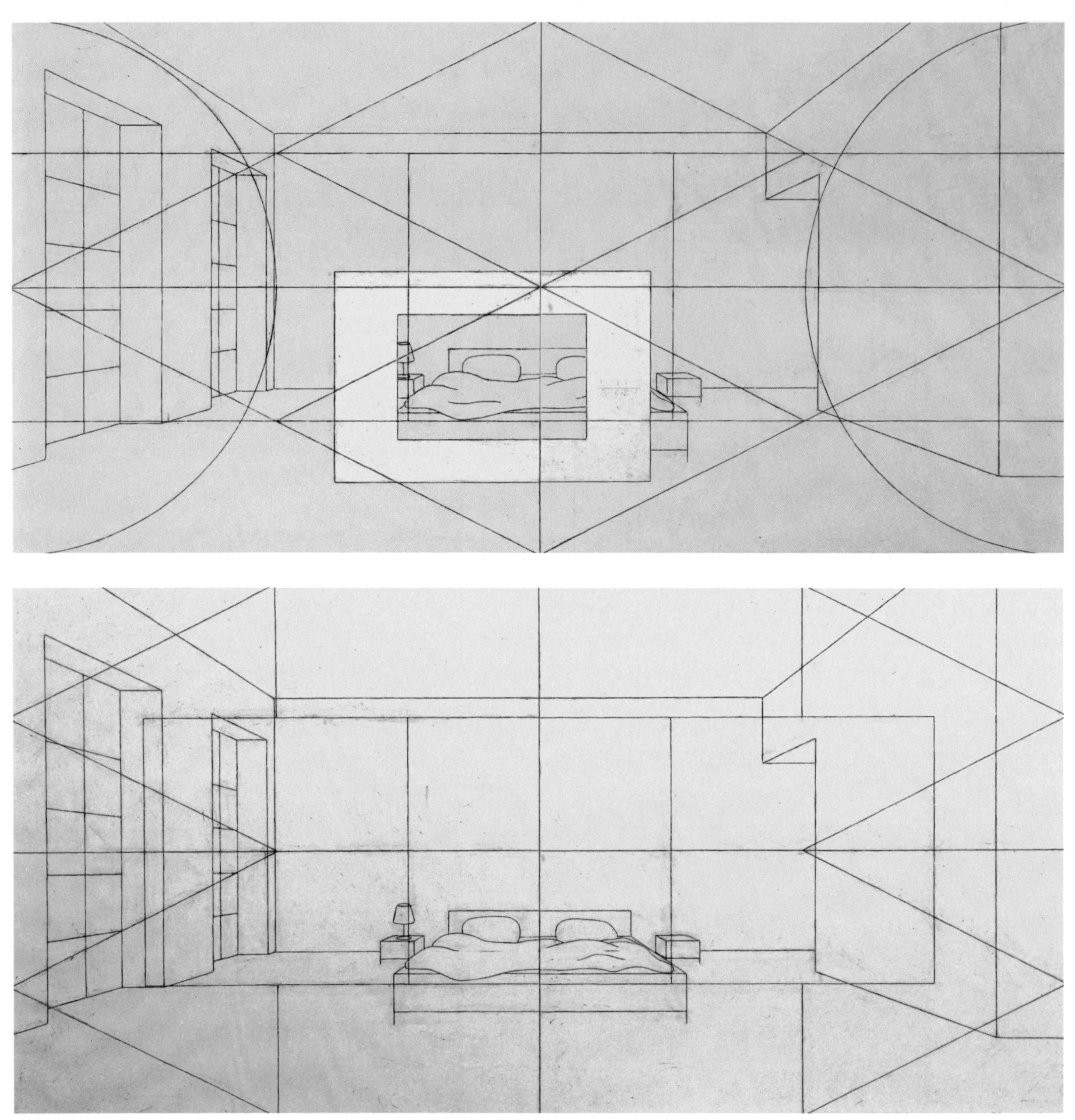

2015.6 Untitled (Interior Frame with Bed), 200 × 400 cm (2 parts)
2015.7 Untitled (Interior World with Bed), 200 × 400 cm (2 parts)

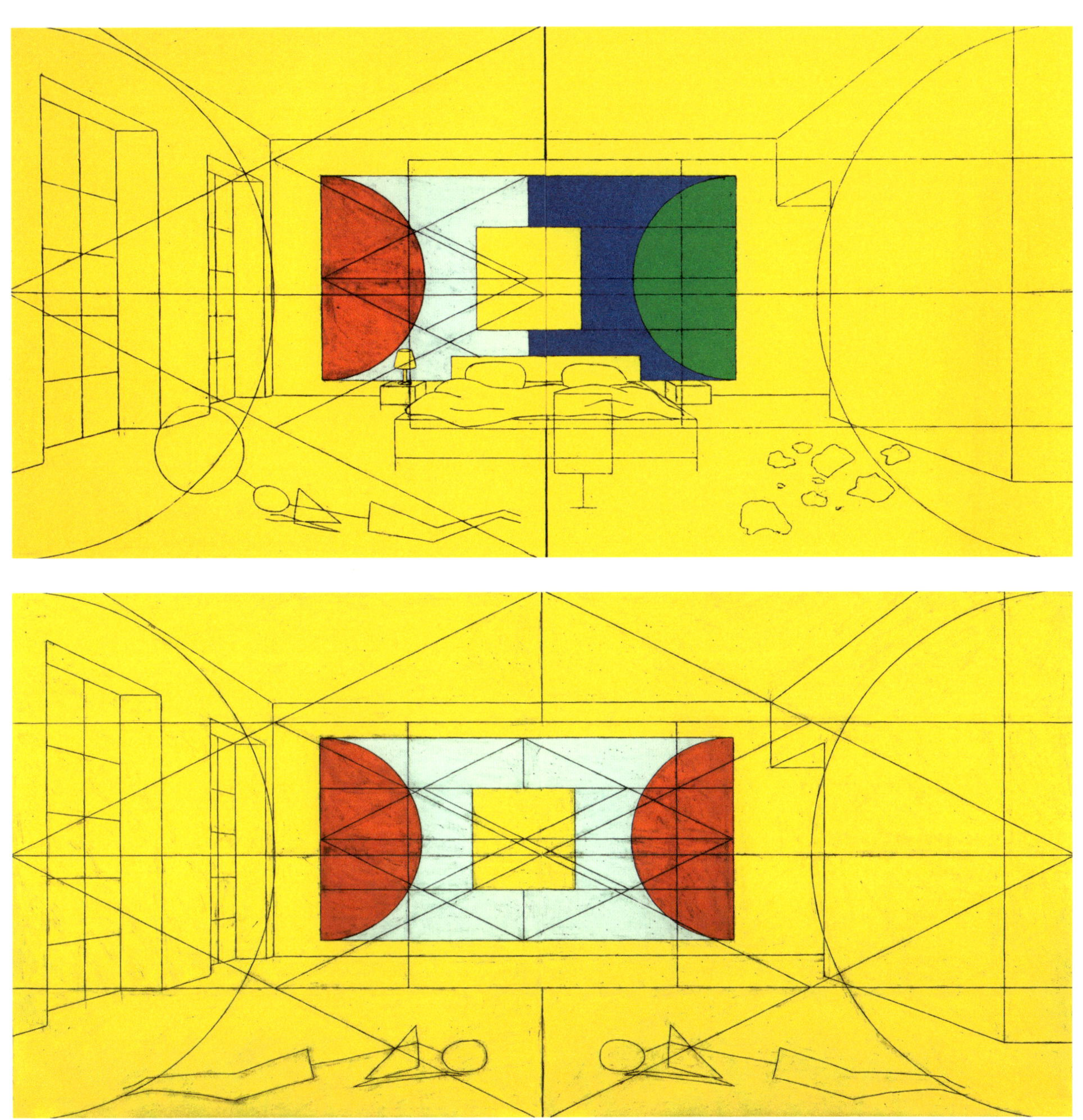

2015.8 Untitled (Overall Chart Room), 200 × 400 cm (2 parts)
2015.9 Untitled (Colored World Frame Chart on Wall), 200 × 400 cm (2 parts)

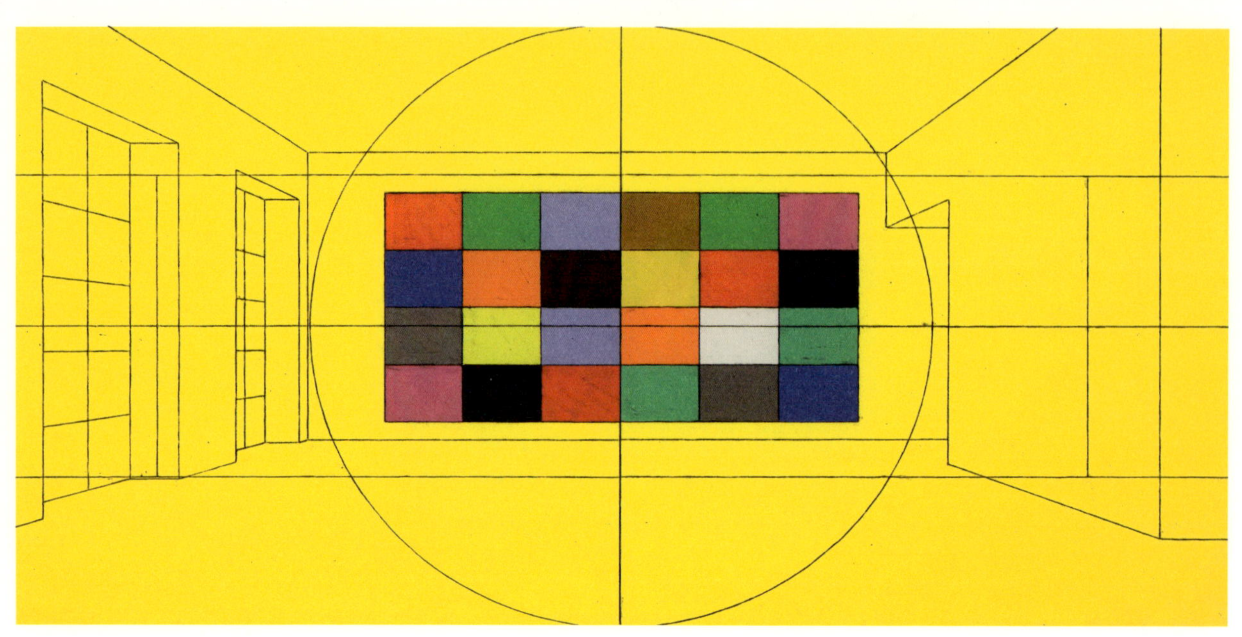

2015.10 Untitled (Interior Element with Light Patterns), 200 × 400 cm (2 parts)

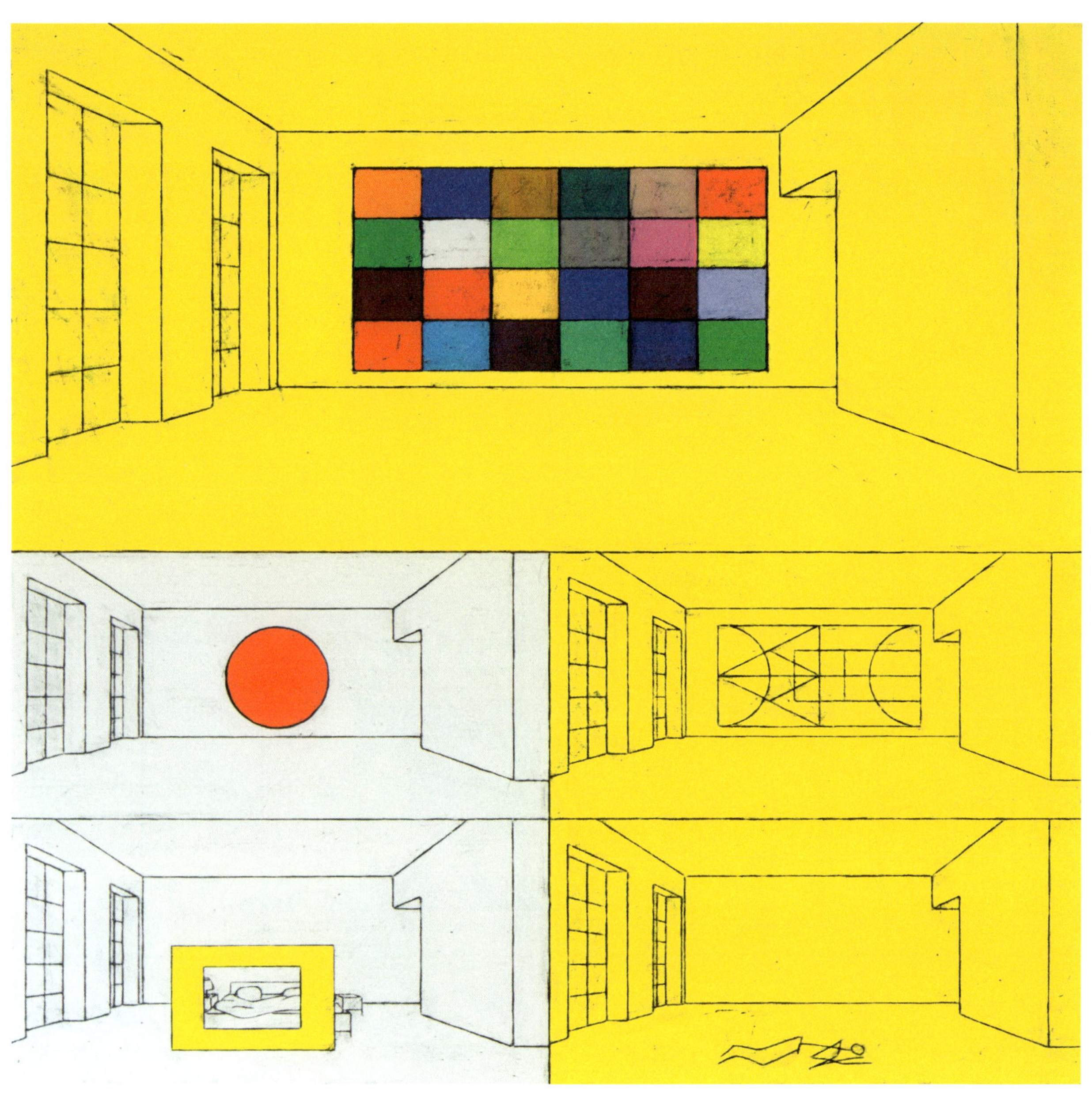

2015.11 Untitled (Elements on Top without Charts), 200 × 200 cm

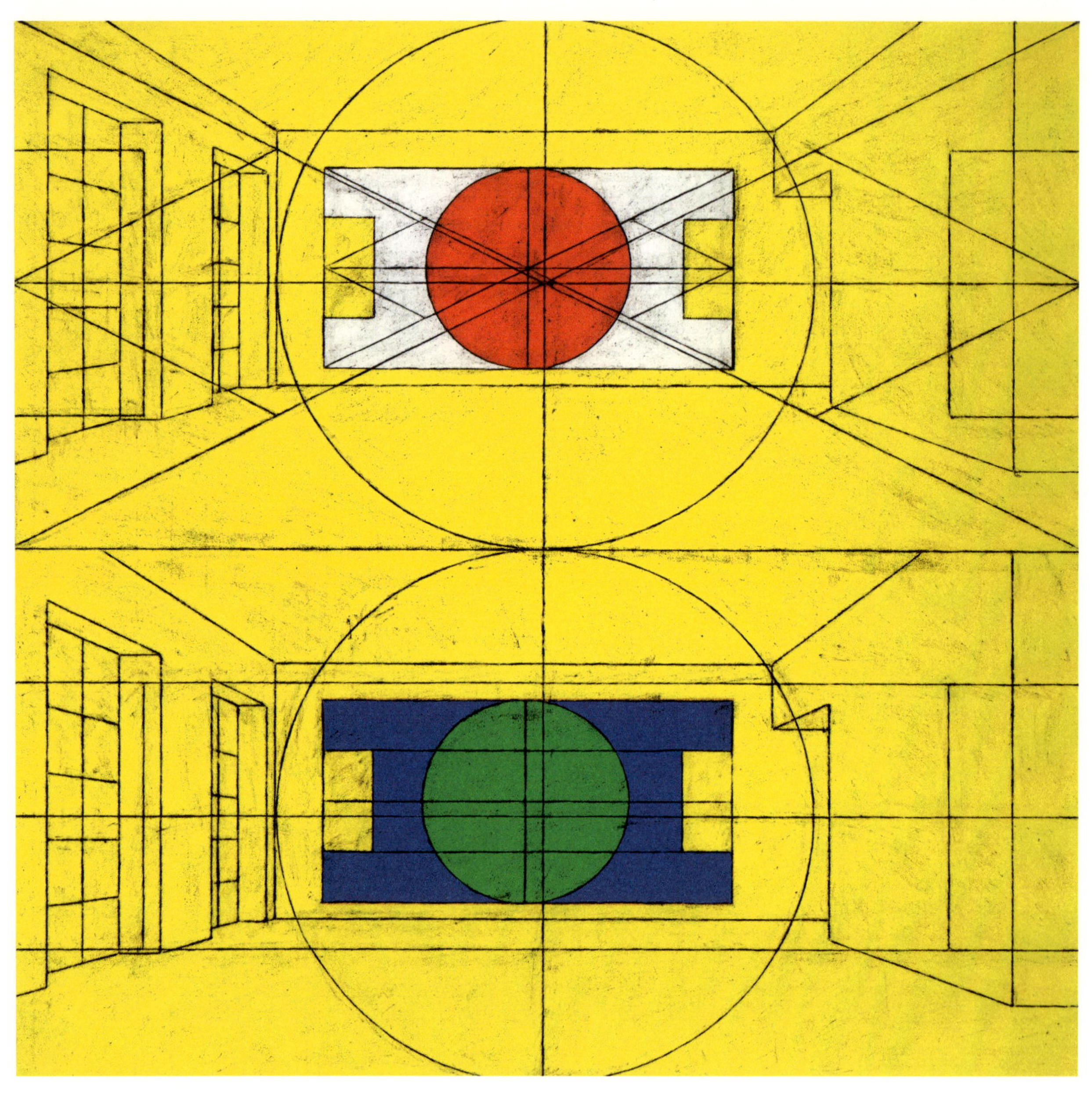

2015.12 Untitled (Subject over Element), 200×200 cm

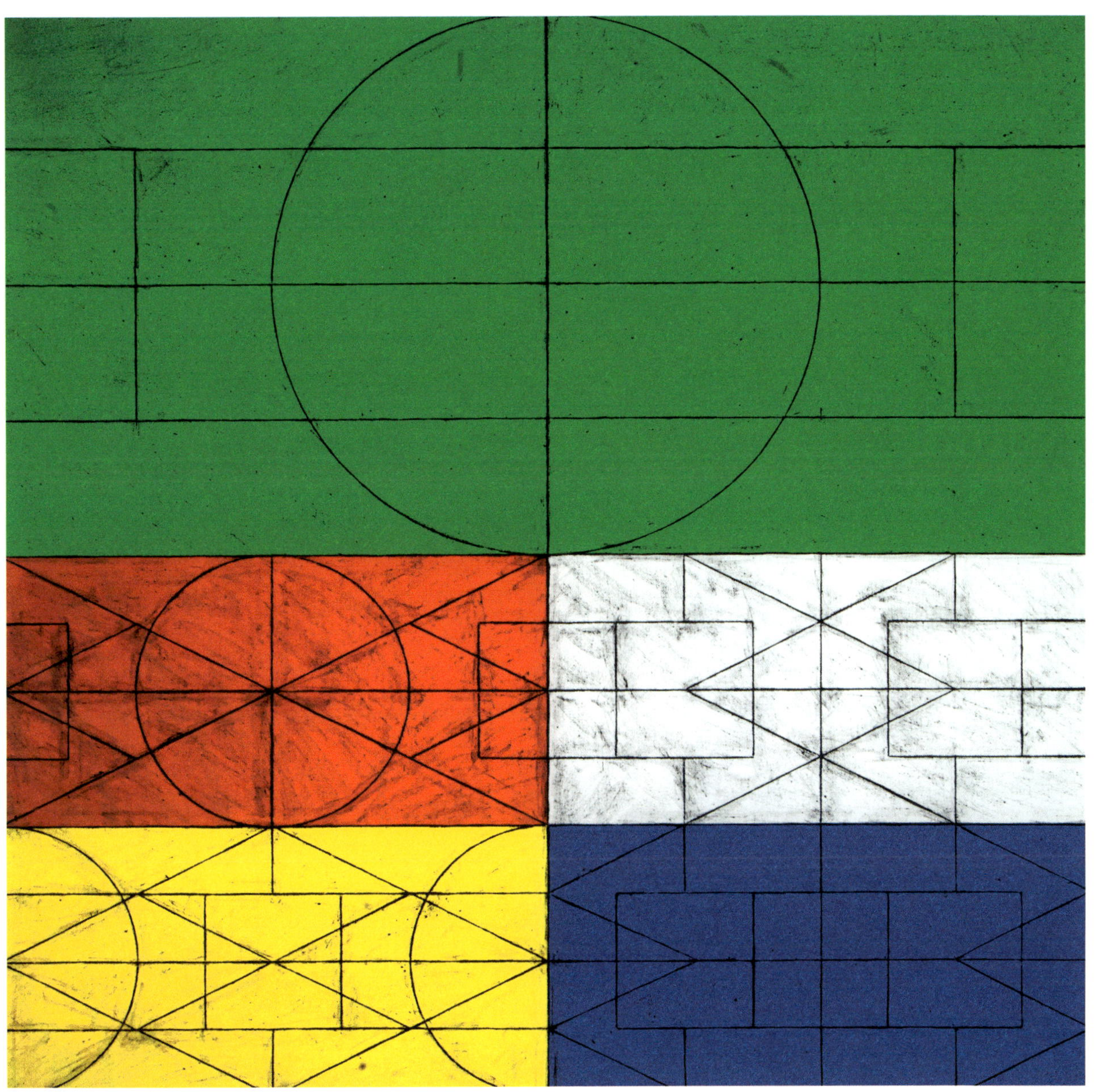

2015.13 Untitled (Elements on Charts), 200 × 200 cm

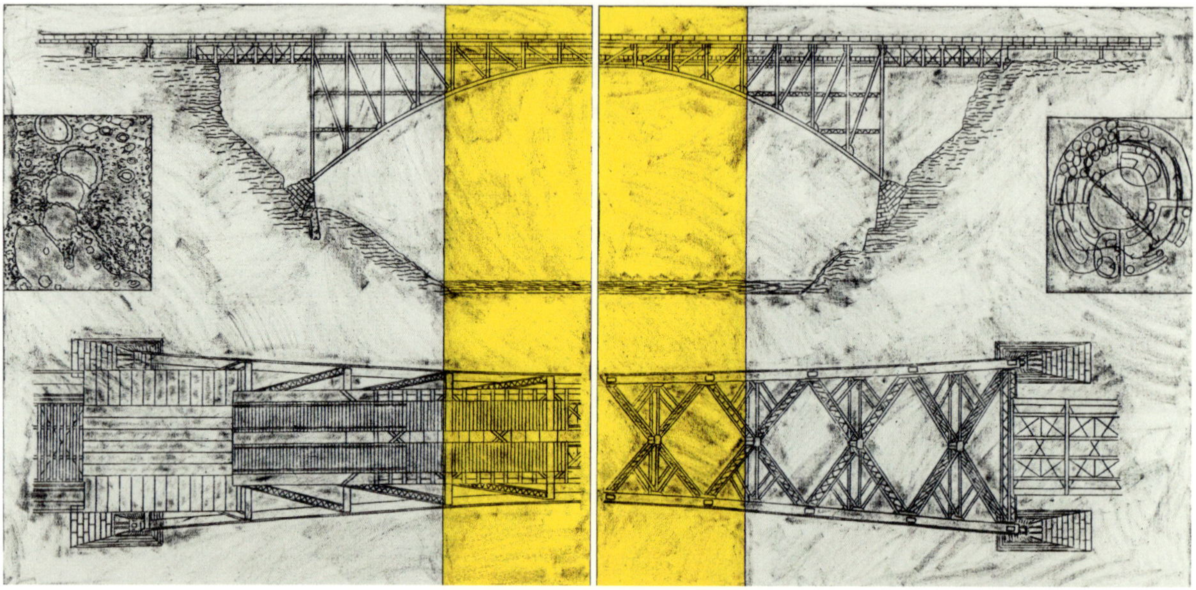

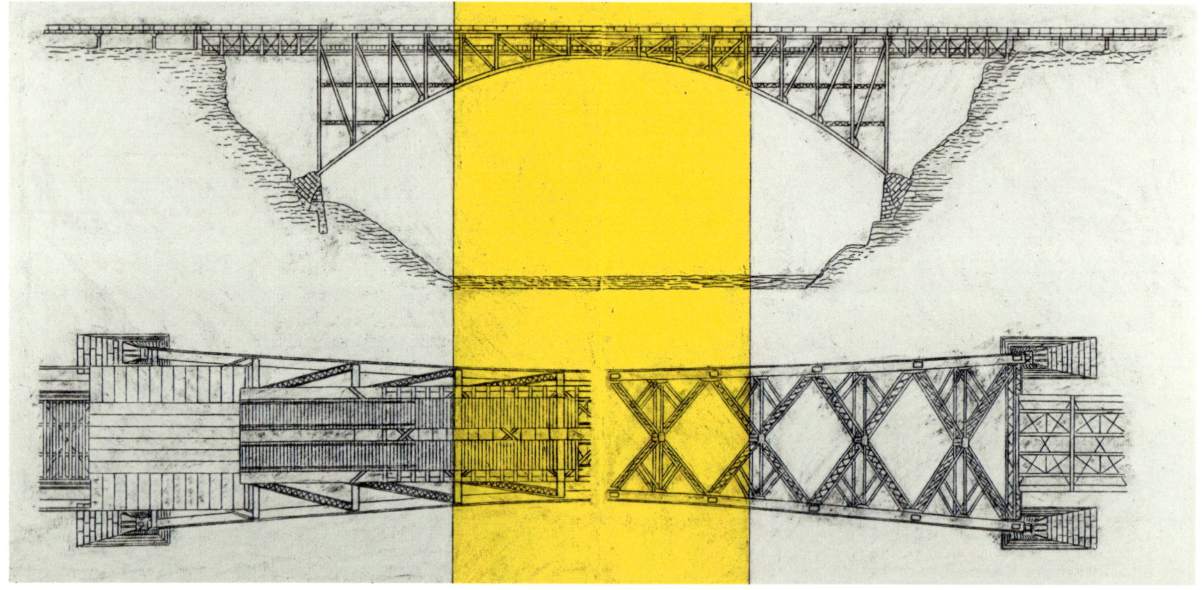

2015.14 Untitled (Railroad Bridge between Subject and Elements), 200 × 400 cm (2 parts)
2015.15 Untitled (Railroad Bridge between Subject and Elements), 200 × 400 cm (2 parts)

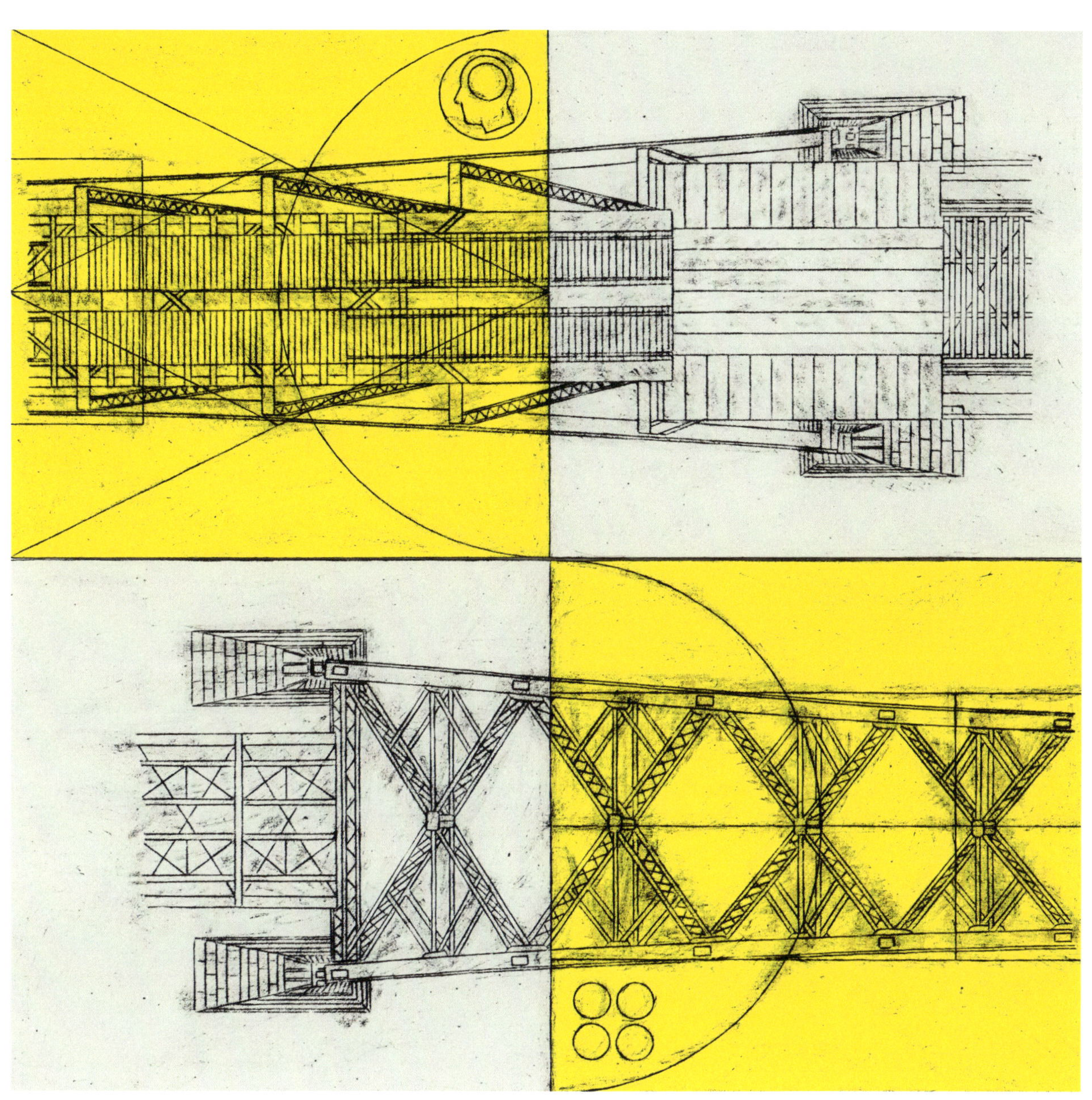

2015.16 Untitled (Yellow Chart and Railroad Bridge), 400 × 400 cm (2 parts)

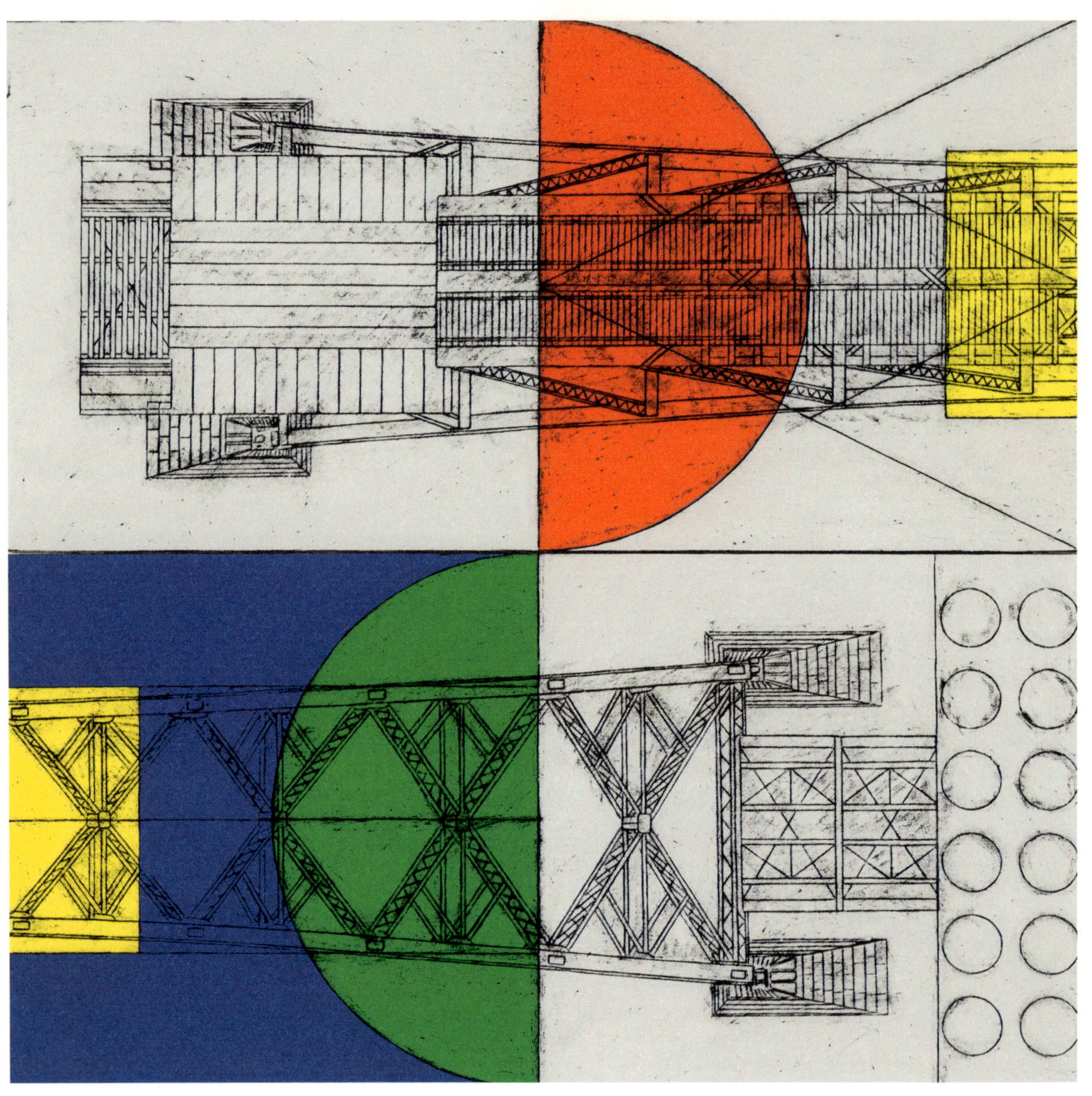

2015.17 Untitled (Five-Colored Chart and Railroad Bridge), 400 × 400 cm (2 parts)

2016

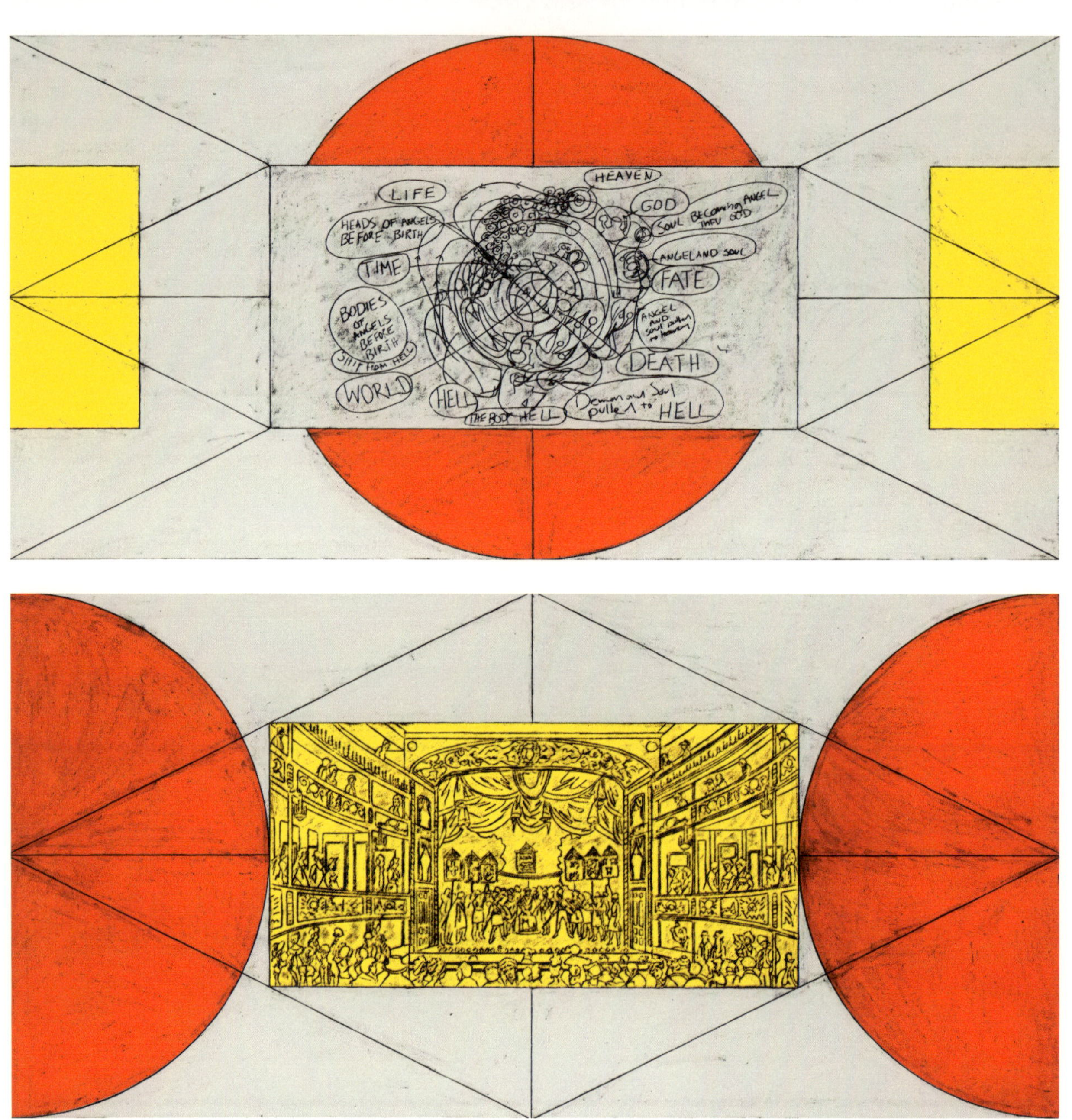

2016.1 Untitled (Subjective Cosmology), 150 × 300 cm
2016.2 Untitled (Subject Frame Theater), 150 × 300 cm

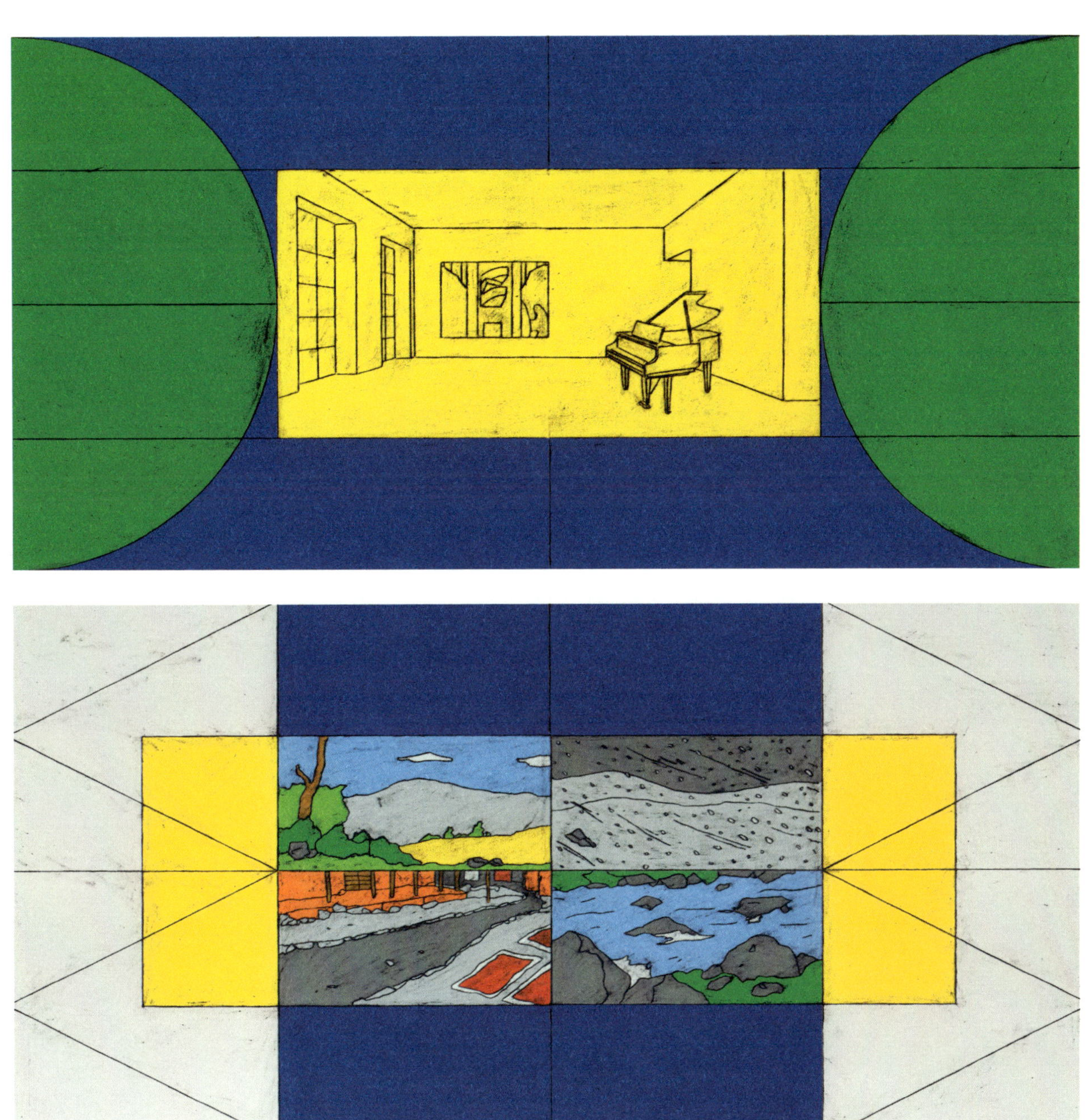

2016.3 Untitled (Piano and Picture), 150 × 300 cm
2016.4 Untitled (World Unframed Landscapes), 150 × 300 cm

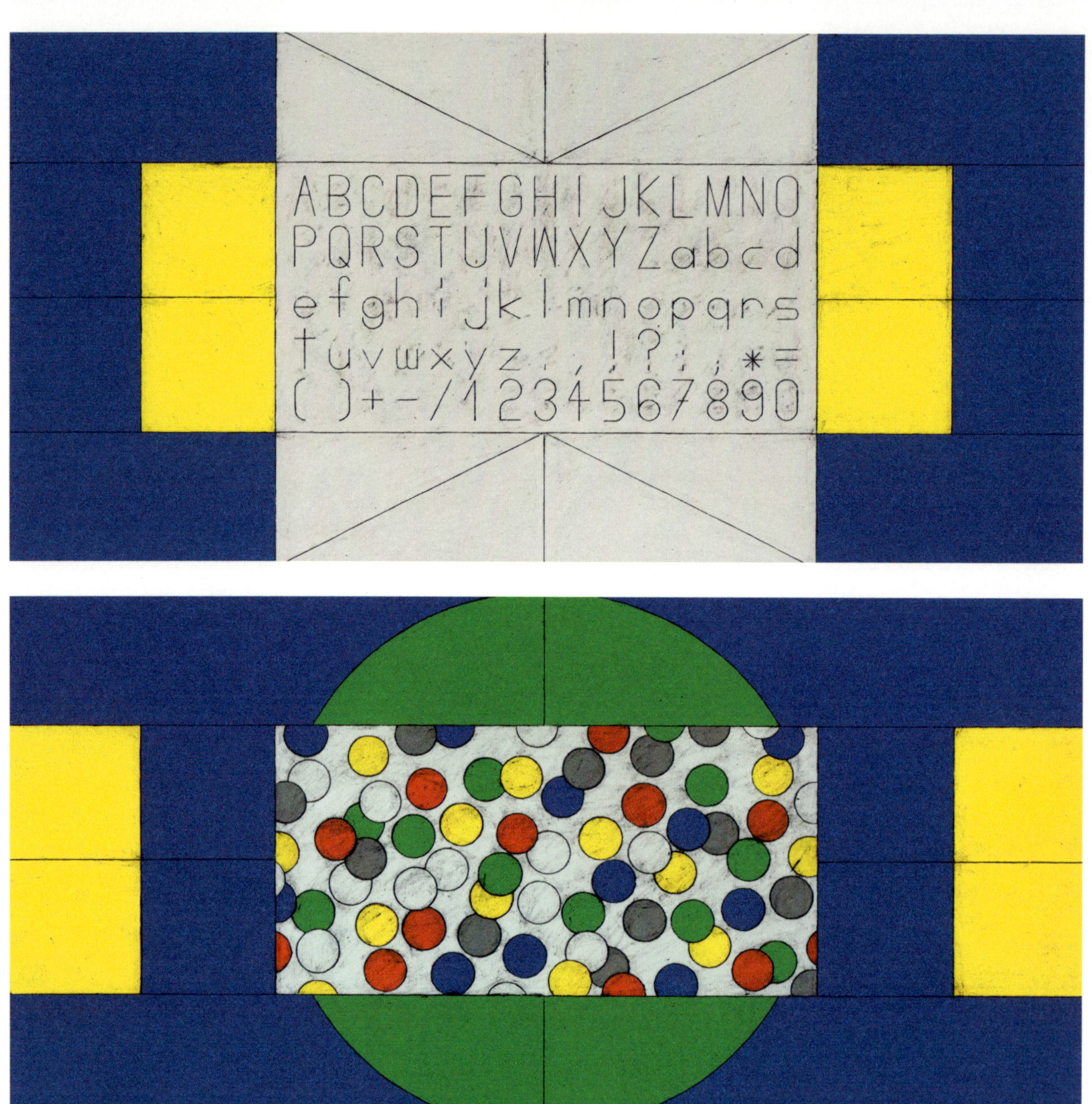

2016.5 Untitled (Sign Typeface), 150 × 300 cm
2016.6 Untitled (Colored Elements), 150 × 300 cm

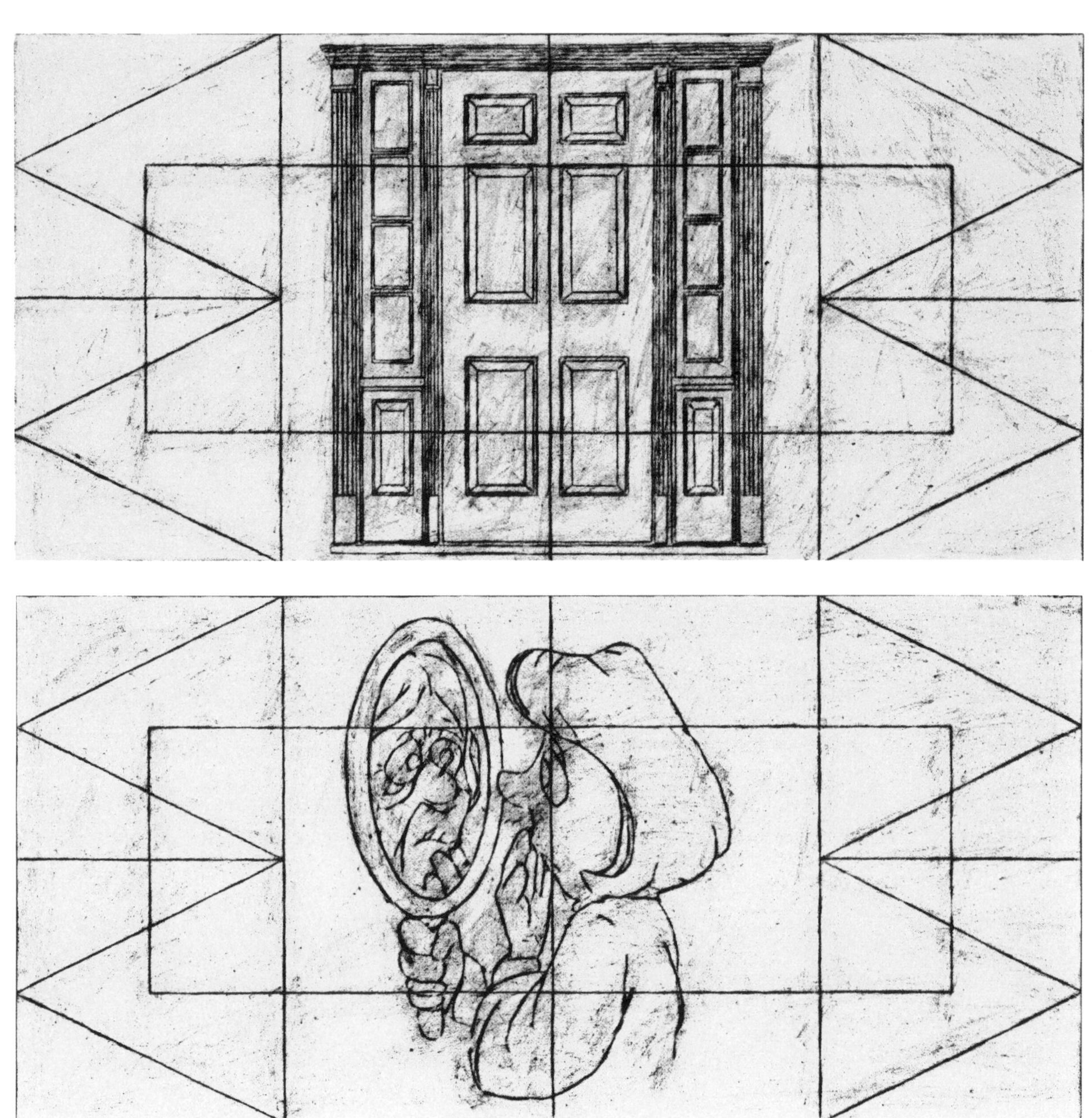

2016.7 Untitled (World Door), 75 × 150 cm
2016.8 Untitled (World Mirror), 75 × 150 cm

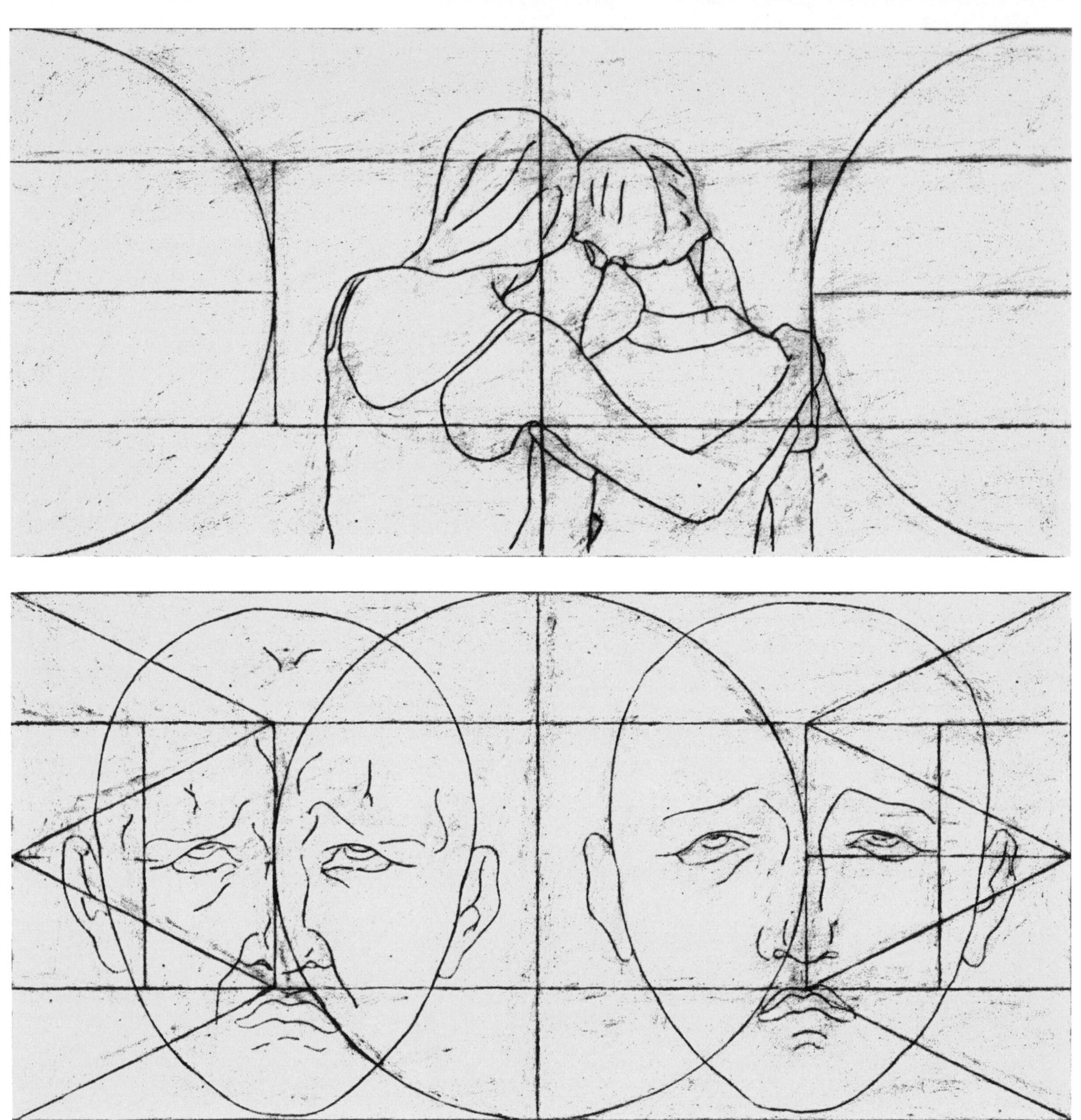

2016.9 Untitled (Frame/Elements Empathy), 75 × 150 cm
2016.10 Untitled (Subjective Heads), 75 × 150 cm

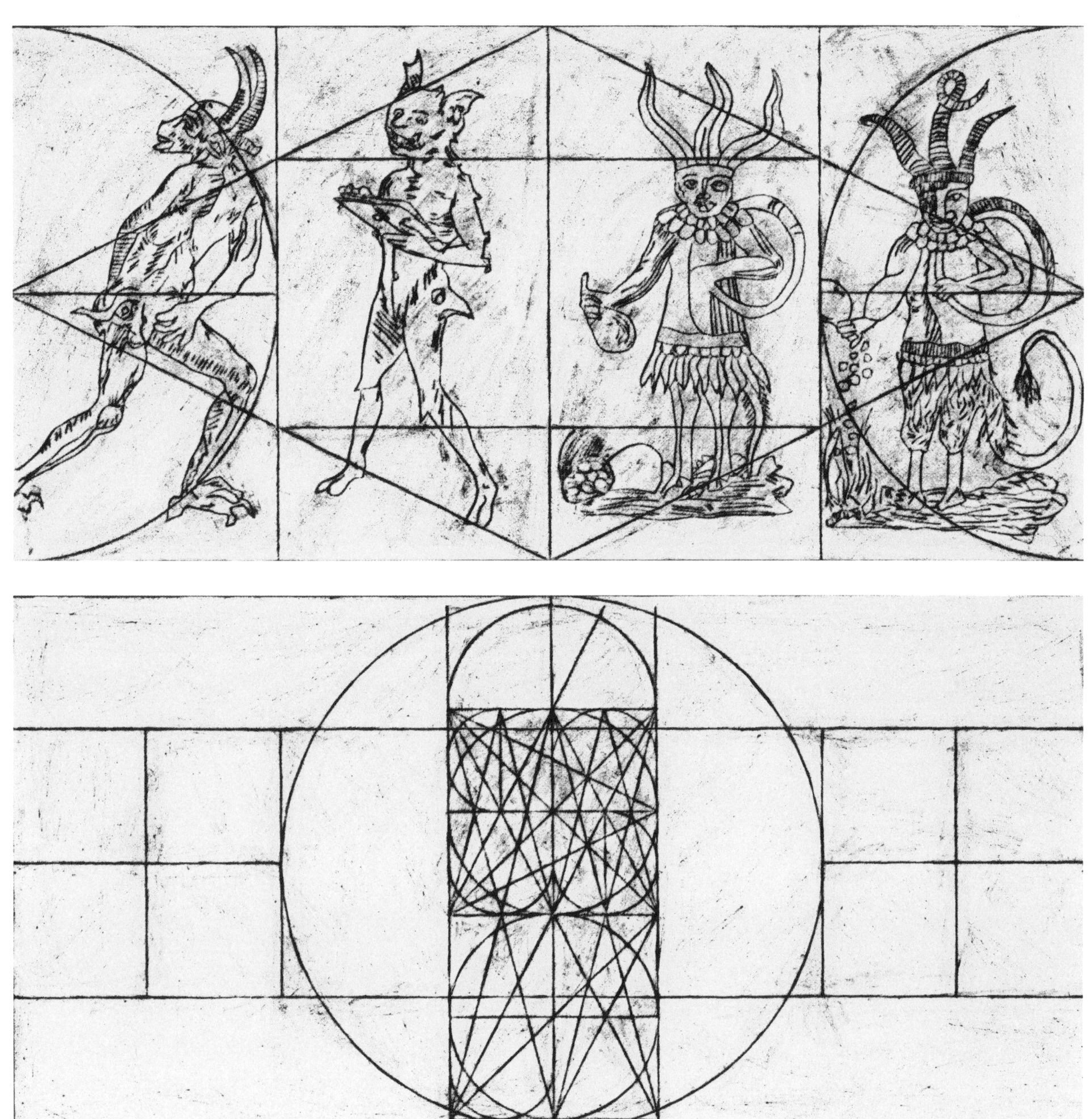

2016.11 Untitled (Frame/Subject Demons), 75 × 150 cm
2016.12 Untitled (Elements Typeface), 75 × 150 cm

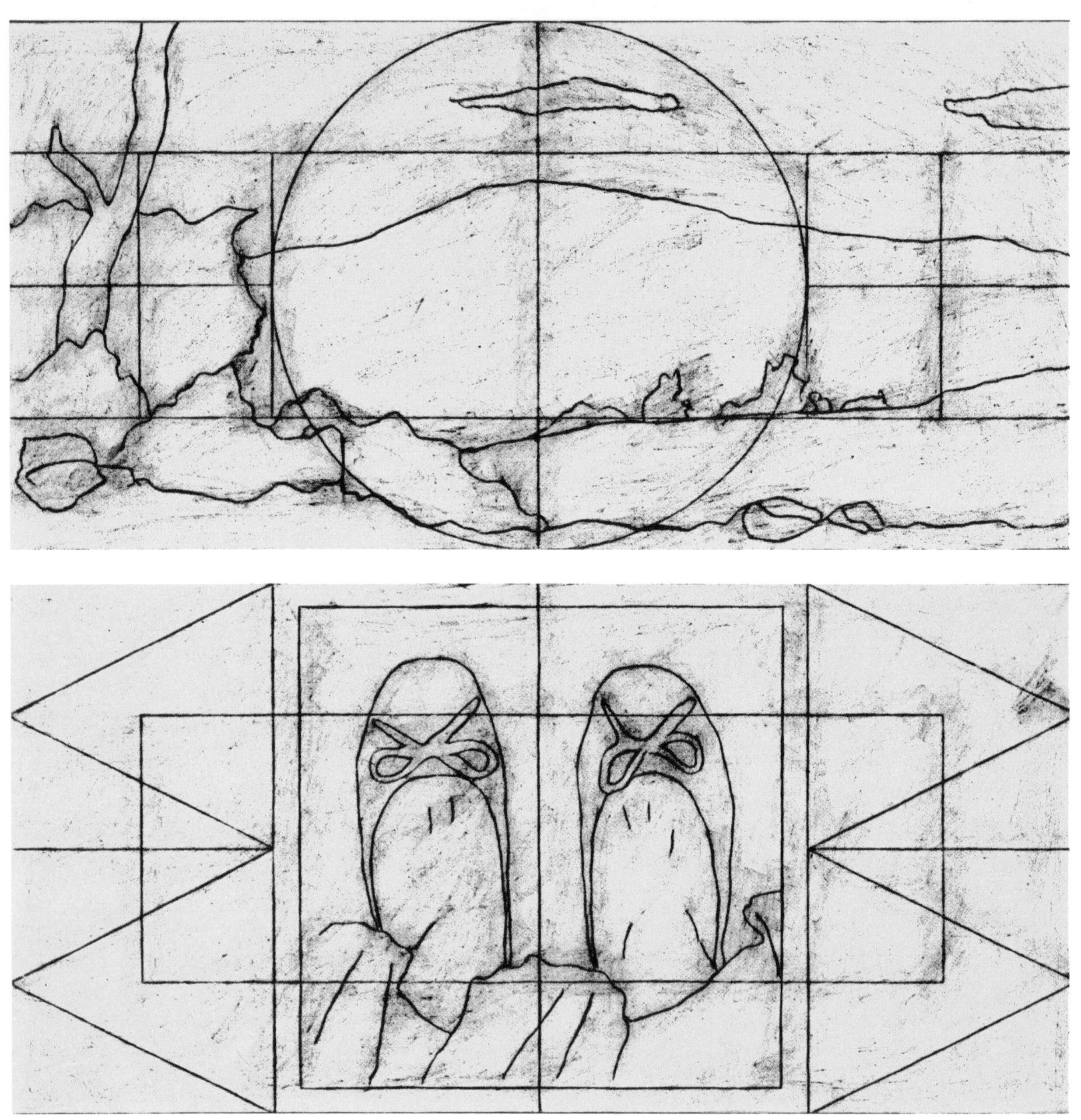

2016.13 Untitled (Elements Landscape), 75 × 150 cm
2016.14 Untitled (World Feet), 75 × 150 cm

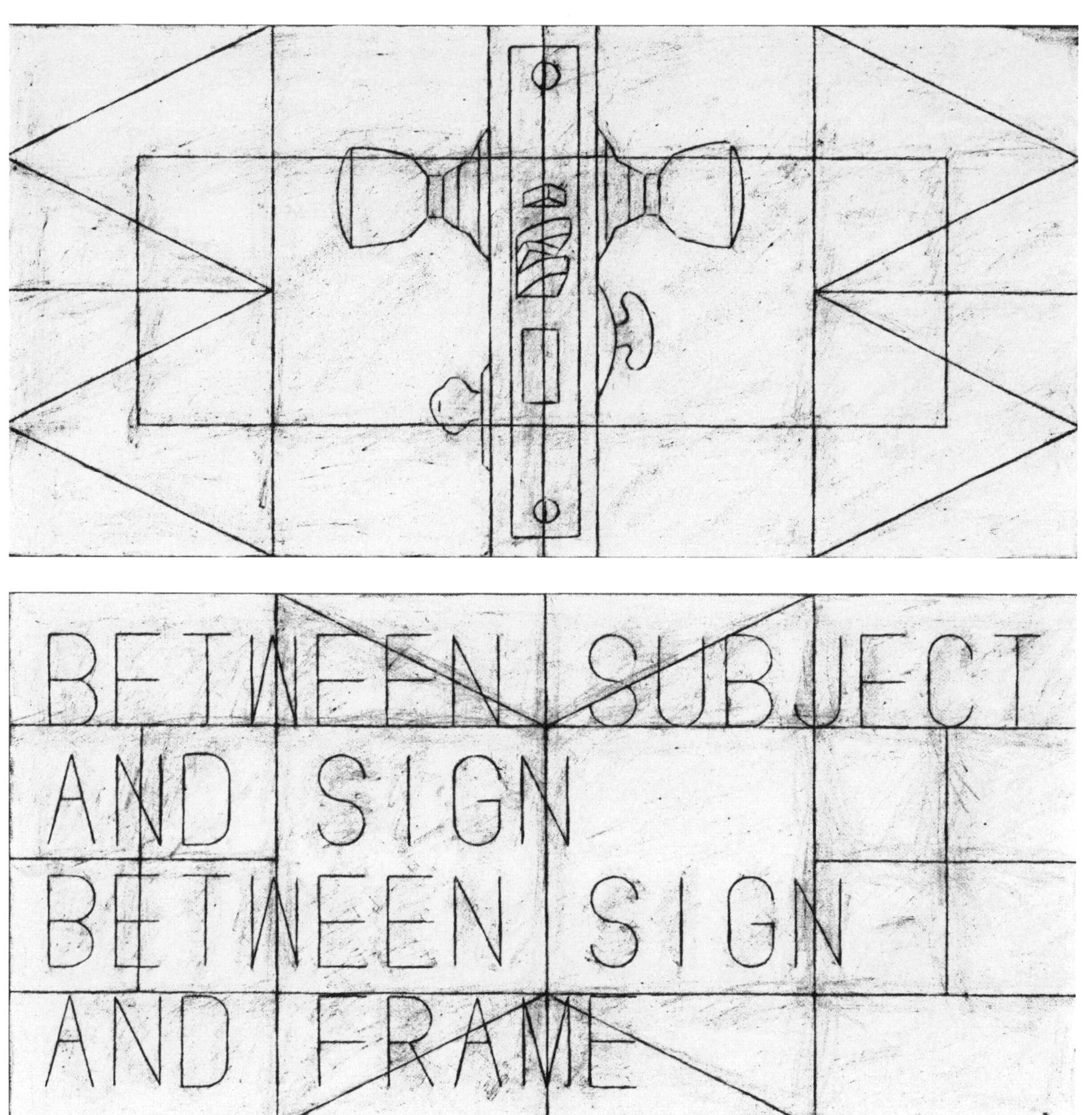

2016.15 Untitled (World Door Lock), 75 × 150 cm
2016.16 Untitled (Sign Test), 75 × 150 cm

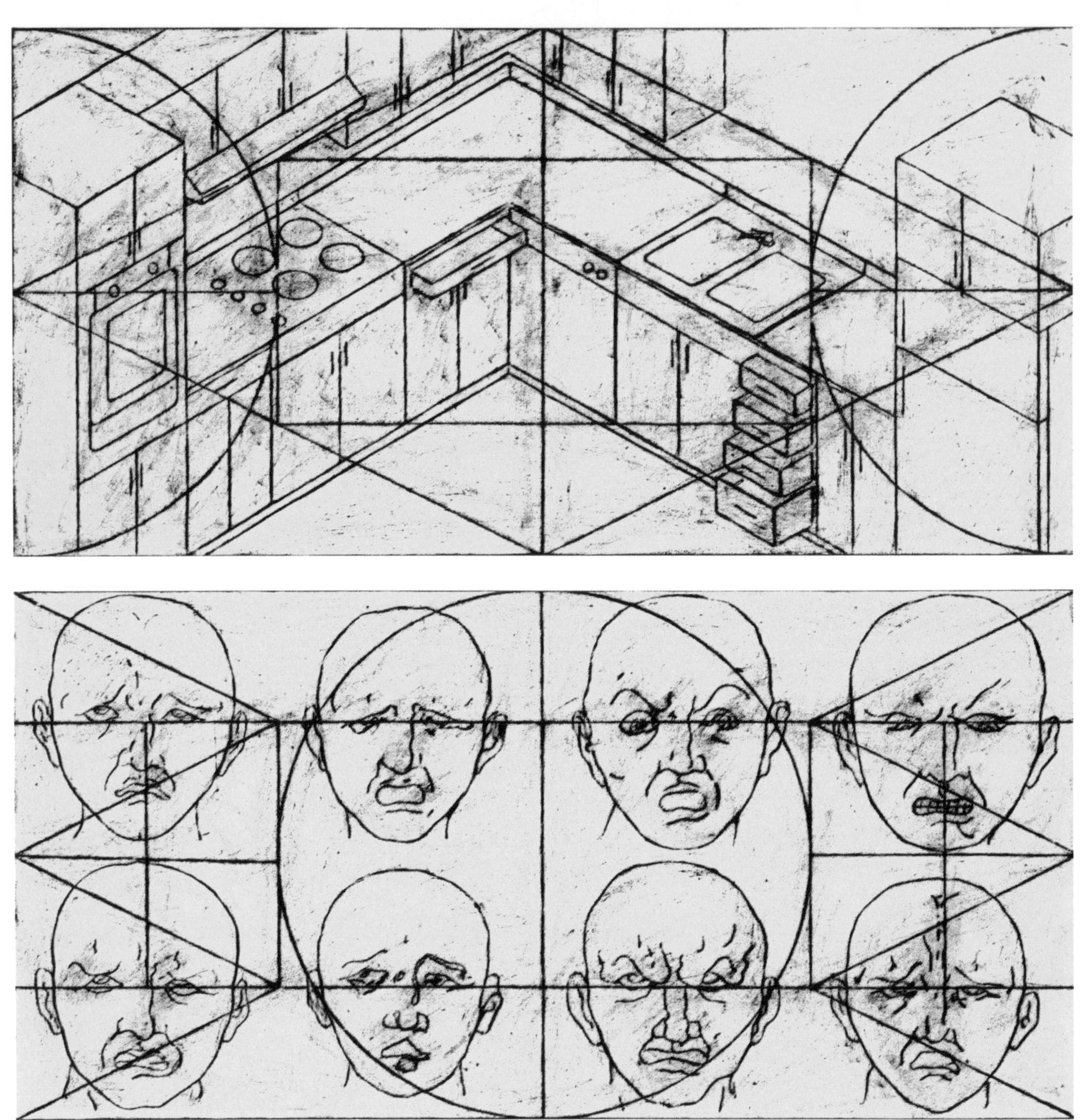

2016.17 Untitled (Frame/Subject Kitchen), 75 × 150 cm
2016.18 Untitled (Subject 8 Heads), 75 × 150 cm

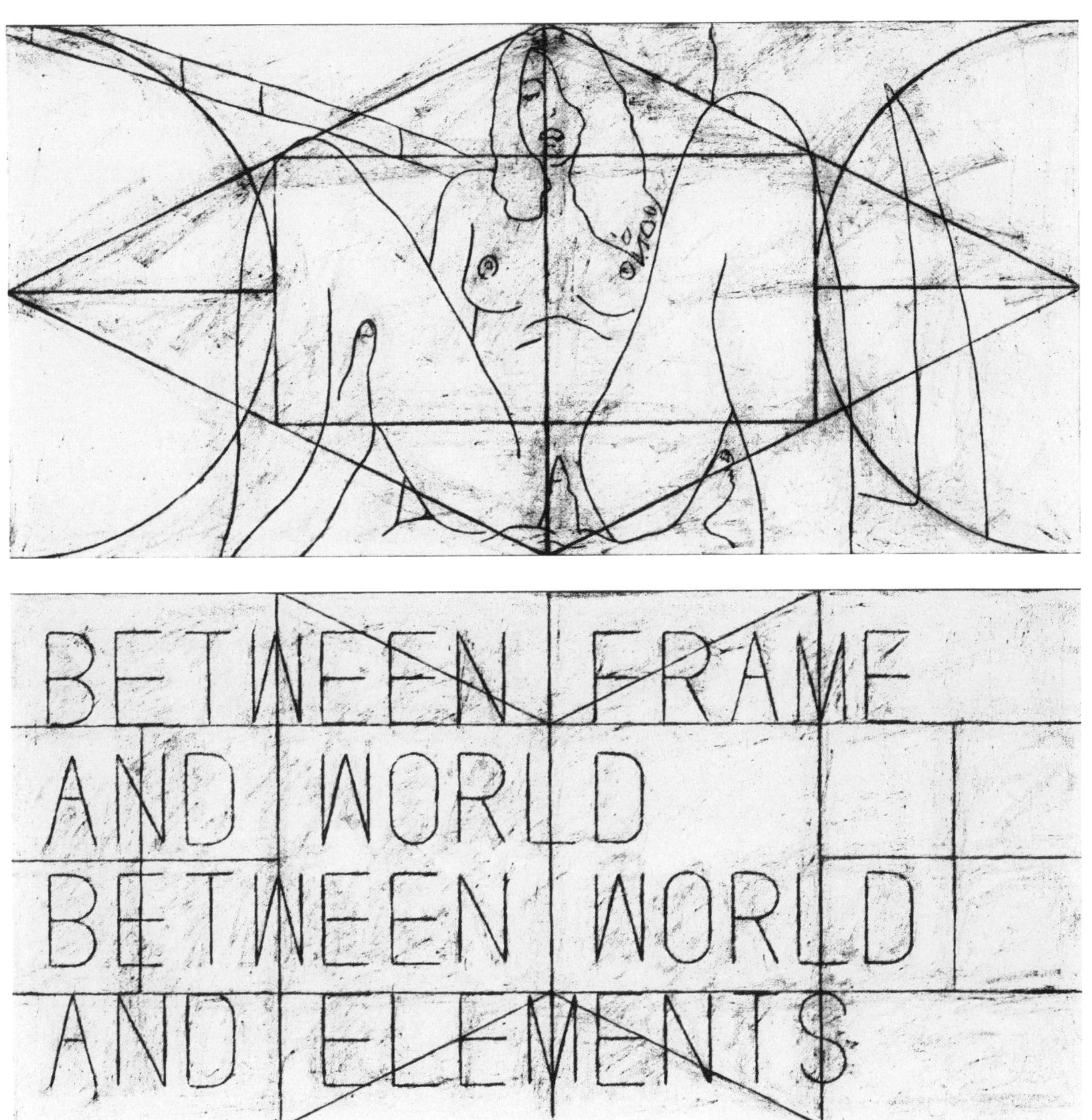

2016.19 Untitled (Frame/Subject 1st Person Sex Porno), 75 × 150 cm
2016.20 Untitled (Sign Test), 75 × 150 cm

The editor and the publisher have made all possible efforts to obtain the best reproduction quality from heterogeneous image material. In order to offer the reader the most complete documentation on Matt Mullican's Rubbings, they have chosen to reproduce all the artworks for which an image was available, even if the quality of the reproduction does not meet the highest standards.

Herausgeber und Verlag haben sich bemüht, aus dem zur Verfügung stehenden Bildmaterial die bestmöglichen Reproduktionen herzustellen. Um dem Leser eine weitgehend vollständige Dokumentation von Matt Mullicans Rubbings vorzulegen, haben sie entschieden, alle Werke abzubilden, von denen Aufnahmen vorhanden waren, selbst wenn deren Qualität im Hinblick auf die Wiedergabe nicht genügend war.

PHOTO CREDITS

All the photographs not listed below are courtesy of the Archives of Matt Mullican, and courtesy of Mai 36 Galerie, Zurich (photo Peter Baracchi).

Actelion Research Center, Allschwil: 2005.1

Brooke Alexander, New York: 1989.1, 1989.2, 1989.6, 1997.1–4, 1997.6–18

Helga de Alvear, Madrid-Cáceres (photo Joaquín Cortés): 2007.2, 2010.1–3

Kunstsammlung AXA Konzern AG: 1987.16

Sebastian Bach, New York: 1986.2

Fotostudio Bartsch, Berlin: 2012.34

Daniel Blau, Munich: 1996.9, 1996.10

Bonhams, Los Angeles: 1985.1

Capitain Petzel, Berlin: 2010.9, 2014.6, 2015.1, 2015.11, 2015.13, 2015.14, 2016.1–20

Christie's: 1985.8, 1989.3, 1989.8, 1989.13, 1997.5, 2014.33

Cornette de Saint-Cyr, Paris: 1992.1

Massimo De Carlo, Milan/London/Hong Kong (photo Alessandro Zambianchi): 2001.1–6, 2013.1–8

Peter Freeman, Inc., New York/Paris: 2009.1, 2009.3, 2009.5, 2009.6, 2009.9, 2009.10, 2011.1, 2012.1, 2012.38, 2012.39, 2012.40, 2012.42, 2012.43, 2012.69, 2013.13, 2013.15, 2013.20

Cristina Guerra Contemporary Art, Lisbon: 2003.2, 2003.7, 2009.8, 2009.11, 2009.13

Peter Heimer, Berlin: 1995.2

Heritage Auctions, Dallas: 1989.17

Hirshhorn Museum and Sculpture Garden, Smithsonian Institution, Joseph H. Hirshhorn Purchase Fund, 1991 (photo Cathy Carver): 1987.4

Georg Kargl, Wien: 1984.1, 1986.1, 1987.23

Kunstmuseum Liechtenstein, Vaduz, purchase with the support of the "Stiftung Freunde des Kunstmuseum Liechtenstein" (photo Stefan Altenburger): 1989.4, 1991.7

LaM–musée d'Art moderne, d'art contemporain et d'art brut, Lille, purchase in 2012, with the support of the FRAC Nord-Pas-de-Calais, Inv. Nr. 2012.9.1 (1–3): 2011.4

Los Angeles County Museum of Art, Gift of Ann and Aaron Nisenson in memory of Michael Nisenson, Digital Image Museum Associates/LACMA/Art Resource NY/Scala, Florence: 1987.7, 1990.2

Los Angeles Modern Auctions (LAMA) (photo Susan Einstein): 1987.20

Middlebury College Museum of Art, Vermont, commissioned by the Committee on Art in Public Places, Middlebury College, with funds provided by the Glenstone Foundation in honor of Charles Gwathmey, and The Edwin Austin Abbey Memorial Fund for Mural Painting in America of The National Academy Museum and School of Fine Arts, New York, 2005.039.1: 2005.2

Öffentliche Versicherung Braunschweig (photo Heiner Koether): 1995.3

ProjecteSD, Barcelona (photo Roberto Ruiz): 1984.7, 1988.6, 2014.2–5, 2015.2–5; (photo Gasull Fotografia): 1989.9, 1991.11, 1991.12, 1991.13, 2011.2, 2012.45

Rago Arts & Auction Center, Lambertville, New Jersey: 1984.11

Santa Barbara Museum of Art, Santa Barbara: 1992.3, 1992.4

Sotheby's: 1988.3, 1989.20, 1989.22

Micheline Szwajcer, Brussels: 1984.3, 1992.16, 2008.3, 2011.9, 2012.9, 2012.15, 2012.24, 2012.28, 2012.29, 2012.30, 2012.31, 2012.32, 2012.33, 2012.35, 2014.17, 2014.20, 2014.21, 2014.23, 2014.26, 2014.27, 2014.30, 2014.36–39, 2014.41, 2015.6, 2015.7, 2015.9.

Tasman Projects, Madrid: 2015.10

Three Star Books, Paris (photo Florian Kleinefenn): 2011.13, 2011.14

UBS Art Collection: 1995.1, 1996.1–6, 1996.8

Whitney Museum of American Art, New York, gift of Eva and Yoel Haller, 2005.157a-b (photo Sheldan C. Collins): 1985.2

Kunsthaus Zürich: 2008.1

This catalogue is published on the occasion
of the exhibition:

Matt Mullican
Nothing Should Exist

EXHIBITION

Kunstmuseum Winterthur
June 12–October 16, 2016

Kunsthalle Vogelmann
Städtische Museen Heilbronn
November 6, 2016–February 19, 2017

Kunstmuseum Winterthur
Museumstr. 52
CH–8400 Winterthur
Tel. + 41 (0) 52 267 51 62
www.kmw.ch

Kunsthalle Vogelmann
Städtische Museen Heilbronn
Allee 28
D–74072 Heilbronn
Tel. + 49 07131/56 4420
www.museen-heilbronn.de/kunsthalle

Curator of the exhibition
Dieter Schwarz

Curator for the Heilbronn venue
Marc Gundel

PUBLICATION

Editor
Dieter Schwarz

Editorial Coordination
Clément Dirié

Proofreading
Clare Manchester (English),
Karin Prätorius (German)

Translation from the German
Fiona Elliott

Design
Nicolas Eigenheer, Noémie Gygax

Color Separation & Print
Musumeci S.P.A., Quart (Aosta)

Typeface
Theinhardt (www.optimo.ch)

Published by JRP|Ringier

Limmatstrasse 270
CH–8005 Zurich
Tel. +41 (0) 43 311 27 50
Fax +41 (0) 43 311 27 51
www.jrp-ringier.com
info@jrp-ringier.com

Printed in Europe

ISBN 978-3-03764-461-4

JRP|Ringier books are available internationally
at selected bookstores and from the following
distribution partners:

Switzerland
AVA Verlagsauslieferung AG
Centralweg 16
CH–8910 Affoltern a. A.
verlagsservice@ava.ch
www.ava.ch

Germany and Austria
Vice Versa Distribution GmbH
Immanuelkirchstrasse 12
D–10405 Berlin
info@vice-versa-distribution.com
www.vice-versa-distribution.com

France
Les presses du réel
35, rue Colson
F–21000 Dijon
info@lespressesdureel.com
www.lespressesdureel.com

UK and other European countries
Cornerhouse Publications HOME
2 Tony Wilson Place
UK–Manchester M15 4FN
ublications@cornerhouse.org
www.cornerhousepublications.org

USA, Canada, Asia, and Australia
ARTBOOK|D.A.P.
155 Sixth Avenue
2nd Floor
USA–New York, NY 10013
orders@dapinc.com
www.artbook.com

For a list of our partner bookshops
or for any general questions, please contact
JRP|Ringier directly at info@jrp-ringier.com,
or visit our homepage www.jrp-ringier.com